GREAT FOOD

❖ *for* ❖

GREAT NUMBERS

Hannelore Dawson

Photography by Dan Gair
Nutrient Analysis by Margaret Merz, R.D.

 VAN NOSTRAND REINHOLD
———————————— New York

Library of Congress Catalog Number
ISBN 0-442-00214-9

Printed in the United States of America

Van Nostrand Reinhold
115 Fifth Avenue
New York, New York 10003

Chapman and Hall
2–6 Boundary Row
London, SE1 8HN, England

Thomas Nelson Australia
102 Dodds Street
South Melbourne 3205
Victoria, Australia

Nelson Canada
1120 Birchmount Road
Scarborough, Ontario M1K 5G4, Canada

16 15 14 13 12 11 10 9 8 7 6 5 4 3 2

Library of Congress Cataloging-in-Publication Data

Dawson, Hannelore.
   Great food for great numbers / Hannelore Dawson : photography by
Dan Gair : nutrient analysis by Margaret Merz.
      p.   cm.
   Includes bibliographical references.
   ISBN 0-442-00214-9 (hardcover)
   1. Quantity cookery.   I. Title.
TX820.D38   1991
641.5'7—dc20   90-38721
                                                                    CIP

(Recipe credits appear on page 547.)

To Sarah, Geoffrey, and to the memory of my mother,
Henny Klages, the first great cook in my life

CONTENTS

———— ❖ ————

v

3   APPETIZERS

6 VEGETARIAN ENTRÉES
UNUSUAL AND TEMPTING

7 SANDWICHES

FOREWORD

❖

There I was, between assignments, with two months on my hands, no books to write or courses to teach, nothing to do but rest. This was a change for me and I was pleased by the prospect, but still looking for something easy and fun to do when the telephone rang. On the other end of the line was a very nice woman who put forth an interesting proposition: Would I consider coming to the University of New Hampshire and cooking dinner for the UNH student body so that they could experience French cuisine? Ah, great, I thought, that should be a challenge and a change from cooking for my usual 75-guest dining room, and even from cooking the occasional 500 cover meals for the American Institute of Wine and Food. I quickly calculated that planning for 1000 would not be that different from 500, and so I said, "Yes, indeed, I would like to come." The idea was all the more appealing because my older son is a graduate of UNH. Then, and only then, did I actually ask for the number of covers. *Five thousand* was the answer. Ah, I had never tackled such a large number before.

Hannelore Dawson came to see me and we had an immediate rapport since she is a native of Germany and I majored in German and have many good friends from Germany. In spite of the lovely atmosphere, I remember nervously devouring a number of biscuits full of butter and heavy cream and slathered with marmalade made from my three decorative calamondin orange trees. The more Hannelore told me about what she had in mind, the more I ate, out of sheer excitement and perhaps the unconscious knowledge that this project would take all my stamina and strength.

We settled on a menu which covered several of the French provinces. There was to be confit, leg of lamb smothered with garlic and parsley, chicken with forty garlic cloves, and an orange tart. It would be easy going, I thought, because I had been serving these in my restaurant for years and was very familiar with the preparations. I knew that nothing could happen.

Well, some things did happen. First, I had to explain to the cooks what I had in mind. I expected to find cooks like students at a cooking school—enthusiastic, bright, and eager to learn new things. Not so here. The cooks were the regular cooks of most university kitchens, some in their late sixties, with habits as old as they were, and those habits were hard to break. Another challenge, I told myself!

To complicate matters, there was not one central kitchen, there were three. I put on my nurse's shoes for the marathon from kitchen to kitchen during the three days we prepared for the big feast. Everything seemed to happen all at once as we redesigned recipes originally created to serve 12 to serve 5000, and just as quickly as the new recipes came off the computer, the food began coming off the kitchen benches at a terrific rate. There were really no problems in the meat kitchen, though we all got a good scare when quarts of valuable lamb pan gravy nearly fell into the dishwasher!

The bake shop was another story. The orange tart which was to be filled with butter and orange curd was in jeopardy! How does one cope with the largest ball of creamed butter ever seen with several gallons of orange juice that refused to emulsify? I ended up heating the whole thing and binding it with cornstarch. And so went the last of our kitchen troubles.

But how would this French cuisine be accepted by the students? And who would honestly tell me whether the food for 5000 had the "Madeleine"-taste and texture. Then, in walked Richard Cattani, editor of the *Christian Science Monitor* and his wife, Jackie, a friend and former graduate of mine, and they gave me the feedback I was looking for: "Incredible, Madeleine," said Richard, "it tastes like your food!" So, the affair turned out to be a success after all. Oh, I am sure that a few students may have been a tad nonplussed by the "weird food." I had heard a few funny comments in passing but, all in all, it was a wonderful experience and a good time, if a bit tiring.

I was pleased when I heard that Hannelore has received an award for her new approach to college dining and I felt gratified to have been a part of such a positive experience.

May Hannelore's book herald a new era for institutional dining. I hope it helps all food service directors and their staffs who read and use it to realize that education need not only take place in libraries and lecture halls but can continue in the dining halls as well.

Madeleine Kamman
Director, School for American Chefs
Beringer Vineyards
St. Helena, California

PREFACE

❖

A quantity production cookbook must reflect major changes in national eating habits. It might be said that in past years food services have simply provided diners with adequate but unimaginative, insufficiently nutritious, and unbalanced meals. Food high in salt and fat but low in freshness and flavor was acceptable in too many dining rooms. In recent years, however, national interest in healthy diet and attractively served food has increased dramatically, and so has the commitment to better quality food and service in industry. I envision this cookbook helping to establish a new standard in quantity food recipes. The recipes call for less fat and salt without compromising taste. They make use of herbs and fresh products to make them more nutritious and more flavorful.

Over the past ten years I have introduced many of the recipes in this book to the University of New Hampshire Dining Services customers. The trend, when I started at UNH, was to more and more commercially prepared food items. At UNH we made the decision to return instead to basic "scratch" cooking. Time has proved we were on the right track, and the best institutions are now following our lead.

There is no excuse for serving bad food. Recipes that are properly developed and clearly written are a major step in eradicating bad food from institutional dining. Training and developing a staff that follows recipes accurately is another important step. This book will provide those recipes and will, I hope, offer some advice on how to begin training a staff to produce the recipes.

During the past 15 years I have poured my energies into taking the "institution" out of institutional dining by providing good food at all times and fine dining on occasion. By educating the staff and customer alike we were able to create a food service where our guests enjoyed different foods, learned to choose a balanced diet from a varied menu, and expected to eat well.

Providing the customer with meals that reflect the national trend toward fresh, wholesome foods, a greater interest in diverse ethnic cuisines, and less fatty and more nutritious meals will be a tremendous challenge. Customers are voicing nutrition concerns and are demanding a menu that is not only varied, but which offers freshness and quality.

Fresh, high quality food properly prepared, presented, and served will be the recipe for a successful food service operation in the next decade. It is my hope that *Great Food for Great Numbers* will provide food service organizations, caterers, and restaurants with a wide selection of quantity recipes to fit their operations and create interest and excitement in good food for great numbers.

Acknowledgments

❖

This book has grown out of 15 years' work with the Nutrition at Work Project, a child-nutrition training program, and with the dining services at the University of New Hampshire. First and foremost, I owe thanks to the many people I worked with, the adult learners I taught, and who, in turn, shared their hands-on knowledge with me, and, of course, to the thousands of students who ate in the UNH dining rooms and challenged my endurance and creativity.

To the UNH dining service staff I give special thanks for their support, cooperative effort, and dedication to implementing my recipes in our dining program. Their many suggestions and ideas improved the recipes and production notes included here, and I am truly grateful to have worked with so many wonderful people who shared my dedication to offering good food and service.

Grateful thanks to Jean Harley, manager of the University of New Hampshire commissary, who relentlessly pursues the best quality products—finding anything from 15 pounds of lemon grass to 4000 boneless breasts of duck. Her support and friendship gave me the courage to persevere; her wit created much needed laughter.

My appreciation to Cheryl Krantz, manager of the University of New Hampshire bakery, who always produces top quality baked goods, for her help in testing and photographing the bakery recipes. And I owe a very special thanks to Margaret Merz, R.D., University of New Hampshire nutritionist. She undertook the enormous task of helping me compile the nutrient data and brought to it the attention-to-detail and hard work needed to complete such a project successfully—without losing her wonderful sense of humor. I value her friendship and love. A thank you to Elizabeth Getts, my son Geoffrey, and my daughter Sarah for their help in the nutrition calculations.

I owe thanks to Pamela Scott Chirls, my sponsoring editor, and Liz Geller, my editorial supervisor at Van Nostrand Reinhold, who guided and encouraged me along the way, and thanks to Luisa Ann Cortissoz and Geraldine McGowan, my respective copy and production editors from Editorial Services of New England, who worked with me during the production stage of the book.

The beautiful photographs were produced in virtual marathon sessions by Dan Gair, who found many inventive ways to show off my food and barely took time out to eat the sets. My thanks to him and his assistants, Michelle Meno and Gary Langley.

A hug to my friends Celeste and Arthur DiMambro, who offered me their hospitality, the use of their kitchen, and even let me turn their house into a studio for part of the photography sessions. I will always cherish their love and friendship.

Thank you Drury Pifer, playwright and friend, who indefatigably tasted many samples and gave this book its name.

I am very lucky to have Chris Fauske, dear friend and writing coach, who edited my German accent out of the text.

I especially want to thank Madeleine Kamman, Margaret and Franco Romagnoli, Ken Hom, Michela Larson, Jim Dodge, and Paula Wolfert for sharing their talents, special gifts of communication, recipes, and good sense with me and the University of New Hampshire dining staff and students. They made it possible to create a link between the daily preparation of large quantities of everyday food and the world of higher cuisine.

Thank you Carl Dawson for living and eating this book with kind forbearance and love.

Technical Notes

Organization

The first part of this book discusses menu planning and offers menus for breakfast, brunch, lunch, and dinner. A three-week cycle menu for a college or university food service is included in the appendix. The large number of theme menus provided make planning for special events easier. Five menus by nationally known great cooks are also included along with detailed production notes.

The second part provides recipes from varied ethnic cuisines that rely on fresh ingredients, herbs, and spices for flavor. Many recipes use low-fat ingredients and oil instead of saturated fats. The recipes are organized in chapters that follow the traditional menu pattern—from appetizers to dessert—including a large chapter on vegetarian entrées. Within chapters the recipes are arranged alphabetically.

Production Notes

The recipes are presented with a brief introductory note followed, when appropriate, by a production note. The production notes provide ingredient and purchasing information, discusses preparation techniques and timing details, and makes suggestions for the creative use of leftover products in encore dishes.

Portions

The number of servings per recipe varies. The institutional standard of 100 servings is used for kettle products such as soups and stews. Many recipe yields are based on production techniques, batch requirements, and on the size of the production pans and serving utensils. For example, a 12″ × 20″ × 2″* pan containing a baked pasta dish such as lasagna, if cut 4″ × 7″ produces 28 standard portions. The servings per recipe will be divisible by either 28 or 14 (for half pans). Quiche is usually cut into six or eight wedges, making the servings per recipe 48 or 96. A recipe based on 50 or 100 portions would prepare enough extra product for 2 to 4 portions to each pan, increasing the cost per portion or not prepare enough product, making the portions skimpy. In some recipes the yield is based on use of a full can or case of a main ingredient, especially when it can be frozen or used as part of another recipe. Most baked goods portions are based on the amount of product the equipment at the University of New Hampshire bakery (where these recipes were tested) can handle at one time.

---

*The standard steam table (hotel pan) is actually closer to 2½″ in depth, but is referred to in the text as 2″ to avoid confusion with the ½ size pan.

Most recipe headers also list portion size, yield, serving utensil required, the serving pan size, cooking or refrigeration temperature, and time. To maintain good portion control, servers should be trained to weigh the food contained in ladles and spoons.

Ingredients

Ingredients are measured in weight rather than volume. This ensures accuracy and prevents "sloppy" mistakes in quantity production, making a standardized yield and an excellent product possible. Ingredient amounts are given as purchased, refuse from paring and trimming has not been deducted from the weight, unless so stated. The dry herbs used are crushed leaves and not the flavorless powdered kind; spices should be no more than 12 months old. Spices and herbs require a reliable ounce portion scale. A spice and herb chart that provides table and teaspoon measures per ounce of spice or herb can be found in the appendix.

Nutritional Information

One purpose of this book has been to provide food services with nutritionally sound recipes that follow recommended dietary goals. Many of the recipes have been fat and sodium modified. Often suggestions for further fat and sodium reductions have been added in the production notes. Each recipe includes nutritional data on calories, protein, fat, and sodium content. The data is based on the *USDA Handbook #8* and in a few instances on data from Bowes and Church's *Food Values of Portions Commonly Used*, 14th edition. Caloric values are given as per-recipe portion listed at the top of the recipe. Protein, carbohydrates, and fat values are listed in grams (one ounce is equivalent to approximately 28 grams.) Each gram of protein and carbohydrate provides four calories, and each gram of fat provides nine calories. The percentage figures show how much each nutrient component contributes to the total caloric value of the food portion. For example, two cottage cheese pancakes contain 259 calories:

    10.9 g protein provides 17% of calories
    37.7 g carbohydrates provide 59% of calories
    6.8 g fat provides 24% of calories

The total here equals 100 percent. This is not always the case. The *USDA Handbook #8* explains why: "The carbohydrate value is the difference between 100 and the sum of the percentages of water, protein, fat and ash. The value for carbohydrates includes crude fiber." In the food's caloric values the indigestible crude fiber has been deducted.

Further data is provided on fats by providing a breakdown of saturated, mono-unsaturated, and polyunsaturated fats in grams to assist menu planners who wish to plan diets low in saturated fats. Recipes low in saturated fats are also low in cholesterol. Notice that this breakdown of component fats will not equal the sum of total fat because of other unspecified components contained in the fat.

The sodium data is stated in milligrams. The daily minimum requirement for adults is 500 milligrams, as recommended in the 10th (1989) edition of the *Recommended*

Dietary Allowances (RDAs). For adults, a daily intake of not more than 3000 milligrams or three grams is a desirable dietary goal.

Encore Presentations

> *"The most common mistake made with leftovers is to try to preserve the food in its original form."* Jacques Pepin, *Everyday Cooking with Jacques Pepin*

I could not agree more with the above quote, and I instituted a rule at UNH that (with very few exceptions) no leftover food was to be served in its original form. That did not mean covering yesterday's baked herb chicken with a barbecue sauce. It meant turning the overproduced food with great creativity into a genuine "encore" dish: *Encore* because the food was so good the first time, it deserved a second appearance.

Any food that can be identified by a guest as yesterday's lunch or dinner reduces in value every item placed next to it, no matter how fresh or good. The customer only notices that, "Aha, they serve old food here," overlooking the effort that has just gone into the 95% of the dishes that are fresh and newly prepared.

Even though some foods taste better reheated, they should not be part of your new offerings. In a college food service they can be set up for self-service in a chafing dish in the dining room. There they take on the aura of a gift—happily enjoyed by the customers, yet still saving the operation money on an all-you-can-eat meal plan system.

One of the first uses of encore foods is in home style soups. Replace the soup cans and dried fatty powders with economical and tasty soups produced from the varied bits of meats, vegetables, and cooked starches always found in abundance in a professional kitchen. See Home Style Soups in Chapter 4 for a detailed discussion.

Breakfast pancake batter can be enriched with eggs and thinned with soda to make thin crepes that can envelope many savory leftovers. Add leftover vegetables to leftover cheese sauce with a few fresh herbs and, *voila*, you have genuinely good vegetarian crepes made from food that might have spoiled in the refrigerator or which if placed, reheated, on the steam table might have spoiled your marketing.

Leftover properly steamed vegetables can be made into pickled salads for the salad bar and moist roast meats into sandwiches or salad plates.

Many recipes require partially-prepared food and the wise manager checks the menu and may purposely steam excess rice for later use. Devise a system of symbols on your weekly menu that draw attention to encore use of foods in recipes. This will save time, labor, and money.

In the recipe text I have made extensive references to appropriate uses of encore foods. I encourage you to think about leftovers not as a chore to deal with but as a stimulating force to creative cooking. I highly recommend Pepin's above-quoted book; he is truly inventive with encore foods.

—1—

THE MENU RUNS THE SHOW

The menu is an all-important component to the success of any food service operation. In this chapter I discuss menu planning and offer some sample menus that use the recipes from this book. A few standard recipes that are found in most recipe files but not in this cookbook are sometimes included.

Menu Planning

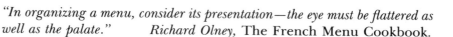

> *"In organizing a menu, consider its presentation—the eye must be flattered as well as the palate."* Richard Olney, The French Menu Cookbook.

Menu planning for large groups of people is a challenging and ultimately rewarding task that demands creativity. The basic requirements of successful menu planning include a solid understanding of food and nutrition, a knowledge of your staff's skills, adequate equipment and facilities to work with, a sense of cost controls, and, most importantly, an understanding of the people to be served. Books that delve into this area of menu planning have already been written and I will not add to that body of work here. Instead, I have made suggestions throughout the book about successful combinations of texture, color, shape, and form of foods and complementary methods of preparation.

The sample menus presented in this chapter keep basic menu planning principles in mind, are nutritionally balanced, and use the recipes found in this book. All the menus provide delicious choices for vegetarians, and I have been careful to specify within the vegetarian menus those recipes that include fish or egg products and those that do not.*

An institutional menu, in contrast to a fixed restaurant menu, completely changes three times a day. This demands a flexible, well-trained, professional staff committed to preparing good food in safe and sanitary kitchens. There should be an emphasis on fresh food, which can be cheaper as well as more flavorful than prepared products. And there should be a dedication to offering dishes with reduced

---

*All breakfast, brunch, appetizers, and dinners have vegetarian choices, but not all the lunches. Lunches that do offer vegetarian choices are marked with a V.

fat, less salt, and no overcooking. Constant vigilance in preventing waste is essential to any food service, and the proper utilization of leftover or over-produced food should be a major concern. The Technical Notes discuss using encore foods in more detail. Such goals as these can only be achieved in a working environment that emphasizes cooperative effort, efficient use of labor, and adequate training.

People living in an institutional setting rely on the food service for their nutritional well-being. The responsibility of the menu planner is therefore grave, and demands menus that will meet the total nutritional requirements of the guests. Planning alone doesn't guarantee success, however. It must be followed through by establishing high standards for procurement, production, and service of quality food.

Cooking from "scratch" may seem a backward move in a world of commercially prepared foods, but freshness and basic preparation is essential to good cooking at any level. Developing menus that balance the use of convenience foods with time-consuming preparations will not overload personnel; rather, it will heighten their interest and foster pride in their work.

Offering a large and varied selection of highly nutritious food items encourages the resident diner to eat a well-balanced diet. If this variety is coupled with an extensive and interesting nutrition awareness program, an institutional food service will have met its responsibilities to its customers.

The sample menus include a cycle menu for a college food service (see the Appendix), and other menus for catering, business, and industrial cafeterias, and for occasional breaks from the cycle menu. The appetizer menus are for parties, receptions, banquets, and special events.

Special events are essential in keeping resident diners happy. Even the most delicious food becomes boring if offered daily. A successful institution will not only feed but entertain its diners. This can be accomplished with such lavish events as described in the Great Cooks on Campus section or with small, inventive, monotony breakers, such as a candlelight breakfast or an unexpected hors d'oeuvre table offered for free grazing. None of this will make any difference, however, unless the food looks and tastes good.

Breakfast Menus

❖

Here are some breakfast menus that offer choices for the light and heavy eater. Some standard egg dishes are included.

❖

Orange Juice/Tomato Juice/Honeydew Melon
Granola
Apple Ginger Whole Wheat Muffins/Brioche Bread
Potato Pancakes with Applesauce
Eggs Diablo

❖

Granola cereal, sweet Georgia muffins, and old-fashioned buttermilk scones provide a breakfast full of complex carbohydrates.

Orange Juice/Cranberry Juice/Fresh Grapefruit Halves
Sunshine Breakfast Drink
Oatmeal Scones/Health Bread
Cottage Cheese Pancakes with Hot Raspberries
Scrambled Eggs

Orange Juice/Grapefruit Juice/Fresh Strawberries
Assorted Dry Cereals
Sweet Georgia Muffins/Oatmeal Bread
Apple Raisin Blintzes
Turkey Sausage Patties with Fried Eggs

Orange Juice/Vegetable Juice/Cantaloupe
Hot Oatmeal/Granola with Banana
Raisin Scones/Multigrain Bread
Warm Cornbread/Boston Baked Breakfast Beans
Poached Eggs

Orange Juice/Apple Juice/Kiwi Fruit
Low-fat Yogurt with Seasonal Berries or Fruit
Sour Cream Coffee Cake/Russian Bread
Johnny Cakes with Hot Blueberry Sauce
Baked Potato Omelet

Assorted Juices/Assorted Fresh Fruit
Bagels with Yogurt Cheese Herb Spread
Buttermilk Scones/Toscano Bread
Buckwheat Cakes with Maple Syrup
Asparagus Tomato Quiche

Brunch Menus

Brunch is a more leisurely meal than breakfast and is especially enjoyed by students in a residential food service. The brunch menu can include any number of lunch or breakfast entrées, as long as they are harmonized, and the kitchen's production capabilities are considered.

I have selected three menus, ranging from simple to a meal for a special occasion. The third menu can be presented buffet style.

Assorted Juices and Fresh Fruits
Sour Cream Coffee Cake and Zucchini Bread
French Toast/Scrambled Eggs/Bacon
Apple Raisin Blintzes
Turkey Divan
Assorted Cereals and Granola

Orange Juice/Tomato Juice
Grapefruit Halves/Honeydew Melon Wedges
Sweet Georgia Muffins/Creamy Yogurt Biscuits
Yeast Pancakes with Bran and Walnuts—served with Maple Syrup and Hot Cinnamon Apple Slices
Eggs Diablo/Fresh Tomato and Pepper Omelet
Alsatian Ham and Onion Pizza/Broccoli Cheese Bagel
Assorted Cereals and Granola

Fruit Platter, Honeydew, Cantaloupe, Fresh Pineapple, and Strawberries
Oatmeal Scones/Whole Wheat Bran Raisin Muffins
Baked Potato Omelet/Turkey Sausage Patties
Spinach Tofu Crepes
Asparagus Tomato Quiche
Buckwheat Cakes with Hot Blueberries
Bagels with Yogurt Walnut Orange Spread

Lunch Menus

For lunch in an institutional setting I like to offer a soup and make-your-own deli sandwich setup, plus one hot dish and one meatless option. This option can be a casserole, a salad, or a sandwich. The labor-saving setup of the make-your-own deli sandwich is accomplished by having the deli attendant serve the customer four ounces of sliced cheeses, cold cuts, a protein salad (such as tuna), or a combination of any thereof. The customers then help themselves to assorted breads, lettuce, tomatoes, and condiments to make their own sandwiches. The menus that follow here are for catered luncheons.

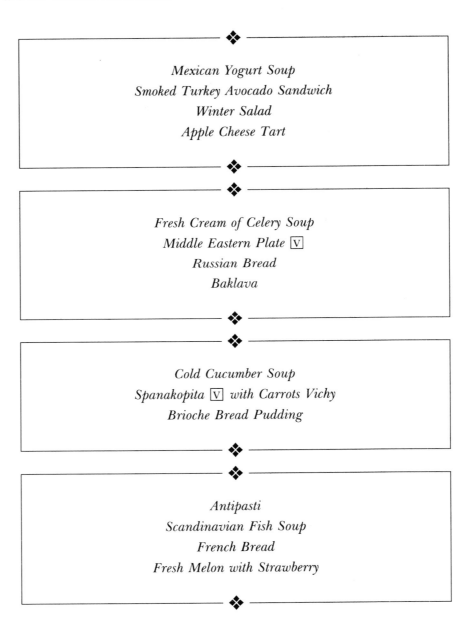

Mexican Yogurt Soup
Smoked Turkey Avocado Sandwich
Winter Salad
Apple Cheese Tart

Fresh Cream of Celery Soup
Middle Eastern Plate [V]
Russian Bread
Baklava

Cold Cucumber Soup
Spanakopita [V] *with Carrots Vichy*
Brioche Bread Pudding

Antipasti
Scandinavian Fish Soup
French Bread
Fresh Melon with Strawberry

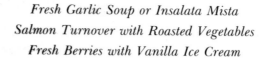

Fresh Garlic Soup or Insalata Mista
Salmon Turnover with Roasted Vegetables
Fresh Berries with Vanilla Ice Cream

Black Bean Salad
Tofu Burger on a Whole Wheat Bun V /*Muffaletta Sandwich*
Sautéed Cherry Tomatoes with Basil
Hazelnut Cookies

Panzanella
Cheese Soufflé V /*Breast of Chicken Tarragon*
Ratatouille V
Multigrain Bread
Poppyseed Cake

Italian Mozzarella amd Tomato Salad V
Tortellini Gratinati V
Wilted Spinach with Lemon
Toscano Bread
Watermelon Slices

Banquet Salad Plate
Fruit and Chicken Caribbean
Stuffed Zucchini V
Fresh Green Beans with Sautéed Peppers
Steamed Rice
Sourdough Bread
Raspberry Yogurt Pie

Dinner Menus

Institutional food services should provide at least three dinner entrée choices, including one for the vegetarian diner. The menu selections must complement each other, should use a variety of equipment, and should balance the labor it takes to produce them. I selected dinner menus suitable for catered functions; the last one is to be served buffet style. All menus provide vegetarian entrée alternatives; I also generally add a starch or vegetable item that would satisfy someone who doesn't eat meat.

Potage Parmentier
Pork Loin Schnitzel/Swiss Breast of Chicken
Cornstuffed Red Bell Pepper
Egg Noodles with Minced Parsley
Italian Broccoli and Cauliflower
Parker House Rolls
Cappuccino Cake/Assorted Fresh Fruit

Zippy Avocado Soup
Chicken Limone/Veal and Sausage Cacciatorra
Polenta with Chunky Marinara Sauce
Asparagus Parmesan/Courgettes a la Latine
Toscano Bread
Meringata/Fresh Fruit Tart

Sesame Dressed Spinach Salad
Marinated Shark Steak/Beef Steak au Pil-Pil
Vegetable Strudel
Delicious Potatoes
Carrots Vichy/Peas and Lettuce
Freshly Baked Rolls
Apple Cheese Tart/Fresh Fruit in Season

Fresh Garlic Soup
Coq au Riesling/Salmon Baked in Lemon Sauce
Mushroom Cakes
Tortino di Verdure
Red and Green Pepper Sauté
Wilted Spinach with Lemon Zest
Multigrain Bread
Bourbon Chocolate Pecan Cake/Orange Slices

Banquet Salad Plate
Greek Lamb Roast/Swiss Breast of Chicken
Tiropita—Greek Three Cheese Strudel
Mushroom Risotto
Artichoke Hearts with Carrots/Fresh Green Beans
with Sautéed Peppers
French Bread
Raspberry Yogurt Pie/Assorted Fresh Fruit

Gazpacho
Roast Beef with Pizzaiola Sauce/Turkey Paillards
Monkfish Fillet Braised with Vegetables/Cream Cheese Soufflé
Riz à L'Americaine
Rutabaga/Stir-fried Vegetables
Buttery Brioche Rolls
Fresh Fruit, Chocolate Mounds, and Hazelnut Cookies*

*Serve this menu buffet style: A cold soup or salad should be placed at the table for the guests. The entrée, rice, and vegetable choices are set up at the buffet table. After plates have been cleared, fruit and cookies can be served family style.

Cycle Menus

❖

Cycle menus can be planned for weeks (three to six is common), a semester, or for the four seasons. Balance is crucial and customer preference must be the foremost guide. See the Appendix for a sample of a three-week cycle for a residential college food service. It takes customer preference into account, by providing a cheeseburger every week, but no other menu entrée is repeated.

Appetizer Menus

❖

I have selected three appetizer menus that offer contrasts in color, texture, and flavor. All have some cold and some hot foods and at least two items are low in calories. These menus make a great buffet for receptions or cocktail parties. They can also be served from trays. If the appetizer menu is followed by a full meal, consider the whole menu when planning appetizers. For example, do not serve chicken as an appetizer if it is part of the main course.

❖ Finger Foods

Presentation

For the tablecloths, choose school, theme or seasonal colors and use flowers, small napkins, and an elevated centerpiece as complements. If serving the menu on page 11, a pyramid of shrimp puff pastries would make a lively centerpiece. Pin ivy runners with flowers that extend from the elevated center to the lower table. Around the centerpiece, place differently-shaped platters of cherry tomatoes, white pizza squares, olives with toothpicks in a bowl, a rectangular platter of cucumber sandwiches, a round platter piled high with chicken wings, neatly displayed melon pieces wrapped with prosciutto, and a bowl of hummus surrounded by zucchini sticks.

MENU PRODUCTION NOTES: Olives and chicken wings can be marinated two to three days in advance. Thaw commercial puff pastry slowly in the refrigerator. Hummus, shrimp filling, and sandwich spread can be made the day before. Select very lean prosciutto and slice it paper thin. Order cherry tomatoes that are about one-inch in diameter and small zucchini. On the day they will be served, stuff tomatoes, chill sandwiches, arrange melon and prosciutto, fill puff pastry, make pizza, and bake-off chicken wings, pastry, and pizza as needed.

Bulgur-stuffed Tomatoes
Cucumber Sandwiches
Hummus Dip with Zucchini Sticks
Black Marinated Olives
Prosciutto e Melone
Chinese Chicken Wings
Shrimp Puff Pastry
White Pizza

❖ Fork and Plate Required

Presentation

A long, narrow table is best to keep food close to the customer with appropriate service utensils to prevent unsightly spills. Plates, silverware, and napkins can be set up on a separate table or placed strategically in small groups. Small glass plates are especially attractive. Attractive jars or pitchers or small baskets could hold the forks.

Lavish flowers make a great centerpiece. A bouquet of helium balloons with potted plants would be another way to call attention to the appetizer buffet. Imaginative centerpieces could also celebrate the purpose of the gathering, for example an antique radio for a communications seminar, a cash register for a marketing group, or a violin or old 78-records for musicians.

A variety of differently shaped dishes and plates add to the presentation. The pot stickers and the yakitori must be served in an open chafing dish to keep them hot. Sushi can be displayed on a lacquered tray or mirror for dramatic effect. The spicy mushrooms are placed on a platter lined with washed pine or fir twigs to complement their woodsy origins and to set off the bright, hot peppers.

MENU PRODUCTION NOTES: Two days ahead, prepare the spicy mushrooms, check the ripeness of the avocados (leave hard ones at room temperature and refrigerate the soft ones). One day ahead, roast vegetables, cook eggs and rice, peel eggs and refrigerate them in cold water, make deviled egg filling (in this timesaving version, yolks are left in the halves). Prepare empañaditas, spicy peanut sauce, and skewer and marinate the yakitori. On the day they will be served, make dipping sauce, stuff eggs and avocados, roll sushi, bake-off empañaditas and yakitori, and roast vegetables.

❖

Avocado Wedges Stuffed with Shrimp
Chilled Roasted Vegetables
Danish Deviled Eggs
Vegetarian Sushi with Wasabi
Empañaditas
Pot Stickers with Dipping Sauce
Spicy Mushrooms
Yakitori

❖

❖ It's Italian!

For an Italian theme dinner, an antipasti table sets the perfect mood. Place the table near the entrance in full view of the arriving guests, as a trattoria would do in Italy. Red, white, and green tablecloths represent the colors of Italy. Posters or pictures of Italy are effective theme decorations. Food focal points are the antipasti with the cold cuts and cheeses, the prosciutto e melone, and the mozzarella tomato platter surrounded with marinated olives and vegetables. The caponata (a cold cooked eggplant dip) is complemented by the crostini. Crostini fontina are excellent hot or at room temperature. A display of very long bread sticks in baskets or earthenware pitchers adds a touch of drama to the presentation.

Nothing on the menu has to be served very hot. I prefer serving the chilled calamari instead, to avoid any last minute preparation. See color plate **1**.

MENU PRODUCTION NOTES: Two days ahead, marinate the black and green olives and roasted peppers. Prepare the caponata and spicy mushrooms. Check avocados and honeydew for ripeness. The day before the event, slice the meats and cheeses, and roast, cover, and refrigerate the vegetables. Clean, blanch, and slice the squid. Bake the bread sticks and store them covered with a clean towel. Do not wrap them in plastic or they will get soft. Toast the bread slices for crostini and cover with parchment paper and store.

On the day they will be served, prepare tomato platters, taking care not to chop the basil until you are ready to take the platters to the buffet. Arrange the melon and antipasti. Top crostini with shredded fontina and bake. Assemble the chilled calamari, caponata, spicy mushrooms, bread sticks, and olives.

Antipasti
Bread Sticks
Caponata
Chilled Calamari or Fried Calamari
Crostini Fontina
Marinated Kalamata Olives
Marinated Green Olives
Mozzarella Tomato Platters
Prosciutto e Melone
Roasted Red Peppers
Spicy Mushrooms

Special Event or Theme Menus

A candlelight breakfast, an appetizer table, a pasta or pizza toppings bar, an unannounced picnic on a beautiful day, or an ice cream smorgasbord feast are all ways to keep the customer in an institutional setting happy.

A special dinner event that sets the mood with festive decorations, theme music, and superb food can be managed at least once a month and is a memorable occasion. Here are a few ideas and menus.

MEXICAN FIESTA MENU

Vegetable Empañaditas
Mexican Yogurt Soup or Sopa de Pollo y Nuez
Beef and Bean Quesadilla/Chicken Tacos
Fish de Lima
Cheese Enchilada Casserole
Rice/Spicy Red Beans
Jalapeño Cheese Biscuits/Warm Flour Tortillas
Fresh Salsa
Shredded Lettuce, Sliced Tomatoes, and Jicama
Melon Wedges

INDIAN SAMPLER MENU

Indian Potato Pastries

Raita (Cucumber Yogurt Salad)

Mulligatawney Soup

Tandoori Murgh/Chicken Curry with Potatoes

Indian Dal/Potato Eggplant Curry

Curried Cucumbers

Steamed Rice

Chapatis, Phulka, or Naan

Almond Cookies

GREEK AND MIDDLE EASTERN MENU

Bulgur-stuffed Tomatoes/Hummus Dip

Lentil Soup

Greek Moussaka/Greek Lamb Roast/Kefta in Yogurt Sauce

Spanakopita/Greek Bean Bake

Eggplant "Mardikian"

Artichoke Hearts with Carrots

Armenian Salad/Greek Salad/Tabouli

Baklava

JAPANESE BENTO BOX MENU*

Udon Noodles in Dashi Broth

Vegetarian Sushi with Wasabi

Yakitori

Grilled Sweet and Sour Tenderloin

Steamed Fish with Vegetables

Fried Rice with Whole Wheat Spaghetti

Japanese Soybeans

Vegetable Tempura

Hot and Sour Cucumber Salad

*Select six recipes for a simpler version of this menu.

SCANDINAVIAN SMORGASBORD MENU

Cucumber Sandwiches/Danish Deviled Eggs
Spicy Mushrooms/Marinated Green Olives
Shrimp Puff Pastry/Chilled Poached Chicken with Green Sauce
Chilled Marinated White Fish/Oven Poached Salmon
Super Hero
Delicious Salad/German Warm Marinated Potato Salad
Currant Buns/Multigrain Bread
Assorted Cheeses and Butter Cookies

VEGETARIAN FEAST MENU

Chilled Roasted Vegetables
Green Velvet Soup
Gateau of Crepes/Pizza Rustica with Spinach
Black Beans Louisiana/Arroz Blanco con Chiles
Peppers with Mushrooms and Onions
Insalata Mista
Health Bread/Oatmeal Bread
Apfelkuchen
Grapes and Pears with Cheese

Great Cooks on Campus

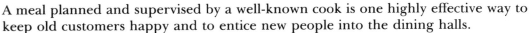

A meal planned and supervised by a well-known cook is one highly effective way to keep old customers happy and to entice new people into the dining halls.

Bringing a nationally known cook or baker into a quantity production kitchen requires flexibility and advanced planning, but the excitement, fun, and learning that are fostered by the event are well worth the effort. Your staff will enjoy working with someone whose book they may own or whose cooking program they watch on television. I initiated just such a program at the University of New Hampshire. Our students enjoyed these events at regular meal prices, the invited public paid from ten to twelve dollars for their meals.

Each event from the Great Cooks on Campus series is described in detail later in the chapter. What follows is a general outline, approximate time sequence, and the necessary steps to take to initiate such a program. I hope it will encourage others to duplicate such an event in their food service.

Identify some cooks with regional or national reputations whom you would like to invite to your kitchen. It is a good idea to select several candidates and contact them no later than six months in advance, sooner if possible. Expect many conflicts in finding a mutually agreeable timetable. Set the date, write a contract, and inform the dining staff of the arrangements. Introduce the great cook to the staff via video, cookbook, or magazine article. Should you select a local cook, display a menu from the cook's restaurant, and then take crucial support staff on a tour of the place, and stay for lunch or dinner. Let your own enthusiasm infect others, and involve everyone as much as possible.

Start the publicity as soon as the contract is signed to foster the anticipation of staff and customers. To advertise the Great Cooks Series at the University of New Hampshire we asked for help from the campus news bureau. They prepared news releases with photos and contacted newspaper editors, food writers, and radio and television stations.

Plan to send information to trade journal editors in the food service business. Prepare table tents, write articles in your menu newsletter (start one if you do not have one), and add notices to your menu boards. Design a logo to establish an identity for the series, and have glossy posters printed up. Two weeks prior to the event hang up the posters in as many prominent places as possible. In a college or university, for example, all residential and academic buildings should be posted. Posters should be put up at off-campus locations, such as local markets and community centers to inform the public of the event.

Scheduling staff training is difficult. It is a complex task to mesh the visiting chef's travel plans with time constraints, staff work schedules, the availability of kitchens and work spaces, and the need to continue regular food production. However, this kind of program greatly motivates the staff to superior performance and all the obstacles can be overcome.

Plan to include a lecture or a food demonstration by the visiting cook. It works both as a public service gesture and as a merchandising tool. One of my goals was to draw attention to the fact that, on a college campus, the dining service is part of the educational environment. It should contribute not only to the students' well-being but also to their education.

UNH Dining presents

GREAT COOKS ON CAMPUS

Asian Influences on American Cuisine
WEDNESDAY　APRIL 20, 1988　7:30 P.M.
Parsons Hall, Room L101
FREE

Lecturer: KEN HOM

Sponsored by:　The President's Office
　　　　　　　Vice President for Academic Affairs Office
　　　　　　　The Student Affairs Office
　　　　　　　Dean of College of Liberal Arts
　　　　　　　Center for International Perspectives
　　　　　　　Whittemore School of Business & Economics - Hotel Administration
　　　　　　　UNH Dining

A Feast Fit for the Last Emperor of China
in the UNH Dining Halls
THURSDAY　APRIL 21, 1988　6:30-7:15 P.M.
Upstairs Huddleston
Public is invited to attend and meet Ken Hom
Price: $12:00

UNH Dining presents

GREAT COOKS ON CAMPUS

Ethnic Influences on French Provincial Cuisine
WEDNESDAY　APRIL 15, 1987　7:30 PM
Parsons Hall, Room L 101
FREE

Lecturer:　MADELEINE KAMMAN

Sponsored by:　　Dean of Student Affairs (Gregg Sanborn)
　　　　　　　　Vice President for Academic Affairs (Richard Hersh)
　　　　　　　　Dean of College of Liberal Arts (Stuart Palmer)
　　　　　　　　Center for International Perspectives
　　　　　　　　Hotel Administration (Raymond Goodman)
　　　　　　　　UNH Dining

Fabulous French Feast for 5,000 in the UNH Dining Halls
THURSDAY　APRIL 16, 1987　6:30-7:30 PM
Upstairs Huddleston
Public is invited to attend and meet Ms. Kamman - $10.00

These posters were designed for the Great Cooks on Campus program.

We brought five Great Cooks on Campus to UNH during my tenure. A brief summary of each event and menu follows. The recipes are identified with a diamond in the table of contents and have been included in the chapters by menu category. Different approaches to training and service will become apparent. All of the events proved popular with the students, brought the community into the university dining rooms, and were exciting and fun for the staff.

Fabulous French Feast for Five Thousand
Madeleine Kamman

Madeleine Kamman, famous for her public television series "Madeleine Cooks," was the first person invited to the Great Cooks series. I contacted Ms. Kamman and explained what I was planning to do. Her superb talent, great reputation, and exacting standards would, I believed, help make the idea work and would inspire the dining services at UNH to move away from an institutional food service mentality.

We planned the menu one January and by February, Ms. Kamman's recipes arrived, written in her clear and precise longhand. Since the recipes generally yielded only four to eight portions, I began converting the recipes to weight measures and expanding the quantities. All of the recipes were added to our computer database. We tested some of the production methods, and the bakery staff tested and adjusted formulas for the expanded recipes.

We made lists of the necessary ingredients and our commissary went to work trying to locate such items as 4,000 duck legs for the confit, and the rendered duck fat in which to bake them. We alerted the produce market in Boston that we would require unusually large amounts of fresh rosemary and basil. We spent a great deal of time with the purchasing staff to ensure their commitment to the project. Their help was to be a major factor in our success.

Three days before the dinner Ms. Kamman came to UNH to train the staff. On Friday evenings UNH's customer count drops significantly and we closed one of our service units to have it available for training. That evening we selected "top your own

Madeleine Kamman instructing bakers in making fougasse.

FABULOUS FRENCH FEAST FOR FIVE THOUSAND

Soupe au Pistou
White bean soup with garlic and parsley

Rolled Leg of Lamb Provençale
Roasted boneless lamb with a garlic and herb stuffing

Magret de Canard aux Noix
Sauteed skinless, boneless duck breast with a creamy nut sauce

Confit of Duck Legs
Duck legs dredged in spices baked in a fat bath

Beefsteak au Pil-Pil
Grilled sirloin strip steaks topped with a herb butter pat

Poulet aux Quarante Gousses d'Ail
Chicken with forty cloves of garlic

Polenta with Creamed Mushrooms—Vegetarian
Cornmeal casserole with fontina cheese and creamed
mushrooms

Courgettes à la Latine
Zucchini with black olives

Wilted Spinach with Lemon Zest

Riz à L'Americaine
Tomato rice with fresh tarragon, parsley and chervil

Fougasse   French Bread   Pogne
Flat bread   Sweet egg dough

Orange Tart

Serpent aux Pommes at aux Prunes
Strudel filled with apples and brandied prunes

Brie   Compeaux   Muenster   Cantal   Boursin
French cheeses

Assorted Fresh Fruit

pizza" for the dinner menu. It is not only popular but can also be easily prepared by student employees. This freed all the cooks and supervisory staff for training.

Ms. Kamman showed us how to debone duck, prepare lamb, bake the polenta, make the confit of duck legs and chicken with forty cloves of garlic. We mixed the herb butter for the beefsteak au pil-pil, simmered the duck bones with veal knuckles for stock, and sautéed the spinach with thin slivers of lemon rind. The cooks gained new skills and learned the methods necessary to produce this feast and appreciated the complexity of the herbs and spices used in French cuisine.

The food sampling at the close of the training session afforded everyone a chance to taste the food as it should be prepared, and provided a rare opportunity for the management and kitchen staff from three units to enjoy a meal together.

Small adjustments had to be made to some of the recipes, but none was large enough to require a change in the purchase orders, and with the help of our computerized menu system the revisions were an easy task. The revised recipes were reprinted and sent to the production staff in all dining units.

A lecture by the visiting great cook was part of this program. It was open to both the campus community and the public and was scheduled the evening before the feast in a centrally located academic building. The lecture was sponsored by the president's office and by four academic departments. Ms. Kamman discussed "Ethnic Influences on French Provincial Cuisine." The lecture drew an enthusiastic crowd of about 100 people and was well-covered by the state and local press.

The dinner the following evening was free to students on a meal plan. The public was invited to attend at a cost of $10.00 per person. We invited the Board of University Trustees and those administrators who had given us support with this project.

Ms. Kamman supervised the preparation in all the dining units the day before the event and on the day itself. As we moved from kitchen to kitchen we reviewed "prep" with the production managers; consulted with the cooks; and instructed the bakers on forming a proper *fougasse*. We admired the table settings, flowers, and room decorations of the service staff; checked the ripeness of the fruit and cheeses; and tasted all dishes when they were ready to be served to the 5,000 guests. The service was cafeteria style, with separate displays of bread and cheese and desserts. Ms. Kamman graciously talked with students during the meal and greeted many of the guests who had joined our regular student diners.

The press gave the event excellent coverage and favorable notices. Sally Tager, reviewing the dinner in the "Living Section" of the *Christian Science Monitor*, wrote: "The food was—dare I say it?—A Fabulous and Fantastic French Feast for Five Thousand."

MENU PRODUCTION NOTES: The recipes are dishes from the Provence, Savoie, and Gascony regions of France. I have added production notes and procurement information where appropriate in the recipe section. Here is an outline of an overall production timetable for this event.

Bakers: Bake off pie shells for orange tart anytime it is feasible as long as they can be stored wrapped and protected from dampness or can be frozen. Four days before the dinner start the leaven for the French bread. Candy the orange slices two to three days ahead of time. The *pogne* can be baked anytime because it freezes very well. One day before the dinner, prepare the filling for *serpent aux pommes et aux prunes*. On the day of the event, fill and bake off the *serpent*. Make the filling for the tart, pour into prebaked shells, and bake until filling is cooked. Prepare and bake the fougasse and French bread (same dough). Thaw the pogne.

Cooks: Anytime beforehand make the herb butter for the beefsteak au pil-pil and freeze it. Prepare the spice mixture for the confit.

On the day before the dinner, make the soup, trim the lamb and spread it with persillade, then roll, tie, and refrigerate it. Make the stock using ribs and trimmings. Rub the duck legs with confit spices and refrigerate overnight. Slice fontina and mushrooms for the polenta. On the day of the event prepare rice to pre-steaming stage and steam as needed; slice zucchini and wash spinach; prepare lemon rind for spinach; cook and assemble the polenta for final baking. Roast the lamb and prepare the gravy. Bake chicken, duck confit, and polenta progressively. Melt butter with lemon juice and rind for spinach. Reheat soup. Make the full amount of sauce for all the duck breasts, but grill duck breasts as needed. Refrigerate the pil-pil butter. Cook beef steaks to order. Sauté zucchini. Steam rice and spinach (barely) as needed throughout the service time.

❖

The Romagnoli's Table
Margaret and G. Franco Romagnoli

The second event in the Great Cooks series took place one October, with Margaret and Franco Romagnoli inviting students and guests to table. The authors of four cookbooks, hosts of the wonderful PBS television program "The Romagnoli's Table," and owners of the restaurant by the same name in Boston, they were uniquely suited to the task. The Romagnolis are very serious about the authenticity of their Italian cuisine but light-hearted when teaching their recipes. The production staff really enjoyed learning with them.

We used the summer downtime to accomplish our training and the Romagnolis worked with the bakers and cooks in an all day session. A classroom was set up in a kitchen that was not being used. We prepared all the dishes that had unfamiliar ingredients or introduced new methods to the staff. We experimented with preparation techniques and adjusted recipes accordingly. For example, the pollo alla cacciatora is usually sautéed first and then braised, but we found that browning the chicken in the oven and then adding the rest of the ingredients to the pan not only saved time and labor but made no difference to the final taste.

The lecture by the Romagnolis included a cooking demonstration that educated and entertained the audience. Entitled "Cucina Italiana: An Historical Perspective," it explained the historical reasons for the development of regional cuisines in Italy and demonstrated the hard "semolina" facts of good pasta-making.

On the day of the dinner, the dining room tables were covered with red, white, and green tablecloths (the colors of the Italian flag) and decorated with red roses and white daisies with green ferns. Posters of Italian cities and landscapes were hung around the room, and the music of Vivaldi played softly.

The Romagnolis gave their considerable attention to all aspects of the preparation and serving of the meal. Antipasti were displayed on the salad bars. Hot food was served from the serving line. Breads and soups were set up separately and the dolce was highlighted on a dessert table with freshly brewed Italian roast coffee. Large buckets of ice kept bottles of sparkling white and red grape juice icy cold.

The menus were printed on blank menu stock from the Romagnolis' restaurant, and they were set on each table so that the diners could read the English translation of the Italian dishes (see the reproduction of the Romagnoli menu on page 22). The staff proudly wore aprons imprinted with the theme title and date of the event. These aprons were given to each staff member to keep as a memento and as a token of appreciation for the hard work which had been both well and cheerfully done.

The Romagnolis graciously greeted students, faculty, and community guests, who all left happy and full of praise for the meal. The next day's student newspaper quoted a freshman's view of the dinner: "It was fantastic. I tried everything there twice. They should come back next year."

MENU PRODUCTION NOTES: The Romagnolis' recipes represent classic Italian dishes from many regions of Italy with some very inventive touches of their own. Large operations can spread the workload over several days, which leaves extra time for decoration and essential last minute preparations.

Bakers: Several days ahead of time, bake meringues and pound cake layers. Toast almonds. Two days beforehand, whip cream and assemble the meringata and

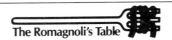

Margaret & Franco Romagnoli

GREAT COOKS ON CAMPUS

UNIVERSITY OF NEW HAMPSHIRE DINING

OCTOBER 12, 1987

MENU

Antipasti

Caponata
sweet and sour eggplant with capers and olives

Mozzarella e pomodori
fresh mozarella and ripe tomatoes

Cima alla Genovese
cold slices of veal stuffed with pork, ham and pistachio nuts

Spuma di fegatini in gelatina
creamy chicken liver mousse in aspic

Prosciutto e Melone
thin slices of Parma ham with honeydew melon

Antipasto di Mare
shrimp, squid and seafood flakes marinated with lemon juice and olive oil

Insalata di Riso alla Torinese
rice salad with tuna, olives, peppers and capers

Insalata di Pasta
pasta salad with shrimp, peppers, cucumber and olives

Roasted Peppers
Charbroiled peppers in olive oil with garlic

Marinated Artichokes, Marinated Mushrooms
in lemon juice with parsley and oregano

Minestre

Pasta e Fagioli
garlic flavored pasta and bean soup

Primi Piatti

Tortellini Gratinati
cheese filled pasta baked in a creamy cheese sauce

Secondi Piatti

Calamari all'Appetitosa
tender rings of squid sauteed in olive oil with garlic, hot pepper and parsley

Pollo alla Cacciatora
chicken baked with rosemary, vinegar and white wine

Manzo alla Pizzaiola
roasted slices of beef with tomatoes, garlic and oregano

Tortiono di Verdure
layers of eggplant, zucchini, potatoes, tomatoes, cheese and toasted bread crumbs

Contorni

Carote al Marsala
carrots glazed with marsala wine

Broccoli e Cavolfiore
broccoli and cauliflower with olive oil and lemon

DOLCE

Cassata alla Siciliana
layered sponge cake with cream and ricotta

Cannoli
pastry filled with ricotta cream and candied fruit or cocoa

Meringata
meringues and toasted almond with frozen whipped cream

The menu from The Romagnoli's Table.

freeze. (Do not freeze for longer than two days.) One day ahead of time, slice pound cake, make ricotta filling, and assemble cassata. Refrigerate. On the day of the event, bake toscano bread, prepare ricotta cream, and fill cannoli.

Cooks: Two to three days beforehand, clean and blanch the squid. Prepare the caponata, roasted peppers, and marinated artichokes. Prepare the chicken liver mousse. Do not attempt the cima alla Genovese unless an experienced chef is available. To save time and ensure quality we had one kitchen prepare this dish for all the other units.

The day before the meal, prepare the rice and pasta salads and the bean soup. Peel and seed the melon. Slice the mozzarella. Cap and trim the roasts.

On the day of the event, prepare the antipasto di mare, slice the tomatoes, and assemble mozzarella platters. Set up antipasti table on a salad bar or on ice. Make the tortellini gratinati, bake off as needed. Roast beef and slice, make the sauce, and arrange neatly in pans. Bake the chicken. Assemble tortiono di verdure and bake all at once to allow the flavors to develop, keep warm. Prepare the carrots and bake as needed. The blanched squid is cooked to order in minutes. Steam broccoli and cauliflower as needed.

A Feast Fit for the Last Emperor of China
Ken Hom

Ken Hom, "one of the world's greatest authorities on Chinese Cooking," according to *The New York Times*, was the third great cook in the series. He is the author of many cookbooks, among them the critically acclaimed, *Ken Hom's East Meets West Cuisine*. His television series, "Ken Hom's Chinese Cookery," was seen worldwide and the accompanying book was a best seller.

As the *San Francisco Examiner* reported in an interview he gave them after the event at UNH: "With all his experience, Hom had never been asked to whip up an 18-course meal for 5,000."

After Mr. Hom had agreed to participate and provided the title for the feast, I met with him in Berkeley, California in February. We discussed and settled on the menu. Upon my return to UNH, the staff and I started to test and expand the recipes for the great numbers we feed. Then the hunt for some of the more exotic ingredients began. Fresh lemongrass had us stumped for a while, but we managed with the help of a Chinese wholesale purveyor to secure the needed 15 pounds.

Mr. Hom's incredible skills and his teaching talent made this event perhaps the most pleasant for the staff. He put everyone at ease with his calm cheerfulness and patience. Because Mr. Hom lived in California, it was impossible to set up a training session in advance of the event. It was decided to have Mr. Hom train the staff in each unit between Monday and Thursday, while they prepared for the event.

A new feature introduced with this event was a Peking duck tasting scheduled for each of the three nights before the feast in the dining units. Mr. Hom demonstrated how Peking duck is prepared for roasting to most of the dinner cooks early on Monday morning. We air dried the ducks with a fan and shipped 12 to each hall. The ducks were roasted hanging from hooks in a convection oven emptied of its racks. In each of the units Mr. Hom taught the cooks how to make Chinese pancakes to serve with the duck and how to make the traditional scallion brushes. At the same time he discussed all the dishes and explained the use of Chinese condiments and spices. He demonstrated how to make beef stir-fry on the griddle and supervised the making of the sauce for the barbecued ribs.

We offered Peking duck as a sample on a specially set up table in each of our three dining halls on successive nights. Each night Mr. Hom was the star in the dining room as he carved the brown, crisp ducks into neat pieces. Student employees quickly rolled the pieces in Chinese pancakes, along with a scallion brush and hoisin sauce, and handed them to the appreciative student crowd. It was not only fun but it advertised the event in such a way as to increase student anticipation for the real feast.

"Asian Influences on American Cuisine" was the title of Mr. Hom's lecture on the night before the feast. As usual it was free and open to the public and sponsored by several academic departments. Mr. Hom took his audience on a culinary tour of the Far East and provided insight into his own East/West cooking style.

To decorate the dining halls for the event, we used landscapes, fans, lanterns, screens and large Oriental-styled flower arrangements. Every diner was given a pair of chopsticks and a menu explaining the dishes. A Chinese employee provided us with signs in Chinese ideograms for the line and salad bars.

A FEAST FIT FOR THE LAST EMPEROR OF CHINA

Tangy Tomato Soup with Lemongrass
Chicken Wings in Black Bean Sauce
Cold Sichuan Noodles
Asparagus with Tangy Mustard Dressing
Green and White Jade Salad
Hot and Sour Cucumber Salad
Cold Green Bean Salad
Sesame-dressed Spinach Salad
Sweet and Sour Fish
Barbecued Ribs with a Spicy Sauce
Home Style Spicy Bean Curd
Stir-fried Orange Beef
Sichuan Fried Eggplant
Corn and Ginger Fried Rice
Fresh Fruit Compote
Almond Cookies
Lemon Tart with Candied Ginger

For four days, Mr. Hom had coached the staff with unflagging energy and enthusiasm and the result was superb food. An appreciative audience, including the president of the university, enjoyed this feast fit for an emperor. At the end of the evening, Mr. Hom graciously autographed copies of his book, which were available for sale in the dining room.

Mr. Hom's visit and the feast were covered in the food section of the *New York Times* and on National Public Radio's news program "All Things Considered."

MENU PRODUCTION NOTES: Mr. Hom's recipes blend Eastern and Western cuisines, which make them distinctly his own. Care was taken to produce for thousands, a product closely resembling the dishes designed to serve four to six people. I have fat-modified them further for this book without, I believe, loss of flavor.

Here again is an approximate timetable that should help alleviate the increased stress placed on the staff by such an event.

Bakers: One day before the feast, bake the pie shells for the lemon tart and sliver or chop the ginger. Prepare the cookie dough.

On the day of the dinner, bake the lemon tart and the almond cookies. A fruit compote of fresh melon, starfruit, strawberries, mangoes, and canned lichee nuts is probably best prepared by the salad department. I have not included a recipe, because the seasonal availability of fruits should dictate what to use.

Cooks: Anytime ahead of time cook the sauce for the barbecued ribs. Cutting the beef for the stir-fry into thin strips may have to be done in the kitchen, unless it can be bought cut properly. Be warned, it took our two butchers two days! Thin, lean flap meat is excellent for this.

One day before the event slice the eggplant, snap the asparagus, and trim the fresh beans. Prepare the mustard and sesame dressings. Toast the Sichuan peppercorns and grind them. Mix the spices for the stir-fry. Steam the rice and chill.

On the day of the feast, bake the ribs slowly. Prepare the chicken wings and reheat them in the oven during service. Prepare the soup but add egg whites just before service. Prepare the spinach and cucumber salad. Steam the salad vegetables and dress them. Cook the noodles and toss them with dressing. Prepare the bean curd. (This keeps well and can be prepared ahead of time.) Stir-fry beef as needed. Broil or barbecue the ribs.

A Taste of Europe
Jim Dodge and Michela Larson with Terry Endow

The next spring we invited Jim Dodge, who at that time was the pastry chef at the Stanford Court Hotel in San Francisco. He suggested that I get in touch with Michela Larson of Michela's restaurant in Cambridge, Massachusetts, to create the savory main part of the dinner. This combination of food and cooks turned out to be irresistible.

Our theme was "A Taste of Europe," because Mr. Dodge was originally trained by Swiss pastry chef Fritz Albecker, of the Strawberry Court restaurant in Portsmouth, New Hampshire, and because Michela's specializes in northern Italian cuisine. We actually had the talents of three cooks, since Michela's executive chef, Terry Endow, brought his skills and knowledge to the recipe discussions and oversaw the food preparations the day of the dinner. We wanted to focus on Mr. Dodge's award-winning book *The American Baker*, so pastries became the highlight of the meal.

On the weekend before the dinner, Mr. Dodge gave a five-hour workshop on cookies and chocolate pastries to our baking staff, students, and faculty from the school's culinary and hotel programs, as well as other interested staff members from the UNH kitchens. Hundreds of cookies were then made and baked for the American Baker's Café lecture and demonstration. Mr. Dodge also gave the staff lessons on how to temper and work with chocolate and how to produce the delectable desserts for the upcoming dinner.

Sunday afternoon, two days before the dinner, Mr. Dodge and Ms. Larson gave a lecture and demonstration to an audience of two hundred on how to prepare antipasti and bake pastries. The lecture took place in a café-like setting—actually a dining room transformed into a café by covering small tables with soft table cloths and putting a rose on each table.

At the end of the demonstration, we served freshly brewed coffee, along with samples of the antipasti and the cookies baked the day before. Chocolate mounds and hussar's loves were the favorites. Happy audience members requested signed copies of Mr. Dodge's book on pastries.

On Monday and Tuesday Mr. Dodge supervised the bakers during the pastry and bread production, while Ms. Larson was busy instructing the dining staff on how to prepare her restaurant's northern Italian dishes. She was joined on Tuesday by Mr. Endow and the "Taste of Europe" moved smoothly into high gear.

The menu was printed on Michela's restaurant paper stock, a lovely marbled, pinkish-grey and pale-green paper. Stiffly starched table linens and pale pink tulips added elegance to the decorations. A few large flower arrangements and soft candlelight enhanced the atmosphere.

The wonderful antipasti and panzanella were the biggest hit, followed closely by the pollo con melanzana fritti. The fried fennel made friends quickly with those brave enough to give this unusual (at least to New England palates) vegetable a try.

The desserts were wonderful and they disappeared as fast as they could be replenished. In addition to hundreds of hussar's love and chocolate mound cookies, 55 cappucino cakes, the same numbers of chocolate beret cakes, 27 hotel pans of brioche bread pudding, and 57 loaves of bourbon cake were enjoyed in the university dining rooms that night.

A TASTE OF EUROPE

Antipasti
Marinated olives, roasted vegetables, cold cuts, and cheese

Insalata Mista
Salad of mixed greens

Panzanella
Bread salad

Zuppa di Cavolo with Fontina Crostini
Cabbage soup with cheese toast

Penne Selvaggio
Baked pasta with goat cheese and wild mushrooms

Agnello di Lucca
Lamb ragout with kalamata olives and fennel

Pollo con Melanzana Fritti
Grilled chicken breast with fried eggplant

Triglie e Gamberetti Arrostiti
Baked red snapper with shrimp

Polenta
Roasted red pepper-flavored cornmeal

Broccoli al Forno
Broccoli with parmesan and garlic

Finocchi Fritti
Deep fried fennel

Sour Dough Bread

Multigrain Bread

Bourbon Pecan Cake

Brioche Bread Pudding

Cappuccino Cake

Chocolate Beret Cake

Hussar's Love

Chocolate Mound Cookies

MENU PRODUCTION NOTES: The recipes from Michela's restaurant feature northern Italian cuisine and ingredients; the quantities were worked out with the help of chef Terry Endow. The dessert recipes, with the exception of the bourbon cake, can be found (in small quantity) in Jim Dodge's book. The cookies served are identified in the dessert section of this book. The following timetable is a guideline for those who want to produce this menu. The chocolate beret is not included because it is difficult to produce and even more difficult to serve in large quantities. We have since substituted eggless wacky cake layers instead of Mr. Dodge's sponge cake layers for the cappuccino cake.

Bakers: A week before the dinner, set the sour dough starter and feed it daily. Bake the brioche bread for the pudding anytime, since it freezes extremely well. Prepare and bake the bourbon cake. Because this very rich cake contains no flour and should be cut very thinly, it has to be frozen to be served or it will be too soft to slice. Slice it while frozen using an electric slicer. Two days ahead of time bake wacky cake sheets and rounds, chocolate mounds, and hussars' loves. One day before, make the cappuccino frosting. On the day of the event bake the two breads. Assemble and frost the cappuccino cake. Assemble and bake the bread pudding. Slice the bourbon pecan cake.

Cooks: Five days before the event, marinate the olives. Toast French or Italian bread slices until very dry, and bag tightly. One day before, slice the cold cuts and cheeses. Pit the olives for the lamb ragout and make the fish sauce. Cook the polenta and let it cool on sheet pans overnight. Cube the fennel for the lamb dish and sauté it with small onions. Slice the eggplant. Peel and seed cucumbers for the panzanella, invert them on a tray, and refrigerate covered. Prepare salad dressing. Clean and trim broccoli and cauliflower. Make the tomato sauce for the chicken. Slice and bread the fennel for deep frying. On the day of the event, cut and roast the antipasti vegetables and arrange them on platters or in pans. Prepare salad greens and make bread salad. Cook the soup. Prepare the penne and bake progressively. Grill eggplant slices and chicken breasts. Top the eggplant with chicken, tomato sauce and cheese, and bake as needed. Garnish with wilted spinach. Cut and bake polenta as needed. Prepare the red snapper in batches, and top with the sautéed shrimp just before serving. Prepare cheese topping for broccoli. Steam broccoli and fry fennel as needed.

❖

A Moroccan Diffa
Paula Wolfert

For our fifth event we went to North Africa for the cuisine and to New York to get help from the foremost authority on Moroccan food, Paula Wolfert. Ms. Wolfert is a cookbook author, restaurant consultant, and food authority who is highly respected and well-known for her intense desire to produce perfect richly flavored food. I had participated in a workshop on Moroccan food she gave at Boston University, and I told her about the Great Cooks series and persuaded her to celebrate a diffa, or feast, with us at the University of New Hampshire.

After discussions with Ms. Wolfert, we selected the menu and the recipes from her books *Couscous and Other Good Food from Morocco* and *Paula Wolfert's World of Food*.

The intensive training methods used to prepare for Ken Hom's meal worked so well we decided to stick with that format. The staff had more time with Ms. Wolfert and were able to learn a great deal from her about the use of spices.

First the bakers got a lesson in making Moroccan ghoriba cookies, fried pastry from the town of Sefrou, and kisra, the anise-flavored whole wheat Moroccan bread. Actually, Moroccans do not eat dessert with their dinners, only fruit, but our customers would have been disappointed without some sweets.

The cooks got their chance to ask questions while Ms. Wolfert explained the recipes and the use of spices used in Moroccan food. The spices were freshly ground around-the-clock—or so it seemed—by student employees in the kitchens, filling the air with the scent of cumin, turmeric, pepper, cinnamon, cardamom, mace, and ginger.

Paula Wolfert proved to be an outstanding teacher who shared her incredible knowledge generously and patiently with the cooks and bakers. For the students and the public she demonstrated *bisteeya*, a wonderful Moroccan pigeon pie, that tasted heavenly when made with chicken. Cooked chicken meat is slowly simmered with garlic, parsley, and many spices. The cooled chicken is layered with sugared ground almonds, flavored with cinnamon and lemon curdled eggs in phyllo crust. The baked pie is dusted with powdered sugar and cinnamon. It was an enlightening taste experience for those in attendance and for the staff who had this spectacular treat for lunch on the feast day.

On the day of the diffa, Ms. Wolfert was tirelessly tasting and spicing until the food met her exacting standards. We had to make one compromise and use instant couscous, which is quite acceptable when serving such a large number of guests. The kitchens were perfumed with the heady scent of spices simmering in the lamb tagine and the harira soup. The aromas were wafting from the ovens where the *djej mechoui* (chicken thighs) and the *kefta* (lamb meatballs) were roasting. The aroma of saffron rose from the steaming spicy vegetables which were waiting to be placed over the fluffy couscous.

The salad bars were filled with Moroccan salads, some garnished with cut-out rutabaga in the shape of a camel. The roasted red peppers were tossed with slivers of preserved lemon peels (which had been pickled in salt weeks before and which were now ready to use) adding flavor and color to this salad. See color plate **16**.

The dining rooms were decorated with potted palms, displays of rugs, brass platters, and pitchers. The staff dressed in fezzes, turbans, and beads; some also wore long robes. In one hall the student supervisors built a life-size camel made out of papier-maché and set it in an oasis of potted plants, where it was tended by a student in an Arab kaftan and headdress. There were belly dancers dancing in one hall.

Mint tea, which is drunk very sweet and hot in Morocco, was set out with sugar and fresh mint leaves. In Morocco, the food is eaten with the first three fingers of the right hand, but we provided silverware.

The atmosphere was certainly Moroccan and so was the food. The diffa was an impressive banquet worthy of its name. The event and Paula Wolfert helped reveal aspects of the culture and wonderful food of a faraway and little-known land.

Ms. Wolfert was pleased and happy about the many compliments the students and guests had for her, the staff, and the food. Though tired, she willingly autographed her books and marveled at the amounts of food a student can consume.

A MOROCCAN DIFFA

Harira
A soup with vegetables, chick peas, lentils, and lamb

Kefta Mkaouara
Lamb and beef meatballs in a spicy tomato sauce

Djej Mechoui
Roasted chicken legs smothered with herbs, garlic, and spices

Mrouzia
Lamb tagine with raisins and almonds

Spicy Vegetables
A creamy medley of winter and summer squashes, carrots,
turnips, and peppers.

Couscous
The Moroccan national dish

Carrot Salad
Cooked carrots dressed with lemon, parsley, and spices

Cucumber Salad
Cucumbers with herbs and cured black olives

"Midway" Olive and Preserved Lemon Salad
Ripe greek olives marinated in olive oil and spices,
with preserved lemon peel

Red Pepper and Preserved Lemon Peel Salad
Marinated peppers with fresh tomatoes and preserved
lemon peel

Spicy Eggplant and Tomato Salad
A strangely spiced eggplant spread

Kisra
Moroccan anise-flavored bread

Fried Pastry from Sefrou
Honey and sugar coated fried dough

Ghoriba
Semolina cookies

Fresh Orange Slices with Ras El Hanout
Ras El Hanout is a mixture of 12 spices

Mint Tea

MENU PRODUCTION NOTES: This complex menu is actually not difficult to prepare because many items can be made ahead of time. The preserved lemons must be pickled at least six weeks in advance. The timetable is for large quantities; if you are only preparing for hundreds, not thousands, of guests, all this can be done in one day.

Bakers: One to two days ahead of time fry the pastry from Sefrou, drizzle with honey, dust with powdered sugar, and store unwrapped at room temperature. Bake the cookies. On the day of the event bake the bread.

Cooks: Pickle the lemon for six weeks! One day before the diffa, prepare the cooked eggplant salad and the red pepper salad. Marinate the olives. Cook the lamb tagine and refrigerate it overnight. Prepare and form the meatballs. Make the paste for the chicken legs. Cook the spicy tomato sauce for the kefta. Cut up the butternut squash, but do not peel it. Grind and mix spices for *ras el hanout.* On the day of the diffa, remove the hardened fat from the tagine. Rub the spicy paste on the chicken legs and let it stand in the refrigerator for 2 to 3 hours. Steam peel oranges, slice them thinly and sprinkle them with *ras el hanout.* Prepare the harira soup and the cucumber and carrot salads. Roast the meatballs on sheet pans and heat them with the sauce. Cook the spicy vegetables, but add cream just before serving. Pour boiling water over the couscous, keep it hot in warmers, and fluff before service. Reheat lamb tagine. Bake chicken progressively.

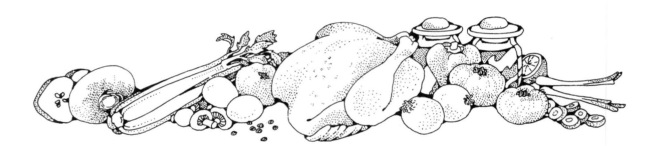

2

BREAKFAST AND BRUNCH ENTRÉES

Nutritious and Delicious

❖

Most institutions offer bacon and eggs every day for breakfast. Institutions should educate their customers about the health hazards of such daily fare and provide attractive alternatives. The recipes below use fewer eggs and more whole grains and vegetables than is typical for breakfast. The turkey sausage contains rice and lean ground turkey meat, an alternative that is lower in fat than pork sausage. Beans can be a main or side dish at breakfast or brunch.

Brunch, especially on college campuses, is a leisurely weekend affair. You can earn rave reviews from your customers by making brunch festive and special with fresh flowers and attractive displays. Brunch allows you to delight your customers with new and different dishes. Many vegetarian entrées can be served at this meal. See the brunch menu section for suggestions.

Breakfast can also be a festive occasion. I used to plan one candlelight breakfast in December or late January in New Hampshire. We drew the curtains, put out white or yellow tablecloths with daffodils, or roses if we could not get daffodils, lit candles, and served fresh strawberries. And it got rid of the winter doldrums every time.

Apple raisin blintzes are a warm treat for brunch on a cold winter morning.

❖ Apple Raisin Blintzes

Blintze is the Yiddish name for a culinary treat of Russian origin. These are filled with cottage cheese, yogurt, and cheddar, and they are sweetened with apples, raisins, and sugar. Serve the blintzes with sour cream and apple sauce. In this recipe yogurt replaces the traditional sour cream to reduce fat and calories.

PRODUCTION NOTES: Drain yogurt in a colander lined with cheesecloth for 30 minutes. Make crepes according to crepe recipes (page 39).

Portions per recipe: 48
Yield: 3 pans/96 blintzes
Portion: 2 blintzes
Serving utensil: spatula

Pan: 12" × 20" × 2"
Temperature: 325° F
Time: 15 minutes

Ingredients	Amounts	
Low-fat yogurt, drained 30 minutes	2 lb.	
Eggs		10 oz.
Small curd, low-fat cottage cheese	6 lb.	
Cheddar cheese, shredded	1 lb.	8 oz.
Cinnamon		½ oz.
Granulated sugar		8 oz.
Raisins	1 lb.	
Apples, peeled, cored, and thinly sliced	3 lb.	
96 cooked crepes	4 lb.	8 oz.
Light cream		12 oz.
Granulated sugar		3 oz.
Cinnamon		¼ oz.

Procedure:

1. Beat eggs, cheeses, yogurt, cinnamon, and sugar until smooth.
2. Fold in raisins and apples.
3. With a #12 scoop place about 2.5 ounces of filling in the center of each crepe.
4. Roll up blintzes and place seam side down in two rows of 16 in a pan.
5. Drizzle 4 ounces of light cream over each pan of blintzes.
6. Mix sugar with cinnamon and sprinkle about 1 ounce over each pan of blintzes.
7. Bake at 325° F for 15 minutes.

Calories: **309**   Protein: **17.0 g (22%)**   Carbohydrates: **31.0 g (40%)**   Sodium: **448 mg**
Total Fat: **13.3 g (39%)**   *Saturated Fat:* **6.5 g**   *Monounsaturated Fat:* **3.0 g**   *Polyunsaturated Fat:* **2.0 g**

❖ Boston Baked Breakfast Beans

Beans for breakfast are not at all uncommon on cold winter mornings in New England. Combined with hot corn bread they provide protein for the vegetarian and with eggs or pancakes they make a very satisfactory early morning meal.

PRODUCTION NOTE: Cook the day before and finish baking the next morning.

Portions per recipe: *50*
Yield: *2 pans*
Portion: *4 ounces*
Serving utensil: *2-ounce ladle*

Pan: *12" × 20" × 2"–½ size*
Temperature: *350° F*
Time: *2 hours and 45 minutes*

Ingredients	Amounts	
White pea beans	5 lb.	
Water	12 lb.	
Salt		2 oz.
Dry mustard		¼ oz.
Cider vinegar		4 oz.
Black strap molasses	1 lb.	
Vegetable oil		4 oz.

Procedure:

1. Sort and wash beans.
2. Place in kettle and cover with cold water. Bring to a simmer and cook two hours. Test to make sure beans are soft.
3. Fold rest of ingredients into hot beans.
4. Pour aproximately 7 pounds of beans into each pan.
5. Cover and refrigerate overnight.
6. Remove cover next morning and bake for 45 minutes at 350° F.

VARIATION: Use a mixture of different legumes, green or yellow split peas, brown lentils, or various types of beans such as lima, pinto, soy, garbanzo, or black. If their cooking times vary too much you may need to cook them separately before combining them to be baked. Most beans cook in 1½ to 2 hours; garbanzo beans and soy beans take at least 3 hours. Split peas and lentils cook in 30 to 45 minutes.

Calories: **192**   Protein: **9.6 g (19%)**   Carbohydrates: **33.4 g (69%)**   Sodium: **454 mg**

Total Fat: **2.8 g (13%)**   *Saturated Fat:* **0.7 g**   *Monounsaturated Fat:* **0.5 g**   *Polyunsaturated Fat:* **1.4 g**

❖ Buckwheat Cakes

Buckwheat flour is high in complex carbohydrates, niacin, calcium, and potassium. These pancakes are high in nutritional value. They are delicious served with a yogurt or sour cream topping and hot raspberries. Blinis, the Russian contribution to haute cuisine, are tiny buckwheat pancakes filled with caviar and sour cream. Try them at an elegant reception.

PRODUCTION NOTES: Part of the batter for these pancakes is prepared at night for breakfast production. In the morning, eggs and very warm milk are beaten into the batter. The heated milk will remove the chill from the batter and activate the yeast. To reduce fat and cholesterol, replace eggs with 2 pounds of whipped egg whites, which contain no cholesterol.

Portions per recipe: 100
Yield: 200 pancakes
Portion: 2 pancakes
Serving utensil: spatula

Griddle temperature: 350° F
Time: 3–4 minutes

Ingredients	Amounts
Warm, low-fat milk (85° F)	12 lb.
Black strap molasses	8 oz.
Dry yeast	1½ oz.
Buckwheat flour	5 lb.
All-purpose flour	3 lb.
Vegetable oil	6 oz.
Eggs	1 lb. 4 oz.
Salt	½ oz.
Baking soda	½ oz.
Very warm, low-fat milk (175° F)	4 lb.

Procedure:

1. Beat milk, molasses, yeast, flours, and oil until well mixed.
2. Cover and let rest at room temperature for 12 hours or overnight.
3. Beat eggs with salt and soda and add to batter.
4. Heat oiled griddle and drop batter (2.1 ounces) using a pancake dropper or a 2-ounce ladle onto grill. Cook until bubbles form on top of pancake and then flip.
5. Pancakes should be nicely browned on both sides.

> Calories: **184**   Protein: **7.5 g (16%)**   Carbohydrates: **30.2 g (65%)**   Sodium: **102 mg**
> Total Fat: **4.5 g (22%)**   *Saturated Fat:* **1.6 g**   *Monounsaturated Fat:* **1.0 g**   *Polyunsaturated Fat:* **1.1 g**

Prepared with egg whites:

> Calories: **187**   Protein: **7.8 g (17%)**   Carbohydrates: **30.1 (64%)**   Sodium: **105 mg**
> Total Fat: **3.9 g (19%)**   *Saturated Fat:* **1.5 g**   *Monounsaturated Fat:* **.9 g**   *Polyunsaturated Fat:* **1.0 g**

❖ Cottage Cheese Pancakes

These cottage cheese pancakes are light, moist, and high in protein. Serve them with cranberry-apple sauce. The bakery at the University of New Hampshire prepares the pancake mix and ships it in 10-pound bags to the various kitchens on campus. This is cheaper than buying pancake mixes, and the kitchens always have some fresh mix on hand.

Pancake Mix (10 lb)

Ingredients	Amounts
Pastry flour	8 lb. 4 oz.
Baking powder	9 oz.
Granulated sugar	1 lb.
Salt	2 oz.

Procedure:

1. Weigh directly into a strong plastic bag, close tightly, and shake.

Pancakes

Portions per recipe: 100
Yield: 200
Portion: 2 pancakes
Serving utensil: spatula

Griddle temperature: 350° F
Time: 5–6 minutes

Ingredients	Amounts
Eggs	6 lb.
Vegetable oil	8 oz.
Low-fat milk	12 lb.
Low-fat cottage cheese, small curd	5 lb.
Pancake mix	10 lb.
Cinnamon	1/4 oz.

Procedure:

1. Beat eggs, oil, milk, and cottage cheese in a large mixing bowl.
2. Add pancake mix and cinnamon and beat at low speed until well blended.
3. Lightly oil hot griddle and portion batter with pancake dropper or a 2-ounce ladle.
4. Cook until bubbles appear on surface. Flip and cook until brown.

Calories: **259**   Protein: **10.9 g (17%)**   Carbohydrates: **37.7 g (59%)**   Sodium: **343 mg**
Total Fat: **6.8 g (24%)**   Saturated Fat: **2.4 g**   Monounsaturated Fat: **1.1 g**   Polyunsaturated Fat: **1.7 mg**

❖ Crepes

Crepes are very easily made on the griddle. They may not be perfectly round, but this does not affect their taste, and appearance is relatively unimportant as they are usually rolled around a filling.

PRODUCTION NOTES: Regular pancake batter can quickly become crepe batter with the addition of eggs and soda water. The formula is 2 parts pancake batter, 1 part beaten eggs, and 1 part soda water. If pancake batter is left over, enrich the batter with eggs and thin with soda water and cook up a batch of crepes for the freezer. Freeze crepes in packages of 32, as this is the number of rolled crepes which fit neatly into a $12 \times 20 \times 2$-inch pan. Cut 8-inch parchment paper squares. Stack the crepes layered with parchment paper, wrap, label, date, and freeze.

Portions per recipe: 80
Yield: 160 crepes/5 stacks
Portion: 2 crepes
Serving utensil: spatula

Griddle temperature: 275° F
Time: 3–4 minutes

Ingredients   Amounts

Ingredients	Amounts
Eggs	3 lb.
Low-fat milk	5 lb.
Pastry flour	1 lb. 12 oz.
Salt	½ oz.
Vegetable oil	8 oz.
Carbonated water (very cold)	1 lb.

Procedure:

1. Beat eggs and milk for 30 seconds.
2. Add flour and salt. Blend briefly. Do not worry about lumps.
3. Add oil and very cold carbonated water. Stir.
4. Heat griddle to 275° F and oil. Portion batter with 1-ounce ladle.
5. Spread quickly into thin round shapes with the bottom of ladle cup. Add more carbonated water if the mix is not thin enough.
6. Flip crepe over as soon as crepes become transparent.
7. Cook until brown spots form.

Calories: **99**   Protein: **3.8 g (15%)**   Carbohydrates: **9.3 g (38%)**   Sodium: **105 mg**
Total Fat: **5.1 g (47%)**   *Saturated Fat:* **1.6 g**   *Monounsaturated Fat:* **0.8 g**   *Polyunsaturated Fat:* **1.8 g**

❖ Eggs Diablo

The fire in the tomato sauce in this dish will rouse even the sleepiest morning customer. Eggs diablo also makes a light vegetarian lunch or dinner when served over rice with broccoli.

PRODUCTION NOTES: The sauce can be prepared in advance, but it tastes fresher if made on the same morning it is to be served. The ingredients can be chopped the day before and refrigerated. The raw eggs are placed into the hot tomato sauce and quickly poached in a steamer. If no steamer is available, cover pan and bake at 300° F for 8 to 10 minutes.

Portions per recipe: 48
Yield: 4 pans/96 eggs
Portion: 2 eggs
Serving utensil: spoon

Pan: 12″ × 20″ × 2″
Cooking method: steam
Time: 6–8 minutes

Ingredients	Amounts
Olive oil	2 oz.
Spanish onions, thinly sliced	1 lb.
Granulated sugar	½ oz.
Green bell peppers, thinly sliced	1 lb.
Yellow bell peppers, thinly sliced	1 lb.
Jalapeno peppers, seeded and thinly sliced	4 oz.
Italian tomatoes, cored and quartered	10 lb.
Salt	1 oz.
Cilantro leaves and stems, chopped	1 oz.
Parsley leaves, chopped	4 oz.
Eggs	12 lb.

Procedure:

1. Heat olive oil in a kettle. Add onions, sprinkle with sugar, and sauté 5 minutes.
2. Add peppers and cook 5 minutes more.
3. Add quartered tomatoes and salt. Bring to a simmer.
4. Add cilantro and parsley.
5. Pour 3 pints of very hot tomato mixture into pan.
6. Crack 24 eggs into rows of 3 × 8 neatly placed on the sauce. Cover.
7. Steam at low pressure 6 to 8 minutes. The eggs will continue to cook after they have been removed from steamer.
8. Serve immediately.

Calories: **194**   Protein: **13.2 g (27%)**   Carbohydrates: **6.9 g (14%)**   Sodium: **410.3 mg**
Total Fat: **12.6 g (59%)**   *Saturated Fat:* **3.5 g**   *Monounsaturated Fat:* **1.8 g**   *Polyunsaturated Fat:* **1.7 g**

❖ Granola

A favorite of the University of New Hampshire breakfast crowd, granola is delicious with bananas, seasonal fruit, and skim milk or low-fat yogurt. Commercial cereal boxes base serving calculations on a 1-ounce portion. We weighed cereal portions taken by customers, and discovered that 2.5 ounces is a more realistic amount. With ¾ cup of skim milk and ¼ cup of fresh fruit this becomes a balanced breakfast which provides approximately 375–400 calories.

Portions per recipe: 270
Yield: 6 pans/42 pounds
Portion: 2.5 ounces
Serving utensil: 4-ounce ladle

Pan: 18" × 26" × 3" cake pan
Temperature: 350° F
Time: 25 minutes

Ingredients

Ingredients	Amounts
Old-fashioned oats	30 lb.
Toasted wheat germ	1 lb. 8 oz.
Sesame seeds	1 lb.
Brown sugar	2 lb. 8 oz.
Walnuts, chopped	1 lb.
Vegetable oil	2 lb.
Honey	1 lb.
Vanilla extract	8 oz.
Raisins	3 lb.

Procedure

1. Mix oats, wheat germ, sesame seeds, brown sugar, and walnuts together.
2. Mix oil, honey, and vanilla; add to oat mixture; and rub together until blended.
3. Transfer 6.5 pounds of the mixture into cake pan.
4. Bake at 350° F for 25 to 30 minutes and stir the mixture twice.
5. When mixture is lightly toasted and dry, remove from oven and let cool.
6. Add raisins and store granola in bags.

Calories: **292**   Protein: **10.1 g (14%)**   Carbohydrates: **44.5 g (61%)**   Sodium: **3.0 mg**
Total Fat: **9.1 g (28%)**   *Saturated Fat:* **1.7 g**   *Monounsaturated Fat:* **2.3 g**   *Polyunsaturated Fat:* **4.3 g**

❖ Johnny Cakes

Old fashioned New England cornmeal pancakes, Johnny cakes are excellent when eaten with maple syrup, hot blueberry sauce, or yogurt and honey.

PRODUCTION NOTE: Prepare the mix in quantity and store until needed in a cool, dry place.

Johnny Cake Mix (30 lb)

Ingredients	Amounts
Cornmeal	15 lb.
Pastry flour	13 lb. 4 oz.
Salt	8 oz.
Baking powder	1 lb. 4 oz.

Pancakes

PRODUCTION NOTES: The cornmeal softens when batter is left to rest overnight but will need additional liquid in the morning. The cornmeal will remain slightly gritty if the batter is mixed and used immediately.

Portions per recipe: 100
Yield: 200 pancakes
Portion: 2 pancakes
Serving utensil: spatula

Griddle temperature: 350° F
Time: 5–6 minutes

Eggs	2 lb.
Low-fat milk	12 lb.
Black strap molasses	4 oz.
Vegetable oil	4 oz.
Johnny cake mix	10 lb.
Low-fat milk	4 lb.

Procedure:

1. Beat eggs with milk, molasses, and oil.
2. Stir in the johnny cake mix.
3. Let rest overnight.
4. In the morning, thin with up to 2 quarts milk.
5. Place 2.25 ounces of mixture on hot oiled griddle using a pancake dropper or 2-ounce ladle.
6. Cook until bubbles appear and then flip.
7. Cook other side 2 to 3 minutes until golden.
8. Serve immediately.

Calories: **203**   Protein: **6.0 g (12%)**   Carbohydrates: **36.2 g (71%)**   Sodium: **381.1 mg**

Total Fat: **3.9 g (17%)**   *Saturated Fat:* **1.2 g**   *Monounsaturated Fat:* **0.8 g**   *Polyunsaturated Fat:* **1.2 g**

❖ Spinach Tofu Crepes

The spinach filling is enriched with high-protein tofu, shredded cheddar cheese, eggs, and flavored with nutmeg.

PRODUCTION NOTES: Soft tofu that is as fresh as possible works best. Crepes can be filled (but not covered with sauce) the night before use and refrigerated. Crepes which have been refrigerated should first be baked for 5 minutes and then covered with sauce.

Portions per recipe: 48
Yield: 3 pans/96 crepes
Portion: 2 crepes
Serving utensil: spatula

Pan: 12" × 20" × 2"
Oven temperature: 325° F
Time: 15–20 minutes

Ingredients

Ingredients	Amounts	
Olive oil		1 oz.
Scallions, chopped		8 oz.
Spinach, washed and coarsely chopped	5 lb.	
Soft tofu	4 lb.	
Cheddar cheese, shredded	1 lb.	
Eggs	2 lb.	
Soy sauce		2 oz.
Nutmeg		1/8 oz.
96 crepes, cooked	4 lb.	8 oz.

Cream Sauce

Ingredients	Amounts	
Oil		1 oz.
All-purpose flour		3 oz.
Milk	2 lb.	
Light cream		8 oz.
Dry sherry		1 oz.
White pepper		1/4 oz.
Italian parsley, minced		1 oz.

(continued)

Procedure:

1. Heat olive oil. Sauté scallions until golden.
2. Add chopped spinach and cook until limp.
3. Beat tofu, cheddar cheese, eggs, soy sauce, and nutmeg in a mixing bowl.
4. Fold in cooked spinach.
5. Place 2 ounces of filling on lower third of crepe with a #16 scoop. Roll up and place seam down in lightly oiled pan.
6. Place 2 rows of 16 crepes in the pan.
7. Make a cream sauce by heating the oil with the flour and slowly stirring in milk. Stir until thickened.
8. Fold in light cream, sherry, pepper, and parsley; pour 1 pint of cream sauce over the crepes in each pan.
9. Bake at 325° F for 15 to 20 minutes.

Calories: **232**   Protein: **12.7 g (22%)**   Carbohydrates: **4.2 g (24%)**   Sodium: **316 mg**

Total Fat: **14.1 g (54%)**   *Saturated Fat:* **5.5 g**   *Monounsaturated Fat:* **3.0 g**   *Polyunsaturated Fat:* **1.8 g**

❖ Sunshine Breakfast Drink

This is a fabulous breakfast on the run—just grab a piece of whole wheat toast or whole grain bread along with the drink.

Portions per recipe: 75   *Serve chilled*
Yield: 4 gallons   *Time: 2–3 minutes*
Portion: 7 ounces
Serving utensil: 8-ounce glass

Ingredients	Amounts
Low-fat yogurt	*20 lb.*
Low-fat, or skim milk	*10 lb.*
Orange juice concentrate	*2 lb.*
Honey	*6 oz.*

Procedure:

1. Whip ingredients in a large mixing bowl 2 to 3 minutes.
2. Serve chilled in an 8-ounce glass or paper cup.

Calories: **128**   Protein: **8.6 g (27%)**   Carbohydrates: **17.9 g (55%)**   Sodium: **115.9 mg**

Total Fat: **2.5 g (17%)**   *Saturated Fat:* **1.6 g**   *Monounsaturated Fat:* **0.7 g**   *Polyunsaturated Fat:* **0.1 g**

❖ Turkey Sausage

These tasty patties are lower in fat than pork or beef breakfast sausages and are much lower in cholesterol.

PRODUCTION NOTES: Form patties by placing scoops of the turkey mixture on a parchment-lined sheet pan (use a #16 scoop). Cover the patties with parchment and set the next sheet pan on top; press lightly to flatten the scoops.

Portions per recipe: 85
Yield: 170 patties
Portion: 2 patties
Serving utensil: tongs

Pan: 18″ × 26″ sheet pan
Griddle temperature: 350° F
Time: 8 minutes

Ingredients

Ingredients	Amounts
Rice, cooked and chilled	3 lb.
Spanish onions, peeled and quartered	1 lb.
Parsley leaves	4 oz.
Ground turkey (raw)	20 lb.
Egg whites	2 lb.
Salt	2 oz.
Black pepper	½ oz.
Poultry seasoning blend	½ oz.
Cayenne pepper	¹⁄₁₆ oz.

Procedure:

1. Chop the rice, onions, and parsley in a food chopper until medium fine.
2. Mix well with turkey, egg whites, salt, and spices.
3. Form 2-ounce patties with a #16 scoop. Refrigerate until needed.
4. Heat griddle to 350° F. Cook patties for 4 minutes on each side.

Calories: **111**   Protein: **17.2 g (62%)**   Carbohydrates: **4.8 g (17%)**   Sodium: **325.7 mg**
Total Fat: **2.1 g (17%)**   *Saturated Fat:* **0.7 g**   *Monounsaturated Fat:* **0.5 g**   *Polyunsaturated Fat:* **0.6 g**

❖ Yeast Pancakes with Bran and Walnuts

These are as fragrant as freshly baked bread and are delicious served with apple sauce or hot blueberries.

PRODUCTION NOTES: The batter need only rise for 1 hour. If this takes too long in the morning, prepare batter the night before, and refrigerate. Allow batter to rise for 30 minutes at room temperature in the morning. Hasten this process by reserving 2 quarts of milk from total amount, heat and fold in to refrigerated batter.

Portions per recipe: *100*
Yield: *200 pancakes*
Portion: *2 pancakes*
Serving utensil: *spatula*

Griddle temperature: *325° F*
Time: *6 minutes*

Ingredients

Ingredients	Amounts	
Eggs	3 lb.	
Granulated sugar		12 oz.
Low-fat milk, warm (85° F)	16 lb.	
All-purpose flour	7 lb.	8 oz.
Oat, wheat, or rice bran	1 lb.	
Dry yeast		6 oz.
Salt		½ oz.
Walnuts, finely chopped	1 lb.	

Procedure:

1. Place eggs with sugar in a mixing bowl; beat well.
2. Add milk, flour, bran, yeast, and salt. Beat well.
3. Let batter rise at room temperature for 1 hour.
4. Stir in chopped walnuts.
5. Drop pancakes onto griddle (2.1 oz) with 2-ounce ladle and cook until bubbles form on surface.
6. Flip and brown on other side.

Calories: **238**   Protein: **9.5 g (16%)**   Carbohydrates: **37.4 g (63%)**   Sodium: **182 mg**

Total Fat: **6.3 g (24%)**   *Saturated Fat:* **2.6 g**   *Monounsaturated Fat:* **1.1 g**   *Polyunsaturated Fat:* **2.3 g**

❖ Yogurt Cheese Herb Spread

A nutritious alternative to cream cheese! One pound of yogurt cheese has approximately 486 calories and 30 grams of fat. One pound of cream cheese has about 1640 calories and 82 grams of fat. See color plate **4**.

PRODUCTION NOTES: Whole milk yogurt is creamier and therefore more effective than non-fat yogurt. If a strict fat-reduced diet is required, non-fat yogurt should be used. The spread with non-fat yogurt is still very tasty when these herbs and spices are used. A teaspoon of sugar can be added to lessen any overly acidic taste. Note: Some low-fat yogurts will not separate if stabilizers and starches have been added to make them taste creamier.

To make yogurt cheese simply line a colander with rinsed cheesecloth or kitchen toweling. Set the colander over a deep bowl to catch the whey. Pour in the yogurt, cover, and refrigerate overnight. Ten pounds of yogurt yields approximately 5 pounds and 10 ounces of yogurt cheese. The whey adds nutrition to bread and other baked goods such as muffins or cakes; use it to replace part of the liquid called for in baked goods recipes.

Portions per recipe: 50   *Pan: 12" × 20" × 2"–¼ size*
Yield: 6 pounds/4 ounces   *Serve chilled*
Portion: 2 ounces   *Time: 24 hours*
Serving utensils: #16 scoop and spreader

Ingredients	Amounts
Whole milk yogurt	*10 lb.*
Scallions	*4 oz.*
Garlic cloves, peeled	*2 oz.*
Italian parsley, flat leaf	*2 oz.*
Fresh thyme	*½ oz.*
Tarragon, crushed	*¼ oz.*
Marjoram, crushed	*¼ oz.*
Black pepper	*¼ oz.*
Salt	*1 oz.*

Procedure:

1. Drain the yogurt overnight. (See production notes above.)
2. In a food chopper mince scallions, garlic, parsley, and thyme.
3. Mix the drained yogurt with the chopped herbs and spices.
4. Chill mixture for at least 1 hour to let the flavors develop.

Calories: **59**   Protein: **3.3 g (22%)**   Carbohydrates: **5.0 g (33%)**   Sodium: **262.7 mg**

Total Fat: **3.0 g (45%)**   *Saturated Fat:* **1.9 g**   *Monounsaturated Fat:* **0.8 g**   *Polyunsaturated Fat:* **0.1 g**

❖ Yogurt Walnut Orange Spread

This sweet spread has the refreshing taste of oranges. It can also be layered like a cream parfait with fresh orange pieces and toasted chocolate cake crumbs. *Lebani* is another name for yogurt cheese.

Portions per recipe: *60*
Yield: *7 pounds 8 ounces*
Portion: *2 ounces*
Serving utensil: *#16 scoop*

Pan: *12″ × 20″ × 2″–¼ size*
Serve chilled

Ingredients	Amounts
Whole milk yogurt	10 lb.
Oranges, peeled, seeds removed, chopped finely	12 oz.
Walnuts, ground or finely chopped	6 oz.
Raisins	8 oz.
Cinnamon	½ oz.
Honey	2 oz.
Orange juice concentrate	2 oz.

Yogurt walnut orange spread on a bagel. Also called *lebani*.

Procedure:

1. Drain yogurt overnight. (See production notes from previous recipe.)
2. Steam oranges for 3 minutes to facilitate peeling. Chop finely.
3. Chop walnuts with raisins and cinnamon.
4. Mix drained yogurt with orange concentrate and honey.
5. Fold in orange pieces and walnut mixture. Chill at least 30 minutes.

VARIATIONS: Lebani can also be mixed with just honey and nuts or with nuts and whole cranberry sauce; fresh or frozen raspberries; or fresh or frozen strawberries. Taste and add honey or sugar to sweeten the lebani spread.

Calories: **84**   Protein: **3.2 g (15%)**   Carbohydrates: **8.8 g (42%)**   Sodium: **36 mg**
Total Fat: **4.3 g (46%)**   *Saturated Fat:* **1.7 g**   *Monounsaturated Fat:* **1.0 g**   *Polyunsaturated Fat:* **1.2 mg**

3

APPETIZERS

Appetizers are a tasty preface to any meal. Whether elaborate or simple, the appetizer must provide the eye with a feast of color and form. Savory, strong flavors and small portions are best. An hors d'oeuvre whets the appetite, it does not satiate it. Careful attention to presentation and garnish is essential, elaborate design is not. Freshness and quality are more important than complicated garnishes, and simple and edible garnishes are best. I often choose a recipe ingredient as a garnish. Not only is it on hand, it can also focus attention on a hidden ingredient. Delicious and unusual appetizers at a special banquet or luncheon set the tone for things to come and increase the guests' anticipation. This chapter makes suggestions that free the menu planner from the banal fresh fruit cup or veggies and dip that are too often standard fare.

Appetizers can be served as a first course, they can be served as an assortment at receptions or cocktail parties, passed by servers, or presented buffet style. Usually people eat eight to ten appetizers from a buffet at a reception or cocktail party, and three to five pieces if a dinner follows. Double the amounts if you are feeding students.

First Course

A first course is often a soup, a savory salad, or one large portion of an appetizer. I like a sampling of several hors d'oeuvres such as the Italian antipasti or Spanish tapas, neatly arranged on a small plate. Appetizers served this way should not exceed three items and they must complement each other in flavor, texture, and color. For example avocado stuffed with shrimp and spicy mushrooms on a lettuce leaf; caponata and crostini fontina; mozzarella with tomatoes and marinated artichokes; yakitori and chilled roasted vegetables; bulgur stuffed tomatoes and chilled calamari; vegetable tempura with dipping sauce and vegetarian sushi. Pairing a hot appetizer with some interesting salad greens makes a simple and attractive first course. It can be quickly assembled and is especially good when a salad is not part of the meal. The possible combinations are endless, but the basic rules of menu planning should be observed. I have included instructions for individual plate presentation in some of the recipes.

Buffet

❖

A self-service appetizer buffet reduces service staff needs and is especially convenient for large banquets. In an institutional dining service an appetizer buffet adds zest to a regular dinner routine. Surprising customers with a beautiful table of hors d'oeuvres breaks the monotony of cafeteria-style dining and is a hit with the college population.

Setting up an appetizer buffet requires careful planning. Consider the distance from the kitchen, the lighting, and the size and shape of the tables. Is there enough floor space to accommodate the expected crowd? Round tables display appetizers attractively and the guest can view and reach food with ease. An elevated center piece and fresh flowers can highlight such a table. Make sure food can be replenished without inconvenience to the guest by leaving ample space between items and building no complicated structures. Short, rectangular tables are also acceptable for self-service meals. Long tables are best if the staff serves the guests or for very large groups, when the tables must be constantly replenished and the guests serve themselves from one side only.

A separate setup for napkins, plates, and utensils keeps the food display uncluttered and neat. Place a cart or table strategically so guests must pass it on their way to the food table.

Cold Appetizers

❖

❖ Antipasti *Michela's*

Excellent presentation and easy advanced preparation make these platters ideal as a salad bar show stopper for luncheon buffets, receptions, or an Italian theme dinner. For a sit-down dinner arrange the antipasti on individual plates and place them on the table before the guests are seated.

Portions per recipe: 48
Yield: 1 platter
Portion: 3 ounces
Serving utensil: tongs

Temperature: 375° F
Time: 20 minutes

Ingredients	Amounts
Mortadella	1 lb.
Cappacola ham	1 lb.
Mozzarella, whole	1 lb.
Provolone cheese	1 lb.
Summer squash	2 lb.
Zucchini	2 lb.
Eggplant, unpeeled	2 lb.
Mushrooms, cleaned	1 lb. 8 oz.
Salt	½ oz.
Black pepper, freshly ground	¼ oz.
Oregano, crushed	⅛ oz.
Olive oil	2 oz.
Balsamic vinegar	1 oz.

Procedure:

1. Slice meats and cheeses into very thin ⅓-ounce slices.
2. Cut vegetables into ¼-inch by 3-inch long sticks.
3. Cut large mushrooms in half.
4. Spread vegetables on sheet pans and sprinkle with salt, pepper, and oregano.
5. Drizzle vegetables with oil and bake at 375° F for 20 minutes.
6. Arrange meats, cheeses, and vegetables on large platter. (See color plate **1**.)
7. Sprinkle vegetables with vinegar just before serving.

Calories: **128**   Protein: **8.8 (27%)**   Carbohydrates: **4.1 (13 %)**   Sodium: **485 mg**
Total Fat: **9.3 (64%)**   *Saturated Fat:* **4.1 g**   *Monounsaturated Fat:* **4.0 g**   *Polyunsaturated Fat:* **.7 g**

❖ Antipasto di Mare   *Romagnoli*

This antipasto is fresh and easy to prepare and has a lively lemon flavor.

Portions per recipe: 96
Yield: 2 platters
Portion: 2 ounces
Serving utensil: spoon

Serve chilled
Time: 1 hour

Ingredients	*Amounts*	
Whole squid, cleaned	5 lb.	
Medium shrimp, shelled	2 lb.	
Seafood flakes, thawed and separated	5 lb.	
Olive oil		8 oz.
Lemon juice		8 oz.
Italian parsley, minced		2 oz.
Salt		½ oz.
White pepper		¼ oz.
Celery stalks, thinly sliced	1 lb.	4 oz.
Romaine lettuce, cleaned 4" pieces	4 lb.	
Lemon, sliced for garnish		8 oz.

Procedure:

1. Wash and remove cartilage from squid.
2. Slice squid into thin rings.
3. Blanch in boiling water 1 minute.
4. Immediately chill in ice water. This keeps squid tender.
5. Steam shrimp for 5 minutes, then chill.
6. Toss chilled squid, shrimp, seafood flakes, and celery.
7. Beat together oil, lemon juice, parsley, salt and pepper.
8. Pour over seafood and marinate 60 minutes.
9. Line a round platter with the romaine lettuce. Mound salad. Garnish with lemon slices.

Calories: **80**   Protein: **9.5 g (48%)**   Carbohydrates: **3.3 g (16%)**   Sodium: **121 mg**

Total Fat: **3.1 g (35%)**   *Saturated Fat:* **.4 g**   *Monounsaturated Fat:* **1.8 g**   *Polyunsaturated Fat:* **.4 g**

❖ Avocado Stuffed with Shrimp

Avocados are cut into quarters for buffet-style service. Arrange wedges like flower petals on round platters with a bowl of cherry tomatoes in the center.

For individual presentation serve half an avocado and stuff it with shrimp using a #16 scoop. Garnish with a lemon wedge.

Portions per recipe: 100 *Serve chilled*
Yield: 200 wedges
Portion: 2 wedges
Serving utensil: cake server

Ingredients	Amounts
Celery, diced	3 lb.
Salad shrimp, cooked and chilled	20 lb.
Eggs, hard boiled and chopped	2 lb.
Lemon juice	6 oz.
Salt	½ oz.
White pepper	⅛ oz.
Mayonnaise	12 oz.
Low-fat yogurt	4 oz.
Picante salsa (hot)	8 oz.
Parsley, minced	2 oz.
Fresh dill weed, finely chopped	1 oz.
50 avocados, ripe	11 lb. 4 oz.

Procedure:

1. Blanch celery for 15 seconds in a steamer at 15 # pressure or dip into boiling water for 1 minute. Chill immediately.
2. Mix shrimp with celery, eggs, lemon juice, salt, and pepper.
3. Fold in mayonnaise, yogurt, picante sauce, and herbs.
4. Cut unpeeled avocado in half, remove pit, cut halves in half again.
5. Dip cut sides into lemon juice.
6. Fill cavity with shrimp salad using a #24 scoop. (Use a #16 scoop for halves.)
7. Garnish with dill or parsley sprigs and lemon wedges.

Calories: **204** Protein: **20.4 g (40%)** Carbohydrates: **4.4 g (8%)** Sodium: **180 mg**
Total Fat: **11.9 g (52%)** *Saturated Fat:* **1.9 g** *Monounsaturated Fat:* **5.4 g** *Polyunsaturated Fat:* **3.4 g**

❖ Bulgur-stuffed Tomatoes

This is an attractive vegetarian appetizer. Be sure to use large cherry tomatoes so they can be filled easily using a scoop. The filling is a healthy mint and lemon flavored tabouli.

PRODUCTION NOTES: Slice the tops off the tomatoes, then scoop the flesh into a colander and let it drain for 30 minutes. Invert tomatoes on plastic trays to drain before filling. Use pulp in the filling. Add diced peeled tomatoes if there is not enough pulp.

Portions per recipe: 50
Yield: 100 tomatoes
Portion: 2 tomatoes
Serving utensil: tongs

Serve chilled
Time: 30 minutes

Ingredients | Amounts

Ingredients	Amounts	
Cherry tomatoes	5 lb.	
Bulgur, medium	1 lb.	
Boiling water	2 lb.	
Celery tops, minced		4 oz.
Italian parsley, minced		4 oz.
Mint leaves, minced		2 oz.
Garlic cloves, crushed		1 oz.
Red onion, finely diced		8 oz.
Pulp from cherry tomatoes, chopped	2 lb.	8 oz.
Lemon juice		6 oz.
Olive oil		1 oz.
Salt		½ oz.
Black pepper		⅛ oz.

Procedure:

1. Scoop pulp out of tomatoes, place pulp in colander, and invert tomato shells on tray.
2. Put bulgur into a mixing bowl and pour boiling water over it.
3. Let bulgur sit covered for 2 to 3 hours. Drain any excess water.
4. Mix bulgur with remaining ingredients. Chill for 30 minutes.
5. Fill tomatoes with bulgur using a #40 scoop.
6. Set in rows or circles on trays and garnish with mint.

Calories: **48**   Protein: **1.6 g (13%)**   Carbohydrates: **9.5 g (79%)**   Sodium: **118 mg**

Total Fat: **.8 g (15%)**   *Saturated Fat:* **.1 g**   *Monounsaturated Fat:* **.5 g**   *Polyunsaturated Fat:* **.2 g**

❖ Caponata *Romagnoli*

A wonderful sweet and sour eggplant appetizer with capers and green olives. See color plate **1**.

Portions per recipe: 150
Yield: 3 pans
Portion: 3.5 ounces
Serving utensil: spoon

Pan: 12″ × 20″ × 2″–½ size
Griddle temperature: 350° F

Ingredients

Ingredients	Amounts
Eggplant, medium-size	15 lb.
Olive oil	8 oz.
Spanish onions, thinly sliced	5 lb.
Celery, thinly sliced	2 lb. 8 oz.
Capers	8 oz.
Olives stuffed with pimento	10 oz.
Red wine vinegar	2 lb.
Salt	1 oz.
Black pepper	½ oz.
Granulated sugar	4 oz.
Canned Italian tomatoes	12 lb. 12 oz.

Procedure:

1. Cut eggplant in half lengthwise, then in ½-inch slices.
2. Place in perforated pan. Salt lightly. Drain for 30 minutes. Rinse.
3. Heat 2 ounces of olive oil in a tilting skillet or griddle. Fry eggplant until golden brown.
4. Keep cooking in batches until all the eggplant is cooked.
5. In remaining oil, sauté onions and celery until soft, then add capers, olives, vinegar, and sugar.
6. Drain tomatoes (reserve juice for another purpose). Select 2 to 3 firm tomatoes for garnish, add the rest (lightly crushed) to the onions.
7. Bring onion and tomato mixture to a simmer, add eggplant, and cook for 8 minutes.
8. Pour into ½ pans. Chill. Garnish with parsley, strips of tomatoes, and green olives.

Calories: **41**   Protein: **1.0 g (10%)**   Carbohydrates: **6.0 g (58%)**   Sodium: **190 mg**
Total Fat: **1.7 g (39%)**   *Saturated Fat:* **.2 g**   *Monounsaturated Fat:* **1.1 g**   *Polyunsaturated Fat:* **.2 g**

❖ Chilled Calamari (Squid)

A simple but very pretty and very inexpensive dish. Serve mounds of calamari surrounded by avocado wedges or cubes. Provide plates and forks or serve as a first course at a sit-down dinner. See color plate **1**.

PRODUCTION NOTES: To prepare the squid, remove cartilage and any viscera, and rinse them in salted water. Bring water to a boil, place the calamari in a flat bottomed colander, and dip the colander for *only* 20 seconds into boiling liquid, remove, and plunge into ice water. This is a fool-proof method that assures tender squid at all times.

Portions per recipe: 50   *Serve chilled*
Yield: 2 trays
Portion: 2 ounces
Serving Utensil: spoon

Ingredients	Amounts
Whole squid	5 lb.
Ripe avocados	3 lb.
Olive oil	4 oz.
Whole garlic cloves	½ oz.
Lime juice	2 oz.
Red wine vinegar	1 oz.
Salt	½ oz.
Black pepper	⅛ oz.
Whole scallions, thinly sliced	8 oz.
Hot red peppers, seeded, diced small	4 oz.
Cilantro leaves, chopped	1 oz.
Parsley, minced	2 oz.

Procedure:

1. Prepare squid, cook, chill, and cut into thin rings.
2. Peel, core, and cube the avocados.
3. Mix the rest of the ingredients together to make dressing and whisk.
4. Pour dressing over avocados and marinate for 20 minutes. Reserve some of the avocados for garnish.
5. Discard garlic cloves and toss squid with rest of the avocados.
6. Mound on platter. Garnish with cilantro sprigs and a small ring of hot red peppers. Surround platter with reserved avocados.

Calories: **97**   Protein: **7.6 g (31%)**   Carbohydrates: **3.6 g (14%)**   Sodium: **133 mg**

Total Fat: **6.0 g (55%)**   *Saturated Fat:* **1.0 g**   *Monounsaturated Fat:* **3.7 g**   *Polyunsaturated Fat:* **.8 g**

❖ Chilled Roasted Vegetables

As delicious as the antipasti, but without the meat. Great also as a vegetable for a summer buffet or meal.

Portions per recipe: 50
Yield: 1 platter
Portion: 3 ounces
Serving utensil: tongs

Pan: 18" × 26" sheet pan
Temperature: 375° F
Time: 15 minutes

Ingredients	Amounts
Summer squash	3 lb.
Eggplant	3 lb.
Whole mushrooms	2 lb.
Asparagus spears, 3–4" long	2 lb.
Carrots, peeled	3 lb.
Olive oil	1½ oz.
Garlic clove, peeled	1 oz.
Salt	½ oz.
Black pepper, freshly ground	⅛ oz.
Oregano, crushed	⅛ oz.
Balsamic vinegar	1 oz.

Procedure:

1. Cut squashes, eggplant, and carrots into 2-inch long sticks.
2. Clean mushrooms, cutting large ones in halves, and break off asparagus ends.
3. Steam or parboil carrots for 3 minutes until still crisp but tender.
4. Oil sheet pans with ½ ounce of olive oil and rub with cut garlic clove.
5. Place vegetables in single layer on sheet pan. Shake to coat with oil.
6. Rub salt, pepper, and oregano together in your hands and sprinkle lightly over vegetables.
7. Roast at 375° F for 15 minutes. Shake pans once after 7 minutes.
8. Cover and cool.
9. Arrange vegetables on a large platter and drizzle with balsamic vinegar just before service. Use lettuce to garnish edges.

VARIATIONS: Other vegetable choices: parsnip, bell peppers (green, red, yellow), turnip, string beans (blanched), white eggplant, shitake mushrooms.

Calories: **36**   Protein: **1.5 g (16%)**   Carbohydrates: **5.7 g (63%)**   Sodium: **120 mg**
Total Fat: **1.1 g (28%)**   *Saturated Fat: .2 g*   *Monounsaturated Fat: .6 g*   *Polyunsaturated Fat: .2 g*

❖ Cima alla Genovese   *Romagnoli*

This is a very attractive cold rolled veal appetizer, excellent for a summer lunch plate, but it is a bit labor intensive.

Portions per recipe: 90   *Pan: 12″ × 20″ × 4″*
Yield: 1 roll   *Temperature: 325° F*
Portion: 2 ounces   *Time: 2 hours*
Serving utensil: tongs or spatula

Ingredients

Ingredients	Amounts
Veal breast, boneless and trimmed	9 lb.
Veal, ground	1 lb.
Pork, lean, ground	8 oz.
Ham, ground	1 lb.
Raw pistachio nuts, blanched and skins removed	4 oz.
Frozen peas	4 oz.
Garlic cloves, crushed	½ oz.
Sweet gherkins, chopped	3 oz.
Eggs	4 oz.
Parmesan cheese, grated	3 oz.
Plain gelatin, dissolved in hot water	¼ oz.
Heavy cream	8 oz.
Eggs, hard-boiled and peeled	12 oz.
Ham 1″ square, long strips	10 oz.
Carrots, quartered	1 lb. 4 oz.
Onions, quartered	12 oz.
Celery stalks with tops	4 oz.
Chicken stock	8 lb.

Procedure:

1. Trim veal into rectangles, pound rectangles to a ½-inch thickness.
2. Mix ground meats with nuts, peas, gherkins, egg, and parmesan.
3. Mix dissolved gelatin with cream, fold into meats.
4. Spread filling on veal breasts.
5. Line up hard boiled eggs and 2 strips of ham down the center of the veal breast.
6. Roll up and tie with butcher string. Wrap in cheese cloth.
7. Place in pan. Add vegetables and chicken stock.
8. Cover and bake at 325° F for 2 hours.
9. Remove from liquid, weigh it down and let cool.
10. Remove cheesecloth and butcher's string, slice the breast into 2-ounce slices. Place on platter, garnish with parsley and gherkins.

Calories: **80**   Protein: **9.3 g (46%)**   Carbohydrates: **1.7 g (8%)**   Sodium: **151 mg**
Total Fat: **3.9 g (43%)**   *Saturated Fat: 1.6 g*   *Monounsaturated Fat: 1.4 g*   *Polyunsaturated Fat: .4 g*

An individual presentation of a cucumber sandwich.

❖ Cucumber Sandwiches

The filling is made with a mixture of cream cheese and lebani (yogurt cheese) to reduce fat content. Yogurt cheese is made by draining yogurt in a colander lined with cheese cloth for at least 24 hours in the refrigerator. See page 47 for yogurt cheese recipe.

PRODUCTION NOTES: The finely shredded cucumber must drain for 1 hour. Use firm whole wheat bread thinly sliced with the crusts trimmed off. The recipe fills 96 small sandwiches and provides extra filling for about 48 Belgian endive spears, which add drama to the presentation. Use the large outer leaves of the endive and save inner leaves for a tossed salad or for peas and lettuce.

For individual servings place two triangles on a small plate, add one filled spear, and garnish with a cherry tomato.

Portions per recipe: 48
Yield: 96 triangles/48 spears
Portion: 2 triangles/1 spear
Serving utensil: tongs

Serve chilled
Time: 1 hour

(continued)

Ingredients	Amounts	
Cucumbers	3 lb.	
Lebani (whole milk yogurt cheese)	3 lb.	
Cream cheese, softened	1 lb.	
Scallions, chopped		8 oz.
Marjoram, crushed		1/8 oz.
Cayenne pepper		1/8 oz.
Salt		1/2 oz.
Whole wheat bread, sliced	3 lb.	8 oz.
Belgian endives	1 lb.	

Procedure:

1. Peel and seed cucumbers, shred finely, salt lightly, drain them for 1 hour.
2. Cream cheeses together and add scallions, spices, and drained cucumbers.
3. Trim bread, spread slices with cream cheese, and cut into triangles.
4. Peel endives into spears, use small pieces for garnish.
5. Fill pastry bag with filling and pipe onto endive spears.
6. Arrange spears around outer edge of a platter and pile bread triangles neatly into the center. Chill until served.
7. See photo on page 61 for individual presentation.

Calories: **165**   Protein: **6.5 g (16%)**   Carbohydrates: **24.6 g (60%)**   Sodium: **373 mg**

Total Fat: **4.4 g (24%)**   *Saturated Fat:* **2.6 g**   *Monounsaturated Fat:* **1.1 g**   *Polyunsaturated Fat:* **.2 g**

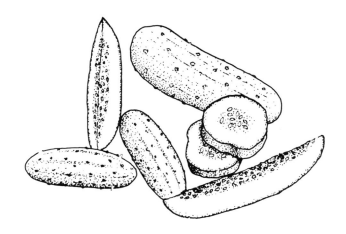

❖ Danish Deviled Eggs

A simple version of deviled eggs. Herb and garlic flavored lebani (yogurt cheese) is piped on halved eggs without removing the yolk. No scooping, no refilling. (See previous recipe for making yogurt cheese on page 47.)

Portions per recipe: 50
Yield: 100 halves
Portion: 2 halves
Serving utensil: spoon

Serve chilled

Ingredients

Ingredients	Amounts	
Eggs, hard-boiled and peeled	6 lb.	4 oz.
Mayonnaise		4 oz.
Yogurt cheese	1 lb.	8 oz.
Parsley, very finely minced		4 oz.
Scallions, very finely minced		2 oz.
Garlic cloves, very finely minced		1 oz.
Dry mustard		½ oz.
Worcestershire sauce		1 oz.
Radish sprouts		1 oz.

Procedure:

1. Remove a thin slice from both ends of the egg, cut egg in half to create a round half and not lengthwise which would make an oval shape.
2. Mix remaining ingredients into a smooth paste.
3. Fit pastry bag with large star tube.
4. Fill bag with cheese filling and pipe onto egg yolk to cover.
5. Cover plate lightly with sprouts, set egg halves neatly on platter, and dust with paprika.

Calories: **112** Protein: **8.1 g (29%)** Carbohydrates: **2.2 g (8%)** Sodium: **103 mg**

Total Fat: **8.2 g (65%)** *Saturated Fat:* **2.5 g** *Monounsaturated Fat:* **2.7 g** *Polyunsaturated Fat:* **2.0 g**

❖ Hummus Dip

A wonderful vegetarian dip from the Middle East, it is a great filling for pita bread and other sandwiches. Low in saturated fats and with good amounts of protein and complex carbohydrates, it can be used as a spread for vegetarian sandwiches.

Portions per recipe: 128
Yield: 8 pounds
Portion: 1 ounce
Serving utensil: #24 scoop

Pan: 12″ × 20″ × 2″–¼ size
Serve chilled
Time: 2 hours

Ingredients	Amounts
Canned chick peas	6 lb. 10 oz.
Tahini paste, oil stirred in	2 lb.
Lemon juice	8 oz.
Garlic cloves, crushed	3 oz.
Cumin	½ oz.
Cayenne pepper	⅛ oz.
Salt to taste	
Fresh parsley, finely chopped	2 oz.

Procedure:

1. Drain chick peas, reserve liquid.
2. Place all ingredients except parsley in food chopper and chop until smooth.
3. If the mixture is too dry, add some of the reserved chick pea liquid.
4. Chill for 2 hours. Arrange dip in a bowl on a platter surrounded by vegetables and pita bread wedges or place on the salad bar.
5. Sprinkle with minced parsley.

Calories: **72**   Protein: **2.4 g (14%)**   Carbohydrates: **7.2 g (40%)**   Sodium: **78 mg**

Total Fat: **4.1 g (51%)**   *Saturated Fat:* **.6 g**   *Monounsaturated Fat:* **1.5 g**   *Polyunsaturated Fat:* **1.8 g**

❖ Italian Mozzarella and Tomato with Fresh Basil

As tasty as it is beautiful to look at, this dish represents the Italian national colors. Fresh mozzarella in brine is preferable, but semi-soft skim mozzarella will do. Use local vine-ripened tomatoes or slice beefsteak tomatoes that have been left to ripen at room temperature. Unripe tomatoes should never be stored below 55°, unfortunately they often have been held at those temperatures enroute to your kitchens. See color plate **1**.

PRODUCTION NOTES: Remove stems from the basil. Cut the basil leaves into strips with a very sharp knife to prevent bruising.

Portions per recipe: 48	*Pan: round trays*
Yield: 2 trays	*Serve chilled*
Portion: 1½ ounces cheese	*Time: 30 minutes*
Serving Utensil: spoon	

Ingredients

Ingredients	Amounts
Fresh mozzarella	4 lb. 8 oz.
Ripe tomatoes, sliced	8 lb.
Olive oil	2 oz.
Oregano, crushed	¼ oz.
Black pepper, freshly ground	¼ oz.
Salt	½ oz.
Basil leaves, cut into thin strips	2 oz.

Procedure:

1. Cut mozzarella into slices that approximate the size of the tomato slices.
2. To serve place three slices of tomato and one slice cheese onto platters, repeat pattern, overlapping slightly into rows or circles.
3. Drizzle with olive oil.
4. Rub oregano, salt, and pepper together in your hands to mix well, sprinkle on platter.
5. Just before serving stack basil leaves neatly and cut into thin strips.
6. Sprinkle cheese and tomatoes liberally with basil.

Calories: **144**   Protein: **8.9 g (25%)**   Carbohydrates: **4.1 g (12%)**   Sodium: **279 mg**
Total Fat: **10.5 g (65%)**   *Saturated Fat:* **5.8 g**   *Monounsaturated Fat:* **3.9 g**   *Polyunsaturated Fat:* **.5 g**

❖ Marinated Artichokes

A strong lemon garlic marinade gives flavor to canned artichokes.

Portions per recipe: *50*
Yield: *1 pan*
Portion: *2 ounces (2 to 3 hearts)*
Serving utensil: *slotted spoon*

Pan: *12" × 20" × 6"–½ size*
Serve chilled
Time: *2–3 days*

Ingredients	Amounts
Artichoke hearts (canned)	12 lb. 12 oz.
Olive oil	3 oz.
Garlic cloves, peeled	2 oz.
Lemon juice	6 oz.
Black pepper	⅛ oz.
Oregano, crushed	⅛ oz.
Italian parsley, minced	4 oz.
Lemon, cut into wedges	8 oz.

Procedure:

1. Drain artichokes in colander for 30 minutes.
2. Beat rest of ingredients together.
3. Pour over drained artichokes. Marinate for 2 to 3 days. Remove garlic cloves.
4. Garnish with minced parsley and lemon wedges.

Calories: **54**   Protein: **1.2 g (9%)**   Carbohydrates: **5.6 g (41%)**   Sodium: **307 mg**

Total Fat: **3.5 g (58%)**   *Saturated Fat:* **.5 g**   *Monounsaturated Fat:* **2.5 g**   *Polyunsaturated Fat:* **.3 g**

❖ Marinated Green Olives

Spanish olives can be surprisingly good if marinated, as in this recipe, for 5 days with lemon zest, fresh hot peppers, marjoram, and garlic. See color plate **1**.

PRODUCTION NOTES: Hot peppers come in many varieties and are not often accurately labeled in the produce market. Ask for hot Hungarian wax peppers or red chili peppers. Handle hot peppers with gloves to avoid coming in contact with the hot oils, which can cause numbness to the hands. The membranes with the seeds carry more fire than the flesh and are removed in this recipe.

Portions per recipe: 60
Yield: 5 pounds
Portion: 4–5 olives
Serving utensil: small tongs

Serve at room temperature
Time: 5 days

Ingredients

Ingredients	Amounts
Large Spanish olives, drained	*5 lb.*
Hot red chili peppers	*4 oz.*
Garlic cloves, sliced	*2 oz.*
Olive oil	*2 oz.*
Marjoram, crushed	*¼ oz.*
Balsamic vinegar	*1 oz.*
Lemon peel	*2 oz.*

Procedure

1. Rinse olives, drain, cover with hot water, soak for 2 hours. Drain.
2. Julienne chili peppers.
3. Toss with olives, garlic, olive oil, balsamic vinegar, and marjoram.
4. Cut thin strips of peel from lemons, julienne them, and add to olives.
5. Toss, cover, and refrigerate for 5 days. Stir once a day.
6. On the day they are served, bring olives to room temperature. Put them on a plate and garnish with lemon slices and rings of red chilies.

Calories: **35**   Protein: **.4 g (5%)**   Carbohydrates: **.9 g (10%)**   Sodium: **481 mg**

Total Fat: **3.5 g (90%)**   *Saturated Fat:* **.1 g**   *Monounsaturated Fat:* **.7 g**   *Polyunsaturated Fat:* **.1 g**

❖ Marinated Kalamata Olives   *Michela's*

These olives are served at Michela's restaurant in Cambridge, Massachusetts. The oranges give a sweet balance to the pungent flavor of the olives. See color plate **1**.

Portions per recipe: 100   *Serve chilled*
Yield: 1 gallon   *Time: 1 day*
Portion: 1 ounce
Serving utensil: small tongs

Ingredients	*Amounts*	
Kalamata olives	*5 lb.*	
Oranges, washed and unpeeled	*2 lb.*	
Garlic cloves, crushed		*1 oz.*
Red pepper flakes		*⅛ oz.*
Fresh rosemary, chopped		*½ oz.*

Procedure:

1. Quarter oranges, remove any seeds, and cut into ¼-inch thick slices.
2. Add to olives.
3. Add garlic and spices. Toss.
4. Cover and marinate for at least 24 hours.

Calories: **65**   Protein: **.5 g (3%)**   Carbohydrates: **1.7 g (10%)**   Sodium: **596 mg**

Total Fat: **6.5 g (90%)**   *Saturated Fat:* **.6 g**   *Monounsaturated Fat:* **4.0 g**   *Polyunsaturated Fat:* **.4 g**

❖ "Midway" Olives and Preserved Lemon   *Wolfert*

Unusual but delightful, these olives are marinated Moroccan style. Freshly ground spices are essential to authentic Moroccan cooking. Invest in an electric coffee grinder and delight in the superb aroma and flavor of spices. Preserved lemons add their unique taste. (See recipe on page 467.) They are simple to make, but need 30 days to pickle. See color plate **16**.

Portions per recipe: 112
Yield: 7 pounds
Portion: 1 ounce
Serving utensil: small tongs

Pan: 12″ × 20″ × 2″– ¼ size
Temperature: 70° F
Time: 3 hours

Ingredients   Amounts

Ingredients	Amounts
Greek Royal olives, drained and rinsed	7 lb.
Garlic cloves	3 oz.
Cilantro, leaves and stems	1 oz.
Parsley leaves	¾ oz.
Hungarian paprika	½ oz.
Cayenne pepper	⅛ oz.
Cumin seed, pulverized	¼ oz.
Olive oil	1 oz.
Lemon juice	6 oz.
Preserved lemon peel	4 oz.

Procedure:

1. Place olives in bowl.
2. Chop garlic with herbs in food chopper until they form a paste.
3. Add spices, oil and juice, pour over olives. Toss.
4. Marinate 3 hours.
5. Rinse preserved lemon, remove pulp, and cut rind into thin slivers.
6. Place olives in serving dishes and sprinkle with lemon rind. Serve at room temperature.

Calories: **82**   Protein: **.6 g (2%)**   Carbohydrates: **2.5 g (12%)**   Sodium: **746 mg**
Total Fat: **8.5 g (92%)**   *Saturated Fat:* **.7 g**   *Monounsaturated Fat:* **5.0 g**   *Polyunsaturated Fat:* **.5 g**

❖ **Panzanella** *Michela's*

A fresh basil flavored cucumber and tomato salad is served on crisp toasted Italian or French bread slices.

PRODUCTION NOTES: Bread can be toasted in advance and stored until needed. This is a good way to salvage day old bread. For individual service, top 2 slices with salad, place on small plate with a sprig of basil.

Portions per recipe: 60
Yield: 120 slices
Portion: 2 slices bread and 2 oz. salad
Serving utensil: spoon and tongs

Temperature: 450° F
Time: 6 minutes

Ingredients	Amounts
Bread, very thinly sliced	1 lb. 8 oz.
Olive oil	2 oz.
Salt	1 oz.
Black pepper	¼ oz.
Ripe tomatoes, diced small	8 lb.
Cucumbers, peeled, seeded, and diced small	8 lb.
Red onions, diced very small	2 lb.
Red wine vinegar	2 oz.
Balsamic vinegar	1 oz.
Olive oil	3 oz.
Salt	¾ oz.
Black pepper, freshly ground	⅛ oz.
Basil leaves, chopped	4 oz.

Procedure:

1. Place slices of bread on sheet pans.
2. Drizzle with oil, sprinkle with salt and pepper.
3. Toast in 450° F oven for 6 minutes. Watch closely. Cool completely and store until needed.
4. Toss prepared vegetables with vinegars, oil, salt, pepper, and basil. Chill.
5. To serve, place salad in glass bowls and the bread in baskets.

Calories: **79**   Protein: **2.0 g (6%)**   Carbohydrates: **11.1 g (56%)**   Sodium: **201 mg**
Total Fat: **3.4 g (38%)**   *Saturated Fat:* **.4 g**   *Monounsaturated Fat:* **2.1 g**   *Polyunsaturated Fat:* **.3 g**

❖ Prosciutto e Melone

An Italian classic, it is good to eat and easy to prepare. See color plate **1**.

PRODUCTION NOTES: The melons must be ripe. Chill the melons before slicing them. The best prosciutto is lean and not too salty with a deep smoky flavor.

Portions per recipe: 64
Yield: 2 platters
Portion: 1 wedge
Serving utensil: tongs

Serve chilled

Ingredients	Amounts
Honeydew melon, ripe	8 lb.
Lean prosciutto	1 lb.

Procedure:

1. Cut melon into quarters, seed and peel.
2. Cut peeled wedges into 4 pieces.
3. Slice prosciutto paper thin.
4. Fold slice like ribbon candy and secure with toothpick to melon wedge.
5. Arrange melon wedges in circles on platter, and place some folded prosciutto slices in the center of the platter or arrange prosciutto slices around platter edge and place plain melon wedges in the center. (The latter method means less preparation time and work.)

Calories: **23**   Protein: **2.0 g (35%)**   Carbohydrates: **2.4 g (42%)**   Sodium: **69 mg**
Total Fat: **.6 g (23%)**   *Saturated Fat:* **.2 g**   *Monounsaturated Fat:* **.3 g**   *Polyunsaturated Fat:* **.1 mg**

❖ Roasted Peppers

This wonderful appetizer would be impossible to produce in large quantities if fresh peppers needed to be grilled and peeled. Nothing quite compares to freshly roasted peppers, and for a small group I recommend them. But, happily for institutions, excellent canned roasted peppers are readily available. See color plate **1**.

Portions per recipe: 100　　　　　　*Pan: 12″ × 20″ × 2″–½ size*
Yield: 2 gallons　　　　　　　　　*Serve chilled*
Portion: 2 ounces　　　　　　　　*Time: 24 hours*
Serving utensil: slotted spoon

Ingredients	Amounts
Canned roasted red peppers	18 lb.
Olive oil, extra virgin	2 oz.
Garlic cloves, halved	1 oz.
Black pepper	¼ oz.

Procedure:

1. Drain peppers in colander. Cut large pieces in half.
2. Place rest of ingredients in bowl. Add peppers. Toss.
3. Refrigerate at least 24 hours.
4. Remove garlic before service, garnish with parsley sprigs.

Calories: **22**　Protein: **.7 g (12%)**　Carbohydrates: **3.4 g (61%)**　Sodium: **894 mg**

Total Fat: **.8 g (32%)**　*Saturated Fat:* **.1 g**　*Monounsaturated Fat:* **.4 g**　*Polyunsaturated Fat:* **.02 g**

❖ Spicy Mushrooms

The hot Hungarian wax peppers give a spicy bite to the pickled mushrooms; their yellow-orange skins also add color. The skin is tender and requires no peeling, which makes the peppers ideal for this dish. See color plate **1**.

PRODUCTION NOTES: The mushrooms should be very fresh and small. Rinse (do not soak) the mushrooms briefly in a colander to remove any dirt, then let them drain for 30 minutes. Remove any blemishes and dark stem ends.

Portions per recipe: *100*
Yield: *2 gallons*
Portion: *2.5 ounces*
Serving utensil: *slotted spoon*

Pan: *12" × 20" × 6"–½ size*
Temperature: *simmer*
Time: *10 minutes*

Ingredients	Amounts
Mushroom buttons	15 lb.
Hot Hungarian wax peppers, seeded	3 lb.
Lemon juice	12 oz.
Garlic cloves, halved	1 oz.
Ginger root, unpeeled and sliced	1 oz.
Dry mustard	¼ oz.
Whole bay leaf	1/16 oz.
Salt	1 oz.
Olive oil	2 oz.

Procedure:

1. Place cleaned mushrooms in kettle.
2. Cut peppers into ½-inch pieces. Add to mushrooms.
3. Add the rest of ingredients except olive oil and bring to a simmer.
4. Simmer for 10 minutes. Pour into pan, cover, and refrigerate.
5. To serve, remove mushrooms from marinade, toss with olive oil and arrange on a plate. Discard garlic and bay leaf.
6. Garnish with lemon slices, a whole Hungarian pepper, and parsley.

Calories: **27**   Protein: **1.6 g (24%)**   Carbohydrates: **3.6 g (53%)**   Sodium: **113 mg**
Total Fat: **.9 g (30%)**   *Saturated Fat:* **.1 g**   *Monounsaturated Fat:* **.4 g**   *Polyunsaturated Fat:* **.2 g**

❖ Spuma di Fegatini—Mousse in Aspic *Romagnoli*

This surprisingly airy paté was developed by Margaret Romagnoli. Offer the paté with melba or Italian bread. A small amount is very satisfying.

PRODUCTION NOTES: Clear chicken broth is required for the aspic. To clear broth, remove all fat, then beat egg white into broth, bring to a simmer. Strain through a double layer of rinsed cheese cloth.

Portions per recipe: 50	Pan: 12″ × 20″ × 2″–¼ size
Yield: 1 loaf	Serve chilled
Portion: 1 ounce	Time: 24 hours
Serving utensil: spreader	

Ingredients	Amounts
Unflavored gelatin	1 oz.
Clear chicken broth, well-seasoned (Reserve 6 ounces of broth for besciamella)	2 lb.
Unsalted butter	1 oz.
All-purpose flour	¾ oz.
Nutmeg, grated	dash
Unsalted butter	1 oz.
Chicken livers, trimmed, all fat removed	1 lb.
Fresh sage leaves	⅛ oz.
Salt	¼ oz.
Black pepper	¼ oz.
Heavy cream, whipped and chilled	4 oz.

Procedure:

1. Soften gelatin in a small amount of broth.
2. Heat broth and add softened gelatin. Heat until dissolved and clear.
3. Refrigerate the gelatin until syrupy. This is the aspic.
4. Melt the butter, add flour and cook for 3 minutes.
5. Stir in reserved broth and nutmeg. Cook to a stiff pudding consistency. Wrap in plastic and chill. This is the besciamella.
6. Heat the butter and sauté chicken livers with sage for 6 to 8 minutes.
7. Add salt and pepper and purée livers in a food processor. Chill.
8. Beat together the cold besciamella, 1 cup of aspic syrup, and the puréed livers. Fold in the chilled whipped cream.
9. Chill pan in freezer. Brush insides with aspic syrup to coat. Repeat the procedure three times, chilling the pan between brushings.
10. Place a decorative pattern of parsley, black olives, red pepper strips on aspic, coat lightly with aspic.
11. Spoon stiff mousse into pan. Level with spatula.
12. Pour aspic over top. Cover and chill for 24 hours.
13. To unmold, dip the pan briefly into hot water. Turn onto platter. Garnish with parsley sprigs.

Calories: **31**   Protein: **2.2 g (28%)**   Carbohydrates: **.8 g (10%)**   Sodium: **63 mg**

Total Fat: **2.1 g (62%)**   *Saturated Fat:* **1.2 g**   *Monounsaturated Fat:* **.6 g**   *Polyunsaturated Fat:* **.1 g**

❖ Vegetarian Sushi with Wasabi

The rice is simmered in dashi broth (*see instructions below*), placed on a nori (toasted seaweed) sheet and rolled up with avocado slices, red pepper strips, stewed shitake mushrooms and a little wasabi paste, a very potent Japanese horseradish.

PRODUCTION NOTES: Sushi mats make these a snap to roll. Mats are available in Asian and health food stores.* To make dashi, put the kombu (seaweed/kelp) in cold water and cook it over low heat. Remove the kombu when the water comes to a boil. (Save the kombu and add it shredded to vegetable soups). Add bonito flakes to the liquid and turn off the heat. Strain the liquid through a cheese cloth for a clear and flavorful dashi. Wasabi is a Japanese horseradish and it is available in powdered form. Mushrooms can be soaked overnight.

Portions per recipe: 40
Yield: 80 pieces
Portion: 2 pieces
Serving utensil: tongs

Serve chilled
Time: 30 minutes

Ingredients	Amounts	
Water	3 lb.	
Kombu (dried seaweed)		¼ oz.
Bonito flakes		¼ oz.
Mirin (Japanese sweet flavoring)		2 oz.
Brown rice, rinsed	1 lb.	8 oz.
Rice vinegar		2 oz.
Dried Shitake (or Chinese) mushrooms		½ oz.
Soy sauce		1 oz.
Mirin (Japanese sweet flavoring)		½ oz.
Red bell peppers, seeded		12 oz.
Avocado, peeled and pitted	1 lb.	
Hoisin sauce		4 oz.
Wasabi powder (Japanese horseradish)		¾ oz.
Nori (toasted seaweed) (10 sheets)		¾ oz.
Pickled ginger		2 oz.
Watercress		4 oz.

Dipping Sauce (10 oz.)–¼ oz. per portion

Ingredients	Amounts
Soy sauce	5 oz.
Rice vinegar	2 oz.
Mirin (Japanese sweet flavoring)	1 oz.
Sake, rice wine	2 oz.

---

*Many Japanese cuisine ingredients can also be found in Asian and health food stores. Sake, the rice wine, can be purchased from a liquor store. The pickled ginger is vacuum packed in plastic bags and can be found in gourmet food stores as well.

Procedure:

1. Bring water with kombu very slowly to a simmer. Remove kombu. Add bonito flakes and strain broth after flakes have settled to the bottom.

2. Cook brown rice in dashi for 30 minutes. Sprinkle with vinegar. Cool.

3. Soak dried mushrooms in lukewarm water for 2 to 3 hours, discard stems, and slice caps into thin strips.

4. Bring soy sauce and mirin to a simmer, add mushroom strips.

5. Simmer until liquid is absorbed. Cool.

6. Cut red peppers into strips.

7. Mix hoisin sauce with wasabi powder to make a paste.

8. Place nori sheet on bamboo mat, rough side down. Spread with 1 cup rice, leaving ½ inch near you and 1 inch away from you uncovered.

9. Near lower edge place rows (1 inch apart) of pepper strips, avocado strips, and mushrooms topped with a teaspoon of the hoisin and wasabi paste.

10. Wet upper edge of nori and using the mat roll nori up away from you.

11. Squeeze roll together gently, lay sushi roll on sealed edge. Roll all sushi.

12. With a wet serrated knife trim edges and cut into 8 pieces.

13. Dipping sauce: Mix soy sauce, vinegar, mirin, and sake. Pour in a small dish in center of platter. Place sushi in neat circles around bowl. Surround sushi with pickled ginger and watercress leaves.

Calories: **85** Protein: **1.8 g (9%)** Carbohydrates: **14.8 g (69%)** Sodium: **165 mg**
Total Fat: **2.0 g (21%)** *Saturated Fat:* **.3 g** *Monounsaturated Fat:* **1.1 g** *Polyunsaturated Fat:* **.4 g**

Hot Appetizers

❖

The aroma of hot appetizers perfumes the air and gets the attention of a hungry crowd. Most of the recipes that follow will keep well and taste good piping hot or at room temperature. Only the fried squid and vegetable tempura need to be kept hot in chafing dishes. Hot appetizers are nice to pass among the guests, accompanied by napkins of course. All the hot appetizers can also be presented alone or in combination with other hot or cold hors d'oeuvres on plates as a first course. They are a splendid beginning to any banquet meal.

❖ Chicken Wings in Black Bean Sauce   *Hom*

In this recipe by Ken Hom, chicken wings are stir-fried with spices and fermented black beans and then braised in soy sauce and sherry. Fermented black beans are available in vacuum packed bags and must be rinsed before use. They only cost a fraction of the price of canned black bean sauce. Use the bean sauce if you cannot find fermented beans.

PRODUCTION NOTES: For a busy banquet prepare wings a day ahead, refrigerate them and reheat them in an oven until hot. They are also good at room temperature.

Portions per recipe: 180	*Pan: 12″ × 20″ × 2″*
Yield: 2 pans	*Skillet temperature: 375° F*
Portion: 3 drummets	*Time: 20 minutes*
Serving utensil: spoon	

Ingredients	Amounts	
Chicken wings, drummets only	40 lb.	
Peanut oil		1 oz.
Sesame oil		1 oz.
Ginger root, peeled, minced		9 oz.
Garlic cloves, crushed		9 oz.
Scallions, chopped		9 oz.
Black fermented beans, rinsed, chopped		12 oz.
Soy sauce		12 oz.
Dry sherry	1 lb.	2 oz.
Water or chicken stock	4 lb.	

Ken Hom's chicken wings sautéed in black bean sauce.

Procedure:

1. Thaw chicken wings, dry with toweling.
2. Heat peanut oil in tilting skillet.
3. Add ginger, and cook for 30 seconds. Add garlic, scallions, and fermented black beans. Cook for 1 minute.
4. Add chicken wings and stir-fry until brown.
5. Lower heat to 300° F. Add soy sauce, dry sherry, and water or stock.
6. Close lid and simmer for 15 minutes. Liquid will almost be evaporated.
7. Place in pan and garnish with scallion flowers.

Calories: **127**   Protein: **10.1 g (32%)**   Carbohydrates: **.9 g (3%)**   Sodium: **148 mg**

Total Fat: **9.1 g (63%)**   *Saturated Fat:* **2.5 g**   *Monounsaturated Fat:* **3.6 g**   *Polyunsaturated Fat:* **2.0 g**

❖ Chinese Chicken Wings

Wings are always popular with the college crowd and at casual receptions. They are an excellent picnic item, since they travel well. Drummets, the fleshy wing sections, are less messy to eat, which makes them a good choice for more formal occasions.

PRODUCTION NOTES: This recipe was designed to use a full 40-pound case of frozen wings. Wings can be kept in marinade and refrigerated for 4 to 5 days.

Portions per recipe: *175*
Yield: *500–540 wings*
Portion: *3 wings*
Serving utensil: *tongs*

Temperature: *325° F*
Time: *30 minutes*

Ingredients | Amounts

Ingredients	Amounts	
Soy sauce	2 lb.	
Hoisin sauce	1 lb.	
Granulated sugar		8 oz.
Ginger		2 oz.
Garlic cloves, crushed		2 oz.
Lemon juice		10 oz.
Sesame oil		1 oz.
Chicken wings	40 lb.	
Cilantro leaves, minced		2 oz.

Procedure:

1. Mix together ingredients for marinade.
2. Pour marinade over chicken wings, toss to cover well, then refrigerate.
3. Place wings on parchment-lined sheet pans.
4. Bake at 325° F for 30 minutes.
5. Sprinkle lightly with minced coriander leaves. Garnish with lemon slices.

Calories: **136**   Protein: **10.8 g (32%)**   Carbohydrates: **2.1 g (6%)**   Sodium: **444 mg**

Total Fat: **9.1 g (60%)**   *Saturated Fat:* **2.5 g**   *Monounsaturated Fat:* **3.6 g**   *Polyunsaturated Fat:* **2.0 g**

❖ Crostini Fontina

Crostini are a wonderful warm appetizer to serve as part of a buffet. They also go especially well with caponata or soup such as zuppa di cavolo. See color plate **1**.

PRODUCTION NOTES: Excellent at room temperature, but take care not to increase the amount of cheese, or it will taste like cold pizza. Sparingly sprinkle the cheese and this will bake to a golden brown and will be dry.

Portions per recipe: 64	*Pan:* 18″ × 26″ sheet pan
Yield: 128 slices	*Temperature:* 325° F
Portion: 2 slices	*Time:* 10 minutes
Serving utensil: tongs	

Ingredients — Amounts

Ingredients	Amounts
French bread, long, thinly sliced	4 lb.
Olive oil	4 oz.
Black pepper	⅛ oz.
Fontina cheese	1 lb.
Basil leaves, freshly chopped (optional)	2 oz.

Procedure:

1. Place bread slices on sheet pans. Drizzle with olive oil.
2. Sprinkle with pepper. Bake at 325° F until toasted golden. Cool.
3. Shred fontina and sprinkle ⅛ ounce on each crostini.
4. Bake for 10 minutes to brown cheese lightly. Sprinkle with basil. Serve.

Calories: **125**   Protein: **4.4 g (14%)**   Carbohydrates: **15.8 g (51%)**   Sodium: **232 mg**

Total Fat: **4.8 g (34%)**   *Saturated Fat:* **1.8 g**   *Monounsaturated Fat:* **2.4 g**   *Polyunsaturated Fat:* **.4 g**

❖ Fried Squid

Surprisingly a favorite with college students, but the squid are a bit tricky to fry.

PRODUCTION NOTES: Use mesh dippers to batter the squid. Let the squid drip for 3 to 4 minutes before dropping them directly into the hot oil of the fryolator.

Portions per recipe: 50		Pan: 12" × 20" × 2"	
Yield: 2 pans		Temperature: 350° F	
Portion: 6 rings/2 ounces		Time: 3 to 4 minutes	
Serving utensil: tongs			

Ingredients / Amounts

Ingredients	Amounts
Squid, cleaned	5 lb.
All-purpose flour	1 lb. 8 oz.
Baking powder	¼ oz.
Salt	¼ oz.
Cayenne pepper	¹⁄₁₆ oz.
Cold water	2 lb. 4 oz.

Procedure:

1. Remove any cartilage from squid and cut into rings.
2. Mix rest of ingredients into a light batter.
3. Rest batter for 15 minutes.
4. Dip 8 ounces of squid rings into batter. Remove with mesh ladle, let excess batter drip off. Repeat in batches.
5. Deep fry for 3 to 4 minutes at 350° F. Drain on paper towels.

Calories: **118**   Protein: **8.5 g (29%)**   Carbohydrates: **11.8 g (40%)**   Sodium: **98 mg**
*Total Fat: **3.8 g (29%)**   *Saturated Fat: .9 g*   *Monounsaturated Fat: .6 g*   *Polyunsaturated Fat:* **1.7 g**

---

*Includes frying oil.

❖ Indian Potato Pastries

Phyllo dough with a healthy filling of curried cauliflower and potatoes result in light and airy pastries.

PRODUCTION NOTES: *Asafoetida* is used in Indian and Iranian cooking. Because of its pronounced garlic and onion flavor, it must be used very sparingly. Asafoetida is available in health food stores and Asian and Indian markets.* These pastries freeze well before they are baked. To prepare frozen pastries, do not thaw them, just lower the oven temperature 50° F and increase the baking time by about 10 minutes.

Portions per recipe: *60*
Yield: *120 pieces*
Portion: *2 pastries*
Serving utensil: *tongs*

Pan: *18″ × 26″ sheet pan*
Temperature: *400° F*
Time: *12 minutes*

Ingredients	Amounts	
Phyllo dough sheets (14″ × 18″)	2 lb.	
Potatoes	5 lb.	
Cauliflower pieces	5 lb.	
Peanut oil		2 oz.
Spanish onion, diced	1 lb.	
Garlic cloves, crushed		½ oz.
Turmeric		¼ oz.
Cumin		¼ oz.
Garam masala		⅛ oz.
Asafoetida		¼ teaspoon
Salt		1 oz.
Unsalted butter		2 oz.

Procedure:

1. Steam potatoes for 12 minutes and mash.
2. Cook cauliflower in hot water for 5 minutes, chop coarsely.
3. Heat peanut oil and sauté onions and spices for 5 minutes.
4. Add the cooked cauliflower and sauté for 3 minutes. Simmer for 10 minutes.
5. Fold in mashed potatoes and cool slightly. Mixture should be dry. If mixture is too moist, raise heat and let liquid evaporate. Be sure to scrape bottom constantly with a spatula to prevent scorching.
6. Cut phyllo sheet into 3 long strips.
7. Melt butter. Brush each strip very lightly.

(continued)

---

*Garam masala, an Indian spice mixture, can also be found in health food stores, Asian markets, and Indian markets.

8. With a #24 scoop place filling onto right upper corner of the strip.

9. Fold lower corner over filling to form a triangle and keep folding from corner to corner, as you would a flag.

10. Place triangles on oiled sheet pan, brush lightly with butter.

11. Bake at 400° F for 10 minutes. Serve warm or at room temperature.

Calories: **99**   Protein: **3.0 g (12%)**   Carbohydrates: **17.7 g (72%)**   Sodium: **252 mg**

Total Fat: **2.1 g (11%)**   *Saturated Fat:* **.6 g**   *Monounsaturated Fat:* **.7 g**   *Polyunsaturated Fat:* **.4 g**

❖ Pot Stickers with Dipping Sauce

This recipe uses prepared wontons. There are several good brands on the market filled with meat or shrimp. Your operation must have a tilting skillet to make these in large quantities.

Portions per recipe: *180*   Pan: *12″ × 20″ × 2″*
Yield: *3 pans*   Temperature: *350° F*
Portion: *2 wontons*   Time: *7 to 8 minutes*
Serving utensil: *spoon*

Ingredients	Amounts	
Frozen wontons, meat filled	30 lb.	
Peanut oil		2 oz.
Sesame oil		1 oz.
Water	1 lb.	
Soy sauce	1 lb.	8 oz.
Rice vinegar		6 oz.
Ginger root, peeled and grated		2 oz.
Scallions (green tops only), chopped		6 oz.

Procedure:

1. Thaw wontons in refrigerator.

2. Heat tilting skillet with 1 ounce peanut and ½ ounce of sesame oil to 350° F.

3. Place about 15 pounds of wontons in one layer into skillet. (Repeat batch.)

4. Pour 8 ounces of water into pan, close lid and steam 7 to 8 minutes.

5. Remove wontons with spatula and place in pan. Only the parts of the wontons that stuck to the skillet will be browned (hence the name).

6. Garnish with scallions.

7. Mix soy sauce, vinegar, ginger, and scallions to make dipping sauce.

8. Serve Japanese dipping sauce (page 465) separately.

Calories: **182**   Protein: **8.3 g (18%)**   Carbohydrates: **26.2 g (57%)**   Sodium: **430 mg**

*Total Fat: **4.6 g (23%)**   *Saturated Fat: **.02 g**   *Monounsaturated Fat: **.06 g**   *Polyunsaturated Fat: **.07 g**

---

*Fat components for wontons were not available.

❖ Shrimp Puff Pastry

Flaky puff pastry is filled with shrimp, cream cheese, red peppers, and dill. Small raw frozen Maine shrimp are very good in this preparation. Fresh dill is available year round and very inexpensive, but use dill weed (⅛ the amount) in an emergency.

Portions per recipe: 120
Yield: 240 pieces
Portion: 2 triangles
Serving utensils: tongs

Pan: 18″ × 26″ sheet pan
Temperature: 375° F
Time: 8 to 10 minutes

Ingredients   Amounts

Ingredients	Amounts	
Puff pastry, prepared commercially	15 lb.	
Small Maine shrimp, thawed	5 lb.	
Cream cheese, softened to room temp.	3 lb.	
Red bell peppers, diced	2 lb.	
Scallions, chopped		4 oz.
Fresh dill, chopped		2 oz.
Salt		½ oz.
White pepper		⅛ oz.
Eggs		2 oz.
Water		8 oz.

Procedure:

1. Cut each pastry sheet into 12 pieces.
2. Mix together the rest of ingredients.
3. Brush pastry with water.
4. With a #40 scoop place filling onto squares.
5. Fold pastry over into triangles. Press edges together.
6. Beat egg with water and brush tops with egg wash.
7. Bake at 375° F for 8 to 10 minutes.
8. Arrange on doily-lined trays.

Calories: **291**   Protein: **7.1 g (10%)**   Carbohydrates: **18.7 g (25%)**   Sodium: **231 mg**
*Total Fat: **21.1 g (65%)**   *Saturated Fat: .3 g*   *Monounsaturated Fat: .2 g*   *Polyunsaturated Fat: .2 g*

---

*Fat components for puff pastry were not available.

❖ Vegetable Empañaditas

The pastry is made with whole wheat and ricotta cheese and spices and filled with a mixture of vegetables and Monterey Jack cheese. Serve with fresh salsa.

PRODUCTION NOTES: In Mexico the dough is made with lard, which makes a very flaky pastry. Chilled vegetable shortening and chilled flour with ice-cold water make this version of the pastry almost as flaky without using lard, which is high in saturated fat.

Portions per recipe: *36*
Yield: *72 pieces*
Portion: *2 pastries*
Serving utensil: *tongs*

Pan: *18" × 26" sheet pan*
Temperature: *350° F*
Time: *10 minutes*

Ingredients	Amounts	
Pastry		
Whole wheat flour	1 lb.	4 oz.
Vegetable shortening		8 oz.
Cumin		1/4 oz.
Turmeric		1/4 oz.
Hungarian paprika		1/4 oz.
Salt		1/4 oz.
Oregano, crushed		1/4 oz.
Skim-milk ricotta cheese		8 oz.
Ice water		4 oz.
Pastry Filling		
Vegetable oil		1 oz.
Spanish onion, diced		8 oz.
Romaine leaves, chopped		8 oz.
Garlic cloves, crushed		1 oz.
Red chili peppers		4 oz.
Red bell pepper, diced	1 lb.	
Whole kernel corn	1 lb.	
Cumin		1/4 oz.
Turmeric		1/4 oz.
Hungarian paprika		1/4 oz.
Salt		1/2 oz.
Monterey Jack cheese, shredded		12 oz.
Egg		2 oz.
Water		8 oz.

(continued)

Procedure:

1. Blend flour with shortening and spices. Add ricotta and ice water.
2. Mix quickly into soft dough. Chill.
3. Heat oil and sauté onions, romaine, and chilies.
4. Add red peppers, corn, and spices and cook at high heat, stirring constantly until liquid has evaporated.
5. Cool slightly and add cheese.
6. Roll out chilled dough and cut into 3 inch circles.
7. Beat egg with water to make an egg wash.
8. Brush dough with egg wash and place filling in center with a #40 scoop. Fold edges together to form a half moon and seal with a fork.
9. Brush with egg wash. Place on oiled sheet pans. Bake at 350° F for 10 to 12 minutes.

Calories: **175**   Protein: **6.2 g (14%)**   Carbohydrates: **16.8 g (38%)**   Sodium: **291 mg**

Total Fat: **11.1 g (57%)**   *Saturated Fat:* **3.7 g**   *Monounsaturated Fat:* **1.9 g**   *Polyunsaturated Fat:* **2.4 g**

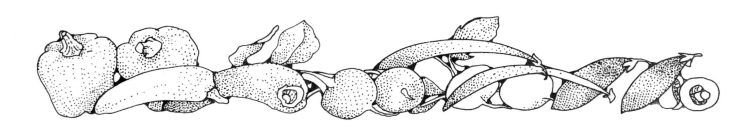

❖ Vegetable Tempura

Light, crisp batter encases winter squash, broccoli and onions. Feel free to substitute other vegetables. This is one of only four deep fried recipes in this book. There have to be exceptions to the rule to keep life interesting, and the dipping sauce and the vegetables are simply delicious.

PRODUCTION NOTES: Serve with dipping sauce and Japanese daikon condiment. Both recipes are in the condiment and sauce chapter.

Portions per recipe: *75*
Yield: *225 pieces*
Portion: *3 pieces*
Serving utensil: *tongs*

Temperature: *340° F*
Time: *4 to 5 minutes*

Ingredients | Amounts

Ingredients	Amounts
Ice water	2 lb. 8 oz.
Egg yolks	2 oz.
Baking powder	¼ oz.
All-purpose flour	1 lb.
Cornstarch	6 oz.
Winter squash, peeled and seeded	3 lb.
Broccoli florets	2 lb.
Large Spanish onions	2 lb.
Water	1 lb.

Procedure:

1. Beat ice water with egg yolks.
2. Mix baking powder with flour and cornstarch. Add to water all at once. Stir briefly, do not beat.
3. Cut winter squash into ¼-inch thick pieces, trim broccoli florets, and split stems, and quarter onions and separate layers.
4. Dust vegetables with flour, dip in batter.
5. Heat fryolators to 340° F and drop vegetables into oil about 15 pieces at a time.
6. Fry for 4 to 5 minutes, then remove to paper lined pans. Skim batter bits from oil. Repeat in batches.
7. Place doily on platter, set dipping sauce in the center, and surround it with tempura vegetables.

Calories: **71**   Protein: **1.3 g (7%)**   Carbohydrates: **9.1 g (50%)**   Sodium: **20 mg**
*Total Fat: **3.4 g (43%)**   Saturated Fat: **1.0 g**   Monounsaturated Fat: **.6 g**   Polyunsaturated Fat: **1.5 g**

---

*Includes frying oil.

❖ White Pizza

This pizza is for garlic and fontina lovers and all those unfortunate people who don't like tomatoes.

PRODUCTION NOTES: Use your own favorite pizza dough recipe, the pizza dough recipe on page 157, or the toscano bread recipe in Chapter 13. (The toscano recipe makes about 22 sheet pan pizzas.) Keep the dough refrigerated while prepping or it will rise too much. Add topping to two pans of pizza at a time (no more than that) and refrigerate until ready to bake.

Portions per recipe: 150   *Pan: 18″ × 26″ sheet pan*
Yield: 5 sheet pans   *Temperature: 400° F*
Portion: 2 pieces   *Time: 12 minutes*
Serving utensil: spatula

Ingredients	Amounts
Pizza dough	7 lb. 8 oz.
Garlic cloves	2 oz.
Oregano, crushed	1 oz.
Red pepper flakes	1/16 oz.
Olive oil	5 oz.
Fontina cheese, shredded	5 lb.
Mozzarella cheese, shredded	2 lb. 8 oz.

Procedure:

1. Divide dough into 12-ounce balls. Roll out to fit pan.
2. Refrigerate until ready to top.
3. Mince garlic with oregano, pepper flakes, and olive oil in food chopper.
4. Ladle 1 ounce onto each pizza.
5. Mix cheeses and sprinkle 1½ pounds on each pizza.
6. Bake at 400° F for 12 minutes.
7. Cut each pan into 60 pieces (3″ × 2.6″). Serve at once.

VARIATION: Chop fresh basil with Italian leaf parsley and sprinkle liberally over baked pizza. It's green, healthy, and delicious.

Calories: **157**   Protein: **7.8 g (20%)**   Carbohydrates: **13.2 g (34%)**   Sodium: **407 mg**
Total Fat: **7.9 g (45%)**   *Saturated Fat:* **4.0 mg**   *Monounsaturated Fat:* **3.0 mg**   *Polyunsaturated Fat:* **.5 g**

❖ Yakitori

Yakitori are sold in Japan as a quick snack by street vendors, and there are yakitori shops everywhere filling the air with their glorious aroma. I suggest you serve them with spicy peanut sauce (recipe on page 469). The sauce is of Thai origin, but I think the two are absolutely delicious together.

Yakitori can also be served as a dinner entrée. Prepare three skewers per person and serve them with steamed sushi rice and sesame spinach.

Portions per recipe: 72
Yield: 72 skewers
Portion: 1 skewer
Serving utensil: tongs

Temperature: 400° F
Time: 12 to 15 minutes

Ingredients	Amounts	
Boneless breasts of chicken	9 lb.	
Scallions, 1-inch pieces, white part only	3 lb.	
Green and red bell peppers	4 lb.	
Sesame oil		2 oz.
Soy sauce		12 oz.
Mirin, Japanese sweet flavoring		4 oz.
Ginger root, peeled and grated		1 oz.
Garlic cloves, crushed		2 oz.

Procedure:

1. Cut up chicken into ½-ounce pieces.
2. Seed peppers and cut into 1-inch pieces.
3. Skewer on 5-inch long bamboo sticks. Skewer a scallion, then a piece of chicken, then a pepper, repeat 3 times.
4. Mix oil, soy sauce, ginger root, and garlic.
5. Pour over skewers, marinate overnight.
6. Bake the skewers in the oven at 400° F for 12 to 15 minutes, or grill them under a broiler for 4 to 5 minutes on each side or over white-hot charcoal for 6 to 7 minutes.

Calories: **62** Protein: **9.4 g (60%)** Carbohydrates: **2.8 g (18%)** Sodium: **295 mg**
Total Fat: **1.4 g (19%)** *Saturated Fat:* **.3 g** *Monounsaturated Fat:* **.4 g** *Polyunsaturated Fat:* **.5 g**

— 4 —

SOUPS

Good cooks make good soups. If the soup is excellent, what follows cannot be bad: This has been my guide when eating out and it has rarely failed me.

Classic cuisine makes a distinction between clear soups and thick soups. In this book, they are divided into cold, hot, and full-course meal soups. I have included only the more unusual or highly nutritious soups. Old familiars can be found in most recipe files.

In Europe, cold soups are popular. In this country the only cold soups most people are familiar with are vichyssoise and gazpacho. Cold soups are especially pleasant in hot weather, but they may need additional marketing to become a successful menu item.

Most people enjoy eating hot soups in all kinds of weather. They are satisfying at lunch or dinner, and at times they can be a whole meal. The soups I call "full-course meals" only need a hunk of bread and a crisp salad to satisfy most appetites.

A soup and sandwich combination is always popular as a daily special and can contribute to repeat business. Combinations that pair the right flavors while using the best production techniques of the staff and the facility can be a rewarding challenge to a menu planner.

Soups are also a great way to use over-produced foods creatively. When making such home-style soups, cooks need to excercise a measure of restraint or they create hodgepodges of leftovers that contain everything but the kitchen sink. I have included a few basic recipes with variations as a guide for the less experienced.

Bases or Stocks: That Is the Question

❖

Most institutions, caterers, and restaurants use bases rather than stocks. Bases are high in salt (even though some manufacturers do offer reduced sodium products) and have very little flavor. They tend to have a nondescript taste, whether beef, poultry, or vegetarian, and are distinguishable only by color. The argument for using bases rests solely on their convenience.

Many people claim that in these days of pre-cut and packaged meat, stocks can no longer be produced successfully. True, large amounts of bones are no longer freely available. However, most kitchens have enough meat scraps, cooked meats, and pan drippings to make excellent stocks that are neither time consuming nor costly. Simmering stocks are the cook's caldrons that perform magic without witchcraft.

Many vegetarians are committed to a simpler and purer lifestyle and we who cook for them should respect this stance. Vegetable stocks should be prepared for vegetarian dishes, instead of using bases and water. Vegetable matter, especially tough and bruised outer lettuce leaves, is abundant in all kitchens and is usually discarded. Why not make it into a tasty and nutritious stock? Stocks are much richer in nutrients and more flavorful than any base, and the sodium content can be controlled by the cooks. Vegetable stock will keep for three to four days in the refrigerator and six months in the freezer.

In an emergency, prepare a Japanese dashi. Dashi, made from kelp, is a flavorful, clear, amber colored broth and can be ready in 12 minutes. It does use bonito flakes, however, and therefore cannot be said to be truly vegetarian. Use it instead of consomme and in place of chicken stock.

Here then are some basic ways to make good stock. Stock recipes do not have to be precise; the rough formula is: double the amount of liquid to meat and vegetable matter.

❖ Chicken Stock

Here are two methods to get good chicken stock. The first method uses all baked, sautéed, or broiled leftover chicken pieces. Pick good meat off the bones for chicken salad and casseroles or to add to a chicken soup. Then brown the bones with a very small amount of chicken fat or oil. To this add the outer leaves of lettuce, celery tops, onion peelings, parsley stalks, carrots, bay leaves, whole cloves, tarragon leaves, and one cup of white vermouth, cover with water and simmer for one hour. Strain the stock and discard the solids. If the stock is too bland, bring it back to a boil and reduce the liquid by a third for a stronger stock. If the stock is too pale add a little soy sauce for color. For the second method collect all pan juices from baked or broiled chicken, refrigerate them, and remove the fat. These drippings make an excellent base for sauces and soups. Add a small amount to the stock made by the other method, which usually is a little more bland.

❖ Beef Stock

Pan drippings alone are usually too dark and strong in flavor to use by themselves for soups. Use them with beef trimmings to make a rich golden stock. The coarsely chopped beef scraps are browned well in a tilting skillet or stock pot with a few onions and a cup of tomato paste. To this add bay leaf, whole allspice, vegetable scraps (no cabbage family members), and water to cover, and let the mixture simmer for two hours. The strained stock needs to be chilled and all fat removed. Again, to make the flavor more concentrated, boil and reduce the liquid's volume.

❖ Meat Stock

If there is a mixture of meat scraps available, make a meat stock. Follow instructions for chicken or beef stock and use all meat bones or scraps available, including ground beef and lean lamb. Lamb can impart a strong taste and I use it sparingly, unless I want to make a scotch broth. For a more intense flavor add to the stockpot the same herbs used in the chicken or beef stock. The stock should simmer no longer than two hours and should be reduced further only after the liquid has been strained.

❖ Fish Stock

If fish stock is necessary—and it rarely is—prepare the stock from chowder fish with dry vermouth, lemon slices, onion, celery, carrots, and spices. Simmer for about 30 minutes. Reserve the fish pieces for a chowder or fish salad. Strain and reduce liquid by one-third. For more flavor add bottled clam juice and freshly squeezed lemon juice. This stock works well for poaching whole salmon or halibut steaks.

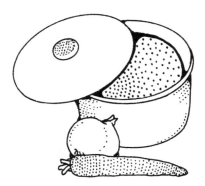

❖ Vegetable Stock

Many of the vegetarian recipes call for vegetable broth, and it is economical and nutritious to make stock. This recipe will make enough to refrigerate or freeze. Don't bother to peel the garlic cloves, but tie the dry herbs and spices into cheese cloth.

After straining the stock, the leftover vegetables can be the used to make green velvet soup.

Portions per recipe: 250
Yield: 10 gallons
Portion: 5 ounces
Serving utensil: 5-ounce ladle

Time: 60 minutes

Ingredients

Ingredients	Amounts	
Olive oil		4 oz.
Spanish onions, diced	2 lb.	
Garlic cloves, unpeeled		8 oz.
Celery tops, coarsely chopped	5 lb.	
Carrots, sliced	5 lb.	
Lettuce leaves, shredded	5 lb.	
Frozen peas	5 lb.	
Water	72 lb.	
Canned Italian tomatoes	6 lb.	6 oz.
Parsley sprigs		4 oz.
Whole black peppercorns		¼ oz.
Whole cloves		⅛ oz.
Bay leaves		⅛ oz.
Oregano, crushed		⅛ oz.

Procedure:

1. Heat olive oil in kettle and sauté onions until golden.
2. Add garlic, celery, carrots, lettuce, and peas and sauté for 5 minutes.
3. Add water, tomatoes with liquid, parsley, and spices tied in cheesecloth.
4. Simmer for 1 hour.
5. Strain broth. Remove spice bag. Save and puree vegetables for green velvet soup (recipe on page 107).
6. Refrigerate or freeze broth in shallow containers.

Calories: **21**   Protein: **.9 g (17%)**   Carbohydrates: **3.5 g (67%)**   Sodium: **39 mg**
Total Fat: **.5 g (21%)**   *Saturated Fat:* **.1 g**   *Monounsaturated Fat:* **.3 g**   *Polyunsaturated Fat:* **.1 g**

❖ Japanese Dashi

A clear broth made with kombu (seaweed) and bonito flakes.

Portions per recipe: 42
Yield: 2 gallons
Portion: 6 ounces
Serving utensil: 6-ounce ladle

Pan: 12″ × 20″ × 6″–½ size
Time: 12 minutes

Ingredients	Amounts
Kombu (seaweed/kelp)	4 oz.
Water (cold)	16 lb.
Dried bonito flakes	2 oz.
Soy sauce	1 oz.

Procedure:

1. Put kombu and cold water in kettle and bring slowly to a boil.
2. Remove kombu from the water and save to add to vegetable soups.
3. Turn off heat and add bonito flakes.
4. When flakes sink to bottom of kettle, strain broth and add soy sauce.

Calories: **2**   Sodium: **45 mg**

Cold Soups

Always chill cold soups very well. Plan ahead or, in an emergency, pop the soup in the freezer. Taste the soup before serving, because the flavors are less pronounced in a cold product and may need adjusting. Chilled soups must never be made with saturated fats; they harden when cold. If not properly amalgamated, the fats will coat the spoon with gritty-tasting residue. Avoid butter and margarine, and use vegetable or olive oil instead.

Serve the soup in iced bowls or cups to keep it well chilled. For a dramatic presentation, freeze the serving pan in a block of ice and place it on a tray decorated with the fruit and vegetable ingredients of the soup.

❖ Blueberry Yogurt Soup

Light and lemon flavored, this soup uses fresh blueberries in season. Frozen Maine blueberries can be used, but the soup will turn light purple because the berries will bleed.

Portions per recipe: 50
Yield: 2.5 gallons
Portion: 7 ounces
Serving utensil: 6-ounce ladle

Pan: 12″ × 20″ × 6″–½ size
Serve chilled
Time: 30 minutes

Ingredients	Amounts	
Lemon peel		2 oz.
Whole cloves		⅛ oz.
Apple juice	6 lb.	
Granulated sugar		4 oz.
Plain low-fat yogurt	15 lb.	
Blueberries, washed and picked over	4 lb.	
Lemon juice		2 oz.

Procedure:

1. Peel lemons thinly, removing only the yellow rind.
2. Place in kettle and add cloves, apple juice, and sugar.
3. Bring mixture to a boil and simmer for 30 minutes.
4. Strain the liquid. Reserve lemon peel and cool the apple juice syrup.
5. Gently beat cold syrup into yogurt. Add blueberries and lemon juice. Taste and chill.
6. Slice lemon peel into very thin slivers and sprinkle over soup before serving.

Calories: **141**   Protein: **7.4 g (21%)**   Carbohydrates: **23.3 g (66%)**   Sodium: **99 mg**

Total Fat: **2.3 g (15%)**   *Saturated Fat:* **1.4 g**   *Monounsaturated Fat:* **.6 g**   *Polyunsaturated Fat:* **.1 g**

The ingredients for chilled borscht and the final product.

❖ Chilled Borscht (Polish Klodnik)

This soup is a favorite of mine. I love the creamy pink color, varied texture, and complexity of flavors. The classic Klodnik contains cooked veal and crayfish. This version is tailored to the meat-avoiding eater and reduces fat by using some yogurt in place of sour cream. If you are not cooking for vegetarians, a good canned consomme can be substituted for the vegetarian stock. For a summer luncheon this is almost a meal if served with warm bite-size turnovers or Russian bread, a green salad, and fruit.

Portions per recipe: *50*
Yield: *2.5 gallons*
Portion: *7 ounces*
Serving utensil: *6-ounce ladle*

Pan: 12″ × 20″ × 6″–½ size
Serve chilled
Time: 1 hour

(continued)

Ingredients	Amounts
Beet greens	4 lb.
Vegetarian stock (chilled)	4 lb.
Dry white wine	1 lb. 12 oz.
Low-fat yogurt	6 lb.
Sour cream	2 lb.
Kosher-style pickles, finely chopped	12 oz.
Cucumber, peeled, seeded, and diced	1 lb. 8 oz.
Salt	1/2 oz.
White pepper	1/8 oz.
Dill, finely chopped	4 oz.
Cooked salad shrimp	2 lb.
Beets, Julienne, canned, drained	2 lb.
Chives, finely chopped	2 oz.
Eggs, hard-boiled and chopped	12 oz.

Procedure:

1. Remove large stems from greens, wash well, and steam or cook for 5 to 8 minutes until tender. Chop finely and chill.
2. Beat together stock, white wine, yogurt, and sour cream.
3. Add pickles, cucumbers, beet greens, salt, pepper, and dill to the stock.
4. Fold in shrimp and julienned beets. Chill.
5. Garnish soup with chopped chives and eggs.

Calories: **115**   Protein: **8.5 g (30%)**   Carbohydrates: **7.5 g (26%)**   Sodium: **345 mg**

Total Fat: **5.8 g (45%)**   *Saturated Fat:* **3.2 g**   *Monounsaturated Fat:* **1.7 g**   *Polyunsaturated Fat:* **.4 g**

❖ Cold Cucumber Soup

Cool mint and cucumber flavors with a touch of curry and fresh coriander make this a very refreshing summer soup. Merchandise this soup as a liquid cucumber salad.

PRODUCTION NOTES: Cut 1 inch off the stem end of the cucumbers to remove possible bitterness. Fresh garlic should be used for this soup. A garlic press saves time and effort. (If commercial garlic crushed in oil is used simmer it with dry vermouth or vegetarian stock before it is added to the rest of the ingredients, to remove the harsh taste.) The white bulbs of scallions are an acceptable alternative to the garlic if a milder flavor is wanted, but use double the quantity of scallions.

Portions per recipe: 50
Yield: 2.5 gallons
Portion: 6 ounces
Serving utensil: 6-ounce ladle

Pan: 12" × 20" × 6"–½ size
Serve chilled
Time: 2 hours

Ingredients	Amounts
Cucumber, peeled, seeded, and finely chopped	8 lb.
Garlic cloves, crushed	2 oz.
Low-fat yogurt	8 lb.
Sour cream	2 lb.
Cayenne pepper	1/16 oz.
Curry powder	1 oz.
Salt	2 oz.
Dill, chopped	2 oz.
Chives, chopped	2 oz.
Mint, chopped	2 oz.
Cilantro, chopped	1 oz.

Procedure:

1. Place cucumbers in a sieve and let drain for 15 minutes.
2. Mix all other ingredients until well blended.
3. Add cucumbers and chill for at least 2 hours.
4. Serve very cold.
5. For individual servings, garnish cup with a thin slice of cucumber and a mint leaf.

Calories: **97**   Protein: **4.9 g (20%)**   Carbohydrates: **8.6 g (35%)**   Sodium: **502 mg**

Total Fat: **5.1 g (47%)**   Saturated Fat: **3.1 g**   Monounsaturated Fat: **1.4 g**   Polyunsaturated Fat: **.2 g**

❖ Gazpacho

This is Spanish liquid salad. Regulate the "heat" by adjusting the amount of tabasco sauce.

Portions per recipe: 50
Yield: 2.5 gallons
Portion: 7 ounces
Serving utensil: 6-ounce ladle

Pan: 12″ × 20″ × 6″–½ *size*
Serve chilled
Time: 2 hours

Ingredients	Amounts	
Spanish onions, chopped		12 oz.
Celery, finely diced	1 lb.	
Cucumbers, peeled, seeded, and finely diced	2 lb.	
Green bell peppers, finely diced	2 lb.	
Italian plum tomatoes, finely diced	4 lb.	
Garlic cloves, crushed		1 oz.
Parsley, minced		4 oz.
Cilantro, chopped		2 oz.
Vegetable stock	4 lb.	
Tomato juice	8 lb.	
Worcestershire sauce		1 oz.
Tabasco sauce		⅛ oz.
Red wine vinegar		2 oz.
Granulated sugar		½ oz.
Freshly ground black pepper		¼ oz.
Salt		¾ oz.
Lemon juice		1 oz.

Procedure:

1. Place all ingredients in mixer and blend well.
2. Chill at least 2 hours. Serve very cold.

Calories: **40**   Protein: **1.6 g (16%)**   Carbohydrates: **8.4 g (83%)**   Sodium: **481 mg**
Total Fat: **.4 g (9%)**   *Saturated Fat:* **.04 g**   *Monounsaturated Fat:* **.03 g**   *Polyunsaturated Fat:* **.1 g**

❖ Zippy Avocado Soup

This soup is creamy smooth; it must be strained through a colander. Substitute vegetable stock or dashi for the chicken stock when cooking for vegetarians.

Portions per recipe: 50
Yield: 2.5 gallons
Portion: 6 ounces
Serving utensil: 6-ounce ladle

Pan: 12″ × 20″ × 6″–½ size
Serve chilled
Time: 4 hours

Ingredients	Amounts	
Chicken stock, all fat removed	12 lb.	
Garlic cloves, crushed		2 oz.
Unflavored gelatin		2 oz.
Ripe avocados, peeled and seeded	4 lb.	
Lemon juice		8 oz.
Salt		2 oz.
Plain low-fat yogurt	4 lb.	
Cayenne pepper		⅛ oz.
Ripe avocados, peeled, seeded, and sliced	1 lb.	8 oz.
Lemon juice		1 oz.
Fresh cilantro leaves		½ oz.

Procedure:

1. Slowly heat chicken stock with garlic and gelatin until stock is clear, do not boil. Remove from heat and let cool.
2. Puree avocados with lemon juice and salt.
3. Mix with cooled stock and yogurt. Add tabasco sauce.
4. Pour through a sieve or china cap.
5. Drizzle avocado slices with lemon juice to prevent discoloring.
6. Place one slice of avocado with a cilantro leaf on top of each serving.

Calories: **98**   Protein: **3.8 g (16%)**   Carbohydrates: **6.0 g (24%)**   Sodium: **470 mg**
Total Fat: **7.2 g (66%)**   *Saturated Fat:* **1.4 g**   *Monounsaturated Fat:* **4.4 g**   *Polyunsaturated Fat:* **.8 g**

Hot Soups

❖

Customers expect to be served bowls of piping hot soup. A soup's temperature should be carefully monitored as it is served. The bowls or cups should be warmed before the soup is ladled into them. Drips or spills from bowl rims should be wiped off with a clean towel before serving. Provide the correct ladle for self-service set-ups and clean the area frequently. Soup garnishes such as grated cheese, croutons, or sour cream should be placed near the serving bowl.

❖ Cream of Cauliflower Soup

A great way to use already cooked cauliflower. Make sure to save the water in which the cauliflower was cooked to use in this recipe. If the cauliflower has been cooked in salted water, omit salt in recipe.

PRODUCTION NOTE: Reduce fat and calories further by substituting evaporated skim milk for the light cream.

Portions per recipe: 50
Yield: 2.5 gallons
Portion: 6 ounces
Serving utensil: 6-ounce ladle

Pan: 12" × 20" × 6"–½ size
Cooking method: steam
Time: 20 minutes

Ingredients	Amounts
Butter or margarine	4 oz.
Spanish onions, finely minced	4 oz.
All-purpose flour	6 oz.
Water cauliflower was cooked in	6 lb.
Low-fat milk	6 lb.
Cauliflower, cooked, and coarsely chopped	5 lb.
Nutmeg	⅛ oz.
White pepper	⅛ oz.
Light cream	8 oz.
Salt	½ oz.
Parsley, minced	2 oz.

Procedure

1. Heat butter and sauté onions until golden.
2. Add flour and cook for 2 minutes.
3. Add cauliflower water slowly, stirring vigorously.

4. Bring to a simmer. Add milk, cauliflower, and spices. Taste.
5. Add cream, salt if needed, and sprinkle with parsley.

> Calories: **77**   Protein: **3.2 g (17%)**   Carbohydrates: **7.8 (41%)**   Sodium: **151 mg**
> Total Fat: **3.9 g (46%)**   *Saturated Fat:* **2.4 g**   *Monounsaturated Fat:* **1.1 g**   *Polyunsaturated Fat:* **.2 g**

❖ Fresh Cream of Celery Soup

This soup provides a welcome use for all the celery tops that are always left over because celery sticks are a constant salad bar item.

Portions per recipe: 50
Yield: 2.5 gallons
Portion: 6 ounces
Serving utensil: 6-ounce ladle

Pan: 12″ × 20″ × 6″–½ size
Time: 45 minutes

Ingredients	Amounts	
Celery stems and leaves, chopped	6 lb.	
Vegetable stock	5 lb.	
Vegetable oil		4 oz.
Garlic cloves, crushed		1 oz.
Spanish onions, chopped		8 oz.
Tarragon, crushed		⅛ oz.
All-purpose flour		6 oz.
Salt		1 oz.
White pepper		⅛ oz.
Nutmeg		¼ oz.
Evaporated skim milk	2 lb.	

Procedure:

1. Cook celery in vegetable stock until tender, about 30 minutes.
2. Heat oil and sauté garlic, onions, and tarragon for 5 minutes.
3. Add flour and cook for 5 minutes more.
4. Stirring constantly add celery stock slowly. Bring to a simmer.
5. Add spices and evaporated skim milk.
6. Garnish with chopped celery leaves.

> Calories: **59**   Protein: **2.2 g (15%)**   Carbohydrates: **7.3 g (49%)**   Sodium: **284 mg**
> Total Fat: **2.5 g (38%)**   *Saturated Fat:* **.7 g**   *Monounsaturated Fat:* **.4 g**   *Polyunsaturated Fat:* **1.2 g**

❖ Fresh Garlic Soup

Don't let the large amount of garlic scare you; simmered, the pungent cloves become mild and sweet. A wonderful creamy soup that uses day old Italian or French bread as a thickener.

Portions per recipe: *50*
Yield: *2.5 gallons*
Portion: *6 ounces*
Serving utensil: *6-ounce ladle*

Pan: *12" × 20" × 6"–½ size*
Time: *45 minutes*

Ingredients	Amounts
Olive oil	2 oz.
Spanish onions, sliced	8 oz.
Celery, diced	12 oz.
Chicken stock	16 lb.
Whole garlic cloves, peeled	12 oz.
Stale Italian or French bread, cubed	2 lb.
Salt	1 oz.
White pepper	¼ oz.
Dry vermouth	8 oz.
Light cream	8 oz.
Fresh parsley, minced	2 oz.
Fresh rosemary, minced	¼ oz.

Procedure:

1. Heat olive oil and sauté onions and celery until golden.
2. Add chicken stock, garlic, bread, salt, pepper, and vermouth.
3. Simmer slowly for 45 minutes.
4. Puree, reheat, and add cream.
5. Top with minced parsley and rosemary.

Calories: **91**   Protein: **3.5 g (15%)**   Carbohydrates: **13.1 g (58%)**   Sodium: **334 mg**

Total Fat: **2.7 g (28%)**   *Saturated Fat:* **.8 g**   *Monounsaturated Fat:* **1.4 g**   *Polyunsaturated Fat:* **.2 g**

❖ Green Velvet Soup

A curry-flavored soup that is delicious hot or cold. Use the vegetable puree reserved from making vegetable stock. Add low-fat yogurt to the cold soup and light cream to the hot soup. Light cream can be omitted altogether to reduce fat calories even further, or substitute evaporated skim milk.

Portions per recipe: 100
Yield: 5 gallons
Portion: 7 ounces
Serving utensil: 6-ounce ladle

Pan: 12" × 20" × 6" – ½ size
Time: 15 minutes

Ingredients

Ingredients	Amounts
Peanut oil	2 oz.
Curry powder	½ oz.
Turmeric	⅛ oz.
Vegetable puree	24 lb.
Vegetable stock	16 lb.
Salt	½ oz.
Light cream	1 lb.
Parsley, minced	4 oz.
Mint, finely chopped	2 oz.

Procedure:

1. Heat peanut oil in kettle, add curry and turmeric, and cook for 5 minutes.
2. Add vegetable puree and stock with salt. Bring to a simmer.
3. Turn off heat and stir in light cream, minced parsley, and chopped mint.
4. Serve hot.

VARIATION: To serve soup cold, refrigerate and stir in cold yogurt (double the amount) and chopped mint just before serving. Sprinkle with mint leaves. Set soup pan in crushed ice. Taste. Cold soup may need a little extra salt and a dash of tabasco.

Calories: **71*** Protein: **2.5 g (14%)** Carbohydrates: **9.8 g (55%)** Sodium: **153 mg**
Total Fat: **3.0 g (38%)** *Saturated Fat:* **.8 g** *Monounsaturated Fat:* **1.4 g** *Polyunsaturated Fat:* **.4 g**

Calories: **65†** Protein: **2.8 g (17%)** Carbohydrates: **9.6 g (59%)** Sodium: **158 mg**
Total Fat: **2.2 g (30%)** *Saturated Fat:* **.3 g** *Monounsaturated Fat:* **1.5 g** *Polyunsaturated Fat:* **.3 g**

---

*With cream.
†With yogurt.

❖ Harira   *Wolfert*

A very substantial soup from Morocco. Ms. Wolfert insists that the spices be freshly ground to get the best flavor possible.

PRODUCTION NOTES: The lemon and egg mixture must be added to the soup at a rolling boil to form strands. After adding the eggs, turn the heat off instantly.

Portions per recipe: *50*
Yield: *3 gallons*
Portion: *8 ounces*
Serving utensil: *6-ounce ladle*

Pan: *12″ × 20″ × 6″–½ size*
Time: *2 hours*

Ingredients	Amounts	
Lamb for stewing, ½″ cubes	4 lb.	
Unsalted butter		2 oz.
Turmeric		1 oz.
Black pepper		½ oz.
Cinnamon		1 oz.
Ginger root, pulverized		½ oz.
Celery, chopped	1 lb.	4 oz.
Spanish onions, chopped	2 lb.	
Parsley, minced		4 oz.
Canned Italian tomatoes, hand crushed	6 lb.	6 oz.
Lentils, rinsed	1 lb.	8 oz.
Canned garbanzo beans with liquid	4 lb.	
Salt		1 oz.
Water (cold)	12 lb.	
Frozen pearl onions	1 lb.	
Eggs		10 oz.
Lemon juice		4 oz.

Procedure:

1. Sauté lamb with butter, spices, celery, onions, and parsley for 5 minutes.
2. Add tomatoes and cook for 15 minutes more.
3. Add rinsed lentils, garbanzo beans, salt, and water. Simmer for 1 hour.
4. Add small onions and simmer for 30 minutes.
5. Beat eggs with lemon juice.
6. Add egg mixture in a slow stream to boiling soup to form thin strands.
7. Keep warm until served but do not boil.

Calories: **182**   Protein: **14.7 g (32%)**   Carbohydrates: **22.3 g (49%)**   Sodium: **275 mg**
Total Fat: **4.3 g (21%)**   *Saturated Fat:* **1.4 g**   *Monounsaturated Fat:* **1.2 g**   *Polyunsaturated Fat:* **.6 g**

❖ Home Style Soups

This is an ideal way to use leftover meats and vegetables. Start all soups by sautéing raw vegetables and cooked meats in oil with herbs or spices. This will give them a stronger taste. If cooked vegetables are the main soup ingredient, sauté some garlic and onions with herbs and add the cooked vegetables just before the soup is served long enough to heat through.

Leftover cooked starches are added to the simmering soup just before it is served. Rice and noodles should be cooked separately and added to the soup in batches to keep them firm and to keep the broth clear. Cooking the starches in the broth makes the soup cloudy. Do not add gravies to clear soups. Meats covered with sauce should be used only in hearty stew-like soups that also contain legumes or potatoes for texture. Pureed vegetables and cheese sauce can be used to make excellent home style cream soup.

The following variations all make 50 portions or 2.5 gallons.

CHICKEN NOODLE SOUP

Ingredients	Amounts
Oil	1 oz.
Onions, celery, carrots, diced	5 lb.
Chicken, cooked and diced	2 lb.
Chicken stock	12 lb.
Noodles (egg noodles, spaghetti, fettucine, angel hair), cooked, cut bite size	5 lb.
Parsley, minced	2 oz.

Procedure:

1. Sauté vegetables in oil until soft.
2. Add chicken and sauté 1 minute.
3. Add stock, bring to a simmer. Add noodles and parsley. Taste.

CHICKEN MINESTRONE

Use olive oil. For vegetables use onions, zucchini, and canned tomatoes. For noodles use elbows, penne, ditaline, or rotini. Add 2 pounds of garbanzo beans or white beans, plus the chicken. Flavor the chicken stock with fresh basil and parmesan cheese. Follow chicken noodle soup procedure.

CHINESE NOODLE SOUP

Omit chicken meat. Use sesame seed oil. For vegetables use sliced onions and celery and carrots cut into ½-inch pieces (or substitute Oriental-style leftover vegetables). Use any type of egg noodles. Flavor the chicken stock with soy sauce, a few spinach leaves, and fold in 10 beaten eggs (20 oz. or 1 egg to 5 portions). Follow chicken noodle soup procedure.

Cook Inger Jensen produces one of her excellent home style chicken noodle soups.

CHICKEN RICE SOUP

Ingredients	Amounts
Oil	1 oz.
Onions, celery	3 lb.
Garlic cloves, crushed	1 oz.
Chicken, cooked and diced	2 lb.
Chicken stock	12 lb.
Rice, cooked	3 lb.
Peas (frozen or cooked)	2 lb.
Red peppers or chopped tomatoes	2 lb.

Procedure:

1. Heat oil and sauté onions and garlic until soft.
2. Add chicken and sauté 1 minute.
3. Add stock and bring to a simmer.
4. Fold in cooked rice, peas, peppers, or tomatoes.
5. Taste and add salt and pepper if needed.

ORIENTAL CHICKEN RICE SOUP

Use sesame seed oil. For the vegetables, use garlic, peapods, and beansprouts. Flavor stock with soy and hot pepper sauces. Garnish with spinach leaves. Follow same procedure as chicken rice soup.

GREEK RICE AND LEMON SOUP

Use olive oil, garlic, chicken, rice, and 16 pounds of stock (no vegetables). Bring to a simmer. Beat 8 egg yolks with 1 cup of lemon juice. Turn off heat and stir into rice soup. Garnish with chopped parsley.

NOTE: All of the above soups can also be made with beef and beef or meat stock, and the Greek soup can be make with beef or lamb.

BEEF VEGETABLE SOUP

Ingredients	Amounts
Oil	1 oz.
Thyme, crushed	1/4 oz.
Oregano, crushed	1/4 oz.
Onions, celery, carrots, broccoli, peas, etc., chopped	8 lb.
Beef, diced or julienned	2 lb.
Beef stock	12 lb.
Fresh chives or parsley, minced	2 oz.

Procedure:

1. Heat oil with spices, add vegetables and beef.
2. Sauté for 5 minutes and add stock.
3. Bring to a simmer and add fresh herbs. Taste.

BEEF LETTUCE SOUP

A superb soup, it uses the dark green outer leaves of lettuce that are not tender enough for salads and leaves that are bruised.

Ingredients	Amounts
Oil	1 oz.
Garlic cloves, crushed	2 oz.
Spanish onions, sliced	1 lb.
Lettuce leaves, sliced into strips	8 lb.
White vermouth	1 lb.
Beef, cooked	2 lb.
Beef stock	10 lb.
Nutmeg, grated	1/4 oz.

Procedure:

1. In the oil, sauté garlic and onions until golden.
2. Fold in lettuce and sauté 1 minute.
3. Add beef, stock, and nutmeg. Taste and add salt and pepper if needed.

VARIATION: This soup can also be made with chicken stock or vegetable stock. For vegetarians omit meat and add 8 ounces of parmesan cheese just before serving.

❖ **Mexican Yogurt Soup**

Spicy with a smooth rich texture, it is low in fat and calories.

PRODUCTION NOTE: Mix yogurt with cornstarch and turn off heat before blending it into hot soup.

Portions per recipe: 50
Yield: 2.5 gallons
Portion: 7 ounces
Serving utensil: 6-ounce ladle

Pan: 12" × 20" × 6"–½ size
Time: 30 minutes

Ingredients / Amounts

Ingredients	Amounts
Vegetable oil	1 oz.
Garlic cloves, crushed	3 oz.
Spanish onions, diced	1 lb.
Granulated sugar	1 oz.
Chili powder	2 oz.
Cumin	¼ oz.
Oregano, crushed	¼ oz.
Canned tomato puree	7 lb.
Vegetarian stock	6 lb.
Canned green chili peppers, diced	1 lb. 14 oz.
Low-fat yogurt	5 lb.
Cornstarch	2 oz.
Salt	1 oz.

Procedure:

1. In oil sauté garlic, onions, sugar, and spices for 5 minutes.
2. Add tomato puree, stock, and canned chilis. Simmer for 10 minutes.
3. Mix yogurt with cornstarch and salt.
4. Turn off heat and blend yogurt mixture into soup.
5. Garnish with a dollop of yogurt and diced chilis.

Calories: **80**   Protein: **4.0 g (20%)**   Carbohydrates: **14.0 g (70%)**   Sodium: **276 mg**
Total Fat: **1.6 g (18%)**   *Saturated Fat: **.6 g***   *Monounsaturated Fat: **.3 g***   *Polyunsaturated Fat: **.4 g***

❖ Mulligatawney Soup

The English contribution to Indian cuisine, a soup flavored with curry and diced apples.

Portions per recipe: **50**
Yield: **2.5 gallons**
Portion: **7 ounces**
Serving utensil: **6-ounce ladle**

Pan: **12″ × 20″ × 6″–½ size**

Ingredients

Ingredients	Amounts
Vegetable oil	2 oz.
Spanish onions, diced	1 lb.
Green bell peppers, diced	1 lb.
Celery, diced	1 lb. 8 oz.
Carrots, diced	1 lb. 8 oz.
Unpeeled apples, cored and diced	2 lb. 8 oz.
All-purpose flour	6 oz.
Curry powder	½ oz.
Ground cloves	⅛ oz.
Salt	1 oz.
Black pepper	¼ oz.
Vegetarian stock, seasoned	12 lb.
Canned tomatoes, diced	6 lb. 6 oz.
Cilantro leaves, chopped	1 oz.

Procedure:

1. Sauté diced vegetables and apples in oil for 5 to 8 minutes.
2. Add flour and spices and cook for 2 minutes.
3. Slowly stir in stock, add tomatoes, and simmer for 30 minutes.
4. Garnish with cilantro leaves.

Calories: **65**   Protein: **1.5 g (9%)**   Carbohydrates: **12.1 g (74%)**   Sodium: **329 mg**

Total Fat: **1.8 g (24%)**   *Saturated Fat:* **.4 g**   *Monounsaturated Fat:* **.3 g**   *Polyunsaturated Fat:* **.7 g**

❖ Pasta e Fagioli *Romagnoli*

A very satisfying soup from Italy. Serve it with grated parmesan or romano cheese.

PRODUCTION NOTES: The salt pork adds to the soup's rich flavor, and the Romagnolis would not be happy if it were left out. However, in consideration of vegetarian and kosher customers you might want to eliminate it. The addition of the spicy oil makes this still a very flavorful soup even without the pork.

Portions per recipe: 100
Yield: 5 gallons
Portion: 8 ounces
Serving utensil: 6-ounce ladle

Pan: 12″ × 20″ × 6″–½ size
Oven temperature: 325° F
Time: 70 min

Ingredients

Ingredients	Amounts	
Olive oil		2 oz.
Spanish onions, diced		10 oz.
Carrots, diced		10 oz.
Celery, diced		8 oz.
Lean salt pork, chopped	1 lb.	
Potatoes, cubed	2 lb.	8 oz.
Garlic cloves, crushed		6 oz.
Canned canellini beans (white kidney beans)	13 lb.	10 oz.
Water	16 lb.	
Canned Italian tomatoes	8 lb.	9 oz.
Macaroni	4 lb.	
Olive oil		4 oz.
Dry rosemary leaves		½ oz.
Whole garlic cloves		3 oz.
Bay leaves		¹⁄₁₆ oz.
Red pepper flakes		⅛ oz.
Lemon rind, grated		2 oz.
Parmesan cheese, grated		10 oz.

Procedure:

1. Heat olive oil and sauté onions, carrots, celery, and salt pork.
2. Add potatoes, garlic, canellini beans, water, and tomatoes. Cook for 30 minutes.
3. Add macaroni and cook for 30 minutes more.
4. Bake oil, spices, and lemon rind in the oven at 325° F for 10 minutes.
5. Strain. Add the oil to soup and stir in well.
6. Soup will be very thick. Add a little hot stock or water to thin if desired.
7. Serve cheese separately or sprinkled over the top.

Calories: **235**   Protein: **10 g (17%)**   Carbohydrates: **34.2 g (58%)**   Sodium: **187 mg**
Total Fat: **7.0 g (27%)**   *Saturated Fat:* **2.3 g**   *Monounsaturated Fat:* **3.3 g**   *Polyunsaturated Fat:* **.9 g**

❖ Potage Parmentier—Leek and Potato Soup

A warm vichyssoise that is very smooth and rich tasting without a lot of cream. The soup is finished with yogurt and light cream.

PRODUCTION NOTES: Leeks must be split in half to ensure that all sand has been rinsed out of them. Use both the white and green parts of the leeks for this soup. Stir arrowroot into yogurt to prevent curdling. Do not let the soup boil after the yogurt has been added. This soup can also be served cold.

Portions per recipe: *100*
Yield: *5 gallons*
Portion: *7 ounces*
Serving utensil: *6-ounce ladle*

Pan: *12″ × 20″ × 6″–½ size*
Time: *45 minutes*

Ingredients	Amounts
Vegetable oil	3 oz.
Leeks, cleaned and chopped	9 lb.
Potatoes, diced	20 lb.
Chicken stock or vegetable stock	20 lb.
Salt	2 oz.
White pepper	¼ oz.
Light cream	1 lb.
Low-fat yogurt	2 lb.
Arrowroot	½ oz.
Nutmeg	⅛ oz.
Chives, chopped	2 oz.

Procedure:

1. Heat olive oil and sauté leeks for about 15 minutes until they are golden.
2. Add potatoes, stock, salt, and pepper.
3. Simmer for 30 minutes.
4. Gently stir light cream, yogurt, arrowroot, and nutmeg together.
5. Turn off heat and stir the cream and yogurt mixture into simmering soup. Taste.
6. Sprinkle with chopped chives.

Calories: **93**   Protein: **3.0 g (13%)**   Carbohydrates: **15.7 g (67%)**   Sodium: **233 mg**
Total Fat: **2.2 g (21%)**   *Saturated Fat:* **1.0 g**   *Monounsaturated Fat: .5 g*   *Polyunsaturated Fat: .5 g*

❖ Soupe au Pistou *Kamman*

This is a hearty vegetable soup with white beans. The pistou, the French version of the Italian pesto, gives the soup its superb flavor.

Portions per recipe: 100
Yield: 5 gallons
Portion: 8 ounces
Serving utensil: 6-ounce ladle

Pan: 12″ × 20″ × 6″–½ size
Time: 2 hours

Ingredients	Amounts	
Dry white pea beans	2 lb.	8 oz.
Water	8 lb.	
Olive oil		3 oz.
Garlic cloves, crushed		4 oz.
Parsley, minced		5 oz.
Salt		1 oz.
Black pepper		¼ oz.
Thyme, crushed		¼ oz.
Bay leaves, finely crushed		1/16 oz.
Carrots, ¼″ cubes	2 lb.	8 oz.
White turnips, ¼″ cubes	2 lb.	8 oz.
Leeks, ¼″ cubes	5 lb.	
Spanish onions, ¼″ cubes	3 lb.	
Potatoes, ¼″ cubes	5 lb.	
Water	16 lb.	
Green beans, ½″ pieces	5 lb.	

Pistou Blend

	Amounts
Garlic cloves	2 oz.
Olive oil	3 oz.
Black pepper	¼ oz.
Parmesan cheese	8 oz.
Basil leaves	6 oz.

(continued)

Procedure:

1. Bring pea beans in water to a boil. Let soak for 1 hour, bring to a boil and simmer until almost tender.
2. Heat olive oil in kettle with garlic and parsley.
3. Add salt and spices.
4. Fold in the diced carrots, turnips, leeks and onions and sauté lightly for 5 minutes.
5. Add water and potatoes, and bring to a boil.
6. After 10 minutes fold in cooked white beans and raw green beans. Simmer soup until potatoes are tender.
7. Make the pistou by blending all ingredients to a smooth paste in a food chopper or processor.
8. Stir pistou into soup just before service.

Calories: **104**   Protein: **4.7 g (18%)**   Carbohydrates: **16.0 g (62%)**   Sodium: **163 mg**

Total Fat: **2.7 g (23%)**   *Saturated Fat:* **.7 g**   *Monounsaturated Fat:* **1.5 g**   *Polyunsaturated Fat:* **.1 g**

❖ Sunny Carrot Cream Soup

Pureed carrot soup gets a dollop of whipped yogurt cream and is sprinkled with toasted sunflower seeds.

PRODUCTION NOTES: Reserve one quarter of the carrot slices and simmer in stock. These are folded into the pureed soup.

Portions per recipe: *100*
Yield: *5 gallons*
Portion: *7 ounces*
Serving utensil: *6-ounce ladle*

Pan: *12″ × 20″ × 6″–½ size*
Time: *35 minutes*

Ingredients

Ingredients	Amounts
Safflower oil	2 oz.
Cajun spice mixture (see page 458)	⅛ oz.
Raw sunflower seeds	8 oz.
Spanish onions, diced	2 lb.
Celery root, peeled and diced	4 lb.
Carrots, thinly sliced	20 lb.
Vegetable stock	16 lb.
Salt	2 oz.
White pepper	¼ oz.
Nutmeg	⅛ oz.
Parsley, minced	4 oz.
Cilantro, finely chopped	2 oz.
Mint, finely chopped	1 oz.
Heavy cream	12 oz.
Low-fat yogurt	1 lb.

Procedure:

1. Heat safflower oil with Cajun spice and roast seeds for 3 to 5 minutes. Stir often.
2. Remove with a slotted spoon. Reserve.
3. Add onions and celery root to oil and sauté for 5 minutes.
4. Take ¼ of carrot slices and add to vegetable stock. Bring to simmer.
5. Add rest of carrots to onions and celery root and sauté for 5 minutes.
6. Strain carrots from stock and reserve.
7. Add hot stock to vegetables and cook for 15 minutes.
8. Puree stock and vegetables and fold in the chopped herbs and reserved carrots. Heat.
9. Whip cream and fold in yogurt.
10. Top each serving with a dollop of yogurt cream and sprinkle with toasted sunflower seeds.

Calories: **69**   Protein: **1.8 g (10%)**   Carbohydrates: **10.7 g (62%)**   Sodium: **267 mg**
Total Fat: **2.7 g (35%)**   *Saturated Fat:* **.9 g**   *Monounsaturated Fat:* **1.0 g**   *Polyunsaturated Fat:* **.9 g**

❖ Tangy Tomato Soup with Lemon Grass   *Hom*

This refreshing soup developed by Ken Hom was first published in his book, *Asian Vegetarian Feast*. I have adapted his recipe to serve 100.

PRODUCTION NOTE: Lemon grass is available whole from Asian markets and some produce purveyors. Use only the soft inside of the stalk.

Portions per recipe: 100   *Pan: 12" × 20" × 6"–½ size*
Yield: 5 gallons   *Time: 20 minutes*
Portion: 6 ounces
Serving utensil: 6-ounce ladle

Ingredients

Ingredients	Amounts
Chicken stock, all fat removed	24 lb.
Lemon grass	4 oz.
Salt	2 oz.
Granulated sugar	4 oz.
Lemon juice	6 oz.
Scallions, finely chopped	8 oz.
Hot red chilies, diced	4 oz.
Cilantro, chopped	2 oz.
Canned tomatoes, diced	12 lb. 6 oz.
Egg whites, beaten with a pinch of salt	1 lb.
Sesame oil	2 oz.
Cilantro leaves	2 oz.

Procedure:

1. Bring chicken stock to a simmer.
2. Split lemon grass, remove white soft center, and finely chop.
3. Add lemon grass to stock with salt, sugar, lemon juice, scallions, chilies, cilantro, and diced tomatoes. Simmer for 10 minutes.
4. Mix beaten egg whites with sesame oil.
5. Pour into simmering soup in a very slow, thin stream.
6. Pull egg whites into long strands by working figure eights through the whites with a fork.
7. Garnish soup with cilantro leaves.

Calories: **30**   Protein: **1.4 g (19%)**   Carbohydrates: **4.2 g (56%)**   Sodium: **321 mg**

Total Fat: **.8 g (24%)**   *Saturated Fat:* **.1 g**   *Monounsaturated Fat:* **.3 g**   *Polyunsaturated Fat:* **.3 g**

Udon noodles in dashi broth.

❖ Udon Noodles in Dashi Broth

In Japan noodles are served by street vendors at all hours of the day or night. The Japanese twirl the noodles around the chopsticks to eat them and slurp the remaining broth from the bowl.

PRODUCTION NOTES: Udon noodles are made with soft flour (unlike pasta which is made with semolina or hard wheat flour) and must be cooked gently. If water comes to a rolling boil, quickly add cold water to return it to a simmer. When serving this soup, it is easier to put the noodles into bowls first, add scallions and tofu, then ladle on the hot broth.

Portions per recipe: 84
Yield: 84 bowls
Portion: 3 ounces noodles and
    4 ounces broth
Serving utensil: 4-ounce ladle

(continued)

Ingredients	Amounts
Dried mushrooms	4 oz.
Dashi broth	16 lb.
Soy sauce	1 oz.
Mirin	1 oz.
Udon noodles	8 lb.
Water	16 lb.
Salt	1 oz.
Scallions, chopped	8 oz.
Tofu, silky, small cubes	2 lb.

Procedure:

1. Soak mushrooms in warm water for 4 to 5 hours.

2. Make dashi broth (page 97) if not on hand.

3. Thinly slice mushroom caps and simmer them in dashi, soy sauce, and mirin for 15 minutes.

4. Cook udon noodles for 7 to 8 minutes until they are al dente. Drain and hold in cold water.

5. Dip noodles into boiling water and ladle 3 ounces into each hot soup bowl.

6. Add a few scallions, and a few cubes of tofu.

7. With a 4-ounce ladle pour hot dashi over noodles making sure that 2 or 3 slices of mushrooms are served.

Calories: **167**   Protein: **6.0 g (14%)**   Carbohydrates: **33.4 g (80%)**   Sodium: **946 mg**

Total Fat: **.9 g (4%)**   *Saturated Fat:* **.1 g**   *Monounsaturated Fat:* **.1 g**   *Polyunsaturated Fat:* **.4 g**

❖ Wonton Soup

This soup uses prepared frozen wontons. There are several good varieties on the market that are filled with beef, pork, or shrimp. Ask your vendor for samples and select the one that suits your operation. Don't neglect to ask for a nutritional analysis.

PRODUCTION NOTE: The broth can be heated and prepared all at once, but the wontons have to be cooked in batches of no more than 200 at a time.

Portions per recipe: *100*
Yield: *200 wontons/3 gallons broth*
Portion: *2 wontons and 5 ounces broth*
Serving utensil: *3-ounce ladle (2 times)*

Pan: *12″ × 20″ × 6″–½ size*
Temperature: *Boiling*
Time: *6 minutes*

Ingredients

Ingredients	Amounts
Chicken stock	32 lb.
Soy sauce	12 oz.
Sesame oil	3 oz.
Frozen wontons	6 lb. 4 oz.
Water (boiling)	40 lb.
Spinach leaves, stems removed	1 lb.

Procedure:

1. Bring chicken stock to a simmer. Add soy sauce and sesame oil.
2. Cook wontons in batches of 200 for 6 to 7 minutes in boiling water.
3. Remove with a skimmer and place 50 into each pan.
4. Add 4 ounces of spinach leaves and 1 gallon of hot chicken stock to each pan.
5. Serve with a 3-ounce ladle, spooning twice.

Calories: **85**   Protein: **3.7 g (17%)**   Carbohydrates: **10.4 g (49%)**   Sodium: **277 mg**

Total Fat: **2.7 g (29%)**   *Saturated Fat:* **.9 g**   *Monounsaturated Fat:* **1.0 g**   *Polyunsaturated Fat:* **.6 g**

❖ Zuppa di Cavolo *Michela's*

A light Italian soup made with two kinds of cabbage.

PRODUCTION NOTES: Pancetta is Italian bacon. Cut from the pig's belly, it is a mixture of lean meat and fat rolled into the size of a big salami and cured but not smoked. It is readily available.

Portions per recipe: *100*
Yield: *5 gallons*
Portion: *7 ounces*
Serving utensil: *6-ounce ladle*

Pan: *12" × 20" × 6"–½ size*
Time: *30 minutes*

Ingredients	Amounts
Pancetta, small cubes	1 lb.
Garlic cloves, crushed	4 oz.
Fresh rosemary, chopped	2 oz.
Spanish onions, thinly sliced	3 lb.
Savoy cabbage, shredded into long strips	7 lb. 8 oz.
Green cabbage, shredded into long strips	7 lb. 8 oz.
Dry white wine or vermouth	12 oz.
Beef stock, defatted	24 lb.
Salt	1 oz.
Black pepper	¼ oz.

Procedure:

1. Sauté pancetta with garlic, rosemary, and onions until pancetta is crisp and onions are golden.
2. Add shredded cabbage and sauté for 10 minutes stirring often.
3. Add white wine and beef stock. Simmer for 15 minutes.
4. Taste and add salt and pepper.
5. Serve this soup with crostini fontina or offer grated cheese separately.

Calories: **51**   Protein: **2.5 g (20%)**   Carbohydrates: **4.3 g (34%)**   Sodium: **154 mg**
Total Fat: **2.8 g (50%)**   *Saturated Fat:* **1.0 g**   *Monounsaturated Fat:* **1.2 g**   *Polyunsaturated Fat:* **.4 g**

Full-Course Meal Soups

❖

Hearty and nutritionally balanced, these soups almost constitute a meal. Complemented by crusty bread and a fruit or mixed green salad they are good for lunch or light supper meals. These soups are served with an 8-ounce ladle.

❖ Beef and Bean Soup

Dried pea beans and fresh green beans add vegetable protein to this soup. It is best made with fresh beans, but frozen Italian beans can be substituted if fresh green beans are of poor quality. Serve with bread and a fresh fruit salad.

PRODUCTION NOTE: Soak the pea beans overnight in 4 times their weight in water.

Portions per recipe: *100*
Yield: *8 gallons*
Portion: *10 ounces*
Serving utensil: *8-ounce ladle*

Pan: *12″ × 20″ × 6″–½ size*
Time: *1½ hours*

Ingredients	*Amounts*	
Pea beans, dry	5 lb.	
Water (cold)	20 lb.	
Olive oil		1 oz.
Lean ground beef	12 lb.	8 oz.
Spanish onions, thinly sliced	1 lb.	
Garlic cloves, crushed		4 oz.
Celery, ½″ pieces	2 lb.	
Carrots, ¼″ slices	2 lb.	
Thyme, crushed		¼ oz.
Marjoram, crushed		¼ oz.
Red pepper flakes		⅛ oz.
Water	16 lb.	
Canned Italian tomatoes	12 lb.	6 oz.
Green beans, 2-inch pieces	4 lb.	
Salt		2 oz.
Parsley, minced		4 oz.

(continued)

Procedure:

1. Simmer or steam the soaked pea beans until tender.
2. Heat oil and brown beef with onions, garlic, celery, carrots, and spices.
3. Add water and tomatoes. Simmer for 60 minutes.
4. Add green beans and salt and cook for 15 minutes.
5. Sprinkle with freshly chopped parsley just before serving.

Calories: **253**   Protein: **15.9 g (25%)**   Carbohydrates: **19.6 g (31%)**   Sodium: **367 mg**
Total Fat: **12.5 g (44%)**   *Saturated Fat:* **4.9 g**   *Monounsaturated Fat:* **5.4 g**   *Polyunsaturated Fat:* **.7 g**

❖ Chicken Gumbo

A specialty of the South made with chicken, ham, okra, and red and green peppers. Traditionally, stewing hens would be used. Simplify the recipe by using boneless chicken meat. Serve with warm cornbread and a green salad.

PRODUCTION NOTES: Frozen chicken pieces (stir-fry) can be used in this recipe, but thaw them before sautéing. Fresh okra is not readily available outside the South. Frozen sliced okra is a good alternative. File powder is ground sassafras.

Portions per recipe: 100   *Pan: 12" × 20" × 6"–½ size*
Yield: 8 gallons   *Time: 1 hour*
Portion: 9 ounces
Serving utensil: 8-ounce ladle

Ingredients	Amounts	
Peanut oil		2 oz.
Spanish onions, thinly sliced	3 lb.	
Green bell peppers, thinly sliced	3 lb.	
Red bell peppers, thinly sliced	3 lb.	
Ham, cubed	2 lb.	
Chicken, uncooked ½" pieces	12 lb.	8 oz.
Raw converted long grain rice	3 lb.	
Thyme, crushed		¼ oz.
Cayenne pepper		⅛ oz.
Salt		1 oz.
Water	32 lb.	
Canned Italian tomatoes, hand crushed	6 lb.	6 oz.
Frozen sliced okra	4 lb.	
File powder		4 oz.

Procedure:

1. Heat peanut oil and sauté onions, peppers, and ham for 10 minutes.
2. Add chicken, rice, thyme, cayenne, and salt. Cook for 10 minutes.
3. Add water, tomatoes, and okra. Simmer for 30 minutes.
4. Mix file powder with a little cold water and stir into soup.
5. Simmer gumbo for 10 minutes longer. Be careful not to let it boil.

Calories: **124**   Protein: **9.3 g (30%)**   Carbohydrates: **14.8 g (48%)**   Sodium: **280 mg**

Total Fat: **2.5 g (18%)**   *Saturated Fat:* **.6 g**   *Monounsaturated Fat:* **.9 g**   *Polyunsaturated Fat:* **.6 g**

❖ Japanese Meat and Shrimp Dumplings Stew

This is a less complicated version of oden nabe, a Japanese beef and chicken stew with shrimp dumplings. It does not contain konnyaku, a gelatin-like product made from seaweed, because it is rarely available in this country. This stew is usually served with hot mustard. Follow the Chinese mustard recipe (page 463), but mix the dry ground mustard with equal parts vinegar and sake.

Portions per recipe: *48*   Pan: *12″ × 20″ × 4″*
Yield: *2 pans*   Time: *2 hours*
Portion: *9 ounce*
Serving utensil: *6-ounce ladle*

Ingredients | Amounts

Ingredients	Amounts	
Beef chuck, 1″ cubes	4 lb.	
Boneless chicken thighs, cut in half	6 lb.	
Chicken stock or water	12 lb.	
Soy sauce		8 oz.
Mirin		4 oz.
Sake		4 oz.
Granulated sugar		2 oz.
Potatoes, quartered	6 lb.	
Tofu, 1″ cubes	2 lb.	
Eggs, hard boiled (48)	5 lb. 4 oz.	

(continued)

Dumplings:

Shrimp, peeled, thawed	*1 lb.*	
Whitefish	*2 lb.*	
French bread, rinds cut off		*3 oz.*
Egg whites		*4 oz.*
Salt		*½ oz.*
White pepper		*⅛ oz.*

Garnish:

Watercress, stems removed	*2 oz.*

Procedure:

1. Put beef, chicken, soy sauce, mirin, sake, sugar, and water into kettle.
2. Bring to a simmer, skimming off any foam that rises to surface. Cook for one hour.
3. Add potatoes and simmer for 30 minutes.
4. Pour 2 gallons into 4" pan.
5. Add 1 pound tofu and 24 eggs to each pan. Fold in gently.
6. Make shrimp dumplings by placing dumpling ingredients into food chopper or processor and blending until very smooth.
7. With a #24 scoop, dip dumplings on to hot stew, 24 per pan.
8. Cover and steam for 10 minutes. Garnish with watercress.
9. Serve each customer 1 egg and 1 dumpling and 1 ladle of soup.

Calories: **245**   Protein: **28.0 g (46%)**   Carbohydrates: **11.2 g (18%)**   Sodium: **548 mg**

Total Fat: **9.2 g (34%)**   *Saturated Fat:* **2.6 g**   *Monounsaturated Fat:* **3.3 g**   *Polyunsaturated Fat:* **1.8 g**

❖ Lentil Soup

Make this soup with vegetable stock for the vegetarian or use meat stock and serve with sliced kielbasa sausage for the meat eater.

PRODUCTION NOTES: Always sort lentils to check for small stones. Lentils do not need soaking, they cook very quickly. Brown lentils keep their shape and are excellent for soups and salads. Red lentils become mushy quickly and are ideal if a creamy lentil soup is wanted.

Portions per recipe: *100*
Yield: *8 gallons*
Portion: *9 ounces*
Serving utensil: *8-ounce ladle*

Pan: *12″ × 20″ × 6″–½ size*
Time: *1 hour*

Ingredients	Amounts	
Olive oil		8 oz.
Spanish onions, diced	2 lb.	
Garlic cloves, crushed		3 oz.
Green bell peppers, diced	2 lb.	
Celery ribs and leaves, chopped	3 lb.	
Brown lentils, sorted and washed	10 lb.	
Curry powder		1 oz.
Red pepper flakes		⅛ oz.
Ground turmeric		¼ oz.
Thyme, crushed		⅛ oz.
Black pepper		¼ oz.
Stock or water	32 lb.	
Potatoes, cubed	8 lb.	
Canned tomatoes, diced	6 lb.	6 oz.
Salt		1 oz.
Yogurt (optional)	3 lb.	2 oz.
Mint, chopped		2 oz.
Kielbasa (optional)	6 lb.	4 oz.

Procedure:

1. Heat olive oil and sauté onions, garlic, peppers, and celery for 5 minutes.
2. Add lentils and spices and sauté for 5 more minutes.
3. Add stock or water and potatoes and simmer for 30 minutes.
4. Add tomatoes and salt and cook for another 15 minutes.
5. Mix yogurt with chopped mint and serve separately as a garnish.

(continued)

VARIATION: Serve topped with thinly sliced kielbasa sausage (1 ounce per person).

Calories: **218***   Protein: **14.6 g (27%)**   Carbohydrates: **35 g (64%)**   Sodium: **185 mg**

Total Fat: **3.2 g (13%)**   *Saturated Fat:* **.6 g**   *Monounsaturated Fat:* **1.8 g**   *Polyunsaturated Fat:* **.5 g**

Calories: **306**†   Protein: **18.4 g (24%)**   Carbohydrates: **35.6 g (46%)**   Sodium: **489 mg**

Total Fat: **10.8 g (32%)**   *Saturated Fat:* **3.4 g**   *Monounsaturated Fat:* **5.5 g**   *Polyunsaturated Fat:* **1.4 g**

❖ Scandinavian Fish Soup

A clear fish chowder full of shrimp and dill. See color plate **5**.

Portions per recipe: 100   *Pan: 12" × 20" × 6"–½ size*
Yield: 8 gallons   *Time: 30 minutes*
Portion: 9 ounces
Serving utensil: 8-ounce ladle

Ingredients	Amounts
Vegetable oil	2 oz.
Leeks, washed well and sliced	6 lb.
Carrots, sliced	4 lb.
Potatoes, peeled and sliced	12 lb.
Water	16 lb.
Salt	1 oz.
White pepper	¼ oz.
White firm fish, 2" pieces	18 lb. 12 oz.
Shrimp, medium (32–40 ct), peeled	5 lb.
Fresh dill weed, chopped	3 oz.

Procedure:

1. Heat oil. Sauté leeks and carrots for 10 minutes.
2. Add potatoes, water, salt, and pepper and simmer for 15 minutes.
3. Add fish and peeled shrimp and simmer for 8 minutes.
4. Add dill weed just before serving.

Calories: **154**   Protein: **22.4 g (58%)**   Carbohydrates: **11.0 g (29%)**   Sodium: **227 mg**

Total Fat: **1.9 g (11%)**   *Saturated Fat:* **.4 g**   *Monounsaturated Fat:* **.3 g**   *Polyunsaturated Fat:* **.9 g**

---

*Soup without kielbasa.
†Soup with kielbasa.

❖ Sopa de Pollo y Nuez— Mexican Chicken and Almond Soup

This creamy chicken soup is flavored with almonds and chilies. Serve it with warm flour tortillas and a grapefruit and avocado salad. Reduce fat calories further by substituting all low-fat yogurt for the cream.

PRODUCTON NOTES: Frozen stir-fry chicken pieces make this recipe a snap to make. Cilantro, also called coriander or Chinese parsley, gives an authentic Mexican taste to this soup. Instead of fresh flour tortillas stale tortillas can be utilized in this fashion. Cut stale tortilla in quarters; brush with oil, sprinkle with Cajun spice and bake at 400° F until crisp and lightly browned.

Portions per recipe: 100　　　　　　　　　*Pan: 12" × 20" × 8"–½ size*
Yield: 8 gallons　　　　　　　　　　　　　*Oven temperature: 300° F*
Portion: 9 ounces　　　　　　　　　　　　*Time: 45 minutes*
Serving utensil: 8-ounce ladle

Ingredients

Ingredients	Amounts
Vegetable oil	2 oz.
Boneless chicken, small pieces	10 lb.
Hungarian paprika	1 oz.
Spanish onions, diced	4 lb.
Hot chilies, halved, seeded, and thinly sliced	12 oz.
Oregano leaves, crushed	½ oz.
Salt	1 oz.
Water or chicken stock	32 lb.
Potatoes, peeled and thinly sliced	10 lb.
Ground almonds	2 lb.
Canned green chilies, diced	6 lb.
Light cream	1 lb.
Low-fat yogurt	1 lb.
Cornstarch	4 oz.
Parsley, chopped	4 oz.
Cilantro, chopped	2 oz.

(continued)

Procedure:

1. Heat oil and sauté chicken pieces with paprika for 5 minutes.
2. Add onions, chilies, and oregano and sauté for 5 minutes more.
3. Add salt, liquid, and potatoes and simmer for 25 minutes.
4. Toast ground almonds until they are light brown in 300° F oven.
5. Add almonds and canned chilies to soup and cook for 5 minutes.
6. Mix light cream with yogurt and cornstarch and stir into hot soup. Simmer for 2 minutes, do not boil.
7. Fold in chopped herbs.

Calories: **110**   Protein: **8.0 g (29%)**   Carbohydrates: **11.7 g (42%)**   Sodium: **130 mg**

Total Fat: **4.2 g (34%)**   *Saturated Fat:* **1.1 g**   *Monounsaturated Fat:* **1.8 g**   *Polyunsaturated Fat:* **.9 g**

❖ Vegetarian Hot and Sour Soup

I have eliminated the traditional pork and used vegetable stock or dashi broth so vegetarians can enjoy this soup.

PRODUCTION NOTES: Cloud ears are tiny black dried mushrooms and golden needles are the dried buds of the tiger lily. If your groceries purveyor does not carry them, call a wholesaler specializing in Oriental food stuffs.

Portions per recipe: *50*
Yield: *4 gallons*
Portion: *9 ounces*
Serving utensil: *8-ounce ladle*

Pan: *12″ × 20″ × 8″–½ size*
Time: *30 minutes*

Ingredients	Amounts
Dried cloud ears	3 oz.
Golden needles (lily buds)	5 oz.
Water (warm)	2 lb.
Vegetable stock or dashi broth	20 lb.
Cellophane noodles	1 lb.
Cornstarch	6 oz.
White pepper	⅛ oz.
Cayenne pepper	⅛ oz.
Rice vinegar	14 oz.
Soy sauce	6 oz.
Dry sherry	4 oz.
Mushrooms, washed and thinly sliced	3 lb.
Silken tofu, cubed small	6 lb.
Eggs, beaten	3 lb.
Scallions, chopped	12 oz.

Procedure:

1. Soak cloud ears and golden needles in warm water for 30 minutes.
2. Bring stock to a simmer. Add cellophane noodles.
3. Add soaked mushrooms and needles with liquid to broth. Discard any sediment. Simmer broth for 10 minutes.
4. Mix cornstarch with peppers. Dissolve in vinegar, soy sauce, and sherry.
5. Stir into broth. Add tofu and mushrooms. Simmer for 5 minutes.
6. Beat eggs with sesame oil and stir into soup. Add scallions.

Calories: **151**   Protein: **8.9 g (24%)**   Carbohydrates: **17.7 g (47%)**   Sodium: **228 mg**
Total Fat: **5.8 g (34%)**   *Saturated Fat:* **2.6 g**   *Monounsaturated Fat:* **1.8 g**   *Polyunsaturated Fat:* **2.2 g**

5

A MELTING POT OF ENTRÉES
Ethnic Dishes, Fresh and Flavorful

Beef and Veal

Americans consume large quantities of red meat, most of it in the form of steaks and hamburgers. A good lean hamburger with a touch of mayonnaise, a ripe tomato slice, and crisp green lettuce is indeed a wonderful sandwich. Lathered with fat-loaded "special sauce" and joined by french fries and milk shakes, however, it is no longer a healthy meal and should definitely not be eaten on a regular basis.

Beef is rich in protein, niacin, B12 and iron but, alas, high in saturated fats. Beef should be trimmed of excess fat and the fat content of ground beef should not exceed 15%. The beef recipes in this chapter include a variety of ethnic dishes that are thrifty, earthy, and very flavorful, plus a few representatives of classic cuisine.

Veal is low in fat and tender; it has a very mild taste and lends itself to a variety of flavorings. Veal is expensive and serving it can be controversial, especially on college campuses, because of the methods used to raise it. The milk-fed veal available so readily in Europe is rarely to be had in this country. I wish that were true for the too-available breaded deep-fried veal cutlet, a poor excuse for food. The two recipes I have included at the end of the beef and veal section are not too high in cost, very tasty, and attractive.

Serve quesadillas topped with lettuce, tomatoes, yogurt/sour cream, and salsa.

❖ Beef and Bean Quesadilla

Flour tortillas are grilled and filled with a warm beef, bean, and cheese mixture. Serve topped with shredded lettuce, diced tomatoes, yogurt and sour cream mixture, and picante salsa. For vegetarians substitute more beans for the beef, and follow the same procedure. To reduce sodium cook your own beans; canned refried beans are high in salt. The nutrient calculations for this recipe are for canned refried beans.

Portions per recipe: 36
Yield: 36 quesadillas
Portion: 1 quesadilla
Serving utensil: spatula

Pan: 12″ × 20″ × 2″
Griddle temperature: 300° F
Time: 3 minutes

Ingredients	Amounts	
Lean ground beef (15% fat)	5 lb.	
Spanish onions, sliced	1 lb.	
Chili powder		2 oz.
Cumin		1/4 oz.
Garlic, crushed		2 oz.
Salsa picante	2 lb.	8 oz.
Canned refried beans	7 lb.	6 oz.
Monterey Jack cheese, shredded	2 lb.	4 oz.
Large flour tortillas	4 lb.	8 oz.
Lettuce, shredded	4 lb.	8 oz.
Tomatoes, diced	4 lb.	8 oz.
Low-fat yogurt		10 oz.
Sour cream		8 oz.
Salsa picante	2 lb.	4 oz.

Procedure:

1. Sauté lean ground beef with onions, spices, and garlic.

2. Add salsa, beans, and cheese. Mix well. Keep warm.

3. Place tortillas on oiled griddle. With a #8 scoop dip filling onto lower half of each tortilla, spreading filling a bit.

4. Cook for 2 to 3 minutes, fold empty half of tortilla over to cover filling, and squeeze lightly.

5. Place in 12 × 20 × 2-inch pan and serve toppings from the salad bar or serve the tortilla on plate topped with lettuce, tomatoes, yogurt and sour cream, and salsa.

6. Garnish with a black olive or avocado wedge.

Calories: **615** Protein: **33.0 g (21%)** Carbohydrates: **66.7 g (43%)** Sodium: **1506 mg**

Total Fat: **25.4 g (37%)** *Saturated Fat:* **11.5 g** *Monounsaturated Fat:* **9.2 g** *Polyunsaturated Fat:* **1.0 g**

❖ Beef Burgundy

A classic French beef stew made with red wine and mushrooms. Serve it over egg noodles or with small red potatoes.

PRODUCTION NOTES: Brown the stew meat in the tilting skillet or in the oven. A steam kettle cannot brown the meat, it just stews it, and the result is an inferior flavor. For large quantities it is therefore worth the trouble to first brown the meat and to transfer it to a large kettle to braise it.

Portions per recipe: 100	*Pan: 12″ × 20″ × 4″*
Yield: 2 pans	*Skillet or oven temperature: 350° F*
Portion: 6 ounces	*Time: 2 hours*
Serving utensil: 4-ounce ladle	

Ingredients

Ingredients	Amounts	
Beef stew meat	25 lb.	
Oil		2 oz.
Spanish onions, sliced	6 lb.	
Garlic, crushed		2 oz.
Bay leaves, crumbled		1/16 oz.
Salt		2 oz.
Black pepper		1/4 oz.
Thyme, crumbled		1/4 oz.
Marjoram, crumbled		1/8 oz.
Burgundy jug wine	4 lb.	
Water	8 lb.	
Mushrooms, washed and sliced	4 lb.	
All-purpose flour		8 oz.
Olive oil		4 oz.
Parsley, chopped		2 oz.

Procedure

1. Brown beef well in oil.
2. Add onions, garlic, and spices and sauté for 5 minutes.
3. Add wine and water, cover, and simmer for 1 hour and 30 minutes.
4. Add mushrooms and simmer for 15 minutes more.
5. Mix flour with oil to make a cold roux. Add 2 pounds of hot stew liquid and blend.
6. Stir into stew and simmer for 15 minutes.
7. Fill 4″ deep steam table pan with 1¾ gallons stew. Sprinkle with chopped parsley.

Calories: **143**   Protein: **17.8 g (50%)**   Carbohydrates: **4.8 g (13%)**   Sodium: **274 mg**
Total Fat: **5.7 g (36%)**   *Saturated Fat:* **1.8 g**   *Monounsaturated Fat:* **2.5 g**   *Polyunsaturated Fat:* **.7 g**

❖ Beef Enchilada Casserole

This is easier than rolling individual enchiladas and is very good. The dish offers a quick way to serve leftover meat in an attractive "encore" dish. This recipe can be used to produce a variety of enchilada casseroles. Substitute ground turkey or shredded cooked chicken or pork roast for the beef and follow the same procedure.

Portions per recipe: *112*
Yield: *4 pans*
Portion: *7 ounces (3" × 2.9" piece)*
Serving utensil: *spatula*

Pan: *12" × 20" × 2"*
Oven temperature: *325° F*
Time: *30 minutes*

Ingredients   Amounts

Ingredients	Amounts
Ground beef (15% fat)	10 lb.
Garlic cloves, crushed	2 oz.
Chili powder	2 oz.
Cumin	1/4 oz.
Oregano, crushed	1/4 oz.
Canned chili salsa	6 lb. 7 oz.
Canned refried beans	7 lb. 6 oz.
Canned green chili, diced	4 lb.
Canned chili salsa	4 lb.
Corn tortillas (132 tortillas)	7 lb.
Monterey Jack cheese, shredded	4 lb.

Procedure:

1. Brown ground beef with garlic and spices.
2. Add chili salsa, refried beans, and chilies. Mix well.
3. Pour 8 ounces salsa in pan.
4. Place 11 tortillas in pan to cover pan completely.
5. Layer approximately 3 pounds of meat and beans on tortillas and top with 8 ounces of cheese.
6. Repeat once and top with another layer of tortillas.
7. Spread tortillas with 8 ounces of salsa and 8 ounces cheese.
8. Bake 30 minutes at 325° F. Let sit for 20 minutes before cutting into 28 pieces.

Calories: **279**   Protein: **17.1 g (24%)**   Carbohydrates: **29.7 g (43%)**   Sodium: **1004 mg**
Total Fat: **12.8 g (41%)**   *Saturated Fat:* **6.0 g**   *Monounsaturated Fat:* **6.2 g**   *Polyunsaturated Fat:* **.5 g**

❖ Beefsteak au Pil-Pil   *Kamman*

In this classic recipe from Madeleine Kamman, small trimmed strip steaks are grilled or broiled until medium rare and topped with herb and garlic butter.

PRODUCTION NOTE: Mix butter ahead of time and, with a large star-tipped pastry tube, pipe ½-ounce rosettes on parchment lined sheet pans and freeze them until ready to serve.

Portions per recipe: *100*	Pan: *12″ × 20″ × 2″*
Yield: *100 steaks*	Griddle temperature: *385° F*
Portion: *1 steak*	Time: *8 minutes*
Serving utensil: *spatula*	

Ingredients	Amounts	
Unsalted butter	1 lb.	8 oz.
Thyme, crushed		¼ oz.
Red pepper flakes, finely chopped		¹⁄₁₆ oz.
Garlic cloves, crushed		2 oz.
Parsley, very finely minced		6 oz.
Sirloin strip steak, all fat removed, 3.5 ounces each	21 lb.	14 oz.
Olive oil		3 oz.

Procedure:

1. Beat butter with herbs until well blended.
2. Pipe ¼-ounce butter rosettes on sheet pans. Freeze.
3. Brush steaks with olive oil and grill on both sides for 3 to 4 minutes.
4. Place a rosette on each hot steak before serving.

Calories: **327**   Protein: **17.4 g (21%)**   Carbohydrates: **.3 g (1%)**   Sodium: **50 mg**

Total Fat: **28.1 g (78%)**   *Saturated Fat:* **12.9 g**   *Monounsaturated Fat:* **12.1 g**   *Polyunsaturated Fat:* **1.1 g**

❖ Bouletten

One of my favorite meals as a kid in Germany were meat patties which Berliners call *bouletten*. These small meat loaves are browned briefly on both sides and braised in a brown onion and mushroom gravy.

Portions per recipe: 105
Yield: 5 pans
Portion: 1 patty
Serving utensil: spoon

Pan: 12″ × 20″ × 2″
Oven temperature: 325° F
Time: 15 minutes

Ingredients

Ingredients	Amounts
Day-old bread	4 lb.
Non-fat dry milk	10 oz.
Salt	2 oz.
Black pepper	¼ oz.
Thyme, crushed	⅛ oz.
Parsley, minced	2 oz.
Lean ground beef	25 lb.
Ground pork	2 lb.
Eggs, beaten	1 lb.
Water	2 lb.

Gravy

Ingredients	Amounts
Vegetable oil	2 oz.
Spanish onions, sliced	2 lb.
Mushrooms, cleaned and sliced	4 lb.
Black pepper	¼ oz.
Thyme, crushed	⅛ oz.
Salt	1 oz.
Dijon-style mustard	4 oz.
All-purpose flour	8 oz.
Red wine	12 oz.
Water	6 lb.
Light cream	1 lb.

Procedure:

1. Place bread, dry milk, spices, and parsley in mixer.
2. Add beef, pork, eggs, and water. Mix at low speed for 5 minutes.
3. Shape meat with #8 scoop and place on lined sheet pan.
4. Cover with parchment paper and press next sheet pan on top to flatten patty. Repeat.
5. Brown patties on griddle on both sides for 2 minutes each.
6. Place 21 patties into pan.
7. Heat oil and sauté onions and mushrooms with spices until golden.

(continued)

8.   Add salt, mustard, and flour. Stir and cook for 5 minutes.

9.   Add red wine, water, and light cream. Bring to simmer.

10. Pour 3 pints of sauce over patties in each pan and bake at 325° F for 15 minutes.

Calories: **339**   Protein: **25.7 g (25%)**   Carbohydrates: **13.1 g (14%)**   Sodium: **511 mg**

Total Fat: **19.9 g (53%)**   *Saturated Fat:* **8.5 g**   *Monounsaturated Fat:* **9.1 g**   *Polyunsaturated Fat:* **1.3 g**

❖ Carbonade à la Flamande— Belgian Beer and Onion Stew

Peasant food at its very best: Beef stew is simmered slowly with lots of onions, parsley, and beer. Serve with boiled potatoes and fresh green beans.

Portions per recipe: 100	*Pan:* 12″ × 20″ × 4″
Yield: 2 pans	*Skillet or oven temperature:* 350° F
Portion: 8 ounces	*Time:* 2 hours
Serving utensil: 6-ounce ladle	

Ingredients	Amounts
Vegetable oil	2 oz.
Beef stew meat, ¾″ *cubes*	25 lb.
Spanish onions, thinly sliced	10 lb.
Carrots, ¼″ *slices*	5 lb.
Garlic cloves, crushed	3 oz.
Thyme, crushed	⅛ oz.
Black pepper	¼ oz.
Bay leaves, crumbled fine	1/16 oz.
Salt	1 oz.
All-purpose flour	6 oz.
Beer, quarts	8 lb.
Water	6 lb.
Parsley, minced	1 lb. 12 oz.

Procedure:

1.   Heat oil and brown beef well.

2.   Add onions, carrots and garlic. Sauté for 5 minutes. Add spices, salt, and flour, and cook 3 minutes.

3.   Stir in beer, water, and half the parsley.

4.   Simmer slowly for 2 hours.

5.   Add rest of chopped parsley and fill pan with 2 gallons plus 1 quart of stew.

Calories: **143**   Protein: **17.7 g (50%)**   Carbohydrates: **7.2 g (20%)**   Sodium: **181 mg**

Total Fat: **4.6 g (29%)**   *Saturated Fat:* **1.7 g**   *Monounsaturated Fat:* **1.7 g**   *Polyunsaturated Fat:* **.6 g**

❖ Greek Moussaka

Layers of meat sauce and eggplants are covered with a ricotta cheese custard and baked.

PRODUCTION NOTES: Eggplant absorbs oil like a sponge, so take care to grease the griddle lightly or bake on lightly oiled sheet pans in the oven. Make this dish with lamb to reduce fat and calories even further.

Portions per recipe: *112*
Yield: *4 pans*
Portion: *8 oz. (3" × 2.9" piece)*
Serving utensil: *spatula*

Pan: *12" × 20" × 2"*
Oven temperature: *325° F*
Time: *50 minutes*

(continued)

Greek moussaka covered with a ricotta custard.

Ingredients	Amounts	
Olive oil		½ oz.
Ground beef (15% fat)	21 lb.	
Spanish onions, chopped	2 lb.	
Garlic cloves, crushed		2 oz.
Cinnamon		¼ oz.
Allspice		¼ oz.
Oregano, crushed		¼ oz.
Black pepper		¼ oz.
Salt		1 oz.
Canned Italian tomatoes, hand crushed	13 lb.	8 oz.
Unpeeled eggplant, ½" slices	16 lb.	
All-purpose flour		8 oz.
Low-fat yogurt	1 lb.	
Ricotta cheese, part skim	4 lb.	
Eggs	2 lb.	
Low-fat milk	6 lb.	
Salt		½ oz.
Nutmeg		⅛ oz.
White pepper		⅛ oz.

Procedure:

1. Heat olive oil and brown beef with onions and spices.
2. Add salt and tomatoes. Simmer for 15 minutes.
3. Grill eggplant at 350° F on both sides until lightly browned.
4. Pour 4 pounds of meat sauce into pan.
5. Cover with grilled eggplant slices. Repeat.
6. Beat flour with yogurt, ricotta, eggs, milk, and spices. Blend well.
7. Pour 3 pints over eggplant. Bake at 325° F for 50 minutes.
8. Let set 20 minutes before cutting each pan into 28 pieces.

Calories: **282**   Protein: **21.7 g (31%)**   Carbohydrates: **9.9 g (14%)**   Sodium: **120 mg**

Total Fat: **17.5 g (56%)**   *Saturated Fat:* **7.9 g**   *Monounsaturated Fat:* **8.1 g**   *Polyunsaturated Fat:* **1.0 g**

❖ Grilled Sirloin Tips with Peppers and Onions

This dish, as quick and easy as a stir-fry, can be served over rice, noodles, or with baked potatoes.

PRODUCTION NOTE: For best results grill beef in 7½-pound batches.

Portions per recipe: *50*
Yield: *2 pans*
Portion: *5.5 ounces*
Serving utensil: *3-ounce ladle*

Pan: *12″ × 20″ × 2″*
Griddle temperature: *400° F*
Time: *6–7 minutes*

Ingredients

Ingredients	Amounts	
Sirloin tips, ½″ × 2″ strips	15 lb.	
Hungarian paprika		½ oz.
Thyme, crushed		¼ oz.
Black pepper		¼ oz.
Garlic cloves, crushed		1 oz.
Green bell peppers, thinly sliced	3 lb.	
Yellow bell peppers, thinly sliced	1 lb.	
Red bell peppers, thinly sliced	1 lb.	
Spanish onions, thinly sliced	2 lb.	
Parsley, minced		2 oz.

Procedure:

1. Toss beef strips with spices and garlic.
2. Heat griddle to 400° F.
3. Oil lightly and stir-fry beef in 7½-pound batches for 3 to 4 minutes.
4. Scatter 2½ pounds of peppers and 1 pound of onions over beef.
5. Stir-fry for 3 to 4 minutes more.
6. Place in pan and garnish with fresh chopped parsley.

Calories: **387**   Protein: **24.3 g (25%)**   Carbohydrates: **3.7 g (4%)**   Sodium: **70 mg**
Total Fat: **30.2 g (70%)**   *Saturated Fat:* **12.9 g**   *Monounsaturated Fat:* **13.6 g**   *Polyunsaturated Fat:* **1.2 g**

❖ Pasta Primavera with Beef

Plenty of vegetables are combined with pasta and spicy beef.

PRODUCTION NOTE: Undercook the pasta. A thin white line should remain in center of noodle.

Portions per recipe: 112	*Pan:* 12″ × 20″ × 2″	
Yield: 4 pans	*Oven temperature:* 325° F	
Portion: 7 ounces	*Time:* 20 minutes	
Serving utensil: 8-ounce ladle		

Ingredients	Amounts	
Olive oil		2 oz.
Mushrooms, sliced	3 lb.	
Lean ground beef	14 lb.	
Garlic cloves, crushed		4 oz.
Oregano, crushed		1/4 oz.
Red pepper flakes		1/16 oz.
Scallions, chopped		8 oz.
Fresh basil, chopped		2 oz.
Italian parsley, minced		4 oz.
Canned Italian tomatoes, hand crushed	6 lb.	12 oz.
Salt		1/2 oz.
Pasta (rotini, bow ties, spirali, or shells)	8 lb.	
Water	40 lb.	
Broccoli pieces	8 lb.	
Zucchini, 1/4″ slices	4 lb.	
Small summer squash, 1/4″ slices	4 lb.	
Red bell peppers, thinly sliced	2 lb.	
Frozen peas, thawed	4 lb.	
Part-skim mozzarella, shredded	2 lb.	
Parmesan cheese, grated		8 oz.

Procedure:

1. Heat olive oil and sauté mushrooms until all liquid has evaporated.
2. Add beef, garlic, oregano, and pepper flakes. Brown for 10 minutes.
3. Add scallions, herbs, tomatoes, and salt. Simmer for 15 minutes.
4. Cook pasta in boiling water for 7 to 8 minutes. Undercook. Test frequently.
5. Drain well.
6. Add to meat sauce immediately.
7. Cook or steam broccoli and squash until tender but crisp.
8. Add to noodles with peppers, thawed peas, and mozzarella.
9. Fold in gently. Ladle 2 gallons into pan. Sprinkle with 2 ounces of parmesan.
10. Bake at 325° F for 20 minutes.

Calories: **317**   Protein: **18.5 g (23%)**   Carbohydrates: **31.6 g (40%)**   Sodium: **196 mg**
Total Fat: **12.0 g (34%)**   *Saturated Fat:* **5.2 g**   *Monounsaturated Fat:* **5.2 g**   *Polyunsaturated Fat:* **1.1 g**

❖ Roast Beef with Pizzaiola   *Romagnoli*

A recipe from the Romagnolis' "Festa Italiana." Roast beef is sliced and covered with pizzaiola sauce to create a very Italian dish.

PRODUCTION NOTES: Trim fat and cap from beef tops to get one lean piece of meat that will slice easily. Save cap meat for stew or soup. Low temperature roasting results in less shrinkage.

Portions per recipe: *100*	Pan: *12″ × 20″ × 2″*
Yield: *200 1¾-ounce slices*	Oven temperature: *275° F*
Portion: *2 slices*	Time: *4–5 hours*
Serving utensil: *spatula*	

Ingredients   Amounts

Ingredients	Amounts
Beef tops, capped	34 lb.

Pizzaiola Sauce

Ingredients	Amounts
Olive oil	2 oz.
Garlic cloves, crushed	3 oz.
Canned Italian tomatoes, coarsely chopped	9 lb. 9 oz.
Oregano, crushed	¼ oz.
Pan drippings, fat removed	2 lb.
Parsley leaves, minced	4 oz.
Black pepper	¼ oz.

Procedure:

1. Rack roasts fatty side up. Leave a 1-inch space between roasts.
2. Insert meat thermometer in thickest part of smallest roast.
3. Remove roasts when thermometer reads 135° F for medium rare. Collect pan drippings, skim off fat.
4. Heat olive oil. Sauté garlic and add tomatoes and oregano.
5. Simmer for 15 minutes. Add pan drippings and simmer for 10 minutes more.
6. Add minced parsley and pepper.
7. Slice beef into 1¾-ounce slices and layer barely overlapping in pan.
8. Top slices generously with pizzaiola sauce.
9. Serve with spatula.

Calories: **204**   Protein: **32.6 g (64%)**   Carbohydrates: **2.3 g (5%)**   Sodium: **144 mg**

Total Fat: **6.4 g (28%)**   *Saturated Fat:* **2.2 g**   *Monounsaturated Fat:* **2.4 g**   *Polyunsaturated Fat:* **.6 g**

❖ Sauerbraten

A German roast that gets its unique flavor from marinating four days in spices and vinegar. When served with potato latkes or semmel knoedel and Pennsylvania red cabbage this meal becomes a German feast.

PRODUCTION NOTE: Begin marinating beef 4 days ahead of serving date, and turn the beef twice daily. Roasts can also be browned and braised in a tilting skillet.

Portions per recipe: *100*
Yield: *100*
Portion: *3 ounces*
Serving utensil: *tongs*

Pan: *12" × 20" × 2"*
Oven temperature: *300° F*
Time: *3–4 hours*

Ingredients	Amounts	
Beef tops	34 lb.	
Cider vinegar	3 lb.	
Water	5 lb.	
Canned tomatoes, diced	6 lb.	6 oz.
Onions, chopped	1 lb.	
Brown sugar	2 lb.	
Dry mustard		1 oz.
Cloves		¼ oz.
Cinnamon		¼ oz.
Allspice		¼ oz.
Ginger		¼ oz.
Nutmeg		⅛ oz.
Pickling brine from dill pickles	8 lb.	
Vegetable oil		4 oz.
All-purpose flour		8 oz.
Sour cream		8 oz.

Procedure:

1. Place roasts in pans deep enough to allow meat to be covered with marinade.
2. Mix vinegar, water, tomatoes, onions, sugar, and spices.
3. Strain pickling brine and add to marinade. Pour over roasts.
4. Refrigerate. (See production note.)
5. Remove meat from marinade and pat dry. Reserve marinade.
6. Place meat in hot oven and roast for 30 minutes.
7. Pour marinade over meat, cover, and roast to 165° F internal temperature.
8. Remove roasts from pan and slice into 3-ounce servings. Reserve pan liquids. Skim off fat.
9. Heat oil with flour to make a roux, stir in hot pan marinade.

(continued)

10. Stir constantly until slightly thickened. Turn off heat and whisk in sour cream.

11. Pour a small amount over sliced beef, serve gravy separately.

Calories: **257**   Protein: **32.7 g (50%)**   Carbohydrates: **20.4 g (32%)**   Sodium: **236 mg**

Total Fat: **7.3 g (26%)**   *Saturated Fat:* **2.4 g**   *Monounsaturated Fat:* **2.7 g**   *Polyunsaturated Fat:* **.9 g**

❖ Sichuan Beef

Sichuan dishes are from the Sichuan province in western China. Fiery seasonings and sesame oil are distinctive features of this regional cuisine.

PRODUCTION NOTES: Make the sauce first. Stir-fry beef as described in the production note for stir-fried beef with orange on page 152. Fold in sauce as needed. Pea pods give the dish more color. If fresh pods are not available, thaw frozen pods and fold in just before serving.

Portions per recipe: 100
Yield: 2 pans
Portion: 5 ounces
Serving utensil: 3-ounce ladle

Pan: 12" × 20" × 4"
Griddle temperature: 400° F
Time: 6 minutes

Ingredients	*Amounts*
Sesame oil	*4 oz.*
Dry sherry	*8 oz.*
Chili bean sauce	*1 oz.*
Ginger root, peeled and grated	*4 oz.*
Soy sauce	*8 oz.*
Sirloin tips, cut ½" × 2" strips	*25 lb.*

Sichuan Sauce

Peanut oil		1 oz.
Garlic cloves, crushed		2 oz.
Carrots, thinly sliced	5 lb.	
Celery, ¾" slices	5 lb.	
Pineapple juice	3 lb.	3 oz.
Cornstarch		3 oz.
Cider vinegar		10 oz.
Five-spice powder		¼ oz.
Salt		1 oz.
Granulated sugar		2 oz.
Fresh pea pods, trimmed	1 lb.	

Procedure:

1. Whisk sesame oil, sherry, chili bean sauce, ginger root, and soy sauce together.

2. Add beef strips and marinate for 4 to 8 hours.

3. Heat peanut oil and sauté garlic, carrots, and celery for 5 to 7 minutes.

4. Add pineapple juice and simmer for 5 minutes.

5. Dissolve cornstarch in cider vinegar and stir into vegetables to thicken slightly.

6. Mix five-spice powder with salt and sugar.

7. Heat griddle to 400° F, oil lightly, and stir-fry beef in 1-pound batches, sprinkling each batch with the five-spice mixture.

8. With spatula place 12 batches of beef in pan. Add 3 quarts vegetables and sauce and 8 ounces of uncooked pea pods.

9. Fold in lightly. Serve at once. Continue to cook in batches.

Calories: **345** Protein: **20.3 g (24%)** Carbohydrates: **6.0 g (7%)** Sodium: **146 mg**
Total Fat: **26.3 g (68%)** *Saturated Fat:* **10.9 g** *Monounsaturated Fat:* **11.8 g** *Polyunsaturated Fat:* **1.5 g**

❖ Stir-fried Beef with Orange   *Hom*

Thinly sliced beef is stir-fried with Sichuan pepper and fresh orange peel in this classic northern Chinese beef specialty adapted by Ken Hom. Sichuan is sometimes spelled Szechuan or Szechwan, I am using Ken Hom's spelling.

PRODUCTION NOTES: Ken Hom tells us in his book *Chinese Cookery* that Sichuan peppercorns are known as "flower pepper" in China and that they are dried berries from a shrub belonging to the citrus family. Sichuan peppercorns must be toasted in the oven or on top of a grill for 5 to 10 minutes before grinding them to a fine powder.

We achieved fabulous results when we stir-fried the marinated beef in the following manner: Heat the griddle to 400° F. Mix Sichuan peppercorns with salt, sugar, and orange peel. Keep mixture near griddle. Brush griddle with sesame oil. Place 10 one-pound batches of beef on the griddle, flatten quickly with spatula, sprinkle lightly with Sichuan pepper mix, flip over once, and remove to serving pan. Repeat. Make scallion brushes for the pan garnish in this manner: Use the white part of the scallion only (about 2″ pieces) and trim off roots. Make about 8 to 10 ¼″ deep cuts at root end. Place in ice water so that cut ends will curl.

Portions per recipe: **100**	*Pan:* **12″ × 20″ × 2″**
Yield: **3 pans**	*Griddle temperature:* **400° F**
Portion: **3 ounces**	*Time:* **6 minutes**
Serving utensil: **spoon**	

Ingredients | Amounts

Ingredients	Amounts
Flap meat, cut into thin strips	25 lb.
Sesame oil	3 oz.
Soy sauce	8 oz.
Dry sherry	8 oz.
Ginger root, finely chopped	6 oz.
Cayenne pepper	¼ oz.
Cornstarch	3 oz.
Orange peel, no pith, thinly sliced	10 oz.
Sichuan peppercorns, toasted and ground	2 oz.
Salt	1 oz.
Granulated sugar	3 oz.
Sesame oil	3 oz.

Procedure:

1. Place meat in pan.
2. Whisk together sesame oil, soy sauce, sherry, ginger root, cayenne, and cornstarch.
3. Pour over meat strips and let marinate for 20 minutes.
4. Mix orange peel with sichuan pepper, salt, and sugar.
5. Heat grill to 400° F and stir-fry meat in batches (see production notes).
6. Garnish pan with orange wedges and scallion brushes.

Calories: **294**   Protein: **28.3 g (39%)**   Carbohydrates: **2.1 g (3%)**   Sodium: **176 mg**

Total Fat: **18.2 g (56%)**   *Saturated Fat:* **7.3 g**   *Monounsaturated Fat:* **7.7 g**   *Polyunsaturated Fat:* **1.1 g**

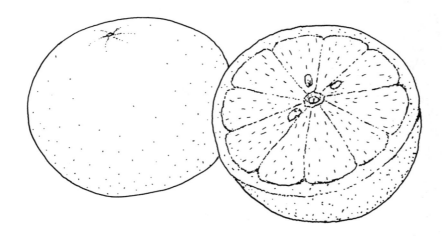

❖ Grilled Veal Provolone

Veal slices are topped with onions, tomatoes, and provolone cheese. Scallops of veal sliced from the loin and leg are best, but institutions with budgetary constraints can use veal cube steaks cut from the shoulder very successfully. The preparation method is the same. See color plate **3**.

PRODUCTION NOTE: Pound veal scallops or steaks between sheets of parchment paper if they are thicker than ¼ inch.

Portions per recipe: *72*
Yield: *4 pans*
Portion: *1 slice*
Serving utensil: *spatula*

Pan: *12″ × 20″ × 2″*
Oven temperature: *325° F*
Time: *6–8 minutes*

Ingredients	Amounts
All-purpose flour	12 oz.
White pepper	¾ oz.
Salt	1 oz.
Marjoram, crushed	¼ oz.
Veal scallops, 4-ounce slices	18 lb.
Olive oil	1 oz.
Spanish onions, very thinly sliced into rings	2 lb.
Garlic, crushed	1 oz.
Canned tomatoes, diced	6 lb. 6 oz.
Rosemary leaves, chopped	1 oz.
Provolone cheese, 1-ounce slices	4 lb. 8 oz.
Rosemary leaves, chopped	1 oz.

Procedure:

1. Mix together flour, pepper, salt, and marjoram.
2. Dredge veal slices in flour just before sautéing.
3. Heat tilting skillet to 325° F with ½ ounce of olive oil.
4. Add first batch of 36 veal slices and sauté 3 minutes on each side.
5. Cook all veal slices in batches of 36, adding more olive oil each time.
6. Place 18 cooked veal slices in 12″ × 20″ × 2″ pan.
7. Add onions and garlic to skillet and sauté for 5 minutes.
8. Add tomatoes and rosemary and simmer for 12 minutes.
9. Cover veal slices with sauce and top each veal scallop with a 1-ounce slice of provolone.
10. Bake at 325° F for 6 to 8 minutes in oven until cheese is melted.
11. Sprinkle with more fresh rosemary before serving.

Calories: **209**   Protein: **21.5 g (41%)**   Carbohydrates: **7.0 g (13%)**   Sodium: **464 g**

Total Fat: **10.3 g (44%)**   *Saturated Fat:* **5.0 g**   *Monounsaturated Fat:* **3.1 g**   *Polyunsaturated Fat:* **.5 g**

❖ Veal and Sausage Cacciatorra

This is a real peasant stew—full of hot Italian sausage and earthy mushroom flavors.

PRODUCTION NOTE: Do not cut the raw sausage. It is easier to slice sausage that has been parboiled and then chilled.

Portions per recipe: 100
Yield: 2 pans
Portion: 7 ounces
Serving utensil: 4-ounce ladle

Pan: 12″ × 20″ × 4″
Skillet temperature: 350° F
Time: 2 hours

Ingredients

Ingredients	Amounts
Hot Italian sausage	12 lb.
Veal stew meat, ¾″ cubes	20 lb.
Spanish onions, sliced	2 lb.
Garlic, crushed	4 oz.
Mushroom buttons, sliced	6 lb.
Oregano, crushed	¼ oz.
Thyme, crushed	¼ oz.
All-purpose flour	8 oz.
Water	6 lb.
Dry vermouth	2 lb.
Whole Italian tomatoes, hand crushed	12 lb. 12 oz.

Procedure:

1. Simmer sausage in water for 12 minutes. Cool.
2. Slice into ½-inch pieces.
3. Heat tilt skillet to 350° F. Brown sausage, then remove from skillet. Keep warm.
4. Add veal, onions, and garlic to pan and brown lightly.
5. Add mushrooms and sauté for 8 minutes.
6. Add spices and flour, and cook for 2 minutes.
7. Stir in water and vermouth. Simmer for 1 hour and 15 minutes.
8. Add sausage and tomatoes to stew and cook for 30 minutes more.
9. Taste and add salt if necessary. Serve over noodles or rice.

Calories: **279**   Protein: **27.1 g (39%)**   Carbohydrates: **7.4 g (11%)**   Sodium: **400 mg**
Total Fat: **16.1 g (51%)**   *Saturated Fat:* **5.6 g**   *Monounsaturated Fat:* **7.1 g**   *Polyunsaturated Fat:* **2.1 g**

Pork and Ham

Americans prefer to eat simply prepared pork dishes such as roasts or chops, BBQ ribs, and lots of bacon and ham. Other cultures have developed more imaginative ways to use pork. There is the whole roasted pig at Hawaiian luaus, the many Chinese stir-frys, the Caribbean stews, and many European pork and ham specialties.

Pork must reach an internal temperature of 150° F to kill any trichinella larvae that may be present in the pork. To cook pork to 170° F has become a common practice, to the detriment of the cooked pork. At this point pork turns grey and dry. For juicy and delicious pork roast, cook the meat to no more than 155° F internal temperature. Microwaves do cook unevenly and pork cooked in this way must register 170° F to be considered safe.

Lean pork is a rich source of the B vitamin thiamin and provides good amounts of iron. A 3-ounce serving of medium lean pork contains 310 to 320 calories, depending on which preparation method has been used.

Pork producers are bringing leaner meat to market. Pork loin can be 85% lean and 15% fat. Boneless ham is usually 76% lean and 24% fat. Remember that curing hams adds a lot of sodium.

I value these recipes for their ethnicity and their versatility. All are easy to prepare and many combine fruits and vegetables with the pork and ham for better nutrition and lower cost.

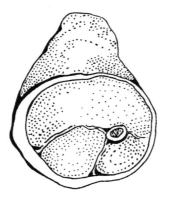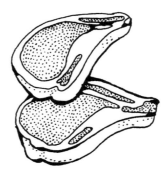

❖ Alsatian Ham and Onion Pizza (Flammkuchen)

Flammkuchen is a specialty of Strasbourg, France. Smoky ham, raw onions, and thick cream are spread on a thin, bread-like crust and baked in an open flame wood-fired oven. I always find time to enjoy this smoky flavored crisp kuchen with a glass of chilled Riesling when in Alsace-Lorraine. This pizza is a version of the flammkuchen. Serve it with a watercress, lettuce, or vegetable soup. The pizza can be served as an appetizer if baked in a ½-size sheet pan and cut into small squares. See color plate **7**.

PRODUCTION NOTES: Use sheet pans if 12″ pizza pans are not available and place two pizzas on each pan. Black Forest-style hams are available from domestic producers and their flavor is fine for this pizza. A smoky Virginia-style ham or lean domestic prosciutto could also be used. The degree of smokiness is important. An imported Black Forest or Westphalian ham would be more authentic and have the best taste. The amount of meat per pizza is only 2 ounces, so the cost will be low. Go for the real thing. The raw onions can be sautéed first for a milder flavor.

Portions per recipe: 60
Yield: 10 12-inch pizzas
*Portion: 1 wedge (12″ pie cut into
    6 pieces)*
Serving utensil: spatula

Pan: 12″ pizza pans
Oven temperature: 400° F
Time: 12–15 minutes

Ingredients / Amounts

Ingredients	Amounts	
Pizza dough		
Water (luke warm)	3 lb.	
Dry yeast		1 oz.
Sugar		½ oz.
All-purpose flour	4 lb.	4 oz.
Olive oil		4 oz.
Salt		1 oz.
Topping		
Smoked ham, julienned	1 lb.	4 oz.
Spanish onions, thinly sliced	5 lb.	
Eggs	1 lb.	4 oz.
Sour cream	1 lb.	4 oz.
Salt		1 oz.
White pepper		¼ oz.
Nutmeg		⅛ oz.

(continued)

Procedure:

1. Make pizza dough by beating all ingredients together and kneading briefly.
2. Let rise once and scale into 12 ounce dough balls.
3. Roll dough into 12-inch circles and press lightly into pans.
4. Cut ham and slice onions. Place onions in ice water until needed.
5. Beat eggs with sour cream, salt, pepper, and nutmeg and spread 8 ounces over dough.
6. Sprinkle 2 ounces of ham evenly over egg and cream mixture.
7. Top ham evenly with 7 ounces of drained, raw onion slices.
8. Bake at 400° F for 12 to 15 minutes. Cut each pizza into 6 wedges.

Calories: **189**   Protein: **6.5 g (14%)**   Carbohydrates: **28.0 g (59%)**   Sodium: **474 mg**

Total Fat: **5.6 g (27%)**   *Saturated Fat:* **2.0 g**   *Monounsaturated Fat:* **2.2 g**   *Polyunsaturated Fat:* **0.6 g**

Apple and onion flavored baked pork chops are complemented with Pennsylvania red cabbage and parsleyed potatoes.

❖ Baked Pork Chops

Deliciously moist and tender pork chops that are a far cry from the usual dry, leathery chops produced in many an institutional kitchen. They are easy to prepare, keep well, and even reheat without loss of texture and taste. Serve these pork chops with boiled potatoes and Pennsylvania red cabbage.

PRODUCTION NOTE: Frozen, unsweetened apple slices can be used instead of fresh apples.

Portions per recipe: *56*
Yield: *4 pans*
Portion: *5-ounce chop*
Serving utensil: *spatula*

Pan: *12″ × 20″ × 2″*
Oven temperature: *325° F*
Time: *40 minutes*

Ingredients

Ingredients	Amounts	
Pork chops, 5 ounces each	17 lb.	8 oz.
Salt		2 oz.
Black pepper		½ oz.
Thyme, crushed		¼ oz.
Apples, peeled and sliced	7 lb.	
Cider vinegar		4 oz.
Apple juice	4 lb.	
Brown sugar		8 oz.
Cinnamon		¼ oz.
Ginger		⅛ oz.
Vegetable oil		2 oz.
Spanish onions, thinly sliced	4 lb.	
Parsley leaves, minced		2 oz.

Procedure:

1. Season pork chops on both sides with salt, pepper, and thyme.
2. Arrange 14 chops in very lightly oiled pan.
3. Top each chop with 2 ounces of apple slices.
4. Mix vinegar with apple juice and pour 1 pint over chops and apples.
5. Mix sugar with cinnamon and ginger and sprinkle evenly over apples.
6. Bake at 325° F for 40 minutes. Add more juice if necessary.
7. Heat vegetable oil and sauté onions until light brown. Fold in parsley.
8. Place hot onions in two neat rows on apples and chops.

Calories: **225**   Protein: **20.8 g (37%)**   Carbohydrates: **17.5 g (31%)**   Sodium: **456 mg**
Total Fat: **7.8 g (31%)**   *Saturated Fat:* **2.6 g**   *Monounsaturated Fat:* **3.2 g**   *Polyunsaturated Fat:* **1.3 g**

❖ Bamberger Cabbage "Hackbraten"

A lot simpler to make than stuffed cabbage, but just as good and easy to serve. Mashed potatoes complement this dish superbly.

Portions per recipe: 56   *Pan: 12″ × 20″ × 2″*
Yield: 2 pans   *Oven temperature: 325° F*
Portion: 7 ounces (3″ × 2.9″ piece)   *Time: 50 minutes*
Serving utensil: spatula

Ingredients	*Amounts*
Vegetable oil	*2 oz.*
Spanish onions, thinly sliced	*4 lb.*
Cloves	*⅛ oz.*
Bay leaves, crumbled	*⅛ oz.*
Caraway seeds	*¼ oz.*
Green cabbage, shredded	*10 lb.*
Water	*2 lb.*
Stale bread, crusts removed	*12 oz.*
Skim milk	*4 oz.*
Ground pork	*10 lb.*
Eggs	*8 oz.*
Thyme, crushed	*⅛ oz.*
Salt	*1 oz.*
Black pepper	*¼ oz.*
Low-fat yogurt	*1 lb.*
Sour cream	*8 oz.*
Eggs	*4 oz.*

Procedure:

1. Heat vegetable oil and sauté onions with spices until soft.
2. Remove half the onions and reserve to use in pork mixture.
3. Add shredded cabbage and water to onions and cook for 10 minutes.
4. Soak bread in skim milk.
5. Mix ground pork with sautéed onions, soaked bread, eggs, thyme, salt, and pepper.
6. Spread 3 pounds of cooked cabbage over bottom of pan and top with 7 pounds of pork mixture.
7. Cover with 3 pounds of cabbage.
8. Mix yogurt with sour cream and eggs. Pour 14 ounces over pan.
9. Bake at 325° F for 45 minutes. Cut each pan into 28 pieces.

Calories: **149**   Protein: **13.3 g (36%)**   Carbohydrates: **9.7 g (26%)**   Sodium: **288 mg**
Total Fat: **6.4 g (38%)**   *Saturated Fat:* **2.3 g**   *Monounsaturated Fat:* **2.2 g**   *Polyunsaturated Fat:* **1.2 g**

❖ **BBQ Ribs with Spicy Sauce** *Hom*

Baked in the oven until most of the fat has been rendered, these ribs are finished on an outdoor grill. Prepared this way the ribs are a first class treat. Baked and finished completely in the oven they are still very, very good. Serve with corn and ginger fried rice and snow peas or broccoli.

PRODUCTION NOTES: Kumquats are available from November to April. The rind is sweet and the pulp is sour. Rinse well in warm water to remove fungicides, cut in half, remove seeds, and chop. For summer cookouts, make the sauce when the kumquats are in season and freeze it, or substitute one-half the specified amount with preserved kumquats and omit the sugar.

Portions per recipe: *100*
Yield: *200 pieces*
Portion: *2 pieces*
Serving utensil: *tongs*

Pan: *18" × 26" sheet pan*
Oven temperature: *250° F*
Time: *90 minutes*

Ingredients

Amounts

Ingredients	Amounts	
Baby spareribs, 4 ounces each (3 riblets)	50 lb.	

Sauce (makes about 1 gallon)

Ingredients		Amounts
Vegetable oil		2 oz.
Spanish onions	2 lb.	
Ginger root, peeled		2 oz.
Garlic cloves, peeled		3 oz.
Kumquats, washed, halved, and seeded	1 lb.	
Canned tomato puree	3 lb.	3 oz.
Hoisin sauce		8 oz.
Dark soy sauce		5 oz.
Chili bean sauce		5 oz.
Granulated sugar		8 oz.
Dry sherry		8 oz.
Water		12 oz.
Sesame oil		1 oz.

Procedure:

1. Bake ribs in 250° F oven for 90 minutes to render fat, discard fat.
2. In food chopper or processor mince onions, ginger root, garlic, and kumquats.
3. Heat oil and sauté mixture.
4. Add tomato puree, hoisin, soy and chili bean sauces, sugar, and sherry.

(continued)

5. Simmer for 30 minutes, add water and sesame oil, and simmer 15 minutes more.

6. Brush baked ribs with sauce and grill outdoors for 3 to 5 minutes on each side. Or finish in 400° F oven until nicely browned (about 10 minutes) or broil 3 to 5 minutes on each side.

Calories: **332**   Protein: **24.6 g (30%)**   Carbohydrates: **5.4 g (7%)**   Sodium: **191 mg**

Total Fat: **23.0 g (62%)**   *Saturated Fat:* **9.0 g**   *Monounsaturated Fat:* **10.2 g**   *Polyunsaturated Fat:* **2.5 g**

❖ Braised Pork "Caribbean"

A sweet and sour fruity pork stew with Caribbean spices and papaya.

PRODUCTION NOTES: Grind the spices together or use *masala garam*, an Indian spice mixture, as a substitute. Whole hot peppers with seeds will add more "heat." If no tilt skillet is available, brown meat in oven and transfer to a steam kettle.

Portions per recipe: 100	*Pan: 12″ × 20″ × 4″*
Yield: 2 pans	*Skillet temperature: 350° F*
Portion: 8 ounces	*Time: 2 hours*
Serving utensil: 6-ounce ladle	

Ingredients	Amounts	
Turmeric		¼ oz.
Black peppercorns		¼ oz.
Cumin seeds		⅛ oz.
Whole cloves		¹/₁₆ oz.
Fenugreek seeds		⅛ oz.
Mustard seeds		¼ oz.
Garlic cloves, peeled		2 oz.
Hot red chili peppers with seeds		2 oz.
Lean pork shoulder, 1″ cubes	24 lb.	
Vegetable oil		1 oz.
Water	8 lb.	
Unripe papaya, peeled, seeded, and cubed	3 lb.	
Peeled sweet potatoes, 1″ pieces	12 lb.	8 oz.
Canned unsweetened coconut milk	4 lb.	
Green bell peppers, thin strips	3 lb.	
Fresh lime juice		12 oz.
Brown sugar		2 oz.
Unsweetened shredded coconut, toasted		2 oz.

Procedure:

1. Grind spices together until pulverized.
2. In food chopper or processor mince garlic and hot peppers to a paste. Add spices.
3. Toss the pork cubes with the spice paste.
4. Heat the vegetable oil in tilt skillet and brown the meat. Add water and simmer for 45 minutes.
5. Add papaya, sweet potatoes, and coconut milk. Simmer for 1 hour.
6. Add salt, green peppers, lime juice, and brown sugar. Taste.
7. Simmer for 10 minutes and serve sprinkled with toasted coconut.

Calories: **172**   Protein: **14.1 g (33%)**   Carbohydrates: **3.7 g (9%)**   Sodium: **71 mg**

Total Fat: **10.9 g (57%)**   *Saturated Fat:* **2.3 g**   *Monounsaturated Fat:* **4.8 g**   *Polyunsaturated Fat:* **.7 g**

❖ Canadian Pork Pie

This French-Canadian pork pie is known as *tourtiere* in Quebec and was added to the UNH recipe file by a French-Canadian cook from Manchester, New Hampshire. Serve it for dinner with gravy and vegetables, or serve it for lunch at room temperature with a tossed green salad.

PRODUCTION NOTE: The filling should cool for at least 12 hours and is best made a day ahead.

Portions per recipe: 210
Yield: 35 pies
Portion: ⅙ pie
Serving utensil: spatula

Pan: 9″ pie pan
Oven temperature: 325° F
Time: 25 minutes

(continued)

Ingredients	*Amounts*	
Potatoes, peeled and cubed	12 lb.	
Lean ground pork	50 lb.	
Spanish onions, diced	3 lb.	
Garlic cloves, crushed		1 oz.
Water	8 lb.	
Salt		3 oz.
Black pepper		½ oz.
Poultry seasoning		¾ oz.
Nutmeg		¼ oz.
Mace		¼ oz.
Pastry, 10″ shell bottom (pre-baked)	17 lb.	8 oz.
Pastry, 10″ shell top (raw)	17 lb.	8 oz.
Eggs		2 oz.
Water		4 oz.

Procedure:

1. Steam or boil potatoes until tender.

2. Brown pork with onions and garlic. Drain excess fat.

3. Add potatoes, water, and seasonings.

4. Simmer for 20 minutes, stirring often.

5. Refrigerate filling overnight or for at least 12 hours.

6. Spoon 24 ounces of filling into pre-baked shell and cover with raw top.

7. Beat 1 egg with 4 oz. of water. Brush pastry top with egg-wash. Prick with fork 4 times to allow steam to escape.

8. Bake at 325° F for 25 minutes.

9. Cut pie into 6 pieces.

Calories: **469**   Protein: **19.1 g (16%)**   Carbohydrates: **37.3 g (32%)**   Sodium: **233 mg**

Total Fat: **26.6 g (51%)**   *Saturated Fat:* **7.0 g**   *Monounsaturated Fat:* **15.5 g**   *Polyunsaturated Fat:* **3.4 g**

❖ Grilled Sweet and Sour Tenderloins

Pork tenderloins are very lean and very tender and should be grilled or broiled briefly. This recipe presents them in a sweet and sour sauce with crisp steamed broccoli florets and peeled and diagonally sliced broccoli stems. Serve with egg noodles or steamed rice and sweet potatoes or carrots.

PRODUCTION NOTE: Cook in batches as needed.

Portions per recipe: *120*
Yield: *3 pans*
Portion: *8 ounces*
Serving utensil: *6-ounce ladle*

Pan: *12" × 20" × 4"*
Griddle temperature: *350° F*
Time: *6–8 minutes*

Ingredients

Ingredients	Amounts	
Sesame oil		1 oz.
Scallions, 1" pieces		4 oz.
Garlic cloves, crushed		1 oz.
Ginger root, peeled and grated		1 oz.
Hot chili pepper, chopped with seeds		1 oz.
White vinegar	2 lb.	
Brown sugar	4 lb.	
Pineapple juice	8 lb.	
Salt		1 oz.
Black pepper		¼ oz.
Canned Italian tomatoes	6 lb.	6 oz.
Green bell peppers, thin strips	6 lb.	
Canned pineapple chunks with liquid	4 lb.	
Sliced water chestnuts, drained	2 lb.	
Cornstarch		6 oz.
Water	2 lb.	
Fresh broccoli	8 lb.	
Trimmed pork tenderloins, ¼" slices	24 lb.	

Procedure:

1. Heat sesame oil and sauté scallions, garlic, ginger, and chili pepper.
2. Add vinegar, brown sugar, pineapple juice, salt, and pepper.
3. Simmer for 5 minutes.
4. Hand crush tomatoes lightly.
5. Add to sauce with peppers, pineapple, and water chestnuts. Simmer.
6. Dissolve cornstarch in water and stir into sauce. Keep hot.
7. Cut broccoli heads into small florets. Peel stems and cut them thinly on bias.
8. Steam 4 pounds of broccoli for 2 to 3 minutes until barely tender.

(continued)

9. Heat oiled griddle to 350° F and brown 8 pounds of tenderloin slices.

10. Place 4 pounds of broccoli and 8 pounds of tenderloins in pan. Fold in 2 quarts of sauce. Serve at once.

Calories: **211**   Protein: **20.2 g (38%)**   Carbohydrates: **26.8 g (51%)**   Sodium: **187 mg**

Total Fat: **2.7 g (12%)**   *Saturated Fat:* **0.8 g**   *Monounsaturated Fat:* **1.1 g**   *Polyunsaturated Fat:* **0.5 g**

❖ Noodles Napoli

A baked pasta dish that tastes as good as it looks.

PRODUCTION NOTES: Undercook the egg noodles or the dish will become too mushy. Frozen chopped broccoli saves labor and can be substituted for the fresh broccoli in this recipe.

Portions per recipe: 112   *Pan: 12″ × 20″ × 2″*
Yield: 4 pans   *Oven temperature: 300° F*
Portion: 7 ounces (3″ × 2.9″ piece)   *Time: 30 minutes*
Serving utensil: spatula

Ingredients	Amounts	
Ham	10 lb.	
Medium egg noodles	7 lb.	8 oz.
Olive oil		4 oz.
Spanish onions, diced	1 lb.	
Garlic cloves, crushed		2 oz.
All-purpose flour		4 oz.
Dry mustard		½ oz.
Salt		1 oz.
Black pepper		¼ oz.
Non-fat dry milk	1 lb.	
Water (hot)	8 lb.	
Nutmeg		⅛ oz.
Ricotta cheese, part skim	4 lb.	
Eggs	1 lb.	
Cheddar cheese, shredded	2 lb.	
Broccoli florets and peeled sliced stems	8 lb.	
Bread crumbs	1 lb.	

Procedure:

1. Slice ham into ¼-inch slices, cut in half, and slice into thin strips.
2. Cook noodles in boiling water until a thin white line is left in center of noodle. Drain immediately.
3. Heat olive oil; sauté onions and garlic.
4. Stir in flour and spices.
5. Reconstitute dry milk with hot water. Stir into onion roux.
6. Turn off heat. Beat in nutmeg, ricotta, eggs, and cheddar cheese.
7. Blanch broccoli for 1 minute in steamer or in boiling water.
8. Fold broccoli, ham, and noodles into cheese sauce.
9. Ladle 1½ gallons of the mixture into pan. Top with 4 ounces of bread crumbs.
10. Bake at 300° F for 30 minutes. Internal temperature should reach 165° F.
11. Let sit for 15 minutes and cut each pan into 28 pieces.

Calories: **260** Protein: **16.8 g (26%)** Carbohydrates: **29.0 g (45%)** Sodium: **614 mg**
Total Fat: **8.4 g (29%)** *Saturated Fat:* **3.6 g** *Monounsaturated Fat:* **3.0 g** *Polyunsaturated Fat:* **0.8 g**

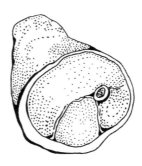

❖ Penne with Ham and Asparagus Sauce

A colorful, low-cost, and quickly prepared dish. Penne are thin pasta tubes with diagonally cut ends. Ziti can be substituted for penne. Reduce calories and fat by substituting light cream for the heavy cream.

PRODUCTION NOTES: Make all the sauce ahead of time, cook penne in batches and sauce only as needed. One pound of dry penne is equal to 2½ pounds cooked. This recipe is calculated to provide 5 ounces of cooked penne per portion. **Do not drown the penne in sauce. The pasta should just be coated lightly.**

Portions per recipe: 100
Yield: 3 pans
Portion: 8 ounces
Serving utensil: 6-ounce ladle

Pan: 12″ × 20″ × 4″
Time: 20 minutes

Ingredients	Amounts	
Ham	6 lb.	4 oz.
Olive oil		1 oz.
Whole garlic cloves		½ oz.
Fresh asparagus, cut diagonally into 1″ pieces	12 lb.	8 oz.
Heavy cream	2 lb.	
Freshly ground black pepper		¼ oz.
Canned roasted red peppers		14 oz.
Fontina cheese, shredded	3 lb.	2 oz.
Romano cheese, grated		4 oz.
Italian parsley, chopped		4 oz.
Penne pasta	12 lb.	8 oz.
Melted butter		1 oz.

Procedure:

1. Slice ham into ¼-inch slices, cut slices in half, and slice into thin strips.
2. Heat olive oil with garlic cloves. Remove garlic after 3 minutes.
3. Add ham strips and sauté until lightly brown, about 5 minutes.
4. Add asparagus pieces and toss with ham. Stir in cream and pepper. Simmer very slowly for 5 minutes.
5. Slice roasted peppers into thin strips and add to sauce.
6. Turn off heat and stir in cheeses and chopped parsley.
7. Cook penne in boiling, salted water with a little oil for 15 minutes.
8. Heat 12″ × 20″ × 2″ pan and brush with melted butter.
9. Place approximately 10 pounds penne in pan and fold in 6 pounds sauce.
10. Serve at once.

Calories: **340***   Protein: **16.4 g (19%)**   Carbohydrates: **44.3 g (52%)**   Sodium: **350 mg**
Total Fat: **10.6 g (29%)**   *Saturated Fat:* **5.5 g**   *Monounsaturated Fat:* **3.1 g**   *Polyunsaturated Fat:* **0.9 g**

Calories: **308†**   Protein: **16.5 g (21%)**   Carbohydrates: **44.4 g (57%)**   Sodium: **350 mg**
Total Fat: **9.0 g (26%)**   *Saturated Fat:* **4.5 g**   *Monounsaturated Fat:* **2.6 g**   *Polyunsaturated Fat:* **0.9 g**

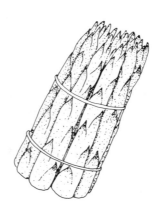

---

*With heavy cream.
†With light cream.

❖ Pork Loin Schnitzel

Everybody knows about the famous Austrian breaded veal cutlet *wiener schnitzel*, which are cut from veal loins. In Germany, schnitzel are also cut from fresh hams. Schnitzel cut from the pork loin are more uniform, which helps with portion control. See color plate **6**.

PRODUCTON NOTES: Pound loin slices lightly between pieces of parchment paper. Breading the schnitzel can be done in advance. The breading will stick better to the cutlets if they are well chilled before they are pan fried.

Portions per recipe: 100
Yield: 200 schnitzel
Portion: 2 schnitzel
Serving utensil: tongs or spatula

Pan: 12″ × 20″ × 2″
Griddle temperature: 325° F
Time: 10–14 minutes

Ingredients	Amounts		
Pork loin, 2-ounce cutlet	25 lb.		
All-purpose flour		2 lb.	4 oz.
Salt			1 oz.
Black pepper			½ oz.
Hungarian paprika			¼ oz.
Eggs		1 lb.	4 oz.
Skim milk			8 oz.
Bread crumbs		2 lb.	4 oz.
Lemons, sliced	8 lb.		
Italian parsley sprigs			1 oz.

Procedure:

1. Place cutlets 1 inch apart on parchment paper.
2. Cover with another sheet and pound lightly with mallet or rolling pin.
3. Mix flour with salt, pepper, and paprika. Place in a 12″ × 20″ × 2″ pan.
4. Beat eggs with milk and pour in another 12″ × 20″ × 2″ pan.
5. Place bread crumbs in third 12″ × 20″ × 2″ pan.
6. Dip pork in flour, then the egg mixture, and then coat with crumbs.
7. Place breaded cutlets on paper lined sheet pan in a single layer.
8. Press crumbs into meat, cover, and refrigerate.
9. Fry on well oiled griddle or in tilt skillet for 5 to 7 minutes on each side.
10. Garnish each schnitzel with a slice of lemon and garnish pan with parsley.

Calories: **180**   Protein: **16.7 g (37%)**   Carbohydrates: **13.2 g (29%)**   Sodium: **213 mg**
Total Fat: **6.1 g (31%)**   *Saturated Fat:* **2.0 g**   *Monounsaturated Fat:* **2.6 g**   *Polyunsaturated Fat:* **0.7 g**

❖ Pork Roast Normandy

The pork is marinated and baked with herbs, spices, and applesauce for a flavorful marriage of East and West. The apples, onions, and thyme are from Normandy. The other spices are Chinese.

Portions per recipe: 100
Yield: 200 2-ounce slices
Portion: 4 ounces
Serving utensil: spatula

Pan: 12″ × 20″ × 2″
Oven temperature: 300° F
Time: 3 hours

Ingredients

Ingredients	Amounts
Vegetable oil	2 oz.
Spanish onions, diced	2 lb.
Garlic cloves, crushed	2 oz.
Fresh thyme (stems removed)	1 oz.
Canned applesauce	2 lb.
Soy sauce	12 oz.
Dry sherry	1 lb.
Ginger root, grated	2 oz.
Black pepper	¾ oz.
Boneless pork roast	40 lb.
Cornstarch	6 oz.
Water	4 lb.

Procedure:

1. Heat oil and sauté onions, garlic, and thyme until soft.
2. Turn off heat. Add applesauce, soy sauce, sherry, ginger, and pepper.
3. Pour over roasts and marinate for 2 hours.
4. Rack roasts, reserve marinade.
5. Roast at 300° F for 3 hours or until internal temperature reaches 155° F.
6. From time to time pour ½ cup marinade over roasts.
7. Remove cooked roasts, deglaze pans with marinade and water and remove fat.
8. Bring pan juices to a boil, dissolve cornstarch with a little water, stir into boiling drippings.
9. Slice pork into 2-ounce portions. Serve with applesauce gravy.

Calories: **216**   Protein: **26.5 g (49%)**   Carbohydrates: **4.7 g (9%)**   Sodium: **273 mg**
Total Fat: **9.1 g (38%)**   *Saturated Fat:* **3.1 g**   *Monounsaturated Fat:* **4.0 g**   *Polyunsaturated Fat:* **1.2 g**

❖ Sausage Tuscany

Simple to prepare, very colorful, and attractive, this Tuscany sausage can be served over rice or noodles or as a hot sandwich filling for a sub or hoagie roll. See color plate **8A**.

PRODUCTION NOTE: Cook sausage the day before serving to make slicing easier. This recipe provides 96 5-ounce servings that would fill 8 dozen rolls.

Portions per recipe: *96*
Yield: *2 pans*
Portion: *5 ounces*
Serving utensil: *3-ounce ladle*

Pan: *12" × 20" × 4"*
Griddle temperature: *375° F*
Time: *6 minutes*

Ingredients	Amounts
Sweet Italian sausage	10 lb.
Hot Italian sausage	10 lb.
Spanish onions, sliced	4 lb.
Green bell peppers, cut in 1" pieces	8 lb.
Basil, crushed	⅛ oz.
Oregano, crushed	⅛ oz.
Tomato juice	1 lb.
Tomatoes, quartered	6 lb.

Procedure:

1. Cook sausage in water, drain, and chill.
2. Slice cold sausage in ¼-inch slices.
3. Heat griddle to 375° F (do not oil).
4. Fry sausage, onions, and peppers with basil and oregano for 6 minutes or until nicely browned.
5. Slowly add tomato juice scraping griddle surface with spatula and scoop into pans, dividing the amount evenly.
6. Add 3 pounds of fresh tomato wedges to each pan. Toss gently and serve.

Calories: **346**   Protein: **14.2 g (16%)**   Carbohydrates: **4.0 g (5%)**   Sodium: **711 mg**
Total Fat: **30.0 g (78%)**   *Saturated Fat:* **10.7 g**   *Monounsaturated Fat:* **13.6 g**   *Polyunsaturated Fat:* **4.0 g**

❖ Szekely Gulyas—Hungarian Sauerkraut Goulash

There are many versions of this Hungarian specialty and this is one I have developed over the years. It might no longer be authentic, but it is delicious. Serve *szekely gulyas* with boiled potatoes, *spaetzle* or *semmelknoedel* (bread dumplings), peas or carrots as a vegetable and offer paprika-flavored yogurt mixed with sour cream as a topping.

PRODUCTION NOTES: Fresh sauerkraut should be used; the texture of canned sauerkraut is too mushy. To lower cholesterol and saturated fat, substitute vegetable oil for the lard: the loss in flavor will only be detected by a gulyas afficionado.

Portions per recipe: *100*
Yield: *2 pans*
Portion: *8 ounces*
Serving utensil: *6-ounce ladle*

Pan: *12″ × 20″ × 4″*
Skillet temperature: *350° F*
Time: *2 hours*

Ingredients

Ingredients	Amounts
Lard	2 oz.
Spanish onions, sliced	4 lb.
Vegetable oil	1 oz.
Lean pork shoulder, 1″ cubes	25 lb.
Hungarian paprika	2 oz.
Tomato paste	1 lb.
Canned peeled Italian tomatoes	6 lb. 6 oz.
Water	8 lb.
Fresh sauerkraut	10 lb.
Caraway seeds	1/3 oz.
Green bell peppers, thinly sliced	3 lb.

Procedure:

1. Heat lard in tilt skillet and sauté onions until golden, about 10 minutes.

2. Remove and save. Add oil and pork to skillet and sprinkle with paprika.

3. Brown well, stir in tomato paste, and cook for 3 minutes more.

4. Add tomatoes, reserved onions, and water and simmer slowly for 45 minutes.

5. Add sauerkraut, caraway seeds, and bell peppers and simmer for 45 minutes more.

6. Taste and add salt if necessary.

Calories: **145**   Protein: **15.1 g (42%)**   Carbohydrates: **6.1 g (17%)**   Sodium: **403 mg**
Total Fat: **6.8 g (42%)**   *Saturated Fat:* **2.2 g**   *Monounsaturated Fat:* **2.8 g**   *Polyunsaturated Fat:* **0.9 g**

Lamb

Lamb is rarely served in institutions, because most Americans do not include it in their diets. Immigrants from the Mediterranean countries are generally the only Americans who regularly use lamb. They do so in a variety of ways and most of the dishes in this chapter are from that corner of the world.

Remove all excess fat from lamb. Lean lamb is an excellent source of B vitamins, especially niacin. It provides good amounts of iron and potassium.

Lamb production has increased in America recently, but most lamb is still imported from New Zealand or Australia. Lamb chops and rack of lamb, the cuts usually eaten in America, are expensive cuts that are served only on special occasions or at catered events. The recipes included here are within the meal cost guidelines institutions follow and are very tasty.

❖ Agnello di Lucca *Michela's*

This grilled lamb is ideal for institutions with long service hours or where meals are cooked to order. The sauce is made in advance and improves in flavor as it sits. The lamb is quickly grilled (pink inside) as needed and is covered with sauce just before it is served.

PRODUCTION NOTES: The lamb should be trimmed of fat and cut into small ¾-inch by ¾-inch cubes from the leg. Grind the trimmings for kefta (lamb meatballs). Frozen small whole onions are an excellent substitute for fresh pearl onions, which are very tedious and time consuming to peel.

Portions per recipe: *100*
Yield: *3 pans*
Portion: *6 ounces*
Serving utensil: *4-ounce ladle*

Pan: *12" × 20" × 2"*
Skillet temperature: *375° F*
Time: *5–7 minutes*

Ingredients

Ingredients	Amounts
Olive oil	1 oz.
Fennel, cut into ¾-inch cubes	8 lb.
Pearl onions, peeled	4 lb.
Olive oil	1 oz.
Garlic cloves, crushed	2 oz.
Burgundy wine	4 lb.
Marsala wine	2 lb.
Meat stock	8 lb.
Cornstarch	2 oz.
Water (cold)	4 oz.
Kalamata olives, drained and pitted	12 oz.
Fresh rosemary leaves, chopped	2 oz.
Lamb, ¾-inch cubes	31 lb. 4 oz.

Procedure:

1. Heat the olive oil until it is almost smoking. Sear fennel and pearl onions. Remove from skillet and reserve.
2. Reduce heat to 300° F. Add olive oil and garlic and sauté until golden.
3. Add red and marsala wines and reduce by a third at a rolling boil.
4. Add stock, bring to a simmer, and stir in dissolved cornstarch. Simmer.
5. Return fennel and onions to sauce and keep warm.
6. Toss lamb cubes with fresh rosemary and grill in batches of approximately 5 pounds.
7. Add 2 ounces of olives to each batch of lamb just to heat. Place two batches or about 10 pounds of lamb into each pan.
8. Pour 1½ quarts of sauce over lamb. Fold in gently. Serve.

Calories: **210**   Protein: **29.1 g (55%)**   Carbohydrates: **3.0 g (6%)**   Sodium: **164 mg**
Total Fat: **8.4 g (36%)**   *Saturated Fat:* **2.8 g**   *Monounsaturated Fat:* **3.4 g**   *Polyunsaturated Fat:* **0.8 g**

❖ Black Forest Lamb "Baeckaoffa"

A wonderful meat and potato casserole. A hot marinade is poured over the meat and allowed to absorb the flavor for 24 hours. This also tenderizes the meat.

In Baden, where this peasant dish originates, it is often covered with bread dough. To do this, bake the casserole for 2 hours, then top with 1-inch-thick dough and bake for 35 minutes. If you have a bakery with a sheeter, have bakers roll out 13" × 11" rectangles to top light half size pans. Individual casseroles make a spectacular entree for a catered meal.

Portions per recipe: 96
Yield: 4 pans
Portion: 6 ounces (2.5" × 2" piece)
Serving utensil: spatula

Pan: 12" × 20" × 2"–½ size
Oven temperature: 350° F
Time: 120 minutes

Ingredients

Ingredients	Amounts	
Lamb stew meat, 1" cubes	16 lb.	
Beef stew meat, 1" cubes	8 lb.	
Water	4 lb.	
Juniper berries		1 oz.
Black peppercorns		½ oz.
Whole cloves		¼ oz.
Bay leaves, crushed		⅛ oz.
White wine	2 lb.	
Vegetable oil		2 oz.
Spanish onions, sliced	4 lb.	
Marjoram, crushed		⅛ oz.
Parsley leaves, minced		4 oz.
Hungarian paprika		¼ oz.
Potatoes, sliced into thin rounds	12 lb.	
Salt		1 oz.
Black pepper		¼ oz.
Margarine		2 oz.
Hungarian paprika		⅛ oz.

Procedure

1. Toss the meat cubes together.
2. Bring the water and spices to a boil. Simmer for 30 minutes, add wine and bring to a simmer. Do not boil.
3. Strain hot marinade over meat. Cover and refrigerate for 24 hours.
4. Heat vegetable oil. Sauté the onions with marjoram until golden, then add parsley and paprika.

5. In oiled pan place a layer of potatoes (1 pound) and cover with meat (3 pounds) and marinade. Top with a layer of onions (8 ounces) and a layer of potatoes. Sprinkle with salt and pepper.

6. Repeat meat and onions, finishing with a layer of neatly overlapping potato rows.

7. Melt margarine with paprika. Brush potatoes generously.

8. Bake for 2½ hours. If potatoes brown too quickly, cover with parchment paper. Cut each pan into 24 pieces.

Calories: **186**   Protein: **22.0 g (47%)**   Carbohydrates: **9.2 g (20%)**   Sodium: **185 mg**
Total Fat: **6.5 g (31%)**   *Saturated Fat:* **2.2 g**   *Monounsaturated Fat:* **2.5 g**   *Polyunsaturated Fat:* **0.9 g**

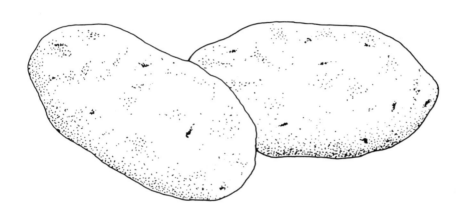

❖ Greek Lamb Roast

The boneless rolled leg of lamb is marinated for 24 hours.

PRODUCTION NOTES: Lamb roasted at a very low temperature is moist and shrinks less. Roasting time for a fully loaded oven is approximately 3 to 4 hours. Always use a thermometer for perfect control. The desired internal temperature for lamb is 150° F.

Portions per recipe: *100*
Yield: *200 1½-ounce slices*
Portion: *3 ounces (2 slices)*
Serving utensil: *tongs*

Pan: *12″ × 20″ × 2″*
Oven temperature: *285° F*
Time: *4 hours*

Ingredients	Amounts
Boneless leg of lamb, well trimmed	31 lb.
Lemon juice	8 oz.
Oregano, crushed	¼ oz.
Fresh rosemary, chopped	2 oz.
Garlic cloves, crushed	2 oz.
Black pepper	¼ oz.
Olive oil	2 oz.
Meat stock	4 lb.
Cornstarch	2 oz.
Water (cold)	4 oz.
Salt	1 oz.
Lemon slices	8 oz.

Procedure:

1. Mix lemon juice, oregano, rosemary, garlic, pepper, and oil.
2. Rub all over lamb, cover, and refrigerate for 24 hours.
3. Drain and reserve marinade.
4. Rack lamb, insert thermometer in smallest roast, and place in 285° F oven. When smallest roast registers 150° F, remove this roast and insert thermometer in next largest roast. Repeat until all roasts are done.
5. Remove cooked roasts and let sit for 20 minutes before slicing.
6. Pour off fat and deglaze roasting pan with marinade and stock.
7. Bring to a simmer and stir in cornstarch dissolved in water.
8. Taste and add salt.
9. Slice lamb into 1½-ounce slices and cover lightly with sauce or serve sauce separately. Garnish with lemon slices.

Calories: **124**   Protein: **18.6 g (60%)**   Carbohydrates: **0.9 g (3%)**   Sodium: **166 mg**
Total Fat: **4.6 g (34%)**   *Saturated Fat:* **1.5 g**   *Monounsaturated Fat:* **2.1 g**   *Polyunsaturated Fat:* **0.4 g**

❖ Grilled Lamb Tips with Green Peppers

Lamb tips cut from the leg are grilled in garlic and marjoram-flavored olive oil and stir-fried with peppers, mushrooms, and onions.

PRODUCTION NOTES: To allow the lamb dry heat in which to brown, the lamb is grilled a few minutes before the vegetables are added. If the grill is crowded, the lamb will stew and get tough.

Portions per recipe: *100*
Yield: *3 pans*
Portion: *6 ounces*
Serving utensil: *4-ounce ladle*

Pan: *12″ × 20″ × 2″*
Oven temperature: *375° F*
Time: *8 minutes*

Ingredients

Ingredients	Amounts
Mushroom buttons	4 lb.
Green bell peppers	3 lb. 8 oz.
Spanish onions, thinly sliced	2 lb. 8 oz.
Olive oil	3 oz.
Garlic cloves, crushed	½ oz.
Marjoram, crushed	⅛ oz.
Lamb tips, ¾″ × 2″ pieces	31 lb. 4 oz.
Tomatoes, cored and cut into wedges	8 lb.
Parsley, finely minced	3 oz.

Procedure:

1. Rinse mushrooms, trim the stems, and slice thin.
2. Cut peppers into 1-inch squares.
3. Toss onions with peppers and mushrooms.
4. Beat olive oil with garlic and marjoram.
5. Heat the grill to 375° F and with a 1-ounce ladle, add olive oil.
6. Spread about 8 pounds of lamb on grill. Brown one side.
7. Add 2 pounds 8 ounces of vegetables and stir-fry for 4 minutes. The lamb should be barely pink at this stage.
8. Place into pan. Add 2 pounds of tomato wedges and 1 ounce of parsley. Toss and serve.
9. Repeat batches as needed.

Calories: **137**   Protein: **16.9 g (50%)**   Carbohydrates: **3.8 g (11%)**   Sodium: **57 mg**
Total Fat: **5.6 g (37%)**   *Saturated Fat:* **1.8 g**   *Monounsaturated Fat:* **2.4 g**   *Polyunsaturated Fat:* **0.6 g**

❖ Herb Roasted Lamb

Mint apple jelly, herbs, and sweet Hungarian paprika glaze this lamb roast.

PRODUCTION NOTES: Lamb roasted at a very low temperature is moist and shrinks less. Roasting time for a fully loaded oven is approximately 3 to 4 hours. Always use a thermometer for perfect control. The desired internal temperature for lamb is 150° F.

Portions per recipe: *100*
Yield: *200 1½-ounce slices*
Portion: *3 ounces (2 slices)*
Serving utensil: *tongs*

Pan: *12″ × 20″ × 2″*
Oven temperature: *285° F*
Time: *4 hours*

Ingredients	Amounts
Mint apple jelly	2 lb.
Garlic cloves, crushed	2 oz.
Rosemary, crushed	¼ oz.
Basil, crushed	⅛ oz.
Hungarian paprika	¾ oz.
Boneless leg of lamb, well-trimmed	31 lb.
Meat stock	4 lb.
Mint apple jelly	8 oz.
Cornstarch	2 oz.
Dry vermouth	4 oz.
Salt	1 oz.
Black pepper	¼ oz.

Procedure:

1. Heat jelly until melted and combine with spices. Cool slightly.
2. Rub each roast with this mixture. Coat well. Let stand at room temperature for 30 minutes.
3. Place roasts on racks in pan. Place thermometer in smallest roast.
4. When smallest roast registers 150° F, remove this roast and insert thermometer into next largest roast. Repeat until all roasts are done.
5. Let the roasts sit for 20 minutes before slicing into 1½ ounce slices.
6. Pour fat off roasting pans. Reserve drippings and deglaze pans with stock.
7. Heat drippings, stock, and jelly. Dissolve cornstarch in vermouth.
8. Stir into boiling stock. Taste.
9. Add salt and pepper. Cover lamb with sauce or serve sauce separately.
10. Garnish with a lemon basket filled with mint jelly.

Calories: **151**   Protein: **18.6 g (49%)**   Carbohydrates: **8.9 g (24%)**   Sodium: **168 mg**

Total Fat: **4.1 g (24%)**   *Saturated Fat:* **1.5 g**   *Monounsaturated Fat:* **1.6 g**   *Polyunsaturated Fat:* **0.4 g**

❖ **Kefta Mkaouara** *Wolfert*

This is a Moroccan meatball recipe from Paula Wolfert. It uses lamb and beef with herbs and spices. The meatballs are browned in the oven and heated in a fragrant tomato sauce and garnished with poached eggs. During the Moroccan Diffa in our dining rooms at UNH we used the poached eggs as a garnish; only a few lucky students got to sample the complete dish. This recipe only includes enough eggs for the garnish; increase the amount to one egg per serving if this is the only entrée served.

PRODUCTION NOTES: With a #32 scoop, form meatballs and place on parchment-lined sheet pans. A meatball forming machine can handle the mixture well; use it if you have got one. Bake at once or refrigerate for no more than one day. Raw meatballs can be frozen for up to three months.

Portions per recipe: 100   *Pan: 12″ × 20″ × 2″*
Yield: 500 meatballs/4 pans   *Oven temperature: 350° F*
Portion: 5 meatballs   *Time: 12 minutes*
Serving utensil: spoon

Ingredients

Ingredients	Amounts
Ground lamb	15 lb.
Ground beef	8 lb.
Parsley, minced	4 oz.
Cilantro, minced	2 oz.
Spanish onions, finely chopped	1 lb. 8 oz.
Cumin seeds, pulverized	½ oz.
Cayenne pepper	⅛ oz.
Salt	4 oz.

Sauce:

Sauce	Amounts
Spanish onion, chopped	12 oz.
Fresh parsley, minced	4 oz.
Garlic cloves, crushed	2 oz.
Canned Italian tomatoes, hand crushed	15 lb. 8 oz.
Cumin seed, pulverized	¼ oz.
Black pepper	¼ oz.
Cinnamon	¼ oz.
Cayenne pepper	¹⁄₁₆ oz.
Eggs (20)	2 lb. 8 oz.

(continued)

Procedure:

1. Combine meatball ingredients and form with a #32 scoop.
2. Place 125 meatballs on each sheet pan.
3. Bake at 350° F for 12 minutes or until well browned.
4. Combine sauce ingredients in kettle and simmer for 30 minutes.
5. Put contents from one sheetpan into 12″ × 20″ × 2″ pan.
6. Cover with ½ gallon sauce.
7. Drop 5 eggs in a row down the center of pan. Cover with foil and return to oven for 8 minutes until eggs are poached. Garnish with parsley and cilantro.

Calories: **184***	Protein: **16.5 g (36%)**	Carbohydrates: **4.3 g (9%)**	Sodium: **621 mg**
Total Fat: **10.9 g (53%)**	*Saturated Fat:* **4.1 g**	*Monounsaturated Fat:* **4.2 g**	*Polyunsaturated Fat:* **0.5**

Calories: **247†**	Protein: **21.3 g (35%)**	Carbohydrates: **4.8 g (8%)**	Sodium: **676 mg**
Total Fat: **15.4 g (56%)**	*Saturated Fat:* **5.5 g**	*Monounsaturated Fat:* **4.6 g**	*Polyunsaturated Fat:* **1.1 g**

❖ Kefta in Yogurt Sauce

For this dish meatballs are made with ground lamb and spiced with turmeric, salt, and pepper. They are baked with spices and finished with yogurt. They are delicious served with steamed rice, baked tomato halves, and curried cucumbers.

PRODUCTION NOTE: The yogurt will curdle when heated to boiling point unless it is mixed with cornstarch or egg whites.

Portions per recipe: *100*
Yield: *300 meatballs/4 pans*
Portion: *3 meatballs*
Serving utensil: *spoon*

Pan: *12″ × 20″ × 2″*
Oven temperature: *350° F*
Time: *12 minutes*

---

*With 20 eggs.
†With 100 eggs.

Ingredients	Amounts
Ground lamb	25 lb.
Turmeric	1 oz.
Salt	4 oz.
Black pepper	½ oz.
Vegetable oil	4 oz.
Spanish onions, finely diced	2 lb.
Freshly ground cumin	¾ oz.
Freshly ground coriander	⅓ oz.
Freshly ground cloves	¼ oz.
Freshly ground cardamom	⅓ oz.
Cinnamon	⅓ oz.
Water (hot)	4 lb.
Salt	1 oz.
Cornstarch	4 oz.
Low-fat yogurt	8 lb.
Fresh mint, chopped	1 oz.
Hungarian paprika	⅛ oz.

Procedure:

1. Heat vegetable oil and sauté onions. Put 8 ounces into each oiled pan.
2. Mix lamb with turmeric, salt, and pepper.
3. With a #24 scoop place 75 meatballs on top of onions.
4. Mix all the spices and sprinkle ½ ounce of mixture over each pan of meatballs.
5. Bake in 350° F oven until brown, about 15 minutes.
6. Pour 1 pint hot water into each pan and bake for another 20 minutes.
7. Mix salt and cornstarch with yogurt. Pour 2 pounds over meatballs.
8. Shake pans to coat meatballs well. Heat for 3 minutes to warm yogurt.
9. Sprinkle with mint and paprika. Serve.

Calories: **130**   Protein: **14.8 g (45%)**   Carbohydrates: **3.8 g (12%)**   Sodium: **610 mg**
Total Fat: **5.9 g (41%)**   *Saturated Fat:* **2.3 g**   *Monounsaturated Fat:* **1.9 g**   *Polyunsaturated Fat:* **1.0 g**

❖ Lamb Navarin

This is a French lamb stew that is simmered with a lot of vegetables. It is ideal served with crusty french bread and a crisp green salad.

PRODUCTION NOTES: Brown lamb in tilting skillet. If none is available and amounts exceed holding capacity of skillet, brown meat in the oven, deglaze pans with water and continue braising in a large steam kettle. Skim off excess fat before adding herbs and vegetables.

Portions per recipe: 100
Yield: 7.5 gallons
Portion: 10 ounces
Serving utensil: 8-ounce ladle

Pan: 12" × 20" × 4"
Time: 1 hour and 45 minutes

Ingredients	Amounts	
Vegetable oil		1 oz.
Lamb stew meat	25 lb.	
Salt		1 oz.
Black pepper		¼ oz.
Water	12 lb.	
Dry vermouth	1 lb.	
Garlic cloves, crushed		2 oz.
Tarragon, crushed		¼ oz.
Thyme, crushed		¼ oz.
Basil, crushed		¼ oz.
Celery with leaves, coarsely chopped	2 lb.	
Carrots, peeled and cut into 1-inch chunks	4 lb.	
Scallions, 1-inch length	1 lb.	
Small red potatoes, unpeeled and quartered	6 lb.	
Canned tomatoes, diced	6 lb.	6 oz.
Cornstarch		3 oz.
Lemon juice		6 oz.
Frozen peas	2 lb.	8 oz.
Fresh parsley, minced		3 oz.

Procedure:

1. Heat the oil and brown the meat.
2. Add salt, pepper, water, and dry vermouth. Simmer for 45 minutes.
3. Skim off excess fat and discard.
4. Add garlic, herbs, celery, carrots, scallions, and potatoes.
5. Simmer for 20 minutes. Add tomatoes and simmer for 30 minutes more.
6. Dissolve cornstarch in lemon juice and stir into stew.
7. Add peas. Ladle stew into 4-inch pans.
8. Sprinkle each pan with 1 ounce of freshly chopped parsley.

Calories: **205**   Protein: **24.6 g (48%)**   Carbohydrates: **9.9 g (19%)**   Sodium: **258 mg**

Total Fat: **6.7 g (29%)**   *Saturated Fat:* **2.3 g**   *Monounsaturated Fat:* **2.5 g**   *Polyunsaturated Fat:* **0.9 g**

❖ Lamb Tagine with Onions and Olives   *Wolfert*

This tagine is redolent with the flavor of Greek olives and ginger, cumin and saffron. Although saffron is a very expensive spice, a very small amount adds a lot of flavor. All spices must be freshly and finely ground.

PRODUCTION NOTES: The lamb is cooked one day ahead, refrigerated overnight, the cold fat removed, and the juices drained and boiled with the olives. The cooked meat is roasted in the oven to crisp it and smothered with the olives and onions. This recipe uses cracked Greek green Royal olives; brandnames available in America are *Krinos* and *Peleponnes*. Please, do not use California green olives. They will ruin the dish.

Portions per recipe: 100
Yield: 3 pans
Portion: 5 ounces
Serving utensil: 3-ounce ladle

Pan: 12" × 20" × 2"
Oven temperature: 400° F
Time: 2 hours and 15–20 min.

(continued)

Ingredients	Amounts
Lamb stew meat (shoulder or neck)	25 lb.
Garlic cloves, crushed	4 oz.
Salt	3/4 oz.
Dry ginger, pulverized	1/2 oz.
Freshly ground black pepper (very fine)	1/2 oz.
Cumin seeds, pulverized	1/2 oz.
Hungarian paprika	3/4 oz.
Saffron, pulverized	1/16 oz.
Olive oil	1 oz.
Spanish onions, peeled and quartered	4 lb.
Italian parsley, stems removed	3 oz.
Cilantro, use stems	1 oz.
Water	6 lb.
Cracked green Greek Royal olives	4 lb.
Lemon juice	12 oz.

Procedure:

1. Remove any excess fat from the lamb.
2. Toss lamb with garlic and spices.
3. Heat oil and brown the spiced lamb for 5 to 8 minutes.
4. Chop the onions with the herbs in food chopper until almost a mush.
5. Add this to the meat with water and simmer for 2 hours.
6. Put in pan and refrigerate overnight.
7. Remove hard fat. Drain juices and reserve.
8. Pit the olives, cover with cold water, bring to a boil, and drain.
9. Bring reserved juices to a boil, add olives, and boil rapidly until thickened.
10. Add lemon juice. Taste and add salt if necessary.
11. Heat meat in a 400° F oven until lightly crisp. Cover with sauce.
12. Garnish with lemon slices, olives, and cilantro sprigs.

Calories: **213*** Protein: **23.6 g (44%)** Carbohydrates: **3.4 g (6%)** Sodium: **635 mg**
Total Fat: **11.5 g (49%)** *Saturated Fat:* **2.6 g** *Monounsaturated Fat:* **5.8 g** *Polyunsaturated Fat:* **.9 g**

*Calories include all fat—no allowance was made for fat removed in step 7.

❖ Lamb Tagine with Raisins and Almonds *Wolfert*

Sweet and spicy, this is a wonderful Moroccan stew from the expert on Moroccan food Paula Wolfert. Adapted from a recipe in her book, *Couscous and Other Good Food from Morocco*. (Published by Harper and Row, 1973.) Serve this tagine with couscous and spicy vegetables.

PRODUCTION NOTES: For best results, all the spices should be freshly ground. An electric coffee grinder does the job well. Clean the grinder by using it to pulverize a ¼ cup of granulated sugar. This tagine can be made a day in advance; it reheats extremely well and the cold fat can be removed further reducing calories and fat.

Portions per recipe: 100
Yield: 2 pans
Portion: 6 ounces
Serving utensil: 4-ounce ladle

Pan: 12″ × 20″ × 4″
Oven temperature: 325° F
Time: 1 hour 45 minutes

Ingredients

Ingredients	Amounts	
Raisins	2 lb.	
Lean lamb stew meat	25 lb.	
Olive oil		1 oz.
Sweet butter		1 oz.
Spanish onions, chopped	5 lb.	
Garlic cloves, crushed		5 oz.
Salt		½ oz.
Freshly ground black pepper		¾ oz.
Turmeric		½ oz.
Dry ginger, pulverized		½ oz.
Cayenne pepper		¼ oz.
Canned Italian tomatoes, hand crushed	6 lb. 12 oz.	
Water	4 lb.	
Parsley, minced		4 oz.
Cilantro, minced		1 oz.
Almonds, sliced		6 oz.

Procedure:

1. Soak raisins in cold water.
2. Remove any extra fat from lamb.
3. Heat oil and butter and add onions, garlic, salt, and spices.
4. Add lamb and toss well. Sauté for 10 minutes.
5. Add crushed tomatoes and water. Simmer for 1 hour.
6. Drain raisins and add with spices to tagine. Cook for 30 minutes more.
7. Ladle 3½ gallons into pan.

(continued)

8. Toast almonds on griddle or in oven with a pat of butter.

9. Sprinkle each pan with 3 ounces of toasted almonds. Serve.

Calories: **205**   Protein: **23.8 g (46%)**   Carbohydrates: **11.0 g (21%)**   Sodium: **135 mg**

Total Fat: **6.9 g (30%)**   *Saturated Fat:* **2.3 g**   *Monounsaturated Fat:* **2.9 g**   *Polyunsaturated Fat:* **.7 g**

❖ Rolled Leg of Lamb Provencal   *Kamman*

Enjoy the taste of the fresh herbs of Provence with every bite of lamb moistened with a wonderful sauce. Even confirmed lamb haters will be converted by this dish.

PRODUCTION NOTES: A day ahead trim the lamb of all fat and gristle. Make the *Persillade* of minced garlic and parsley, roll it into the boneless lamb, and tie the lamb with butcher string. Refrigerate for 24 hours. Use any of the meatscraps and the lamb ribs for stock. Refrigerate the stock and remove all fat.

Portions per recipe: *100*   Pan: *12″ × 20″ × 2″*
Yield: *200 2-ounce slices*   Oven temperature: *350° F*
Portion: *2 slices*   Time: *45 minutes*
Serving utensil: *spatula*

Ingredients | Amounts

Ingredients	Amounts	
Boneless leg of lamb	32 lb.	
Lamb ribs, 1″ pieces	5 lb.	
Fennel seeds		½ oz.
Meat stock	4 lb.	
Garlic cloves, peeled and chopped		6 oz.
Parsley, chopped		12 oz.
Fresh rosemary leaves		1 oz.
Thyme, crushed		¼ oz.
Salt		1 oz.
Freshly ground black pepper		½ oz.
Olive oil		4 oz.
Broth	4 lb.	
Cornstarch		1 oz.

Procedure:

1. A day ahead trim the boneless leg and remove all gristle and fat one day before serving.

2. Add trimmings but not the fat to lamb ribs and roast in 350° F oven until brown. Put in kettle.

3. Add fennel seeds and meat stock and simmer for 2 hours. Strain and refrigerate. Remove all fat before using.

4. Next day chop garlic and parsley in food chopper or processor to make persillade.

5. Reserve ¼ cup of persillade per 100 servings of sauce.

6. Mix the remainder of persillade with rosemary, thyme, salt, and pepper.

7. Coat inside of roast with persillade, roll, and tie with butcher twine.

8. Brush the outside with oil and rub with more persillade. Refrigerate for 24 hours.

9. Let roast sit at room temperature for 30 minutes. Heat oven to 350° F.

10. Roast for 45 to 60 minutes, let sit for 20 minutes, and slice into 2-ounce slices.

11. Deglaze roasting pans with refrigerated lamb broth. Strain broth into kettle.

12. Bring to a simmer, dissolve cornstarch in cold water, and stir into broth.

13. Add reserved persillade and serve with lamb slices.

Calories: **153**   Protein: **21.4 g (56%)**   Carbohydrates: **1.3 g (3%)**   Sodium: **287 mg**

Total Fat: **6.4 g (37%)**   *Saturated Fat:* **2.0 g**   *Monounsaturated Fat:* **2.9 g**   *Polyunsaturated Fat:* **0.6 g**

THYME

GARLIC

ROSEMARY

Poultry

Poultry has become very popular in American homes, institutions, and restaurants. This is partially due to the lower cost of poultry, but has also been prompted by public awareness of its high nutritional value. The skinless white meat is a low-fat protein source surpassed only by lean white fish. (See nutrient values on page 191.) The meat's mild taste can be enjoyed for its own flavor, yet this mildness allows cooks to create wonderful dishes flavored with wines, herbs, and spices. Poultry can be equally delicious delicately flavored with lemon or prepared with such strong flavors as curry or cilantro.

Many restaurants and institutions are using frozen prepared chicken products. Food manufacturers tempt the institutional buyer with a large array of poultry dishes under the banner of portion and labor control. Little is gained in labor savings; poultry is not difficult to prepare and is easily portioned. Many prepared poultry entrées contain large amounts of added fat and sodium, reducing poultry's most important dietary value. In comparing costs I have generally found poultry entrées prepared from scratch cost less and taste better.

The poultry recipes are grouped by species and product cut to facilitate the task of menu planning.

Whole Chicken

The use of whole chickens may not be practical for very large food service operations, but smaller institutions and caterers can use whole chickens to great advantage. Use large fryers rather than roasting hens; they cook in a much shorter time and can be easily cut up with poultry shears or can be pulled apart with gloved hands after they have been cooked.

PRODUCTION NOTES: Nothing is more simple to roast than a whole chicken. Rub the inside and skin with lemon juice, place a bouquet of fresh herbs such as thyme, parsley, tarragon, or sage in the cavity and just pop it in the oven for between 40 minutes and 1 hour, depending on size. Roasted chicken breast sandwiches are terrific and could become a signature item at a deli counter.

A three to 3½ pound fryer provides about 11 ounces of roasted white meat, 6 ounces of dark meat, 2 wings and 2 drumsticks.

Drumsticks and wings paired with pasta, rice or potato salad make a good daily special and can also be packaged for take-out. Small chicken bits can be turned into a chicken salad for salad plates or sandwiches and the bones lend themselves to use in flavorful stocks.

I am always amazed that small cafeterias and snackbars don't take advantage of whole chicken in the manner described above. There is very little labor involved and, of course, the price is right.

Nutrient values are for roasted 100 grams (3.5 ounce) servings from the USDA Agricultural Handbook No. 8.

Light meat w/o skin:
CALORIES: 182   PROTEIN: 32.3 g (71%)   FAT: 4.9 g (24%)*

Dark Meat w/o skin:
CALORIES: 184   PROTEIN: 29.3 g (64%)   FAT: 6.5 g (32%)*

Drumstick with skin:
CALORIES: 235   PROTEIN: 32.6 g (56%)   FAT: 10.2 g (39%)*

❖ Chilled Poached Chicken with Green Sauce

An ideal catering entrée, this chicken recipe can be poached in advance, and covered with sauce and served when needed. The green sauce is made with an egg white mayonnaise base to reduce cholesterol and it gets its bright green color from pureed fresh watercress, sorrel, parsley, and scallions. It is a dish that can be made ahead of time to be served on warm summer days, but it is equally good on winter buffets. Use white and dark meat.

PRODUCTION NOTE: Let the cooked chicken cool in the stock. It will be easier to work with.

Portions per recipe: 75
Yield: approx. 14 pounds cooked
    boneless pulled chicken
Portion: 3 ounces
Serving utensil: spoon

Cooking method: simmer
Time: 30 minutes

Ingredients	Amounts	
Water	64 lb.	
Carrot, unpeeled and cut into chunks	1 lb.	
Spanish onions, quartered	1 lb.	
Bay leaves, crumbled		1/16 oz.
Parsley sprigs		1 oz.
Black peppercorns, bruised		1/8 oz.
Tarragon, crushed		1/8 oz.
Whole chicken fryers, rinsed (12)	36 lb.	
Scallions, minced		8 oz.
Watercress, minced		8 oz.
Parsley leaves, minced		4 oz.
Fresh tarragon, minced		4 oz.
Sorrel, minced		2 oz.
Egg white mayonnaise (page 460)	1 lb.	8 oz.
Low-fat yogurt	1 lb.	

(continued)

*Data for fat components not available.

Procedure:

1. Bring water to a boil with vegetables, spices, and herbs.
2. Add chickens and simmer for 45 minutes. Let cool in stock. Use stock for soups or sauces.
3. Pull off cooked meat. Remove skin. Arrange neatly on large platter.
4. Fold fresh herbs into the egg white mayonnaise and yogurt. Pour over chicken.
5. Garnish and serve.

Calories: **232**   Protein: **29.6 g (51%)**   Carbohydrates: **2.0 g (3%)**   Sodium: **128 mg**

Total Fat: **11.2 g (43%)**   *Saturated Fat:* **2.3 g**   *Monounsaturated Fat:* **2.2 g**   *Polyunsaturated Fat:* **5.6 g**

❖ Coq au Riesling

A white wine coq au vin from the peasant cuisine of Alsace-Lorraine. See color plate **9**.

PRODUCTION NOTE: Procure whole, cut-up fryers (1 chicken for 4 servings). Cut split breasts in half. Each serving should contain 3 pieces of chicken—breast, thigh or drumstick, and wing or backbone piece.

Portions per recipe: 60
Yield: 2 pans
Portion: 12 ounces
Serving utensil: spoon

Pan: 12″ × 20″ × 2″
Oven temperature: 375° F
Time: 45 minutes

Ingredients	Amounts
Whole chicken, cut up (12 pieces)	45 lb.
Salt	1 oz.
Black pepper	¼ oz.
Thyme, crushed	⅛ oz.
Spanish onions, quartered	5 lb.
Mushroom buttons, whole	3 lb.
Water (hot)	2 lb.
Riesling wine	4 lb.
Dijon mustard	2 oz.
Lemon juice	2 oz.
Cornstarch	1 oz.

Procedure:

1. Rub the chicken pieces with salt, pepper, and thyme.
2. Place in a single layer into 4 pans. Add the onions and bake at 350° F for 15 minutes.
3. When nicely browned, pour off the fat and combine the chicken and onions from two pans into one. Deglaze the empty pans with 1 pint hot water.
4. Mix the pan juices with wine, mustard, lemon juice, and cornstarch.
5. Add 1½ pounds of mushrooms to pan of chicken. Pour 3 pints liquid over chicken.
6. Bake uncovered for 30 minutes.

Calories: **519***   Protein: **44.0 g (34%)**   Carbohydrates: **4.4 g (4%)**   Sodium: **324 mg**

Total Fat: **35.0 g (60%)**   *Saturated Fat:* **10.0 g**   *Monounsaturated Fat:* **14.3 g**   *Polyunsaturated Fat:* **7.6 g**

Breast of Chicken

❖

White chicken meat is not as flavorful as dark meat, but it is by far the most popular. Boneless breast of chicken has become the fast food of restaurant kitchens. At home it is favored by many a working parent for its convenience and speed of preparation.

❖ Boneless Breast of Chicken in Pastry

A turnover pastry envelops a boneless breast of chicken topped with a cream and yogurt cheese herb and garlic mixture. This dish should be reserved for special occasions, as it is fairly high in fat. An excellent banquet entrée, because the chicken transports well and stays moist and hot. It is absolutely delicious.

PRODUCTION NOTES: Drain 2 quarts of whole milk yogurt in a cheese cloth lined colander to make yogurt cheese. Beat 1 egg with 1 cup water to make an egg wash to brush the pastry with, before it is baked.

Portions per recipe: 100
Yield: 100 pastries
Portion: 1 pastry
Serving utensil: spatula

Pan: 18" × 26" sheet pan
Oven temperature: 325° F
Time: 25 minutes

(continued)

---

*Calories include all fat—no allowance was made for fat removed in Step 3.

The ultimate banquet entrée: Boneless breast of chicken in pastry.

Ingredients	Amounts
Garlic cloves	4 oz.
Parsley	4 oz.
Scallions	4 oz.
Cornstarch	2 oz.
Basil, crushed	1/4 oz.
Black pepper	1/4 oz.
Cream cheese	1 lb.
Yogurt cheese	2 lb.
Pastry circles, 4 ounces each	25 lb.
Boneless, skinless chicken breasts, 6 ounces each	37 lb. 8 oz.

Procedure:

1. Mince garlic, parsley, and scallions in a food processor or chopper.
2. Add cornstarch, basil, pepper, cream cheese, and yogurt cheese and blend until smooth.
3. Remove to a bowl.
4. Place 10 pastry circles on table. With a #40 scoop place herb filling in center, then set raw chicken breast on filling. Fold pastry edges up over chicken. Squeeze edges together to close pastry.

5. Place about 20 pastries on sheet pan. Brush with whole milk egg wash.
6. Bake at 325° F for 25 minutes.

Calories: **683**   Protein: **32.5 g (19%)**   Carbohydrates: **48.9 g (29%)**   Sodium: **189 mg**

Total Fat: **38.9 g (51%)**   *Saturated Fat:* **10.1 g**   *Monounsaturated Fat:* **21.2 g**   *Polyunsaturated Fat:* **4.4 g**

❖ Breast of Chicken Tarragon

Tarragon has a real affinity for chicken meat. In this recipe the skin and underside of the breast are thoroughly rubbed with a paste made with safflower oil, scallions, fresh parsley, and dried tarragon.

Portions per recipe: 60
Yield: 60 breast halves
Portion: 1 half breast
Serving utensil: tongs

Pan: 12" × 20" × 2"
Oven temperature: 325° F
Time: 35 to 40 minutes

Ingredients

Ingredients	Amounts
Chicken breasts	25 lb.
Safflower oil	2 oz.
Scallions	12 oz.
Italian parsley	9 oz.
Tarragon, crushed	1 oz.
Black pepper	¼ oz.
Lemon juice	2 oz.
Canned Italian tomatoes	6 lb. 6 oz.

Procedure:

1. Trim any excess skin or fat off chicken breasts.
2. In a food chopper or processor blend oil, scallions, parsley, tarragon, pepper, and lemon juice to a paste.
3. Rub chicken breasts all over with paste and let marinate about 30 minutes.
4. Crush tomatoes and put about 1½ pounds in each pan. Set 15 breasts on top of tomatoes.
5. Bake at 325° F for 35 to 40 minutes.
6. Serve each breast with a little tomato sauce.

Calories: **284**   Protein: **32.3 g (45%)**   Carbohydrates: **3.1 g (5%)**   Sodium: **175 mg**

Total Fat: **15.9 g (50%)**   *Saturated Fat:* **4.1 g**   *Monounsaturated Fat:* **5.9 g**   *Polyunsaturated Fat:* **3.7 g**

❖ Cajun Style Chicken

Spicy and very simple to prepare, serve this chicken breast with rice, black beans, and a crisp salad.

Portions per recipe: *96*
Yield: *4 pans*
Portion: *1 breast half*
Serving utensil: *tongs*

Pan: *18″ × 26″ sheet pan*
Oven temperature: *325° F*
Time: *22 minutes*

Ingredients	Amounts
Boneless, skinless chicken breasts, 6 ounces each	36 lb.
Margarine, melted	4 oz.
Cajun spice (recipe page 458)	2 oz.

Procedure:

1. Place 24 chicken breasts flat on oiled sheet pan.
2. Brush chicken with margarine and sprinkle lightly with spices.
3. Bake at 325° F for 22 minutes or until done.

> Calories: **132**   Protein: **25.6 g (78%)**   Carbohydrates: **.4 g (1%)**   Sodium: **87 mg**
>
> Total Fat: **2.4 g (16%)**   *Saturated Fat:* **.2 g**   *Monounsaturated Fat:* **.8 g**   *Polyunsaturated Fat:* **.4 g**

❖ California Chicken Veronique

Baked with white wine, mushrooms, artichokes, orange pieces, and grapes, this chicken dish celebrates the best of California.

PRODUCTION NOTES: Frozen artichoke quarters are fine for this dish. The grapes can be red or green but must be seedless. Steam oranges in 5# pressure steamer for 2 minutes, this will make peeling them a snap.

Portions per recipe: *60*
Yield: *4 pans*
Portion: *1 breast*
Serving utensil: *spoon*

Pan: *12″ × 20″ × 2″*
Oven temperature: *350° F*
Time: *45 minutes*

Ingredients	Amounts	
Olive oil		2 oz.
Garlic cloves, crushed		1 oz.
Cayenne pepper		$\frac{1}{16}$ oz.
Orange juice		4 oz.
Chicken breasts, split	25 lb.	
Frozen artichoke quarters	4 lb.	
Whole mushroom buttons	3 lb.	
California chablis	4 lb.	
Cornstarch		2 oz.
Seedless grapes, stems removed	2 lb.	
Oranges, peeled and cut into		
$\frac{1}{2}$" pieces	2 lb.	

Procedure:

1. Mix together oil, garlic, cayenne, and orange juice. Rub chicken pieces with mixture. Place 15 pieces in each pan.
2. Bake at 350° F for 15 minutes or until nicely browned. Pour off excess fat.
3. Add 1 pound of artichoke quarters and 12 ounces of whole mushrooms to each pan.
4. Pour 1 pound of chablis over chicken and bake 20 minutes.
5. Toss cornstarch with grapes and orange pieces. Add 1 pound to each pan.
6. Bake for 10 more minutes or until meat thermometer registers 185° F.

Calories: **307**   Protein: **34.0 g (44%)**   Carbohydrates: **7.8 g (10%)**   Sodium: **133 mg**

Total Fat: **15.4 g (45%)**   *Saturated Fat:* **4.3 g**   *Monounsaturated Fat:* **6.5 g**   *Polyunsaturated Fat:* **3.4 g**

❖ Chicken Limone

Boneless breast of chicken is pounded lightly between floured sheets of parchment paper and grilled in lemon butter. The final touch is a heaping spoonful of lemon and rosemary flavored mushrooms.

Portions per recipe: *48*   Pan: *12" × 20" × 2"*
Yield: *3 pans*   Griddle temperature: *350° F*
Portion: *1 breast half*   Time: *10 minutes*
Serving utensil: *spatula*

Ingredients	Amounts	
Butter blend (60% margarine/ 40% butter)		4 oz.
Lemon juice		2 oz.
Mushrooms, thinly sliced	3 lb.	
Rosemary leaves, minced		1 oz.
Parsley, minced		2 oz.
All-purpose flour		4 oz.
Salt		1 oz.
White pepper		1/4 oz.
Boneless, skinless chicken breasts, 6 ounces each	18 lb.	

Procedure:

1. Melt butter blend with lemon juice.

2. Pour 1 ounce of lemon butter on griddle. Add mushrooms, toss and add rosemary, parsley, and another ladle of butter. Sauté for 5 minutes. Remove and hold warm.

3. Mix flour with salt and pepper. Flour parchment paper and place chicken breast on paper, sprinkle with more flour, cover with parchment, and pound to flatten chicken slightly.

4. Pour lemon butter on grill and sauté chicken breasts for 5 minutes on each side.

5. Place 16 breasts in pan and top each breast with 1 ounce of mushrooms.

Calories: **155**   Protein: **26.4 g (68%)**   Carbohydrates: **3.4 g (9%)**   Sodium: **317 mg**

Total Fat: **3.4 g (20%)**   *Saturated Fat:* **1.1 g**   *Monounsaturated Fat:* **1.1 g**   *Polyunsaturated Fat:* **.8 g**

❖ Chicken Teriyaki

Marinated in a teriyaki sauce and broiled, grilled, or baked, this chicken breast is moist and flavorful. Surprise people by serving it at a picnic with cold sichuan noodles and green and white jade salad or with any of the other Far Eastern salads in this book.

PRODUCTION NOTES: The recipe gives baking instructions, however, the chicken can also be broiled or grilled indoors or outdoors. Conference groups who wanted to have a picnic away from campus loved to take the raw marinated chicken breasts and cook them outdoors. The acidic marinade helps keep the chilled chicken safe from bacteria during its transit in coolers. The boneless breasts cook very quickly over a charcoal fire.

Portions per recipe: 105		Pan: 12" × 20" × 2"	
Yield: 7 pans		Oven temperature: 325° F	
Portion: 1 breast half		Time: 30 minutes	
Serving utensil: tongs			

Ingredients — Amounts

Ingredients	Amounts
Vegetable oil	2 oz.
Sesame oil	1 oz.
Scallions, minced	4 oz.
Garlic cloves, crushed	2 oz.
Ginger root, peeled and grated	3 oz.
Soy sauce	8 oz.
Lemon juice	8 oz.
Brown sugar	4 oz.
Boneless, skinless chicken breasts, 6 ounces each	39 lb. 6 oz.
Pineapple chunks, drained, reserve juice	6 lb. 12 oz.
Green bell pepper, ½" pieces	3 lb.

Procedure:

1. Heat oils and sauté scallions, garlic, and ginger for 5 minutes.
2. Add soy sauce, lemon juice, and sugar and bring to a boil. Remove from heat and cool.
3. Brush chicken with marinade and place 15 breasts into each pan.
4. Bake at 325° F for 20 minutes.
5. Add about 1 pound of pineapple chunks with juice and 6 ounces of peppers to pan.
6. Bake for 10 more minutes.

Calories: **157**   Protein: **26.0 g (66%)**   Carbohydrates: **7.0 g (18%)**   Sodium: **199 mg**

Total Fat: **2.3 g (13%)**   *Saturated Fat:* **.6 g**   *Monounsaturated Fat:* **.5 g**   *Polyunsaturated Fat:* **.7 g**

❖ Cold Marinated Chicken

This beautiful dish is great for outdoor weddings, picnics, catered summer luncheons and dinners. It is a refreshing and elegant entrée for a self-service buffet, especially if paired with lemon pasta, roasted vegetables or new potatoes. See color plate **10**.

Portions per recipe: 48
Yield: 2 pans or platter
Portion: 1 breast half
Serving utensil: spoon

Pan: 12″ × 20″ × 4″
Cooking method: steam
Time: 12 minutes

Ingredients	Amounts	
Boneless, skinless chicken breasts	18 lb.	
Celery with tops		8 oz.
Spanish onions, quartered		8 oz.
Bay leaves (4)		
Water (hot)	2 lb.	
White vermouth		4 oz.
Olive oil		2 oz.
Red wine vinegar		2 oz.
Whole garlic cloves, cut in half		1 oz.
Salt		½ oz.
White pepper		⅛ oz.
Basil leaves, sliced into strips		2 oz.
Olive oil		1 oz.
Green bell peppers, cut into wedges	2 lb.	
Red bell peppers, cut into wedges	2 lb.	
Yellow bell peppers, cut into wedges	2 lb.	

Procedure:

1. Remove all fat from chicken, and put it into 4″ pan with celery, onions, bay leaves, water, and vermouth.
2. Steam at low pressure for 12 minutes. Test chicken to make sure it is done.
3. Let chicken cool in liquid.
4. Beat together oil, vinegar, garlic, salt, and pepper. Let steep for 30 minutes. Remove garlic cloves. Add fresh basil. Set dressing aside.
5. Heat olive oil and sauté peppers for 2 to 3 minutes (should be crisp).
6. Toss peppers with dressing.
7. Place 24 chicken breasts on platter or in pan overlapping slightly. Top with 3 pounds of marinated peppers. Chill for 30 minutes before serving.

Calories: **152**   Protein: **26.0 g (68%)**   Carbohydrates: **3.2 g (8%)**   Sodium: **191 mg**

Total Fat: **3.4 g (20%)**   *Saturated Fat:* **.6 g**   *Monounsaturated Fat:* **1.7 g**   *Polyunsaturated Fat:* **.6 g**

Pollo con melanzane fritte—grilled eggplant and boneless chicken breast topped with fresh tomato sauce and fontina.

❖ Pollo con Melanzane Fritte   *Michela's*

Chicken with grilled eggplant, a wonderful combination that is topped with a light tomato sauce and fontina cheese and garnished with barely sautéed spinach. Salt, rinse, and drain the eggplant, that way it will absorb less fat in the grilling.

PRODUCTION NOTE: Eggplant and chicken can also be brushed with oil and broiled.

Portions per recipe: 60
Yield: 4 pans
Portion: 1 breast half
Serving utensil: spatula

Pan: 12" × 20" × 2"
Oven temperature: 325° F
Time: 8 minutes

(continued)

Ingredients	Amounts
Eggplant, unpeeled and sliced ¼" thick	5 lb.

Sauce

Olive oil	2 oz.
Garlic cloves, crushed	2 oz.
Spanish onions, diced	1 lb. 8 oz.
Oregano, crushed	⅛ oz.
Canned tomatoes, diced	3 lb. 3 oz.
Salt	½ oz.
Black pepper	⅕ oz.
Boneless, skinless chicken breasts	22 lb. 8 oz.
Fontina cheese, ½-ounce slices	1 lb. 12 oz.
Olive oil	1 oz.
Spinach, washed, large stems removed	2 lb.

Procedure:

1. Put eggplant slices in perforated pans and sprinkle lightly with salt.
2. After 30 minutes rinse well, drain, and pat dry with toweling.
3. Heat griddle to 375° F, oil lightly, and cook eggplant until soft.
4. Place 15 slices in pan.
5. Heat 1 ounce oil with garlic, add onions and oregano, and sauté for 10 minutes.
6. Drain tomatoes and toss with onions. Keep warm.
7. Brown chicken breast on both sides on 375° F griddle for about 4 minutes.
8. Place cooked chicken on eggplant slice, top with 1-ounce tomato and onion mixture and one slice of fontina cheese.
9. Bake at 325° F for 8 minutes until cheese is melted.
10. Sauté spinach for about 15 seconds until just barely wilted.
11. Place spinach in 2 rows alongside chicken. Serve at once.

Calories: **207**   Protein: **30.4 g (59%)**   Carbohydrates: **4.4 g (9%)**   Sodium: **332 mg**

Total Fat: **7.1 g (30%)**   *Saturated Fat:* **3.2 g**   *Monounsaturated Fat:* **2.2 g**   *Polyunsaturated Fat:* **2.9 g**

❖ Swiss Breast of Chicken

A breast of chicken rests on a bed of spinach and is baked in a nutmeg flavored white sauce.

PRODUCTION NOTES: Rub the chicken with spices and let it sit for 30 minutes before browning it. If fresh chives are not available, use scallion tops or 3 tablespoons of freeze-dried chives.

Portions per recipe: *60*
Yield: *4 pans*
Portion: *1 breast half*
Serving utensil: *spoon*

Pan: *12″ × 20″ × 2″*
Oven temperature: *325° F*
Time: *20 minutes*

Ingredients

Ingredients	Amounts	
Butter blend (60% margarine/ 40% butter)		5 oz.
All-purpose flour		4 oz.
Low-fat milk	5 lb.	8 oz.
Fresh chives, chopped		4 oz.
Nutmeg		⅛ oz.
Swiss cheese, shredded	2 lb.	
Boneless, skinless chicken breasts (6 oz.)	22 lb.	8 oz.
Olive oil		2 oz.
Thyme, crushed		¹⁄₁₀ oz.
Cayenne pepper		¹⁄₁₆ oz.
Spinach, washed, large stems removed	8 lb.	

Procedure:

1. Melt butter, add flour, cook for 2 minutes, slowly wisk in low-fat milk to make a white sauce. Add chives, nutmeg, and Swiss cheese. Keep warm.
2. Toss chicken breasts with oil, thyme, and cayenne.
3. Brown chicken on 350° F unoiled griddle for about 4 minutes on each side or broil.
4. Steam or blanch spinach for 1 minute until barely wilted. Drain.
5. Put about 2# spinach in each pan. Place 15 browned chicken breasts on top of the spinich.
6. Pour 1 quart cheese sauce over the chicken and bake at 325° F for 20 minutes.

Calories: **232**   Protein: **31.7 g (55%)**   Carbohydrates: **5.0 g (9%)**   Sodium: **395 mg**
Total Fat: **8.7 g (34%)**   *Saturated Fat:* **2.9 g**   *Monounsaturated Fat:* **3.7 g**   *Polyunsaturated Fat:* **1.3 g**

Chicken Legs and Thighs

❖

Legs and thighs are much more economically priced than is the chicken breast. They are also very succulent and have more flavor because they contain a little more fat than the white chicken meat. The drumsticks are fun finger food, much liked by the college crowd. Boneless thighs are becoming increasingly available in large quantities. They can be substituted for boneless breast of chicken in many of the recipes above at a substantial saving.

❖ BBQ Chicken Legs—Marinated

Whole chicken legs are marinated overnight, baked in the oven, and cooked outside over charcoal; this guarantees a fully cooked barbequed chicken in a very short time, even if you are preparing for thousands. If rain interferes with your plans you can, of course, serve the dish baked without loss of appeal.

Portions per recipe: 100
Yield: 100 chicken legs
Portion: 1 leg
Serving utensil: tongs

Pan: 18″ × 26″ sheet pan
Oven temperature: 325° F
Time: 25 minutes

Ingredients	Amounts
Olive oil	4 oz.
Garlic cloves, crushed	2 oz.
Soy sauce	2 lb.
Honey	2 oz.
Catsup	12 oz.
Lemon juice	12 oz.
Cayenne pepper	1/8 oz.
Oregano, crushed	1/8 oz.
Black pepper	1/8 oz.
Whole chicken legs, trimmed of excess fat	75 lb.

Procedure:

1. Blend oil, garlic, soy sauce, honey, catsup, lemon juice, cayenne, oregano, and black pepper.
2. Pour half over chicken legs, toss, and let marinate overnight.
3. Bake legs on sheet pans at 325° for 20 minutes.
4. Transfer chicken to outdoor grills and brush with reserved marinade.
5. Grill until browned and hot through, 3 to 4 minutes on each side.

Calories: **488**   Protein: **46.0 g (38%)**   Carbohydrates: **2.0 g (2%)**   Sodium: **491 mg**
Total Fat: **31.3 g (58%)**   Saturated Fat: **8.6 g**   Monounsaturated Fat: **13.0 g**   Polyunsaturated Fat: **6.7 g**

❖ Chicken Parmesan

Baked in creamy yogurt and parmesan, this chicken is fabulous.

Portions per recipe: 100
Yield: 5 pans
Portion: 2 drumsticks
Serving utensil: spoon

Pan: 12" × 20" × 2"
Oven temperature: 350° F
Time: 40 minutes

Ingredients	Amounts
Low-fat yogurt	4 lb.
Honey	2 oz.
Hungarian paprika	½ oz.
Salt	1 oz.
Cornstarch	8 oz.
Parmesan cheese, grated	10 oz.
Chicken drumsticks	60 lb.
Parmesan cheese, grated	5 oz.

Procedure:

1. Blend yogurt with paprika, salt, cornstarch, and parmesan.
2. Toss with drumsticks and place 20 drumsticks (alternating bony end in and out) into pan.
3. Sprinkle drumsticks in each pan with 1 ounce of grated parmesan.
4. Bake at 350° F for 35 minutes. Stir the pan juices and serve some juice with each drumstick.

Calories: **324**   Protein: **37.9 g (47%)**   Carbohydrates: **4.0 g (5%)**   Sodium: **353 mg**
Total Fat: **17.4 g (48%)**   Saturated Fat: **5.4 g**   Monounsaturated Fat: **6.6 g**   Polyunsaturated Fat: **3.6 g**

❖ Djej Mechoui—Roasted Chicken Thighs   *Wolfert*

Heavenly melt-in-your-mouth chicken redolent of the spices of Morocco. See color plate **16**.

PRODUCTION NOTE: Grind cumin fresh and allow 24 hours for herbs and spices to penetrate meat.

Portions per recipe: *50*
Yield: *100 thighs*
Portion: *2 thighs*
Serving utensil: *tongs*

Pan: *18″ × 26″ sheet pan*
Oven temperature: *400° F*
Time: *20 minutes*

Ingredients	Amounts
Parsley leaves	8 oz.
Cilantro leaves	4 oz.
Scallions, white parts only	12 oz.
Garlic cloves, crushed	4 oz.
Salt	1 oz.
Hungarian paprika	½ oz.
Cayenne pepper	⅛ oz.
Cumin seed, pulverized	½ oz.
Butter blend (60% margarine/ 40% butter)	4 oz.
Vegetable oil	4 oz.
Chicken thighs with skin, 5 ounces each	31 lb. 4 oz.

Procedure:

1. Place herbs, scallions, spices, butter, and oil in food chopper or processor and turn into a paste.
2. Rub paste all over chicken thighs, cover, and refrigerate 24 hours.
3. Place thighs on sheet pans and bake at 400° F for 20 minutes.
4. Place 50 thighs in neat rows into 12″ × 20″ × 2″ pan. Keep warm until ready to serve.
5. Garnish with sprigs of cilantro.

Calories: **529**   Protein: **40.1 g (30%)**   Carbohydrates: **1.5 g (1%)**   Sodium: **188 mg**
Total Fat: **39.1 g (67%)**   *Saturated Fat:* **11.2 g**   *Monounsaturated Fat:* **15.5 g**   *Polyunsaturated Fat:* **9.2 g**

❖ Fruit and Chicken "Caribbean"

Boneless chicken thighs are cooked with vegetables, mango chutney, papaya, and bananas. This dish is a capricious fantasy, and it is quite likely that no such dish exists in the Caribbean. Serve with rice and ginataan (sweet potatoes).

PRODUCTION NOTES: The papayas and bananas should be slightly underripe. It is sometimes difficult to get boneless thighs. Use 100 thighs with bones if necessary, but the skin must be removed.

Portions per recipe: *60*
Yield: *5 pans*
Portion: *2 thighs*
Serving utensil: *spoon*

Pan: *12″ × 20″ × 2″*
Oven temperature: *325° F*
Time: *50 minutes*

Ingredients

Ingredients	Amounts
Vegetable oil	2 oz.
Allspice	⅛ oz.
Mango chutney	1 lb.
Salt	½ oz.
Boneless, skinless chicken thighs (4 oz.)	30 lb.
Spanish onions, quartered	4 lb.
Green bell peppers, cut into wedges	4 lb.
Red bell peppers, cut into wedges	2 lb.
Hot chilies, with seeds, chopped	2 oz.
Pineapple juice	2 lb. 14 oz.
Lime juice	4 oz.
Bananas, ½″ slices	6 lb.
Papaya, peeled, seeds removed, and thinly sliced	4 lb.

Procedure:

1. Blend oil with allspice, chutney, and salt. Toss chicken thighs in the mixture and let stand for 30 minutes.

2. Place 24 thighs in lightly oiled pan. Bake at 325° for 20 minutes.

3. Toss vegetables together and add 2 pounds to each pan. Mix pineapple and lime juice and add 10 ounces of juice to each pan.

4. Bake for 15 minutes. Fold in bananas and papaya slices and cook for 15 more minutes.

Calories: **232**   Protein: **30.1 g (52%)**   Carbohydrates: **18.0 g (31%)**   Sodium: **317 mg**
Total Fat: **3.5 g (14%)**   *Saturated Fat:* **.9 g**   *Monounsaturated Fat:* **.7 g**   *Polyunsaturated Fat:* **1.1 g**

Fruit and chicken "Caribbean" with papayas and bananas is sweet and spicy.

❖ Jambalaya

A Creole classic, this dish tastes better when reheated. For best results it should be cooked in two stages. This also makes it easier to remove excess fat from the dish.

PRODUCTION NOTES: Bake the chicken with the sauce a day ahead of time. Refrigerate. The next day fold in shrimp and bake until shrimp is cooked. Shrimp pieces are much lower priced than whole peeled shrimp and they are perfectly fine for this dish.

Portions per recipe: 96
Yield: 4 pans
Portion: 1 thigh and 6 ounces sauce
Serving utensil: 4-ounce ladle

Pan: 12″ × 20″ × 2″
Oven temperature: 350° F
Time: 35 minutes first baking/25 minutes
    second baking

Ingredients	Amounts		
Chorice or hot Italian sausage	*5 lb.*		
Olive oil		*1 oz.*	
Garlic cloves, crushed		*2 oz.*	
Spanish onions, sliced	*2 lb.*		
Celery, ½" pieces	*4 lb.*		
Green bell peppers, sliced thick	*6 lb.*		
Canned Italian tomatoes	*19 lb.*	*2 oz.*	
Cayenne pepper		*⅛ oz.*	
White vermouth		*8 oz.*	
Skinless chicken thighs, 5 ounces each	*31 lb.*	*4 oz.*	
Frozen shrimp pieces	*10 lb.*		
Parsley, minced		*4 oz.*	

Procedure:

1. Simmer sausage for 15 minutes, drain, and chill.

2. Heat olive oil with garlic, add onions, celery, and peppers. Sauté for 10 minutes.

3. Add tomatoes, cayenne, and vermouth and simmer for 30 minutes.

4. Cut cold sausage into ¼-inch pieces.

5. Place 24 chicken thighs in pan and add about 1 pound of sausage slices.

6. Brown in 350° F oven for 15 minutes. Add 3 quarts of tomato mixture.

7. Bake for 20 minutes. Refrigerate.

8. Remove hard fat from surface.

9. Add 2½ pounds of shrimp to each pan, stir in, and bake at 300° F for 20 minutes. Sprinkle each pan with fresh parsley.

Calories: **274*** Protein: **32.3 g (47%)** Carbohydrates: **7.2 g (11%)** Sodium: **977 mg**
Total Fat: **12.3 g (40%)** *Saturated Fat:* **4.0 g** *Monounsaturated Fat:* **5.1 g** *Polyunsaturated Fat:* **2.1 g**

---

*No fat reduction has been made in the calculations for the possible fat removal in step 8.

❖ Pollo alla Cacciatora *Romagnoli*

This is the Romagnolis' delicious version of hunter's chicken.

PRODUCTION NOTE: If you need to substitute dry rosemary, crush or chop it and soak it overnight in the olive oil to soften it.

Portions per recipe: 100
Yield: 4 pans
Portion: 1 thigh and 1 drumstick
Serving utensil: spoon

Pan: 12″ × 20″ × 2″
Oven temperature: 325° F
Time: 40 minutes

Ingredients	Amounts
Olive oil	4 oz.
Garlic cloves, crushed	4 oz.
Fresh rosemary, minced	2 oz.
Salt	½ oz.
Chicken thighs with skin, 5 ounces each	31 lb. 4 oz.
Chicken drumsticks, 4 ounces each	25 lb.
Red wine vinegar	1 lb. 8 oz.
Dry Italian white wine	2 lb. 8 oz.
Rosemary, minced	½ oz.

Procedure:

1. Blend together olive oil, garlic, rosemary, and salt.
2. Rub chicken with mixture and place 25 pieces in each pan.
3. Bake chicken at 325° F for 20 minutes until nicely browned.
4. Pour off fat and combine chicken pieces from two pans into one.
5. Mix vinegar and wine and pour 1 pint over chicken in each pan.
6. Bake for 20 minutes. Garnish with chopped rosemary.

Calories: **372*** Protein: **34.7 g (37%)** Carbohydrates: **.7 g (1%)** Sodium: **275 mg**
Total Fat: **27.3 g (66%)** *Saturated Fat:* **7.0 g** *Monounsaturated Fat:* **17.3 g** *Polyunsaturated Fat:* **.5 g**

*In the caloric calculations, no fat reduction (see step 4) was made. If ⅓ of the fat per portion has been discarded, the fat percentage per portion would be 44% (18.2 g).

❖ Poulet aux Quarante Gousses d'Ail (Provence)— Chicken with 40 Cloves of Garlic *Kamman*

This dish uses 40 whole garlic cloves for every 10 pounds of chicken. Plan on spending a lot of time peeling garlic cloves if Ms. Kamman is looking over your shoulder. We have cheated with success and used the commercial whole garlic packed in oil—not a bad substitute for a labor intensive task. Chicken thighs, drumsticks, or whole legs are best. The chicken coated with a persillade to which fresh rosemary and thyme have been added makes this dish a feast to remember.

Portions per recipe: 100
Yield: 200 thighs
Portion: 2 thighs
Serving utensil: spoon

Pan: 18″ × 26″ sheet pan
Oven temperature: 350° F
Time: 30 minutes

Ingredients

Ingredients	Amounts
Olive oil	1 oz.
Italian parsley	4 oz.
Garlic cloves, crushed	4 oz.
Fresh rosemary	1 oz.
Thyme, crushed	1/8 oz.
Black pepper	1/4 oz.
Chicken thighs with skin, 5 to 6 ounces each	68 lb.
Whole garlic cloves, peeled	2 lb.
Water (boiling)	1 lb.

Procedure:

1. Brush sheet pans with olive oil.

2. Mince parsley, garlic, rosemary, thyme, and pepper in food chopper or processor.

3. Coat chicken thighs with herbs and place on sheet pans. Add garlic cloves.

4. Bake at 350° for 30 minutes. Transfer 50 thighs to 12″ × 20″ × 2″ pans.

5. Pour off excess fat from sheet pans, add ½ cup boiling water, and scrape pans. Pour liquid through a sieve and collect juices.

6. Pour about 1 pint of the juices over chicken and bake for 15 minutes more.

7. Garnish with chopped parsley. Serve garlic cloves with each thigh.

Calories: **529**   Protein: **42.6 g (32%)**   Carbohydrates: **2.7 g (2%)**   Sodium: **189 mg**
Total Fat: **37.5 g (63%)**   *Saturated Fat:* **10.6 g**   *Monounsaturated Fat:* **15.5 g**   *Polyunsaturated Fat:* **8.1 g**

❖ Tandoori Murgh

In India these chicken legs are cooked in the very hot tandoori oven, baked in a regular oven they are still excellent.

Portions per recipe: 100
Yield: 200 drumsticks
Portion: 2 drumsticks
Serving utensil: spoon

Pan: 12" × 20" × 2"
Oven temperature: 350° F
Time: 40 minutes

Ingredients	Amounts
Low-fat yogurt	4 lb.
Garlic cloves, crushed	4 oz.
Cumin	1 oz.
Ginger	1/2 oz.
Chili powder	2 oz.
Cayenne pepper	1/8 oz.
Salt	2 oz.
Lemon juice	2 oz.
Chicken drumsticks, 4 to 5 ounces each	55 lb.

Procedure:

1. Blend yogurt with spices, salt, and lemon juice.
2. Pour over drumsticks, toss to coat, and let marinate overnight.
3. Place on sheet pans and bake at 350° F for 40 minutes, or place under broiler and broil 10 minutes on each side.
4. Place 50 drumsticks in a pan and garnish with parsley sprigs.

Calories: **284**   Protein: **33.4 g (47%)**   Carbohydrates: **2.0 g (2%)**   Sodium: **167 mg**
Total Fat: **17.1 g (54%)**   *Saturated Fat:* **4.2 g**   *Monounsaturated Fat:* **5.7 g**   *Polyunsaturated Fat:* **3.3 g**

Chicken Pieces (Boneless)

In these recipes frozen chicken pieces are used. They are usually sold as stir-fry chicken. Since the weight of the chicken decreases after it thaws, the amount of chicken called for in the recipes has been adjusted upwards. If fresh chicken is used, the amounts can be reduced by 12 to 15 percent.

❖ Chicken Broccoli Stir-fry

This is a very colorful and light stir-fry with a touch of tarragon.

PRODUCTION NOTES: Use a hot grill to stir-fry batches of no more than 6 pounds of chicken and 7 pounds of vegetables. Julienned carrots are available frozen, they are sometimes called "shoestring" carrots.

Portions per recipe: *50*
Yield: *2 pans*
Portion: *7 ounces*
Serving utensil: *4-ounce ladle (2 dips)*

Pan: *12" × 20" × 2"*
Oven temperature: *400° F*
Time: *10 minutes*

Ingredients

Ingredients	Amounts
Chicken pieces, (³⁄₄" × ³⁄₄" × ¹⁄₄"), thawed	13 lb. 12 oz.
Garlic cloves, crushed	1 oz.
Black pepper	¹⁄₈ oz.
Tarragon, crushed	¹⁄₁₆ oz.
Cornstarch	2 oz.
Soy sauce	3 oz.
Peanut oil	4 oz.
Spanish onions, sliced	1 lb.
Broccoli florets and stems peeled and sliced	8 lb.
Mushrooms, thinly sliced	3 lb.
Frozen carrots, julienne or shoestring	3 lb.
Lemon juice	2 oz.

Procedure:

1. Toss chicken pieces with garlic, pepper, tarragon, cornstarch, and soy sauce to coat pieces well.

2. Pour 2 ounces of peanut oil on a hot grill. Stir-fry chicken with onions for 5 minutes.

3. Add broccoli and mushrooms and stir-fry for 3 minutes.

4. Add thawed carrots and stir-fry for 2 minutes.

5. Toss with 1 ounce lemon juice and scoop with two large spatulas into serving pan.

Calories: **136**   Protein: **18.4 g (54%)**   Carbohydrates: **8.0 g (23%)**   Sodium: **173 mg**
Total Fat: **3.8 g (25%)**   *Saturated Fat:* **1.3 g**   *Monounsaturated Fat:* **1.3 g**   *Polyunsaturated Fat:* **1.1 g**

Chicken curry with potatoes becomes an Indian special event when served with curried cucumbers and dal.

❖ Chicken Curry with Potatoes

An Indian potato curry strongly flavored with Madras curry powder.

PRODUCTION NOTES: The best piece of equipment to use is the tilting skillet, but a griddle will do. This dish can be kept warm without loss of flavor or texture, just add a little fresh cilantro before service.

Portions per recipe: 50
Yield: 2 pans
Portion: 7 ounces
Serving utensil: spoon

Pan: 12″ × 20″ × 2″
Skillet temperature: 350° F
Time: 10 minutes

Ingredients	Amounts
Potatoes, ½″ cubes	10 lb.
Chicken pieces (¾″ × ¾″ × ¼″), thawed	13 lb. 12 oz.
Madras blend curry powder	¾ oz.
Salt	1 oz.
Peanut oil	4 oz.
Spanish onions, thinly sliced	6 lb.
Cilantro, chopped	4 oz.

Procedure:

1. Cook or steam potatoes until barely tender; they need to hold their shape. Drain and keep hot.
2. Toss chicken pieces with curry powder and salt.
3. Heat peanut oil and stir-fry chicken with onions for 5 minutes.
4. Add potato cubes and stir-fry 5 minutes longer.
5. Toss with cilantro and put in serving pan.

Calories: **141** Protein: **17.5 g (50%)** Carbohydrates: **13.1 g (37%)** Sodium: **275 mg**

Total Fat: **1.9 g (12%)** *Saturated Fat:* **.4 g** *Monounsaturated Fat:* **.7 g** *Polyunsaturated Fat:* **.3 g**

❖ Chicken Geschnetzeltes—Swiss

In Switzerland this dish is made with milkfed veal. It is just as delicious made with chicken pieces, and it takes only about 8 minutes to prepare. This is excellent with spaetzle, pasta, rice, or oven browned new potatoes.

Portions per recipe: 80
Yield: 2 pans
Portion: 6 ounces
Serving utensil: 4-ounce ladle

Pan: 12" × 20" × 2"
Skillet temperature: 350° F
Time: 8 minutes

Ingredients	Amounts
Safflower oil	2 oz.
Spanish onions, thinly sliced	2 lb.
Chicken pieces (¾" × ¾" × ¼"), thawed	22 lb.
All-purpose flour	2 oz.
Sage	⅛ oz.
White pepper	⅛ oz.
Salt	½ oz.
Mushrooms, thinly sliced	6 lb.
White vermouth	4 oz.
Water	2 lb.
Fresh thyme, chopped	1 oz.
Light cream	2 lb.
Parsley leaves, minced	2 oz.

Procedure:

1. Heat oil and sauté onions with chicken pieces until golden.
2. Mix flour with sage, pepper, and salt. Dust over chicken.

(continued)

3. Stir in mushrooms and sauté for 2 minutes.

4. Add vermouth and water and bring to a simmer.

5. Add fresh thyme and light cream. Simmer another minute.

6. Put in serving pan and sprinkle with minced parsley.

Calories: **128**   Protein: **17.4 g (54%)**   Carbohydrates: **4.7 g (15%)**   Sodium: **60 mg**

Total Fat: **4.2 g (30%)**   *Saturated Fat:* **1.8 g**   *Monounsaturated Fat:* **1.0 g**   *Polyunsaturated Fat:* **1.0 g**

Rock Cornish Game Hens

❖

A cross between rock cornish and white rock birds, rock cornish game hens are a small breed weighing between 12 and 14 ounces when eviscerated. Heavy breasted, very tender and juicy, they can be roasted, stuffed, and split for broiling.

The fresh birds which are available already split are far preferable to the frozen whole ones. A 3-ounce serving of roasted light meat without skin provides 123 calories, 15 grams of protein (49%), and 6.9 grams of fat (50%).

❖ Rock Cornish Game Hens Broiled with Chinese Marinade

Split rock cornish hens are dipped in marinade and broiled. Serve them with steamed rice and stir-fried vegetables or with creamed spinach and oven-browned red potatoes.

PRODUCTION NOTE: Order the hens already split, or cut them in half with poultry shears.

Portions per recipe: 100	*Pan: 12" × 20" × 2"*
Yield: 100 halves	*Cooking method: broil*
Portion: 1 split hen	*Time: 12–15 minutes*
Serving utensil: tongs	

Ingredients	Amounts
Rock cornish hens, split	*43 lb. 12 oz.*
Chinese marinade (pages 458–459)	*4 lb.*

Procedure:

1. Heat broilers. Dip split hens in marinade and place on broiler pans.
2. Broil for 6 to 7 minutes on each side. Place neatly in pans and garnish with scallions.

Calories: **466**   Protein: **29.1 g (25%)**   Carbohydrates: **2.5 g (3%)**   Sodium: **280 mg**

Total Fat: **36.7 g (71%)**   *Saturated Fat:* **12.9 g**   *Monounsaturated Fat:* **14.9 g**   *Polyunsaturated Fat:* **4.8 g**

❖ Rock Cornish Game Hens L'Orange

These game hens are split and basted with a ginger-flavored orange glaze in a very hot oven.

Portions per recipe: 100
Yield: 100 split hens
Portion: 1 split hen
Serving utensil: spatula

Pan: 12″ × 20″ × 2″
Oven temperature: 400° F
Time: 25 to 30 minutes

Ingredients

Ingredients	Amounts	
Rock cornish hens, split	43 lb.	12 oz.
Lemon juice		12 oz.
Salt		1 oz.
Apple jelly	2 lb.	
Orange juice concentrate	1 lb.	
Water	1 lb.	
Ginger root, grated		3 oz.
White pepper		¼ oz.
Cardamom		⅛ oz.
Unpeeled oranges, thinly sliced	4 lb.	

Procedure:

1. Rinse birds, rub with lemon juice, and sprinkle lightly with salt.
2. Place 12 per pan and brown in oven for 10 minutes.
3. Melt apple jelly and add orange juice, water, and spices. Simmer for 10 minutes.
4. Pour glaze over hens, top each hen with a slice of orange, and bake for 15 to 20 minutes.

Calories: **482**   Protein: **28.4 g (24%)**   Carbohydrates: **8.5 g (7%)**   Sodium: **112 mg**

Total Fat: **36.4 g (68%)**   *Saturated Fat:* **13.0 g**   *Monounsaturated Fat:* **14.9 g**   *Polyunsaturated Fat:* **4.7 g**

Duck

The duck marketed in America as Long Island duckling is actually the domesticated Peking duck. While most people think of duck as being very fatty, duck meat itself is not at all fatty; the layer of fat is located under the skin and will baste the meat as it roasts. Low temperature roasting will draw out more fat and keep the meat moist.

During the "Feast Fit for the Last Emperor of China" Ken Hom taught the UNH staff to prepare Peking duck. This crisp and succulent duck is dipped in boiling water to which honey has been added, air-dried for several hours and then baked hanging from hooks (we rigged up a coathanger contraption which worked fine) at 450° F for between 45 minutes and one hour. We managed to hang six ducks in each convection oven. To read more about the feast see pages 23 to 25 and to read about more elaborate preparation of Peking duck (we did not, for example, inflate it), read Ken Hom's book *Chinese Technique*.

❖ Confit of Duck Legs   *Kamman*

The duck legs are flavored with a very fragrant mixture of spices and baked very slowly in a fat bath which has also been flavored with the same spices. The legs stay very moist and lose a lot of fat. The skin is dark brown and absolutely delicious.

In Gascony confit was used to preserve ducks in an age when refrigeration and freezing were unknown. Ms. Kamman describes the method used to make confit and its origin in her book *In Madeleine's Kitchen*.

Legs covered with fat and then refrigerated keep for weeks. At UNH confit of duck became a wonderful catering item. We used it in picnic hampers and for VIP luncheons. A special French winter event could feature a cassoulet with duck confit added as a special treat.

This dish could be daunting if ducks had to be cut and fat had to be rendered. Luckily, duck legs and already rendered duck fat are available from several vendors in any quantity.

PRODUCTION NOTES: Rub spices over legs and let them penetrate for 24 hours. Peel garlic cloves one day ahead of time. On the day the dish will be served heat the duck fat with the spices and pour it through a china cap lined with a rinsed cheese cloth. IMPORTANT: Blot any moisture from pans before covering them with hot fat. One gallon of duckfat will be enough to get the first 100 portions baked; more fat will bake out of the legs. Bake in batches of 25 legs per pan. Pour fat through cheese cloth after all the legs are baked. Cool the fat and freeze it for later use. If you plan to make confit only once, don't throw the fat away. Instead use a little duck fat when braising red cabbage or preparing German fried potatoes. It's high in cholesterol but has a remarkable flavor.

Portions per recipe: 200
Yield: 200 legs
Portion: 1 leg
Serving utensil: tongs

Pan: 12" × 20" × 2"
Oven temperature: 300° F
Time: 50 minutes

Ingredients

Ingredients	Amounts	
Cinnamon		½ oz.
Allspice		½ oz.
Nutmeg		¼ oz.
Cloves		¼ oz.
Cardamon		½ oz.
Ginger		½ oz.
Cumin		¼ oz.
Black pepper		¼ oz.
Dry thyme, crushed		¼ oz.
Bay leaves, crumbled		¹⁄₁₆ oz.
Salt		3 oz.
Duck legs, (8–10 oz. each)	100 lb.	
Whole garlic cloves	2 lb.	8 oz.
Duck fat	16 lb.	

Procedure:

1. Mix spices and salt. Coat duck legs well.
2. Place 20 legs in each pan and add 40 garlic cloves. Refrigerate for 24 hours.
3. The next day blot any liquid from pans with kitchen toweling.
4. Heat duck fat and pour ½ gallon over legs. Bake at 300° F until garlic is golden and a thermometer inserted away from bone reads 160° F.
5. Drain fat and pour over next batch until all legs are baked.

Calories: **321*** Protein: **19.1 g (24%)** Carbohydrates: **1.9 g (2%)** Sodium: **269 mg**
Total Fat: **25.7 g (72%)** *Saturated Fat:* **8.6 g** *Monounsaturated Fat:* **12.2 g** *Polyunsaturated Fat:* **3.3 g**

---

*Calculation based on approximate 60% fat loss in baking process.

❖ Magret de Canard aux Noix   *Kamman*

A very juicy and flavorful grilled breast of duck—its dark gamey meat perfectly complements the brandy and walnut sauce.

PRODUCTION NOTE: The small filet strips that are attached with a tough tendon to the breast are removed and reserved for the duck stock that is used in the walnut cream sauce. Take care to grill the breast only to medium rare, it should still be slightly pink inside. For large quantities it is best to cook 50 breast filets to get sauté juices for the sauce. Prepare the sauce for the entire quantity to be served but grill or broil the rest of the breasts as needed. Barely coat the breasts with sauce.

Portions per recipe: 200
Yield: 8 pans
Portion: 1 breast half
Serving utensil: spoon

Pan: 12″ × 20″ × 2″
Tilting skillet temperature: 350° F
Time: 5–6 minutes

Ingredients

Ingredients	Amounts	
Boneless duck breasts (5 oz.)	62 lb.	8 oz.
Spanish onions, quartered		8 oz.
Celery stalks and tops		8 oz.
Unpeeled carrots, cut into pieces		4 oz.
Water	8 lb.	
White vermouth		4 oz.
Walnut pieces	1 lb.	8 oz.
Olive oil		1 oz.
Brandy		8 oz.
Heavy cream	3 lb.	
Salt		1 oz.
Garlic cloves, crushed		½ oz.
Parsley, minced		3 oz.

Procedure:

1. Remove skin and strip the small filet with tendon from breasts (reserve skins to render duckfat for confit). Remove all fat.

2. Chop breast strips with the bits of fat and sauté with onions, celery, and carrots. Add water and simmer for 2 hours until reduced by a third. Drain.

3. Sauté the walnut pieces in olive oil for 2 to 3 minutes. Reserve.

4. In the same tilting skillet, sauté 50 duck breast halves for 3 minutes on each side. Cook the rest as needed on a 350° F griddle brushed with olive oil.

5. Remove 25 breasts to each pan and keep warm.

6. Deglaze the skillet with duck stock and brandy. Simmer 10 minutes. Stir in cream, salt, pepper, garlic, parsley, and reserved walnuts.

7. Taste and correct seasoning if necessary. Pour 1 cup of sauce over each pan.

Calories: **282**   Protein: **29.8 g (42%)**   Carbohydrates: **.5 g (1%)**   Sodium: **68 mg**
Total Fat: **17.1 g (55%)**   *Saturated Fat:* **6.9 g**   *Monounsaturated Fat:* **8.6 g**   *Polyunsaturated Fat:* **2.2 g**

Turkey

❖

In large quantity food operations the pre-cooked boneless breast of turkey is most useful and profitable. Portions can be well controlled and there are no dry legs and carcasses to deal with. The disadvantage of the pre-cooked turkey is that usually it is high in sodium and has no roasting flavor. Smaller operations that want to roast their own turkeys should remove the breasts and roast them separately. Roast or braise the drumsticks and thighs and use the wings and backs for stock production.

To cut your own paillards, remove the breast from the bone and slice thin against the grain. Ground fresh turkey is now readily available from most poultry purveyors.

❖ Turkey Chili con Carne

Chili made with turkey instead of beef is much lower in fat and just as tasty. Chili is excellent with a sandwich for lunch or served over rice for dinner. Complete the meal with warm flour tortillas and a crisp green salad.

Portions per recipe: 100
Yield: 5 gallons
Portion: 8.5 ounces
Serving utensil: 6-ounce ladle

Pan: 12″ × 20″ × 6″–½ size
Tilting skillet temperature: 350° F
Time: 60 minutes

Ingredients	Amounts	
Olive oil		2 oz.
Spanish onions, sliced	2 lb.	
Turkey, ground	12 lb.	8 oz.
Garlic cloves, crushed		4 oz.
Chili powder		4 oz.
Cumin		¼ oz.
Cinnnamon		1/16 oz.
Black pepper		¼ oz.
Salt		1 oz.
Green bell peppers, diced	4 lb.	
Jalapeno peppers, diced		4 oz.
Canned kidney beans	13 lb.	5 oz.
Canned tomatoes, diced	6 lb.	4 oz.
Canned tomato puree	13 lb.	
Canned green chili, diced	2 lb.	8 oz.

Procedure:

1. Heat olive oil and sauté onions until golden.
2. Add turkey, garlic, and spices and brown well.
3. Add salt and rest of ingredients and simmer for 1 hour.

(continued)

Variation: Cook 6 pounds of dried beans instead of using canned kidney beans. Do not limit yourself to one bean. My favorite combination is pinto beans, baby lima beans, and yellow split peas.

Calories: **134**   Protein: **14.9 g (44%)**   Carbohydrates: **16.3 g (48%)**   Sodium: **57 mg**

Total Fat: **2.3 g (15%)**   *Saturated Fat:* **.5 g**   *Monounsaturated Fat:* **.7 g**   *Polyunsaturated Fat:* **.6 g**

❖ Turkey Divan

An attractive dish for a light brunch, lunch, or dinner.

PRODUCTION NOTE: Fresh stalks of broccoli are tastier but thawed frozen spears are acceptable.

Portions per recipe: 80
Yield: 5 pans
Portion: 1 folded slice
Serving utensil: spatula

Pan: 12″ × 20″ × 2″
Oven temperature: 300° F
Time: 18–20 minutes

Ingredients	Amounts	
Pre-cooked boneless turkey breast	12 lb.	8 oz.
Broccoli spears, blanched	10 lb.	
Safflower oil		4 oz.
All-purpose flour		6 oz.
White pepper		⅛ oz.
Non-fat dry milk	1 lb.	
Water (hot)	7 lb.	8 oz.
Cheddar cheese, grated	3 lb.	
Nutmeg		⅛ oz.

Procedure:

1. Slice turkey breast into 2½-ounce slices.
2. Fold turkey slice over 2 broccoli stalks and place 16 slices per pan.
3. Heat oil and flour with pepper.
4. Reconstitute milk powder with water. Add to roux and stir until thickened, then add cheese and nutmeg.
5. Pour 3 cups of cheese sauce over turkey. Bake at 300° F for 18 minutes.

Calories: **219**   Protein: **21.5 g (39%)**   Carbohydrates: **5.3 g (10%)**   Sodium: **783 mg**

Total Fat: **11.7 g (48%)**   *Saturated Fat:* **5.0 g**   *Monounsaturated Fat:* **3.5 g**   *Polyunsaturated Fat:* **2.3 g**

❖ **Turkey Paillards**

Raw turkey breast is thinly sliced, pounded lightly, covered with a herb and spice paste, and baked in a spicy sweet and sour sauce.

PRODUCTION NOTES: Place turkey slices between two sheets of parchment paper and pound lightly with a mallet. The paillards can also be broiled or sautéed and served without the sauce.

Portions per recipe: 100	*Pan: 12″ × 20″ × 2″*
Yield: 5 pans/200 slices	*Oven temperature: 350° F*
Portion: 2 slices	*Time: 10 minutes*
Serving utensil: spatula	

Ingredients   Amounts

Ingredients	Amounts	
Cilantro leaves		8 oz.
Italian parsley		12 oz.
Olive oil		4 oz.
Salt		2 oz.
Dijon mustard		4 oz.
Cumin		1/4 oz.
Turmeric		1/4 oz.
White pepper		1/8 oz.
Raw turkey breast slices, 2 ounces each	25 lb.	
Garlic cloves, crushed		2 oz.
Hot red chilies, minced		2 oz.
Cider vinegar	2 lb.	
Brown sugar		8 oz.
White vermouth		8 oz.
Mushrooms, thinly sliced	2 lb.	

Procedure:

1. Mince cilantro with parsley very finely in a food chopper or processor. Add olive oil, salt, mustard, and spices and blend into a paste.

2. Coat pounded turkey slices with spice paste and place 40 slices into pan, overlapping them slightly.

3. Heat together garlic, chilies, vinegar, brown sugar, and vermouth until sugar has dissolved.

4. Scatter mushrooms slices over paillards, pour in 1 cup boiling sauce, and bake at 350° F for 8 to 10 minutes. Time accurately or turkey will be dry.

Calories: **125**   Protein: **22.9 g (73%)**   Carbohydrates: **4.0 g (13%)**   Sodium: **290 mg**

Total Fat: **1.9 g (13%)**   *Saturated Fat:* **.4 g**   *Monounsaturated Fat:* **.9 g**   *Polyunsaturated Fat:* **.3 g**

Fish

❖

Fish consumption in the United States has steadily increased in recent years, and the oceans unfortunately have been over-fished for certain species such as haddock. This unsound practice has meant very high fish prices and does not bode well for a healthy fish population. Food services should actively support ecologically sound fishing regulations and work with their customers to increase acceptance of unfamiliar fish species that are still available at lower cost.

Some formerly under-utilized species have, however, become fad foods for nouvelle cuisine restaurants. As a result formerly cheap monkfish and mahi mahi are now fetching higher prices. Pollock or hake can be substituted for haddock or cod if the price is right. Tilefish steaks or fillets are relatively cheap all the way down the Atlantic coast. Rockfish like tilefish is reasonably priced year round on the west coast. Both these fish can be used when firm white fish steaks or fillets are called for in the recipes that follow. Fish suppliers are very helpful and they will find the quantity and species you need.

Fresh fish is available everywhere thanks to excellent interstate transportation. Fresh fish is much superior to frozen so use the fresh fish in most recipes. Farm raised catfish and rainbow trout are plentiful and reasonably priced. Even farmed salmon production, especially in Norway, has increased so much in recent years that salmon prices have dropped substantially and become affordable to institutions.

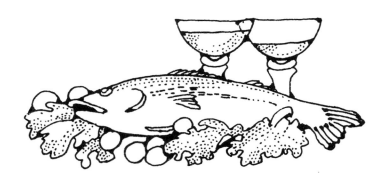

❖ Baked Fresh Pollock "Persillade"

Pollock or other white firm fish fillets are brushed with melted lemon margarine and covered with a parsley and garlic mixture.

PRODUCTION NOTE: Fish should go directly from the oven to the serving line. Do not keep it in warmers. Bake as needed to keep fish as moist as possible.

Portions per recipe: *100*
Yield: *5 pans*
Portion: *6 ounces*
Serving utensil: *spatula*

Pan: *12″ × 20″ × 2″*
Oven temperature: *325° F*
Time: *15 minutes*

Ingredients	Amounts
Margarine	8 oz.
Lemon juice	12 oz.
White pepper	⅛ oz.
Salt	½ oz.
Pollock fillets (6 oz.)	37 lb. 8 oz.
Parsley leaves	8 oz.
Garlic cloves	4 oz.
Lemon slices	2 lb.

Procedure:

1. Melt margarine with lemon juice, pepper, and salt.
2. Brush pan with lemon margarine and place 20 fish fillets in pan.
3. Brush fillets generously on top.
4. Mince parsley with garlic in food chopper or processor.
5. Sprinkle over fish fillets.
6. Cover with foil and bake at 325° F for 15 minutes, or until fish flakes.
7. Slice lemon thinly and garnish each fillet with a slice.

Calories: **175**   Protein: **33.2 g (75%)**   Carbohydrates: **.7 g (2%)**   Sodium: **224 mg**
Total Fat: **3.5 g (18%)**   *Saturated Fat:* **.4 g**   *Monounsaturated Fat:* **1.0 g**   *Polyunsaturated Fat:* **1.4 g**

❖ Beacon Hill Bluefish

This Atlantic coast fish is available all year and abundant from April to September. It is very oily and good to grill indoors and outdoors; marinate the steaks or fillets first. This recipe is an elegant baked concoction with scallops and crab meat.

PRODUCTION NOTES: Bluefish have a dark oily layer of tissue under their skin. Trim this layer from fillets, as it has a rather strong fishy taste. Marinate the fish overnight and broil bluefish after it has been topped with seafood. This dish can also be baked uncovered at 350° F for 18 minutes.

Portions per recipe: *96*
Yield: *6 pans*
Portion: *5-ounce fillet*
Serving utensil: *spatula*

Pan: *12" × 20" × 2"*
Cooking method: *broil*
Time: *7–8 minutes*

Ingredients	Amounts
Butter blend (60% margarine/ 40% butter)	4 oz.
Spanish onions, diced	1 lb.
Celery tops, finely chopped	1 lb.
Mushrooms, sliced	6 lb.
White vermouth	1 lb.
Lemon juice	8 oz.
Salt	½ oz.
White pepper	⅛ oz.
Dry thyme, crushed	1/16 oz.
Bluefish, dark oily layer removed (5 ounces each)	30 lb.
Scallops	6 lb.
Butter blend, melted	8 oz.
Crab meat, picked over and free of cartilage	2 lb.
Bread crumbs	1 lb.
Parsley, minced	4 oz.

Procedure:

1. Heat butter blend and sauté onions, celery tops, and mushrooms until golden.
2. Add vermouth, lemon juice, salt, pepper, and thyme. Simmer for 10 minutes. Cool slightly.
3. Place 16 fillets in oiled pan. Pour 3 cups vegetable marinade over fillets.
4. Refrigerate overnight.
5. Heat broilers.
6. Add 1 pound scallops to each pan.
7. Mix butter blend with crab meat, bread crumbs and parsley.

8. Top each fillet with crab mixture using a #30 scoop and spread lightly.

9. Broil 5 inches from broiler unit for 7 to 8 minutes. Test fish to see if it is done. Fish should flake easily, do not overcook.

Calories: **262**   Protein: **36.2 g (55%)**   Carbohydrates: **6.1 g (9%)**   Sodium: **276 mg**

Total Fat: **9.5 g (32%)**   *Saturated Fat:* **2.5 g**   *Monounsaturated Fat:* **3.8 g**   *Polyunsaturated Fat:* **2.3 g**

❖ Broiled or Grilled Mahi Mahi

Mahi mahi is the Hawaiian name for dolphin. Mahi mahi is not related to the mammalian dolphin. The fish has a meaty texture. If no mahi mahi is available, shark, swordfish, and fresh tuna can be substituted.

PRODUCTION NOTES: Barbecue steaks for 4 minutes on each side, cook on a 350° F oiled griddle for 5 minutes on each side, or place under a broiler 3 inches from flame for 6 to 8 minutes.

Portions per recipe: 100　　　　　　　*Pan: 12″ × 20″ × 2″*
Yield: 100 steaks　　　　　　　　　*Griddle temperature: 350° F*
Portion: 7-ounce steak　　　　　　*Time: 10 minutes*
Serving utensil: spatula

Ingredients

Ingredients	Amounts
Lime peel, grated	1 oz.
Lime juice	8 oz.
Scallions	8 oz.
Tomatoes, seeded	1 lb.
Worcestershire sauce	4 oz.
Tabasco sauce	1/6 oz.
Mace	1/8 oz.
Peanut oil	8 oz.
Mahi mahi steaks with skin, 3/4″ thick, 7 ounces each	43 lb. 12 oz.
Limes, cut into wedges	2 lb.

Procedure:

1. Puree first eight ingredients in a blender or work to a sauce in a food chopper or processor.

2. Pour a thin layer of marinade into a shallow pan.

3. Dip mahi mahi into marinade and place on oiled griddle. Cook for 5 minutes.

(continued)

4. Brush top side with more marinade, turn over, and grill for 5 more minutes.

5. Place neatly into pan and garnish with lime wedges to serve.

Calories: **193**   Protein: **37.8 g (78%)**   Carbohydrates: **.5 g (1%)**   Sodium: **193 mg**

Total Fat: **3.7 g (17%)**   *Saturated Fat:* **.8 g**   *Monounsaturated Fat:* **1.3 g**   *Polyunsaturated Fat:* **1.1 g**

❖ Cajun Baked Catfish

Blackened catfish has spawned blackened everything on the culinary scene. Cajun spiced food is popular with the college crowd. Here is a baked catfish that has the flavor but needs no frying.

PRODUCTION NOTE: Commercially available Cajun spice mixes are basically a high-priced salt. Make your own mixture and save money and reduce the salt content. Follow the Cajun spice mixture recipe in the condiment section.

Portions per recipe: 96   *Pan:* 12" × 20" × 2"
Yield: 6 pans   *Temperature:* 350° F
Portion: 5 ounces   *Time:* 12 minutes
Serving utensil: spatula

Ingredients	Amounts
Catfish fillets, 5 ounces each	30 lb.
Margarine	8 oz.
Lemon juice	12 oz.
Cajun spice mixture (see page 458)	3 oz.
Lemon slices	2 lb.

Procedure:

1. Place 16 fillets into oiled pan.

2. Melt margarine with lemon juice and brush fillets generously.

3. Sprinkle each pan with ½ ounce of cajun spice.

4. Bake at 350° F uncovered for 12 minutes. Test for doneness, fish should flake easily.

5. Garnish each fillet with a thin slice of lemon, or garnish with a thin slice of a green chili pepper.

Calories: **185**   Protein: **25.9 g (56%)**   Carbohydrates: **.7 g (2%)**   Sodium: **121 mg**

Total Fat: **8.2 g (39%)**   *Saturated Fat:* **1.8 g**   *Monounsaturated Fat:* **3.2 g**   *Polyunsaturated Fat:* **2.0 g**

❖ Chilled Marinated White Fish

Here is an ideal picnic dish for warm summer evenings. It can, of course, be just as happily eaten indoors. This dish was inspired by Edward Giobbi's catfish in carpione in his book *Eat Right, Eat Well—The Italian Way* published by Knopf, 1985. Carpione is the name of the onion marinade.

PRODUCTON NOTES: Tilefish, rockfish, pollock, cod, or any other firm white fish can be used. This also can make a wonderful sandwich, placed on a bulky roll with lettuce and tomato, or serve it as a salad plate with a variety of lettuce greens and cherry tomatoes and cucumber slices.

Portions per recipe: 105
Yield: 5 pans
Portion: 6 ounces
Serving utensil: spatula

Pan: 12" × 20" × 2"
Temperature: 325° F
Time: 12 minutes

Ingredients	Amounts	
Olive oil		4 oz.
Pignolia (pine) nuts		5 oz.
Spanish onions, thinly sliced	10 lb.	
Golden muscat raisins		15 oz.
Red pepper flakes		$1/16$ oz.
Water	2 lb.	
Cider vinegar	6 lb.	
Salt		1 oz.
Firm white fish fillets (6 oz.)	39 lb.	6 oz.
Parsley leaves, minced		5 oz.

Procedure:

1. Heat olive oil and sauté pignolia nuts until light brown.
2. Remove nuts and reserve.
3. Add onions and sauté slowly for 10 minutes.
4. Add raisins, pepper flakes, water, vinegar, and salt. Simmer for 5 minutes.
5. Place 21 fish fillets close together in three rows in oiled pan.
6. Pour 3 pints of marinade over fish and sprinkle with 1 ounce of pignolia nuts.
7. Bake at 325° F for 12 minutes. Test fish for doneness.
8. Cover and refrigerate overnight.
9. Sprinkle each pan generously with 1 ounce minced parsley just before serving.

Calories: **200**   Protein: **33.9 g (68%)**   Carbohydrates: **7.8 g (15%)**   Sodium: **201 mg**
Total Fat: **3.4 g (15%)**   *Saturated Fat:* **.3 g**   *Monounsaturated Fat:* **1.2 g**   *Polyunsaturated Fat:* **1.2 g**

❖ Fish de Lima

White, firm-fleshed fish is marinated overnight and baked to create a moist poached fish flavored with limes and green chili peppers perfect for a Mexican fiesta. Serve it with Mexican rice, baked winter squash, warm flour tortillas, and fresh salsa.

PRODUCTION NOTE: Order thick fish fillets for this dish. If you must use thin fillets, fold them over.

Portions per recipe: *48*
Yield: *3 pans*
Portion: *6 ounces*
Serving utensil: *spatula*

Pan: *12" × 20" × 2"*
Temperature: *325° F*
Time: *15 minutes*

Ingredients	Amounts
White, firm fish fillets, 6 ounces each	18 lb.
Olive oil	4 oz.
Garlic cloves, crushed	2 oz.
Canned green chilies, diced	2 lb. 8 oz.
Canned pimento, diced	1 lb. 12 oz.
Jalapeño with seeds, freshly chopped	1 oz.
Oregano, crushed	1/8 oz.
Lime juice	8 oz.
Lime slices	8 oz.
Parsley, minced	2 oz.

Procedure:

1. Place 16 fish fillets in lightly oiled pan.
2. Mix together rest of ingredients except parsley.
3. Pour 1 pint over fish.
4. Cover with plastic wrap and refrigerate overnight.
5. Bake uncovered as needed at 325° F for 15 minutes.
6. Sprinkle with parsley and serve at once.

Calories: **192**   Protein: **33.6 g (70%)**   Carbohydrates: **3.8 g (8%)**   Sodium: **156 mg**
Total Fat: **4.2 g (20%)**   *Saturated Fat:* **.3 g**   *Monounsaturated Fat:* **2.0 g**   *Polyunsaturated Fat:* **1.1 g**

❖ Fresh Tuna Kabobs

Four types of tuna are available fresh: yellow and bluefin tuna, bonito and albacore. Fresh tuna is sold as steaks or in chunks. Raw tuna meat is dark reddish in color and of a dense meaty texture when cooked. Tuna steaks can be cooked like mahi mahi or shark, recipes for which are elsewhere in this chapter. The mahi mahi and shark can also be cut into chunks and used for this kebab recipe. See color plate **8B**.

PRODUCTION NOTES: Marinate fish chunks in lemon juice, herbs, and oil for at least two hours before grilling or broiling them. Leave the tail on the shrimp for an attractive presentation.

Portions per recipe: 24
Yield: 24 skewers
Portion: 1 skewer
Serving utensil: tongs

Pan: 12" × 20" × 2"
Temperature: broil
Time: 8 minutes

Ingredients	Amounts
Tuna, loin fillet or 1-ounce chunks	4 lb. 8 oz.
Lemon juice	4 oz.
Fresh thyme, chopped	½ oz.
Parsley leaves, minced	1 oz.
Olive oil	2 oz.
White pepper	¹⁄₁₆ oz.
Shrimp, 28–36 ct, peeled, deveined	3 lb.
Mushrooms, stem trimmed short	1 lb. 8 oz.
Green bell peppers, 1" squares	1 lb.
Red bell peppers, 1" squares	1 lb.

Procedure:

1. Cut loin fillet into 1-ounce pieces if necessary.
2. Mix lemon juice with fresh thyme, parsley, olive oil, and white pepper.
3. Pour over tuna, toss and marinate 2 hours in the refrigerator.
4. Using flat metal skewers or 12 inch bamboo skewers skewer in any order 3 pieces of tuna, 3 shrimp with tails, 3 mushrooms, and 4 pieces of bell pepper.
5. Brush with marinade.
6. Place under broiler and broil 4 minutes, turn once and broil 4 minutes longer.

Calories: **209**   Protein: **32.1 g (61%)**   Carbohydrates: **3.0 g (6%)**   Sodium: **119 mg**
Total Fat: **7.7 g (33%)**   *Saturated Fat:* **.8 g**   *Monounsaturated Fat:* **3.1 g**   *Polyunsaturated Fat:* **2.1 g**

❖ Grilled Rainbow Trout

Rainbow trout meat is high in fat content, which gives it a rich flavor. The high fat content also causes it to spoil rapidly and most farmed trout is immediately frozen. Rainbow trout are available with or without heads, boneless, and butterflied. Select the type your customers prefer. College students do not find heads appealing and their appetites are frightened off by such a sight, therefore this recipe caters to student demands.

PRODUCTION NOTE: Pat lightly thawed trout with paper towels to dry them, or the flour and moisture will form a sticky paste.

Portions per recipe: 96
Yield: 4 pans
Portion: 1 trout, 5 ounces
Serving utensil: spatula

Pan: 12″ × 20″ × 2″
Griddle temperature: 350° F
Time: 10 minutes

Ingredients	Amounts	
Flour	1 lb.	
Salt		1 oz.
Black pepper		¼ oz.
Thyme, crushed		⅛ oz.
Trout (without heads, boneless, and thawed) (5 oz.)	30 lb.	
Lemons, sliced	2 lb.	
Parsley leaves, minced		2 oz.

Procedure:

1. Mix flour with salt, pepper, and thyme.
2. Dry trout with paper towels.
3. Dredge lightly in flour mixture.
4. Grill on oiled griddle for 5 to 7 minutes on each side, 3 minutes if butterflied fillets are used.
5. Place 24 fish in pan. Garnish with lemon slices and minced parsley before serving.

Calories: **185**   Protein: **29.6 g (64%)**   Carbohydrates: **3.7 g (8%)**   Sodium: **95 mg**
Total Fat: **4.8 g (23%)**   *Saturated Fat:* **.9 g**   *Monounsaturated Fat:* **1.5 g**   *Polyunsaturated Fat:* **1.7 g**

❖ Italian Baked Fish

White, firm fish is topped with fresh tomatoes and peppers flavored with olive oil, oregano, and garlic and baked. This is wonderful with rice or pasta.

PRODUCTION NOTE: Leave Italian tomatoes at room temperature to ripen fully. They will develop a richer color and flavor. Unripe tomatoes (and that is what arrives in most high quantity kitchens) should never be refrigerated. Refrigerate them once they are ripe and after they have been sliced or diced.

Portions per recipe: 100
Yield: 5 pans
Portion: 6 ounces
Serving utensil: spatula

Pan: 12″ × 20″ × 2″
Temperature: 300° F
Time: 15–20 minutes

Ingredients

Ingredients	Amounts
Olive oil*	10 oz.
Garlic cloves, crushed	2 oz.
Oregano leaves, crushed	⅛ oz.
Black pepper	⅛ oz.
Salt	1 oz.
Italian plum tomatoes, diced	6 lb.
Green bell peppers, diced	2 lb. 8 oz.
Parsley leaves, minced	4 oz.
White, firm fish fillet (6 oz.)	37 lb. 8 oz.

Procedure:

1. Mix olive oil with garlic, oregano, pepper, salt, tomatoes, peppers, and parsley.
2. Pour 1 cup tomato mixture into pan.
3. Place 20 fillets on top. Pour 2 cups tomato mixture over fish.
4. Bake at 300° F uncovered for 15 minutes. Test for doneness.

Calories: **190**   Protein: **33.4 g (70%)**   Carbohydrates: **1.9 g (4%)**   Sodium: **206 mg**
Total Fat: **4.6 g (22%)**   *Saturated Fat:* **.4 g**   *Monounsaturated Fat:* **2.2 g**   *Polyunsaturated Fat:* **3.4 g**

---

*To reduce fat and calories further, cut amount of oil in half: (Calories: **197**   Total Fat: **3.2 g (16%)**).

❖ Korean Fish Stew

This is a very simple cabbage stew with shrimp and fish. Serve it with plain steamed white rice. Konchu chang is a Korean chili paste available from Asian food stuffs purveyors and Asian specialty markets.

Portions per recipe: *48*
Yield: *2 pans*
Portion: *8 ounces*
Serving utensil: *6-ounce ladle*

Pan: *12" × 20" × 2"*
Cooking method: *steam*
Time: *25 minutes*

Ingredients	Amounts
Dried Chinese mushrooms	4 oz.
Vegetable oil	1 oz.
Chinese cabbage, shredded	5 lb.
Fresh mushrooms, halved or quartered	2 lb.
Scallion bulbs and tops, ½" pieces	2 lb.
Garlic cloves, crushed	2 oz.
Water and mushroom liquid	12 lb.
Soy sauce	2 oz.
Kochu chang (chili paste)	½ oz.
Small shrimp	2 lb.
Tofu, ½" cubes	2 lb.
Firm, white fish, 2-ounce pieces	6 lb.
Kochu chang (Korean chili paste)	⅛ oz.
Rice vinegar or lemon juice	2 oz.
Scallions, chopped	2 oz.

Procedure:

1. Soak dried mushrooms in hot water for 30 minutes.
2. Drain and reserve liquid. Discard stems. Slice caps thinly.
3. Heat oil in kettle or tilt skillet and sauté cabbage, mushrooms (fresh and dried), scallions, and garlic for 3 minutes.
4. Add water, reserved liquid, and soy sauce and simmer for 10 minutes.
5. Mix kochu chang with 1 cup soup liquid and stir in. Fold in shrimp and tofu.
6. Ladle 5 quarts into pan. Top with 24 fish pieces.
7. Mix kochu chang with vinegar and brush fish.
8. Cover and steam at high pressure for 5 minutes or bake in 325° F for 10–12 minutes. Garnish with scallions.
9. Serve carefully to keep pieces of fish from breaking up.

Calories: **115**   Protein: **18.2 g (63%)**   Carbohydrates: **5.6 g (19%)**   Sodium: **175 mg**
Total Fat: **2.6 g (19%)**   *Saturated Fat:* **.9 g**   *Monounsaturated Fat:* **.4 g**   *Polyunsaturated Fat:* **1.3 g**

❖ Marinated Mako Shark Steak

Mako shark is the most popular and perhaps the best tasting shark. The raw steaks are quite pink but turn white when cooked. Shark is not unlike swordfish in texture, meaty but more moist. It is less expensive than swordfish, but shark must be very fresh. See color plate **8B**.

Portions per recipe: *100*
Yield: *6 pans*
Portion: *1 steak, 7 ounces*
Serving utensil: *spatula*

Pan: *12″ × 20″ × 2″*
Griddle temperature: *350° F*
Time: *10–14 minutes*

Ingredients / Amounts

Ingredients	Amounts
Peanut oil	3 oz.
Sesame oil	1 oz.
Ginger root, grated	2 oz.
Garlic cloves, crushed	2 oz.
Chili bean sauce	1 oz.
Brown sugar	1 oz.
Soy sauce	8 oz.
Lemon juice	4 oz.
Shark steaks, 7 ounces each	42 lb.
Scallions, minced	12 oz.

Procedure:

1. Beat first eight ingredients together well.
2. Dip both sides of steaks into marinade. Set on sheet pans and refrigerate for 1 hour.
3. Heat griddle to 350° F and cook shark for 5 to 7 minutes on each side.
4. Place 16 steaks into pan and sprinkle shark with scallions.

Calories: **263** Protein: **40.3 g (61%)** Carbohydrates: **1.0 g (3%)** Sodium: **281 mg**
Total Fat: **9.7 g (33%)** *Saturated Fat:* **2.0 g** *Monounsaturated Fat:* **3.4 g** *Polyunsaturated Fat:* **3.3 g**

❖ Monkfish Braised with Vegetables

Monkfish is sweet and meaty. Some people even claim it tastes like lobster, but if you have enjoyed Maine lobster fresh from a lobsterman's boat you will find monkfish wanting. Sold as "lotte" in some parts of the country only the tail of the very ugly monkfish is used. The flesh must be fully cooked so it is completely firm, and this makes it tricky to broil or grill monkfish without overcooking it, which turns the meat tough and dry. I prefer poaching or braising monkfish in quantity; it keeps the flesh moist and tender. Serve this recipe with rice, pasta, or over a biscuit split in half and a crisp green salad.

PRODUCTION NOTE: Remove all membranes from the fillet before cutting it, they turn tough and stringy.

Portions per recipe: *100*
Yield: *3 pans*
Portion: *7.5 ounces*
Serving utensil: *6-ounce ladle*

Pan: *12″ × 20″ × 2″*
Temperature: *300° F*
Time: *25 minutes*

Ingredients	Amounts
Vegetable oil	2 oz.
Leeks, split, cleaned well, and thinly sliced	4 lb.
Garlic cloves, crushed	1 oz.
Mushrooms, trimmed and thinly sliced	6 lb.
Italian plum tomatoes, diced	4 lb.
Yellow bell peppers, thinly sliced	2 lb.
Parsley, minced	4 oz.
White vermouth	1 lb.
Light cream	4 lb.
Hungarian paprika	½ oz.
Salt	1 oz.
Capers, drained	2 oz.
Monkfish, ¾″ slices	30 lb.

Procedure:

1. In vegetable oil sauté leeks, garlic, and mushrooms for 5 minutes.
2. Add tomatoes, peppers, parsley, vermouth, and cream. Bring to a simmer.
3. Stir in paprika, salt, and capers and simmer 5 minutes.
4. Place 10 pounds of monkfish in each pan. Pour 3 quarts of vegetable sauce over fish.
5. Bake at 300° F for 25 minutes.

Calories: **161**   Protein: **21.1 g (52%)**   Carbohydrates: **4.4 g (11%)**   Sodium: **151 mg**
Total Fat: **6.4 g (36%)**   *Saturated Fat:* **2.3 g**   *Monounsaturated Fat:* **3.5 g**   *Polyunsaturated Fat:* **.5 g**

❖ Oven Poached Salmon

The abundance of farm raised whole salmon is a real boon for catering departments. A whole poached salmon makes a classy centerpiece for cold buffets. Here is a simple poaching method that produces moist and flavorful salmon in less than 30 minutes. It requires a hot court bouillon. Make court bouillon by simmering chowder fish pieces with white vermouth, water, bay leaf, onions, carrots, and parsley stems for 30 minutes. Serve cold salmon with cucumber mint dressing (p. 389) or green sauce (p. 191).

PRODUCTION NOTES: Salmon should weigh 6 to 7 pounds and fit into 12" × 20" × 4" pan. Leave head on. One salmon serves 18 to 20 people at a self-service buffet. Staff will need to remove the backbone after the top layer has been served.

Portions per recipe: *108*
Yield: *6 whole salmons*
Portion: *5 ounces*
Serving utensil: *spoon and fork*

Pan: *12" × 20" × 4"*
Temperature: *350° F*
Time: *30 minutes*

Ingredients | Amounts

Ingredients	Amounts	
Court bouillon	12 lb.	
Whole Norwegian salmon	40 lb.	
Long European cucumber	2 lb.	
Lemon, slices	1 lb.	
Italian parsley		2 oz.
Fresh dill or sorrel leaves		½ oz.

Procedure:

1. Bring court bouillon to a simmer.
2. Place 2 salmons on their sides in pan.
3. Pour 2 quarts boiling hot court bouillon over fish.
4. Cover tightly with foil and poach in 350° F oven.
5. After 30 minutes remove from oven and let cool in liquid.
6. To serve, remove skin and place on large platter with head on.
7. Garnish with thin cucumber and lemon slices, parsley, fresh dill or sorrel leaves.
8. Offer sauce separately.

Calories: **245**   Protein: **36.3 g (60%)**   Carbohydrates: **0.0**   Sodium: **78 g**
Total Fat: **10.0 g (40%)**   *Saturated Fat:* **1.9 g**   *Monounsaturated Fat:* **3.5 g**   *Polyunsaturated Fat:* **2.9 g**

❖ Salmon Baked in Lemon Sauce

Light and very lemony, this sauce complements the rich salmon taste.

Portions per recipe: *60*
Yield: *5 pans*
Portion: *8-ounce fillet*
Serving utensil: *spatula*

Pan: *12″ × 20″ × 2″*
Temperature: *300° F*
Time: *12 minutes*

Ingredients	Amounts
Salmon fillets, 8 ounces each	30 lb.
Unsalted butter, melted	4 oz.
Lemon juice	9 oz.
Fresh rosemary leaves	1 oz.
Fresh thyme leaves	1 oz.
White pepper	1/16 oz.
Parsley leaves, minced	4 oz.
Lemon wedges	2 lb.

Procedure:

1. Place 12 fillets neatly into pan.
2. Mix melted butter with lemon juice, herbs, and white pepper.
3. With a 3-ounce ladle pour lemon butter over fillets in each pan.
4. Bake at 325° F for 12 minutes or until fish flakes easily.
5. Sprinkle fillets with fresh parsley and top each piece with lemon.

Calories: **346**   Protein: **49.1 g (57%)**   Carbohydrates: **.4 g (1%)**   Sodium: **106 mg**

Total Fat: **16.1 g (42%)**   *Saturated Fat:* **3.5 g**   *Monounsaturated Fat:* **5.1**   *Polyunsaturated Fat:* **4.4 g**

❖ Salmon Turnover

This is a great way to use extra cooked salmon or canned salmon, which in this case is quite satisfactory.

PRODUCTION NOTES: If a turnover press is used, cut 3-ounce pieces of dough and press into circles, otherwise roll dough and cut into 4-inch squares. Beat 1 egg with 1 cup water to make an egg wash.

Portions per recipe: 96
Yield: 96 turnovers
Portion: 1 turnover
Serving utensil: tongs

Pan: 18″ × 26″ sheet pan
Temperature: 350° F
Time: 20–25 minutes

Ingredients

Ingredients	Amounts	
Salmon, cooked	12 lb.	
Vegetable oil		2 oz.
Spanish onions, diced	2 lb.	
Garlic cloves, crushed		2 oz.
Frozen spinach, thawed and chopped	6 lb.	
Sour cream	1 lb.	
Yogurt	2 lb.	
Nutmeg		1/8 oz.
Black pepper		1/4 oz.
Salt		1 oz.
Pastry dough circles (3 ounces each)	18 lb.	
Low-fat yogurt	1 lb.	
Fresh dill, chopped		1 oz.

Procedure:

1. Check salmon for bones, and break into chunks.
2. Heat oil and sauté onions and garlic until golden.
3. Squeeze spinach lightly to remove liquid.
4. Add sautéed onions to spinach. Cool slightly.
5. Add sour cream, yogurt, and spices to spinach mixture. Fold in salmon.
6. With a #16 scoop place filling in center of pastry dough.
7. Close with turnover press or fold by hand and seal edges with prongs of a fork.
8. Brush with egg wash and prick 3 times with fork.
9. Bake at 325° F for 20 to 25 minutes.
10. Serve with a dollop of yogurt mixed with fresh dill.

Calories: **515**   Protein: **18.4 g (14%)**   Carbohydrates: **38.8 g (30%)**   Sodium: **559 mg**

Total Fat: **31.9 g (56%)**   *Saturated Fat:* **8.5 g**   *Monounsaturated Fat:* **16.8 g**   *Polyunsaturated Fat:* **3.6 g**

❖ Smoked Salmon Fettuccine

Quick, easy, tasty, and very pretty to look at.

PRODUCTION NOTES: Smoked Norwegian or Scottish salmon is preferred but Nova Scotia lox can be used successfully. Drain noodles briefly, so that cooking water still clings to them, or it will be difficult to toss fettucine with sauce. Reserve some of the hot pasta water just in case.

Portions per recipe: *24*
Yield: *1 pan*
Portion: *7 ounces*
Serving utensil: *tongs or spoon*

Pan: *12″ × 20″ × 2″*
Cooking method: *boil*
Time: *10 minutes*

Ingredients	Amounts	
Olive oil		2 oz.
Garlic cloves, crushed		1 oz.
Spanish onions, thinly sliced		8 oz.
Smoked salmon	1 lb.	
Light cream	1 lb.	
Frozen peas	2 lb.	
Fresh dill, chopped		4 oz.
Freshly ground black pepper		⅛ oz.
Fettuccine	4 lb.	
Lightly salted water (boiling)	16 lb.	

Procedure:

1. Heat olive oil and sauté onions and garlic until golden.
2. Slice salmon into thin julienne strips.
3. Add salmon with cream to onions. Bring to a simmer.
4. Fold in peas, dill and black pepper. Keep warm.
5. Boil fettuccine in water until barely tender.
6. Drain very briefly and toss immediately with salmon sauce.
7. Serve at once.

Calories: **335**   Protein: **13.1 g (16%)**   Carbohydrates: **52.4 g (63%)**   Sodium: **169 mg**
Total Fat: **7.8 g (21%)**   *Saturated Fat:* **2.6 g**   *Monounsaturated Fat:* **3.5 g**   *Polyunsaturated Fat:* **1.0 g**

❖ Steamed Fish with Vegetables

A simple and very colorful way to serve any white fish fillet.

Portions per recipe: 96
Yield: 6 pans
Portion: 6-ounce fillet
Serving utensil: spatula

Pan: 12″ × 20″ × 2″
Cooking method: steam
Time: 7 minutes

Ingredients

Ingredients	Amounts
White fish fillet	36 lb.
Green bell peppers, thinly sliced	2 lb.
Yellow bell peppers, thinly sliced	1 lb.
Red bell peppers, thinly sliced	1 lb.
Butter blend (60% margarine/ 40% butter)	6 oz.
Garlic cloves, crushed	1 oz.
Lemon juice	4 oz.
Dry vermouth	12 oz.
Cayenne pepper	$\frac{1}{16}$ oz.
Chives, freeze dried	$\frac{1}{4}$ oz.

Procedure:

1. Place 16 pieces of fish neatly in oiled pan.
2. Mix pepper strips and sprinkle 10 ounces evenly over fillets.
3. Melt butter and sauté garlic until golden.
4. Add rest of ingredients and simmer for 10 minutes.
5. Pour ½ cup over fish fillets in each pan.
6. Steam for 7 minutes at 5# pressure, or 12 minutes in convection steamer, or cover and bake for 15 minutes in a 325° F oven.
7. Serve at once.

Calories: **173**   Protein: **33.3 g (77%)**   Carbohydrates: **1.0 g (2%)**   Sodium: **157 mg**
Total Fat: **3.1 g (16%)**   *Saturated Fat:* **.5 g**   *Monounsaturated Fat:* **.8 g**   *Polyunsaturated Fat:* **1.2 g**

Steamed fish with vegetables is very low in calories, colorful, and easy to prepare.

❖ Stuffed Fillet of Sole with Shrimp Sauce

A savory shrimp stuffing is rolled into fillets of sole and baked and served with a creamy shrimp sauce.

Portions per recipe: *105*
Yield: *5 pans*
Portion: *1 fillet*
Serving utensil: *spatula*

Pan: *12″ × 20″ × 2″*
Temperature: *325° F*
Time: *20 minutes*

Ingredients

Ingredients	Amounts
Spanish onions	1 lb.
Celery, tops only	1 lb.
Garlic cloves, crushed	2 oz.
Parsley leaves, minced	2 oz.
Vegetable oil	2 oz.
Black pepper	¼ oz.
Sage	⅛ oz.
Salt	½ oz.
Salad shrimp, raw	3 lb.
Lemon juice	4 oz.
Dry vermouth	8 oz.
Bread crumbs	12 oz.
Sole or flounder fillets (4 ounces each)	26 lb. 4 oz.
Cold shrimp sauce (see page 459–460)	

Procedure:

1. In food chopper or processor mince onions, celery, garlic, and parsley.
2. Sauté in oil until soft. Add spices, shrimp, lemon juice, and vermouth.
3. Cook for 3 minutes and fold in bread crumbs. Add more bread crumbs if too loose.
4. Place a #40 scoop of filling on tail end of the fish and roll up.
5. Place 21 fillets seam side down in oiled pan.
6. Bake fish at 325° F for 20 minutes.
7. Make shrimp sauce. Pour 1 ounce sauce over each fillet.

Calories: **138**   Protein: **24.5 g (71%)**   Carbohydrates: **3.3 g (10%)**   Sodium: **139 mg**
Total Fat: **2.3 g (15%)**   *Saturated Fat:* **.5 g**   *Monounsaturated Fat:* **.5 g**   *Polyunsaturated Fat:* **.8 g**

❖ Sweet and Sour Fish   *Hom*

This is a recipe from "A Feast Fit for the Last Emperor of China." This recipe is exceptionally good and it is included here even though the fish is deep fried. Occasionally it is acceptable to take a break and indulge, especially if you usually serve a low-fat, healthy menu.

PRODUCTION NOTES: Prepare sauce in advance, but steam vegetables and fry fish as needed. Frozen shoestring carrots save time and labor and are more uniform.

Portions per recipe: 100
Yield: 5 pans
Portion: 6 ounces
Serving utensil: spatula

Pan: 12″ × 20″ × 2″
Oil temperature: 360° F
Time: 6 minutes

Ingredients	Amounts
Sesame oil	1 oz.
Scallions, chopped	12 oz.
Ginger root, chopped	3 oz.
Frozen shoestring carrots	5 lb.
Chicken stock	4 lb.
Soy sauce	6 oz.
Dry sherry	12 oz.
Tomato paste	10 oz.
Cider vinegar	12 oz.
Granulated sugar	6 oz.
Cornstarch	3 oz.
Pollock fillets, 6 ounces each	37 lb. 8 oz.
Cornstarch	1 lb.
Frozen peas	5 lb.
Frozen pea pods	2 lb. 8 oz.
Green or yellow bell peppers, thinly sliced	2 lb.

Procedure:

1. Heat sesame oil and sauté scallions and ginger briefly.
2. Add carrots, stock, soy sauce, sherry, paste, and vinegar.
3. Simmer for 10 minutes. Mix sugar with cornstarch and stir in to thicken.
4. Keep warm.
5. Make cross slashes in top of fish fillets.
6. Dip fish in cornstarch, dust off excess.
7. Deep fry for about 6 minutes until brown and crisp. Do not crowd baskets.
8. Place 20 pieces lightly overlapping in pan.
9. Steam peas, pods, and pepper strips for 1 minute at high pressure.
10. Top each pan of fish with 2 pounds vegetables and 1½ pints of sauce.
11. Serve at once.

Calories: **250*** Protein: **35.2 g (56%)** Carbohydrates: **14.0 g (22%)** Sodium: **286 mg**

Total Fat: **5.2 g (19%)** *Saturated Fat:* **1.1 g** *Monounsaturated Fat:* **2.3 g** *Polyunsaturated Fat:* **2.1 g**

---

*Total includes fat from deep-frying.

❖ Triglie e Gambaretti Arrostiti—Red Snapper with Shrimp *Michela's*

This recipe was part of "The Taste of Europe" special event. I have modified the procedure since that event so the dish can be baked or broiled successfully, giving the shrimp more flavor. The recipe uses red snapper, an Atlantic and Gulf Coast fish, but any firm white fish fillets such as grouper or Pacific red snapper rockfish can be substituted.

PRODUCTION NOTES: Peel large shrimp, but do not remove tails. Fillets should be fairly thick and with the red skin left on.

Portions per recipe: *100*
Yield: *5 pans*
Portion: *5-ounce fillet and*
    1 large shrimp
Serving utensil: *spatula*

Pan: *12" × 20" × 2"*
Oven temperature: *325° F*
Time: *12 minutes*

Ingredients	Amounts
Green Greek Royal olives, unpitted	8 oz.
Italian tomatoes, ripe	10 lb.
Lemons	3 lb.
Sweet butter	4 oz.
Garlic cloves, crushed	3 oz.
Fresh rosemary, chopped	2 oz.
Red snapper fillets, 5 ounces each	31 lb. 4 oz.
Shrimp, peeled with tail attached	3 lb. 8 oz.
Olive oil	2 oz.
Garlic cloves, crushed	1 oz.
Fresh rosemary, chopped	1 oz.

Procedure:

1. Pit olives and chop coarsely.
2. Peel and seed tomatoes and dice into small pieces.
3. Slice lemons as thinly as possible with electric slicer.
4. Heat butter and sauté garlic and tomatoes for 5 minutes.
5. Add rosemary and olives. Simmer for 10 minutes.
6. Pour 2 cups of sauce into pan.
7. Place 20 fillets, skin side up, in two neat rows in pan.
8. Top each fillet with a slice of lemon.
9. Bake at 325° F for 12 minutes.
10. Sauté shrimp in olive oil with garlic and rosemary until pink but not curled.
11. Place one shrimp on each fillet. Serve at once.

Calories: **182**   Protein: **32.7 g (71%)**   Carbohydrates: **2.2 g (4%)**   Sodium: **156 mg**
Total Fat: **3.9 g (19%)**   *Saturated Fat:* **1.1 g**   *Monounsaturated Fat:* **1.1 g**   *Polyunsaturated Fat:* .9 g

❖ Tuna all'Arrabbiata—Pasta with Tuna

A "mad," fiery tuna sauce with ziti. Very simple but subtle; a small amount will moisten the ziti. For a truly Italian taste do not drown the ziti in sauce.

PRODUCTION NOTES: Use canned albacore tuna. Stir ziti several times while they are boiling. The tubes tend to stick together. Cooked ziti break up easily, therefore they should be handled as little as possible and are better served with 2 scoops from a shallow 4-ounce ladle.

Portions per recipe: 35
Yield: 1 pan
Portion: 7 ounces (ladle twice)
Serving utensil: 4-ounce ladle

Pan: 12″ × 20″ × 4″
Cooking method: simmer
Time: 15 minutes

Ingredients

Ingredients	Amounts	
Olive oil		2 oz.
Garlic cloves, crushed		2 oz.
Oregano, crushed		1/8 oz.
Basil, crushed		1/4 oz.
Red pepper flakes		1/16 oz.
Canned chunk white albacore tuna, drained	4 lb.	4 oz.
Canned Italian tomatoes	6 lb.	6 oz.
Parsley, minced		4 oz.
Ziti	5 lb.	
Water (boiling)	24 lb.	
Salt		1 oz.

Procedure:

1. Heat olive oil and sauté garlic, oregano, basil, pepper flakes, and tuna for 5 minutes.

2. Drain tomatoes and crush whole tomatoes lightly by hand. Reserve tomato juice.

3. Add to tuna and fold in gently. Simmer for 10 minutes. Add parsley.

4. Pour ziti into boiling water and add salt and a few drops of olive oil.

5. Cook for about 12 minutes, stirring every few minutes.

6. Drain ziti briefly, add to sauce, and fold in gently. If too dry, heat reserved tomato juice, and fold into pasta.

Calories: **349** Protein: **23.9 g (27%)** Carbohydrates: **52.7 g (61%)** Sodium: **329 mg**
Total Fat: **4.3 g (11%)** *Saturated Fat:* **.8 g** *Monounsaturated Fat:* **1.7 g** *Polyunsaturated Fat:* **1.2 g**

Canned albacore tuna is served in a spicy hot tomato sauce with ziti.

Shellfish

Americans are fond of shellfish. Too often, however, they favor it breaded and deep fried. The recipes in this chapter combine seafood with vegetables and sauces that keep fat to a minimum, but that are, nonetheless, full of flavor.

Shrimp is almost always frozen and, happily, peeled frozen shrimp is both excellent and saves time and labor. Bay scallops are usually less expensive than sea scallops. Buy all scallops fresh not frozen. Squid is very inexpensive, and properly blanched it is tender and delicious. Mussels are becoming more popular and are reasonably priced. Steamed clams are also very popular with student diners. No recipe is needed, just steam and serve with hot lemon butter and clam juice. I have included a simple clam sauce recipe for spaghetti, vermicelli, or linguine.

❖ Calamari all'Appetitosa—Savory Squid *Romagnoli*

Squid—so simple and so good! One of the most popular dishes from the "Festa Italiana."

PRODUCTION NOTES: Remove cartilage and any viscera from shrimp. Rinse in salted water. Bring water to a boil, place squid in a flat bottomed colander, dip for only 20 seconds into boiling liquid, remove, and plunge into ice water. This is a foolproof method that assures tender squid at all times.

Portions per recipe: *80*
Yield: *2 pans*
Portion: *3 ounces*
Serving utensil: *spoon*

Pan: *12″ × 20″ × 2″–½ size*
Skillet temperature: *350° F*
Time: *1 minute*

Ingredients

Ingredients	Amounts
Squid, with tentacles	15 lb.
Olive oil	8 oz.
Garlic cloves, crushed	3 oz.
Sweet butter	4 oz.
Bread crumbs	12 oz.
Italian parsley, minced	4 oz.
Lemon juice	12 oz.
Red pepper sauce (Tabasco)	½ oz.

Procedure:

1. Cut blanched squid into ¼″ rings and half or quarter tentacles.
2. Refrigerate until ready to cook.
3. Heat olive oil in tilting skillet and sauté garlic 30 seconds.
4. Add squid and sauté for one minute.
5. Add butter, bread crumbs, lemon juice, and red pepper sauce.
6. Toss briefly and place in pans. Garnish with lemon wedges.

Calories: **133**   Protein: **13.9 g (42%)**   Carbohydrates: **6.4 g (19%)**   Sodium: **69 mg**
Total Fat: **5.4 g (36%)**   *Saturated Fat:* **1.4 g**   *Monounsaturated Fat:* **2.6 g**   *Polyunsaturated Fat:* **.8 g**

❖ Clam Sauce with Spaghetti

This flavorful sauce is white and delicately flavored. It can be prepared in about 10 minutes. If a robust red sauce is wanted, eliminate the cream, lemon juice, and vermouth and add canned Italian plum tomatoes instead. The tomatoes must be simmered for 30 to 45 minutes (sauce should be thick) before adding the clams.

PRODUCTION NOTE: Thaw frozen clams in the refrigerator overnight.

Portions per recipe: *64*
Yield: *1 gallon*
Portion: *3 ounces*
Serving utensil: *2-ounce ladle*

Pan: *12″ × 20″ × 4″–½ size*
Temperature: *325° F*
Time: *10 minutes*

Ingredients	Amounts
Boiling water lightly salted	*32 lb.*
Spaghetti	*8 lb.*
Olive oil	*3 oz.*
Spanish onions, diced	*2 lb.*
Garlic cloves, crushed	*4 oz.*
Oregano, crushed	*⅛ oz.*
White pepper	*1/16 oz.*
All-purpose flour	*2 oz.*
Dry white vermouth	*1 lb.*
Lemon juice	*4 oz.*
Light cream	*1 lb.*
Frozen clams, chopped	*8 lb.*
Italian parsley, minced	*4 oz.*

Procedure:

1. Cook spaghetti al dente in boiling water. Drain and hold.
2. In olive oil sauté onions, garlic, oregano, and pepper for 5 minutes.
3. Stir in the flour. Add vermouth and lemon juice and bring to a simmer.
4. Add cream and clams and simmer for 3 to 5 minutes.
5. Stir in fresh parsley and serve at once over spagetti.

Calories: **78***   Protein: **7.8 g (40%)**   Carbohydrates: **4.1 g (21%)**   Sodium: **36 mg**
Total Fat: **3.3 g (38%)**   *Saturated Fat:* **1.1 g**   *Monounsaturated Fat:* **1.4 g**   *Polyunsaturated Fat:* **.4 g**

Calories: **288†**   Protein: **15.1 g (21%)**   Carbohydrates: **46.4 g (65%)**   Sodium: **40 mg**
Total Fat: **4.2 g (13%)**   *Saturated Fat:* **1.2 g**   *Monounsaturated Fat:* **1.5 g**   *Polyunsaturated Fat:* **.7 g**

---

*Nutrient values are for sauce only.
†Nutrient values for sauce and pasta.

❖ Dutch Steamed Shrimp

Shrimp are steamed in their shells and the customer does the peeling. No complaints were heard from the student diners.

PRODUCTION NOTE: Cook shrimp in batches in a vegetable fond that will become a shellfish fond as soon as the first batch of shrimp has been steamed in it.

Portions per recipe: *70*
Yield: *2 pans*
Portion: *8 to 9 shrimp*
Serving utensil: *slotted spoon*

Pan: *12″ × 20″ × 2″*
Cooking method: *simmer*
Time: *5 minutes*

Ingredients

Ingredients	Amounts
Olive oil	2 oz.
Garlic cloves, crushed	2 oz.
Carrots, coarsely chopped	2 lb.
Spanish onions, diced	2 lb.
Bay leaves, crumbled	¼ oz.
Dry vermouth	2 lb.
Lemon juice	4 oz.
Water	8 lb.
Salt	½ oz.
Black pepper	¼ oz.
Green shrimp, unpeeled (28–32 count)	20 lb.

Procedure:

1. Heat olive oil in kettle. Add garlic, vegetables, and bay leaves.
2. Sauté for 5 minutes. Add vermouth, lemon juice, water, salt, and pepper. Simmer for 30 minutes.
3. Add 10 pounds of shrimp at a time to kettle. Close lid and steam for 5 minutes. Time carefully.
4. Remove shrimp to a pan. Some of the vegetables will stick to shrimp.
5. Add next batch.
   Note: Add more lemon juice and pepper to kettle if you steam more than 6 batches.

Calories: **161**   Protein: **26.7 g (66%)**   Carbohydrates: **4.1 g (10%)**   Sodium: **285 mg**
Total Fat: **3.5 g (20%)**   *Saturated Fat:* **.6 g**   *Monounsaturated Fat:* **1.2 g**   *Polyunsaturated Fat:* **1.0 g**

❖ Mediterranean Seafood Sauce

A creamy pasta sauce with seafood, monkfish, and fresh tomatoes.

Portions per recipe: 120
Yield: 3 pans
Portion: 5 ounces
Serving utensil: 4-ounce ladle

Pan: 12″ × 20″ × 2″
Temperature: 300° F
Time: 10 minutes

Ingredients	Amounts	
Olive oil		2 oz.
Scallions, chopped	2 lb.	
Garlic cloves, crushed		4 oz.
Red pepper flakes		⅛ oz.
Rosemary leaves, chopped		2 oz.
Bay scallops	10 lb.	
All-purpose flour		4 oz.
Dry vermouth		8 oz.
Lemon juice		4 oz.
Frozen shrimp, peeled and thawed	15 lb.	
Monkfish, membranes removed, ½″ pieces	10 lb.	
Italian plum tomatoes, diced	6 lb.	
Salt		1 oz.
Light cream	3 lb.	

Procedure:

1. In olive oil sauté scallions, garlic, and pepper flakes for 5 minutes.
2. Add rosemary and scallops and sauté for 2 minutes.
3. Dust with flour and toss well.
4. Add vermouth, lemon juice, shrimp, monkfish, and fresh tomatoes.
5. Bring to a simmer stirring gently.
6. Turn heat off. Add salt and cream. Taste and pan.

Calories: **159**   Protein: **24.1 g (61%)**   Carbohydrates: **4.2 g (11%)**   Sodium: **250 mg**

Total Fat: **4.6 g (26%)**   *Saturated Fat:* **1.7 g**   *Monounsaturated Fat:* **1.2 g**   *Polyunsaturated Fat:* **.6 g**

❖ Mussels with Linguine

Mussels are now available from mussel farms. These mussels, because they are raised in deep water, have no pearls, which makes them more appealing than shore-harvested mussels.

PRODUCTION NOTE: Check mussels and discard any that are not tightly closed and discard any mussels that do not open after they have been steamed.

Portions per recipe: *100*
Yield: *4 pans*
Portion: *6 ounces mussels and*
    4 ounces linguine
Serving utensil: *spoon and tongs*

Pan: *12" × 20" × 4"*
Cooking method: *steam*
Time: *5 minutes*

Ingredients

Ingredients	Amounts	
Maine mussels	50 lb.	
Sweet butter	1 lb.	
Olive oil		8 oz.
Garlic cloves, crushed		4 oz.
Shallots, finely minced		8 oz.
Red pepper flakes		¼ oz.
Thyme, crumbled		⅛ oz.
Lemon juice		12 oz.
Dry vermouth or white wine	2 lb.	
Parsley, minced		4 oz.
Fresh oregano, minced		½ oz.
Linguine	12 lb.	8 oz.
Water	40 lb.	
Salt		1 oz.
Olive oil		⅛ oz.

Procedure:

1. Melt butter with oil and garlic. Cook for 3 minutes.
2. Add shallots, pepper flakes, and thyme. Cook for 3 minutes.
3. Pour in the lemon juice and vermouth and simmer slowly until liquid has been reduced by one third.
4. Add mussels, toss, close lid, and steam for 5 minutes or until mussels open. Monitor carefully, mussels should be plump, shrivelled looking mussels are overcooked.
5. Mix parsley with fresh oregano. Sprinkle over mussels.
6. Cook linguine until it is al dente. Serve 4 ounces of linguine topped with 6 ounces of mussels in their shells, making sure to ladle mussel broth over each serving.

Calories: **462**   Protein: **34.4 g (30%)**   Carbohydrates: **51.6 g (45%)**   Sodium: **763 mg**
Total Fat: **12.0 g (23%)**   *Saturated Fat:* **3.7 g**   *Monounsaturated Fat:* **4.0 g**   *Polyunsaturated Fat:* **2.1 g**

❖ Oriental Scallops and Shrimp

A very colorful dish that can be quickly prepared in small batches. A tilting skillet is the ideal piece of equipment for this.

Portions per recipe: 50
Yield: 2 pans
Portion: 5 ounces
Serving utensil: spoon

Pan: 12" × 20" × 2"
Skillet temperature: 350° F
Time: 6–8 minutes

Ingredients	Amounts	
Peanut oil		1 oz.
Sesame oil		1 oz.
Ginger root, peeled and grated		½ oz.
Garlic cloves, crushed		1 oz.
Cayenne pepper		¹⁄₁₆ oz.
Frozen shrimp, peeled and thawed	10 lb.	
Yellow bell peppers, cut into strips	1 lb.	
Red bell peppers, cut into strips	1 lb.	
Sea scallops	5 lb.	
Soy sauce		1 oz.
Lemon juice		4 oz.
Fresh snow peas, trimmed	2 lb.	
Scallions, chopped		2 oz.

Procedure:

1. Heat oils and stir in ginger root, garlic, and cayenne.
2. Add shrimp and bell peppers and stir-fry for 4 minutes.
3. Add scallops, soy sauce, and lemon juice and bring to a simmer.
4. Fold in snow peas and cook for 1 minute.
5. Ladle into serving pan and garnish with chopped scallions.
6. Serve with steamed white or brown rice or with egg noodles.

Calories: **157**   Protein: **26.7 g (68%)**   Carbohydrates: **4.0 g (10%)**   Sodium: **241 mg**

Total Fat: **3.1 g (18%)**   *Saturated Fat:* **.5 g**   *Monounsaturated Fat:* **.7 g**   *Polyunsaturated Fat:* **1.2 g**

❖ Seafood Chop Suey

I am not at all fond of Surimi (seafood flakes), but it can be used quite successfully in this dish. Serve chop suey with steamed rice or Chinese noodles.

Portions per recipe: 72
Yield: 2 pans
Portion: 6 ounces
Serving utensil: 4-ounce ladle

Pan: 12″ × 20″ × 2″
Skillet temperature: 325° F
Time: 15 minutes

Ingredients

Ingredients	Amounts	
Peanut oil		1 oz.
Sesame oil		1 oz.
Garlic cloves, crushed		2 oz.
Chili bean paste		½ oz.
Celery, 1″ pieces	5 lb.	
Carrots, ¼″ slices	3 lb.	
Canned bamboo shoots, drained	2 lb.	8 oz.
Canned water chestnuts, sliced and drained	2 lb.	8 oz.
Granulated sugar		½ oz.
Cornstarch		1 oz.
Dry sherry		8 oz.
Lemon juice		8 oz.
Soy sauce		4 oz.
Frozen shrimp, peeled and thawed	7 lb.	8 oz.
Fresh bay scallops	7 lb.	8 oz.
Seafood flakes (surimi), shredded	4 lb.	
Red bell pepper, diced	1 lb.	
Frozen pea pods, thawed	2 lb.	
Scallions, chopped		8 oz.
Cilantro, chopped		2 oz.

Procedure:

1. Heat oils in tilting skillet. Add garlic and chili bean paste.
2. Stir-fry celery and carrots for 5 minutes.
3. Add bamboo shoots and water chestnuts and close lid. Simmer for 5 minutes.
4. Mix sugar and cornstarch and dissolve in sherry, lemon juice, and soy sauce.
5. Stir into vegetables. Add shrimp, scallops, and seafood flakes.
6. Bring to a simmer, stirring constantly.
7. Fold in red peppers and pea pods. Turn off heat.
8. Ladle chop suey in pans and top with scallions and cilantro.

Calories: **158**   Protein: **22.7 g (57%)**   Carbohydrates: **10.9 g (27%)**   Sodium: **306 mg**
Total Fat: **2.4 g (14%)**   *Saturated Fat: .4 g*   *Monounsaturated Fat: .5 g*   *Polyunsaturated Fat: .8 g*

❖ Seafood Crepes

These crepes are filled with shrimp, scallops, halibut pieces, and crab meat. Halibut pieces are sold as tidbits and are reasonably priced and available frozen from fish wholesalers.

PRODUCTION NOTES: The white sauce for the filling should be thick. Reserve 1 quart of the thick sauce before folding in the shellfish and fish. Thin the reserved sauce with yogurt, and pour it over the crepes before they are baked.

Portions per recipe: 96
Yield: 6 pans/192 crepes
Portion: 2 crepes
Serving utensil: spatula

Pan: 12″ × 20″ × 2″
Temperature: 325° F
Time: 15 minutes

Ingredients	Amounts	
Bay scallops	5 lb.	
Halibut tidbits	10 lb.	
Cooked salad shrimp	5 lb.	
Crab meat, picked over	1 lb.	8 oz.
Margarine		8 oz.
All-purpose flour		12 oz.
Hungarian paprika		¼ oz.
Cayenne pepper		¹⁄₁₆ oz.
Thyme, crushed		¹⁄₁₆ oz.
Salt		½ oz.
Whole milk and seafood cooking liquids	8 lb.	
Dry sherry		2 oz.
Lemon juice		2 oz.
Crepes (cooked)	9 lb.	
Low-fat yogurt	2 lb.	
Parmesan cheese, grated		1 oz.

Procedure:

1. Steam scallops and halibut tidbits for 5 minutes at low pressure. Drain the cooking liquid into a gallon container and reserve.
2. Add shrimp and crabmeat to cooked scallops and halibut.
3. Melt margarine and add flour, spices, and salt. Cook for 3 minutes.
4. Stir in the milk with cooking liquids, sherry, and lemon juice.
5. Bring to a simmer. Reserve 1 quart for sauce. Fold rest into seafood.
6. Fill crepes with a #16 scoop, roll, and place 22 crepes in each pan.

7. Mix yogurt and parmesan cheese with reserved sauce and pour 1 cup over each pan.

8. Bake at 325° F for 15 minutes.

Calories: **167** Protein: **24.0 g (57%)** Carbohydrates: **6.3 g (15%)** Sodium: **232 mg**
Total Fat: **5.3 g (29%)** *Saturated Fat:* **1.6 g** *Monounsaturated Fat:* **1.4 g** *Polyunsaturated Fat:* **1.4 g**

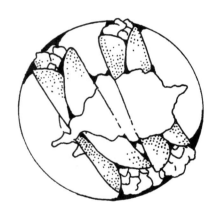

6

VEGETARIAN ENTRÉES
Unusual and Tempting

More and more, people enjoy eating meatless entrées for lunch or dinner and institutions, especially college dining services, must offer diners meatless alternatives. Though many vegetarians will not eat red meat at all, many willingly include fish and shellfish in their diets, and most will eat eggs and dairy products. Though grain, bean, and tofu dishes are less popular than the egg and dairy dishes, they are gaining acceptance as meatless alternatives and can be quite appealing when prepared wih imaginative spicing.

In developing meatless entrées I have resisted the temptation to cover everything with cheese. Students will try almost anything smothered in melted cheese, but the high saturated fat content of cheese must be considered when preparing vegetarian dishes.

The recipes in this chapter are presented in four categories according to the main ingredient.

- Eggs and Cheese
- Tofu
- Legumes
- Grains, Nuts, and Vegetables

Eggs and Cheese

Eggs and cheeses are excellent protein foods and cheeses are a good calcium source. Unfortunately they are also high in saturated fat and cholesterol. The recipes that follow have been modified to take account of this as much as possible. The menu planner for a residential institution should be careful to offer vegetarian egg and cheese dishes for lunch and dinner no more than three or four times a week and to choose the rest of the meatless entrées from the other three categories.

❖ Asparagus Tomato Quiche

Fresh asparagus and tomatoes add taste and color to this quiche.

PRODUCTION NOTES: Always use prebaked pie shells for quiche or they will be soggy. To prebake, set another pie pan inside the one filled with raw dough. Bake upside down for 8 to 10 minutes, turn over and remove the empty pie pan, bake for 2 minutes, and cool.

Portions per recipe: 84
Yield: 14 pies
Portion: ⅙ pie
Serving utensil: spatula

Pan: 9" pie shell
Oven temperature: 325° F
Time: 30 minutes

Ingredients	Amounts	
Vegetable oil		1 oz.
Spanish onions, finely diced	1 lb.	
Asparagus, cut diagonally into 1" pieces	4 lb.	
Basil, crushed		⅛ oz.
Prebaked pastry bottom, 9"	7 lb.	
Eggs, beaten	5 lb.	4 oz.
All-purpose flour		8 oz.
Non-fat dry milk	2 lb.	
Water	5 lb.	
Cheddar cheese, shredded	2 lb.	8 oz.
Swiss cheese, shredded	2 lb.	8 oz.
Salt		½ oz.
White pepper		¹⁄₁₆ oz.
Nutmeg		¹⁄₁₆ oz.
Ripe Italian tomatoes, seeded and diced	4 lb.	

Procedure:

1. Heat vegetable oil. Add onions and sauté until golden.
2. Add asparagus and basil and stir-fry for 2 minutes.
3. Pour one cup of the onions and asparagus into prebaked pie shell.
4. Beat eggs, flour, milk powder, and water together.
5. Fold in cheeses and spices.
6. Pour 20 ounces of quiche filling over the vegetables in pie shell.
7. Sprinkle one cup diced tomatoes over filling.
8. Bake at 325° F for 30 minutes.
9. Let cool 10 minutes before cutting quiche in 6 pieces.
10. Garnish each slice on the center of the quiche with parsley and tomato slice.

Calories: **380**   Protein: **18.6 g (20%)**   Carbohydrates: **19.9 g (21%)**   Sodium: **294 mg**
Total Fat: **24.9 g (59%)**   *Saturated Fat:* **9.0 g**   *Monounsaturated Fat:* **9.2 g**   *Polyunsaturated Fat:* **2.3 g**

❖ Baked Potato Omelet

A wonderful entrée for breakfast, brunch, lunch, or dinner and excellent for a buffet because it keeps very well. The potatoes are somewhat like Swiss roesti topped with a creamy omelet.

PRODUCTION NOTE: Use leftover baked potatoes for this dish or boil potatoes in their jackets, peel, and shred coarsely.

Portions per recipe: 42
Yield: 2 pans
Portion: 7 ounces (3" × 4" piece)
Serving utensil: spatula

Pan: 12" × 20" × 2"
Oven temperature: 350° F
Time: 35 minutes

Ingredients

Ingredients	Amounts	
Vegetable oil		2 oz.
Spanish onions, thinly sliced	4 lb.	
Fresh sage, chopped		1 oz.
Salt		1 oz.
Potatoes, cooked, peeled, and coarsely shredded	8 lb.	
Eggs	4 lb.	8 oz.
Heavy cream		8 oz.
Low-fat yogurt	1 lb.	
Salt		½ oz.
Black pepper		⅛ oz.
Italian plum tomatoes, diced	1 lb.	

Procedure:

1. Heat oil and sauté onions with sage for 10 minutes. Cool slightly.
2. Toss onions with salt and shredded potatoes.
3. Spread 6 pounds of potato mixture evenly over bottom of oiled pan. Bake at 350° F for 15 min.
4. Beat eggs with cream, yogurt, salt, and pepper. Fold in tomatoes.
5. Pour about 2 quarts over roasted potatoes and bake for 20 minutes.
6. Cut each pan into 21 pieces.

Calories: **145**   Protein: **7.2 g (19%)**   Carbohydrates: **13.5 g (37%)**   Sodium: **564 mg**
Total Fat: **7.0 g (43%)**   *Saturated Fat:* **2.4 g**   *Monounsaturated Fat:* **1.5 g**   *Polyunsaturated Fat:* **1.5 g**

❖ Broccoli Cheese Crepes

Broccoli is sautéed in olive oil and garlic for flavorful cheese-filled crepes.

PRODUCTON NOTES: The crepe recipe can be found on page 39. If crepes are prepared in advance and the filling is cold, bake for 5 minutes, then pour on the sauce and finish baking.

Portions per recipe: 48	*Pan: 12″ × 20″ × 2″*
Yield: 3 pans	*Oven temperature: 325° F*
Portion: 2 crepes	*Time: 15 minutes*
Serving utensil: spatula	

Ingredients

Ingredients	Amounts
Olive oil	1 oz.
Garlic cloves, crushed	3 oz.
Frozen chopped broccoli	7 lb. 8 oz.
Eggs	1 lb.
Ricotta cheese	2 lb.
Cheddar cheese, shredded	4 lb.
Nutmeg	1/16 oz.
Black pepper	1/4 oz.
Crepes (cooked)	4 lb. 8 oz.
Light cream	1 lb. 8 oz.
Parmesan cheese, grated	4 oz.
Cornstarch	1 oz.

Procedure:

1. Heat olive oil with garlic. Add broccoli and sauté for 5 minutes.
2. Beat eggs, ricotta, and cheddar cheese together with spices.
3. Fold in sautéed broccoli.
4. Portion filling onto lower third of crepe with a #12 scoop.
5. Roll up crepe and place seam side down in two rows of 16 in each pan.
6. Mix low-fat yogurt with light cream, parmesan and cornstarch.
7. Pour 1 cup over each pan.
8. Bake at 325° F for 15 minutes.
9. Garnish with steamed broccoli florets.

Calories: **308**   Protein: **19.3 g (25%)**   Carbohydrates: **14.8 g (19%)**   Sodium: **433 mg**

Total Fat: **19.3 g (57%)**   *Saturated Fat:* **12.6 g**   *Monounsaturated Fat:* **4.6 g**   *Polyunsaturated Fat:* **1.4 g**

❖ Cheese Enchilada Casserole

Spicy and cheesey, this is a simple-to-prepare Mexican casserole.

PRODUCTION NOTES: Each pan contains 24 tortillas, 3 pounds of beans, 2 pounds of cheese, and 1 cup and 4 pints of salsa and chilies. After assembling the casserole, bake it immediately or the tortillas will get soggy. Refried vegetarian beans contain no lard.

Portions per recipe: 112
Yield: 4 pans
Portion: 6 ounces (3" × 2.9" piece)
Serving utensil: spatula

Pan: 12" × 20" × 2"
Oven temperature: 325° F
Time: 20 minutes

Ingredients

Ingredients	Amounts
Chili salsa	12 lb.
Green chilies	10 lb.
Canned vegetarian refried beans	7 lb. 6 oz.
Flour tortillas, 12"	9 lb.
Monterey Jack cheese, shredded	8 lb.

Procedure:

1. Mix 8 pounds of salsa with chilies and 4 pounds of salsa with the refried beans.

2. Cover bottom of oiled pan with 1 cup of the salsa and chilies mixture.

3. Place a layer of 6 flour tortillas on top of the mixture and spread with approximately 3 pounds of refried beans. Sprinkle with 8 ounces of Jack cheese.

4. Place 6 flour tortillas over beans and cheese.

5. Cover with 1 pint salsa and chilies and sprinkle with 8 ounces jack cheese.

6. Repeat tortilla, salsa and chilies, cheese layers two more times.

7. Bake at 325° F until cheese has melted.

8. Let rest for 20 minutes before cutting each pan into 28 portions.

Calories: **299** Protein: **14.4 g (19%)** Carbohydrates: **37.5 g (50%)** Sodium: **1138 mg**
Total Fat: **12.6 g (37%)** *Saturated Fat:* **5.1 g** *Monounsaturated Fat:* **4.1 g** *Polyunsaturated Fat:* **.3 g**

❖ Cream Cheese Soufflé

This is a very rich soufflé, but fabulous for quantity food service since it will only collapse slightly and stays light and fluffy. It even reheats well if placed covered in a steamer or in a low temperature (250° F) oven. This soufflé goes well with ratatouille, baked or stewed tomatoes, or wilted spinach. See color plate **11**.

PRODUCTION NOTES: It is very important to beat the egg whites to a soft peak and to fold them in very gently. Bake the soufflé at once. For very large quantities prepare all the cheese batter at once, but beat and fold in the egg whites in batches.

Portions per recipe: *30*
Yield: *2 pans*
Portion: *4 ounces (4" × 2" piece)*
Serving utensil: *spatula*

Pan: *12" × 20" × 2"–½ size*
Oven temperature: *350° F*
Time: *35 minutes*

Ingredients	Amounts
Large eggs	1 lb. 8 oz.
Cream cheese, softened at room temperature	5 lb.
Sour cream	2 lb.
Cream of tartar	⅛ oz.

Procedure:

1. Separate eggs carefully.
2. Beat egg yolks with cream cheese and sour cream until smooth.
3. Beat egg whites with cream of tartar until they form soft peaks.
4. Fold beaten egg whites very, very gently into cheese mixture.
5. Pour 3½ pounds into lightly oiled half pan.
6. Bake at 350° F for 35 minutes.
7. Immediately cut each pan into 15 pieces. Serve at once.

Calories: **365**   Protein: **9.1 g (10%)**   Carbohydrates: **3.5 g (4%)**   Sodium: **267 mg**

Total Fat: **34.9 g (86%)**   *Saturated Fat:* **21.2 g**   *Monounsaturated Fat:* **9.4 g**   *Polyunsaturated Fat:* **1.5 g**

❖ **Eggplant Frittata**

A little more work than eggplant parmigiana, but worth the effort.

PRODUCTION NOTES: Use this recipe when fried eggplant was on yesterday's menu and was over-produced and leftover. Ignore the first 3 steps and continue with the rest of the recipe to prepare eggplant frittata in a jiffy.

Portions per recipe: 112
Yield: 4 pans
Portion: 6 ounces (3″ × 2.9″ piece)
Serving utensil: spatula

Pan: 12″ × 20″ × 2″
Oven temperature: 325° F
Time: 40 minutes

Ingredients	Amounts	

Batter for Frying:

Eggs	2 lb.	
Water (cold)	1 lb.	
All-purpose flour		12 oz.
Black pepper		¼ oz.
Salt		1 oz.
Eggplant, unpeeled and sliced ½″ thick	30 lb.	
Bread crumbs	1 lb.	8 oz.

Topping:

Ricotta cheese	2 lb.	
Parmesan cheese, grated		8 oz.
Eggs	3 lb.	
Low-fat milk	4 lb.	
Basil, crushed		¼ oz.
Cayenne pepper		1/16 oz.
Nutmeg		⅛ oz.

Procedure:

1. Beat eggs with water, flour, pepper, and salt to make a thin batter.
2. Dip eggplant slices in batter and place in colander to drain.
3. Coat dipped slices with bread crumbs.
4. Cook both sides on well-oiled 300° F griddle for 4 minutes.
5. Place 3 layers of cooked slices in unoiled pan.
6. Beat ricotta, parmesan, eggs, milk, and spices together until blended.
7. Pour 1 quart over each pan.
8. Bake at 325° F for 40 minutes. Cut each pan into 28 pieces.

Calories: **120**   Protein: **6.6 g (22%)**   Carbohydrates: **14.3 g (48%)**   Sodium: **224 mg**
Total Fat: **4.4 g (33%)**   *Saturated Fat:* **2.0 g**   *Monounsaturated Fat:* **.6 g**   *Polyunsaturated Fat:* **.4 g**

❖ Empañadas—Mexican Cheese Turnovers

Creamy and spicy, these turnovers are wonderful for lunch or dinner. Serve them with cold or warmed salsa. See color plate **12**.

Portions per recipe: 75
Yield: 75 turnovers
Portion: 1 turnover
Serving utensil: spatula

Pan: 18″ × 26″ sheet pan
Oven temperature: 350° F
Time: 20 minutes

Ingredients	Amounts
Garlic cloves	2 oz.
Cilantro leaves and stems	3 oz.
Parsley leaves	2 oz.
Jalapeño peppers with seeds	2 oz.
Low-fat yogurt, drained 30 minutes	3 lb.
Cream cheese, softened	5 lb.
Eggs	12 oz.
Canned green chilies, diced	1 lb.
Chili salsa	8 oz.
Salt	½ oz.
Pastry dough	7 lb.

Procedure:

1. In food chopper or processor mince garlic, cilantro, parsley, and jalapeño pepper.
2. Place with other ingredients except dough into mixer bowl.
3. Beat until smooth.
4. Roll dough out to about ⅛″ thickness and cut dough into 5″ squares.
5. Place a #16 scoop of filling in center.
6. Brush edges of dough squares with egg wash and fold into triangles.
7. Press edges down with a fork and pierce tops. Brush with egg wash.
8. Place on sheet pans and bake at 350° F for 20 minutes.

NOTE: Form dough into ⅛-inch-thick circles (1.5 ounces) and press close with turnover machine if available, or fold and close pastry edges with a fork.

Calories: **326**   Protein: **6.7 g (8%)**   Carbohydrates: **22.2 g (27%)**   Sodium: **176 mg**
Total Fat: **23.7 g (65%)**   *Saturated Fat:* **10.0 g**   *Monounsaturated Fat:* **10.6 g**   *Polyunsaturated Fat:* **2.1 g**

❖ Garden Lasagna

Lasagna noodles are layered with three kinds of cheese, fresh vegetables, and a bechamel sauce. This is labor intensive, but well worth the effort. Prepare the separate layers and set up an assembly line for large productions.

PRODUCTION NOTE: Replace the more difficult to handle lasagna noodles with pot noodles and just smooth the noodles into layers.

Portions per recipe: *96*	Pan: *12″ × 20″ × 2″*
Yield: *4 pans*	Temperature: *350° F*
Portion: *7 ounces (3″ × 3.3″ piece)*	Time: *35 minutes*
Serving utensil: *spatula*	

Ingredients	Amounts
Water, lightly salted	40 lb.
Lasagna noodles	5 lb.

Filling

Ingredients	Amounts
Low-fat ricotta cheese	10 lb.
Part-skim mozzarella cheese, shredded	5 lb.
Parmesan cheese, grated	8 oz.
Skim milk	2 lb.
Eggs	1 lb.
Cinnamon	$1/16$ oz.
White pepper	$1/8$ oz.
Basil, crushed	$1/4$ oz.
Italian parsley, minced	4 oz.

Sauce

Ingredients	Amounts
Vegetable oil	4 oz.
All-purpose flour	6 oz.
Salt	$1/2$ oz.
Nutmeg	$1/8$ oz.
Low-fat milk	8 lb.

Vegetables

Ingredients	Amounts
Olive oil	1 oz.
Garlic cloves, crushed	1 oz.
Broccoli florets and peeled stems, sliced	8 lb.
Zucchini, coarsely shredded	6 lb.
Carrots, coarsely shredded	4 lb.

(continued)

Procedure:

1. Bring lightly salted water to a rolling boil and add lasagna noodles a few at a time. This keeps noodles in one piece.

2. Cook for 7 to 8 minutes. Drain and cover with cold water.

3. Beat together cheeses, eggs, milk, spices, and herbs.

4. To make a bechamel sauce heat oil and stir in flour, salt, and nutmeg until smooth, 2 to 3 minutes. Do not brown.

5. Slowly stir in the milk in a thin stream. Stir until thickened.

6. Stir-fry garlic and vegetables in olive oil for 5 minutes. Place in bowl.

7. To assemble, place 6 to 7 cooked noodles in a pan, layer 1½ pounds of cheese on top of the noodles, and cover cheese with 1½ pounds of vegetables. Repeat twice.

8. Top with 6 to 7 more noodles and cover with 1 quart of sauce.

9. Bake at 350° F for 35 minutes. Let settle for 20 minutes before cutting each pan into 24 pieces.

Calories: **288**   Protein: **20.5 g (29%)**   Carbohydrates: **28.6 g (40%)**   Sodium: **295 mg**

Total Fat: **11.6 g (36%)**   *Saturated Fat:* **6.2 g**   *Monounsaturated Fat:* **3.4 g**   *Polyunsaturated Fat:* **1.1 g**

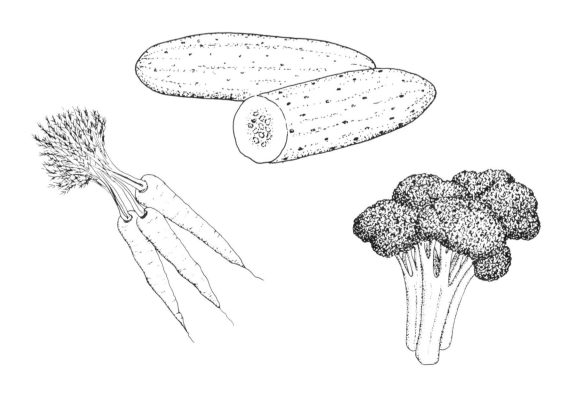

❖ Gateau of Crepes

This is a simpler, fat-modified version of a Julia Child recipe.

PRODUCTION NOTES: Twenty-four crepes are needed for each pan. Make your own (see recipe on page 39) or use prepared frozen crepes. For a less labor-intensive version fold all vegetables into cheese mixture and layer with crepes. Not quite as pretty to look at, but quicker to make.

Portions per recipe: *112*
Yield: *4 pans*
Portion: *6 ounces (3" × 2.9" piece)*
Serving utensil: *spatula*

Pan: *12" × 20" × 2"*
Oven temperature: *325° F*
Time: *45 minutes*

Ingredients

Ingredients	Amounts
Frozen broccoli, chopped	16 lb.
Carrots, shredded	8 lb.
Scallions, chopped	2 lb.
Lemon juice	4 oz.
Low-fat ricotta cheese	6 lb.
Low-fat yogurt	2 lb.
Eggs	4 lb.
Low-fat milk	2 lb.
Nutmeg	1/8 oz.
White pepper	1/4 oz.
Salt	1 oz.
Swiss cheese, shredded	2 lb.
Crepes (cooked)	4 lb. 8 oz.

Procedure:

1. Steam broccoli at 5# pressure for 4 minutes in perforated pan. Drain.
2. Cook shredded carrots with scallions and lemon juice for 5 minutes.
3. In a mixer bowl beat together ricotta, eggs, yogurt, milk, and spices.
4. Fold in shredded Swiss cheese.
5. Place 8 crepes in bottom of ungreased pan.
6. Cover with 2 pounds of broccoli. Top broccoli with 3 cups of cheese mixture.
7. Layer 8 more crepes on top. Cover with 2½ pounds of carrots.
8. Top carrots with 3 cups cheese mixture and another layer of crepes.
9. Cover crepes with 2 pounds of broccoli. Pour 2 pints of cheese mixture over broccoli, starting around the edges of pan. Make sure the broccoli is completely covered.
10. Bake at 325° F for 45 minutes. Cut each into 28 servings.

Calories: **171**   Protein: **11.3 g (26%)**   Carbohydrates: **13.2 g (31%)**   Sodium: **236 mg**
Total Fat: **8.9 g (46%)**   Saturated Fat: **4.0 g**   Monounsaturated Fat: **1.3 g**   Polyunsaturated Fat: **1.3 g**

❖ Italian Ricotta Torte

This dish evokes the flavor of pizza in a quiche filled with ricotta and sautéed peppers.

Portions per recipe: 60	*Pan:* 9" pie pan
Yield: 10 pies	*Oven temperature:* 300° F
Portion: ⅙ pie	*Time:* 50 minutes
Serving utensil: pie server	

Ingredients   *Amounts*

Ingredients	Amounts
Olive oil	1 oz.
Garlic cloves, crushed	2 oz.
Red onions, thinly sliced	1 lb. 8 oz.
Green bell peppers, seeded and thinly sliced	5 lb.
Red bell peppers, seeded and thinly sliced	2 lb.
Yellow bell peppers, seeded and thinly sliced	2 lb.
Oregano, crushed	¼ oz.
Basil, crushed	⅛ oz.
Ricotta cheese	8 lb.
Eggs	1 lb. 4 oz.
Skim milk	2 lb.
Salt	½ oz.
Black pepper	⅛ oz.
Italian parsley, minced	8 oz.
Pastry shells, 10" bottoms, prebaked	5 lb.

Procedure:

1. Heat olive oil with garlic. Add onions, peppers, and spices and sauté for 5 minutes.
2. In mixing bowl beat together ricotta, eggs, milk, salt, and pepper at low speed.
3. Fold in sautéed vegetables and minced parsley.
4. Pour 2 pounds of cheese filling into prebaked shell.
5. Bake at 300° F for 50 minutes or until done. Cut into 6 pieces.

Calories: **302**   Protein: **11.4 g (15%)**   Carbohydrates: **23.6 g (31%)**   Sodium: **181 mg**
Total Fat: **20.3 g (59%)**   *Saturated Fat:* **8.1 g**   *Monounsaturated Fat:* **7.4 g**   *Polyunsaturated Fat:* **2.0 g**

❖ Mexican Rice

Layered like lasagna but very easy to assemble, this is a filling and satisfying dish. It can also be made with brown rice.

Portions per recipe: 56
Yield: 2 pans
Portion: 7 ounces (3″ × 2.9″ piece)
Serving utensil: spatula

Pan: 12″ × 20″ × 2″
Oven temperature: 325° F
Time: 30–40 minutes

Ingredients

Ingredients	Amounts
Converted rice	3 lb.
Water	6 lb.
Salt	¼ oz.
Egg whites	1 lb.
Jalapeño peppers, chopped	1 oz.
Sour cream	2 lb.
Low-fat yogurt	3 lb.
Salsa picante	2 lb.
Canned vegetarian refried beans	4 lb.
Cumin	¼ oz.
Canned tomatoes, diced	3 lb. 3 oz.
Canned green chilies, diced	14 oz.
Monterey Jack cheese, shredded	2 lb.

Procedure:

1. Steam or boil rice until barely tender.
2. Beat egg whites with chopped jalapeño, sour cream, yogurt, and salsa.
3. Mix beans with cumin, tomatoes and green chilies.
4. Oil pan lightly and spread 2 pounds of cooked rice over bottom of pan.
5. Cover with 1 quart of sour cream sauce. Top with 4 pounds of beans.
6. Sprinkle with 1 pound of shredded cheese. Cover with 2 pounds of cooked rice.
7. Top rice with 1 quart of sour cream sauce. Start pouring around edges.
8. Bake at 325° F for 30 minutes or until set. Cut each pan into 28 pieces.

Calories: **260**   Protein: **18.3 g (28%)**   Carbohydrates: **29.8 g (45%)**   Sodium: **572 mg**
Total Fat: **9.3 g (32%)**   *Saturated Fat:* **5.0 g**   *Monounsaturated Fat:* **2.8 g**   *Polyunsaturated Fat:* **.4 g**

❖ Mushroom and Broccoli Cheese Spaetzle

A favorite in southern Germany, this version is from Bavaria.

PRODUCTION NOTES: The spaetzle are a little time consuming to make, but well worth the effort. They are like a lumpy fresh pasta. Do not attempt to serve too many portions at one time, since to prepare 5 pounds of spaetzle takes about 15 minutes of scraping and cutting. Spaetzle can also be served as a starch by themselves. This recipe makes 5 pounds of cooked spaetzle. They can be made ahead of time and refrigerated for 24 hours. They also freeze well.

Portions per recipe: *28*	Pan: *12″ × 20″ × 2″*
Yield: *1 pan*	Oven temperature: *325° F*
Portion: *6 ounces*	Time: *10 minutes*
Serving utensil: *spoon*	

Ingredients / Amounts

Dough

Ingredients	Amounts
Eggs	14 oz.
Low-fat milk	1 lb.
Salt	½ oz.
Nutmeg	⅛ oz.
Flour	2 lb.

Filling

Ingredients	Amounts
Butter	2 oz.
Spanish onions, thinly sliced	1 lb.
Mushrooms, sliced	1 lb.
Parsley, minced	2 oz.
Swiss cheese, shredded	8 oz.
Broccoli florets	4 lb.
Swiss cheese, shredded	8 oz.

Procedure:

1. Beat eggs with milk, salt, nutmeg, and flour to a smooth, soft dough.
2. Beat until dough feels elastic.
3. In a small kettle bring salted water to a simmer. Add 1 teaspoon of oil to prevent foaming.
4. Wet a narrow cutting board and place 1 pound of dough near edge.
5. Dip a knife into boiling water and scrape ¼″ thick by 2″ wide strips of dough into boiling water. (See photo on page 273.)

6. Spaetzle will rise to the surface when done. Skim with colander and drain.

7. Heat butter in skillet and sauté onions and mushrooms until golden and soft. Toss with parsley, Swiss cheese, and spaetzle.

8. Steam broccoli until barely tender. Place in three long rows evenly in buttered pan.

9. Spoon 2 rows of spaetzle between broccoli. Top with grated cheese and cook briefly under broiler or bake at 325° F until cheese melts.

Calories: **227**   Protein: **11.7 g (20%)**   Carbohydrates: **29.1 g (51%)**   Sodium: **276 mg**
Total Fat: **8.0 g (32%)**   *Saturated Fat:* **4.6 g**   *Monounsaturated Fat:* **1.9 g**   *Polyunsaturated Fat:* **.7 g**

Spaetzle noodle dough is pushed into boiling water.

❖ Noodle Kugel

Not quite the traditional noodle kugel, but just as delicious. It is very high in protein but, alas, also in fat. The kugel can be enjoyed with vegetables for lunch or dinner, or with stewed fruit, applesauce, or fresh raspberry sauce as a warm dessert. If you plan to serve it for dessert increase the sugar to one pound and substitute cinnamon for paprika.

Portions per recipe: 120
Yield: 4 pans
Portion: 6 ounces
Serving utensil: 4-ounce ladle

Pan: 12″ × 20″ × 2″
Oven temperature: 325° F
Time: 25 minutes

Ingredients

Ingredients	Amounts	
Egg noodles, medium-size	10 lb.	
Water	40 lb.	
Cream cheese, at room temperature	6 lb.	
Low-fat cottage cheese	15 lb.	
Sour cream	2 lb.	8 oz.
Low-fat yogurt	7 lb.	8 oz.
Egg whites		8 oz.
Salt		½ oz.
Granulated sugar		2 oz.
Hungarian paprika		⅛ oz.

Procedure:

1. Cook noodles in boiling water until almost done. Drain.
2. Beat cheeses with sour cream, yogurt, egg whites, salt, and sugar.
3. Fold in cooked noodles. Blend well.
4. Oil pan lightly and pour in approximately 14 pounds of kugel mixture.
5. Dust the top with paprika and bake at 325° F for 25 minutes.

Calories: **316**   Protein: **16.7 g (21%)**   Carbohydrates: **32.4 g (41%)**   Sodium: **376 mg**

Total Fat: **13.0 g (37%)**   *Saturated Fat:* **7.2 g**   *Monounsaturated Fat:* **3.7 g**   *Polyunsaturated Fat:* **.8 g**

❖ Noodles Florentine

A very creamy casserole loaded with iron-rich spinach.

Portions per recipe: 60
Yield: 2 pans
Portion: 6 ounces
Serving utensil: 4-ounce ladle

Pan: 12″ × 20″ × 2″
Oven temperature: 350° F
Time: 20 minutes

Ingredients / Amounts

Ingredients	Amounts	
Egg noodles, medium	5 lb.	
Water	16 lb.	
Olive oil		1 oz.
Spanish onions, chopped	1 lb.	
Garlic cloves, crushed		1 oz.
Frozen chopped spinach, thawed	7 lb.	8 oz.
White pepper		⅛ oz.
Tarragon, crushed		1/16 oz.
Nutmeg, grated		⅛ oz.
Lemon juice		8 oz.
Low-fat yogurt	4 lb.	
Cornstarch		2 oz.
Swiss cheese, shredded	6 lb.	
Sour cream	1 lb.	
Bread crumbs, toasted	2 lb.	
Parmesan cheese, grated		2 oz.

Procedure:

1. Cook noodles in boiling water for 7 minutes. They must be undercooked.
2. Heat olive oil and sauté onions, garlic, and spinach until most of the liquid has evaporated.
3. Turn off heat. Fold in spices, lemon juice, and cooked noodles.
4. Mix yogurt with cornstarch, Swiss cheese, sour cream, and toasted bread crumbs.
5. Fold into spinach noodle mixture and blend well.
6. Pour approximately 12 pounds of mixture into oiled pan. Sprinkle with 1 ounce of parmesan cheese.
7. Bake at 350° F for 20 minutes.

Calories: **434** Protein: **23.6 g (22%)** Carbohydrates: **45.1 g (41%)** Sodium: **197 mg**
Total Fat: **17.7 g (37%)** *Saturated Fat:* **10.0 g** *Monounsaturated Fat:* **5.2 g** *Polyunsaturated Fat:* **1.2 g**

❖ Penne Selvaggio—Pasta with Wild Mushrooms
Michela's

This unusual pasta dish was part of the "Taste of Europe" special event. I have added fresh porcini mushrooms, which are readily available and more reasonably priced than oyster or shitake mushrooms. American goat cheese is excellent and readily available.

PRODUCTION NOTE: The distinct flavor of this sauce is derived from cooking the onions slowly in one thin layer and turning them only once to allow the natural sugars to caramelize; use the tilting skillet or the griddle.

Portions per recipe: 36	*Pan: 12″ × 20″ × 4″*
Yield: 1 pan	*Skillet temperature: 300° F*
Portion: 7 ounces	*Time: 15 minutes*
Serving utensil: 4-ounce ladle (2 dips)	

Ingredients	Amounts
Olive oil	½ oz.
Spanish onions, thinly sliced	1 lb.
Unsalted butter	2 oz.
Porcini mushrooms, thinly sliced	1 lb.
Oyster mushrooms, quartered	5 oz.
Shitake mushrooms	5 oz.
Garlic cloves, crushed	1 oz.
Salt	1 oz.
Freshly ground black pepper	¼ oz.
Fresh goat cheese	10 oz.
Light cream	1 lb.
Penne noodles	5 lb.
Water	16 lb.

Procedure:

1. Cook onions according to production note for about 15 minutes at 300° F in a tilting skillet.
2. Remove and reserve. Add butter to skillet.
3. Sauté the sliced mushrooms with garlic until golden.
4. Stir in salt, pepper, goat cheese, and light cream. Lower heat.
5. Keep sauce warm.
6. Cook penne in lightly salted water that has reached a rolling boil until al dente.
7. Drain briefly and pour into pan. Fold in about 1 quart of sauce. Serve.

Calories: **293**   Protein: **18.5 g (25%)**   Carbohydrates: **49.9 g (68%)**   Sodium: **323 mg**

Total Fat: **4.8 g (15%)**   *Saturated Fat:* **3.0 g**   *Monounsaturated Fat:* **1.0 g**   *Polyunsaturated Fat:* **.7 g**

❖ Pizza Rustica with Spinach

A tasty, double pie crust, deep dish pizza. This dish was inspired by a recipe from *The Vegetarian Epicure*, by Anna Thomas. The pie reheats and freezes extremely well.

Portions per recipe: *144*
Yield: *24 pies*
Portion: *⅙ pie*
Serving utensil: *pie server*

Pan: *9″ pie pan*
Oven temperature: *350° F*
Time: *35 minutes*

Ingredients | Amounts

Ingredients	Amounts
Olive oil	1 oz.
Garlic cloves, crushed	2 oz.
Frozen chopped spinach, thawed	10 lb.
Eggs	3 lb.
Part skim ricotta cheese	12 lb.
Canned Italian tomatoes, drained	12 lb. 12 oz.
Green bell peppers, diced	5 lb.
Parmesan cheese, grated	8 oz.
Oregano, crushed	¼ oz.
Low-fat mozzarella, shredded	6 lb.
10″ pastry shell bottom, pre-baked	12 lb.
10″ pastry shell top, raw dough	12 lb.

Procedure:

1. Heat olive oil with garlic, add spinach, and cook for 10 minutes. Cool.
2. In a large mixing bowl beat eggs with ricotta. Fold in spinach.
3. Crush canned tomatoes with your hands and fold in diced bell peppers, parmesan, and oregano.
4. Spread 1 pound of spinach mixture on the prebaked pie bottom.
5. Top with a cup of crushed tomatoes. Sprinkle with 4 ounces of mozzarella.
6. Place raw pastry shell on top. It is not necessary to crimp it.
7. Bake at 325° F for 35 minutes.
8. Let rest for 20 minutes before cutting into 6 pieces.

Calories: **486**   Protein: **16.4 g (14%)**   Carbohydrates: **38.6 g (32%)**   Sodium: **272 mg**
Total Fat: **29.6 g (54%)**   *Saturated Fat:* **9.8 g**   *Monounsaturated Fat:* **15.6 g**   *Polyunsaturated Fat:* **3.2 g**

❖ Polenta with Creamed Mushrooms   *Kamman*

Creamy French polenta from the Savoie was another triumph of the fabulous French feast.

PRODUCTION NOTE: To avoid lumps, mix corn meal with water (slurry) before stirring it into the boiling water or broth.

Portions per recipe: *56*
Yield: *2 pans*
Portion: *8 ounces*
Serving utensil: *spoon*

Pan: *12″ × 20″ × 2″*
Oven temperature: *325° F*
Time: *12 minutes*

Ingredients

Ingredients	Amounts	
Yellow corn meal	3 lb.	8 oz.
Water or vegetarian stock	16 lb.	
Salt		1 oz.
White pepper		1/16 oz.
Nutmeg		1/8 oz.
Unsalted butter		4 oz.
Mushrooms, cleaned and sliced	6 lb.	
Garlic cloves, crushed		1 oz.
Rosemary, chopped		1/2 oz.
Parsley, minced		3 oz.
Light cream	4 lb.	
Fontina cheese, 1-ounce slices	3 lb.	

Procedure:

1. Mix corn meal with enough cold water to make a slurry.
2. Bring rest of water with salt and spices to a boil in a kettle.
3. Add corn meal to boiling water, stirring until thickened.
4. Mixture should bubble sluggishly. Keep warm.
5. Heat butter in tilting skillet and sauté mushrooms for 5 minutes.
6. Add garlic, rosemary, parsley, and cream and simmer uncovered until mixture has reduced enough to coat the back of a spoon.
7. Butter pan lightly and pour 4 pounds of polenta into pan and spread to a ¾″ thickness.
8. Cover with 2 pounds of mushroom sauce. Top with 12 slices of fontina cheese.
9. Repeat layers once and bake at 325° F for 12 minutes or until cheese has melted.

Calories: **289**   Protein: **10.5 g (15%)**   Carbohydrates: **26.0 g (36%)**   Sodium: **461 mg**
Total Fat: **16.7 g (52%)**   *Saturated Fat:* **9.7 g**   *Monounsaturated Fat:* **4.7 g**   *Polyunsaturated Fat:* **1.2 g**

❖ Spanakopita—Greek Spinach Strudel

This classic spinach strudel from Greece can be eaten hot or cold. The fat content in this recipe is greatly reduced by layering the phyllo so it is fan shaped and hanging over the sides of the pan instead of separating each phyllo layer with melted butter.

PRODUCTION NOTE: Thaw phyllo pastry in the refrigerator overnight. Score the portions before baking for a better appearance.

Portions per recipe: *56*
Yield: *2 pans*
Portion: *5 ounces (3" × 2.9" piece)*
Serving utensil: *spatula*

Pan: *12" × 20" × 2"*
Oven temperature: *350° F*
Time: *45 minutes*

Ingredients

Ingredients	Amounts
Spanish onions, diced	1 lb.
Garlic cloves, crushed	2 oz.
Spinach, frozen, chopped	5 lb.
Eggs, beaten	5 lb.
Feta cheese, rinsed and crumbled	4 lb.
Nutmeg	⅛ oz.
Phyllo pastry (14" × 18" size)	2 lb. 8 oz.
Butter blend, melted (60% margarine/40% butter)	4 oz.

Procedure:

1. Mix onions, garlic, spinach, eggs, feta cheese, and nutmeg.
2. Brush pan with melted butter blend.
3. Place 10 sheets of phyllo, fan-like, overhanging sides of pan.
4. Drizzle with ½ ounce of butter blend. Repeat with 10 more sheets.
5. Pour 7½ pounds of spinach filling into each pan.
6. Fold overhanging sheets toward center of pan. Brush with butter blend.
7. Cover mixture with 6 squarely placed phyllo sheets. Brush very lightly with butter blend.
8. Score portions into 28 pieces with a sharp knife.
9. Bake at 350° F for 45 minutes, cut and serve.

Calories: **231**   Protein: **10.8 g (19%)**   Carbohydrates: **17.2 g (30%)**   Sodium: **172 mg**
Total Fat: **12.8 g (50%)**   *Saturated Fat:* **6.7 g**   *Monounsaturated Fat:* **2.5 g**   *Polyunsaturated Fat:* **1.0 g**

❖ Stuffed Zucchini

A light dish for hot summer days. Serve stuffed zucchini with polenta and chunky marinara sauce.

Portions per recipe: *100*
Yield: *200 halves*
Portion: *2 halves*
Serving utensil: *spatula*

Pan: *12" × 20" × 2"*
Oven temperature: *325° F*
Time: *20 minutes*

Ingredients | Amounts

Ingredients	Amounts
Zucchini, medium size	37 lb.
Garlic cloves, crushed	4 oz.
Spanish onions	2 lb.
Olive oil	2 oz.
Basil	¼ oz.
Marjoram	⅛ oz.
Black pepper	¼ oz.
Low-fat mozzarella, shredded	4 lb.
Fontina cheese, shredded	2 lb.
Parmesan cheese, grated	8 oz.
Bread crumbs	1 lb. 4 oz.

Procedure:

1. Trim stem end and cut zucchini in half (boats). Scoop out the soft insides with a sharp spoon.
2. Chop zucchini pulp with garlic and onions in food processor or chopper.
3. Heat olive oil and sauté chopped vegetables with spices until soft.
4. Cool mixture slightly and blend in cheeses and bread crumbs.
5. Stuff zucchini halves with about 2 ounces of stuffing.
6. Place halves in oiled pan in rows. Pour ½ cup of water in pan and bake uncovered at 325° F for 20 minutes.

Calories: **170**   Protein: **10.6 g (25%)**   Carbohydrates: **12.0 g (29%)**   Sodium: **223 mg**

Total Fat: **7.5 g (40%)**   *Saturated Fat:* **4.2 g**   *Monounsaturated Fat:* **2.4 g**   *Polyunsaturated Fat:* **.4 g**

1. Italian appetizers tempt guests for a festive reception. Clockwise from the top: bread sticks, spicy mushrooms, crostini fontina, mozzarella and tomato, marinated kalamata olives, chilled calamari, marinated green olives, antipasti, roasted peppers, prosciutto e melone, and caponata. Pages **498, 73, 81, 65, 68, 58, 67, 53, 72, 71, 57**.

2. Green and white jade salad, cold Sichuan noodle salad, and hot and sour cucumber salad, are three Chinese dishes from the Feast Fit for the Last Emperor of China. Pages **374, 368, 375**.

3. Grilled veal provolone and mushrooms rosemary. Page **154**.

4. Lebani on a garlic bagel. Page **47**.

5. This Scandanavian fish soup is a full course meal. Page **130**.

6. Pork loin schnitzel are served with a slice of lemon. Page **170**.

7. Flammkuchen is an Alsatian ham and onion pizza. Page **157**.

8A. Sausage Tuscany can be served over pasta or in a sub roll. In New Hampshire they sell this type of sandwich at autumn country fairs. Page **172**.

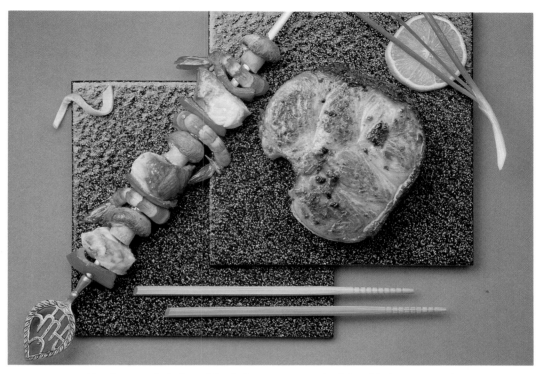

8B. Fresh tuna kabobs with shrimp are wonderful grilled or broiled as is the marinated mako shark steak. Pages **231, 235**.

9. Coq au Riesling from Alsace-Lorraine—chicken pieces cooked in white wine with mushrooms, small onions, and thyme. Page **192**.

10. A cold chicken dish that can go on picnics. Page **200**.

11. A velvety smooth souffle best served with colorful, crisp vegetables such as asparagus or a sauté of peppers. Page **264**.

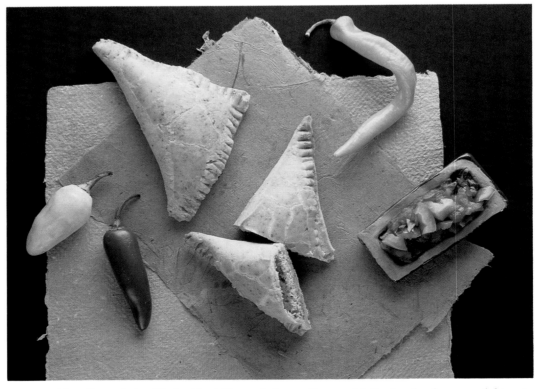

12. Empañadas filled with chilies and cheese. Serve with fresh salsa for a special treat. Page **266**.

13. Black beans Louisiana with basmati rice. Page **299**.

14. Pasta and lentils are delicious warm or cold. Page **308**.

15. The garden sandwich is popular for lunch and supper. Page **341**.

16. A Moroccan diffa that includes djej mechoui (roasted chicken legs) with couscous and spicy vegetables surrounded by (from left to right) "Midway"olives, orange slices with ras el hanout, red pepper and preserved lemon peel salad, cucumber salad, lamb tagine smothered with olives, preserved lemons, and kisra. Pages **206, 437, 69, 519, 379, 187, 467, 493**.

❖ Tiropita—Greek Three Cheese Strudel

A rich cheese pastry, absolutely delicious, but not for people who have to watch their cholesterol intake.

PRODUCTION NOTE: Tiropita and spanakopita are ideal for deli counter sales and take-out operations. They can be eaten at room temperature or reheated quickly for individual orders. Tiropita and spanakopita are easy to take on picnics and go well with any other form of al fresco dining.

Portions per recipe: 56
Yield: 2 pans
Portion: 5 ounces (3" × 2.9" piece)
Serving utensil: spatula

Pan: 12" × 20" × 2"
Oven temperature: 350° F
Time: 30–40 minutes

Ingredients	Amounts	
Garlic cloves, crushed		2 oz.
Fresh parsley, stems removed		8 oz.
Scallions		8 oz.
Fresh rosemary, leaves only		1 oz.
Feta cheese, rinsed and crumbled	4 lb.	
Low-fat ricotta cheese	4 lb.	
Parmesan cheese, grated		12 oz.
Eggs, beaten	6 lb.	
White pepper		1/16 oz.
Phyllo pastry (14" × 18")	2 lb.	8 oz.
Butter blend		4 oz.

Procedure:

1. In food chopper or processor mince garlic, parsley, scallions, and rosemary.
2. Mix cheeses with eggs, herbs, and pepper.
3. Brush pan with melted butter blend.
4. Place 10 sheets of phyllo, fan-like, overhanging sides of pan.
5. Drizzle with ½ ounce of butter blend. Repeat with 10 more sheets.
6. Pour 7½ pounds of cheese filling into each pan.
7. Fold overhanging sheets toward center of pan. Brush with butter blend.
8. Cover mixture with 6 squarely placed phyllo sheets. Brush very lightly with butter blend.
9. Score with a sharp knife into 28 portions per pan.
10. Bake at 350° F for 30–40 minutes.

Calories: **284**   Protein: **18.4 g (24%)**   Carbohydrates: **18.4 g (24%)**   Sodium: **339 mg**
Total Fat: **18.0 g (52%)**   *Saturated Fat:* **9.0 g**   *Monounsaturated Fat:* **3.4 g**   *Polyunsaturated Fat:* **1.3 g**

❖ Tomato Eggplant Casserole

This colorful eggplant casserole is a variation of the familiar eggplant parmigiana and was inspired by a recipe and picture in *The Victory Garden Cookbook*, by Marian Morash, published by Knopf (1982).

PRODUCTION NOTES: Grill the slices of eggplant on both sides until they are almost cooked. They will not soften much more during baking. The size of the eggplant slices and tomatoes should not exceed 2 inches, which is the depth of the pan.

Portions per recipe: 48	*Pan: 12″ × 20″ × 2″*
Yield: 2 pans	*Oven temperature: 325° F*
Portion: 5 ounces	*Time: 35 minutes*
Serving utensil: spatula	

Ingredients	Amounts
Olive oil	1 oz.
Spanish onions, thinly sliced	5 lb.
Garlic cloves, crushed	1 oz.
Italian parsley, minced	4 oz.
Eggplant, unpeeled, sliced	8 lb.
Basil, crushed	⅛ oz.
Oregano, crushed	¼ oz.
Salt	½ oz.
Black pepper	¼ oz.
Tomatoes, sliced	3 lb.
Monterey jack cheese, 1-ounce slices	3 lb.
Provolone, 1-ounce slices	1 lb. 8 oz.

Procedure:

1. Heat olive oil and sauté onions with garlic until soft and golden.
2. Mix in parsley.
3. Cut large eggplant slices in half, leave small ones whole.
4. Grill slices on lightly oiled grill for 4 to 5 minutes on each side.
5. Mix basil, oregano, salt, and pepper and sprinkle on eggplant slices.
6. Cover bottom of pan with 1 pound of onions.
7. Cut cheese slices in half.
8. Stand slices almost upright, lean them first against the pan and then against each other, make 3 rows of eggplant, tomato, eggplant, alternating the two cheeses between rows. Repeat until pan is full.
9. Arrange 1 pound of onion mixture between rows.
10. Bake at 325° F for 35 minutes.

Calories: **198**   Protein: **15.7 g (31%)**   Carbohydrates: **9.1 g (18%)**   Sodium: **285 mg**

Total Fat: **13.2 g (60%)**   *Saturated Fat:* **7.0 g**   *Monounsaturated Fat:* **4.2 g**   *Polyunsaturated Fat:* **.5 g**

Serve this layered tomato eggplant casserole with rice.

❖ Tortellini di Fiesoli

This dish was inspired by a memorable meal in La Terrazza in Fiesoli while overlooking the lovely Tuscan hills.

PRODUCTION NOTES: For large numbers, cook fresh or frozen tortellini in 20-pound batches. Do not use a dried product. Dried tortellini are only good when cooked in a rich chicken or vegetable broth.

Portions per recipe: 100
Yield: 3 pans
Portion: 5 ounces
Serving utensil: 4-ounce ladle

Pan: 12″ × 20″ × 2″
Time: 12 minutes

Ingredients	Amounts	
Sauce		
Margarine		6 oz.
All-purpose flour		6 oz.
Vegetarian stock	6 lb.	
Tomato puree	3 lb.	
Light cream	1 lb.	
Salt		1 oz.
White pepper		1/8 oz.
Basil, crushed		1/4 oz.
Tortellini		
Olive oil		1 oz.
Garlic cloves, crushed		1 oz.
Red pepper flakes		1/8 oz.
Green bell peppers, cut into strips	2 lb.	
Red bell peppers, cut into strips	2 lb.	
Small zucchini, sliced 1/4″ thick	5 lb.	
White cheese tortellini	5 lb.	
Green cheese tortellini	5 lb.	
Water, lightly salted	40 lb.	
Parmesan cheese		3 oz.

Procedure:

1. Make a white sauce by melting the margarine and cooking the flour in it for 2 to 3 minutes. Do not brown.
2. Stir in the stock and bring to a simmer. Add tomato puree, cream, salt, pepper, and basil.
3. Heat olive oil with garlic. Sauté peppers and zucchini for 5 minutes.
4. Cook the tortellini in boiling water for about 12 minutes. Drain.

5. Toss tortellini with vegetables and sauce.
6. Ladle into serving pans and sprinkle each pan with 1 ounce parmesan cheese.

Calories: **151**   Protein: **7.7 g (20%)**   Carbohydrates: **16.0 g (42%)**   Sodium: **236 mg**
Total Fat: **7.7 g (45%)**   *Saturated Fat:* **1.4 g**   *Monounsaturated Fat:* **3.1 g**   *Polyunsaturated Fat:* **1.4 g**

❖ Tortellini Gratinati *Romagnoli*

If you like pasta Alfredo, you'll like this entrée. It was very popular at the Romagnolis' "Festa Italiana" celebration.

Portions per recipe: *120*
Yield: *4 pans*
Portion: *6 ounces*
Serving utensil: *4-ounce ladle*

Pan: *12″ × 20″ × 2″*
Oven temperature: *325° F*
Time: *7 minutes*

Ingredients

Ingredients	Amounts
Heavy cream	4 lb.
Light cream	8 lb.
Parmesan cheese, grated	1 lb. 4 oz.
Unsalted butter	6 oz.
White pepper	¼ oz.
Nutmeg	¼ oz.
Fontina cheese, shredded	5 lb.
White cheese tortellini	20 lb.
Water, lightly salted	80 lb.

Procedure:

1. Bring the two creams to a boil. Slowly stir in the parmesan cheese.
2. Add the butter and stir vigorously. Beat in the spices. Turn off heat.
3. Slowly add all but 16 ounces of fontina to the sauce, stirring constantly.
4. Cook the tortellini in boiling water for 12 minutes.
5. Fold tortellini gently into cheese sauce. Place 8 quarts per pan.
6. Sprinkle each pan with 4 ounces of shredded fontina.
7. Bake at 325° F until cheese has melted, about 5 to 7 minutes.

Calories: **390**   Protein: **19.8 g (20%)**   Carbohydrates: **23.5 g (24%)**   Sodium: **435 mg**
Total Fat: **27.8 g (64%)**   *Saturated Fat:* **13.0 g**   *Monounsaturated Fat:* **9.2 g**   *Polyunsaturated Fat:* **3.0 g**

❖ Tortino di Verdure *Romagnoli*

The Romagnolis suggested this vegetarian entrée for "Festa Italiana." It is a special treat indeed, and a great side dish for banquets. Serve it with chicken or lamb.

PRODUCTION NOTES: In this dish it's advisable to salt the eggplant to extract some of the water before cooking. After 20 minutes rinse and drain the eggplant slices.

Portions per recipe: 56
Yield: 2 pans
Portion: 6 to 7 ounces (3" × 2.9" piece)
Serving utensil: spatula

Pan: 12" × 20" × 2"
Oven temperature: 325° F
Time: 50 minutes

Ingredients	Amounts		
Eggplant	4 lb.		
Bread crumbs	1 lb.	8 oz.	
Fresh basil, cut into thin shreds		2 oz.	
Italian parsley, minced		4 oz.	
Salt		1 oz.	
Black pepper		¼ oz.	
Unsalted butter		1 oz.	
Potatoes, peeled and thinly sliced	4 lb.		
Mozzarella cheese, shredded	1 lb.	8 oz.	
Eggs, beaten	1 lb.	8 oz.	
Zucchini, ¼" thick slices	4 lb.		
Canned Italian tomatoes	6 lb.	6 oz.	
Olive oil		1 oz.	

Procedure:

1. Cut eggplant lengthwise into ⅓" thick slices. Salt and drain.
2. Mix breadcrumbs with herbs and spices.
3. Butter sides and bottom of pans and coat heavily with crumbs.
4. Place a layer of eggplant slices in pan. Sprinkle with 2 ounces of crumbs.
5. Sprinkle with 6 ounces of cheese and drizzle with 6 ounces of beaten eggs.
6. Cover with a layer of potato slices, 2 ounces of crumbs, and 6 ounces of cheese.
7. Drizzle with 6 ounces of beaten eggs.
8. Cover with a layer of zucchini slices.
9. Drain the canned tomatoes. Crush tomatoes lightly and spread evenly on top of zucchini. Sprinkle with crumbs.
10. Drizzle with ½ ounce of olive oil. Bake at 325° F for 50 minutes. Test and bake until potatoes are fully cooked.

Calories: **142**   Protein: **7.7 g (22%)**   Carbohydrates: **15.1 g (42%)**   Sodium: **386 mg**
Total Fat: **5.3 g (33%)**   *Saturated Fat:* **2.1 g**   *Monounsaturated Fat:* **1.1 g**   *Polyunsaturated Fat:* **.3 g**

❖ Zucchini Frittata

This is essentially a baked zucchini omelet.

Portions per recipe: *42*
Yield: *2 pans*
Portion: *8 ounces (3" × 4" piece)*
Serving utensil: *spatula*

Pan: *12" × 20" × 2"*
Oven temperature: *325° F*
Time: *25 minutes*

Ingredients	Amounts
Olive oil	1 oz.
Garlic cloves, crushed	1 oz.
Spanish onions, thinly sliced	1 lb.
Zucchini, 1/4" thick slices	12 lb.
Oregano, crushed	1/8 oz.
Bread crumbs	4 oz.
Cheddar cheese, shredded	1 lb.
Low-fat mozzarella, shredded	1 lb.
Eggs	5 lb.
Skim milk	8 oz.
Salt	1/2 oz.
Black pepper	1/8 oz.
Nutmeg	1/16 oz.

Procedure:

1. Brush hot griddle with olive oil and stir-fry garlic, onions, and zucchini for 3 to 4 minutes. Sprinkle with oregano.

2. Brush pans with remaining olive oil and cover bottom with 2 ounces of crumbs.

3. Top with about 6 pounds of vegetables. Combine cheeses and sprinkle 1 pound over vegetables.

4. Beat eggs with milk and spices. Pour 3 pints over each pan.

5. Bake at 325° F for 25 minutes or until set. Cut each pan into 21 pieces.

Calories: **169**   Protein: **11.8 g (28%)**   Carbohydrates: **8.7 g (20%)**   Sodium: **337 mg**
Total Fat: **11.6 g (61%)**   *Saturated Fat:* **5.2 g**   *Monounsaturated Fat:* **2.5 g**   *Polyunsaturated Fat:* **1.0 g**

Tofu (Bean Curd)

❖

Tofu, or bean curd, is made from soy beans that have been soaked, pureed, cooked, and strained to make soy milk. The soy milk, in a process very similar to that used in making cheese, is curdled and pressed into cakes. In Japan (tofu) and in China (doufu), bean curd is a dietary staple. Many different types are available, from fresh to spiced, pressed, deep-fried, and freeze-dried.

The most common tofu types sold in America are silken, soft, firm, and extra firm. Tofu should be very fresh. It can be kept for about a week in the refrigerator submerged in fresh water. The water should be changed once or twice a day.

Nutritionally, tofu is packed with protein. It is not as low in fat as we might assume. For example, an average 2-ounce serving of very firm tofu (70 calories) contains 8 grams of protein, 4 grams of fat, and less than 1 gram of carbohydrates. This means that 50% of calories are from fat. The fat is however mostly polyunsaturated, and tofu is cholesterol free. Tofu is high in iron and provides good amounts of calcium. Although tofu is low in sodium, it is not really significant, because its bland taste means most preparation methods use soy sauce to give it flavor. It is easily digestable and is a dietary boon to people who are lactose intolerant.

Tofu acceptance is relatively low, but can be much improved with taste samples and educational tabletents.

Other tofu recipes are given in the index.

❖ Broccoli Tofu Lasagne

The tofu blends in so very well that it will be acceptable to everyone.

Portions per recipe: 56
Yield: 2 pans
Portion: 8 ounces (3″ × 2.9″ piece)
Serving utensil: spatula

Pan: 12″ × 20″ × 2″
Oven temperature: 325° F
Time: 30 minutes

Ingredients	Amounts	
Lasagna noodles	2 lb.	8 oz.
Water, lightly salted	24 lb.	
Olive oil		1 oz.
Garlic cloves, crushed		2 oz.
Red pepper flakes		$1/16$ oz.
Broccoli florets and peeled stems	6 lb.	
Canned roasted peppers, cut into strips	1 lb.	4 oz.
Salt		$1/2$ oz.
Soft tofu	4 lb.	
Parmesan cheese, grated		4 oz.
Part-skim ricotta cheese	1 lb.	
Provolone cheese, shredded	1 lb.	
Egg whites	1 lb.	
Nutmeg, grated		$1/16$ oz.
Canned Italian tomatoes	6 lb.	6 oz.
Oregano, crushed		$1/8$ oz.
Part-skim mozzarella, shredded	1 lb.	

Procedure:

1. Place a few lasagna noodles at a time into boiling salted water and cook for 10 minutes. Drain and cover with cold water.
2. Heat olive oil with garlic and pepper flakes and add broccoli.
3. Stir-fry for 4 minutes. Fold in roasted peppers and salt. Set aside.
4. Mix soft tofu with parmesan, ricotta, provolone, eggs, and nutmeg.
5. Drain tomatoes (reserve the liquid), crush lightly, and toss with oregano.
6. Assemble lasagna:
   a. Pour ½ cup of tomato liquid in pan. Place 6 cooked noodles on top.
   b. Spread 2 pounds of tofu mixture evenly over them, followed by 6 noodles.
   c. Top with 1½ pounds of vegetables and 6 noodles.
   d. Spread 2 pounds of tofu mixture over them, top with 1½ pounds of vegetables, and cover with 6 noodles.
   e. Cover with 2 pounds of tomatoes and bake at 325° F for 40 minutes.
7. Sprinkle with 4 ounces of shredded mozzarella and bake for 5 minutes or until cheese has melted.
8. Let rest for 20 minutes. Cut each pan into 28 pieces.

Calories: **178**   Protein: **11.9 g (27%)**   Carbohydrates: **19.2 g (44%)**   Sodium: **266 mg**
Total Fat: **6.0 g (30%)**   *Saturated Fat:* **3.1 g**   *Monounsaturated Fat:* **1.3 g**   *Polyunsaturated Fat:* **1.2 g**

❖ Home Style Spicy Bean Curd   *Hom*

Ken Hom suggested this vegetarian entrée for the "Feast Fit for the Last Emperor of China" event. It replaced our old hot and spicy tofu recipe, which was not too popular, and became the favorite tofu dish in our menu cycle. Serve this dish with steamed rice and stir-fried vegetables.

Portions per recipe: *50*
Yield: *1 pan*
Portion: *4 ounces*
Serving utensil: *3-ounce ladle*

Pan: *12″ × 20″ × 2″*
Cooking method: *Steam*
Time: *7 minutes*

Ingredients	Amounts
Vegetable oil	1 oz.
Ginger root, peeled and chopped	4 oz.
Garlic cloves, crushed	4 oz.
Chili bean sauce	6 oz.
Yellow bean sauce	6 oz.
Granulated sugar	1 oz.
Vegetarian stock	2 lb.
Dry sherry	8 oz.
Cornstarch	1 oz.
Soft tofu, 1″ cubes	10 lb.
Sesame oil	1 oz.
Scallions, finely chopped	8 oz.

Procedure:

1. Heat oil with ginger, garlic, and the bean sauces in a steam kettle.
2. Add sugar, stock, and sherry. Simmer for 5 minutes.
3. Dissolve cornstarch in a little cold vegetable stock. Stir in to thicken sauce.
4. Add tofu cubes and stir gently. Cook for 5 more minutes.
5. Drizzle with sesame seed oil and sprinkle with scallions.

Calories: **88**   Protein: **7.6 g (34%)**   Carbohydrates: **3.9 g (18%)**   Sodium: **7 mg**
Total Fat: **5.5 g (56%)**   *Saturated Fat:* **.9 g**   *Monounsaturated Fat:* **1.3 g**   *Polyunsaturated Fat:* **3.0 g**

Spicy bean curd is shown here with fried rice and whole wheat spaghetti.

❖ Hot and Sour Tofu Dumplings

Protein-packed vegetarian meatballs are simmered with vegetables in a Chinese hot and sour sauce. Serve with rice, soba noodles, and stir-fried vegetables.

Portions per recipe: 42
Yield: 210 dumplings
Portion: 5 dumplings
Serving utensil: 4-ounce ladle

Pan: 12" × 20" × 2"
Time: 12 minutes

Ingredients

	Amounts
Dumplings:	
Sesame oil	1 oz.
Chili bean sauce	2 oz.
Scallions, minced	8 oz.
Garlic cloves, crushed	2 oz.
Ginger root, peeled and chopped	2 oz.
Frozen peas	2 lb.
Soy sauce	1 oz.
Soft tofu	8 lb.
Eggs	12 oz.
Cornstarch	4 oz.
Sauce:	
Dried Chinese mushrooms	2 oz.
Sesame oil	1 oz.
Chili bean sauce	2 oz.
Scallions, 1" pieces	8 oz.
Carrots, very thinly sliced	1 lb.
Vegetarian broth or dashi	2 lb.
Cider vinegar	8 oz.
Soy sauce	2 oz.
Brown sugar	1 oz.
Dry sherry	4 oz.
Cornstarch	2 oz.
Fresh bean sprouts, rinsed	12 oz.
Fresh snow peas, trimmed	1 lb.

Procedure:

1. Heat sesame oil with chili bean sauce and sauté scallions, garlic, ginger, and peas. Cook for 5 minutes, then mash in food chopper or processor.

2. Beat together soy sauce, tofu, eggs, vegetable puree, and cornstarch. Refrigerate.

3. Soak mushrooms in water for 2 hours. Drain and slice into ¼" strips.

4. Heat sesame oil with chili bean sauce, add mushroom slices, scallions, and carrots. Stir-fry for 3 minutes.

5. Add broth, cider vinegar, soy sauce, and sugar and bring to a simmer.

6. Mix sherry and cornstarch and stir into hot liquid.

7. Pour 2 pints of vegetable sauce into pan. With a #40 scoop place 70 dumplings in sauce.

8. Cover and steam for 12 minutes at low pressure.

9. Fold in peas and bean sprouts.

Calories: **146**   Protein: **10.6 g (29%)**   Carbohydrates: **13.3 g (36%)**   Sodium: **166 mg**
Total Fat: **6.8 g (41%)**   *Saturated Fat:* **1.3 g**   *Monounsaturated Fat:* **1.5 g**   *Polyunsaturated Fat:* **3.2 g**

❖ Scrambled Tofu

This is a cousin to scrambled eggs with one difference: The tofu reduces the cholesterol content but not the fat. Serve this dish for brunch or as a simple dinner entrée with baked tomato halves. It should be served quite moist and, like scrambled eggs, must be prepared in small batches.

Portions per recipe: 24   *Pan: 12″ × 20″ × 2″–½ size*
Yield: 1 pan   *Griddle temperature: 325° F*
Portion: 4 ounces   *Time: 8–10 minutes*
Serving utensil: spatula

Ingredients | Amounts

Ingredients	*Amounts*
Vegetable oil	*1 oz.*
Mushrooms, washed and sliced	*8 oz.*
Green peppers, cut into thin strips	*1 lb.*
Italian plum tomatoes, seeded and diced	*1 lb. 8 oz.*
Soft tofu, crumbled	*3 lb.*
Soy sauce	*2 oz.*
Eggs, beaten	*1 lb.*

Procedure:

1. Heat griddle and spread with oil. Sauté mushrooms, peppers, and tomatoes.

2. Beat tofu with soy sauce and eggs.

3. Fold into vegetables and cook until set.

4. Garnish with thinly sliced scallions. Serve at once.

Calories: **92**   Protein: **7.4 g (32%)**   Carbohydrates: **3.8 g (17%)**   Sodium: **165 mg**
Total Fat: **5.9 g (57%)**   *Saturated Fat:* **.9 g**   *Monounsaturated Fat:* **1.0 g**   *Polyunsaturated Fat:* **2.5 g**

❖ Sichuan Tofu Triangles

Crisp brown tofu triangles are smothered with a hot and sour vegetable sauce. Serve with brown rice or Chinese noodles.

PRODUCTION NOTES: Use very firm tofu and press out additional liquid by the following method: Place tofu between two plastic cutting boards and weigh it down with a 12″×20″×4″ pan filled with water. Drain liquid for 30 minutes.

Portions per recipe: 30
Yield: 60 triangles
Portion: 2 triangles
Serving utensil: spatula

Pan: 12″×20″×2″
Skillet temperature: 350° F
Time: 8 minutes

Ingredients	Amounts	
Tofu, 1 pound cakes	6 lb.	
Peanut oil		1 oz.
Sesame oil		1 oz.
Ginger root, peeled and grated		1 oz.
Dry mustard		¼ oz.
Chili bean sauce		2 oz.
Green bell peppers, cut into thin strips	2 lb.	
Red bell peppers, cut into thin strips	1 lb.	
Scallions, 1″ pieces	2 lb.	
Dry sherry		8 oz.
Water	2 lb.	
Cider vinegar		4 oz.
Soy sauce		4 oz.
Cornstarch		2 oz.

Procedure:

1. Press tofu for 30 minutes. Cut each cake into 5 long slices, then cut each slice diagonally to form an elongated triangle.
2. Heat oils in tilting skillet and fry triangles until crisp, 4 minutes on each side.
3. Put 30 triangles into each pan. Keep warm.
4. Add ginger, mustard, and chili bean sauce to skillet and stir for 30 seconds.
5. Add peppers and scallions and stir-fry for 3 minutes. Add sherry.
6. Blend water, vinegar, soy sauce, and cornstarch, stir in, and bring to a simmer.
7. Pour 1 quart over tofu triangles.

Calories: **112** Protein: **8.5 g (30%)** Carbohydrates: **7.5 g (26%)** Sodium: **225 mg**
Total Fat: **6.4 g (51%)** Saturated Fat: **1.0 g** Monounsaturated Fat: **1.7 g** Polyunsaturated Fat: **3.2 g**

❖ Tofu Burger on a Whole Wheat Bun

A spicy tofu pattie is presented like a burger on a health bread bun.

PRODUCTION NOTES: Using the health bread dough (recipe on page 491) bake 9 dozen buns, 2 ounces of raw dough each, or use the type of bun available to you. Chili bean and hoisin sauces are available from Asian wholesale houses or retail markets.

Portions per recipe: *108*
Yield: *9 dozen*
Portion: *1 burger*
Serving utensil: *spatula*

Pan: *12" × 20" × 2"*
Griddle temperature: *325° F*
Time: *10 minutes*

Ingredients	Amounts
Peanut oil	2 oz.
Garlic cloves, crushed	1 oz.
Chili bean sauce	2 oz.
Hoisin sauce	4 oz.
Marjoram, crushed	¼ oz.
Spanish onions, chopped	3 lb.
Firm tofu, crumbled	15 lb.
Soy sauce	2 oz.
Tahini paste	8 oz.
Eggs	3 lb.
Bread crumbs	2 lb.
Health bread buns (1 dozen, 1½ ounces each)	10 lb. 4 oz.
Ripe tomatoes, sliced	5 lb.
Romaine lettuce, cut to fit buns	3 lb.

Procedure:

1. Heat oil with garlic. Stir in chili bean and hoisin sauce.
2. Add marjoram and onions. Stir-fry in spices until onions are soft.
3. Turn off heat. Fold in tofu.
4. Beat soy sauce with tahini and eggs in large mixing bowl.
5. Add tofu mixture and enough bread crumbs to form patties.
6. Form tofu into 3½ ounce patties with a #8 scoop on parchment-lined trays.
7. Grill patties at 325° F for 5 minutes on each side.
8. Place 15 bun bottoms in pan, and top with lettuce leaf.
9. Slide patties onto lettuce, add tomato slices, and cover with bun tops.

Calories: **232**   Protein: **12.3 g (21%)**   Carbohydrates: **31.6 g (54%)**   Sodium: **351 mg**
Total Fat: **7.6 g (29%)**   *Saturated Fat:* **1.1 g**   *Monounsaturated Fat:* **1.7 g**   *Polyunsaturated Fat:* **2.2 g**

❖ Tofu Noodles

Firm tofu is cut into small cubes and simmered in a spicy soy sauce and then tossed with bite-size cellophane noodles and lots of julienned carrots. It should be eaten with a spoon and served in deep plates or bowls or served over steamed rice.

PRODUCTION NOTES: Cover cellophane noodle bundles with warm water for 5 minutes. Cut into 2-inch-long pieces. Frozen julienned carrots are uniform and excellent for this dish.

Portions per recipe: *60*
Yield: *1 pan*
Portion: *8 ounces*
Serving utensil: *8-ounce ladle*

Pan: *12″ × 20″ × 4″*
Time: *10 minutes*

Ingredients	Amounts
Sesame oil	1 oz.
Hot red chilies, unseeded and sliced thin	2 oz.
Soy sauce	4 oz.
Rice vinegar	2 oz.
Vegetarian stock or dashi	4 lb.
Firm tofu, ¼″ cubes	7 lb. 8 oz.
Frozen julienned carrots	10 lb.
Cellophane noodles	2 lb.
Water (warm)	6 lb.
Very fresh mushrooms, washed and sliced	1 lb.
Scallions, thinly sliced	8 oz.

Procedure:

1. Heat sesame oil with chilies, soy sauce, rice vinegar, and stock.
2. Add tofu and simmer slowly for 5 minutes.
3. Steam carrots at low pressure for 7 minutes.
4. Soak and cut cellophane noodles into 2″ length.
5. Fold carrots and cellophane noodles gently into tofu. Simmer 5 minutes.
6. Pour into pan and top with raw mushrooms and scallions.

Calories: **131**   Protein: **5.5 g (16%)**   Carbohydrates: **21.7 g (66%)**   Sodium: **137 mg**

Total Fat: **3.3 g (22%)**   *Saturated Fat:* **.5 g**   *Monounsaturated Fat:* **.8 g**   *Polyunsaturated Fat:* **1.8 g**

❖ Tofu Stir-fry

The trick to tasty tofu lies in frying the tofu separately from the vegetables in spicy sesame oil.

Portions per recipe: 50
Yield: 2 pans
Portion: 7 ounces
Serving utensil: 6-ounce ladle

Pan: 12" × 20" × 2"
Griddle temperature: 375° F
Time: 12 minutes

Ingredients

Ingredients	Amounts
Sesame oil	1 oz.
Almonds, slivered	8 oz.
Chili bean sauce	1 oz.
Firm tofu, cut into ½" cubes	8 lb.
Hoisin sauce	1 oz.
Peanut oil	1 oz.
Scallions, 1" pieces	1 lb.
Zucchini, ¼" thick slices	8 lb.
Green bell peppers, sliced thin	3 lb.
Spinach, washed, large stems removed	3 lb.
Soy sauce	2 oz.
Tomato wedges	2 lb.

Procedure:

1. Heat griddle to 375° F with sesame oil, add almonds, and fry 2 minutes.

2. Add chili bean sauce and tofu, and stir-fry for 5 minutes. Divide equally into 2 pans. Toss gently with ½ ounce of hoisin sauce. Keep warm.

3. Add peanut oil to grill and stir-fry scallions, zucchini, and peppers for 4 minutes. Add spinach and soy sauce and stir-fry for 3 minutes.

4. Divide equally into pans. Add 1 pound of tomato wedges to each pan. Toss. Serve at once.

Calories: **120**   Protein: **8.7 g (29%)**   Carbohydrates: **8.1 g (27%)**   Sodium: **264 mg**

Total Fat: **7.2 g (54%)**   *Saturated Fat:* **1.0 g**   *Monounsaturated Fat:* **2.8 g**   *Polyunsaturated Fat:* **3.0 g**

Legumes

❖

Plants that have pods, such as peas and beans, are legumes. Dried legumes are vital to a vegetarian diet. They are excellent sources of protein, complex carbohydrates, B vitamins, calcium, and iron. The protein in plants is not, however, a complete protein source; it is usually lacking in one or two essential (human cell building) amino acids. Some plant proteins complement each other. Whole grains and beans eaten together will contain all essential amino acids. Nutritionists call the tactic of combining two or more plant proteins in a dish or at one meal *protein complementation*. Protein complementation can also be achieved by combining plant protein with dairy products, for instance by drinking a glass of skim milk during the meal or by adding a small amount of cheese to the recipe.

Many people have problems digesting beans because they contain complex sugars (oligosaccharides) that cannot be broken down by the human digestive system, causing gas formation in the large intestine. If beans are eaten frequently, the body seems to tolerate them with less trouble. The University of California, Berkeley Wellness Letter, which is a reliable source of information, suggests soaking legumes overnight and discarding the (soaking) liquid. This method improves digestion of the complex sugars contained in legumes with only small losses of water solubles, vitamins, and minerals.

Most of the recipes that follow have been devised with protein complementation in mind. Vegetarians should be encouraged to eat a slice of whole wheat bread or drink a glass of milk with all dishes to provide all essential amino acids.

❖ Baked Chick Peas

A simple-to-prepare dish. Serve with mashed or au gratin potatoes, brown rice, or couscous.

Portions per recipe: 60
Yield: 2 pans
Portion: 8 ounces
Serving utensil: 6-ounce ladle

Pan: 12″ × 20″ × 2″
Oven temperature: 325° F
Time: 50 minutes

Ingredients	Amounts
Olive oil	2 oz.
Garlic cloves, crushed	3 oz.
Spanish onions, sliced	4 lb.
Green bell peppers, thinly sliced	4 lb.
Tarragon, crushed	⅛ oz.
Fresh basil, chopped	2 oz.
Parsley, minced	4 oz.
Salt	½ oz.
Black pepper	¼ oz.
Canned tomatoes, diced	6 lb. 6 oz.
Canned chick peas (garbanzo beans)	12 lb. 12 oz.
Parmesan, grated	2 oz.

Procedure:

1. Heat olive oil with garlic and sauté onions and peppers for 5 minutes.
2. Add herbs, spices, and tomatoes. Drain chick peas and fold in.
3. Divide equally between 2 pans. Cover and bake at 325° F for 50 minutes.
4. Uncover and sprinkle each pan with 1 ounce of parmesan cheese. Serve.

> Calories: **153**　Protein: **6.8 g (17%)**　Carbohydrates: **27.1 g (70%)**　Sodium: **502 mg**
> Total Fat: **2.7 g (15%)**　*Saturated Fat:* **.5 g**　*Monounsaturated Fat:* **1.1 g**　*Polyunsaturated Fat:* *.4 g*

❖ Black Beans Louisiana

Black beans with collard greens, bell peppers, and tomatoes go perfectly with fluffy short grain rice. For a special treat use basmati or texmati rice. See color plate **13**.

Portions per recipe: 100
Yield: 2 pans
Portion: 6 ounces
Serving utensil: 4-ounce ladle

Pan: 12″ × 20″ × 4″
Time: 2 hours

Ingredients	Amounts	
Black beans	5 lb.	
Water	24 lb.	
Olive oil		2 oz.
Spanish onions, chopped	2 lb.	
Frozen chopped collard greens	5 lb.	
Red bell peppers, diced	1 lb.	
Canned Italian tomatoes	6 lb.	6 oz.
Cayenne pepper		⅛ oz.
Cider vinegar		8 oz.
Salt		2 oz.

Procedure:

1. Soak beans overnight. Next day bring beans to a simmer and cook for 1½ hours.
2. Heat olive oil and sauté onions for 10 minutes. Add collard greens, peppers, tomatoes, cayenne, vinegar, and salt. Simmer for 30 minutes.
3. Fold in cooked black beans. Taste and adjust seasoning if necessary.

> Calories: **100**　Protein: **5.9 g (24%)**　Carbohydrates: **16.5 g (66%)**　Sodium: **283 mg**
> Total Fat: **1.1 g (10%)**　*Saturated Fat:* **.2 g**　*Monounsaturated Fat:* **.5 g**　*Polyunsaturated Fat:* *.2 g*

❖ Chili con Queso

Garden-style chili is layered with cooked bulgur and Monterey jack cheese.

PRODUCTION NOTE: This is an ideal encore dish for overproduced garden-style chili.

Portions per recipe: *112*
Yield: *4 pans*
Portion: *7 ounces (3″ × 2.9″ piece)*
Serving utensil: *spatula*

Pan: *12″ × 20″ × 2″*
Oven temperature: *325° F*
Time: *12 minutes*

Ingredients

Ingredients	Amounts
Vegetable oil	2 oz.
Spanish onions, chopped	2 lb.
Celery, thinly sliced	4 lb.
Green bell peppers, diced	4 lb.
Chili powder	½ oz.
Oregano, crushed	⅛ oz.
Salt	1 oz.
Canned kidney beans	6 lb. 6 oz.
Canned tomatoes, diced	13 lb. 4 oz.
Canned green chilies, diced	2 lb. 8 oz.
Salsa picante	2 lb.
Bulgur	5 lb.
Water	8 lb.
Monterey Jack cheese, shredded	6 lb.
Low-fat yogurt	4 lb.

Procedure:

1. Heat oil and sauté onions, celery, peppers, and spices.
2. Add beans with liquid, tomatoes, chilies, and salsa. Simmer for 15 minutes.
3. Place 5 pounds of bulgur in a 12″ × 20″ × 4″ pan. Add 1 gallon of water and steam at 5# pressure for 12 minutes.
4. Mix two pounds of the shredded cheese with the yogurt.
5. Oil 12″ × 20″ × 2″ pan lightly and spread 3 pounds of cooked bulgur in bottom.
6. Top with 1 pint of yogurt mixture.
7. Cover with 8 pounds of chili. Sprinkle with 1 pound of shredded cheese.
8. Bake at 325° F for 12 minutes. Cut each pan into 28 pieces.

Calories: **228**   Protein: **11.3 g (20%)**   Carbohydrates: **27.4 g (48%)**   Sodium: **447 mg**
Total Fat: **8.7 g (34%)**   *Saturated Fat:* **4.1 g**   *Monounsaturated Fat:* **2.5 g**   *Polyunsaturated Fat:* **.7 g**

❖ Garbanzo Casserole

The red lentils give a smooth, rich texture to this dish.

Portions per recipe: *64*
Yield: *2 pans*
Portion: *7 ounces*
Serving utensil: *6-ounce ladle*

Pan: *12" × 20" × 2"*
Oven temperature: *350° F*
Time: *10 minutes*

Ingredients	Amounts	
Vegetable oil		2 oz.
Spanish onions, chopped	1 lb.	
Celery, thinly sliced	3 lb.	
Mushrooms, thinly sliced	3 lb.	
Red lentils	1 lb.	
Cumin		1/4 oz.
Turmeric		1/8 oz.
Oregano, crushed		1/8 oz.
Cayenne pepper		1/16 oz.
Canned chick peas (garbanzo beans)	6 lb.	10 oz.
Frozen whole kernel corn	2 lb.	
Canned tomatoes, diced	6 lb.	6 oz.
Croutons		12 oz.
Cheddar cheese, shredded	1 lb.	
Parsley, minced		2 oz.
Cilantro, chopped		2 oz.

Procedure:

1. Heat oil and sauté onions, celery, mushrooms, and lentils with spices.
2. Add chick peas with liquid, corn, and tomatoes. Simmer for 30 minutes.
3. Pour 2 gallons into pan.
4. Sprinkle each pan with 6 ounces of croutons and 8 ounces of shredded cheese.
5. Bake at 350° F for 10 minutes. Sprinkle with the fresh herbs and serve.

Calories: **159**   Protein: **7.8 g (20%)**   Carbohydrates: **24.9 g (62%)**   Sodium: **219 mg**

Total Fat: **4.2 g (24%)**   *Saturated Fat:* **1.8 g**   *Monounsaturated Fat:* **1.0 g**   *Polyunsaturated Fat:* **1.0 g**

❖ Garden Style Chili

This simple vegetable chili is excellent served over steamed bulgur.

PRODUCTION NOTE: Serve chili and bulgur (or rice) from half size pans on the steam table.

Portions per recipe: 100	*Pan:* 12″ × 20″ × 4″–½ size
Yield: 3 pans	*Cooking method:* steam
Portion: 6 ounces	*Time:* 30 minutes
Serving utensil: 4-ounce ladle	

Ingredients	*Amounts*
Olive oil	2 oz.
Spanish onions, chopped	2 lb.
Celery, thinly sliced	4 lb.
Green bell peppers, diced	4 lb.
Chili powder	½ oz.
Cumin	⅛ oz.
Oregano, crushed	⅛ oz.
Granulated sugar	½ oz.
Canned kidney beans	13 lb. 4 oz.
Canned tomatoes, diced	12 lb. 12 oz.
Celery tops, finely chopped	2 oz.

Procedure:

1. Heat olive oil in steam kettle and sauté onions, celery, and bell peppers with chili powder and cumin for 5 minutes.
2. Add oregano, sugar, beans, and tomatoes. Simmer for 25 minutes.
3. Pour 1½ gallons of mixture into each pan.
4. Garnish with chopped celery leaves.

Calories: **78**   Protein: **4.0 g (20%)**   Carbohydrates: **14.2 g (72%)**   Sodium: **117 mg**

Total Fat: **1.1 g (11%)**   *Saturated Fat:* **.1 g**   *Monounsaturated Fat:* **.5 g**   *Polyunsaturated Fat:* **.3 g**

❖ Greek Bean Bake

Bulgur and white kidney beans (canned cannellini) are baked with tomatoes and feta cheese.

PRODUCTION NOTES: If you prefer to use dry beans, bring 2 pounds of white kidney beans covered with cold water to a boil. Let them sit for 1 hour, then simmer them slowly for 1½ hours.

Portions per recipe: *56*　　　　　　Pan: *12″ × 20″ × 2″*
Yield: *2 pans*　　　　　　　　　　Oven temperature: *325° F*
Portion: *6 ounces*　　　　　　　　Time: *35 minutes*
Serving utensil: *spatula or spoon*

Ingredients

Ingredients	Amounts
Water	1 lb. 10 oz.
Bulgur	2 lb.
Olive oil	2 oz.
Garlic cloves, crushed	1 oz.
Spanish onions, diced	1 lb.
Celery with tops, chopped	2 lb.
Carrots, chopped	2 lb.
Oregano, crushed	⅛ oz.
Cayenne pepper	¹⁄₁₆ oz.
Canned cannellini	5 lb. 15 oz.
Canned Italian tomatoes	6 lb. 6 oz.
Parsley, minced	2 oz.
Feta cheese, rinsed and crumbled	4 lb.

Procedure:

1. Pour boiling water over bulgur and set aside.
2. Heat olive oil with garlic. Add onions, celery, carrots, and spices and sauté for 15 minutes.
3. Stir in cannellini with liquid and bulgur.
4. Crush whole tomatoes lightly and stir in parsley.
5. Spread 2 quarts of bean mixture in oiled pan.
6. Cover with 1 pound of crumbled feta cheese. Distribute 1 pint of crushed tomatoes evenly over cheese.
7. Repeat bean and cheese layer. Top with 2 pints of tomatoes.
8. Bake at 325° F for 35 minutes.

Calories: **165**　Protein: **10.0 g (24%)**　Carbohydrates: **25.8 g (63 %)**　Sodium: **634 mg**
Total Fat: **1.5 g (8%)**　*Saturated Fat:* **5.1 g**　*Monounsaturated Fat:* **2.3 g**　*Polyunsaturated Fat:* **.5 g**

❖ Hawaiian Beans

A sweet and sour pineapple and chick pea stew that is excellent served over fluffy white rice.

Portions per recipe: *100*
Yield: *3 pans*
Portion: *6 ounces*
Serving utensil: *4-ounce ladle*

Pan: *12" × 20" × 4"–½ size*
Time: *30 minutes*

Ingredients	Amounts
Vegetable oil	2 oz.
Garlic, crushed	1 oz.
Ginger root, chopped	3 oz.
Cayenne pepper	⅛ oz.
Dry mustard	¼ oz.
Carrots, ¼" thick slices	5 lb.
Canned chick peas (garbanzo beans)	19 lb. 14 oz.
Pineapple juice	3 lb.
Honey	15 oz.
Soy sauce	4 oz.
Pineapple chunks	6 lb. 12 oz.
Green bell peppers, 1" pieces	4 lb.
Cider vinegar	1 lb.
Cornstarch	5 oz.

Procedure:

1. Heat vegetable oil with garlic, ginger, mustard, and cayenne.
2. Stir in carrots, chick peas, pineappple juice, honey, and soy sauce.
3. Simmer for 30 minutes.
4. Add pineapple chunks with liquid and bell peppers.
5. Mix vinegar with cornstarch and stir in to thicken stew slightly.

Calories: **171**   Protein: **5.1 g (12%)**   Carbohydrates: **33.1 g (77%)**   Sodium: **343 mg**

Total Fat: **1.7 g (9%)**   *Saturated Fat:* **.3 g**   *Monounsaturated Fat:* **.3 g**   *Polyunsaturated Fat:* **.8 g**

Chick peas are simmered with pineapple chunks and peppers to make Hawaiian beans.

❖ Indian Dal

Dal is the Indian name for legumes and arhar dal, also called toovar dal, are brown lentils. Do not use red lentils (masoor dal) because they will cook to mush. In India lentils are cooked with ghee, which is clarified butter. This recipe uses oil instead. Serve dal with rice and curries.

Portions per recipe: 100
Yield: 2 pans
Portion: 4 ounces
Serving utensil: 4-ounce ladle

Pan: 12″ × 20″ × 2″
Time: 30 minutes

Ingredients	*Amounts*
Vegetable oil	4 oz.
Spanish onions, thinly sliced	2 lb.
Garlic cloves, crushed	4 oz.
Brown lentils	8 lb.
Cumin	½ oz.
Turmeric	½ oz.
Cayenne pepper	⅛ oz.
Asafoetida	dash
Salt	2 oz.
Water	24 lb.

Procedure:

1. In vegetable oil sauté onions and garlic for 5 minutes.
2. Add lentils and spices and cook for 2 minutes.
3. Add salt and water and simmer covered for 30 minutes.
4. Dal should be soupy.

Calories: **138**   Protein: **10.4 g (30%)**   Carbohydrates: **21.8 g (63%)**   Sodium: **224 mg**

Total Fat: **1.6 g (10%)**   *Saturated Fat:* **.3 g**   *Monounsaturated Fat:* **.6 g**   *Polyunsaturated Fat:* **.8 g**

❖ Japanese Soybeans

Soybeans contain the eight essential amino acids the adult body needs for cell growth but can't produce. Although they are a complete protein source, soybeans lack histidine, an amino acid that children need. Therefore, vegetarian children cannot rely on soybeans alone. They must complement soybeans with dairy products.

This recipe braises soybeans with dashi, a Japanese bonito broth. If you are serving a strict vegetarian diet, use a miso broth or vegetarian stock instead.

PRODUCTION NOTES: Soak the soybeans overnight in cold water. Look for the dashi recipe in the soup section (on page 97).

Portions per recipe: *100*	Pan: *12″ × 20″ × 2″*
Yield: *2 pans*	Oven temperature: *300° F*
Portion: *4 ounces*	Time: *2 hours and 30 minutes*
Serving utensil: *4-ounce ladle*	

Ingredients	Amounts
Dry soybeans	8 lb.
Dashi broth	16 lb.
Granulated sugar	8 oz.
Mirin (Japanese syrup)	8 oz.
Soy sauce	12 oz.
Rice vinegar	8 oz.

Procedure:

1. Soak soybeans overnight covered with cold water.
2. Drain and divide evenly into pans.
3. Make dashi, reserve seaweed. Cut seaweed into thin 1″ long strips.
4. Mix dashi with sugar and mirin. Pour 6 quarts over beans.
5. Cover and bake 2 hours in 300° F oven.
6. Remove cover. Mix soy sauce with vinegar and seaweed strips. Add about 2 cups to each pan. Stir gently and bake uncovered 30 minutes longer.

Calories: **172**   Protein: **13.5 g (31%)**   Carbohydrates: **15.4 g (36%)**   Sodium: **195 mg**
Total Fat: **7.2 g (37%)**   *Saturated Fat:* **1.1 g**   *Monounsaturated Fat:* **1.6 g**   *Polyunsaturated Fat:* **4.1 g**

❖ Pasta and Lentils

A great combination that is delicious hot or cold. See color plate **14**.

PRODUCTION NOTES: Short ditalini pasta is perfect for this dish. Small elbow noodles will do. Always sort and check lentils for stones.

Portions per recipe: *100*
Yield: *3 pans*
Portion: *6 ounces*
Serving utensil: *8-ounce ladle*

Pan: *12″ × 20″ × 4″*
Time: *30 minutes*

Ingredients	Amounts
Brown lentils	6 lb.
Water	18 lb.
Salt	½ oz.
Olive oil	4 oz.
Balsamic vinegar	4 oz.
Lemon juice	4 oz.
Garlic cloves, crushed	2 oz.
Salt	1 oz.
Black pepper	¼ oz.
Water	36 lb.
Salt	½ oz.
Ditalini	6 lb.
Ripe Italian plum tomatoes, diced	8 lb.
Fresh rosemary, chopped finely	2 oz.
Scallions, chopped	12 oz.

Procedure:

1. In a kettle place sorted lentils, cover with cold water and bring to a simmer. Cook for 30 minutes until lentils are barely tender.
2. In a large bowl blend together oil, vinegar, lemon juice, garlic, salt, and pepper.
3. Bring water with salt to a rolling boil. Add ditalini, stir and cook for 10–12 minutes. Stir occasionally. Drain.
4. Toss drained hot pasta immediately with the dressing.
5. Add tomatoes, the boiling hot lentils, rosemary, and scallions. Toss.
6. If pasta is served cold, more vinegar and salt may be needed to taste.

Calories: **211** Protein: **11.5 g (21%)** Carbohydrates: **37.7 g (71%)** Sodium: **279 mg**

Total Fat: **1.9 g (8%)** *Saturated Fat:* **.3 g** *Monounsaturated Fat:* **.9 g** *Polyunsaturated Fat:* **.4 g**

❖ Vegetarian Stew

A vegetable stew full of protein-rich legumes. Offer grated parmesan separately. Serve this stew with warm corn bread, jalapeño biscuits, or steamed rice.

Portions per recipe: 100
Yield: 3 pans
Portion: 9 ounces
Serving utensil: 8-ounce ladle

Pan: 12" × 20" × 4"
Time: 1 hour and 15 minutes

Ingredients | Amounts

Ingredients	Amounts	
Olive oil		4 oz.
Garlic cloves, crushed		2 oz.
Thyme, crushed		¼ oz.
Savory, crushed		¼ oz.
Spanish onions, sliced	4 lb.	
Celery with tops, chopped	5 lb.	
Carrots, ¼" slices	5 lb.	
Green split peas	1 lb.	
Water	16 lb.	
Potatoes, peeled and cut into 1" cubes	5 lb.	
Frozen lima beans	2 lb.	8 oz.
Whole kernel corn, frozen	2 lb.	8 oz.
Canned tomatoes, diced	6 lb.	6 oz.
Canned red kidney beans	6 lb.	10 oz.
Soy sauce		2 oz.
Worcestershire sauce		2 oz.
Black pepper		⅛ oz.
Fresh parsley, minced		3 oz.

Procedure:

1. Heat olive oil and sauté garlic, herbs, and onions for 5 minutes.
2. Add celery, carrots, and split peas and sauté for 5 minutes.
3. Add water and potatoes and simmer for 45 minutes.
4. Add rest of the ingredients except parsley and simmer for 20 minutes.
5. Transfer to serving pans and sprinkle each pan with 1 ounce of parsley.

Calories: **127**   Protein: **5.9 g (18%)**   Carbohydrates: **23.7 g (74%)**   Sodium: **143 mg**
Total Fat: **1.6 g (11%)**   *Saturated Fat:* **.2 g**   *Monounsaturated Fat:* **.9 g**   *Polyunsaturated Fat:* **.3 g**

Grains, Nuts, and Vegetables

❖

Whole grains are excellent sources of complex carbohydrates, fiber, B vitamins, vitamin E, most essential minerals, and essential fatty acids.

In the preceding sections grains were a part of the cheese, egg, tofu, and legume recipes. In this section, they are either the major ingredient or are combined with vegetables.

The protein value of nuts can significantly contribute to a strict vegetarian diet. Unfortunately nuts are very high in fat, so I use them sparingly in some of the recipes that follow.

Vegetables provide complex carbohydrates, fiber, large amounts of vitamin C, small amounts of protein (legumes excepted) and hardly any fat. Dark green, leafy, and orange or yellow vegetables are the best source of beta carotene, a nutrient the body converts to vitamin A. Beta carotene is an antioxidant and is thought to assist in the prevention of cancer. All vegetables are good sources of a variety of minerals.

❖ Amaranth-stuffed Acorn Squash

Acorn squash is baked with a stuffing made with leeks, mushrooms, carrots, and amaranth. Amaranth grains are just a little bit larger than poppy seeds and are a superb protein source. Amaranth is especially high in amino acids, particularly lysine. The grain was grown by the Aztecs centuries ago and is now farmed in America.

PRODUCTION NOTES: Amaranth becomes very mushy if cooked without toasting it first. In this recipe amaranth is prepared like rice for risotto so it will have texture and a nutty taste.

Portions per recipe: 50
Yield: 50 halves
Portion: ½ squash
Serving utensil: spatula

Pan: 12" × 20" × 2"
Oven temperature: 350° F
Time: 25 minutes

Ingredients	Amounts
Olive oil	2 oz.
Amaranth	3 lb.
Mushrooms, sliced	2 lb.
Leeks, chopped, washed, and drained	2 lb.
Carrots, shredded	2 lb.
Salt	1 oz.
Black pepper	⅛ oz.
Water	8 lb.
Acorn squash, halved and seeded	25 lb.

Amaranth-stuffed acorn squash takes advantage of a high protein grain.

Procedure:

1. Heat olive oil. Add amaranth and stir until it starts to pop.
2. Add mushrooms, leeks, carrots, salt, and pepper and sauté for 5 minutes.
3. Stir in ½ gallon of water and simmer for about 8 minutes, if liquid is absorbed, stir in a quart of water.
4. Simmer until liquid is absorbed and add another quart. Amaranth should be soft after 25 minutes.
5. Steam, bake, or broil (brush with oil) squash halves for 10 minutes.
6. Fill cavity with a #8 scoop of the amaranth mixture. Brush rim with oil and bake uncovered at 350° F for 15 minutes.

Calories: **197**   Protein: **6.0 g (12%)**   Carbohydrates: **39.6 g (80%)**   Sodium: **123 mg**
Total Fat: **2.9 g (13%)**   *Saturated Fat:* **.7 g**   *Monounsaturated Fat:* **1.2 g**   *Polyunsaturated Fat:* **1.0 g**

❖ Arroz Blanco con Chilies

A delicious casserole that is layered with corn tortillas, rice, and chilies stuffed with cheese.

PRODUCTION NOTES: Let this dish sit for 15 minutes before cutting. Take care to place stuffed chilies neatly in 4 rows of 7 so that you will be able to serve a whole chili to each customer. If no cooked rice is on hand, steam 2 pounds, 10 ounces of raw rice with 1 gallon (8 pounds) water and ¼ ounce of salt.

Portions per recipe: *56*
Yield: *2 pans*
Portion: *5 ounces (3" × 2.9" piece)*
Serving utensil: *spatula*

Pan: *12" × 20" × 2"*
Oven temperature: *325° F*
Time: *55 minutes*

Ingredients	Amounts
Corn tortillas, small	10 oz.
Canned salsa picante	2 lb.
Rice (cooked)	8 lb.
Canned whole green chilies	6 lb. 6 oz.
Monterey Jack cheese	3 lb. 8 oz.
Sour cream	1 lb.
Low-fat yogurt	3 lb.
Eggs	8 oz.
Salt	¼ oz.

Procedure:

1. Oil pan and line with 6 corn tortillas.
2. Cover with 8 ounces of salsa and a layer of 2 pounds of cold rice.
3. Cut Jack cheese into long 1-ounce sticks.
4. Slit open chilies, remove any seeds, and stuff with cheese.
5. Place neatly into 4 rows of 7 chilies. Cover with 2 pounds of rice.
6. Spread with 8 ounces of salsa.
7. Beat sour cream with yogurt, eggs, and salt. Pour 1 quart over casserole.
8. Bake at 325° F for 55 minutes.

Calories: **269**   Protein: **11.7 g (17%)**   Carbohydrates: **30.1 g (45%)**   Sodium: **455 mg**
Total Fat: **11.5 g (38%)**   *Saturated Fat:* **5.8 g**   *Monounsaturated Fat:* **3.3 g**   *Polyunsaturated Fat:* **.4 g**

❖ Barley Bake

Whole-hulled barley rather than pearl barley provides the whole grain goodness inherent in this dish. The dish can be served as a vegetarian entreé when combined with a bean dish. It is especially good with lamb or baked chicken.

Portions per recipe: *60*
Yield: *2 pans*
Portion: *7 ounces*
Serving utensil: *spoon*

Pan: *12″ × 20″ × 2″*
Oven temperature: *325° F*
Time: *20 minutes*

Ingredients	Amounts	
Spanish onions	1 lb.	
Mushrooms, trimmed	2 lb.	
Carrots		8 oz.
Celery with tops		8 oz.
Olive oil		2 oz.
Garam masala powder		1/4 oz.
Turmeric		1/4 oz.
Whole-hulled barley	4 lb.	
Water	18 lb.	
Ripe Italian plum tomatoes, diced	2 lb.	
Basil, crushed		1/8 oz.
Parsley, minced		4 oz.
Coriander, chopped		2 oz.

Procedure:

1. In a food chopper or processor coarsely chop onions, mushrooms, carrots, and celery.

2. Heat olive oil with spices and sauté vegetables and barley for 5 minutes.

3. Add water and simmer for 25 minutes.

4. Fold in tomatoes and herbs.

5. Place approximately 12 pounds of mixture into pan. Bake at 325° F for 20 minutes.

Calories: **127**   Protein: **3.7 g (12%)**   Carbohydrates: **26.2 g (83%)**   Sodium: **41 mg**

Total Fat: **1.5 g (11%)**   *Saturated Fat:* **.2 g**   *Monounsaturated Fat:* **.8 g**   *Polyunsaturated Fat:* **.3 g**

❖ Celery Root with Hazelnuts

My German mother invented this recipe when I brought a friend home from college who turned out to be a vegetarian. My mother had planned to make pork schnitzel for dinner, so she breaded thinly sliced celery root to make a meatless cutlet for my friend. This is simply wonderful. Serve with cheesey pasta or the baked potato omelet (page 261) to provide more protein.

PRODUCTION NOTES: Celery root is also sold under the name celeriac. To prepare celeriac, trim the root end, peel the brown skin, and slice it on an electric slicer.

Portions per recipe: 40
Yield: 80 slices
Portion: 2 slices
Serving utensil: tongs

Pan: 12″ × 20″ × 2″
Oven temperature: 350° F
Time: 10 minutes

Use strips of red and yellow peppers as garnish to celery root slices with hazelnut breading.

Ingredients	Amounts
Celeriac, trimmed and washed	6 lb.
Salt	½ oz.
All-purpose flour	4 oz.
Eggs	10 oz.
Skim milk	2 oz.
Bread crumbs	10 oz.
Hazelnuts, finely ground	8 oz.
Whole roasted hazelnuts	4 oz.

Procedure:

1. Cut trimmed celeriac into 1-ounce slices.
2. Mix salt and flour. Beat eggs with milk. Mix bread crumbs with hazelnuts.
3. Dredge celeriac slices in flour.
4. Dip into egg and coat with crumbs. Press crumbs lightly to make them stick well.
5. Heat well-oiled grill and cook each slice for 5 minutes on each side.
6. Place in a pan and keep warm.
7. Roast hazelnuts at 325° F in the oven for 10 minutes. Roll in a kitchen towel to loosen skins. Discard the skins, chop the nuts coarsely, and sprinkle over pan.

Calories: **98**   Protein: **3.5 g (14%)**   Carbohydrates: **13.8 g (56%)**   Sodium: **261 mg**

Total Fat: **3.7 g (33%)**   *Saturated Fat:* **.4 g**   *Monounsaturated Fat:* **2.2 g**   *Polyunsaturated Fat:* **.4 g**

❖ Corn-stuffed Red Bell Peppers

A very colorful and nutritious combination. Serve these with brown rice and broccoli.

Portions per recipe: *48*
Yield: *2 pans*
Portion: *1 pepper half*
Serving utensil: *spoon*

Pan: *12″ × 20″ × 2″*
Oven temperature: *325° F*
Time: *30 minutes*

Ingredients	Amounts	
Red large bell peppers	10 lb.	
Safflower oil		2 oz.
Spanish onions, chopped	1 lb.	
Garlic cloves, crushed		1 oz.
Jalapeño pepper, seeded and chopped		2 oz.
Cumin		⅛ oz.
Paprika		¼ oz.
Frozen whole kernel corn	8 lb.	
Baby lima beans	2 lb.	8 oz.
Eggs	1 lb.	
Monterey jack cheese, shredded	3 lb.	
Tomato juice	1 lb.	

Procedure:

1. Cut peppers in half and seed carefully.
2. Heat oil and sauté onions, garlic, jalapeño, and spices for 5 minutes.
3. Add corn and lima beans and simmer for 10 minutes.
4. Cool slightly and fold in eggs and shredded cheese.
5. Fill pepper halves using a #8 scoop.
6. Pour 1 cup of tomato juice in pan. Place 24 peppers on top.
7. Cover and bake at 325° F for 30 minutes.

Calories: **299**   Protein: **16.0 g (21%)**   Carbohydrates: **36.3 g (48%)**   Sodium: **223 mg**
Total Fat: **11.9 g (35%)**   *Saturated Fat:* **5.0 g**   *Monounsaturated Fat:* **3.1 g**   *Polyunsaturated Fat:* **1.8 g**

❖ Eggplant "Mardikian"

This is an eggplant stew inspired by the Egyptian stew in George Mardikian's out-of-print cookbook *Dinner at Omar Khayyam's*, published by Viking, New York (1942). Serve with bulgur, brown rice, or orzo noodles and herb yogurt topping (page 462) to provide more protein.

Portions per recipe: *100*
Yield: *2 pans*
Portion: *8 ounces*
Serving utensil: *8-ounce ladle*

Pan: *12″ × 20″ × 4″*
Time: *1 hour*

Ingredients

Ingredients	Amounts
Olive oil	2 oz.
Garlic cloves, minced	1 oz.
Spanish onions, sliced	6 lb.
Mushrooms, sliced	3 lb.
Eggplant, diced 1″ cubes	16 lb.
Allspice, ground	½ oz.
Frozen lima beans	4 lb.
Canned peeled Italian tomatoes	12 lb. 12 oz.
Water	2 lb.
Salt	1 oz.
Black pepper	¼ oz.
Frozen corn	2 lb.
Green bell peppers, 1″ pieces	2 lb.
Fresh parsley, minced	4 oz.
Honey	3 oz.

Procedure

1. Heat olive oil in a kettle. Add garlic and onions and sauté for 10 minutes.

2. Add mushrooms, eggplant, and allspice and sauté for 5 minutes more.

3. Crush tomatoes lightly by hand. Add to kettle with lima beans, water, salt, and pepper. Simmer 40 minutes.

4. Add corn, diced peppers, and fresh parsley and cook for 5 minutes more.

5. Offer herb yogurt topping (see recipe on page 462) separately.

Calories: **118**   Protein: **2.2 g (8%)**   Carbohydrates: **23.1 g (78%)**   Sodium: **213 mg**
Total Fat: **1.2 g (9%)**   *Saturated Fat:* **.2 g**   *Monounsaturated Fat:* **.7 g**   *Polyunsaturated Fat:* **.2 g**

❖ Mushroom Cakes

Top these mushroom cakes with a mushroom sauce or sautéed mushrooms. Serve them with noodle kugel and broccoli or as a sandwich on a whole wheat bun with lettuce and tomatoes. They are wonderful with mashed potatoes.

Portions per recipe: *50*
Yield: *50 cakes*
Portion: *1 cake*
Serving utensil: *spatula*

Pan: *12" × 20" × 2"*
Griddle temperature: *350° F*
Time: *8 minutes*

Ingredients	Amounts
Vegetable oil	4 oz.
Mushrooms, thinly sliced	5 lb.
Garlic cloves, crushed	2 oz.
Spanish onions, chopped	10 oz.
Rosemary, crushed	⅛ oz.
Black pepper	¼ oz.
Celery stems and leaves, finely chopped	10 oz.
Green bell peppers, chopped	10 oz.
Carrots, finely shredded	8 oz.
Lemon juice	4 oz.
Sour cream	8 oz.
Eggs, beaten	12 oz.
Bread crumbs	1 lb. 8 oz.
Provolone cheese, shredded	2 lb.

Procedure:

1. Heat oil and sauté mushrooms with garlic, onions, and spices until mushrooms are brown.

2. Add celery, peppers, carrots, and lemon juice. Simmer for 5 minutes.

3. Cool to room temperature. Fold in sour cream, eggs, bread crumbs, and cheese.

4. Mix well and refrigerate for 1 to 2 hours.

5. With a #8 scoop place mushroom mixture directly on oiled griddle.

6. Flatten to form pattie. Cook both sides for 4 minutes; each side should be well browned.

7. Place neatly into serving pans. Garnish with sautéed mushrooms or cover with mushroom sauce.

Calories: **165**   Protein: **8.4 g (20%)**   Carbohydrates: **14.3 g (35%)**   Sodium: **306 mg**

Total Fat: **8.4 g (45%)**   *Saturated Fat:* **4.5 g**   *Monounsaturated Fat:* **2.2 g**   *Polyunsaturated Fat:* **1.1 g**

❖ Okra Beignet

A vegetable griddle cake or fritter—I have misnamed them—since they are not unlike a beignet, though they are not deep-fried, they are just as light and airy as the famous New Orleans pastry specialty.

Portions per recipe: 24
Yield: 72 beignets
Portion: 3 beignets
Serving utensil: spatula

Pan: 12″ × 20″ × 2″
Griddle temperature: 350° F
Time: 6 minutes

Ingredients

Ingredients	Amounts	
Fresh okra	4 lb.	
Scallions, chopped		12 oz.
Green bell peppers, diced		12 oz.
Red bell peppers, diced		8 oz.
All-purpose flour		4 oz.
Cajun spice (page 458)		1 oz.
Bread crumbs		8 oz.
Eggs, separated	1 lb.	4 oz.
Light cream		4 oz.
Lemons		8 oz.

Procedure:

1. Cut off stem end and slice okra into very thin slices.
2. Toss with scallions, peppers, flour, cajun spice, and bread crumbs.
3. Beat egg yolks with cream and stir into okra mixture.
4. Whip egg whites until they form soft peaks and fold gently into okra mix.
5. Heat well-oiled griddle and drop batter onto it with a #24 scoop.
6. Cook for 3 minutes on each side. Put in a pan and garnish with lemon slices.

Calories: **139**   Protein: **6.2 g (18%)**   Carbohydrates: **18.4 g (53%)**   Sodium: **264 mg**
Total Fat: **4.0 g (26%)**   *Saturated Fat:* **1.4 g**   *Monounsaturated Fat:* **.8 g**   *Polyunsaturated Fat:* **.5 g**

❖ Polenta with Chunky Marinara Sauce

A very low-cost entrée with great eye appeal. The polenta is served at Michela's in Cambridge, Massachusetts. I have added the marinara sauce.

PRODUCTION NOTES: You can make the polenta a day ahead. To reheat it, sprinkle with fontina cheese and bake. Cook the tomatoes very briefly to keep their fresh taste.

Portions per recipe: 78	Pan: 18″ × 26″ sheet pan
Yield: 156 triangles	Oven temperature: 325° F
Portion: 2 triangles	Time: 8–10 minutes
Serving utensil: spatula	

Ingredients	Amounts
Polenta	
Water	6 lb.
Salt	½ oz.
White pepper, ground	⅛ oz.
Marjoram, crushed	⅛ oz.
Hungarian paprika	⅙ oz.
Yellow cornmeal	2 lb.
Water	4 lb.
Canned roasted red peppers	1 lb.
Olive oil (for brushing)	1 oz.
Sauce	
Olive oil	1 oz.
Spanish onions, finely diced	12 oz.
Garlic cloves, crushed	2 oz.
Parsley, minced	2 oz.
Basil, chopped	1 oz.
Bay leaves, crumbled	1/16 oz.
Thyme, crushed	⅛ oz.
Cayenne pepper	1/16 oz.
Ripe Italian plum tomatoes, chopped	3 lb.
Green bell peppers, chopped	1 lb.
Carrots, thinly sliced	1 lb.
Fontina cheese, shredded	12 oz.
Parmesan cheese, grated	4 oz.

Procedure:

1. Bring water with salt, pepper, marjoram, and paprika to a boil.

2. Mix cornmeal with cold water to make a slurry. Add slowly to boiling water, stirring vigorously to prevent lumps from forming. Stir till thickened.

3. Brush 18″ × 26″ sheet pan with olive oil. Pour in 12 pounds of polenta, spread evenly, brush with olive oil, and cover with parchment paper.

4. Refrigerate until well-chilled. (Overnight is best.)

5. Cut into 78 3″ × 2″ rectangles and cut them again diagonally to form triangles.

6. Arrange 78 triangles in four rows in a 12″ × 20″ × 2″ pan.

7. Sprinkle with cheeses and bake for 8 minutes at 325° F.

8. Marinara sauce: Heat olive oil. Sauté onions, garlic, herbs, and spices for 15 minutes.

9. Add tomatoes, red peppers, and salt. Cook for 5 minutes more.

10. Pour 1 quart of sauce over triangles before serving.

Calories: **84**   Protein: **2.9 g (13%)**   Carbohydrates: **11.5 g (54%)**   Sodium: **150 mg**
Total Fat: **3.0 g (32%)**   *Saturated Fat:* **1.3 g**   *Monounsaturated Fat:* **1.2 g**   *Polyunsaturated Fat:* **.4 g**

Polenta is served with a chunky marinara sauce.

❖ Potato Eggplant Curry

White eggplants and potatoes combine to make a complete meal. White eggplants are small and slender with a tender skin. If they are not available you may use purple eggplant, but they will need to be peeled.

Portions per recipe: *50*
Yield: *2½ gallons*
Portion: *8 ounces*
Serving utensil: *6-ounce ladle*

Cooking method: *steam*
Time: *30 minutes*

Ingredients	Amounts
Vegetable oil	2 oz.
Garlic cloves, crushed	1 oz.
Spanish onions, thickly sliced	2 lb.
White eggplant, unpeeled and cut into 1" pieces	6 lb.
Red potatoes, quartered	8 lb.
Curry powder	1 oz.
Turmeric	¼ oz.
Salt	1 oz.
Water	4 lb.
Green bell peppers, 1" pieces	2 lb.
Yellow bell peppers, 1" pieces	2 lb.
Italian parsley, minced	4 oz.

Procedure:

1. Heat oil in kettle. Add garlic, onions, eggplant, and potatoes, and stir.
2. Add curry powder and turmeric. Sauté for 5 minutes.
3. Add salt and water, cover, and simmer for 15 minutes.
4. Add peppers and simmer for 10 minutes more.
5. Ladle into serving pan and sprinkle with parsley.

Calories: **84**   Protein: **2.2 g (10%)**   Carbohydrates: **16.0 g (76%)**   Sodium: **229 mg**
Total Fat: **1.5 g (16%)**   *Saturated Fat:* **.3 g**   *Monounsaturated Fat:* **.2 g**   *Polyunsaturated Fat:* **.7 g**

❖ Stuffed Acorn Squash

I developed this recipe especially for vegetarians at the UNH Thanksgiving dinner. Until then vegetarians had to make do with three items: mashed potatoes, squash, and peas!

PRODUCTION NOTE: The squashes should be dark green. If they are turning orange, they are over-ripe and will be less sweet and unpleasantly stringy.

Portions per recipe: 50
Yield: 50 halves
Portion: ½ squash
Serving utensil: spatula

Pan: 12" × 20" × 2"
Oven temperature: 325° F
Time: 30 minutes

Ingredients	Amounts	
Safflower oil		2 oz.
Spanish onions, chopped		12 oz.
Celery, diced	2 lb.	
Brown rice	2 lb.	
White pepper		¹⁄₁₆ oz.
Salt		½ oz.
Water	6 lb.	
All-purpose apples, peeled and shredded	3 lb.	
Walnuts, chopped		8 oz.
Cheddar cheese, shredded	3 lb.	2 oz.
Cinnamon		¼ oz.
Allspice		⅛ oz.
Fresh sage, chopped		1 oz.
Large acorn squash (25 squashes)	22 lb.	
Unsalted butter		4 oz.

Procedure:

1. Heat oil and sauté onions for 5 minutes. Stir in the rice and celery and sauté for 5 more minutes.
2. Add salt, pepper, and water and cook at low temperature for 30 minutes or until the water is absorbed and rice is tender. Turn off heat.
3. Stir in apples, walnuts, cheddar cheese, spices, and sage.
4. Cut squashes in half, remove seeds, and steam at low pressure for 10 minutes.
5. Brush squash rim with melted butter and fill cavity with rice stuffing using a #8 scoop.
6. Set the squash in pan with ½ cup of water. Bake uncovered at 325° F for 30 minutes.

Calories: **300**   Protein: **10.2 g (14%)**   Carbohydrates: **35.3 g (47%)**   Sodium: **306 mg**
Total Fat: **14.4 g (43%)**   *Saturated Fat:* **7.5 g**   *Monounsaturated Fat:* **3.8 g**   *Polyunsaturated Fat:* **2.3 g**

❖ Summer Squash Casserole

Squash is baked au gratin, with a crunchy layer of cornbread stuffing mix. I used a traditional New England squash recipe and improvised, adding enough protein for a meatless entrée.

Portions per recipe: *100*
Yield: *4 pans*
Portion: *7 ounces*
Serving utensil: *6-ounce ladle*

Pan: *12″ × 20″ × 2″*
Oven temperature: *325° F*
Time: *35 minutes*

Ingredients	Amounts
Safflower oil	8 oz.
Garlic cloves, crushed	2 oz.
All-purpose flour	12 oz.
Non-fat dry milk	2 lb.
Water (hot)	15 lb.
Salt	1 oz.
Black pepper	¼ oz.
Sage	⅛ oz.
Oregano, crushed	⅛ oz.
Cheddar cheese, shredded	2 lb.
Corn bread stuffing mix	6 lb.
Wheat germ, toasted	12 oz.
Yellow summer squash, ¼″ slices	20 lb.

Procedure:

1. Heat oil with garlic and flour and cook for 2 minutes.
2. Beat milk powder with hot water and stir slowly into a roux. Simmer.
3. Add spices, herbs, and cheddar cheese.
4. Toss corn stuffing mix with wheat germ.
5. Place 2 pounds 8 ounces of squash slices in an oiled pan. Cover with 1 quart of cheese sauce and 12 ounces of cornbread mix. Repeat.
6. Cover and bake at 325° F for 25 minutes.
7. Remove cover and bake for 10 more minutes. Serve at once.

Calories: **229**   Protein: **8.0 g (14%)**   Carbohydrates: **32.4 g (57%)**   Sodium: **511 mg**

Total Fat: **6.5 g (26%)**   *Saturated Fat:* **2.4 g**   *Monounsaturated Fat:* **1.4 g**   *Polyunsaturated Fat:* **2.1 g**

❖ Vegan Stir-fry

Peanuts and fermented black beans add a new twist to a familiar stir-fry. The peanuts add protein, but also fat and calories (105 per oz/10 calories per serving). Please weigh oil and nuts carefully. More is neither merrier nor better here.

PRODUCTION NOTES: This recipe calls for young corn on the cob. These miniature cobs are available canned. Frozen kernel corn can be substituted if necessary. Chinese black bean sauce can be used instead of fermented black beans.

Portions per recipe: 60	*Pan: 12" × 20" × 2"*
Yield: 2 pans	*Griddle temperature: 375° F*
Portion: 5 ounces	*Time: 8 minutes*
Serving utensil: spoon	

Ingredients	Amounts
Broccoli florets and stems, peeled and thinly sliced	6 lb.
Cauliflower, cored and cut into bite-size pieces	6 lb.
Red bell peppers, sliced into thin strips	2 lb.
Scallions, 1" pieces	12 oz.
Canned miniature corn cobs, drained	3 lb. 12 oz.
Peanut oil	1 oz.
Unsalted roasted Virginia peanuts, chopped	6 oz.
Chinese fermented black beans, rinsed and chopped	4 oz.
Yellow bean sauce	4 oz.
Soy sauce	2 oz.
Lemon juice	2 oz.

Procedure:

1. Mix the cut vegetables together and divide into 2 batches.
2. Heat griddle with ½ ounce of oil, 3 ounces of peanuts, and 2 ounces of black beans.
3. Stir-fry for 1 minute and add 1 batch of vegetables.
4. Stir-fry for 5 minutes. Mix together yellow bean sauce, soy sauce, and lemon.
5. Drizzle 4 ounces over vegetables and toss well.
6. Transfer to pan. Start next batch.

Calories: **42**   Protein: **2.3 g (21%)**   Carbohydrates: **5.2 g (49%)**   Sodium: **66 mg**

Total Fat: **1.9 g (40%)**   *Saturated Fat:* **.3 g**   *Monounsaturated Fat:* **.7 g**   *Polyunsaturated Fat:* **.6 g**

❖ Vegetable Strudel

Loved by all the UNH students, these beta-carotene rich vegetables in puff pastry make these strudel triangles a very special treat, alas high in fat. The same filling can be placed in two strips of phyllo dough (see Indian potato pastries, page 83 for instructions). Substitute 4 pounds of phyllo and 4 ounces of butter for puff pastry and it will reduce the calories to 125 and the fat to 3.8 grams (27%) per serving.

Portions per recipe: 120	Pan: 18″ × 26″ sheet pan
Yield: 120 triangles	Oven temperature: 425° F
Portion: 1 strudel	Time: 8–10 minutes
Serving utensil: spatula	

Ingredients

Ingredients	Amounts
Frozen puff pastry, thawed	15 lb.
Canned sweet potatoes, drained	6 lb. 10 oz.
Low-fat cottage cheese	4 lb.
Cheddar cheese, shredded	2 lb. 8 oz.
Frozen chopped broccoli, thawed and drained	5 lb.
Garlic cloves, crushed	1 oz.
Ground cloves	1/8 oz.
Black pepper	1/4 oz.
Salt	1/2 oz.
Eggs	2 oz.
Water	8 oz.

Procedure:

1. Cut each puff pastry sheet into six squares.
2. Mash sweet potatoes with paddle in mixer. Fold in rest of ingredients.
3. Place one #16 scoop of filling in center of pastry.
4. Brush edges of pastry with beaten egg and water and fold over to form a triangle. Press edges with fork to seal.
5. Line sheet pans with parchment paper. Place 24 triangles on sheet pan.
6. Prick twice with fork and bake at 425° F for 8 to 10 minutes.

Calories: **333**   Protein: **7.5 g (9%)**   Carbohydrates: **24.3 g (29%)**   Sodium: **307 mg**

Total Fat: **23.3 g (62%)**   *Saturated Fat: *   *Monounsaturated Fat: *   *Polyunsaturated Fat: *

---

*Incomplete data since no fat component data was available from puff pastry manufacturer.

❖ Vegetarian Chow Mein

This dish was developed for quantity production from a recipe in Ken Hom's book, *Asian Vegetarian Feast*. I added the yellow pepper strips for color and the chili bean sauce for "heat."

PRODUCTION NOTE: Cilantro has a strong taste loved by afficionados. However, for all but the keenest tastes, temper the cilantro by mixing it with parsley.

Portions per recipe: 60	*Pan: 12" × 20" × 2"*
Yield: 2 pans	*Griddle temperature: 375° F*
Portion: 7 ounces	*Time: 7 minutes*
Serving utensil: 6-ounce ladle	

Ingredients

Ingredients	Amounts
Medium egg noodles	5 lb.
Water	24 lb.
Peanut oil	2 oz.
Garlic cloves, crushed	2 oz.
Ginger root, peeled and chopped	2 oz.
Chili bean sauce	2 oz.
Celery, sliced diagonally into ½" pieces	3 lb.
Mushroom buttons, trimmed and cut into halves	3 lb.
Canned bamboo shoots, drained	2 lb. 2 oz.
Fresh bean sprouts, rinsed	5 lb.
Soy sauce	4 oz.
Dry sherry	4 oz.
Cilantro leaves, chopped	2 oz.
Parsley, minced	4 oz.

Procedure:

1. Cook noodles for about 7 minutes in boiling lightly salted water.
2. Drain and hold in cold water until needed.
3. Heat oil with garlic, ginger, and chili bean sauce.
4. Add celery, mushrooms, and bamboo shoots. Stir-fry for 5 minutes.
5. Add noodles with bean sprouts and stir-fry for 2 minutes.
6. Sprinkle with sherry sauce, soy sauce, and herbs. Toss well and transfer to serving pan.

Calories: **180**   Protein: **7.6 g (17%)**   Carbohydrates: **31.8 g (70%)**   Sodium: **139 mg**

Total Fat: **3.3 g (17%)**   *Saturated Fat: .6 g*   *Monounsaturated Fat: .9 g*   *Polyunsaturated Fat: .8 g*

—7—

SANDWICHES

Preparing sandwiches in large quantities is time consuming, but can be streamlined if done assembly-line fashion. Most customers prefer to have sandwiches made to order, but this is a slow and annoying task in a large cafeteria where speed of service is essential. In a college or other residential food service operation, a make-your-own sandwich bar is an effective solution. Sandwich fillings are controlled by a server, but the bread and fixings are available for self-service. The diners make the selection and prepare the sandwich themselves—a tremendous labor saving device with perfect control on the high cost components.

Cold cuts, cheeses, egg, meat, and fish salad combinations can be placed on various rolls and breads with or without lettuce and tomatoes. There are the classic sandwiches such as the Reuben, Grilled Cheese, and Tuna, but creative sandwich making has no limit other than good taste.

I have included a few meat sandwich combinations and a larger number of meatless sandwiches, hot and cold.

Sandwiches with Meat and Fish

❖

❖ Beef and Cheese Sub

Sautéed vegetables with browned beef and a little melted cheese make this sub a very satisfying meal.

PRODUCTION NOTES: Leftover beef patties or roast beef can make an encore appearance in disguise. Just sauté chopped or crumbled cooked beef briefly with a little oil and the vegetables. The bran is added to absorb moisture and prevent the sub from getting soggy, and adds fiber.

Portions per recipe: 96
Yield: 8 dozen subs
Portion: 1 sub
Serving utensil: tongs

Pan: 12" × 20" × 2"
Oven temperature: 325° F
Time: 5–6 minutes

Ingredients	Amounts
Lean ground beef (15% fat)	15 lb.
Garlic cloves, crushed	2 oz.
Oregano, crushed	¼ oz.
Basil, crushed	¼ oz.
Salt	2 oz.
Black pepper	⅛ oz.
Spanish onions, thinly sliced	4 lb.
Celery stalks and tops, chopped	2 lb.
Green bell peppers, chopped	3 lb.
Wheat, rice, or oat bran	4 oz.
Tomatoes, coarsely chopped	5 lb.
Part skim mozzarella cheese, shredded	3 lb.
Sub rolls (about 2.7 ounces each)	16 lb.

Procedure:

1. Brown ground beef with garlic and spices. Drain excess fat.
2. Add onions, celery, and peppers and stir-fry for 10 minutes.
3. Remove from heat. Fold in bran, tomatoes, and cheese.
4. Fill sub rolls wih 4 ounces of meat mixture.
5. Heat uncovered at 325° F for 5 to 7 minutes or until cheese has melted.

Calories: **409**   Protein: **24.5 g (24%)**   Carbohydrates: **41.0 g (40%)**   Sodium: **796 mg**
Total Fat: **17.1 g (38%)**   *Saturated Fat:* **7.8 g**   *Monounsaturated Fat:* **7.1 g**   *Polyunsaturated Fat:* **.8 g**

❖ Marinated Fish on a Bun

Grilled fish fillets are marinated for two days with red wine vinegar, onions, celery, and roasted peppers and served on a bun with lettuce and tomato.

PRODUCTION NOTES: Fish fillets should be thick and fit inside the bun. Cod, haddock, pollock, tilefish and rockfish are all excellent for this sandwich. This is a good way to make use of leftover baked or fried fish. Just cut the cooked fish portions to fit the buns.

Portions per recipe: *96*
Yield: *8 dozen sandwiches*
Portion: *3-ounce fish fillet on a bun*
Serving utensil: *spatula*

Pan: *12" × 20" × 2"*
Griddle temperature: *350° F*
Time: *10 minutes*

Ingredients | Amounts

Ingredients	Amounts
Hungarian paprika	¹/₂ oz.
All-purpose flour	8 oz.
Firm, white fish fillets (3 ounces each)	18 lb.
Olive oil	2 oz.
Spanish onions, thinly sliced	3 lb.
Celery stalks, very thinly sliced	3 lb.
Canned roasted red peppers	3 lb.
Red wine vinegar	2 lb.
Salt	1 oz.
Black pepper	¹/₄ oz.
Basil, crushed	¹/₈ oz.
Romaine lettuce, bun size pieces	1 lb. 8 oz.
Tomatoes, sliced	4 lb.
Whole wheat buns	10 lb. 8 oz.

Procedure:

1. Mix paprika with flour and dredge fish fillets in the flour.
2. Grill fillets on a well-oiled griddle for 5 minutes on each side.
3. Place in one layer in pan.
4. Heat olive oil and sauté onions and celery for 5 minutes only. Vegetables should be crisp.
5. Slice roasted peppers into strips and add with vinegar and spices to onions and celery.
6. Pour vegetables over fish and let marinate for 2 days.
7. Place 15 bun bottoms in pan. Top with lettuce leaf and tomato slice.
8. With slotted spoon, place fish fillets on buns.
9. Top with extra vegetables and cover with bun tops. Serve at once.

Calories: **227**   Protein: **21.9 g (38%)**   Carbohydrates: **29.2 g (51%)**   Sodium: **246 mg**

Total Fat: **2.9 g (11%)**   *Saturated Fat:* **.2 g**   *Monounsaturated Fat:* **.6 g**   *Polyunsaturated Fat:* **.6 g**

❖ Muffaletta

This version of the famous New Orleans sandwich uses fresh vegetables rather than the traditional pickled vegetables.

PRODUCTION NOTES: Slice 1-pound loaves of Italian bread in half. Hollow out the bottom half by removing the soft center, leaving the crust. Dry the removed bread and make into bread crumbs. Buy economical salad olives for this recipe.

Portions per recipe: 60
Yield: 12 loaves
Portion: ⅕ loaf
Serving utensil: plate

Ingredients	Amounts	
Italian bread	12 lb.	
Celery, thinly sliced	2 lb.	
Carrots, coarsely shredded	2 lb.	
Cauliflower, chopped	2 lb.	
Scallions, chopped	1 lb.	
Green olives with pimentos, chopped		8 oz.
Olive oil		1 oz.
Lemon juice		2 oz.
Black pepper		⅛ oz.
Oregano, crushed		⅛ oz.
Red pepper flakes		¹⁄₁₆ oz.
Italian parsley, minced		4 oz.
Mortadella, ½-ounce slices	1 lb.	14 oz.
Cooked ham, 1-ounce slices	3 lb.	12 oz.
Genoa salami, ¼-ounce slices		15 oz.
Provolone cheese, 1-ounce slices	3 lb.	12 oz.

Procedure:

1. Prepare loaves of bread.
2. Mix the vegetables with olives, oil, lemon juice, spices, and parsley.
3. Fill loaf bottoms with 10 ounces of vegetable salad.
4. Top with 5 slices each of mortadella, ham, salami, and provolone.
5. Cover with bread crust and slice into 5 pieces. Place on plate to serve.

Calories: **498**   Protein: **25.0 g (20%)**   Carbohydrates: **56.0 g (45%)**   Sodium: **1496 mg**

Total Fat: **18.1 g (33%)**   *Saturated Fat:* **7.1 g**   *Monounsaturated Fat:* **6.6 g**   *Polyunsaturated Fat:* **1.3 g**

❖ Shrimp Salad Boat

Shrimp and eggs mixed with a lemony yogurt mayonnaise and minced lima beans result in a surprisingly creamy texture. European cucumber slices tucked into the frankfurter roll make this a light, refreshing sandwich.

PRODUCTION NOTES: Celery should be blanched to kill any bacteria. To save time and labor, crack eggs into oiled pan and steam at low pressure for 7 minutes. 12 pounds of cooked salad shrimp can be substituted for raw shrimp.

Portions per recipe: 96
Yield: 8 dozen rolls
Portion: 1 Roll
Serving utensil: tongs

Pan: 12″ × 20″ × 2″
Serve chilled

Ingredients

Ingredients	Amounts	
Maine shrimp	15 lb.	
Cooked eggs (see production note)	4 lb.	
Celery stalks, blanched	2 lb.	
Lima beans, cooked	2 lb.	8 oz.
Lemon juice		2 oz.
Italian parsley		4 oz.
Salt		1 oz.
White pepper		1/8 oz.
Mayonnaise		8 oz.
Low-fat yogurt, drained 30 minutes	2 lb.	
Frankfurter rolls	9 lb.	
European cucumbers, thinly sliced	6 lb.	

Procedure:

1. Steam raw Maine shrimp for 5 to 7 minutes at low pressure. Drain.
2. Place eggs, celery, lima beans, lemon juice, and parsley in food processor and mince.
3. Remove to a bowl and fold in shrimp, salt, pepper, mayonnaise, and drained yogurt. Chill for 30 minutes.
4. Open frankfurter roll, insert 4 cucumber slices and two #24 scoops of shrimp salad. Keep chilled until ready to serve.

Calories: **259**   Protein: **21.5 g (33%)**   Carbohydrates: **25.9 g (40%)**   Sodium: **512 mg**
Total Fat: **7.3 g (25%)**   *Saturated Fat:* **1.1 g**   *Monounsaturated Fat:* **.7 g**   *Polyunsaturated Fat:* **2.1 g**

❖ Smoked Turkey and Avocado Sandwich

The mild smokey flavor of the turkey is complemented by grapefruit and avocado slices on Russian, health, or whole wheat bread.

PRODUCTION NOTES: A 2-pound sandwich loaf provides about 28 slices of bread, or 14 sandwiches. The creamy avocado takes the place of mayonnaise, and even though it is relatively high in oil, the fatty acids are mostly mono- and polyunsaturated.

Portions per recipe: 84
Yield: 84 sandwiches
Portion: 1 sandwich
Serving utensil: plate

Pan: 18″ × 26″ sheet pan

Ingredients	Amounts
Grapefruit	4 lb.
Ripe avocados	8 lb.
Olive oil	1 oz.
Black pepper	⅛ oz.
Whole wheat sandwich bread	12 lb.
Radish sprouts	2 lb.
Smoked turkey, thinly sliced	13 lb. 2 oz.

Procedure:

1. Peel and section grapefruit, place in colander, and let juices drain for about 5 minutes.
2. Peel and pit avocado and slice thinly. Pour 4 oz. of drained juice over avocado slices to prevent discoloration.
3. Toss grapefruit with olive oil and pepper. Fold in avocado.
4. Place bread in 4 rows of 6 slices on sheet pan. Top each slice with ⅓ ounce of sprouts and 1½ ounces of avocado salad.
5. Place 2 ounces of thinly sliced turkey on top.
6. Top with a slice of bread. Secure each sandwich with 2 frilled picks.
7. Cut sandwich in half diagonally. Serve on plate.

Calories: **335**   Protein: **22.2 g (26%)**   Carbohydrates: **37.6 g (44%)**   Sodium: **830 mg**
Total Fat: **12.1 g (32%)**   Saturated Fat: **2.9 g**   Monounsaturated Fat: **4.9 g**   Polyunsaturated Fat: **2.1 g**

The super hero is a super sandwich.

❖ Super Hero

There is a story behind this basically ordinary sandwich. On one April Fools' Day we presented the UNH students at lunch with an absolutely empty serving line and large signs saying "April Fools!" Inside the dining room we had set up long tables with six-foot long loaves of the super hero and the servers were cutting the sandwich according to the students' requests. The sandwiches became a favorite even when presented in regular loaves.

PRODUCTION NOTES: You will need a rotary oven to produce six-foot loaves. However, 36-inch loaves can have their ends removed and aligned. Setting up the loaves this way they will extend as long as your line.

(continued)

Portions per recipe: 96
Yield: 12 loaves
Portion: ¹/₈ loaf
Serving utensil: serrated knife

Ingredients	Amounts
French bread, long (36")	15 lb.
Cooked ham	6 lb.
Cooked turkey breast	6 lb.
Genoa salami	1 lb. 8 oz.
Swiss cheese	3 lb.
Processed American cheese	3 lb.
Romaine, cleaned	6 lb.
Tomatoes, sliced	5 lb.
Green bell peppers, shredded	3 lb.

Procedure:

1. Split bread in half.
2. Slice ham and turkey into 1-ounce slices and shave salami into ¹/₈-ounce slices.
3. Cut Swiss cheese into 1-ounce slices and American cheese into ½-ounce slices.
4. On the bottom half of the French loaf place a layer of romaine.
5. Place a row of tomatoes on top of romaine.
6. Top with a row each of ham, turkey, salami, and Swiss cheese.
7. Place American cheese on an angle (see photo).
8. Slice into 8 portions.

Calories: **448**   Protein: **25.0 g (22%)**   Carbohydrates: **44.0 g (39%)**   Sodium: **1381 mg**
Total Fat: **15.7 g (32%)**   *Saturated Fat:* **7.1 g**   *Monounsaturated Fat:* **5.8 g**   *Polyunsaturated Fat:* **.8 g**

Sandwiches with Cheeses and Vegetables

❖

The sandwiches below are meatless. Some could have small amounts of meat added if desired. For example, the bagel could easily become a ham, broccoli, and cheese bagel. Be creative and adapt any of these sandwiches to your specific operation. Remember that you must recalculate the food values if you want to post them for your customers.

❖ Broccoli Cheese Bagel

Slightly crunchy broccoli smothered with melted cheese tops this bagel.

Portions per recipe: 72
Yield: 144 bagel halves
Portion: 2 bagel halves
Serving utensil: spatula

Pan: 12" × 20" × 2"
Oven temperature: 325° F
Time: 6 minutes

Ingredients	Amounts
Olive oil	1 oz.
Garlic cloves, crushed	1 oz.
Mushrooms, thinly sliced	4 lb. 8 oz.
Marjoram, crushed	⅛ oz.
Frozen chopped broccoli	10 lb.
Plain bagel, sliced	9 lb.
Alfalfa sprouts	1 lb.
Provolone cheese, 1-ounce slices	9 lb.

Procedure:

1. Heat olive oil with garlic. Sauté mushrooms for 7 minutes.

2. Add marjoram and thawed broccoli to mushrooms and sauté for 2 minutes.

3. Using a #16 scoop place vegetables onto bagel halves, add a few sprouts, and top with provolone cheese.

4. Bake at 325° F for 6 minutes or until cheese is melted.

> Calories: **386**   Protein: **22.9 g (24%)**   Carbohydrates: **35.8 g (37%)**   Sodium: **706 mg**
> Total Fat: **17.2 g (40%)**   *Saturated Fat:* **9.8 g**   *Monounsaturated Fat:* **4.5 g**   *Polyunsaturated Fat:* **.6 g**

❖ Eggplant Sandwich

Sautéed eggplant slices are placed on a bed of shredded vegetables and covered with cheese and a tomato concasse. *Concassé* is a French term for briefly sautéed chopped tomatoes to distinguish it from a long cooking tomato sauce.

PRODUCTION NOTES: Salt eggplant slices and let them drain before sautéing them on the griddle. They must be fully cooked. Peel tomatoes by dipping them in boiling water for 20 seconds. Cut plum tomatoes in half and squeeze out seeds before chopping them coarsely.

Portions per recipe: 96	*Pan: 12″ × 20″ × 2″*
Yield: 8 dozen sandwiches	*Griddle temperature: 350° F*
Portion: 1 sandwich	*Time: 8 minutes*
Serving utensil: spatula	

Ingredients	Amounts	
Unpeeled eggplant, ½″ thick slices	12 lb.	
Salt		2 oz.
Carrots, finely shredded	2 lb.	
Chinese cabbage, finely shredded	2 lb.	
Celery, finely shredded	1 lb.	
Zucchini, finely shredded	1 lb.	
Scallions, minced		8 oz.

Tomato Concassé:

Olive oil		1 oz.
Spanish onions, chopped		8 oz.
Italian plum tomatoes, peeled, seeded and chopped	4 lb.	
Oregano, crushed		⅛ oz.
Salt		½ oz.
Black pepper		⅕ oz.
Whole wheat buns (1¾ ounces)	10 lb.	8 oz.
Provolone cheese, shredded	3 lb.	

Procedure:

1. Place eggplant slices in colander and sprinkle with salt. After 20 minutes rinse with cold water and drain.

2. Heat griddle to 350° F. Oil lightly and grill eggplant for 4 minutes on each side.

3. Toss all the vegetables together.

4. Heat olive oil and sauté onions and tomatoes with oregano for 5 minutes.

The eggplant sandwich can be served open-faced or closed.

5. Place 15 bun bottoms in pan and top with about 1 ounce of vegetables using a #16 scoop.

6. Set hot eggplant slice on vegetables and ladle 1 ounce of tomato concassé over eggplant.

7. Top with provolone and bun halves. Serve at once.

8. Variation: Present an openfaced sandwich with shredded vegetable on one bun half and eggplant topped with provolone and hot tomato concassé on the other.

Calories: **194**   Protein: **9.2 g (18%)**   Carbohydrates: **29.6 g (61%)**   Sodium: **400 mg**
Total Fat: **5.4 g (25%)**   *Saturated Fat:* **2.4 g**   *Monounsaturated Fat:* **1.3 g**   *Polyunsaturated Fat:* **.2 g**

❖ Falafel in a Pita Pocket

Falafel balls mixed with potatoes and baked, not deep-fried, are served in a pita pocket with a cucumber yogurt sauce. They are wonderful!

Portions per recipe: 96
Yield: 48 pita breads
Portion: 1 half pocket with 5 falafel
Serving utensil: plastic gloves

Pan: 18" × 26" sheet pan
Oven temperature: 350° F
Time: 10 minutes

Ingredients	Amounts
Olive oil	2 oz.
Garlic cloves, crushed	4 oz.
Spanish onions, finely chopped	1 lb.
Canned chick peas (garbanzo beans), drained	9 lb. 15 oz.
Peeled potatoes, cooked	5 lb.
Tahini	2 lb.
Eggs, beaten	2 lb.
Cumin	¼ oz.
Cayenne pepper	⅛ oz.
Turmeric	⅛ oz.
Salt	1 oz.
Cilantro, chopped	2 oz.
Syrian bread	9 lb.
Cucumber yogurt sauce (see recipe on page 370)	12 lb.
Tomatoes, cut into wedges	3 lb.

Procedure:

1. Heat olive oil with garlic and sauté onions until very soft.
2. Place chick peas, potatoes and tahini in food chopper or processor and mash until smooth.
3. Remove to a bowl. Add onions, eggs, spices, and cilantro and mix well.
4. With a #50 scoop set mounds of chick pea batter on oiled sheet pan.
5. Bake at 350° F for 10 minutes.
6. Cut pockets in half, stuff with 5 falafel, and with a #16 scoop top falafel with 2 ounces of cucumber salad.
7. Garnish with tomato wedge and serve at once.

Calories: **279**   Protein: **10.5 g (15%)**   Carbohydrates: **41.1 g (59%)**   Sodium: **545 mg**
Total Fat: **7.8 g (25%)**   *Saturated Fat:* **1.3 g**   *Monounsaturated Fat:* **4.7 g**   *Polyunsaturated Fat:* **1.1 g**

❖ Garden Sandwich

The original recipe was given to us by Smith College in Massachusetts. It has gone through many changes over the years. This is a very popular sandwich. See color plate **15**.

PRODUCTION NOTE: Use the Russian bread recipe to bake sandwich loaves that yield 28 slices per loaf.

Portions per recipe: *112*
Yield: *112 sandwich slices*
Portion: *1 sandwich slice*
Serving utensil: *spatula*

Pan: *18" × 26" sheet pan*
Oven temperature: *325° F*
Time: *5 minutes*

Ingredients

Ingredients	Amounts	
Chopped frozen spinach	12 lb.	8 oz.
Safflower oil		2 oz.
Scallions, chopped		12 oz.
Mushrooms, thinly sliced	6 lb.	
Green bell peppers, chopped	2 lb.	
Swiss cheese, shredded	2 lb.	
Sunflower seeds, toasted		8 oz.
Mayonnaise		4 oz.
Low-fat yogurt	1 lb.	
Lemon juice		4 oz.
Black pepper		¼ oz.
Russian bread, sliced	8 lb.	
Tomatoes, sliced	5 lb.	
Provolone cheese, 1-ounce slices	8 lb.	

Procedure:

1. Cook spinach without water for 10 minutes, drain, and squeeze dry.
2. Heat oil and sauté scallions, mushrooms, and bell peppers for 5 minutes.
3. Remove to bowl and add spinach, Swiss cheese, sunflower seeds, mayonnaise, yogurt, lemon juice, and pepper. Blend well.
4. Oil sheet pan lightly. Arrange bread in 4 rows of 6 slices.
5. With a #12 scoop dip spinach mixture onto bread.
6. Spread slightly and top with 1 tomato slice and 1 provolone cheese slice.
7. Bake at 325° F for 5 minutes or until cheese has melted.

Calories: **251**   Protein: **14.7 g (23%)**   Carbohydrates: **22.4 g (36%)**   Sodium: **283 mg**
Total Fat: **12.3 g (44%)**   *Saturated Fat:* **6.6 g**   *Monounsaturated Fat:* **3.0 g**   *Polyunsaturated Fat:* **1.7 g**

❖ Hummis and Cheese Pocket

Pita pockets are filled with hummis, Swiss cheese, sprouts, cucumbers, and tomatoes.

PRODUCTION NOTE: Pita pockets open with ease if they are cut in half and then warmed up.

Portions per recipe: 96
Yield: 96 pockets/48 pita breads
Portion: 1 pocket
Serving utensil: #24 scoop

Ingredients	Amounts
Canned chick peas (garbanzo beans), drained	6 lb. 10 oz.
Tahini paste, oil stirred in	2 lb.
Lemon juice	4 oz.
Low-fat yogurt	1 lb.
Garlic cloves, crushed	2 oz.
Cayenne pepper	1/8 oz.
Salt	1 oz.
Curry powder	1/2 oz.
Whole wheat syrian bread	9 lb.
Swiss cheese, 1-ounce slices	6 lb.
European cucumber, thinly sliced	6 lb.
Tomatoes, sliced	8 lb.
Alfalfa sprouts	1 lb. 8 oz.

Procedure:

1. In a food chopper or processor mash chick peas to a smooth paste.
2. Add tahini, lemon juice, yogurt, garlic, and spices. Blend well.
3. Cut pouches in half, open, and fill with 1 slice Swiss cheese, a #24 scoop of hummis, 3 cucumber slices, 2 tomato slices, and ¼ cup of sprouts.
4. Serve at once.

Calories: **336**   Protein: **16.3 g (19%)**   Carbohydrates: **33.8 g (40%)**   Sodium: **441 mg**

Total Fat: **14.1 g (38%)**   *Saturated Fat:* **5.9 g**   *Monounsaturated Fat:* **6.2 g**   *Polyunsaturated Fat:* **1.6 g**

❖ Open Face Bean Sprout Sandwich

Three kinds of sprouts add texture and flavor to this melted cheese sandwich.

Portions per recipe: 24
Yield: 48 slices
Portion: 2 slices
Serving utensil: spatula

Pan: 18" × 26" sheet pan
Oven temperature: 350° F
Time: 3–5 minutes

Ingredients

Ingredients	Amounts	
Whole wheat or rye bread	*4 lb.*	
Prepared yellow mustard		*8 oz.*
Tomatoes, sliced	*6 lb.*	
Bean sprouts, rinsed	*3 lb.*	
Radish sprouts, rinsed	*1 lb.*	
Alfalfa sprouts		*12 oz.*
Swiss cheese, 1-ounce slices	*3 lb.*	

Procedure:

1. Spread bread lightly with mustard.
2. Place 4 rows of 6 slices on sheet pan.
3. Arrange 3 tomato slices on each piece of bread.
4. Mix sprouts by tossing them gently. Top tomatoes with 1½ ounces of sprouts.
5. Cover with Swiss cheese.
6. Bake at 350° F for 3 to 5 minutes or until cheese has melted.

Calories: **370**   Protein: **24 g (25%)**   Carbohydrates: **18 g (43%)**   Sodium: **481 mg**
Total Fat: **18.0 g (43%)**   *Saturated Fat:* **10.3 g**   *Monounsaturated Fat:* **4.3 g**   *Polyunsaturated Fat:* **1.0 g**

❖ Sprout and Mushroom Melt

The oatmeal bread adds sweetness to this delightful grilled cheese sandwich.

Portions per recipe: 96
Yield: 96 sandwiches
Portion: 1 sandwich
Serving utensil: spatula

Pan: 18″ × 26″ sheet pan
Griddle temperature: 350° F
Time: 8 minutes

Ingredients	Amounts
Olive oil	2 oz.
Garlic cloves, crushed	2 oz.
Mushrooms, thinly sliced	6 lb.
Soy sauce	2 oz.
Fresh bean sprouts, rinsed	4 lb.
Tomatoes, chopped	4 lb.
Part skim mozzarella, shredded	3 lb.
Oatmeal bread, sliced	12 lb.
Gouda cheese, 1-ounce slices	6 lb.

Procedure:

1. Heat olive oil with garlic. Sauté mushrooms for 10 minutes.
2. Remove to large bowl. Fold in soy sauce, bean sprouts, tomatoes, and shredded mozzarella.
3. With #12 scoop ladle mixture onto oatmeal bread. Top with gouda and another slice of oatmeal bread. Press together lightly.
4. Grill sandwich on both sides for 4 minutes.

Calories: **329**   Protein: **17.7 g (22%)**   Carbohydrates: **34.0 g (41%)**   Sodium: **279 mg**

Total Fat: **13.4 g (37%)**   Saturated Fat: **6.9 g**   Monounsaturated Fat: **3.7 g**   Polyunsaturated Fat: **1.8 g**

❖ Tofu Egg Salad on Seeded Rye

The flavor and taste of egg salad made with cholesterol free tofu.

Portions per recipe: 36
Yield: 36 sandwiches
Portion: 1 sandwich
Serving utensil: plate

Ingredients	Amounts	
Scallions, minced		12 oz.
Celery stalks and tops, finely chopped		12 oz.
Soft tofu, crumbled	5 lb.	
Mayonnaise		12 oz.
Dry mustard		1/4 oz.
Dijon-style mustard		2 oz.
Salt		1 oz.
Hungarian paprika		1/4 oz.
Turmeric		1/8 oz.
Seeded rye bread, sliced	5 lb.	
Boston lettuce leaves	1 lb.	

Procedure:

1. Blend together scallions, celery, tofu, mayonnaise, and spices.
2. Place rye slices on cutting board and top each slice with a lettuce leaf.
3. With a #12 scoop dip tofu salad onto lettuce and spread lightly.
4. Top with another slice of rye. Secure with two frilled picks. Cut in half.

Calories: **276**   Protein: **11.4 g (16%)**   Carbohydrates: **35.6 g (51%)**   Sodium: **742 mg**

Total Fat: **11.4 g (37%)**   *Saturated Fat:* **1.3 g**   *Monounsaturated Fat:* **2.2 g**   *Polyunsaturated Fat:* **7.2 g**

❖ Vegetarian Sub

I developed this hot vegetarian sandwich for cookouts, but because it was so popular we served it frequently for lunch or as a sandwich supper.

PRODUCTION NOTE: Split the top of the sub roll like a hotdog bun. Do not slice it.

Portions per recipe: 96
Yield: 8 dozen subs
Portion: 1 sub
Serving utensil: plastic wrap

Pan: 12″ × 20″ × 2″
Oven temperature: 325° F
Time: 8 minutes

Ingredients	Amounts	
Olive oil		2 oz.
Garlic cloves, crushed		1 oz.
Zucchini, thinly sliced	10 lb.	
Mushrooms, sliced	3 lb.	
Green bell peppers, shredded	6 lb.	
Bean sprouts, rinsed and drained	4 lb.	
Tomatoes, cut in wedges	6 lb.	
Oregano, crushed		¼ oz.
Red pepper flakes		⅛ oz.
Salt		1 oz.
Italian parsley, minced		4 oz.
Basil, shredded		2 oz.
Large whole wheat hoagie rolls, split	16 lb.	
Cheddar cheese, shredded	3 lb.	
Part skim mozzarella, shredded	6 lb.	

Procedure:

1. Heat oil with garlic. Sauté zucchini, mushrooms, and peppers for 10 minutes.
2. Fold in tomatoes, bean sprouts, spices, and herbs.
3. Fill each hoagie roll with 4 ounces of vegetables.
4. Mix cheeses together and sprinkle 1½ ounces over vegetables.
5. Set rolls split side up in pan. Bake at 325° F for 8 minutes.
6. Wrap in plastic for take-out. Keep warm.

Calories: **363**   Protein: **18.5 g (20%)**   Carbohydrates: **43.5 g (48%)**   Sodium: **761 mg**

Total Fat: **13.6 g (34%)**   *Saturated Fat:* **6.5 g**   *Monounsaturated Fat:* **4.0 g**   *Polyunsaturated Fat:* **1.9 g**

8

SALADS

Colorful salads put together from crisp greens and vegetables or from combinations of starch, meat, eggs, cheese, or fish are becoming more and more popular. Nutrition conscious customers select salads as lunch or dinner entrées or as a part of their meals. Well-presented and displayed salad plates enhance deli case offerings and speed up service on made-to-order sandwich lines. Lunch and dinner banquet menus that include salad plate presentations that can be put together assembly-line fashion are easy on the serving staff and please most guests.

Salad bars are now firmly established in college and university dining halls, restaurants, school lunch rooms, staff cafeterias, and even in fast food places. Many diners will make a meal from the salad bar in the mistaken notion that the rest of the food offered is too high in calories. They carefully select low-calorie greens and vegetables and then drown them in oily dressings and top them with such high-calorie items as shredded cheese, sunflower seeds, and croutons. They end up with a lot of calories from fat and hardly any carbohydrates. Institutions need to inform and educate their customers about the nutritional value of salad bar items with displays or menu newsletters and table tents.

Salad Plates

❖

Serve salads on well-chilled plates, neatly arranged with simple edible garnishes if needed. Robust greens such as spinach, escarole, radicchio, or Belgian endive can be dressed in advance. Tender greens wilt too fast to be dressed before serving. Salad dressings should be served separately from cruets on the table or from self-service stations. Many calorie conscious guests prefer this in any case.

Below are just a few of my favorite salad combinations. Imaginative cooks and menu planners will use encore foods to produce salad plates, not only to enhance the menu but also to reduce food waste and generate additional revenue. Produce a riot of colors and textures with your salad plates to keep your customers content and your staff challenged.

❖ Banquet Salad Plate

A beautiful and sturdy salad that can wait for the guests.

PRODUCTION NOTES: Slice bottom end of Belgian endive to loosen leaves as often as necessary. Use large outer leaves for plate design and add the small center leaves to the romaine and escarole. If fresh chives are not available, substitute thinly sliced scallion greens, not freeze-dried chives.

Portions per recipe: 150
Yield: 150 plates
Portion: 1 plate
Serving utensil: plate

Serve chilled
Time: 30 minutes

Ingredients	Amounts
Romaine lettuce, cleaned	10 lb.
Escarole, cleaned	6 lb.
Belgian endive	14 lb.
Mushrooms, washed and thinly sliced	5 lb.
Red onions, sliced into rings	4 lb.
Red bell peppers, sliced into rings	6 lb.
Olive oil	3 lb.
Red wine vinegar	12 oz.
Water (cold)	4 oz.
Garlic cloves, peeled and halved	1 oz.
Salt	2 oz.
Black pepper	½ oz.
Parsley, minced	4 oz.
Fresh chives, finely chopped	2 oz.

Procedure:

1. Cut romaine and escarole into bite-size pieces.
2. Separate endive leaves and place 5 large leaves in a star shape on the plate. (See photo.) Add small leaves to greens.
3. Fill center of star with 2 ounces of greens.
4. Top with ½ ounce of mushroom slices, 3 onion rings, and one red pepper ring.
5. Mix olive oil with vinegar, water, garlic, salt, and pepper.
6. Let dressing flavors develop for 30 minutes. Remove garlic. Beat dressing with herbs.
7. Pour ½ ounce of dressing over greens or serve dressing separately.

Calories: **123**   Protein: **.6 g (2%)**   Carbohydrates: **9.6 g (31%)**   Sodium: **171 mg**
Total Fat: **9.3 g (68%)**   *Saturated Fat:* **1.3 g**   *Monounsaturated Fat:* **6.7 g**   *Polyunsaturated Fat:* **.9 g**

The banquet salad plate pleases both the eye and the palate.

❖ Cheese Salad Plate

This is a fruit and cheese salad plate. With a hunk of crusty French or dark Russian bread it makes a good lunch or light supper.

PRODUCTION NOTES: The apple wedger and corer gadget comes in handy here. To prevent apple slices from oxidizing dip them in acidulated water or simply use pineapple juice.

Portions per recipe: 100   *Serve chilled*
Yield: 100 plates
Portion: 1 plate
Serving utensil: #12 scoop

(continued)

Ingredients	Amounts
Swiss cheese, shredded	6 lb. 8 oz.
Cheddar cheese, shredded	6 lb. 8 oz.
Radishes, finely shredded	2 lb.
Carrots, shredded	2 lb.
Green bell peppers, diced	1 lb.
Celery, blanched 10 seconds and diced	2 lb.
Scallions, chopped	1 lb.
Walnuts, chopped	8 oz.
Low-fat yogurt	2 lb.
Parsley, minced	4 oz.
Chicory, cleaned, leaves separated	5 lb.
Green grapes, seedless	10 lb.
Red delicious apples	5 lb.

Procedure:

1. Mix cheeses with vegetables, nuts, yogurt, and parsley.

2. Place one #12 scoop of cheese salad onto chicory leaf on luncheon plate.

3. Add a 1½-ounce cluster of grapes.

4. Cut apples into wedges (dip to prevent oxidixing) and place 3 slices neatly next to chicory.

VARIATION: Omit the cheddar cheese and walnuts in the recipe below. Substitute julienned salami for the cheeses and diced pickles for the walnuts and add 1 ounce of dijon-style mustard. Presentation is the same.

Calories: **296**   Protein: **16.8 g (23%)**   Carbohydrates: **15.3 g (21%)**   Sodium: **281 mg**

Total Fat: **19.7 g (59%)**   *Saturated Fat:* **11.7 g**   *Monounsaturated Fat:* **5.0 g**   *Polyunsaturated Fat:* **1.1 g**

❖ Chunky Chicken Salad

Ripe tomato slices surround a crisp mound of lettuce greens topped with a chunky chicken salad fragrant with freshly chopped tarragon.

PRODUCTION NOTES: The chicken is steamed with dried tarragon and tossed hot with lemon juice, salt, and pepper to produce a delectable flavor. Still warm, it is quickly finished with the cold, fresh tarragon yogurt dressing and served at once without chilling the chicken. However, if the salad has to be kept for more than 20 minutes before it is served, the chicken must be refrigerated. Cook the chicken uncovered in a steamer or simmer it with a small amount of water in a kettle with the lid down.

Portions per recipe: 100
Yield: 100 plates
Portion: 5 ounces of chicken salad
Serving utensil: #8 scoop

Cooking method: simmer
Time: 10–15 minutes

Ingredients	Amounts		
Ripe tomatoes, sliced	18 lb.		
Romaine, bite-size pieces	8 lb.		
Chicory, bite-size pieces	2 lb.		
Small summer squash, thinly sliced	3 lb.		
Chicken meat, raw cubes or strips	25 lb.		
Water	2 lb.		
Tarragon, crushed		¼ oz.	
Lemon juice		8 oz.	
Salt		2 oz.	
White pepper		⅛ oz.	
Celery, diced and blanched	3 lb.		
Low-fat yogurt	1 lb.	8 oz.	
Mayonnaise	1 lb.	8 oz.	
Fresh tarragon, chopped		3 oz.	

Procedure:

1. Edge the plate with a round of tomato slices.
2. Toss lettuce greens with squash slices and place 2 ounces in center of plate.
3. Cook chicken pieces with water and tarragon until tender but still moist, 10 to 15 minutes. Drain and reserve broth.
4. In large bowl mix lemon juice, salt, and pepper.
5. Stir in no more than 1 pint of broth. Toss with hot chicken and celery.
6. Blend yogurt, mayonnaise, and half the chopped tarragon.
7. Fold into cooled chicken.
8. With a #8 scoop place chicken salad in center of greens.
9. Garnish with the rest of fresh tarragon.

Calories: **145**   Protein: **19.4 g (54%)**   Carbohydrates: **6.2 g (17%)**   Sodium: **322 mg**

Total Fat: **5.0 g (17%)**   *Saturated Fat:* **.8 g**   *Monounsaturated Fat:* **.9 g**   *Polyunsaturated Fat:* **2.8 g**

❖ Cold Stuffed Vegetables

A nutritious vegetarian trio of zucchini stuffed with onions and pignolia nuts, a yellow pepper filled with tabouli, and a tomato half topped with a spinach cheese mixture.

PRODUCTION NOTES: Prepare and cook zucchini and make tabouli the day before serving. Drain yogurt overnight to make yogurt cheese and thaw spinach. Remove a thin slice from the top and bottom of ripe tomatoes and cut into two thick slices.

Portions per recipe: 100　　　　*Oven temperature: 350° F*
Yield: 100 plates　　　　　　*Time: 30 minutes*
Portion: 1 plate with 3 vegetable halves
Serving utensil: #24 scoop

Ingredients	Amounts	
Stuffed zucchini		
Small zucchini	12 lb.	8 oz.
Pignolia nuts		12 oz.
Garlic cloves, crushed		4 oz.
Spanish onions	2 lb.	
Olive oil		2 oz.
Thyme, crushed		1/8 oz.
Black pepper		1/4 oz.
Eggs, beaten		8 oz.
Bread crumbs		14 oz.
Stuffed peppers		
Yellow pepper, cut in half vertically and seeded	15 lb.	
Tabouli (see page 382)	12 lb.	8 oz.
Low-fat yogurt	1 lb.	
Sour cream		8 oz.
Mint leaves		1 oz.
Cheese tomatoes		
Tomatoes, halved	12 lb.	8 oz.
Whole milk yogurt	10 lb.	
Olive oil		1 oz.
Spanish onions, minced		8 oz.
Chopped frozen spinach, thawed	5 lb.	
Salt		1 oz.
White pepper		1/8 oz.
Nutmeg		1/16 oz.
Lettuce leaves	3 lb.	

Procedure:

1. Trim stem end and cut zucchini in half. Scoop out the soft insides with a sharp tablespoon.

2. Chop zucchini pulp with nuts, garlic, and onions in food chopper or processor.

3. Heat olive oil and sauté chopped vegetables with spices until soft.

4. Fold in eggs and bread crumbs.

5. Stuff zucchini halves with about 2 ounces of stuffing.

6. Place in oiled pan. Pour ½ cup of water in pan and bake uncovered at 325° F for 20 minutes. Chill overnight.

7. Prepare tabouli. Fold in yogurt and sour cream. Chill overnight.

8. Drain yogurt overnight. You should have about 5 pounds 10 ounces of yogurt cheese.

9. Heat oil and sauté onions until soft. Squeeze spinach dry, add to onions, and cook for 8 minutes. Cool.

10. Mix yogurt cheese, spinach, and spices. With a #24 scoop place spinach mixture onto tomato.

11. With #16 scoop place chilled tabouli in raw pepper halves. Garnish with mint leaves.

12. Arrange chilled zucchini, pepper, and tomato with a leaf of lettuce.

Calories: **186**   Protein: **8.0 g (17%)**   Carbohydrates: **26.6 g (57%)**   Sodium: **404 mg**
Total Fat: **5.4 g (26%)**   *Saturated Fat:* **1.4 g**   *Monounsaturated Fat:* **2.3 g**   *Polyunsaturated Fat:* **1.0 g**

❖ Middle Eastern Plate

A cold rice-stuffed eggplant, hummus with pita bread triangles, and broccoli florets and one egg slice topped with cucumber yogurt salad combine on one plate for a cool, nutritious meal on a hot summer's day.

PRODUCTION NOTES: Purchase very small eggplants or cut medium sized ones in half horizontally as well as vertically. Fill and cook eggplants one day ahead.

Portions per recipe: *64*
Yield: *64 plates*
Portion: *1 plate*
Serving utensil: *#8 and #24 scoop*

Oven temperature: *350° F*
Time: *35 minutes*

Ingredients	Amounts	
Stuffed Eggplant:		
Small eggplant	15 lb.	
Spanish onions, diced	1 lb.	
Garlic cloves, crushed		2 oz.
Green bell peppers	1 lb.	
Olive oil		2 oz.
Tomatoes, diced	6 lb.	
Canned tomato puree	2 lb.	
Salt		1 oz.
Black pepper		¼ oz.
Parsley, minced		4 oz.
Rice, cooked	4 lb.	
Walnuts, chopped		8 oz.
Hummus:		
Hummus dip (see recipe on page 342)	4 lb.	
Pita bread, cut into triangles	4 lb.	8 oz.
Egg Salad:		
Broccoli florets	4 lb.	
Eggs, hard boiled	8 lb.	
Boston lettuce leaves, washed	2 lb.	
Cucumber yogurt salad (see recipe page 370)	12 lb.	

Procedure:

1. Slice off stalk end and cut eggplants in half.
2. Scoop out flesh, leaving about ½ inch all around.
3. Chop flesh with onions, garlic, and bell peppers.
4. Heat olive oil and sauté vegetable mixture until soft.
5. Add diced tomatoes and puree and cook for 5 minutes.
6. Add salt, pepper, and parsley. Reserve 2 quarts of sauce.
7. Mix rice and walnuts with rest of sauce and place filling with a #8 scoop into eggplant.
8. Place into oiled pan, cover, and bake for 25 minutes.
9. Uncover pan, top each eggplant with a tablespoon of reserved sauce, and bake for 10 more minutes. Chill overnight.
10. On a plate assemble 1 baked eggplant half, 1 #24 scoop of hummis with 4 pita triangles, 3 broccoli florets, and one sliced hard boiled egg, set on a lettuce leaf and topped with 3 ounces of cucumber yogurt salad.

Calories: **433**   Protein: **17.6 g (16%)**   Carbohydrates: **57.2 g (53%)**   Sodium: **566 mg**
Total Fat: **12.4 g (26%)**   *Saturated Fat:* **2.8 g**   *Monounsaturated Fat:* **3.1 g**   *Polyunsaturated Fat:* **3.3 g**

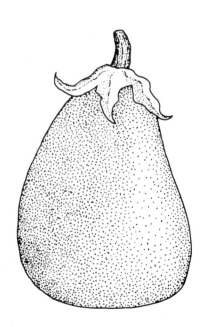

❖ Oriental Basket

Sichuan spicy noodles are topped with teriyaki chicken slices and complemented with refreshing hot and sour cucumber salad. Place the noodles in a large bowl and the cucumber salad in a small bowl and set them in a basket with a napkin and chop sticks. Of course, they taste just as good on a plain plate with the cucumber salad served in a lettuce leaf.

Portions per recipe: 100
Yield: 100 baskets
Portion: 4 ounces noodles, 4 ounces
chicken, 3 ounces cucumber salad,
2 ounces watermelon
Serving utensil: baskets

Pan: 12-ounce and 4-ounce bowls

PRODUCTION NOTES: Prepare 100 portions of all 3 recipes, but do not add pineapples and peppers to the chicken. Chill the chicken breast before slicing.

Ingredients	Amounts
Cold sichuan noodle salad (see recipe on page 368)	25 lb.
Chicken teriyaki (see recipe on pages 198–199)	25 lb.
Hot and sour cucumber salad (see recipe on page 375)	18 lb. 12 oz.
Watermelon slices	12 lb. 8 oz.

Procedure:

1. Prepare noodles, chicken, and cucumbers according to recipes.
2. Slice cold chicken breast into 8 slices against the grain.
3. Place noodles into 12-ounce bowl and arrange chicken slices on top.
4. Spoon cucumbers into small bowl.
5. Line basket with doily, set bowls inside and add a slice of watermelon, a napkin, and chop sticks.

Calories: **527**   Protein: **38.7 g (29%)**   Carbohydrates: **75.1 g (56%)**   Sodium: **617 mg**

Total Fat: **8.7 g (15%)**   *Saturated Fat:* **1.9g**   *Monounsaturated Fat:* **2.3 g**   *Polyunsaturated Fat:* **3.8 g**

❖ Tortellini Salad

White and green tortellini are tossed with red and green peppers and served on a bed of radicchio and escarole with Genoa salami cornucopias. For a vegetarian plate substitute tomato slices around edge of plate and subtract 55 calories, 3 grams of protein (16%) and 5 grams of fat (30%) from each portion.

Portions per recipe: 100
Yield: 100 plates
Portion: 6 ounces tortellini and
    5 salami slices
Serving utensil: plate

Cooking method: rolling boil
Time: 12 minutes

Ingredients / Amounts

Ingredients	Amounts
Green cheese tortellini	10 lb.
White cheese tortellini	10 lb.
Water, lightly salted	80 lb.
Olive oil	4 oz.
Garlic cloves, crushed	1 oz.
Lemon juice	14 oz.
Salt	1 oz.
Black pepper	¼ oz.
Light cream	1 lb.
Red onions, minced	2 lb.
Green bell peppers, thinly sliced	3 lb. 8 oz.
Red bell peppers, thinly sliced	3 lb. 8 oz.
Fresh basil, chopped	4 oz.
Italian parsley, minced	8 oz.
Salami, ⅕-ounce slices	3 lb. 2 oz.
Radicchio, cut into bite-size pieces	3 lb.
Escarole, cut into bite-size pieces	4 lb.
Romaine, cut into bite-size pieces	8 lb.

Procedure:

1. Cook tortellini in boiling salted water for 12 minutes. Drain.
2. In a large bowl beat together olive oil, garlic, vinegar, salt, and pepper. Toss hot tortellini with this dressing. Fold in cream. Cool.
3. Add onions, peppers, and herbs. Fold in gently.
4. Wrap each salami slice cornucopia fashion.
5. Line plate with lettuce and with a 6-ounce ladle, place salad into center, and arrange salami around edge of plate.

Calories: **392**   Protein: **16.9 g (17%)**   Carbohydrates: **19.2 g (22%)**   Sodium: **788 mg**
Total Fat: **16.6 g (38%)**   Saturated Fat: **3.2 g**   Monounsaturated Fat: **10.1 g**   Polyunsaturated Fat: **2.3 g**

❖ Tostada Salad Plate

Refried beans, crisp lettuce, and tomatoes are piled high on a tostada and topped with avocado slices, shredded cheese, and fresh salsa.

PRODUCTION NOTES: Instead of fresh avocado slices, frozen guacamole can be used. The fresh salsa makes this salad special, however if labor and time constraints force you to substitute canned salsa add fresh parsley and cilantro (2 ounces each) to salsa.

Portions per recipe: 100
Yield: 100
Portion: 1 tostada
Serving utensil: plate

Oven temperature: 325° F
Time: 20 minutes

Ingredients

Ingredients	Amounts
Low-fat yogurt	3 lb.
Sour cream	12 oz.
Tostadas	3 lb. 5 oz.
Canned refried beans	7 lb. 6 oz.
Canned green chilies, diced	2 lb. 8 oz.
Iceberg lettuce, shredded	12 lb. 8 oz.
Ripe tomatoes, diced	6 lb. 4 oz.
Avocados (20 medium)	5 lb. 8 oz.
Cheddar cheese, shredded	6 lb. 4 oz.
Fresh salsa (see recipe on page 461)	8 lb.

Procedure:

1. Drain yogurt for 30 minutes and mix with sour cream.
2. Place tostada in center of plate.
3. Mix refried beans with chopped chilies, cover and bake at 325° F for 20 minutes. Place a level #16 scoop on tostada, and spread lightly.
4. Top with 2 ounces of shredded lettuce and 1 ounce of chopped tomatoes.
5. Peel avocado, cut into 12 slices, and add 3 slices to each tostada.
6. Sprinkle with 1 ounce of shredded cheddar. Top with a #40 scoop of yogurt and a heaping 1-ounce ladle of fresh salsa. Serve at once.

Calories: **245**   Protein: **13.0 g (21%)**   Carbohydrates: **19.7 g (32%)**   Sodium: **379 mg**

Total Fat: **15.0 g (55%)**   *Saturated Fat:* **7.2 g**   *Monounsaturated Fat:* **6.5 g**   *Polyunsaturated Fat:* **.5 g**

This vegetarian salad is packed to go anywhere.

❖ Vegetarian Salad

Barbecues and picnics are a welcome break from the routine of institutional dining rooms and are especially enjoyed by students. Unfortunately, vegetarian eaters are often left to fend for themselves among the steaks, hamburgers, and hot dogs. Here is a salad in a box that will please and satisfy vegetarians and will complement potato and pasta salads, which are popular outdoor fare.

PRODUCTION NOTE: Use clear plastic bowls with lids to display salad well. Serve with a crusty French roll or whole wheat bread.

(continued)

Portions per recipe: *100*   Serve chilled
Yield: *100 bowls*
Portion: *1 bowl*
Serving utensil: *bowl*

Ingredients | Amounts

Ingredients	Amounts
Carrots, shredded	3 lb.
Very fresh mushrooms, thinly sliced	3 lb.
Zucchini, thinly sliced	3 lb.
Romaine, cleaned and cut into 1" pieces	8 lb.
Spinach, cleaned and cut into 1" pieces	4 lb.
Olive oil	2 lb.
Wine vinegar, red	12 oz.
Garlic cloves, crushed	¾ oz.
Salt	2 oz.
Black pepper	¼ oz.
Parsley leaves, minced	2 oz.
Swiss cheese, ½-ounce cubes	6 lb. 4 oz.
Fontina cheese, ½-ounce cubes	6 lb. 4 oz.
Feta cheese, ½-ounce cubes	3 lb. 2 oz.
Green bell peppers, cut into rings	2 lb. 8 oz.
Eggs, hard boiled and halved	6 lb. 4 oz.
Black olives	2 lb.
Cherry tomatoes	4 lb.

Procedure:

1. Toss shredded carrots and sliced vegetables with greens.
2. Mix oil, vinegar, garlic, salt, pepper, and parsley.
3. Fill bowl with 3 ounces of salad.
4. Arrange two cubes each of Swiss and fontina cheese and one cube of feta cheese around edge of bowl.
5. Place green pepper ring in center of bowl and egg half inside ring.
6. Garnish with 5 black olives and two cherry tomatoes.
7. Pour ¾ ounce of salad dressing over all.
8. Cover and keep chilled until needed.

Calories: **406**   Protein: **22.3g (22%)**   Carbohydrates: **7.7g (8%)**   Sodium: **1024 mg**

Total Fat: **34.4 g (75%)**   *Saturated Fat:* **10.0 g**   *Monounsaturated Fat:* **13.5 g**   *Polyunsaturated Fat:* **.2 g**

Salad Bar Salads

❖

Salad bars should offer a good selection of plain and marinated vegetables and tossed greens with some composed salads added for variety. Restaurants can offer a very large selection that need not change very much on a daily basis, but cafeterias in institutions where customers eat every day will keep their diners' interest if a smaller but varied selection with daily surprises and changes is offered. The basic lettuce—fresh and crisp—and tomatoes must always be available along with at least two popular dressings.

❖ Armenian Salad

A refreshing zucchini yogurt salad that does not weep as cucumber salad is wont to do.

Portions per recipe: **100**   *Pan:* **12" × 20" × 4"–¼ size**
Yield: **4 pans**   *Serve chilled*
Portion: **3 ounces**
Serving utensil: **slotted spoon**

Ingredients	Amounts
Zucchini, thinly sliced	15 lb.
Red onions, thinly sliced	1 lb.
Low-fat yogurt	3 lb.
Mayonnaise	1 lb.
Cider vinegar	4 oz.
Granulated sugar	½ oz.
Salt	1 oz.
White pepper	¹⁄₁₆ oz.
Mint leaves, minced	2 oz.
Italian parsley, minced	4 oz.

Procedure:

1. Toss zucchini with onions. Chill.
2. Combine the rest of ingredients. Chill for 30 minutes.
3. Just before serving pour dressing over vegetables and fold in.

Calories: **55**   Protein: **1.6g (11%)**   Carbohydrates: **4.1g (29%)**   Sodium: **147 mg**
Total Fat: **3.9g (63%)**   *Saturated Fat:* **.6 g**   *Monounsaturated Fat:* **.7 g**   *Polyunsaturated Fat:* **2.5 g**

❖ Asparagus Salad with Mustard Dressing   *Hom*

A salad from "A Feast Fit for the Last Emperor of China" celebration, but it's good enough for common folks.

Portions per recipe: *100*
Yield: *3 pans*
Portion: *3 ounces*
Serving utensil: *tongs*

Pan: *12″ × 20″ × 2″*
Cooking method: *steam*
Time: *5–7 minutes*

Ingredients	Amounts
Fresh asparagus	30 lb.
Egg yolks	1 lb.
Dry mustard	2 oz.
Water (hot)	10 oz.
Soy sauce	6 oz.
Ginger root, peeled and grated	8 oz.

Procedure:

1. Break woody ends of asparagus, the stalk will snap at the right place.
2. Cut stalks diagonally into 3-inch pieces. Place 10 pounds in perforated pan.
3. Steam at low pressure for 5 to 7 minutes. Plunge pan into ice water and drain.
4. Beat egg yolks with mustard, hot water, soy sauce, and ginger.
5. Transfer asparagus into solid pans and pour 1 pint of dressing over each pan.

Calories: **41**   Protein: **3.2 g (31%)**   Carbohydrates: **3.3 g (32%)**   Sodium: **101 mg**

Total Fat: **1.8 g (39%)**   *Saturated Fat:* **.5 g**   *Monounsaturated Fat:* **.7 g**   *Polyunsaturated Fat:* **.3 g**

❖ Black Bean Salad

Unusual and very nutritious.

PRODUCTION NOTES: Cover beans with cold water, refrigerate, and let soak overnight.

Portions per recipe: *100*
Yield: *4 pans*
Portion: *3 ounces*
Serving utensil: *spoon*

Pan: *12″ × 20″ × 4″–¼ size*
Cooking method: *simmer*
Time: *2 hours*

Ingredients

Ingredients	Amounts
Black beans, soaked overnight	5 lb.
Water	16 lb.
Bay leaves	¹⁄₁₆ oz.
Allspice	¼ oz.
Salt	½ oz.
Olive oil	2 oz.
Garlic cloves, crushed	1 oz.
Red wine vinegar	8 oz.
Black pepper	⅛ oz.
Salt	1 oz.
Jalapeño peppers with seeds, chopped	1 oz.
Scallions, chopped	1 lb.
Ripe Italian plum tomatoes, seeded and diced	8 lb.
Parsley, minced	2 oz.
Cilantro, minced	1 oz.
Avocados, peeled, seeded, and diced	1 lb. 12 oz.
Lemon juice	4 oz.

Procedure:

1. Put soaked beans in a kettle. Add water, bay leaves, allspice, and salt and simmer very slowly for 2 hours. Beans must keep their shape.
2. Beat olive oil with garlic, vinegar, spices, and jalapeño peppers.
3. Add hot cooked beans to dressing. Discard bay leaves.
4. Fold in scallions, tomatoes, and parsley. Transfer to serving pan.
5. Toss avocados with lemon juice and cilantro and place on top of beans.

Calories: **100**   Protein: **5.4 g (22%)**   Carbohydrates: **16.5 g (66%)**   Sodium: **120 mg**
Total Fat: **1.9 g (17%)**   *Saturated Fat:* **.2 g**   *Monounsaturated Fat:* **1.0 g**   *Polyunsaturated Fat:* **.3 g**

❖ Carrot Salad *Wolfert*

The complex flavors of Moroccan meals call for simple salads that refresh the palate. This carrot salad performs that function superbly.

Portions per recipe: *100*
Yield: *4 pans*
Portion: *3 ounces*
Serving utensil: *spoon*

Pan: *12″ × 20″ × 2″–¼ size*
Cooking method: *simmer*
Time: *12 minutes*
Serve chilled

Ingredients	Amounts
Carrots, peeled	20 lb.
Garlic cloves, peeled	1 oz.
Cinnamon	½ oz.
Cumin seed, pulverized	1 oz.
Hungarian paprika	½ oz.
Cayenne pepper	⅛ oz.
Lemon juice	1 lb.
Salt	1 oz.
Granulated sugar	1 oz.
Olive oil	4 oz.
Parsley, minced	8 oz.

Procedure:

1. Cover carrots and garlic cloves with water and boil for 12 minutes. Drain.
2. Discard garlic, and slice cooled carrots into ¼-inch-thick coins.
3. Combine spices with lemon juice, salt, and sugar. Pour over carrots and chill for at least 2 hours.
4. Toss with oil and parsley just before serving. Transfer into ¼ pans for the salad bar.

Calories: **49**   Protein: **1.0 g (8%)**   Carbohydrates: **9.3 g (75%)**   Sodium: **139 mg**
Total Fat: **1.4 g (25%)**   *Saturated Fat:* **.3 g**   *Monounsaturated Fat:* **.8 g**   *Polyunsaturated Fat:* **.1 g**

❖ Cold Green Bean Salad *Hom*

Green beans marinating in a lively sesame dressing are a wonderful addition to any salad bar. The beans should be crisp.

PRODUCTION NOTES: Fish sauce is a condiment readily available from oriental markets. The Tiparos brand from Thailand comes in a 23-ounce bottle and costs a little more than a dollar.

Portions per recipe: *100*
Yield: *4 pans*
Portion: *3 ounces*
Serving utensils: *tongs*

Pan: *12" × 20" × 2"–¼ size*
Serve chilled
Time: *2 hours*

Ingredients | Amounts

Ingredients	Amounts	
Fresh whole green beans	20 lb.	
Vegetable oil		4 oz.
Spanish onions, chopped	2 lb.	
Fish sauce		6 oz.
Sesame seed		5 oz.
Lemon juice		8 oz.
Sesame oil		2 oz.
Salt		1 oz.
Tabasco sauce		¼ oz.

Procedure:

1. Trim ends of fresh beans.
2. Steam or cook until crisp but tender. Plunge into ice water, then drain well.
3. Heat vegetable oil. Sauté onions until golden and soft.
4. Add rest of ingredients to onions and blend well.
5. Pour dressing over cold beans.
6. Chill for two hours before serving.

Calories: **52**   Protein: **1.7 g (13%)**   Carbohydrates: **7.6 g (58%)**   Sodium: **115 mg**

Total Fat: **2.1 g (36%)**   *Saturated Fat:* **.4 g**   *Monounsaturated Fat:* **.4 g**   *Polyunsaturated Fat:* **.9 g**

❖ Cold Sichuan Noodle Salad   *Hom*

This spicy noodle salad is wonderful with chicken teriyaki. It will keep very well and can safely be taken on picnics. See color plate **2**.

Portions per recipe: 100
Yield: 2 pans
Portion: 4 ounces
Serving utensil: tongs

Pan: 12″ × 20″ × 4″
Serve chilled

Ingredients

Ingredients	Amounts
Medium egg noodles	20 lb.
Vegetable oil	4 oz.
Scallions, finely chopped	8 oz.
Garlic cloves, crushed	4 oz.
Yellow bean sauce	12 oz.
Chili bean sauce	8 oz.
Ginger root, peeled and minced	4 oz.
Dry sherry	12 oz.
Soy sauce	12 oz.
Sesame oil	4 oz.
Cilantro leaves, minced	4 oz.
Red bell peppers, seeded and cut into long, thin strips	12 oz.
Scallions (green tops only), chopped	4 oz.

Procedure:

1. Cook noodles in salted water until barely done, 5 to 6 minutes.
2. Drain and rinse with warm water.
3. Heat oil and stir-fry scallions, garlic, bean sauces, ginger root, and sherry. Remove from heat.
4. Add soy sauce, sesame oil, and minced cilantro.
5. Toss drained noodles with warm dressing.
6. Garnish with red pepper strips and scallion greens.

Calories: **373**   Protein: **13.1 g (14%)**   Carbohydrates: **65.9 g (71%)**   Sodium: **195 mg**

Total Fat: **6.3 g (15%)**   *Saturated Fat:* **1.3 g**   *Monounsaturated Fat:* **1.8 g**   *Polyunsaturated Fat:* **2.2 g**

❖ Cucumber Salad *Wolfert*

A simple but delightful salad with a touch of cured black olives. See color plate **16**.

PRODUCTION NOTE: Peel and seed cucumbers a day ahead of time and place them cut-side-down on parchment-lined sheet pans to drain.

Portions per recipe: 100
Yield: 3 pans
Portion: 2 ounces
Serving utensil: perforated spoon

Pan: 12″ × 20″ × 2″–¼ size
Serve chilled

Ingredients	Amounts
Cucumbers	20 lb.
Granulated sugar	8 oz.
Cider vinegar	3 oz.
Olive oil	4 oz.
Marjoram, crushed	¼ oz.
Thyme, crushed	¹/₁₆ oz.
Salt	2 oz.
Oil cured black olives, cut in slivers from the pit	2 oz.
Cherry tomatoes	4 oz.
Parsley sprigs	1 oz.

Procedure:

1. Peel, seed, and coarsely shred cucumbers.
2. Place in colander and let drain for 15 minutes.
3. Beat together rest of ingredients, mix with cucumbers, and chill for 1 hour.
4. Pit and slice cured olives into slivers.
5. Put salad into pans and sprinkle with cured olive slivers.
6. Garnish with cherry tomatoes and parsley sprigs.

Calories: **32**   Protein: **.6 g (6%)**   Carbohydrates: **4.9 g (61%)**   Sodium: **236 mg**
Total Fat: **1.4 (39%)**   *Saturated Fat: .2 g   Monounsaturated Fat: .9 g   Polyunsaturated Fat: .2 g*

❖ Cucumber Yogurt Salad

Cucumber yogurt salad is known as raita in India and as cazik in Turkey. Many variations exist in the hot eastern Mediterranean and Asian countries.

Portions per recipe: 100
Yield: 1½ gallons
Portion: 2 ounces
Serving utensil: spoon

Pan: 12" × 20" × 2"
Serve chilled

Ingredients   Amounts

Ingredients	Amounts	
Unpeeled cucumbers, washed	20 lb.	
Salt		4 oz.
Black pepper		¼ oz.
Granulated sugar		1 oz.
Cider vinegar		4 oz.
Garlic cloves, crushed		1 oz.
Low-fat yogurt	2 lb.	
Parsley, minced		2 oz.
Mint, minced		2 oz.

Procedure:

1. Cut cucumbers in half and seed with a sharp spoon.

2. Shred with a coarse blade and place in colander to drain for 30 minutes.

3. Mix salt, pepper, sugar, vinegar, garlic, yogurt, and herbs in a large bowl.

4. Add drained cucumbers, fold in, and chill well before serving.

Calories: **19**   Protein: **1.0 g (21%)**   Carbohydrates: **3.7 g (78%)**   Sodium: **478 mg**

Total Fat: **.3 g (14%)**   *Saturated Fat:* **.1 g**   *Monounsaturated Fat:* **.01 g**   *Polyunsaturated Fat:* **.06 g**

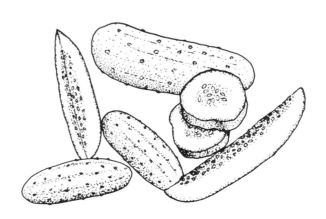

❖ Delicious Salad

Bacon adds crunch and a pleasant saltiness to this sweet, orange-flavored spinach and apple salad.

PRODUCTION NOTE: Use unpeeled yellow Delicious apples for this salad.

Portions per recipe: 100
Yield: 3 pans
Portion: 3 ounces
Serving utensil: tongs

Pan: 12" × 20" × 4"

Ingredients	Amounts	
Bacon, sliced	2 lb.	
Spinach, washed	12 lb.	
Yellow Delicious apples, unpeeled	5 lb.	
Frozen orange juice concentrate		12 oz.
Mayonnaise		8 oz.
Low-fat yogurt	2 lb.	
Black pepper		⅛ oz.

Procedure:

1. Bake, drain, and chop bacon.
2. Remove large stems and cut spinach into bite-size pieces.
3. Core and thinly slice apples.
4. Toss spinach with apples and bacon. Chill.
5. Blend concentrate with mayonnaise, yogurt, and pepper.
6. Just before serving pour 2 cups of dressing over salad in each pan and toss.

Calories: **99**   Protein: **2.5 g (10%)**   Carbohydrates: **6.6 g (27%)**   Sodium: **112 mg**

Total Fat: **7.4 g (67%)**   *Saturated Fat:* **2.3 g**   *Monounsaturated Fat:* **2.7 g**   *Polyunsaturated Fat:* **1.9 g**

❖ German Warm Marinated Potato Salad

A picnic potato salad that can be served outside without worrying about refrigeration. Use uncut tiny red or new potatoes if they are available.

PRODUCTION NOTES: Potatoes and vinegar broth should be hot for the very best flavor. Always marinate potatoes (works for pasta and rice too) while they are hot in order to develop a deeper flavor, especially when making a mayonnaise-based salad.

Portions per recipe: 100   Pan: 12″ × 20″ × 4″
Yield: 2 pans   Cooking method: simmer
Portion: 4 ounces   Time: 20 minutes
Serving utensil: slotted spoon

Ingredients

Ingredients	Amounts	
Red potatoes, cut into 1″ pieces	25 lb.	
Scallions, thinly sliced	2 lb.	
Cider vinegar	1 lb.	
Salt		1 oz.
Black pepper		½ oz.
Chicken or vegetable stock	2 lb.	
Soy sauce		1 oz.
Safflower oil		3 oz.
Parsley, minced		4 oz.
Eggs, hard boiled		8 oz.
Radishes, sliced		2 oz.

Procedure:

1. Cook potatoes gently until tender but firm, about 30 minutes.
2. Mix rest of ingredients and toss gently with hot potatoes.
3. Garnish with cooked egg slices and radishes.

VARIATION: Substitute 4 pounds of crisp cooked green beans cut into 2-inch pieces for 4 pounds of potatoes.

Calories: **83**   Protein: **2.2 g (11%)**   Carbohydrates: **18.1 g (87%)**   Sodium: **137 mg**
Total Fat: **1.2 g (13%)**   *Saturated Fat:* **.2 g**   *Monounsaturated Fat:* **.03 g**   *Polyunsaturated Fat:* **.7 g**

❖ Greek Salad

A classic combination of crisp greens, feta cheese, and Greek olives.

PRODUCTION NOTE: Several types of Greek olives are available from importers. I prefer Atalanti, also called Royal or Kalamata olives.

Portions per recipe: 100
Yield: 3 pans
Portion: 3 ounces
Serving utensil: tongs

Pan: 12″ × 20″ × 4″

Ingredients	Amounts	
Romaine, cut into bite-size pieces	14 lb.	
Red onions, thinly sliced	2 lb.	
Green bell peppers, thinly sliced	3 lb.	
Feta cheese, crumbled	3 lb.	2 oz.
Olive oil		4 oz.
Lemon juice		10 oz.
Black pepper		⅛ oz.
Greek olives	2 lb.	

Procedure:

1. Toss first 3 ingredients. Chill.
2. Blend feta cheese with oil, lemon juice, and pepper.
3. Pour 1 pint over salad greens in each pan. Scatter 12 ounces of olives over salad and serve at salad bar.

Calories: **86**   Protein: **3.3 g (15%)**   Carbohydrates: **3.4 g (16%)**   Sodium: **244 mg**
Total Fat: **6.9 g (72%)**   *Saturated Fat:* **2.5 g**   *Monounsaturated Fat:* **3.1 g**   *Polyunsaturated Fat:* **.4 g**

❖ Green and White Jade Salad   *Hom*

Crisp steamed broccoli and cauliflower are complemented by a creamy sesame dressing. See color plate **2**.

PRODUCTION NOTE: Dress salad as needed. It does not keep.

Portions per recipe: *100*
Yield: *3 pans*
Portion: *3 ounces*
Serving utensil: *spoon*

Pan: *12" × 20" × 2"*
Cooking method: *steam*
Time: *10 minutes*

Ingredients	Amounts
Broccoli	*10 lb.*
Cauliflower	*10 lb.*
Tahini	*12 oz.*
Cider vinegar	*8 oz.*
Tabasco sauce	*¹⁄₈ oz.*
Vegetable oil	*2 oz.*
Sesame oil	*2 oz.*
Soy sauce	*4 oz.*
Granulated sugar	*2 oz.*

Procedure:

1. Cut broccoli in florets. Peel stalks and slice diagonally into ¼-inch-thick pieces.

2. Cut cauliflower into bite-size florets. Put 3 pounds of broccoli and cauliflower in each pan.

3. Steam broccoli and cauliflower in perforated pans for 10 minutes at low pressure. Plunge into ice water. Drain well. Transfer to solid pans.

4. Beat together the dressing ingredients. Pour 1 cup of dressing over each pan of vegetables.

Calories: **53**   Protein: **1.9 g (14%)**   Carbohydrates: **3.8 g (29%)**   Sodium: **46 mg**

Total Fat: **3.1 g (52%)**   *Saturated Fat:* **.5 g**   *Monounsaturated Fat:* **1.0 g**   *Polyunsaturated Fat:* **1.4 g**

❖ Hot and Sour Cucumber Salad *Hom*

Thin slivers of red hot pepper add heat and color to this cool cucumber salad. See color plate **2**.

Portions per recipe: 100
Yield: 4 pans
Portion: 3 ounces
Serving utensil: slotted spoon

Pan: 12″ × 20″ × 2″–¼ size
Serve chilled
Time: 4 hours

Ingredients

Ingredients	Amounts
Medium cucumbers	25 lb.
Cider vinegar	1 lb. 14 oz.
Granulated sugar	5 oz.
Salt	2 oz.
Red chili peppers, seeded and finely sliced	6 oz.
Garlic cloves, crushed	5 oz.

Procedure:

1. Peel and slice cucumbers in half lengthwise. Seed.
2. Cut halves into ½-inch slices.
3. Combine the rest of ingredients well.
4. Toss with cucumber pieces and let marinate for 4 hours.
5. Drain before placing cucumber salad into pans.

Calories: **23**   Protein: **.7 g (12%)**   Carbohydrates: **5.6 g (86%)**   Sodium: **223 mg**

Total Fat: **.1 g (4%)**   *Saturated Fat: **.04 g***   *Monounsaturated Fat: —*   *Polyunsaturated Fat: **.06 g***

❖ Insalata di Pasta *Romagnoli*

Pasta with cucumbers and shrimp in a lemony dressing.

Portions per recipe: 100
Yield: 2 pans
Portion: 3½ ounces
Serving utensil: spoon or 4-ounce ladle

Pan: 12″ × 20″ × 4″
Serve chilled
Time: 1 hour

Ingredients | Amounts

Ingredients	Amounts	
Small elbow macaroni	6 lb.	
Water, lightly salted	32 lb.	
Unpeeled cucumbers, seeded and diced	3 lb.	
Spanish onions, finely minced		6 oz.
Celery stalks, thinly sliced		8 oz.
Green bell peppers, diced		12 oz.
Red bell peppers, diced		12 oz.
Black olives, pitted and chopped		8 oz.
Mayonnaise	1 lb.	
Low-fat yogurt		8 oz.
Lemon juice		8 oz.
Salt		½ oz.
White pepper		⅛ oz.
Salad shrimp, cooked	2 lb.	8 oz.

Procedure:

1. Cook macaroni until tender but firm (*al dente*). Drain and rinse with cold water.
2. Mix together rest of ingredients except shrimp.
3. Toss with pasta, fold in shrimp. Place 20 pounds of salad in each pan. Chill for 1 hour before serving.

Calories: **155**   Protein: **6.5 g (17%)**   Carbohydrates: **20.7 g (54%)**   Sodium: **167 mg**

Total Fat: **5.2 g (30%)**   *Saturated Fat:* **.8 g**   *Monounsaturated Fat:* **1.1 g**   *Polyunsaturated Fat:* **2.9 g**

❖ Insalata di Riso alla Torinese   *Romagnoli*

Present this salad in a large glass bowl to show off its color and texture.

Portions per recipe: 100
Yield: 2 pans
Portion: 4 ounces
Serving utensil: spoon

Pan: 12″ × 20″ × 2″
Cooking method: steam
Time: 30 minutes

Ingredients

Ingredients	Amounts
Converted rice	4 lb.
Water (boiling)	10 lb.
Olive oil	4 oz.
Lemon juice	1 lb.
Salt	1 oz.
Black olives, pitted, chopped	4 oz.
Green olives with pimiento, chopped	4 oz.
Small capers	6 oz.
Green bell peppers, diced	1 lb. 8 oz.
Red bell pepprs, diced	1 lb. 8 oz.
Chunk white tuna in water, drained	3 lb. 10 oz.
Frozen peas	2 lb.
Frozen shoestring carrots	2 lb.
Italian parsley	4 oz.

Procedure:

1. Steam rice with hot water at low pressure for 30 minutes. Rinse.
2. Beat together oil, lemon juice, salt, olives, capers, and peppers. Add warm rice and toss well.
3. Steam peas and carrots until barely tender, 2 to 3 minutes.
4. Add to rice salad with tuna and parsley. Toss and chill.

Calories: **114**   Protein: **6.3 g (22%)**   Carbohydrates: **17.5 g (61%)**   Sodium: **207 mg**
Total Fat: **1.9 g (15%)**   *Saturated Fat: **.3 g***   *Monounsaturated Fat: **1.1 g***   *Polyunsaturated Fat: .4 g*

❖ Insalata Mista *Michela's*

Perfect greens are dressed with red wine and balsamic vinegar.

Portions per recipe: 100
Yield: 3 pans
Portion: 2 ounces
Serving utensil: tongs

Pan: 12" × 20" × 4"
Serve chilled

Ingredients	Amounts	
Romaine lettuce	10 lb.	
Radicchio	1 lb.	8 oz.
Belgian endive	3 lb.	
Red wine vinegar		3 oz.
Balsamic vinegar		1 oz.
Red onions, very finely minced		2 oz.
Olive oil, extra virgin		12 oz.
Salt		½ oz.
Freshly ground black pepper		⅛ oz.

Procedure:

1. Tear romaine into large pieces.
2. Remove whole radicchio leaves gently from core. Tear large leaves in half.
3. Break off endive leaves whole from core. Keep cutting core from the bottom to make removing leaves easier. Cut heart in half.
4. Beat vinegars with onions, oil, salt, and pepper.
5. Put 3 pounds romaine, 8 ounces radicchio and 1 pound endives into each pan.
6. Toss salad in each pan with ⅔ cup dressing.

Calories: **47**   Protein: **.9 g (8%)**   Carbohydrates: **3.3 g (28%)**   Sodium: **65 mg**

Total Fat: **3.5 g (67%)**   *Saturated Fat:* **.4 g**   *Monounsaturated Fat:* **2.8 g**   *Polyunsaturated Fat:* **.3 g**

❖ Red Pepper and Preserved Lemon Peel Salad
Wolfert

Another refreshing and unusual Moroccan salad with zesty preserved lemon peel and the heat of cayenne pepper. See color plate **16**.

PRODUCTION NOTE: Preserved lemon peel is an essential ingredient in this salad. See the recipe on page 467 for instructions on how to pickle lemons.

Portions per recipe: 100
Yield: 3 pans
Portion: 2 ounce
Serving utensil: spoon

Pan: 4″ × 20″ × 2″ salad
Serve chilled
Time: 1 hour

Ingredients

Ingredients	Amounts
Tomatoes, seeded	10 lb.
Canned roasted red peppers	4 lb.
Red onions, finely chopped	1 lb.
Olive oil	2 oz.
Lemon juice	2 oz.
Cumin seed, pulverized	¼ oz.
Hungarian paprika	¾ oz.
Cayenne pepper	1/16 oz.
Preserved lemon peel	3 oz.

Procedure:

1. Cut seeded fresh tomatoes into ¾-inch pieces.
2. Slice peppers into strips.
3. Combine with rest of ingredients except lemon peel.
4. Mix well and refrigerate for 1 hour.
5. Rinse preserved lemon and remove pulp.
6. Dice the peel into ⅛- to 1/16-inch pieces.
7. Place chilled salad in pans and sprinkle 1 ounce of peel over salad.

Calories: **20**   Protein: **.6 g (12%)**   Carbohydrates: **3.2 g (64%)**   Sodium: **25 mg**
Total Fat: **.8 g (36%)**   *Saturated Fat:* **.1 g**   *Monounsaturated Fat:* **.6 g**   *Polyunsaturated Fat:* **.3 g**

❖ Sesame Dressed Spinach Salad *Hom*

Barely cooked spinach and toasted sesame seeds—a tasty combination.

PRODUCTION NOTES: Steam spinach in perforated 12″ × 20″ × 2″ inserts for just 1 minute. If no steamer is available, plunge spinach in small batches into boiling water, remove after 1 minute, and immerse at once in ice water.

Portions per recipe: *80*
Yield: *2 pans*
Portion: *3 ounces*
Serving utensil: *tongs*

Pan: *12″ × 20″ × 4″*
Cooking method: *steam*
Time: *1 Minute*

Ingredients	Amounts
Fresh spinach	15 lb.
Soy sauce	10 oz.
Granulated sugar	2 oz.
Cider vinegar	4 oz.
Vegetable oil	6 oz.
Sesame oil	1 oz.
Sesame seeds	6 oz.

Procedure:

1. Wash spinach at least twice and remove large stems.
2. Steam or cook for 1 minute. Leaves should barely wilt.
3. Plunge into ice water. Drain well and shake gently.
4. Mix soy sauce, sugar, vinegar and oils. Beat well.
5. Toss with spinach and refrigerate for at least 2 hours.
6. Toast sesame seeds in 300° F oven until light brown.
7. Transfer spinach to pans and sprinkle each pan with 3 ounces of sesame seeds.

Calories: **53**   Protein: **2.6 g (19%)**   Carbohydrates: **3.4 g (25%)**   Sodium: **252 mg**
Total Fat: **3.8 g (64%)**   *Saturated Fat:* **.7 g**   *Monounsaturated Fat:* **.7 g**   *Polyunsaturated Fat:* **1.5 g**

❖ Spicy Eggplant and Tomato Salad   *Wolfert*

This cooked Moroccan salad is more like a condiment and should have the consistency of fruit butter. This salad can also be served as an appetizer.

PRODUCTION NOTES: This is best made on the wide surface of a tilting skillet. This salad keeps for 3 to 4 days.

Portions per recipe: *150*
Yield: *1 gallon*
Portion: *1.5 ounces*
Serving utensil: *#24 scoop*

Skillet temperature: *375° F*
Time: *20 minutes*

Ingredients

Ingredients	Amounts	
Unpeeled eggplant, sliced	10 lb.	
Olive oil		1 oz.
Canned Italian tomatoes, drained	6 lb.	6 oz.
Garlic cloves, crushed		2 oz.
Cayenne pepper		1/16 oz.
Hungarian paprika		1/2 oz.
Cumin seed, pulverized		1/4 oz.
Lemon juice		4 oz.

Procedure:

1. Deep fry eggplant slices. Drain on paper towels.

2. On a tilting skillet heat olive oil, add drained tomatoes, and sauté for 5 minutes.

3. Chop eggplant with spices in food chopper or processor. Add to skillet.

4. Stir until moisture evaporates and oil forms around the edges. Be careful not to scorch.

5. Add lemon juice and refrigerate.

6. Line a punch bowl with lettuce leaves and spoon salad onto leaves. Serve with Kisra, a whole wheat Moroccan bread (see recipe on page 493), or with pita bread wedges.

Calories: **51**   Protein: **.5 g (4%)**   Carbohydrates: **2.6 g (21%)**   Sodium: **33 mg**
Total Fat: **4.3 g (77%)**   *Saturated Fat:* **.4 g**   *Monounsaturated Fat:* **2.8 g**   *Polyunsaturated Fat:* **.9 g**

❖ Tabouli

A Middle Eastern salad that has even found its way into the American supermarket. This bulgur salad is made with lots of parsley, lemon juice, and fresh tomatoes.

Portions per recipe: 100
Yield: 2 pans
Portion: 4 ounces
Serving utensil: spoon

Pan: 12″ × 20″ × 2″
Serve chilled
Time: 2 hours

Ingredients	Amounts
Medium bulgur	7 lb.
Water (boiling)	12 lb.
Olive oil	8 oz.
Lemon juice	14 oz.
Salt	2 oz.
Black pepper	¼ oz.
Dry mint, crushed	⅛ oz.
Red onions	1 lb.
Garlic cloves, crushed	1 oz.
Italian parsley	12 oz.
Fresh mint leaves	8 oz.
Celery, tops only	12 oz.
Italian plum tomatoes, seeded and chopped	6 lb.

Procedure:

1. Pour boiling water over bulgur. Cover and let soak for 45 minutes.
2. Pour off any excess water.
3. Beat oil with lemon juice, salt, pepper, and dry mint.
4. Chop onions, parsley, mint, and celery tops in food processor until finely minced.
5. Add to dressing. Fold in bulgur and tomatoes. Chill for 2 hours before serving.

Calories: **137**   Protein: **4.3 g (12%)**   Carbohydrates: **26.1 g (76%)**   Sodium: **231 mg**

Total Fat: **2.8 g (18%)**   *Saturated Fat:* **.4 g**   *Monounsaturated Fat:* **1.7 g**   *Polyunsaturated Fat:* **.4 g**

❖ Winter Salad

During the winter months, when lettuce is often of poor quality and expensive, this salad makes a fresh and cost effective addition to your salad bar offerings.

Portions per recipe: 100
Yield: 3 pans
Portion: 2 ounces
Serving utensil: tongs

Pan: 12″ × 20″ × 4″
Serve chilled
Time: 30 minutes

Ingredients

Ingredients	Amounts	
Zucchini	4 lb.	
Green bell peppers	2 lb.	
Red bell peppers	2 lb.	
Olive oil		8 oz.
Cider vinegar		4 oz.
Garlic cloves, crushed		1 oz.
Marjoram, crushed		⅛ oz.
Salt		1 oz.
Black pepper		¼ oz.
Spinach, washed well	8 lb.	

Procedure:

1. Shred zucchini and peppers coarsely.
2. Beat oil with vinegar, garlic, marjoram, salt, and pepper.
3. Toss with shredded vegetables. Chill and let marinate for 30 minutes.
4. Coarsely chop spinach and toss with marinated vegetables.

Calories: **31**   Protein: **.9 g (11%)**   Carbohydrates: **2.3 g (29%)**   Sodium: **111 mg**
Total Fat: **2.4 g (69%)**   *Saturated Fat:* **.3 g**   *Monounsaturated Fat:* **1.7 g**   *Polyunsaturated Fat:* **.2 g**

—9—

SALAD DRESSINGS

Out of the Ordinary and Low Calorie, Too

❖

The salad dressings in this chapter are an alternative to powdered salad dressing mixes. Some are oil- or mayonnaise-based but are modified to reduce fat. They are strongly flavored and even when used sparingly will impart good taste to salads. For cholesterol restricted diets substitute egg white mayonnaise (see recipe on pages 460–461) for regular mayonnaise; it will reduce both cholesterol and saturated fats.

I have never found a commercially prepared low calorie dressing I have liked. I hope that your customers will like mine. With one exception these are all yogurt dressings I developed for Colombo Yogurt, Incorporated. I have made adjustments to the original recipes, some of which were only household-size.

❖ Avocado Dressing

This dressing is zesty and creamy. Only a small amount of oil is added to the already oil-rich mashed avocado. Serve this dressing with fruit or greens, or with a mixture of both.

PRODUCTION NOTES: Keep avocados at room temperature to ripen. Avocados are ripe, when stem end feels soft when gently squeezed. Refrigerate them until needed. It is necessary to pour the oil over the dressing before chilling it. This prevents discoloration of the dressing exposed to air. If the oil is eliminated to save fat calories, press a sheet of plastic film directly on dressing to prevent the avocado from oxidizing.

Portions per recipe: 128   *Serve chilled*
Yield: 1 gallon   *Time: 1 hour*
Portion: 1 ounce
Serving utensil: 1-ounce ladle

Ingredients   Amounts

Ingredients	Amounts
Low-fat yogurt	2 lb.
Ripe avocados	7 lb.
Mayonnaise	8 oz.
Garlic cloves, crushed	1 oz.
Red pepper sauce	1/4 oz.
Curry powder	1/2 oz.
Lemon juice	4 oz.
Salt	1 oz.
Sunflower seed oil	2 oz.

Procedure:

1. Drain yogurt in a colander for 30 minutes. It will lose 1 cup of whey.
2. Peel and pit avocados.
3. Mash avocados in mixer with mayonnaise and garlic until smooth.
4. Add drained yogurt, pepper sauce, curry powder, juice, and salt. Fold in.
5. Pour into pans, cover with sunflower oil. Chill for 1 hour.
6. Stir in oil just before serving.

Calories: **56**   Protein: **.8 g (6%)**   Carbohydrates: **2.1 g (15%)**   Sodium: **18 mg**
Total Fat: **5.3 g (85%)**   *Saturated Fat:* **.8 g**   *Monounsaturated Fat:* **2.6 g**   *Polyunsaturated Fat:* **1.6 g**

❖ Balsamic Vinaigrette

Dark and aromatic balsamic vinegar flavors this magnificent vinaigrette. My friend Arthur DiMambro, from whom I learned this recipe, tosses his salad greens with this dressing and everybody loves it.

PRODUCTION NOTES: The subtle garlic flavor is achieved by steeping barely bruised peeled cloves in the oil and vinegar mixture for no more than one hour. To bruise garlic, just press the unpeeled clove with the flat side of a French knife; this will also loosen the skin.

Portions per recipe: 256
Yield: 1 gallon
Portion: ½ ounce
Serving utensil: tablespoon

Serve at room temperature
Time: 1 hour

Ingredients

Ingredients	Amounts
Balsamic vinegar	1 lb.
Olive oil	7 lb.
Garlic cloves, bruised slightly	3 oz.
Freshly ground black pepper	½ oz.
Salt	2 oz.
Dijon mustard	2 oz.

Procedure:

1. Mix vinegar with oil and add garlic. Let stand for 1 hour at room temperature.
2. Remove garlic cloves. Add pepper, salt, and mustard and beat to amalgamate oil and vinegar.
3. Toss with salad greens (½ ounce per 3 ounces of salad) or serve on the salad bar.

Calories: **111**   Protein: **trace**   Carbohydrates: **.2 g (1%)**   Sodium: **86 mg**
Total Fat: **12.3 g (99%)**   *Saturated Fat:* **1.7 g**   *Monounsaturated Fat:* **9.1 g**   *Polyunsaturated Fat:* **1.0 g**

❖ Creamy Dill

A rich yogurt and sour cream dressing with fresh dill.

PRODUCTION NOTES: Dry dill weed can be substituted, but it will not be nearly as tasty. Substitute ½ ounce dry dill weed to fresh dill and add 2 ounces finely minced parsley for color.

Portions per recipe: 128
Yield: 1 gallon
Portion: 1 ounce
Serving utensil: 1-ounce ladle

Serve chilled
Time: 1 hour

Ingredients

Ingredients	Amounts	
Low-fat yogurt	6 lb.	
Sour cream	2 lb.	
Salt		2 oz.
Granulated sugar		1 oz.
Lemon juice		6 oz.
Cider vinegar		3 oz.
White pepper		⅛ oz.
Dill, ferns only, chopped		5 oz.

Procedure:

1. Combine all ingredients in a mixing bowl and blend at low speed.
2. Refrigerate for 1 hour to let the flavor develop.

Calories: **30**   Protein: **1.1 g (15%)**   Carbohydrates: **2.2 g (36%)**   Sodium: **18 g**
Total Fat: **1.8 g (54%)**   *Saturated Fat:* **1.1 g**   *Monounsaturated Fat:* **.5 g**   *Polyunsaturated Fat:* **.1 g**

❖ Cucumber Mint Dressing

A hint of garlic and a faint taste of fresh mint and dried sweet marjoram add flavor to this creamy cucumber dressing.

PRODUCTION NOTES: Drain the grated cucumber in a colander for 30 minutes. This dressing will only keep 24 hours.

Portions per recipe: 128
Yield: 1 gallon
Portion: 1 ounce
Serving utensil: 1-ounce ladle

Serve chilled
Time: 1 hour

Ingredients

Ingredients	Amounts
Cucumbers, peeled	5 lb.
Mayonnaise	2 lb.
Low-fat yogurt	2 lb.
Lemon juice	4 oz.
Garlic cloves, crushed	1 oz.
Marjoram	1/8 oz.
Hungarian paprika	1/4 oz.
Cayenne pepper	1/16 oz.
Salt	2 oz.
Mint leaves, finely minced	2 oz.

Procedure:

1. Seed and finely shred cucumbers. Drain in colander for 30 minutes.
2. Combine all the other ingredients until well blended.
3. Fold in drained cucumbers and chill for 1 hour.

Calories: **59**   Protein: **.6 g (4%)**   Carbohydrates: **1.4 g (10%)**   Sodium: **218 mg**
Total Fat: **5.8 g (88%)**   *Saturated Fat:* **.6 g**   *Monounsaturated Fat:* **1.0 g**   *Polyunsaturated Fat:* **3.9 g**

❖ Fresh Herb House Dressing

We called this our house dressing to avoid mentioning yogurt in its name, because we found many male students responded negatively to the word.

PRODUCTION NOTES: The herbs in this dressing are available year-round, but other fresh herb combinations in season such as thyme, tarragon, sage, lemon balm, basil, oregano and cress can be substituted.

Portions per recipe: *128*   Serve chilled
Yield: *1 gallon*   Time: *1 hour*
Portion: *1 ounce*
Serving utensil: *1-ounce ladle*

Ingredients	Amounts
Whole milk yogurt	8 lb.
Dijon-style mustard	8 oz.
Prepared horseradish	1 oz.
Salt	1 oz.
Granulated sugar	½ oz.
White pepper	1/16 oz.
Scallions	8 oz.
Garlic cloves	1 oz.
Parsley leaves, stems removed	4 oz.

Procedure:

1. Optional: For a thicker dressing drain yogurt for 30 minutes.
2. Blend yogurt gently with mustard, horseradish, salt, sugar, and pepper.
3. In a food chopper or processor chop scallions, garlic, and parsley until very finely minced.
4. Fold into dressing and chill for 1 hour.

Calories: **21**   Protein: **1.1 g (21%)**   Carbohydrates: **1.9 g (36%)**   Sodium: **37 mg**
Total Fat: **1.0 g (43%)**   *Saturated Fat:* **.6 g**   *Monounsaturated Fat:* **.3 g**   *Polyunsaturated Fat:* **.1 g**

❖ Honey Cream Dressing for Fruits

This is a simple topping for fresh fruit salads.

PRODUCTION NOTE: Yogurt is drained for two hours to make the dressing creamier and stiffer.

Portions per recipe: 128
Yield: 1 gallon
Portion: 1 ounce
Serving utensil: 1-ounce ladle

Serve chilled
Time: 1 hour

Ingredients	Amounts
Whole milk yogurt	8 lb.
Honey	8 oz.
Orange juice concentrate	12 oz.
Lemon rind, freshly grated	1 oz.
Nutmeg	1/16 oz.

Procedure:

1. Line colander with cheesecloth and drain yogurt for 2 hours.
2. Blend yogurt with honey, orange concentrate, lemon rind, and nutmeg.
3. Chill for 1 hour before serving.
   Variation: Omit orange concentrate and add 1 ounce French vanilla extract and use 1 pound more yogurt.

> Calories: **29** Protein: **1.1 g (15%)** Carbohydrates: **4.0 g (55%)** Sodium: **13 mg**
> Total Fat: **0.9 g (28%)** *Saturated Fat:* **0.6 g** *Monounsaturated Fat:* **0.3 g** *Polyunsaturated Fat:* **trace**

❖ Honey Poppy Seed

This recipe was originally developed by Linda Holzhauser, former chef at University of New Hampshire Dining Services. I have made some changes to the recipe.

PRODUCTION NOTE: Toast poppy seeds on an oiled sheet pan for 5 to 6 minutes in a 325° F oven.

Portions per recipe: 128
Yield: 1 gallon
Portion: 1 ounce
Serving utensil: 1-ounce ladle

Serve at room temperature
Time: 4 hours

(continued)

Ingredients	Amounts	
Honey	12 oz.	
Water (boiling)	4 oz.	
Cider vinegar	12 oz.	
Prepared yellow mustard	8 oz.	
Dijon-style mustard	8 oz.	
Safflower oil	1 lb.	
Olive oil	2 lb.	
Poppy seeds, slightly toasted	4 oz.	

Procedure:

1. In a large mixing bowl blend honey with the boiling hot water.
2. Add rest of ingredients and whip at low speed until well blended.
3. Let sit for 4 hours at room temperature to allow the flavor to develop.

Calories: **114**   Protein: **.5 g (2%)**   Carbohydrates: **3.4 g (12%)**   Sodium: **89 mg**

Total Fat: **10.9 g (86%)**   *Saturated Fat:* **.4 g**   *Monounsaturated Fat:* **6.1 g**   *Polyunsaturated Fat:* **1.3 g**

❖ Jade Dressing

Watercress adds bite to this very green dressing.

PRODUCTION NOTE: Dry washed herbs well. Excess water could make the dressing runny.

Portions per recipe: *128*
Yield: *1 gallon*
Portion: *1 ounce*
Serving utensil: *1-ounce ladle*

Serve chilled
Time: *1 hour*

Ingredients	Amounts	
Low-fat yogurt	8 lb.	
Olive oil		1 oz.
Balsamic vinegar		2 oz.
Salt		1 oz.
Cayenne pepper		$1/16$ oz.
Oregano, crushed		$1/8$ oz.
Watercress, thick stems removed		8 oz.
Scallions		8 oz.
Garlic cloves		1 oz.
Parsley leaves		4 oz.

Procedure:

1. Blend together yogurt, olive oil, vinegar, salt, and cayenne.
2. In food chopper or porcessor finely mince watercress, scallions, garlic, and parsley.
3. Fold into dressing and chill for 1 hour before serving.

> Calories: **56**   Protein: **.6 g (26%)**   Carbohydrates: **1.6 g (31%)**   Sodium: **101 mg**
> Total Fat: **1.2 g (49%)**   *Saturated Fat: .6 g*   *Monounsaturated Fat: .3 g*   *Polyunsaturated Fat: .1 g*

❖ Lemon Dressing with Fresh Chives

A fresh and lively dressing for tender greens, this is especially good with bib and Boston lettuce or with any type of cress. Mix a bit of arugula and radicchio into the greens. They will enhance both the dressing and the tender greens with their slightly bitter flavors and brilliant colors.

Portions per recipe: 128
Yield: 1 gallon
Portion: 1 ounce
Serving utensil: 1-ounce ladle

Serve chilled
Time: 30 minutes

Ingredients	Amounts
Lemon juice	5 lb.
Water	2 lb.
Honey	8 oz.
Dijon-style mustard	8 oz.
Thyme, crushed	1/8 oz.
Salt	1/2 oz.
Freshly ground black pepper	1/4 oz.
Walnut or almond oil	2 oz.
Fresh chives, chopped	12 oz.

Procedure:

1. Blend together lemon juice, water, honey, mustard, and spices.
2. Chill for 30 minutes.
3. Just before serving beat in the nut oil and chives.

❖ Orange Walnut Dressing

Toasted walnuts and orange rind give zest to this dressing.

Portions per recipe: 128
Yield: 1 gallon
Portion: 1 ounce
Serving utensil: 1-ounce ladle

Serve chilled
Time: 1 hour

Ingredients	Amounts
Whole milk yogurt	8 lb.
Dijon mustard	2 oz.
Orange rind, grated	1 oz.
Freshly squeezed orange juice	8 oz.
White pepper	1/8 oz.
Turmeric	1/8 oz.
Cumin	1/4 oz.
Walnuts, toasted	8 oz.

Procedure:

1. Blend all ingredients except walnuts and chill for 1 hour.
2. Chop walnuts coarsely and fold into dressing.
3. Serve at once.

Calories: **25**   Protein: **.6 g (10%)**   Carbohydrates: **2.0 g (32%)**   Sodium: **13 mg**

Total Fat: **1.5 g (54%)**   *Saturated Fat:* **.6 g**   *Monounsaturated Fat:* **.4 g**   *Polyunsaturated Fat:* **.3 g**

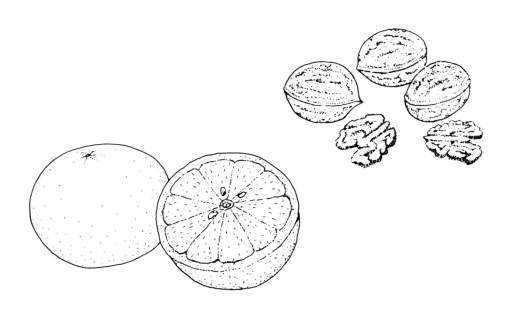

❖ Sweet and Sour Sesame Dressing

An Oriental-style dressing with just a touch of toasted sesame oil.

Portions per recipe: 128
Yield: 1 gallon
Portion: 1 ounce
Serving utensil: 1-ounce ladle

Serve chilled
Time: 1 hour

Ingredients

Ingredients	Amounts
Sesame oil	1 oz.
Sesame seeds	3 oz.
Ginger root, grated	1 oz.
Garlic cloves, crushed	1 oz.
Soy sauce	1 oz.
Honey	4 oz.
Lemon juice	8 oz.
Cayenne pepper	$1/16$ oz.
Low-fat yogurt	8 lb.

Procedure:

1. Heat sesame oil and toast sesame seeds for 2 minutes.
2. Add ginger, garlic, soy sauce, honey, lemon juice, and cayenne.
3. Simmer slowly for 5 minutes. Cool
4. Stir mixture gently into yogurt and chill for 1 hour.

Calories: **56**   Protein: **.8 g (6%)**   Carbohydrates: **2.1 g (15%)**   Sodium: **18 mg**

Total Fat: **5.3 g (85%)**   *Saturated Fat:* **.8 g**   *Monounsaturated Fat:* **2.6 g**   *Polyunsaturated Fat:* **1.6 g**

—10—

VEGETABLES

Beyond Corn and Peas

❖

Here is my vegetable philosophy in a nutshell: Fresh is best, frozen is good, and canned is almost always unacceptable. I use only a few canned vegetables: beets, Italian tomatoes, legumes, and a few ethnic specialties.

The plants we eat as vegetables (some, such as the tomato, are actually fruits) provide us with carbohydrates, fiber, vitamins, minerals, some protein, and water. Vegetables are, with a few exceptions, low in fat and low in calories. Americans still do not include enough vegetables in their diet. The hospitality industry, and especially residential food service institutions, can effect real change by providing an abundance of fresh and properly prepared vegetable choices.

Perfectly steamed frozen vegetables are quick and easy and should be offered daily without spices and margarine. The guests can choose to add butter, salt, and pepper or, if an herb and spice bar is available, anything else that strikes their fancy. It is boring and repetitive, however, to offer only steamed vegetables. I have included vegetable recipes that go beyond corn and peas. Interesting and colorful vegetable combinations flavored with herbs and spices and prepared in a variety of ways should be offered alongside the basic steamed vegetables to give the diner a choice. The amounts of fat added are kept to a minimum and will add fewer fat calories to a meal than the addition of butter patties on plain vegetables would.

Please note that the undigestible vegetable fiber is *not* included in the USDA caloric calculations, but is included in the carbohydrate weight. This will make the percentage contribution of the carbohydrates from 10% to 20% more in very high fiber vegetables distorting the overall percentage points.

❖ Artichoke Hearts with Carrots

Cooked a la Grecque they are delicious hot and any leftovers can be chilled and added to the salad bar offerings or can garnish a salad plate.

Portions per recipe: *100*
Yield: *3 pans*
Portion: *4 ounces*
Serving utensil: *spoon*

Pan: *12" × 20" × 2"*
Cooking method: *simmer*
Time: *22 minutes*

Ingredients	Amounts
Olive oil	1 oz.
Carrots, 1" pieces	18 lb.
Garlic cloves, crushed	4 oz.
Granulated sugar	½ oz.
Frozen artichoke hearts, quartered	8 lb.
Lemon juice	12 oz.
Tarragon, crushed	¼ oz.
Salt	1 oz.
Black pepper	⅛ oz.

Procedure:

1. Heat olive oil in kettle. Add carrots, garlic, and sugar. Close lid and cook for 10 minutes.
2. Fold in rest of ingredients and simmer for 12 minutes.

Calories: **50**   Protein: **1.8 g (14%)**   Carbohydrates: **10.9 g (86%)**   Sodium: **152 mg**

Total Fat: **.6 g (10%)**   *Saturated Fat:* **.09 g**   *Monounsaturated Fat:* **.2 g**   *Polyunsaturated Fat:* **.2 g**

❖ Asparagus Parmesan

Serve this when fresh asparagus is plentiful and cheap.

Portions per recipe: **100**
Yield: **3 pans**
Portion: **4 ounces**
Serving utensil: **tongs**

Pan: **12" × 20" × 2"**
Cooking method: **steam**
Time: **3 minutes**

Ingredients

Ingredients	Amounts
Green asparagus	30 lb.
Olive oil	3 oz.
Lemon juice	6 oz.
White pepper	⅛ oz.
Parmesan cheese, grated	3 oz.

Procedure:

1. Break the ends off asparagus stalks. They will snap at the edible part. (Trim and peel ends and add to vegetable soup.)

2. Place in perforated pans and steam for 3 to 4 minutes. Transfer to solid pans.

3. Heat lemon juice with olive oil and pepper. Pour 2 ounces over each pan.

4. Sprinkle each pan of asparagus with 1 ounce of grated parmesan.

Calories: **28**   Protein: **2.6 g (37%)**   Carbohydrates: **2.8 g (40%)**   Sodium: **17 mg**
Total Fat: **1.3 g (41%)**   *Saturated Fat:* **.3 g**   *Monounsaturated Fat:* **.7 g**   *Polyunsaturated Fat:* **.2 g**

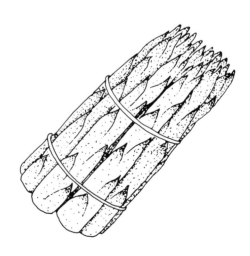

❖ Baked Acorn Squash Rings

Attractive to look at, these are a welcome change from the usual brown sugar-packed halves. Acorn squash, like all winter squash, is an excellent source of vitamin A.

PRODUCTION NOTES: Remove a slice from stem end and scoop out seeds with a spoon. Set slicer blade to ½-inch thickness and slice squash into rings. Some people find it easier to slice squash first and then remove the seeds from each slice.

Portions per recipe: 100	*Pan: 18″ × 26″ sheet pan*
Yield: 200 rings	*Oven temperature: 350° F*
Portion: 2 rings	*Time: 25 minutes*
Serving utensil: spatula	

Ingredients	Amounts
Acorn squash	40 lb.
Margarine	1 lb.
Honey	4 oz.
Hungarian paprika	¼ oz.
Nutmeg	¹⁄₁₆ oz.

Procedure:

1. Cut squash into rings. (See production notes.)
2. Melt margarine with honey and spices.
3. Pour ¼ cup of water into sheet pan.
4. Dip rings in melted margarine and place on sheet pan.
5. Bake at 350° F for 25 minutes.
6. Transfer rings to 12″ × 20″ × 2″ pan, overlapping them slightly.

Calories: **91**   Protein: **1.1 g (5%)**   Carbohydrates: **15.4 g (68%)**   Sodium: **6 mg**

Total Fat: **3.8 g (37%)**   *Saturated Fat:* **.7 g**   *Monounsaturated Fat:* **1.7 g**   *Polyunsaturated Fat:* **1.2 g**

❖ Baked Winter Squash

Though winter squash is usually served mashed, in this recipe partially steamed squash cubes are baked with ginger and honey.

PRODUCTION NOTES: Hubbard squash is best, because its large size makes it easier to cut into cubes. Butternut and buttercup (turban) also can be used. Many produce houses will peel and seed squash. The quantity used in this recipe is based on peeled and seeded winter squash.

Portions per recipe: *100*
Yield: *3 pans*
Portion: *3 ounces*
Serving utensil: *spoon*

Pan: *12″ × 20″ × 2″*
Oven temperature: *350° F*
Time: *20 minutes*

Ingredients

Ingredients	Amounts
Winter squash, prepared	20 lb.
Vegetable oil	3 oz.
Unsalted butter	1 oz.
Ginger root, peeled and chopped	3 oz.
Lemon juice	4 oz.
Honey	2 oz.

Procedure:

1. Cut squash into 1-inch cubes. Steam at low pressure for 5 minutes.
2. Heat oil, butter, ginger, lemon juice, and honey.
3. Place about 7 pounds of steamed squash in each pan.
4. Pour 4 ounces of honey butter over each pan of squash and bake 20 minutes.

Calories: **36**   Protein: **.9 g (10%)**   Carbohydrates: **5.9 g (65%)**   Sodium: **226 mg**

Total Fat: **1.2 g (30%)**   *Saturated Fat:* **.4 g**   *Monounsaturated Fat:* **.2 g**   *Polyunsaturated Fat:* **.5 g**

❖ Bayou Lima Beans

A tasty alternative to succotash.

Portions per recipe: 100
Yield: 3 *pans*
Portion: 3 *ounces*
Serving utensil: 2-ounce ladle

Pan: 12″ × 20″ × 2″
Cooking method: braise
Time: 25 minutes

Ingredients	Amounts
Spanish onions	3 lb.
Peanut oil	3 oz.
Cajun spice mixture (see recipe on page 458)	1 oz.
Carrots, ¼″ thick slices	2 lb.
Frozen lima beans	20 lb.
Water	2 lb.
Lemon juice	4 oz.
Parsley leaves, minced	3 oz.

Procedure:

1. Cut small onions into quarters, large onions into eighths.
2. Heat oil and sauté onions with cajun spices for 5 minutes.
3. Add carrots, lima beans, and water. Simmer for 20 minutes.
4. Stir in lemon juice and minced parsley.

Calories: **112**   Protein: **6.1 g (22%)**   Carbohydrates: **20.0 g (71%)**   Sodium: **56 mg**

Total Fat: **1.3 g (10%)**   *Saturated Fat:* **.2 g**   *Monounsaturated Fat:* **.4 g**   *Polyunsaturated Fat:* **.5 g**

❖ Black-eyed Peas

In this country, black-eyed peas remind us of the South, where they are cooked with salt pork and are also known as cow peas. They were brought to the United States by slaves. Black-eyed peas are native to India and this recipe cooks them in northern Indian style.

PRODUCTION NOTES: This recipe uses frozen black-eyed peas, but dried peas can be used. Soak ½ the amount of dry peas in water and extend cooking time by 45 minutes. Asafoetida is an Indian spice with a strong onion flavor, it is available from health food and Indian stores.

Portions per recipe: *100*
Yield: *2 pans*
Portion: *3 ounces*
Serving utensil: *2-ounce ladle*

Pan: *12″ × 20″ × 2″*
Cooking method: *simmer*
Time: *30 minutes*

Ingredients

Ingredients	Amounts
Vegetable oil	4 oz.
Cumin seed, whole	¼ oz.
Asafoetida	Pinch
Spanish onions, diced	1 lb.
Hot green chilies	1 oz.
Frozen black-eyed peas	20 lb.
Turmeric	¼ oz.
Chili powder	½ oz.
Salt	1 oz.
Water	4 lb.
Lemon juice	4 oz.
Yogurt	2 lb.
Cilantro leaves, chopped	1 oz.
Parsley leaves, minced	2 oz.

Procedure:

1. Heat oil with cumin seed and asafoetida until seeds start to pop.
2. Add onions and chilies and sauté for 5 minutes.
3. Stir in the black-eyed peas, turmeric, chili powder, salt, and water.
4. Simmer for 25 minutes. Stir in lemon juice and yogurt.
5. Mix together cilantro and parsley. Transfer peas to pans and sprinkle with herbs.

Calories: **88**   Protein: **4.9 g (22%)**   Carbohydrates: **13.6 g (62%)**   Sodium: **390 mg**
Total Fat: **1.8 g (18%)**   *Saturated Fat:* **.5 g**   *Monounsaturated Fat:* **.3 g**   *Polyunsaturated Fat:* **.8 g**

❖ Bok Choy

Bok choy is a thick-ribbed Chinese cabbage with dark green leaves. It tastes best stir-fried. Any leftover bok choy can be served cold as a salad with the addition of a little lemon juice.

PRODUCTION NOTES: Prepare bok choy for cooking by cutting a slice from the bottom and removing the outer leaves (chop them fine for soup); they are a little tough. Split the stems and cut them diagonally into 2-inch pieces. Stir-fry in 10 pound batches. Five-spice powder is a Chinese spice blend that contains star anise, fennel, cloves, toasted Sichuan peppercorns, and cinnamon. Can also be stir-fried on a griddle.

Portions per recipe: *100*	Pan: *12″ × 20″ × 4″*
Yield: *2 pans*	Skillet temperature: *375° F*
Portion: *3 ounces*	Time: *5–7 minutes*
Serving utensil: *spoon*	

Ingredients

Ingredients	Amounts
Peanut oil	4 oz.
Garlic cloves, crushed	2 oz.
Five-spice powder	$^{1}/_{16}$ oz.
Bok choy, trimmed and cut into 2″ pieces	20 lb.
Soy sauce	1 oz.

Procedure:

1. Heat 2 ounces of peanut oil in tilting skillet.
2. Stir 1 ounce of garlic and 1 teaspoon of five-spice powder into oil. Immediately add 10-pound batch of bok choy.
3. Stir-fry for 5 to 7 minutes. Fold in 1 tablespoon of soy sauce.
4. Ladle into serving pan. Bok choy should be slightly crunchy.
5. Repeat with second 10-pound batch.

Calories: **21**   Protein: **1.2 g (23%)**   Carbohydrates: **1.9 g (36%)**   Sodium: **68 mg**

Total Fat: **1.3 g (56%)**   *Saturated Fat:* **.2 g**   *Monounsaturated Fat:* **.5 g**   *Polyunsaturated Fat:* **.4 g**

Celery quarters braised with shredded carrots.

❖ Braised Celery Quarters

Celery hearts are split into quarters and baked with shredded carrots in vegetarian or chicken stock and vermouth.

PRODUCTION NOTES: This recipe can also be prepared in a tilting skillet. Follow the first 2 steps then place celery quarters in one layer in skillet, add bay leaves, close lid, and simmer for 30 minutes.

Portions per recipe: 150
Yield: 4 pans
Portion: 3½ ounces
Serving utensil: spoon

Pan: 12″ × 20″ × 2″
Oven temperature: 350° F
Time: 30 minutes

Ingredients	Amounts
Margarine	4 oz.
Spanish onions, diced small	2 lb.
Carrots, finely shredded	2 lb.
Thyme	1/16 oz.
White pepper	1/8 oz.
Salt	1 oz.
Vegetarian or chicken stock	7 lb.
Dry vermouth	1 lb.
Celery hearts, trimmed and quartered	30 lb.
Bay leaves (2 per pan)	

(continued)

Procedure:

1. Melt margarine and sauté onions and carrots with thyme for 6 to 8 minutes.
2. Add salt, pepper, stock, and vermouth. Simmer for 2 minutes.
3. Place celery quarters in two tight rows of 18 to 19 pieces.
4. Pour 3 pints of vegetable sauce over each pan of celery.
5. Add 2 bay leaves to each pan, cover, and bake at 350° F for 30 minutes.

Calories: **20**   Protein: **.6 g (12%)**   Carbohydrates: **3.4 g (68%)**   Sodium: **241 mg**
Total Fat: **.7 g (32%)**   Saturated Fat: **.1 g**   Monounsaturated Fat: **.3 g**   Polyunsaturated Fat: **.2 g**

❖ Broccoli al Forno   *Michela's*

A toasted bread crumb and parmesan cheese topping adds flavor (and fat) to steamed broccoli. I have reduced the butter and the parmesan cheese from the original "Taste of Europe" version. Now it is less rich but not less tasty.

Portions per recipe: *100*   Pan: *12″ × 20″ × 2″*
Yield: *3 pans*   Cooking method: *steam*
Portion: *3 ounces*   Time: *5 minutes*
Serving utensil: *spoon*

Ingredients

Ingredients	Amounts
Unsalted butter	4 oz.
Garlic cloves, crushed	1 oz.
Bread crumbs	12 oz.
Parmesan cheese, grated	2 oz.
Broccoli florets	25 lb.

Procedure:

1. Heat butter to light brown stage. Add garlic and bread crumbs and toast to a medium brown.
2. Remove from heat and stir in parmesan cheese.
3. Steam broccoli until crisp but tender in 12″ × 20″ × 2″ pan. Drain off any liquid.
4. Top each pan with 8 ounces of sautéed bread crumbs.

Calories: **44**   Protein: **2.7 g (24%)**   Carbohydrates: **6.2 g (56%)**   Sodium: **54 mg**
Total Fat: **1.5 g (31%)**   Saturated Fat: **.8 g**   Monounsaturated Fat: **.4 g**   Polyunsaturated Fat: **.2 g**

❖ Broccoli with Garlic and Celeriac

Fresh trimmed broccoli is steamed briefly and topped with sautéed garlic and celeriac (celery root). Celeriac has a sweet, nutty flavor that softens the taste of broccoli.

PRODUCTION NOTES: Use florets and stems. Peel and quarter stems and cut them into 3-inch-long pieces.

Portions per recipe: *100*
Yield: *3 pans*
Portion: *3 ounces*
Serving utensil: *spoon*

Pan: *12″ × 20″ × 2″*
Cooking method: *steam*
Time: *12 minutes*

Ingredients | Amounts

Ingredients	Amounts
Olive oil	2 oz.
Celeriac, peeled and julienned	3 lb.
Garlic cloves, crushed	4 oz.
Salt	½ oz.
Broccoli, trimmed	25 lb.

Procedure:

1. Heat olive oil and sauté celeriac and garlic for 12 minutes. Celeriac should be golden brown and tender, not mushy. Add salt.

2. Steam broccoli until crisp but tender in 12″ × 20″ × 2″ pan. Drain off any liquid.

3. Top each pan with 1-pound celeriac-garlic sauté.

Calories: **30**   Protein: **2.3 g (30%)**   Carbohydrates: **5.0 g (66%)**   Sodium: **85 mg**

Total Fat: **.8 g (24%)**   *Saturated Fat:* **.1 g**   *Monounsaturated Fat:* **.4 g**   *Polyunsaturated Fat:* **.1 g**

❖ Carrots Vichy

A classic rendition, sweet and lemony. These carrots are smothered with fresh parsley and chives.

PRODUCTION NOTES: Carrots can also be steamed and ½ cup of lemon butter poured over them. Butter is used for flavor and safflower oil to reduce saturated fat.

Portions per recipe: *100*   Pan: *12″ × 20″ × 2″*
Yield: *2 pans*   Oven temperature: *325° F*
Portion: *4 ounces*   Time: *30 minutes*
Serving utensil: *spoon*

Ingredients | Amounts

Ingredients	Amounts
Unsalted butter	2 oz.
Safflower oil	2 oz.
Lemon juice	4 oz.
Salt	½ oz.
White pepper	⅛ oz.
Carrots, ¼″ thick slices	25 lb.
Parsley, minced	4 oz.
Fresh chives, chopped	2 oz.

Procedure:

1. Melt butter with lemon juice and spices.
2. With a 2-ounce ladle pour hot lemon butter in each pan.
3. Add sliced carrots and pour another ladle of lemon butter over them.
4. Cover tightly and bake in a 325° F oven for 30 minutes.
5. Uncover, add fresh herbs, and toss gently. Serve at once.

Calories: **53**   Protein: **1.1 g (8%)**   Carbohydrates: **10.3 g (78%)**   Sodium: **35 mg**

Total Fat: **1.2 g (20%)**   *Saturated Fat:* **.4 g**   *Monounsaturated Fat:* **.2 g**   *Polyunsaturated Fat:* **.5 g**

❖ Carrots with Marsala Wine *Romagnoli*

The Italian way to serve carrots. The marsala wine gives sweetness and a special taste to a simple vegetable.

PRODUCTION NOTE: Frozen shoestring carrots are an attractive alternative to sliced carrots.

Portions per recipe: *100*
Yield: *2 pans*
Portion: *4 ounces*
Serving utensil: *spoon*

Pan: *12″ × 20″ × 2″*
Oven temperature: *325° F*
Time: *20 minutes*

Ingredients

Ingredients	Amounts
Unsalted butter	8 oz.
Granulated sugar	2 oz.
Salt	1 oz.
Black pepper	¼ oz.
Marsala wine	2 lb.
Carrots, ¼″ thick slices	25 lb.
Parsley leaves, minced	2 oz.

Procedure:

1. Simmer butter, sugar, salt, pepper, and marsala wine slowly for 15 minutes.
2. Put carrot slices into pans and pour 1 pint of marsala sauce over each pan.
3. Cover and bake at 325° F for 20 minutes.

Calories: **62**   Protein: **1.1 g (7%)**   Carbohydrates: **10.9 g (70%)**   Sodium: **145 mg**
Total Fat: **2.0 g (29%)**   Saturated Fat: **1.2 g**   Monounsaturated Fat: **.6g**   Polyunsaturated Fat: **.2 g**

❖ Cauliflower Milanese

Partially steamed cauliflower is baked in a marinara sauce sprinkled with parmesan cheese. An excellent encore presentation of leftover sauce.

Portions per recipe: *100*
Yield: *3 pans*
Portion: *4 ounces*
Serving utensil: *spoon*

Pan: *12″ × 20″ × 2″*
Oven temperature: *325° F*
Time: *20 minutes*

Ingredients   Amounts

Cauliflower, cored and broken into large florets	30 lb.

Sauce

Ingredient	Amount
Olive oil	1 oz.
Spanish onions, finely diced	12 oz.
Garlic cloves, crushed	2 oz.
Carrots, thinly sliced	1 lb.
Parsley, minced	2 oz.
Fresh basil leaves, chopped	1 oz.
Bay leaves, crumbled	1/8 oz.
Thyme	1/8 oz.
Cayenne pepper	1/16 oz
Plum tomatoes, ripened and chopped	3 lb.
Green peppers, seeded and chopped	1 lb.
Salt	1/2 oz.
Parmesan cheese, grated	6 oz.

Procedure:

1. Steam 10 pounds of cauliflower at low pressure in perforated pans for 5 minutes. Drain.
2. For marinara sauce heat olive oil and cook onions, garlic, carrots, herbs, and spices for 15 minutes.
3. Add tomatoes, green peppers, and salt and simmer for 5 minutes.
4. Transfer cauliflower to solid pan. Pour 1 quart marinara sauce over it.
5. Sprinkle with parmesan and bake at 325° F for 20 minutes.

Calories: **31**   Protein: **2.1 g (27%)**   Carbohydrates: **4.4 g (57%)**   Sodium: **97 mg**

Total Fat: **1.0 g (29%)**   *Saturated Fat: **.4 g**   Monounsaturated Fat: **.4 g**   Polyunsaturated Fat: **.1 g***

❖ Cheese-baked Tomato Halves

For banquet dinners I often included this vegetable along with a green one as the garnish. Baked tomatoes are excellent with mild white fish, roasted lamb, or beef.

Portions per recipe: 160
Yield: 4 pans, 160 halves
Portion: ½ tomato
Serving utensil: spoon

Pan: 12″ × 20″ × 2″
Oven temperature: 350° F
Time: 12 minutes

Ingredients

Ingredients	Amounts
Tomatoes	20 lb.
Bread crumbs	1 lb.
Garlic cloves, crushed	1 oz.
Basil leaves, chopped	1 oz.
Italian parsley, chopped	3 oz.
Swiss cheese, shredded medium-fine	2 lb. 8 oz.
Parmesan, grated	4 oz.
Black pepper	¼ oz.

Procedure:

1. Core, stem, and cut tomatoes in half. Place tightly in 4 rows of 10 in oiled pans.

2. Blend together all the other ingredients.

3. Sprinkle 8 ounces of the mixture over tomatoes in each pan.

4. Bake at 350° F for 12 minutes.

Calories: **52**   Protein: **3.2 g (25%)**   Carbohydrates: **4.8 g (37%)**   Sodium: **57 mg**
Total Fat: **2.4 g (41%)**   *Saturated Fat:* **1.4 g**   *Monounsaturated Fat:* **.7 g**   *Polyunsaturated Fat:* **.1 g**

❖ Chinese Cabbage with Two Kinds of Mushrooms

Dried red chilies and toasted sesame seeds flavor the Chinese cabbage and the mushrooms.

PRODUCTION NOTES: Straw mushrooms are available canned. Soak dry mushrooms overnight.

Portions per recipe: *100*
Yield: *3 pans*
Portion: *3 ounces*
Serving utensil: *spoon*

Pan: *12″ × 20″ × 2″*
Tilt skillet temperature: *375° F*
Time: *7 minutes*

Ingredients

Ingredients	Amounts
Dry Chinese mushrooms soaked overnight	4 oz.
Peanut oil	4 oz.
Dried red chilies, small whole pods	¼ oz.
Sesame seeds	½ oz.
Chinese cabbage (nappa), 4″ pieces	20 lb.
Canned whole straw mushrooms, drained	1 lb. 14 oz.
Soy sauce	1 oz.

Procedure:

1. Squeeze soaked mushrooms lightly, remove any tough stems, and slice caps into strips.
2. Heat oil and fry chilies and sesame seed for about 1 minute.
3. Add Chinese cabbage and both kinds of mushrooms and stir-fry for 6 minutes.
4. Stir in soy sauce and transfer into serving pans.

Calories: **27**   Protein: **1.5 g (22%)**   Carbohydrates: **3.1 g (46%)**   Sodium: **68 mg**
Total Fat: **1.4 g (47%)**   *Saturated Fat:* **.2 g**   *Monounsaturated Fat:* **.6 g**   *Polyunsaturated Fat:* **.5 g**

❖ Corn Pudding

A creamy pudding that provides a protein complement to such meatless entrées as celery root with hazelnuts, mushroom cakes, or okra beignets.

Portions per recipe: 96
Yield: 6 pans
Portion: 5 ounces
Serving utensil: spatula or spoon

Pan: 12″ × 20″ × 2″–½ size
Oven temperature: 275° F
Time: 50 minutes

Ingredients

Ingredients	Amounts	
Vegetable oil		1 oz.
Scallions, chopped	2 lb.	
Red bell peppers, chopped	1 lb.	8 oz.
Frozen whole kernel corn	12 lb.	8 oz.
Canned cream-style corn	6 lb.	6 oz.
Eggs, separated	1 lb.	14 oz.
Light cream	4 lb.	
Salt		½ oz.
Nutmeg		⅛ oz.
Cayenne pepper		¹⁄₁₆ oz.

Procedure:

1. Heat oil and cook scallions until soft, about 5 minutes.
2. Place in mixing bowl and add red peppers, corn, egg yolks, cream, salt, nutmeg, and cayenne. Blend well.
3. Whip egg whites to soft peak stage and fold gently into corn mixture.
4. Lightly oil pan and pour in corn mixture until pan is ¾ full.
5. Bake at 275° F for 40 minutes, raise heat to 350° F, and bake for 10 minutes more to brown top.

Calories: **129**   Protein: **4.0 g (12%)**   Carbohydrates: **19.3 g (60%)**   Sodium: **163 mg**

Total Fat: **5.4 g (38%)**   *Saturated Fat:* **2.7 g**   *Monounsaturated Fat:* **1.6 g**   *Polyunsaturated Fat:* **.7 g**

❖ Courgettes a la Latine (Zucchini) *Kamman*

Another dish from the "French Feast for 5,000" special event. Zucchini is sautéed with garlic and cured olives and finished with a sprinkling of grated lemon rind.

PRODUCTION NOTES: Cook in small batches using no more than 6 pounds of zucchini at any one time. Cooking time is very short to keep zucchini very crisp. Can also be stir-fried on griddle.

Portions per recipe: *100*
Yield: *3 pans*
Portion: *3 ounces*
Serving utensil: *spoon*

Pan: *12″ × 20″ × 2″*
Skillet temperature: *350° F*
Time: *3 minutes*

Ingredients	Amounts
Olive oil	6 oz.
Garlic cloves, crushed	3 oz.
Oil cured Greek olives, seeded and chopped	6 oz.
Zucchini, ⅛″ thick slices	20 lb.
Salt	¾ oz.
Black pepper	¼ oz.
Parsley, minced	2 oz.

Procedure:

1. Heat 2 ounces olive oil with 1 ounce garlic and 2 ounces chopped olives.

2. Add 6 pounds of zucchini slices. Stir-fry for 2 minutes.

3. Mix salt and pepper. Sprinkle ⅓ ounce over zucchini and stir-fry for 1 minute.

4. Place in pan and sprinkle with minced parsley.

Calories: **34**   Protein: **1.1 g (13%)**   Carbohydrates: **3.0 g (35%)**   Sodium: **130 mg**

Total Fat: **2.3 g (61%)**   *Saturated Fat:* **.3 g**   *Monounsaturated Fat:* **1.6 g**   *Polyunsaturated Fat:* **.2 g**

❖ Curried Cucumbers

Braised cucumbers are one of my favorite vegetables. Even cooked they taste cool and refreshing. Curried cucumbers are wonderful with Indian dishes, such as tandoori murgh or chicken potato curry. See photo on 208. They are also a good accompaniment to barbecued chicken or lamb.

PRODUCTION NOTE: Large cucumbers are fine for this dish. The tilting skillet produces golden brown cucumbers, but a steam kettle can be used with good results.

Portions per recipe: *100*
Yield: *3 pans*
Portion: *3 ounces*
Serving utensil: *3-ounce ladle*

Pan: *12" × 20" × 2"*
Skillet temperature: *350° F*
Time: *12 minutes*

Ingredients

Ingredients	Amounts
Cucumbers	25 lb.
Olive oil	2 oz.
Scallions, chopped	1 lb.
Salt	1/2 oz.
Cayenne pepper	1/16 oz.
Turmeric	1/4 oz.
Curry powder	1/2 oz.
Mint leaves, chopped	2 oz.

Procedure:

1. Peel cucumbers, cut in half lengthwise, seed, and cut into 1" thick pieces.
2. Heat olive oil in tilt skillet, add cucumbers, and sauté for 5 minutes.
3. Stir in scallions, salt, and spices. Cover and simmer for 5 minutes. Cucumbers should be tender but firm.
4. Toss with chopped mint just before serving.
5. Optional: Top with yogurt dollops.

Calories: **22**   Protein: **.7 g (13%)**   Carbohydrates: **3.8 g (69%)**   Sodium: **57 mg**
Total Fat: **.8 g (33%)**   *Saturated Fat:* **.11 g**   *Monounsaturated Fat:* **.4 g**   *Polyunsaturated Fat:* **.1 g**

❖ Delicious Red Potatoes

Because timing is not crucial, these potatoes are ideal for institutions with long service periods. Held at 300° F in the oven they will get crisper but will not dry out.

PRODUCTION NOTE: Slice potatoes directly into a deep pan filled with water so they will not become discolored.

Portions per recipe: 100
Yield: 3 pans
Portion: 3 ounces
Serving utensil: spoon

Pan: 12″ × 20″ × 2″
Oven temperature: 375° F
Time: 25 minutes

Ingredients	Amounts
Red potatoes, unpeeled	25 lb.
Salt	1 oz.
Black pepper	¼ oz.
Olive oil	8 oz.
Unsalted butter, melted	9 oz.

Procedure:

1. Wash potatoes well and cut out any blemishes.
2. Cut into ¼-inch slices and place in water-filled pan. Wash and drain.
3. Toss potato slices with salt, pepper, and olive oil.
4. Place approximately 8 pounds of potatoes in each pan. Drizzle with 3 ounces of melted butter.
5. Bake at 375° F for 25 minutes or until crisp and brown on top.

Calories: **106**   Protein: **1.8 g (7%)**   Carbohydrates: **15.3 g (58%)**   Sodium: **115 mg**
Total Fat: **4.4 g (37%)**   *Saturated Fat:* **1.6 g**   *Monounsaturated Fat:* **2.3 g**   *Polyunsaturated Fat:* **.3 g**

❖ Finocchi Fritti *Michela's*

Fennel is a bulbous plant native to the Mediterranean. It has a slight licorice flavor. Fennel can be eaten raw in salads or added to crudites. It is often braised with stock or prepared au gratin. Here it is deep fried.

PRODUCTION NOTES: Prepare fennel by cutting off the feathery tops. Keep some to garnish pans. Trim a thin slice off the base and remove the tough outer stalk. Cut the bulbs into strips along the grain.

Portions per recipe: *100*	Pan: *12″ × 20″ × 2″*
Yield: *3 pans*	Fat temperature: *350° F*
Portion: *2 ounces*	Time: *3–4 minutes*
Serving utensil: *Slotted spoon*	

Ingredients

Ingredients	Amounts
*Fennel	15 lb.
Eggs, beaten	2 lb.
Skim milk	8 oz.
Bread crumbs	3 lb.

Procedure:

1. Prepare fennel (see production notes), wash, and drain.
2. Beat eggs with milk and pour into shallow pan. Drop in 24 oz. fennel. Remove to colander, drain briefly, and toss in bread crumbs.
3. Deep fry at 350° F for 3 to 4 minutes. Do not crowd baskets.
4. Drain fried fennel on paper towels before putting into serving pans.

---

*No nutritional data for fennel.

❖ Fresh Green Beans with Sautéed Peppers

This is my favorite way to prepare and eat green beans. They can be eaten hot or at room temperature.

Portions per recipe: *100*
Yield: *2 pans*
Portion: *3 ounces*
Serving utensil: *spoon*

Pan: *12" × 20" × 2"*
Cooking method: *steam*
Time: *5 minutes*

PRODUCTION NOTE: Prepare dressing 30 minutes before steaming the green beans. Sauté bell pepper strips on the griddle with a small amount of olive oil.

Ingredients	Amounts
Dressing	
Olive oil	2 oz.
Balsamic vinegar	2 oz.
Garlic cloves, whole	½ oz.
Salt	1 oz.
Freshly ground black pepper	⅛ oz.
Olive oil	1 oz.
Red bell peppers, thin strips	2 lb.
Green beans	20 lb.

Procedure:

1. Beat together olive oil and balsamic vinegar.
2. Bruise the garlic with the blade of a cleaver. Add to oil and vinegar with the salt and pepper. Let sit for 30 minutes.
3. Heat the olive oil and sauté the bell pepper strips for 4 minutes. Hold.
4. Snip stem end of beans, leave tips on. Steam for 5 minutes at low pressure in a perforated pan. Beans should be crisp but tender, not soft.
5. Discard garlic cloves, beat dressing again, and pour over hot beans.
6. Toss and place into pan. Garnish with sautéed red peppers.

Calories: **34**   Protein: **1.5 g (18%)**   Carbohydrates: **6.2 g (73%)**   Sodium: **115 mg**

Total Fat: **1.0 g (26%)**   *Saturated Fat:* **.14 g**   *Monounsaturated Fat:* **.6 g**   *Polyunsaturated Fat:* **.14 g**

Green beans with sautéed peppers and balsamic vinegar.

❖ German Fried Potatoes

Bacon and onions make these potatoes hard to resist.

PRODUCTION NOTES: Boil the potatoes in their jackets, let them cool, and slice them unpeeled, or use frozen stew-cut potatoes and boil or steam them until they are tender but firm. For production of more than 500 portions it is advisable to cook bacon and onions ahead of time. Fry the potatoes in batches of about 10 pounds with about 1 pound of cooked bacon and 2 pounds of onions.

Portions per recipe: *100*	Pan: *12″ × 20″ × 2″*
Yield: *3 pans*	Grill temperature: *375° F*
Portion: *3 ounces*	Time: *7–8 minutes*
Serving utensil: *spoon*	

Ingredients	Amounts
Raw bacon, diced	2 lb.
Spanish onions, diced	4 lb.
Cooked potatoes, ¼″ thick slices	20 lb.
Parsley, minced	3 oz.

Procedure:

1. Fry bacon on hot griddle until almost crisp, add cooked potato slices, and fry for 4 minutes, turning the potatoes once.
2. Top potatoes with onions and turn over. Fry until onions are golden.
3. Place in serving pans and sprinkle with 1 ounce of chopped parsley.

Calories: **134**   Protein: **2.5 g (8%)**   Carbohydrates: **19.4 g (58%)**   Sodium: **67 mg**

Total Fat: **5.3 g (35%)**   *Saturated Fat:* **2.0 g**   *Monounsaturated Fat:* **2.4 g**   *Polyunsaturated Fat:* **.7 g**

❖ German Hot Potato Salad

A warm potato salad that is excellent with pork chops, hot dogs, kielbasa, or fried fish.

PRODUCTION NOTES: Use precooked bacon in this recipe. If raw bacon is used, bake or microwave about 1 pound, 12 ounces and discard the fat. Cook and cut potatoes close to serving time. Potatoes should not be cold when added to the dressing.

Portions per recipe: 150	*Pan: 12" × 20" × 4"*
Yield: 3 pans	*Cooking method: simmer*
Portion: 4 ounces	*Time: 20 minutes*
Serving utensil: 3-ounce ladle or #8 scoop	

Ingredients

Ingredients	Amounts
Olive oil	2 oz.
Frozen pre-cooked lean bacon	1 lb.
Spanish onions, chopped	2 lb.
Celery stalks, thinly sliced	5 lb.
Water	4 lb.
Salt	1 oz.
Black pepper	½ oz.
Cider vinegar	4 lb.
Red potatoes, cooked and quartered (warm)	30 lb.
Parsley, minced	4 oz.

Procedure:

1. Heat olive oil. Finely chop bacon and add to olive oil.
2. Stir in onions and celery and sauté for 5 minutes.
3. Add water, salt, pepper, and vinegar and simmer for 2 minutes.
4. Turn off heat and toss potatoes in hot dressing.
5. Transfer to serving pans and sprinkle generously with parsley.

Calories: **118**   Protein: **2.6 g (9%)**   Carbohydrates: **23.6 g (80%)**   Sodium: **113 mg**
Total Fat: **2.2 g (17%)**   *Saturated Fat: .7 g*   *Monounsaturated Fat: 1.1 g*   *Polyunsaturated Fat: .3 g*

❖ Ginataan (Sweet Potatoes with Coconut)

Sweet potatoes Caribbean style.

Portions per recipe: 100
Yield: 3 pans
Portion: 3 ounces
Serving utensil: spoon

Pan: 12″ × 20″ × 2″
Oven temperature: 325° F
Time: 20 minutes

Ingredients	Amounts
Canned sweet potatoes	26 lb. 8 oz.
Lemon juice	6 oz.
Brown sugar	1 lb. 8 oz.
Coconut, shredded	12 oz.

Procedure:

1. Drain sweet potatoes and place in one layer in pans.
2. Pour 2 ounces of lemon juice over potatoes in each pan.
3. Mix brown sugar and coconut and sprinkle 12 ounces evenly on potatoes.
4. Bake at 325° F for 20 minutes.

Calories: **153**   Protein: **2.1 g (5%)**   Carbohydrates: **33.7 g (88%)**   Sodium: **75 mg**
Total Fat: **1.4 g (8%)**   *Saturated Fat:* **1.1 g**   *Monounsaturated Fat:* **.1 g**   *Polyunsaturated Fat:* **.1 g**

❖ Glazed Carrots

The Cape Neddick Inn in Maine serves ginger-flavored carrots as one of their side dishes. This interpretation is based on my memory of that dish.

Portions per recipe: 100
Yield: 3 pans
Portion: 4 ounces
Serving utensil: spoon

Pan: 12″ × 20″ × 2″
Oven temperature: 350° F
Time: 15 minutes

Ingredients	Amounts
Carrots, sliced diagonally into 1″ pieces	25 lb.
Unsalted butter	2 oz.
Ginger root, peeled and grated	2 oz.
Apricot nectar	3 lb.
Brown sugar	6 oz.
Cayenne pepper	$1/16$ oz.
Salt	$1/2$ oz.

Procedure:

1. Steam carrots in perforated pans at high pressure for 3 minutes.
2. Heat butter with ginger root. Add nectar, sugar, cayenne, and salt.
3. Simmer for 10 minutes.
4. Transfer about 8 pounds of steamed carrots into each pan and pour 1 pound of sauce over them.
5. Bake at 350° F for 15 minutes until well glazed.

Calories: **62**   Protein: **1.1 g (7%)**   Carbohydrates: **13.9 g (90%)**   Sodium: **106 mg**

Total Fat: **.7 g (10%)**   *Saturated Fat: .3 g*   *Monounsaturated Fat: .2 g*   *Polyunsaturated Fat: .1 g*

❖ Italian Broccoli and Cauliflower

Portions per recipe: 100
Yield: 3 pans
Portion: 3 ounces
Serving utensil: spoon

Pan: 12″ × 20″ × 2″
Temperature: Steam (15 lb.)
Time: 2–4 minutes

Ingredients

Ingredients	Amounts
Broccoli, trimmed florets	10 lb.
Cauliflower, trimmed florets	10 lb.
Olive oil	4 oz.
Lemon juice	2 oz.
Salt	1 oz.
Freshly ground black pepper	¼ oz.

Procedure:

1. Steam broccoli and cauliflower in separate perforated pans.
2. Put equal amounts into pan.
3. Beat oil with lemon juice, salt, and pepper. Drizzle ¼ cup over vegetables.

Calories: **22**   Protein: **1.2 g (22%)**   Carbohydrates: **2.4 g (44%)**   Sodium: **120 mg**

Total Fat: **1.3 g (53%)**   *Saturated Fat: .2 g*   *Monounsaturated Fat: .8 g*   *Polyunsaturated Fat: .2 g*

❖ Italian Potatoes for Buffets or Cookouts

This is an excellent dish to accompany barbecued chicken or steak. It keeps very well and can serve as a vegetarian entrée.

Portions per recipe: 36
Yield: 1 pan
Portion: 5 ounces
Serving utensil: spoon

Pan: 12″ × 20″ × 2″
Oven temperature: 375° F
Time: 35 minutes

Ingredients	*Amounts*
Olive oil	2 oz.
Spanish onions, thinly sliced	2 lb.
Garlic cloves, crushed	1 oz.
Marjoram, crushed	¼ oz.
Potatoes, thinly sliced	6 lb.
Vegetarian stock or chicken broth	1 lb.
Salt	½ oz.
Tomatoes, thinly sliced	3 lb.
Fontina cheese, shredded	12 oz.
Fresh basil leaves, cut into strips	½ oz.
Italian parsley leaves, chopped	½ oz.

Italian potatoes for buffets or cookouts.

Procedure:

1. Heat olive oil and sauté onions with garlic and marjoram.
2. Put in 2-inch pan and add raw potato slices, stock, salt, and pepper.
3. Cover with foil and bake 20 minutes. Remove foil.
4. Add a layer of tomato slices. Sprinkle with basil and parsley.
5. Sprinkle with cheese and bake 15 minutes more.

Calories: **111**   Protein: **4.2 g (15%)**   Carbohydrates: **13.8 g (50%)**   Sodium: **195 mg**

Total Fat: **4.7 g (38%)**   *Saturated Fat:* **2.1 g**   *Monounsaturated Fat:* **2.0 g**   *Polyunsaturated Fat:* **.4 g**

❖ Latkes—Potato Pancakes

Traditionally served at Hanukkah, latkes are so good they deserve to be served more often. Try them for breakfast, brunch, or for dinner with sauerbraten.

PRODUCTION NOTES: The top layer of the potato batter will become discolored if left exposed to the air. Press plastic wrap directly onto the batter. Batter should be runny, not stiff. If the batter is too thin, add more bread crumbs.

Portions per recipe: 60
Yield: 120 pancakes
Portion: 2 pancakes
Serving utensil: spatula

Pan: 12″ × 20″ × 2″
Griddle temperature: 360° F
Time: 6–7 minutes

Ingredients

Ingredients	Amounts	
Potatoes, peeled	15 lb.	
Spanish onions		12 oz.
Eggs		10 oz.
Bread crumbs	1 lb.	
Salt		1 oz.
Vegetable oil for griddle		4 oz.

Procedure:

1. Chop raw potatoes and onions to a mush in food processor or blender.
2. Beat in rest of ingredients.
3. Drop batter with a 2-ounce ladle on well oiled hot griddle.
4. Flatten to even thickness.
5. Fry until golden brown on each side. Serve at once.

Calories: **116**   Protein: **2.8 g (10%)**   Carbohydrates: **21.2 g (73%)**   Sodium: **245 mg**

Total Fat: **2.4 g (18%)**   *Saturated Fat:* **.6 g**   *Monounsaturated Fat:* **.6 g**   *Polyunsaturated Fat:* **1.1 g**

❖ Mushrooms Rosemary

Fragrant fresh rosemary flavors grilled button mushrooms.

Portions per recipe: 100
Yield: 3 pans
Portion: 2 ounces
Serving utensil: spoon

Pan: 12″ × 20″ × 2″
Griddle temperature: 350° F
Time: 6 minutes

Ingredients	Amounts
Button mushrooms	15 lb.
Olive oil	2 oz.
Unsalted butter, melted	2 oz.
Rosemary leaves, chopped	4 oz.
Salt	½ oz.
Freshly ground black pepper	¼ oz.

Procedure:

1. Wash, drain, and trim mushrooms. Cut any large ones in half.

2. Stir together olive oil, melted butter, rosemary, salt, and pepper.

3. With a 1-ounce ladle pour herb butter on hot griddle.

4. Add 5 pounds of mushrooms and sauté, adding more butter if griddle gets too dry.

5. Mushrooms should be golden brown all over.

Calories: **26** Protein: **1.4 g (21%)** Carbohydrates: **3.1 g (48%)** Sodium: **57 mg**

Total Fat: **1.3 g (45%)** *Saturated Fat: .4 g* *Monounsaturated Fat: .6 g* *Polyunsaturated Fat: .2 g*

❖ Parsnip Fritters

Parsnips are a nut-flavored root vegetable. They are excellent if sautéed with a small amount of oil and finished with lemon juice and honey. In this recipe shredded parsnips and carrots are made into a fritter batter.

PRODUCTION NOTE: Parsnips should be small. Large parsnips often have a woody core.

Portions per recipe: 48
Yield: 96 fritters
Portion: 2 fritters
Serving utensil: spatula

Pan: 12" × 20" × 2"
Griddle temperature: 350° F
Time: 8 minutes

Ingredients

Ingredients	Amounts
Vegetable oil	1 oz.
Spanish onions, minced	8 oz.
Parsnips, peeled and shredded	8 lb.
Carrots, shredded	2 lb.
Lemon rind	1/4 oz.
Salt	1/2 oz.
White pepper	1/8 oz.
Eggs, beaten	12 oz.
All-purpose flour	8 oz.
Vegetable oil for griddle	2 oz.

Procedure:

1. Heat oil and sauté onions, parsnips, and carrots until barely tender.
2. Remove to a large bowl and cool slightly.
3. Stir in lemon rind, salt, pepper, eggs, and flour.
4. Drop batter with a 2-ounce ladle on 350° F, well-oiled grill. Flatten lightly.
5. Cook for 4 minutes on each side. Place 3 rows of 16 slightly overlapping fritters in pan. Garnish with parsnip and carrot coins, that have been cut into the shape of a windmill.

Calories: **100**   Protein: **2.2 g (9%)**   Carbohydrates: **17.2 g (69%)**   Sodium: **135 mg**

Total Fat: **2.8 g (25%)**   Saturated Fat: **.7 g**   Monounsaturated Fat: **.7 g**   Polyunsaturated Fat: **1.1 g**

❖ Peas and Lettuce

Peas are briefly braised with lettuce. This is a great way to use the tough but vitamin- and mineral-rich outer leaves of various lettuces, such as romaine, iceberg, and Boston.

Portions per recipe: *100*
Yield: *3 pans*
Portion: *3 ounces*
Serving utensil: *spoon*

Pan: *12″ × 20″ × 2″*
Cooking method: *braise*
Time: *15 minutes*

Ingredients	Amounts
Lettuce leaves	3 lb.
Garlic cloves	2 oz.
Scallions	12 oz.
Olive oil	1 oz.
Dry vermouth	8 oz.
Lemon juice	6 oz.
Salt	½ oz.
White pepper	1/16 oz.
Nutmeg	⅛ oz.
Frozen peas	20 lb.

Procedure:

1. Chop lettuce leaves with garlic and scallions in food processor or chopper.
2. Heat olive oil and add chopped lettuce mixture. Stir-fry for 2 minutes.
3. Add vermouth, lemon juice, salt, pepper, and nutmeg. Simmer for 15 minutes.
4. Stir in frozen peas and simmer for 3 minutes, just until heated.
5. Transfer to serving pan.

Calories: **76**   Protein: **5.0 g (26%)**   Carbohydrates: **13.2 g (69%)**   Sodium: **158 mg**

Total Fat: **.6 g (7%)**   *Saturated Fat:* **.1 g**   *Monounsaturated Fat:* **.2 g**   *Polyunsaturated Fat:* **.2 g**

❖ Pennsylvania Red Cabbage (Rotkohl)

A sweet and sour braised red cabbage, this is the perfect vegetable for duck, roast pork, and Cornish game hens.

PRODUCTION NOTE: Vinegar is not only important to this recipe for its sour taste, it also restores the color of the cabbage.

Portions per recipe: *100*
Yield: *2 pans*
Portion: *3 ounces*
Serving utensil: *slotted spoon*

Pan: *12″ × 20″ × 4″*
Cooking method: *braise*
Time: *40 minutes*

Ingredients

Ingredients	Amounts
Vegetable oil	3 oz.
Spanish onions, diced	2 lb.
Red cabbage, coarsely shredded	20 lb.
Cooking apples, peeled and chopped	5 lb.
Brown sugar	12 oz.
Water	2 lb.
Cider vinegar	2 lb.
Salt	1 oz.
Black pepper	¼ oz.

Procedure:

1. Heat vegetable oil and sauté onions for 5 minutes.
2. Add cabbage, apples, brown sugar, and water. Stir and bring to a simmer.
3. Stir in vinegar, salt, and pepper and cook slowly for 30 minutes.
4. Taste and add more vinegar if not sour enough.

Calories: **57**   Protein: **1.1 g (8%)**   Carbohydrates: **12.1 g (85%)**   Sodium: **119 mg**
Total Fat: **1.1 g (17%)**   *Saturated Fat:* **.3 g**   *Monounsaturated Fat:* **.2 g**   *Polyunsaturated Fat:* **.6 g**

❖ Peppers with Mushrooms and Onions

A colorful stir-fry that can accompany many entrées. Any leftovers can be mixed with shredded cheese. Placed between 2 slices of whole wheat bread the leftovers then become an improved grilled cheese sandwich.

PRODUCTION NOTES: The amounts given are for one batch of stir-fry. Prepare in batches. Stack seeded pepper halves and use slicer attachment to cut them.

Portions per recipe: *32*   Pan: *12″ × 20″ × 2″*
Yield: *1 pan*   Griddle temperature: *375° F*
Portion: *3 ounces*   Time: *5–7 minutes*
Serving utensil: *spoon*

Ingredients

Ingredients	Amounts	
Green bell peppers	4 lb.	
Red bell peppers		8 oz.
Vegetable oil		1 oz.
Spanish onions, thinly sliced	1 lb.	
Mushrooms, washed and sliced	1 lb.	
Oregano, crushed		⅛ oz.

Procedure:

1. Halve and seed peppers and cut into thin, long strips.
2. Heat grill to 375° F. Add oil.
3. Toss vegetables together and stir-fry for 5 to 7 minutes.
4. Sprinkle oregano over vegetables. Toss briefly and transfer to serving pan.

Calories: **29**   Protein: **.9 g (13%)**   Carbohydrates: **4.3 g (59%)**   Sodium: **2 mg**

Total Fat: **1.2 g (37%)**   *Saturated Fat: .3 g*   *Monounsaturated Fat: .32 g*   *Polyunsaturated Fat: .6 g*

❖ Primavera Vegetables

Serve primavera vegetables separately or toss penne, ziti, or rotini pasta with these vegetables for a light lunch or dinner entrée. The amount is adequate for 5 pounds of uncooked pasta.

Portions per recipe: 50
Yield: 1 pan
Portion: 4 ounces
Serving utensil: 4-ounce ladle

Pan: 12″ × 20″ × 4″
Cooking method: simmer
Time: 10 minutes

Ingredients	Amounts
Olive oil	2 oz.
Garlic cloves, crushed	1 oz.
Scallions, 1″ pieces	12 oz.
Celery stalks, thinly sliced	1 lb.
Mushrooms, washed, trimmed, and sliced	1 lb.
Green bell peppers, seeded and cut into strips	1 lb.
Italian plum tomatoes, diced	3 lb.
Broccoli, florets and peeled stems, thinly sliced	4 lb.
Frozen peas	2 lb.
Basil, crushed	¼ oz.
Salt	½ oz.
Light cream	1 lb.
Parmesan cheese, grated	3 oz.

Procedure:

1. Heat olive oil with garlic. Sauté scallions, celery, mushrooms, and bell peppers for 5 minutes.
2. Add tomatoes, broccoli, peas, and basil and simmer for 5 minutes.
3. Stir in cream and parmesan cheese. Serve at once or toss with cooked pasta.

Calories: **70**   Protein: **3.3 g (19%)**   Carbohydrates: **7.1 g (40%)**   Sodium: **181 mg**
Total Fat: **3.7 g (47%)**   *Saturated Fat:* **1.6 g**   *Monounsaturated Fat:* **1.5 g**   *Polyunsaturated Fat:* **.3 g**

❖ Ratatouille

This is my version of a very popular French Mediterranean vegetable stew.

Portions per recipe: 100
Yield: 2 pans
Portion: 4 ounces
Serving utensil: 4-ounce ladle

Pan: 12" × 20" × 4"
Time: 35 minutes

Ingredients	Amounts	
Olive oil		4 oz.
Garlic cloves, crushed		3 oz.
Bay leaves, crumbled		1/16 oz.
Spanish onions, thinly sliced	3 lb.	
Granulated sugar		1 oz.
Oregano, crushed		1/2 oz.
Cayenne pepper		1/16 oz.
Eggplant, unpeeled, cut into 1/2" cubes	8 lb.	
Zucchini, 1/4" thick slices	5 lb.	
Summer squash, small, sliced 1/2" thick	5 lb.	
Canned tomatoes, diced	6 lb.	6 oz.
Green bell peppers, seeded, 1" square pieces	3 lb.	
Tomato paste	1 lb.	
Romano cheese, grated		4 oz.

Procedure:

1. Heat olive oil with garlic and bay leaves.
2. Add onions, sugar, oregano, and cayenne pepper. Cook for 5 minutes.
3. Stir in eggplant and squash slices, add tomatoes, and simmer for 20 minutes.
4. Add bell peppers and tomato paste and simmer for 10 minutes more.
5. Transfer to serving pan and sprinkle each pan with 2 ounces of romano cheese.

Calories: **48**   Protein: **1.9 g (16%)**   Carbohydrates: **7.6 g (63%)**   Sodium: **123 mg**
Total Fat: **1.7 g (32%)**   *Saturated Fat: .2 g*   *Monounsaturated Fat: .9 g*   *Polyunsaturated Fat: .23 g*

❖ Rutabaga—Swedish Turnips

Rutabaga is a much neglected starchy vegetable that contributes fiber and vitamin A to our diet. Raw, sliced, or shredded it is also a good addition to the offerings of the salad bar.

Portions per recipe: *100*	Pan: *12″ × 20″ × 2″*
Yield: *3 pans*	Oven temperature: *350° F*
Portion: *3 ounces*	Time: *30 minutes*
Serving utensil: *spoon*	

Ingredients | Amounts

Ingredients	Amounts
Rutabagas, waxed	25 lb.
Unsalted butter	1 oz.
Vegetable oil	2 oz.
Salt	1 oz.
White pepper	⅛ oz.
Water	1 lb. 8 oz.

Procedure:

1. Pare rutabagas, cut into ½-inch thick slices, then cut into sticks. They should be the shape of fat french fries.
2. Melt butter with oil, salt, and pepper.
3. Put approximately 7 pounds of rutabaga sticks into each pan.
4. Add 1 cup of water and 1 ounce of melted butter mixture to each pan.
5. Cover and bake for 25 minutes.
6. Uncover and bake for 10 minutes more.

Calories: **42**   Protein: **1.1 g (10%)**   Carbohydrates: **7.8 g (74%)**   Sodium: **129 mg**

Total Fat: **1.0 g (21%)**   *Saturated Fat:* **.3 g**   *Monounsaturated Fat:* **.2 g**   *Polyunsaturated Fat:* **.4 g**

❖ Sautéed Cherry Tomatoes with Fresh Basil

A quick and easy recipe that goes well with baked chicken and roast lamb.

PRODUCTION NOTE: Cook in tilting skillet or on griddle in 5- to 10-pound batches.

Portions per recipe: 150
Yield: 4 pans
Portion: 2 ounces
Serving utensil: spoon

Pan: 12″ × 20″ × 2″
Skillet temperature: 350° F
Time: 2–3 minutes

Ingredients	Amounts
Olive oil	2 oz.
Garlic cloves, crushed	4 oz.
Cherry tomatoes	20 lb.
Basil leaves, chopped	2 oz.
Parsley, stems removed, minced	2 oz.

Procedure:

1. Heat olive oil with garlic and sauté tomatoes, tossing them gently for 2 to 3 minutes. Do not overcook or tomatoes will pop.

2. Mix basil and parsley. Place tomatoes in pans and sprinkle each pan with 1 ounce of herbs.

Calories: **15**   Protein: **.5 g (13%)**   Carbohydrates: **2.6 g (69%)**   Sodium: **5 mg**

Total Fat: **.5 g (30%)**   *Saturated Fat:* **.1 g**   *Monounsaturated Fat:* **.3 g**   *Polyunsaturated Fat:* **.1 mg**

❖ Sichuan Fried Eggplant   *Hom*

Eggplant fried in batter and served with a hot and spicy sauce. This was a hit during the "Feast Fit for the Last Emperor of China." It is another of Ken Hom's wonderful recipes.

Portions per recipe: 100
Yield: 4 pans
Portion: 2 slices
Serving utensil: spoon

Pan: 12″ × 20″ × 2″
Fryolator temperature: 350° F
Time: 3–4 minutes

Ingredients

Ingredients	Amounts	
Eggplant, unpeeled, sliced	30 lb.	
All-purpose flour	1 lb.	4 oz.
Ice water	6 lb.	12 oz.
Salt		¾ oz.
Vegetable oil		2 oz.
Scallions, chopped		8 oz.
Ginger root, chopped		2 oz.
Chili bean sauce		4 oz.
Vegetable stock	2 lb.	
Dry sherry		10 oz.
Cider vinegar		8 oz.
Tomato paste		12 oz.
Granulated sugar		2 oz.
Soy sauce		8 oz.
Cornstarch		2 oz.

Procedure:

1. Mix flour with ice water and salt to make a light batter.
2. Strain through a fine sieve and let rest for 20 minutes.
3. Heat oil and add scallions, ginger, and chili bean sauce and sauté for 1 minute.
4. Add stock, sherry, vinegar, tomato paste, sugar, and soy sauce. Simmer.
5. Dissolve the cornstarch in a little water. Stir into simmering liquid until sauce has thickened.
6. Dip eggplant slices in batter and deep fry at 350° F in fryolator. Do not overload the baskets.
7. Fry until golden and drain on paper.
8. Arrange overlapping slices in pans. Pour 1 pint of sauce over each pan. Serve.

Calories: **91**   Protein: **2.2 g (10%)**   Carbohydrates: **13.5 g (59%)**   Sodium: **248 mg**

Total Fat: **3.8 g (37%)**   *Saturated Fat:* **.4 g**   *Monounsaturated Fat:* **.9 g**   *Polyunsaturated Fat:* **1.6 g**

❖ Spicy Red Beans

Southern beans with a distinctively Cajun flavor. Red beans are smaller than kidney beans and are closer in shape to black beans.

Portions per recipe: 100	*Pan:* 12″ × 20″ × 4″
Yield: 2 pans	*Cooking method:* simmer
Portion: 5 ounces	*Time:* 2 hours
Serving utensil: 3-ounce ladle	

Ingredients / Amounts

Ingredients	Amounts	
Dry red beans	6 lb.	
Water	12 lb.	
Peanut oil		4 oz.
Spanish onions, diced	2 lb.	
Garlic cloves, crushed		4 oz.
Bay leaves		$^{1}/_{16}$ oz.
Celery, chopped	3 lb.	
Canned tomatoes, diced	6 lb.	6 oz.
Cajun spice mix (see recipe on page 458)		2 oz.

Procedure:

1. Soak beans in water overnight in refrigerator.
2. Heat peanut oil. Sauté onions, garlic, and bay leaves for 5 minutes.
3. Add celery and sauté for 5 minutes longer.
4. Stir tomatoes and soaked beans with water. Simmer for 1 hour.
5. Add Cajun spice and more water if necessary and simmer for 1 hour more.

Calories: **114**   Protein: **7.0 g (24%)**   Carbohydrates: **19.2 g (67%)**   Sodium: **81 mg**

Total Fat: **1.5 g (12%)**   *Saturated Fat:* **.3 g**   *Monounsaturated Fat:* **.6 g**   *Polyunsaturated Fat:* **.6 g**

❖ Spicy Vegetables for Couscous *Wolfert*

Colorful and full of flavor, this creamy Moroccan vegetable dish is piled high on top of fluffy couscous. The serving is very generous because it also constitutes a vegetarian entrée. For extra zip serve it with harissa sauce (see recipe on page 466). See color plate **16**.

PRODUCTION NOTES: Do not peel butternut squash. Wash well, seed, cut into 1-inch chunks, and steam separately.

Portions per recipe: *100*
Yield: *3 pans*
Portion: *8 ounces*
Serving utensil: *4-ounce ladle*

Pan: *12″ × 20″ × 2″*
Cooking method: *braise*
Time: *45 minutes*

Ingredients	Amounts	
Butternut squash, unpeeled, 1″ pieces	12 lb.	
Olive oil		4 oz.
Carrots, 1″ pieces	6 lb.	
White turnips, unpeeled, trimmed and quartered	9 lb.	
Hot red chili peppers		3 oz.
Saffron		1/16 oz.
Water	8 lb.	
Zucchini, 1″ pieces	6 lb.	
Summer squash, 1″ pieces	6 lb.	
Red bell peppers, 1″ pieces	2 lb.	
Tomato puree	1 lb.	
Heavy cream	2 lb.	
Parsley, minced		3 oz.
Cilantro, chopped		1 oz.
Freshly ground black pepper		1/4 oz.
Salt		1 oz.

Procedure:

1. Heat olive oil. Add carrots and turnips and sauté for 10 minutes.
2. Seed chili peppers and slice thinly. Add with saffron and water to vegetables and simmer 15 minutes.
3. Steam butternut squash for 10 minutes in steamer at 5 pound pressure.
4. Add summer and butternut squash, tomato puree, and cream. Simmer for 10 minutes.
5. Add herbs and spices, fold in gently. Serve piled high on couscous or serve separately.

Calories: **97**   Protein: **2.0 g (8%)**   Carbohydrates: **13.4 g (55%)**   Sodium: **149 mg**

Total Fat: **4.9 g (45%)**   *Saturated Fat:* **2.3 g**   *Monounsaturated Fat:* **1.9 g**   *Polyunsaturated Fat:* **.4 g**

❖ Stir-fried Vegetables

The combination of stir-fried vegetables given here should be a starting point. Use any fresh and colorful assortment of vegetables. Cook the ones that need most time to become tender first. Stir-fry in a tilting skillet or on the griddle in small batches using a scant amount of oil each time.

PRODUCTION NOTE: A tilting skillet or a griddle produces excellent stir-fried vegetables. Take care to cook in 8-pound batches.

Portions per recipe: *100*	Pan: *12" × 20" × 4"–½ size*
Yield: *3 pans*	Tilting skillet temperature: *375° F*
Portion: *4 ounces*	Time: *6 minutes*
Serving utensil: *spoon*	

Ingredients / Amounts

Ingredients	Amounts
Vegetable oil	2 oz.
Sesame oil	½ oz.
Celery, 1" pieces	3 lb.
Broccoli, florets and peeled sliced stems	3 lb.
Zucchini, ½" slices	6 lb.
Summer squash, ½" slices	6 lb.
Mushrooms, thinly sliced	3 lb.
Tomatoes, wedges	3 lb.
Scallion, green tops only, chopped	3 oz.
Parsley, minced	3 oz.
Soy sauce	2 oz.

Procedure:

1. Mix vegetable oil with sesame oil, and use ¾ ounce per batch.
2. Heat skillet with oil and add one third of each vegetable except tomatoes, scallions and parsley.
3. Stir-fry for about 5 minutes.
4. Add tomatoes, scallion greens, parsley, and soy sauce. Fold in.
5. Place in pans and serve at once.

Calories: **26**   Protein: **1.4 g (18%)**   Carbohydrates: **4.0 g (61%)**   Sodium: **48 mg**
Total Fat: **.9 g (31%)**   *Saturated Fat:* **.2 g**   *Monounsaturated Fat:* **.2 g**   *Polyunsaturated Fat:* **.5 g**

❖ Tasty Turnips

Braised or steamed turnips are pleasant. Students often object to their strong flavor, but mashed and mixed with potatoes they are mild and delicious.

Portions per recipe: 100
Yield: 2 pans
Portion: 4 ounces
Serving utensil: #8 scoop

Pan: 12" × 20" × 2"
Cooking method: steam
Time: 12 minutes

Ingredients

Ingredients	Amounts
Turnips, white purple top	12 lb.
Potatoes, peeled	10 lb.
Unsalted butter	2 oz.
Low-fat milk	2 lb.
Granulated sugar	½ oz.
Salt	1 oz.
White pepper	⅛ oz.
Nutmeg	¹⁄₁₆ oz.

Procedure:

1. Steam or cook vegetables until soft. Drain.

2. Mash in mixer with rest of ingredients. Transfer to pan.

3. Garnish with chopped turnip leaves, if available, or parsley.

Calories: **48**   Protein: **1.4 g (12%)**   Carbohydrates: **9.4 g (78%)**   Sodium: **146 mg**
Total Fat: **.7 g (13%)**   *Saturated Fat: .4 g*   *Monounsaturated Fat: .2 g*   *Polyunsaturated Fat: .1 g*

❖ Wilted Spinach with Lemon Zest *Kamman*

The spinach only barely touches the skillet in this very brief sauté and is tossed with lemon juice and a touch of lemon rind. Spinach should look wilted, not cooked.

PRODUCTION NOTES: Prepare in small batches. Set up batch amounts in advance because the cook has to work very quickly. Brush skillet with butter before adding the first batch of spinach. If no tilting skillet is available, steam 3 pounds of spinach for 30 seconds and toss with hot lemon butter.

Portions per recipe: 100
Yield: 5 pans
Portion: 2 ounces
Serving utensil: tongs

Pan: 12″ × 20″ × 2″
Skillet temperature: 350° F
Time: 15 seconds

Ingredients

Ingredients	Amounts
Spinach, washed well	15 lb.
Unsalted butter	3 oz.
Lemon juice	3 oz.
Salt	1 oz.
Freshly ground black pepper	¼ oz.
Freshly grated lemon rind	½ oz.

Procedure:

1. Remove blemishes and very thick stems from spinach.
2. Melt butter and brush tilting skillet. Heat skillet to 350° F.
3. To the remaining butter add lemon juice, salt, pepper and lemon rind.
4. Toss 3 lb. of spinach in hot skillet for 30 seconds.
5. Add 1 ounce of lemon butter. Toss briefly, transfer to pan, and serve at once.
6. Repeat as needed. Do not keep in warmers.

Calories: **17**   Protein: **1.4 g (33%)**   Carbohydrates: **1.8 g (42%)**   Sodium: **148 mg**

Total Fat: **.9 g (48%)**   *Saturated Fat:* **.5 g**   *Monounsaturated Fat:* **.2 g**   *Polyunsaturated Fat:* **.1 g**

❖ Zucchini Italiano

A wonderful combination that is excellent with the cheese soufflé in the vegetarian section or with baked fish and poultry, along with rice and pasta. It should have just a hint of garlic and basil.

Portions per recipe: **80**
Yield: **2 pans**
Portion: **4 ounces**
Serving utensil: **4-ounce ladle**

Pan: **12″ × 20″ × 2″**
Skillet temperature: **350° F**
Time: **10 minutes**

Ingredients / Amounts

Ingredients	Amounts
Olive oil	2 oz.
Spanish onions, diced	2 lb.
Garlic cloves, crushed	½ oz.
Bay leaves	1/16 oz.
Basil leaves, crushed	⅛ oz.
Zucchini, ¼″ thick slices	17 lb.
Italian plum tomatoes, chopped	7 lb.
Salt	1 oz.
Black pepper	⅛ oz.
Parmesan cheese, grated	2 oz.

Procedure:

1. Heat olive oil. Sauté onions and garlic with bay leaves and basil for 5 minutes. Remove bay leaves.
2. Add zucchini and sauté for 5 minutes, stirring constantly.
3. Add tomatoes, salt, and pepper and simmer for 5 minutes.
4. Transfer to serving pan and sprinkle 1 ounce of grated parmesan over the top.

Calories: **34**   Protein: **1.8 g (21%)**   Carbohydrates: **5.1 g (60%)**   Sodium: **156 mg**

Total Fat: **1.1 g (29%)**   *Saturated Fat:* **.3 g**   *Monounsaturated Fat:* **.6 g**   *Polyunsaturated Fat:* **.2 g**

—11—

GRAINS AND OTHER STARCHES

Good Fiber and Protein Sources

❖

Grains are a high-fiber food if they have been minimally processed. Some grains, such as amaranth and quinoa, are very good sources of protein. Because they are so high in protein, grains, combined with beans, are the basis for a meatless diet. Other starches on the menu are potatoes, rice, and pasta. Choose a variety and complement the entrées with different textures and flavors to keep your customers' interest and educate them about the alternatives available to them.

❖ Amaranth and Rice Risotto

Amaranth seeds are toasted, sautéed with rice and leeks, and cooked like risotto. The tiny amaranth seed is packed with protein.

Portions per recipe: *100*
Yield: *2 pans*
Portion: *4 ounces*
Serving utensil: *#8 scoop*

Pan: *12" × 20" × 2"*
Skillet temperature: *350° F*
Time: *25 minutes*

Ingredients	Amounts
Safflower oil	4 oz.
Chili powder	¼ oz.
Amaranth	3 lb.
Converted long grain rice	4 lb.
Leeks, cleaned and thinly sliced	4 lb.
Mushrooms, thinly sliced	2 lb.
Water	12 lb.
Salt	1 oz.
Hungarian paprika	1 oz.
Basil leaves, chopped	2 oz.

Procedure:

1. Heat oil with chili powder and toast amaranth until it starts to make popping noises.
2. Stir in rice, leeks, and mushrooms.
3. Add ½ gallon of water, stir, and simmer for about 8 minutes.
4. Add another ½ gallon of water, salt, basil, and paprika. Simmer until water is absorbed. Test and if not tender add more water 1 quart at a time.

Calories: **134**   Protein: **3.5 g (11%)**   Carbohydrates: **25.1 g (75%)**   Sodium: **224 mg**

Total Fat: **2.2 g (15%)**   *Saturated Fat: .4 g*   *Monounsaturated Fat: .8 g*   *Polyunsaturated Fat: .9 g*

❖ Apple Brown Rice

A brown rice casserole that is layered with savory onions and sweet apples. Serve this recipe with roast pork, baked chicken, lamb, or pork chops.

Portions per recipe: 100
Yield: 3 pans
Portion: 3 ounces
Serving utensil: spoon

Pans: 12″ × 20″ × 2″
Oven temperature: 350° F
Time: 45 minutes

Ingredients

Ingredients	Amounts
Brown rice	6 lb.
Water	10 lb.
Salt	1 oz.
Vegetable oil	2 oz.
Spanish onions, thinly sliced	6 lb.
Granulated sugar	2 oz.
Marjoram, crushed	1/8 oz.
Apples, unpeeled, quartered and sliced	9 lb.
Cinnamon	1/4 oz.
Ground cloves	1/8 oz.
Lemon juice	4 oz.

Procedure:

1. Cook or steam the rice with water and salt for 35 to 45 minutes.
2. Heat vegetable oil and sauté onions with sugar and marjoram until golden.
3. Toss apples with cinnamon, cloves, and lemon juice.
4. Oil pan and spread 8 ounces of cooked onions evenly in bottom of pan.
5. Cover with 2½ pounds of cooked rice, 1 pound of apple slices and 8 ounces of sautéed onions. Repeat one more time.
6. Bake at 350° F for 45 minutes.
7. Garnish with unpeeled red apple slices dipped in lemon juice.

Calories: **137**   Protein: **2.4 g (7%)**   Carbohydrates: **29.6 g (86%)**   Sodium: **112 mg**

Total Fat: **1.5 g (10%)**   *Saturated Fat:* **.3 g**   *Monounsaturated Fat:* **.4 g**   *Polyunsaturated Fat:* **.6 g**

❖ Bread Dumplings—Semmelknödel

Knödel in German and Austrian cuisine are large dumplings made from raw and cooked potatoes, farina, yeast dough or from stale bread. Bread dumplings are delicious with all kinds of roasts and are traditionally served with sauerbraten. For a variation, when time allows, stuff each dumpling with a pitted prune soaked in brandy or calvados for 20 minutes.

PRODUCTION NOTE: Dip the scoop into hot water when forming dumplings, this will give them a smoother surface.

Portions per recipe: 60
Yield: 3 pans/60 dumplings
Portion: 1 (4 ounces) dumpling
Serving utensil: spatula

Pan: 12″ × 20″ × 2″ perforated
Cooking method: steam
Time: 15 minutes

Ingredients

Ingredients	Amounts
Margarine	1 lb.
Onions, chopped	2 lb.
Sage	¼ oz.
Black pepper	¼ oz.
Freshly grated nutmeg	⅛ oz.
Salt	¾ oz.
Stale bread, cubed	6 lb.
Water (warm)	4 lb.
Dry non-fat milk powder	10 oz.
Eggs	1 lb. 12 oz.
Italian parsley, chopped	4 oz.
Bread crumbs	6 oz.
Italian parsley, chopped	3 oz.

Procedure:

1. Heat margarine and sauté onions with spices and salt.
2. Place in large mixing bowl, add rest of ingredients and mix on low speed until well blended.
3. Chill for 2 hours or overnight.
4. Oil perforated pans and with a #8 scoop place 20 dumplings into each pan.
5. Steam 15 minutes at low pressure. Sprinkle with chopped parsley. Serve.

Calories: **215**   Protein: **6.5 g (12%)**   Carbohydrates: **31.4 g (58%)**   Sodium: **203 mg**
Total Fat: **6.6 g (28%)**   *Saturated Fat:* **1.2 g**   *Monounsaturated Fat:* **3.1 g**   *Polyunsaturated Fat:* **2.1 g**

❖ Corn and Ginger Fried Rice   *Hom*

This dish is both attractive and very tasty. It also provides vegetarians with an excellent protein complement.

PRODUCTION NOTES: The rice must be cold before it is stir-fried. Stir-fry in 3 batches, each made up of 5 pounds of cold cooked rice and 4 pounds of corn. The rice is best stir-fried in a tilting skillet or commercial size wok, but a griddle will do fine. Stir-fry in batches of 5 pounds of rice.

Portions per recipe: *100*
Yield: *3 pans*
Portion: *4 ounces*
Serving utensil: *spoon*

Pans: *12" × 20" × 2"*
Skillet/wok temperature: *375° F*
Time: *7 minutes*

Ingredients   Amounts

Ingredients	Amounts	
Converted long grain rice	5 lb.	
Water	12 lb.	
Vegetable oil		½ oz.
Salt		1 oz.
Peanut oil		3 oz.
Ginger root, peeled and chopped		3 oz.
Scallions, chopped		9 oz.
Soy sauce		3 oz.
Dry sherry		12 oz.
Frozen whole kernel corn, thawed	12 lb.	
Black pepper		¾ oz.
Sesame oil		3 oz.
Scallions, green tops only, sliced		3 oz.

Procedure:

1. Steam rice with salt and oil. Chill.
2. Per batch, heat 1 ounce peanut oil. Add 1 ounce ginger and 3 ounces scallions and cook for 1 minute.
3. Add 1 ounce soy sauce and 4 ounces of sherry and stir. Add 5 pounds of cold rice. Stir-fry for 5 minutes.
4. Add 4 pounds of corn, and about ⅛ ounce pepper. Cook for 3 minutes.
5. Add sesame oil and stir-fry another 2 minutes.
6. Pan and sprinkle with scallion greens.

Calories: **147**   Protein: **3.2 g (9%)**   Carbohydrates: **29.6 g (81%)**   Sodium: **271 mg**
Total Fat: **2.4 g (15%)**   *Saturated Fat:* **.4 g**   *Monounsaturated Fat:* **.9 g**   *Polyunsaturated Fat:* **.9 g**

❖ Couscous

Excellent any time, this is absolutely delicious with spiced vegetables as a vegetarian entrée or with both lamb tagine recipes adapted from Paula Wolfert's book *Couscous and Other Good Food from Morocco*.

PRODUCTION NOTES: Instant couscous is simple to use and, when made from 100% semolina, is quite good. Regular couscous needs to be rinsed, dried, fluffed, and steamed for 20 minutes. Paula Wolfert then sprinkles it with milk, lets it rest, and then fluffs and steams it one more time. For small numbers take the time to make regular couscous by Ms. Wolfert's method. The texture and taste are worth the effort but too time consuming and difficult for large crowds.

Portions per recipe: 100	*Pan: 12″ × 20″ × 4″*
Yield: 2 pans	*Temperature: 212° F*
Portion: 3.5 ounces	*Time: 5 minutes*
Serving utensil: #8 scoop	

Ingredients

Ingredients	Amounts
Vegetable stock (see recipe on page 96)	16 lb.
Saffron	1/16 oz.
Instant couscous	6 lb.
Parsley, minced	4 oz.
Cilantro leaves, minced	2 oz.

Procedure:

1. Heat vegetarian stock, add saffron, and simmer for 5 minutes.
2. Pour 3 pounds of couscous into pan and add 8 pounds of the boiling stock.
3. Stir, cover, and keep warm.
4. Just before serving, fluff couscous with fork and sprinkle with the mixture of fresh herbs.

Calories: **107**   Protein: **2.4 g (9%)**   Carbohydrates: **22.1 g (82%)**   Sodium: **3 mg**

Total Fat: **.2 g (2%)**   *Saturated Fat:* **.03 g**   *Monounsaturated Fat:* **.03 g**   *Polyunsaturated Fat:* **.07 g**

❖ Fried Rice with Whole Wheat Spaghetti

Almost a meal in itself, this recipe is especially good when served with home-style spicy bean curd or BBQ ribs with spicy sauce. The dish is also useful as a quick encore offering when leftover cold rice is in the refrigerator.

PRODUCTION NOTES: Cold rice and spicy whole wheat spaghetti are stir-fried with vegetables. To make omelets for this dish spread the beaten egg thinly as for crepes on hot griddle, cook on one side only, roll up and cut into thin pieces, unrolled the egg will be in long noodle-like strands.

Portions per recipe: 144	*Pan: 12″ × 20″ × 4″*
Yield: 3 pans	*Skillet or griddle temperature: 325° F*
Portion: 4 ounces	*Time: 10 minutes*
Serving utensil: 4-ounce ladle	

Ingredients   Amounts

Rice

Ingredients	Amounts
Converted long grain rice	6 lb.
Oil	½ oz.
Salt	1 oz.
Water	15 lb.

Noodles

Ingredients	Amounts
Whole wheat spaghetti, broken into 2″ pieces	3 lb.
Water	8 lb.
Salt	½ oz.
Sesame oil	1 oz.
Chili garlic sauce	1 oz.

Omelets

Ingredients	Amounts
Eggs, beaten	3 lb.
Water	4 oz.
Peanut oil	3 oz.
Spanish onions, thinly sliced	3 lb.
Green bell peppers, thinly sliced	3 lb.
Celery, thinly sliced	2 lb.
Fresh bean sprouts	1 lb.
Iceberg lettuce, shredded	12 oz.
Soy sauce	6 oz.
Scallions, chopped	8 oz.

(continued)

Procedure:

1. Steam rice with oil, salt, and water. Chill.
2. Cook noodles until barely tender. Toss with sesame oil and chili garlic sauce.
3. Beat eggs with water. Make thin rolled omelets, slice into thin strips.
4. Heat peanut oil. Stir-fry onions, peppers, and celery.
5. Add cooked cold rice, sprouts, lettuce, and soy sauce.
6. Stir-fry for 3 minutes. Fold in egg strips and noodles, and fry for 3 more minutes.
7. Place in pans and garnish with chopped scallions.

Calories: **132**   Protein: **3.9 g (12%)**   Carbohydrates: **23.8 g (72%)**   Sodium: **187 mg**

Total Fat: **2.2 g (15%)**   *Saturated Fat:* **.5 g**   *Monounsaturated Fat:* **.4 g**   *Polyunsaturated Fat:* **.6 g**

❖ Harvest Quinoa

This round white South American seed is technically not a grain, but it has grain-like properties. Extremely high in protein and calcium, it is a valuable diet component for strict vegetarians. Serve this dish with baked bananas and broccoli or with corn stuffed peppers.

PRODUCTION NOTES: The quinoa seed is coated with saponin, which is removed before packaging: however, it is advisable to rinse the seeds in cold water to remove any possible traces of the saponin, to avoid a soapy aftertaste. Quinoa turns rancid very quickly because of its high oil content, and is best stored in the freezer.

Portions per recipe: 100
Yield: 3 pans
Portion: 5 ounces
Serving utensil: spoon

Pans: 12" × 20" × 2"
Cooking method: simmer
Time: 30 minutes

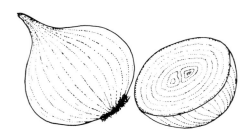

Ingredients	Amounts	
Quinoa	4 lb.	
Water	8 lb.	
Tomato juice	2 lb.	
Vegetable oil		1 oz.
Spanish onions, chopped	1 lb.	
Sunflower seeds		4 oz.
Cumin		½ oz.
Jalapeño peppers, chopped		4 oz.
Red bell peppers, chopped	1 lb.	
Winter squash, peeled, seeded, and cubed	10 lb.	
Canned kidney beans	6 lb. 10 oz.	
Water	2 lb.	
Cilantro, chopped		1 oz.
Parsley, minced		4 oz.

Procedure:

1. Rinse quinoa in cold water, and drain well.
2. Bring water and tomato juice to a boil. Add quinoa and simmer for 20 minutes.
3. Heat oil and sauté onions until golden. Add sunflower seeds and cumin and cook for 3 minutes.
4. Stir in peppers, squash, beans, and water. Simmer for 20 minutes.
5. Fold in hot quinoa and chopped herbs and serve.

Calories: **133**   Protein: **5.9 g (18%)**   Carbohydrates: **24.8 g (75%)**   Sodium: **170 mg**

Total Fat: **2.0 g (13%)**   *Saturated Fat: .2 g*   *Monounsaturated Fat: .4 g*   *Polyunsaturated Fat: .9 g*

❖ **Mushroom Risotto**

The rich, earthy taste of dried porcini mushrooms and saffron make this risotto very special.

PRODUCTION NOTES: Use the tilting skillet or prepare in 4-inch pans in the oven. Use hot vegetarian broth for a meatless meal. Dried porcini mushrooms are usually sold sliced.

Portions per recipe: 100	*Pan:* 12″ × 20″ × 4″
Yield: 2 pans	*Skillet temperature:* 300° F
Portion: 4 ounces	*Time:* 20–25 minutes
Serving utensil: #8 scoop	

Ingredients	Amounts	
Dried porcini mushrooms, sliced		8 oz.
Water (warm)	1 lb.	8 oz.
Olive oil		2 oz.
Butter		8 oz.
Leeks, white part, washed and sliced	4 lb.	
Garlic cloves, crushed		2 oz.
Italian arborio or American short grain rice	5 lb.	8 oz.
Chicken stock	20 lb.	
Saffron (optional)		1/16 oz.
Salt		2 oz.
Black pepper		1/4 oz.
Parmesan, grated		7 oz.
Olive oil		1 oz.
Mushrooms, sliced	4 lb.	
Italian parsley, minced		4 oz.

Procedure:

1. Soak mushrooms in warm water until soft (about 20 minutes).
2. Heat oil with butter and sauté mushrooms and leeks until golden.
3. Add garlic and rice and fry until rice crackles.
4. Heat stock with saffron, salt, and pepper.
5. Pour 2½ quarts of stock and water from mushrooms into rice mixture. Be careful to strain out any sediment which could be sand.
6. Stir, letting rice absorb the liquid. Stir in another 2½ quarts every 5 minutes.
7. Taste rice for tenderness after all liquid has been absorbed. It should be tender; if not, add a little hot water and cook until done.
8. Fold in grated parmesan. Ladle into pans.
9. In olive oil, sauté the fresh mushrooms, toss with parsley, and top each pan with 2 pounds of sautéed mushrooms.

Calories: **134**   Protein: **3.1 g (9%)**   Carbohydrates: **22.2 g (66%)**   Sodium: **260 mg**

Total Fat: **3.6 g (24%)**   *Saturated Fat:* **1.7 g**   *Monounsaturated Fat:* **1.3 g**   *Polyunsaturated Fat:* **.2 g**

❖ Riz à L'Americaine *Kamman*

A glorious rice dish, this was the starch for the elegant "French Feast for 5,000." Long grain rice is flavored with garlic, shallots, brandy, and lots of fresh tarragon, chervil, and chives.

PRODUCTION NOTES: Sauté the rice with garlic, shallots, and onions. Prepare to this point, place in pans (approximately 4 pounds of rice in each pan) and hold until it needs to be steamed.

Portions per recipe: 100　　　　　　*Pan: 12" × 20" × 4"*
Yield: 2 pans　　　　　　　　　　　*Cooking method: steam*
Portion: 4 ounces　　　　　　　　　*Time: 20 minutes*
Serving utensil: spoon

Ingredients	Amounts
Olive oil	2 oz.
Garlic cloves, crushed	4 oz.
Shallots, chopped	8 oz.
Spanish onions, diced	2 lb.
Long grain converted rice	6 lb.
Chicken stock, well-seasoned	12 lb.
Canned tomato puree	4 lb.
Brandy	8 oz.
Parsley, minced	4 oz.
Fresh chives, chopped	4 oz.
Fresh tarragon, chopped	4 oz.

Procedure:

1. Heat olive oil and sauté garlic, shallots, and onions for 10 minutes.
2. Fold in rice and stir until well coated with oil.
3. Mix seasoned chicken stock with tomato puree and brandy.
4. Place 4 pounds of rice mixture in pan. Pour 1 gallon of stock over rice.
5. Steam at low pressure until fully cooked, about 20 minutes.
6. Gently fold in 6 ounces of fresh herbs. Serve at once.

Calories: **119**　Protein: **2.3 g (8%)**　Carbohydrates: **24.6 g (83%)**　Sodium: **4 mg**

Total Fat: **1.1 g (8%)**　*Saturated Fat:* **.2 g**　*Monounsaturated Fat:* **.7 g**　*Polyunsaturated Fat:* **.1 g**

❖ Roasted Wheat and Vegetables

Ordinary bulgur combined with sautéed radicchio and Belgian endives becomes something out of the ordinary.

PRODUCTION NOTES: Bulgur is available in fine, medium, and coarse grind. Use coarse grind for this recipe. Do not substitute cracked wheat for bulgur. Both are wheat, but bulgur has been steamed, dried, and ground and will become edible with just a soaking of hot water. Cracked wheat is raw ground wheat and requires long cooking.

Portions per recipe: 100	*Pan: 12″ × 20″ × 2″*
Yield: 3 pans	*Oven temperature: 325° F*
Portion: 5 ounces	*Time: 20 minutes*
Serving utensil: spoon	

Ingredients	Amounts	
Coarse bulgur	5 lb.	
Water (hot)	6 lb.	
Low-fat milk	2 lb.	
Low-fat yogurt	4 lb.	
Parmesan cheese, grated		8 oz.
Tarragon, crushed		⅛ oz.
Olive oil		2 oz.
Garlic cloves, crushed		4 oz.
Celery, chopped	4 lb.	
Radicchio, chopped	3 lb.	
Belgian endives, thinly sliced	3 lb.	
Salt		1 oz.
Black pepper		⅛ oz.
Dry vermouth	1 lb.	

Procedure:

1. Put bulgur in mixing bowl. Pour in hot water and soak for 10 minutes.
2. Stir in milk, yogurt, parmesan cheese, and tarragon.
3. Heat olive oil with garlic. Add celery, radicchio, and Belgian endives and sauté for 5 minutes.
4. Pour in vermouth, add salt and pepper, and simmer for 10 minutes.
5. Fold vegetables into bulgur.
6. Transfer about 9 pounds into each pan. Bake at 325° F for 20 minutes.

Calories: **128**   Protein: **5.2 g (16%)**   Carbohydrates: **22.3 g (69%)**   Sodium: **190 mg**

Total Fat: **2.6 g (18%)**   *Saturated Fat:* **.9 g**   *Monounsaturated Fat:* **1.2 g**   *Polyunsaturated Fat:* **.3 g**

—12—

CONDIMENTS AND SAUCES

Complements

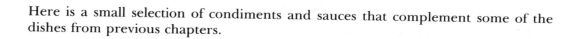

Here is a small selection of condiments and sauces that complement some of the dishes from previous chapters.

❖ Cajun Spice Mixture

Not as salty as the commercial offerings but with just as much flavor. This may not be authentic Cajun but it's a version I have worked with during the past year and I like it a lot.

Ingredients	Amounts
Bay leaves	¼ oz.
Thyme leaves	3 oz.
Oregano leaves	2 oz.
Black peppercorns	3 oz.
Hungarian paprika	7 oz.
Cayenne pepper	7 oz.
Garlic powder	4 oz.
Dry mustard	2 oz.
Salt	2 oz.

Procedure:

1. In a spice or coffee grinder pulverize the first four ingredients.
2. Blend in the rest of the dry ingredients, stirring gently.
3. Store in an airtight jar until needed.

> *Calories: **38**   Protein: **2.8 g (15%)**   Carbohydrates: **13.2 g (69%)**   Sodium: **692 mg**
> Total Fat: **2.0 g (23%)**   *Saturated Fat: **.4 g**   Monounsaturated Fat: **.6 g**   Polyunsaturated Fat: **.8 g***

❖ Chinese Marinade

A simple marinade that gives a Chinese flavor to grilled or broiled fish, chicken, beef, or pork. Use this marinade to flavor tofu cubes or slices.

PRODUCTION NOTE: Marinate tofu, chicken, beef, and pork for 2 hours or more. Brush marinade on fish fillets or steaks.

Yield: 1 gallon

---

*Nutrient analysis for 1 ounce.

Ingredients	Amounts
Soy sauce	4 lb.
Tomato juice	2 lb.
Brown sugar	12 oz.
Lemon juice	8 oz.
Ginger root, grated	4 oz.
Garlic cloves, crushed	4 oz.
Chili bean sauce	2 oz.
Sesame oil	2 oz.

Procedure:

1. Beat ingredients together until sugar has been dissolved.
2. Store in clean gallon jar in the refrigerator.

Nutrient Analysis for 1 pint (1 pound).

Calories: **427**   Protein: **22 g (20%)**   Carbohydrates: **63 g (59%)**   Sodium: **6993 mg**

Total Fat: **8 g (18%)**   *Saturated Fat:* **1.3 g**   *Monounsaturated Fat:* **2.9 g**   *Polyunsaturated Fat:* **3.1 g**

❖ Cold Shrimp Sauce

Serve this sauce with poached salmon, baked sole, or broiled fish steaks.

PRODUCTION NOTE: The sauce will be watery unless the yogurt and cucumbers are drained.

Portions per recipe: 200	Pan: 12″ × 20″ × 4″–½ size
Yield: 1½ gallons	Serve chilled
Portion: 1 ounce	Time: 2 hours
Serving utensil: 1-ounce ladle	

Ingredients	Amounts
Yogurt	4 lb.
Cucumbers, peeled and seeded	4 lb.
Fresh dill	4 oz.
Parsley, stems removed	3 oz.
Scallions, trimmed	8 oz.
Mayonnaise	1 lb. 8 oz.
White pepper	⅛ oz.
Worcestershire sauce	1 oz.
Lemon juice	2 oz.
Salad shrimp, cooked	5 lb.

(continued)

Procedure:

1. Drain yogurt for 30 minutes in a cheese-cloth-lined sieve.
2. Finely shred cucumbers and drain for 30 minutes in a colander.
3. Mince herbs and scallions in a food processor.
4. Blend drained yogurt with mayonnaise, pepper, worcestershire sauce, lemon juice, minced herbs, and shredded cucumber.
5. Fold in cooked salad shrimp. Chill for at least 2 hours before serving.

Calories: **44**   Protein: **2.9 g (26%)**   Carbohydrates: **1.2 g (11%)**   Sodium: **45 mg**

Total Fat: **3.1 g (63%)**   *Saturated Fat:* **.4 g**   *Monounsaturated Fat:* **.5 g**   *Polyunsaturated Fat:* **2.0 g**

❖ Egg White Mayonnaise

No egg yolks are used in this light and fluffy mayonnaise, which is excellent for those who must follow a low-cholesterol diet.

PRODUCTION NOTES: Beat the egg whites until they are very soft—barely stiff—before adding the lemon juice, vinegar, and spices. Then slowly beat in the oil for a very airy, light mayonnaise. Stir the mayonnaise after it has been chilled for 2 hours. It will lose about ¼ of its volume. A 1-cup measure weighs about 5 ounces. This mayonnaise can be stored for about a week. It might separate and collect liquid egg white on the bottom, so just stir before using.

Portions per recipe: 280   *Serve chilled*
Portion: ⅓ ounce
Serving utensil: 1 tablespoon

Ingredients	Amounts
Egg whites	*1 lb. 8 oz.*
Salt	*½ oz.*
White pepper	*⅛ oz.*
Lemon juice	*2 oz.*
Cider vinegar	*2 oz.*
Dijon mustard	*1 oz.*
Safflower oil	*3 lb.12 oz.*

Procedure:

1. In a large mixing bowl whip egg whites to a very soft stage.
2. Beat in salt, pepper, lemon juice, vinegar, and mustard.
3. Switch to high speed and add safflower in a slow stream.

4. Beat until creamy and refrigerate.

5. Stir briefly before adding to foods or cold sauces.

Calories: **56**   Protein: **.3 g (1%)**   Carbohydrates: **.1 g (½%)**   Sodium: **69 mg**

Total Fat: **6.1 g (98%)**   *Saturated Fat:* **.6 g**   *Monounsaturated Fat:* **.7 g**   *Polyunsaturated Fat:* **4.5 g**

❖ Fresh Salsa Sauce

Serve fresh salsa with your Mexican dishes and beat the competition.

PRODUCTION NOTES: Ripe beefsteak tomatoes are best, fresh Italian plum tomatoes also work well. Seed the tomatoes by cutting them in half and gently squeezing seeds out.

Portions per recipe: 200　　*Pan: 12″ × 20″ × 4″–½ size*
Yield: 1½ gallons　　*Serve chilled*
Portion: 1 ounce　　*Time: 1 hour*
Serving utensil: 1-ounce ladle

Ingredients	Amounts
Tomatoes, seeded	*6 lb.*
Yellow peppers, seeded	*3 lb.*
Jalapeño peppers with seeds	*6 oz.*
Scallions, trimmed and chopped	*3 lb.*
Cilantro leaves, minced	*3 oz.*
Parsley leaves, minced	*3 oz.*
Salt	*1 oz.*
Olive oil	*2 oz.*

Procedure:

1. Dice tomatoes, peppers, and jalapeños to a uniformly small size.

2. Mince scallions, cilantro, and parsley in food chopper or processor.

3. Toss all ingredients together with salt and olive oil.

4. Refrigerate and let flavors develop for 1 hour.

Calories: **21**   Protein: **.8 g (15%)**   Carbohydrates: **2.8 g (53%)**   Sodium: **30 mg**

Total Fat: **.7 g (30%)**   *Saturated Fat:* **trace**   *Monounsaturated Fat:* **.4 g**   *Polyunsaturated Fat:* **.1 g**

❖ Herb Yogurt Topping

Serve this sauce in place of sour cream. It is especially good with vegetarian vegetable stews.

PRODUCTION NOTES: Sorrel is a sour grass herb and will give a very different taste from the more peppery watercress. Sorrel is harder to procure than watercress.

Portions per recipe: 128	*Pan: 12" × 20" × 4"–¼ size*
Yield: 1 gallon	*Serve chilled*
Portion: 1 ounce	*Time: 30 minutes*
Serving utensil: 1-ounce ladle	

Ingredients	Amounts
Whole milk yogurt	10 lb.
Garlic cloves	4 oz.
Italian parsley	8 oz.
Sorrel or watercress	4 oz.
Scallions, greens	8 oz.
Salt	½ oz.
White pepper	⅛ oz.
Granulated sugar	½ oz.
Light cream (optional)	4 oz.

Procedure:

1. Drain yogurt in a cloth-lined colander for 30 minutes.
2. In food chopper or processor mince garlic and herbs.
3. Blend together with rest of ingredients and chill.

Calories: **26*** Protein: **1.4 g (22%)** Carbohydrates: **1.5 g (23%)** Sodium: **61 mg**

Total Fat: **1.3 g (45%)** *Saturated Fat:* **.8 g** *Monounsaturated Fat:* .4 g *Polyunsaturated Fat:* **trace**

---

*Nutritional calculations are based using light cream in the recipe.

❖ Hot Chinese Mustard

This mustard is served with Chinese dumplings (dim sum) or fried foods such as shrimp. Serve with the pot stickers in the appetizer section.

Portions per recipe: *768*
Yield: *1 gallon*
Portion: *⅙ ounce*
Serving utensil: *teaspoon*

Pan: *12" × 20" × 2"–¼ size*
Serve chilled
Time: *1 hour*

Ingredients

Ingredients	Amounts
Dry mustard	2 lb.
Salt	½ oz.
Sugar	12 oz.
White pepper	½ oz.
Water	5 lb.
White vinegar	3 lb.

Procedure:

1. Whip all ingredients in mixer until smooth.
2. Chill for 1 hour to let flavors develop.

Calories: **8**   Protein: **.3 g (15%)**   Carbohydrates: **1.0 g (50%)**   Sodium: **7 mg**

Total Fat: **.3 g (34%)**   *Saturated Fat:* **trace**   *Monounsaturated Fat:* **.2 g**   *Polyunsaturated Fat:* **.1 g**

❖ Japanese Daikon or Cucumber Condiment

Serve this with tempura, vegetarian sushi, and with Japanese meat and shrimp dumplings. It should always be available at a Japanese special event.

PRODUCTION NOTES: Daikons are sweet, mild oriental radishes. If crisp and fresh it need not be peeled. Reject flabby daikons—they have lost their moisture and flavor.

Portions per recipe: 64
Yield: 4 pounds
Portion: 1 ounce
Serving utensil: spoon

Serve chilled

Ingredients

Ingredients	Amounts
Daikon or cucumber	4 lb.
Scallions	12 oz.
Nori seaweed, toasted, cut into thin strips	1 oz.
Wasabi (green horseradish) powder	¼ oz.
Soy sauce	1 oz.

Procedure:

1. Shred daikon or grate finely. If using cucumber, peel, seed, shred. Let drain in colander 10 minutes.
2. Mix scallions with nori, wasabi powder, and soy sauce.
3. Fold in daikon and chill.

Calories: **5**   Protein: **.2 g (16%)**   Carbohydrates: **1.1 g (88%)**   Sodium: **18 mg**

Total Fat: **trace**   *Saturated Fat:* **trace**   *Monounsaturated Fat:* **trace**   *Polyunsaturated Fat:* **trace**

❖ Japanese Dipping Sauce

Excellent for sushi, fried fish, or tempura.

Portions per recipe: 64
Yield: 1 quart
Portion: ¹/₂ ounce
Serving utensil: 1 tablespoon

Ingredients	Amounts
Dark soy sauce	1 lb. 12 oz.
Sake	4 oz.
Mirin	4 oz.
Bonito flakes	¹/₄ oz.
Scallions	4 oz.

Procedure:

1. Combine soy sauce, sake, and mirin.
2. Simmer until slightly reduced and alcohol has boiled off.
3. Remove from heat, add bonito flakes, and let stand 2 hours.
4. Strain and serve with very, very thinly sliced scallions.

Calories: **12**   Protein: **1.0 g (33%)**   Carbohydrates: **2.0 g (67%)**   Sodium: **473 mg**

Total Fat: **trace**   *Saturated Fat:* **trace**   *Monounsaturated Fat:* **trace**   *Polyunsaturated Fat:* **trace**

❖ **Moroccan Harissa**   *Wolfert*

This red pepper sauce can flavor couscous or be served as a relish with Moroccan salads.

PRODUCTION NOTES: Harissa paste from Tunisia is available but is sometimes hard to find. Make your own paste and freeze the extra. The recipe below is to be used as a relish. For couscous thin paste with broth from the tagine or the spicy vegetables, eliminate the olive oil, and boil rapidly for 5 minutes. To make 1 pound of harissa paste, soak 12 ounces of dried red chili peppers in hot water for one hour. Drain. In a food chopper or processor work soaked chilies and 4 ounces of garlic cloves and ½ ounce salt into a paste.

Portions per recipe: 64
Yield: 1 quart
Portion: ½ ounce
Serving utensil: 1 tablespoon

Ingredients	Amounts
Lemon juice	1 lb.
Harissa paste (see production notes)	2 oz.
Cumin seed, ground	¼ oz.
Parsley, minced	2 oz.
Olive oil	12 oz.

Procedure:

1. Blend all ingredients together and serve.

Calories: **50** Protein: **.1 g (1%)** Carbohydrates: **.7 g (1%)** Sodium: **1 mg**	
Total Fat: **5.4 g (98%)** *Saturated Fat:* **.7 g** *Monounsaturated Fat:* **4.4 g** *Polyunsaturated Fat:* **.5 g**	

❖ **Moroccan Preserved Lemons** *Wolfert*

Preserved lemons are used in some of the salads in this book and, as Paula Wolfert says in *Couscous and Other Food from Morocco*, they are one of the indispensable ingredients of Moroccan cooking. When the lemon is ready to use, remove lemons, rinse well, scrape off fleshy inside and cut the peel into very thin strips. See color plate **16**.

Yield: 1 gallon

Serve at room temperature
Time: 30 days

Ingredients	*Amounts*
Lemons	6 lb.
Salt	12 oz.
Lemon juice	1 lb.

Procedure:

1. Quarter lemons from the top to within ½ inch of bottom.
2. Sprinkle salt on exposed flesh and reshape fruit.
3. Place 2 ounces of salt in clean gallon jar.
4. Pack in lemon tightly, adding salt between layers.
5. Add enough lemon juice to cover lemons completely. Close lid tightly.
6. Keep at room temperature for 30 days. Shake jar daily.

Nutrition note: Lemon peel contains mostly indigestible fiber and minute amounts of oil.

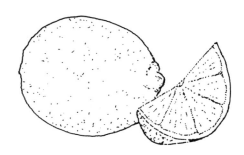

❖ Mushroom Sauce Varesa

I first had this wonderful mushroom sauce in Varesa, Italy, where it was served with potato gnocchi. The fresh sage gives the sauce a subtle, earthy taste. It is excellent with gnocchi, tortellini, and just about any pasta. A small amount of sauce will flavor a lot of pasta.

PRODUCTION NOTES: The mushrooms are cooked until all liquid has evaporated and oil is showing around the edges of the pan. Add the sage at this point and sauté very briefly, being careful not to burn it. Dried porcini mushrooms add extra flavor but can be omitted.

Portions per recipe: *128*
Yield: *1 gallon*
Portion: *1 ounce*
Serving utensil: *1-ounce ladle*

Pan: *12" × 20" × 4"–½ size*
Skillet temperature: *350° F*
Time: *20 minutes*

Ingredients	Amounts	
Dried porcini mushrooms		1 oz.
Warm water		8 oz.
Medium-size mushrooms	6 lb.	
Garlic cloves, crushed		2 oz.
Olive oil		4 oz.
Fresh sage leaves, cut into thin strips		2 oz.
Black pepper		⅛ oz.
Salt		½ oz.
All-purpose flour		2 oz.
White vermouth	1 lb.	
Light cream	3 lb.	
Parmesan cheese, grated		2 oz.

Procedure:

1. Soak dried porcini mushrooms in warm water for 1 hour. Drain and reserve liquid.
2. Chop fresh mushrooms with garlic, until fine but not mushy in a food chopper or processor.
3. Heat olive oil in tilting skillet and sauté mushrooms until brown and dry.
4. Mince porcini mushrooms. Add sage leaves and sauté for 2 minutes.
5. Add spices and flour and fold in.
6. Stir in reserved soaking liquid, making sure to discard sediment.
7. Stir in vermouth and cream. Simmer for 5 minutes and stir in parmesan.
8. Toss with pasta or serve separately.

Calories: **41**   Protein: **1.1 g (11%)**   Carbohydrates: **2.4 g (23%)**   Sodium: **13 mg**

Total Fat: **3.2 g (70%)**   *Saturated Fat:* **1.5 g**   *Monounsaturated Fat:* **1.3 g**   *Polyunsaturated Fat:* **.2 g**

❖ Spicy Peanut Butter Dipping Sauce

Serve this dip with yakatori or crisp vegetables.

Portions per recipe: *128*   *Pan:* *12" × 20" × 4"–¼ size*
Yield: *2 quarts*
Portion: *½ ounce*
Serving utensil: *tablespoon*

Ingredients	*Amounts*	
Garlic cloves, crushed		2 oz.
Sesame oil		1 oz.
Ginger		1 oz.
Cumin		½ oz.
Turmeric		½ oz.
Red pepper flakes		¼ oz.
Soy sauce		4 oz.
Lemon juice		4 oz.
Water	3 lb.	
Creamy peanut butter	2 lb.	8 oz.
Brown sugar		4 oz.

Procedure:

1. Cook garlic in oil. Add spices, soy sauce, lemon juice, and water and simmer for 10 minutes.

2. Whisk in peanut butter and brown sugar. Simmer for 5 minutes.

3. Serve warm.

> Calories: **60**   Protein: **2.2 g (14%)**   Carbohydrates: **3.2 g (21%)**   Sodium: **94 mg**
>
> Total Fat: **4.6 g (69%)**   *Saturated Fat:* **.8 g**   *Monounsaturated Fat:* **2.2 g**   *Polyunsaturated Fat:* **1.4 g**

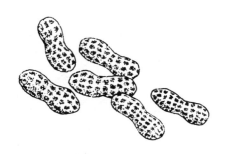

—13—

BAKED GOODS

Biscuits, Coffee Cakes, Granola, Muffins, and Scones

❖

Muffins and quick breads are a wonderful American tradition. Combined with a steaming hot mug of coffee they help start many a day. Nutritionally better than the fried doughnut, they can, however, still be very high in fats. I have included some recipes here that pack in a bit more nutrition, but that still satisfy the sweet tooth. The more savory biscuits and scones, of course, are also excellent dinner breads and go well with jam or cheese for an afternoon tea.

A note about ingredients: The recipes will specify different types of flour. All purpose flour will not give the same results and should not be substituted without further testing. Whole eggs, when they are fresh, will usually give a little more volume but frozen pasteurized eggs are fine and are being used at UNH, where these recipes were tested. For bread recipes the margarine or shortening can be changed to vegetable oil but reduce the amount used by 10 per cent and expect a denser product in some cases.

❖ Apple Ginger Whole Wheat Muffin

This old-fashioned muffin combines a zippy ginger taste with the goodness of unpeeled apples and molasses.

PRODUCTION NOTE: Use unwaxed apples and wash them well.

Portions per recipe: 60
Yield: 5 dozen muffins
Portion: 1 muffin
Serving utensil: tongs

Pan: muffin pan
Oven temperature: 350° F
Time: 18 minutes

Ingredients	Amounts
Margarine	8 oz.
Granulated sugar	8 oz.
Eggs	12 oz.
Ginger	$\frac{1}{2}$ oz.
Cinnamon	$\frac{1}{4}$ oz.
Black strap molasses	2 lb.
Buttermilk	2 lb.
Baking soda	$1\frac{1}{2}$ oz.
Whole wheat flour	3 lb. 8 oz.
Apples, unpeeled, cored and coarsely chopped	2 lb.

Procedure:

1. Cream margarine and sugar. Add eggs and beat for 2 minutes.
2. Add spices, molasses, and buttermilk.
3. Add baking soda, flour, and chopped apples. Mix in lightly.
4. Fill lined muffin tins with batter using a #16 scoop.
5. Bake at 350° F for 18 to 20 minutes.

Calories: **187**   Protein: **4.8 g (10%)**   Carbohydrates: **34.5 g (74%)**   Sodium: **40 mg**
Total Fat: **4.3 g (21%)**   *Saturated Fat:* **.9 g**   *Monounsaturated Fat:* **1.7 g**   *Polyunsaturated Fat:* **1.3 g**

❖ Buttermilk Scones

Very low in fat but still light and flaky. Serve this delightful scone warm.

Portions per recipe: 48
Yield: 4 dozen scones
Portion: 1 scone
Serving utensil: tongs

Pan: 18″ × 26″ sheet pan
Oven temperature: 400° F
Time: 15 minutes

Ingredients	*Amounts*
All-purpose flour	3 lb.
Vegetable shortening	5 oz.
Baking soda	½ oz.
Baking powder	3 oz.
Granulated sugar	1 oz.
Salt	½ oz.
Buttermilk	2 lb.

Procedure:

1. Mix together the first 6 ingredients to a coarse crumb stage.
2. Add buttermilk to make soft dough. Do not knead.
3. Roll out 1-inch thick on floured surface. Cut into 3″ × 2″ squares and then cut again diagonally to make triangles.
4. Wash with buttermilk or melted butter. Place 24 on a sheet pan.
5. Bake at 400° F for 15 minutes.

Calories: **141**   Protein: **3.6 g (10%)**   Carbohydrates: **23.7 g (67%)**   Sodium: **417 mg**

Total Fat: **3.4 g (22%)**   *Saturated Fat:* **.9 g**   *Monounsaturated Fat:* **1.8 g**   *Polyunsaturated Fat:* **.5 g**

❖ Creamy Yogurt Biscuits

James Beard, in his autobiographical cookbook, *Delights and Prejudices*, recalls a cream biscuit recipe made by Let, the Chinese cook Beard's mother employed in her Portland, Oregon hotel. The biscuits are wonderful when made with heavy cream, but still very good (and much lower in fat) when made with 1 part cream and 2 parts yogurt.

Portions per recipe: 180
Yield: 15 dozen biscuits
Portion: 1 biscuit
Serving utensil: tongs

Pan: 18″ × 26″ sheet pan
Oven temperature: 380° F
Time: 12–15 minutes

Ingredients	Amounts	
All-purpose flour	12 lb.	
Granulated sugar		4 oz.
Salt		1 oz.
Baking powder		5 oz.
Baking soda		2 oz.
Low-fat yogurt	8 lb.	
Heavy cream	4 lb.	
Butterblend, melted		8 oz.

Procedure:

1. Place all ingredients in mixing bowl and with paddle blend to a soft dough.
2. Dump on floured bench and roll out dough to a 1-inch thickness.
3. Cut by hand into 2-ounce biscuits.
4. To use automatic dough cutter, weigh out 4 pounds 8 ounces of dough for every 3 dozen biscuits.
5. Place on sheet pan and brush tops with melted butterblend.
6. Bake at 380° F for 12 to 15 minutes.

Note: For variety, the biscuits can be sprinkled with sugar or with parmesan cheese before baking.

> Calories: **170**   Protein: **4.5 g (11%)**   Carbohydrates: **25.6 g (60%)**   Sodium: **206 mg**
> Total Fat: **5.4 g (28%)**   *Saturated Fat:* **2.9 g**   *Monounsaturated Fat:* **1.6 g**   *Polyunsaturated Fat:* **.5 g**

❖ Jalapeño Cheese Biscuits

This biscuit is excellent with eggs diablo for breakfast or with turkey chili for lunch or dinner. Because this biscuit provides extra protein, it is a fine companion to garden-style chili.

PRODUCTION NOTES: Use canned diced green chilies for this. Add more cold water if dough is too dry.

Portions per recipe: *504*	Pan: *18″ × 26″ sheet pan*
Yield: *42 dozen biscuits*	Oven temperature: *380° F*
Portion: *1 biscuit*	Time: *15 minutes*
Serving utensil: *tongs*	

Ingredients	Amounts
Pastry flour	25 lb.
Baking powder	2 lb.
Salt	4 oz.
Cayenne pepper	⅛ oz.
Vegetable shortening	10 lb.
Non-fat dry milk	3 lb.
Water (very cold)	16 lb.
Parmesan cheese, grated	8 oz.
Cheddar cheese, shredded	1 lb. 4 oz.
Cottage cheese	3 lb.
Canned green chilies, diced	2 lb. 8 oz.

Procedure:

1. Place all dry ingredients and shortening in mixer bowl.
2. Mix with paddle until mixture resembles small crumbs.
3. Add water and blend. Do not overmix.
4. Weigh out 4 pounds 8 ounces of dough for every 3 dozen biscuits.
5. Use automatic dough cutter or cut by hand.
6. Bake at 380° F for 15 minutes.

Calories: **183**   Protein: **3.8 g (8%)**   Carbohydrates: **19.8 g (43%)**   Sodium: **417 mg**
Total Fat: **9.8 g (48%)**   *Saturated Fat:* **2.7 g**   *Monounsaturated Fat:* **5.4 g**   *Polyunsaturated Fat:* **1.2 g**

❖ Kernel Cornbread

This corn bread is nice and moist with extra texture provided by whole kernels of corn. Serve it for breakfast with baked beans and ham or with eggs diablo. Warm cornbread is delicious with chicken dinners and is especially good with turkey chili.

Portions per recipe: 600
Yield: 10 pans
Portion: 3" × 2.5" piece
Serving utensil: spatula

Pan: 18" × 26" × 3" cake pan
Oven temperature: 400° F
Time: 20 minutes

Ingredients

Ingredients	Amounts
Whole kernel corn	15 lb.
Granulated sugar	10 lb.
Non-fat dry milk	10 lb.
Salt	1 lb.
Baking powder	6 oz.
Baking soda	2 oz.
Yellow cornmeal	15 lb.
Bread flour	10 lb.
Corn liquid	5 lb.
Vegetable oil	5 lb.
Sour cream	10 lb.
Eggs	10 lb.

Procedure:

1. Drain corn and reserve liquid. Place kernels in mixing bowl.
2. Add sugar, milk powder, salt, baking powder, soda, cornmeal, and flour. Beat for 1 minute.
3. Add corn liquid, oil, sour cream, and eggs. Beat at medium speed for 2 to 3 minutes.
4. Pour 9 pounds of batter into each pan. Bake at 400° F for 20 minutes.
5. Keep warm until ready to serve.

Calories: **195** Protein: **5.9 g (12%)** Carbohydrates: **28.5 g (58%)** Sodium: **396 mg**

Total Fat: **7.9 g (36%)** *Saturated Fat:* **2.3 g** *Monounsaturated Fat:* **1.6 g** *Polyunsaturated Fat:* **2.4 g**

❖ Oatmeal Scones

Oatmeal and oat bran together with a touch of almond extract give these scones their nutty taste. Serve them with orange marmalade and jam for breakfast. They are also especially good at an afternoon tea with lebani and hot pepper jelly.

Portions per recipe: 72
Yield: 6 dozen scones
Portion: 1 scone
Serving utensil: tongs

Pan: 18″ × 26″ sheet pan
Oven temperature: 375° F
Time: 15 minutes

Ingredients

Ingredients	Amounts
Vegetable shortening	1 lb. 8 oz.
Brown sugar	1 lb.
Black strap molasses	8 oz.
Eggs	1 lb. 8 oz.
Almond extract	1 oz.
Quick cooking oats	3 lb.
Oat bran	8 oz.
Low-fat milk	1 lb. 12 oz.
Whole wheat flour	1 lb.
Pastry flour	2 lb.
Baking powder	12 oz.
Salt	½ oz.

Procedure:

1. Cream shortening with sugar, molasses, eggs, and almond extract.
2. Add oats and oat bran. Mix well.
3. Add milk and blend.
4. Add whole wheat flour, baking powder, and salt. Mix to form a very soft dough.
5. Very slowly add the pastry flour—just enough to clean sides of mixing bowl.
6. Sprinkle bench with remainder of the pastry flour and dump dough.
7. Roll dough until it is ¾-inch thick and cut into 2-inch rounds or squares.
8. Brush with milk and sprinkle with a few oats.
9. Place 36 scones on each sheet pan and bake at 375° F for 15 minutes.

Calories: **284**   Protein: **6.8 g (9%)**   Carbohydrates: **38.7 g (54%)**   Sodium: **853 mg**

Total Fat: **12.2 g (39%)**   *Saturated Fat:* **3.1 g**   *Monounsaturated Fat:* **6.4 g**   *Polyunsaturated Fat:* **1.9 g**

❖ Raisin Scones

Spread orange walnut yogurt cheese on these scones for a tasty breakfast in a hurry.

Portions per recipe: 360
Yield: 30 dozen scones
Portion: 1 scone
Serving utensil: tongs

Pan: 18″ × 26″ sheet pan
Oven temperature: 380° F
Time: 15 minutes

Ingredients	Amounts
Pastry flour	20 lb.
Whole wheat flour	5 lb.
Baking powder	1 lb. 8 oz.
Salt	4 oz.
Granulated sugar	6 lb.
Vegetable shortening	1 lb. 8 oz.
Margarine	4 lb. 8 oz.
Water (cold)	5 lb.
Eggs, beaten	6 lb.
Raisins	3 lb. 8 oz.

Procedure:

1. Place all dry ingredients in large mixing bowl. With paddle blend for 1 minute.
2. Add shortening and margarine. Blend to crumb consistency.
3. Add water and eggs and mix until just blended, 2 to 3 minutes. Do not over mix.
4. If you have an automatic roll cutter, weigh out 4 pounds of dough for 3 dozen scones. Otherwise, roll out on floured bench ¾″ thick. Cut into squares and cut squares diagonally to form a triangle.
5. Each triangle should weigh approximately 1¾ ounces.
6. Place on greased sheet pans. Bake at 380° F for 15 minutes.

Calories: **225**   Protein: **3.9 g (7%)**   Carbohydrates: **35.9 g (64%)**   Sodium: **436 mg**
Total Fat: **7.6 g (30%)**   *Saturated Fat:* **1.6 g**   *Monounsaturated Fat:* **3.6 g**   *Polyunsaturated Fat:* **2.0 g**

❖ Sour Cream Coffee Cake

A moist, delicious cake made with sour cream and yogurt. This recipe was sent to me by a parent when I ran a recipe from home contest. The yogurt is my addition.

PRODUCTION NOTE: Vary this basic cake with seasonal fresh fruits and berries. See suggestions below.

Portions per recipe: *180*
Yield: *3 pans*
Portion: *3" × 2.5" piece*
Serving utensil: *spatula*

Pan: *18" × 26" × 3" cake pan*
Oven temperature: *350° F*
Time: *40–45 minutes*

Ingredients	Amounts
Sour cream	3 lb.
Low-fat yogurt	3 lb.
Margarine	3 lb.
Granulated sugar	6 lb.
Eggs	2 lb. 8 oz.
Vanilla extract	3 oz.
Lemon juice	3 oz.
Freshly grated lemon rind	1 oz.
Pastry flour	8 lb. 12 oz.
Baking powder	3 oz.
Baking soda	1 oz.
Brown sugar	1 lb. 8 oz.
Walnuts, finely chopped	1 lb. 8 oz.
Cinnamon	¾ oz.

Procedure:

1. Beat together sour cream, yogurt, margarine, sugar, eggs, vanilla, and lemon juice.
2. Add lemon rind, flour, baking powder, and soda. Mix until smooth.
3. Pour 8½ pounds of batter into greased pan.
4. Mix sugar, walnuts, and cinnamon. Sprinkle on top.
5. With a spatula swirl sugar into batter to form spirals.
6. Bake at 350° F for 40 minutes.
7. Cool slightly. Cut into 6" × 10" pieces.

VARIATIONS:
a. Mix 3 pounds fresh berries with 8 ounces of sugar and 2 ounces of lemon juice. Fold into batter.
b. Shred 3 pounds of apples. Mix with ¼ ounce of ginger, ¼ ounce of cinnamon, 8 ounces of brown sugar, and a dash of nutmeg. Fold in.
c. Mix 3 pounds pitted sliced plums, peaches, nectarines, or cherries with 1 ounce of vanilla, 3 ounces of brandy, and 8 ounces of sugar. Fold in.

Calories: **242** Protein: **3.4 g (6%)** Carbohydrates: **37.2 g (61%)** Sodium: **97 mg**
Total Fat: **9.1 g (34%)** *Saturated Fat:* **2.4 g** *Monounsaturated Fat:* **3.7 g** *Polyunsaturated Fat:* **2.5 g**

❖ Sweet Georgia Muffin

Spicy, moist, and made with sweet potatoes, this muffin is ideal for weekend brunches if your bakery closes down on Friday or Saturday. It also freezes well!

PRODUCTION NOTES: This recipe was developed to use a case (six #10 cans) of sweet potatoes. All muffin batter must be just barely blended and should look lumpy. A tough muffin with tunnels is a sure sign of overbeating.

Portions per recipe: 576   Pan: lined muffin tins
Yield: 48 dozen muffins   Oven temperature: 350° F
Portion: 1 muffin   Time: 25 minutes
Serving utensil: tongs

Ingredients	Amounts
Granulated sugar	24 lb.
Vegetable oil	12 lb.
Eggs	6 lb.
Sweet potatoes* or yams, drained and mashed	39 lb. 12 oz.
Bread flour	12 lb.
Pastry flour	10 lb. 8 oz.
Salt	3 oz.
Baking soda	6 oz.
Baking powder	3 oz.
Ground cloves	2 oz.
Cinnamon	3 oz.
Nutmeg	2 oz.

Procedure:

1. Beat together sugar, oil, and eggs.
2. Beat in sweet potatoes.
3. Combine dry ingredients and add to sweet potato mixture.
4. Mix until just blended. Do not beat.
5. Portion with a #16 scoop into muffin tins.
6. Bake at 350° F for 25 minutes.

Calories: **257**   Protein: **2.8 g (4%)**   Carbohydrates: **39.0 g (61%)**   Sodium: **104 g**
Total Fat: **10.3 g (36%)**   *Saturated Fat:* **2.6 g**   *Monounsaturated Fat:* **1.9 g**   *Polyunsaturated Fat:* **5.1 g**

---

*Sweet potatoes have 22,680 units of vitamin A per pound. Yams only have a trace of vitamin A but are higher in potassium.

❖ Whole Wheat Bran Raisin Muffin

A tasty fiber-rich muffin made with safflower oil.

Portions per recipe: 432
Yield: 36 muffins
Portion: 1 muffin
Serving utensil: tongs

Pan: muffin tins
Oven temperature: 400° F
Time: 20 minutes

Ingredients

Ingredients	Amounts
Granulated sugar	6 lb.
Non-fat dry milk	2 lb.
Baking powder	6 oz.
Baking soda	4 oz.
Salt	4 oz.
Eggs	4 lb.
Safflower oil	4 lb.
Black strap molasses	6 lb.
All-Bran cereal	5 lb.
Water	10 lb.
Whole wheat flour	10 lb.
Pastry flour	10 lb.
Raisins	8 lb.

Procedure:

1. Mix sugar, milk powder, baking powder, soda, and salt for 2 minutes.
2. Add eggs and oil and beat for 3 minutes.
3. Add molasses, All-Bran, and water. Mix for 1 minute.
4. Add flours and raisin and fold in until blended. Do not overmix.
5. Drop into papered muffin tins with a #16 scoop.
6. Bake in 400° F oven for 20 minutes.

Calories: **203**　Protein: **4.5 g (9%)**　Carbohydrates: **37.7 g (74%)**　Sodium: **244 mg**
Total Fat: **5.0 g (22%)**　*Saturated Fat:* **.8 g**　*Monounsaturated Fat:* **.7 g**　*Polyunsaturated Fat:* **3.3 g**

❖ Zucchini Bread

Speckled with flecks of green zucchini and orange peel, this is an attractive, as well as a tasty, sweet bread.

PRODUCTION NOTES: Peel oranges, removing all white pith, and cut thinly. If you use the commercial product orange fruitex, you'll need 4 times as much orange peel as is called for.

Portions per recipe: 203
Yield: 7 loaves (29 count)
Portion: 1 slice
Serving utensil: tongs

Pan: 2 pound loaf pan
Oven temperature: 350° F
Time: 1 hour and 20 minutes

Ingredients	Amounts	
Cake flour	8 lb.	8 oz.
Salt		2 oz.
Baking powder		4 oz.
Baking soda		½ oz.
Granulated sugar	2 lb.	4 oz.
Eggs	1 lb.	8 oz.
Walnuts, finely chopped	1 lb.	
Zucchini, shredded	5 lb.	
Orange peel, cut thin		8 oz.
Vegetable oil	1 lb.	
Water (warm)	4 lb.	

Procedure:

1. Mix at low speed flour, salt, baking powder, soda, and sugar.
2. Mix together eggs, walnuts, zucchini, orange peel, oil, and water.
3. Add slowly to dry ingredients and mix only until moistened.
4. Pour about 3 pounds of dough into each pan.
5. Bake at 350° F for about 1 hour and 20 minutes.

Calories: **118**   Protein: **2.2 g (7%)**   Carbohydrates: **20.4 g (69%)**   Sodium: **202 mg**

Total Fat: **3.0 g (23%)**   *Saturated Fat:* **.7 g**   *Monounsaturated Fat:* **.6 g**   *Polyunsaturated Fat:* **1.5 g**

Yeast Breads and Rolls

❖

The aroma of baking bread brightens wet and gloomy days and fills people with nostalgic longings—even if they've grown up on store bought bread. Gladden the hearts of your customers and bake them some bread. The University of New Hampshire Dining Service is one of few large quantity food operations that bakes most of its breads (with the exception of buns, English muffins, pita bread, and bagels) on the premises. Fresh from the oven, the bread and rolls are displayed on the bread board for dinner, a variety of sandwich breads are offered for lunch, and tempting hot breads are available in the morning to give the UNH students a unique dining experience.

PRODUCTION NOTES: Drizzle a very small amount of oil around the edge of the mixing bowl during the final minute of kneading; it will help gather the dough and leave a clean bowl. The yeast specified is instant dry. Non-fat milk powder can be replaced with fresh low-fat milk. The bread is kneaded by machine and proofed in a moist proof box. The breads are baked either in a rotating or rack oven. Convection oven times may vary somewhat. Load bread in convection ovens on 2 racks, 3 maximum.

Yeast breads. Back row from the left: Buttery brioche rolls, the basket is filled with Russian bread, kisra, toscano, and the split Irish bread. Middle row: Whole wheat sandwich loaf and sliced brioche. Front row from left: Braided sourdough, Italian loaf, and bread sticks.

❖ Anadama Bread

There are a variety of stories about how this bread got its name. I personally like the one about the New England fisherman who apparently had to do his own baking because of a lazy wife, and who, while kneading the dough, kept cursing, "Anna, damn her." But whatever the source of the name, this bread is delicious.

Portions per recipe: 1200
Yield: 40 loaves (1¾ pound each—
    28 slices per loaf)
Portion: 1 slice
Serving utensil: bag

Pan: 2-pound loaf pans
Oven temperature: 400° F
Time: 30 minutes

Ingredients	*Amounts*	
Granulated sugar	1 lb.	6 oz.
Black strap molasses	6 lb.	10 oz.
Yellow cornmeal	5 lb.	
Vegetable oil	5 lb.	
Salt		8 oz.
Water (100° F)	32 lb.	
Dry yeast	1 lb.	8 oz.
Bread flour	50 lb.	

Procedure:

1. Beat together sugar, molasses, cornmeal, oil, salt, and water.
2. Sprinkle the yeast over mixture and fold in. Let rise 30 minutes.
3. Add flour and mix for 10 minutes.
4. Cover with cloth and let rise in the bowl for 1 hour.
5. Use 2 pounds 4 ounces of dough for each loaf. Form and place in bread pans.
6. Place bread in proof box until slightly raised.
7. Brush tops with lightly salted water and sprinkle with cornmeal.
8. Complete proofing until double in size.
9. Bake at 400° F for 30 minutes.

Calories: **107**   Protein: **2.8 g (11%)**   Carbohydrates: **17.1 g (64%)**   Sodium: **83 mg**
Total Fat: **2.4 g (20%)**   *Saturated Fat:* **.6 g**   *Monounsaturated Fat:* **.4 g**   *Polyunsaturated Fat:* **1.2 g**

❖ Brioche Bread   *Dodge*

This rich and feathery bread recipe from Jim Dodge is the basis for his wonderful bread pudding.

Portions per recipe: 336
Yield: 12 loaves (1½ pounds each,
   28 slices per loaf)
Portion: 1 slice
Serving utensil: tongs

Pan: 2-pound loaf pan
Oven temperature: 375° F
Time: 45 minutes

Ingredients	Amounts
Instant dry yeast	4 oz.
Granulated sugar	15 oz.
Water (100° F)	2 oz.
Eggs	7 lb. 2 oz.
Salt	6 oz.
Bread flour	12 lb. 8 oz.
Unsalted butter, cut into 1" pieces	6 lb.

Procedure:

1. Mix yeast with sugar and water.
2. Add eggs, salt, and flour. Mix until smooth.
3. Slowly add ½ the butter. Scrape bowl and paddle.
4. Add rest of butter slowly. Beat at medium speed for 16 to 20 minutes, until dough is elastic.
5. Chill dough overnight.
6. Form dough into 2-pound loaves.
7. Proof until loaves have doubled in size, about 1 hour.
8. Bake at 375° F until golden brown, about 45 minutes.

Calories: **140**   Protein: **3.3 g (9%)**   Carbohydrates: **14.0 g (40%)**   Sodium: **208 mg**
Total Fat: **7.8 g (50%)**   *Saturated Fat:* **4.4 g**   *Monounsaturated Fat:* **2.3 g**   *Polyunsaturated Fat:* **.5 g**

Buttery brioche rolls and the brioche loaf used for Jim Dodge's delectable bread pudding.

❖ Buttery Brioche Rolls

This very rich yeast dough makes absolutely mouth-watering rolls that will boost your coffee counter sales. They are also excellent for buffets—make them half the size—because they need no butter.

PRODUCTION NOTE: Scrape down the paddle and sides of the bowl when necessary.

Portions per recipe: 72
Yield: 6 dozen rolls
Portion: 1 roll
Serving utensil: tongs

Pan: muffin tins
Oven temperature: 350° F
Time: 20 minutes

Ingredients	Amounts
Bread flour	6 lb. 8 oz.
Granulated sugar	9 oz.
Instant dry yeast	2 oz.
Salt	½ oz.
Eggs	3 lb. 8 oz.
Unsalted butter, cut into small pieces	2 lb. 8 oz.

Procedure:

1. Place flour in bowl with sugar, yeast, and salt. Blend briefly.
2. Add eggs and mix until smooth.
3. Slowly add ½ the butter. Scrape bowl and paddle.
4. Add rest of butter slowly. Beat at medium speed for 16 to 20 minutes, until dough is elastic.
5. Chill dough for ½ hour or overnight if you want these fresh for breakfast.
6. Weigh dough into 3-ounce pieces. Roll into balls and place in ungreased muffin tins.
7. Proof until double in size, about 45 minutes.
8. Bake at 350° F for 20 minutes.

Calories: **307**   Protein: **7.7 g (10%)**   Carbohydrates: **33.8 g (44%)**   Sodium: **104 mg**

Total Fat: **15.6 g (46%)**   *Saturated Fat:* **8.7 g**   *Monounsaturated Fat:* **4.6 g**   *Polyunsaturated Fat:* **1.1 g**

❖ Currant Buns

Currants and grated lemon rind give these buns a memorable taste.

Portions per recipe: 252
Yield: 21 dozen rolls
Portion: 1 roll
Serving utensil: tongs

Pan: 18" × 26" sheet
Oven temperature: 375° F
Time: 12 minutes

Ingredients	Amounts	
Low-fat milk (100° F)	5 lb.	
Instant dry yeast		4 oz.
Pastry flour	6 lb.	
Margarine (soft)	5 lb.	
Granulated sugar	3 lb.	
Salt		1 oz.
Eggs, beaten	3 lb.	8 oz.
Vanilla extract		½ oz.
Currants	2 lb.	8 oz.
Freshly grated lemon rind		3 oz.
Bread flour	9 lb.	
Unsalted butter		12 oz.
Honey		8 oz.

(continued)

Procedure:

1. Beat together milk, yeast, and flour. Let ferment until volume doubles. (This is also called a *yeast sponge*.)
2. Cream margarine, sugar, and salt until light and fluffy.
3. Add eggs, vanilla, and yeast sponge. Beat for 1 minute at low speed.
4. Add currants, lemon rind, and flour. Mix for 6 minutes.
5. Let rise in bowl for 1 hour.
6. Weigh out 5-pound pieces. Let rest 10 minutes. Cut into 3 dozen buns with automatic dough cutter or by hand.
7. Place 3 dozen buns on parchment-lined sheet pan. Proof for 30 minutes.
8. Bake at 375° F for 12 minutes.
9. Melt butter with honey. Brush rolls with honey butter while warm.

Calories: **212**   Protein: **4.1 g (8%)**   Carbohydrates: **27.2 g (52%)**   Sodium: **60 mg**

Total Fat: **9.5 g (40%)**   *Saturated Fat:* **2.0 g**   *Monounsaturated Fat:* **4.1 g**   *Polyunsaturated Fat:* **2.8 g**

❖ French Bread   *Kamman*

The thin loaves have a slightly sour taste and a slightly salty crust. This dense, fragrant bread is made with a sugarless leaven. The leaven must be started four days in advance, so plan accordingly. It's well worth the effort.

PRODUCTION NOTES: The bread is started with a leaven made without sugar over a 4 day period. Plan to start 4 days before baking. Use a bread flour with a high gluten content (12–14%). The dough should be tacky, do not knead for more than 10 minutes. Use French bread pans with rounded bottoms if you own some. If your oven is equipped with a steam valve, give the bread a good blast right after you have placed the loaves in the oven. If not, place a pan of hot water on the bottom shelf while the bread is baking. Bake at 450° F and brush or spray with salted water once during the baking.

Leaven

This yields about 2 gallons of leaven, enough for thirty 12-ounce (baked) loaves.

Day 1: Mix 1½ pounds of flour with 2 ounces of dry yeast and 2 quarts of lukewarm water. Cover with cheese cloth. Let ferment overnight at room temperature.

Day 2: Add 1½ pounds of flour and 2 quarts of lukewarm water to leaven. Stir. Cover. Let ferment overnight at room temperature.

Day 3: Add 1½ pounds of flour and 2 quarts of lukewarm water to leaven. Stir. Cover. Let ferment overnight at room temperature.

Portions per recipe: *288*
Yield: *24 loaves (12 ounces each)*
    (12 slices per loaf)
Portion: *1 slice*
Serving utensil: *serrated knife*

Pan: *18" × 26" sheet*
Oven temperature: *400° F*
Time: *25 minutes*

Ingredients

Ingredients	Amounts
Bread flour	14 lb.
Leaven	16 lb.
Salt	3 oz.
Water, lightly salted	2 lb.

Procedure:

1. Put flour into mixing bowl. Add leaven and salt.
2. Knead at low speed for 5 to 6 minutes. Dough will be tacky.
3. Let rise in bowl for 1 hour. Punch down and let rise again for 30 minutes.
4. Weigh out 20-ounce balls. Let rest 10 minutes. Form into long thin loaves.
5. Brush with salted water. Let rise for 30 minutes.
6. With a very sharp, thin blade make 3 long slashes in each loaf. Brush with water.
7. Bake at 400° F for 10 minutes. Brush with salted water and bake for another 10 minutes.
8. Place on bread board with serrated knife.

Calories: **106**   Protein: **3.6 g (14%)**   Carbohydrates: **21.2 g (80%)**   Sodium: **115 mg**

Total Fat: **.5 g (4%)**   *Saturated Fat:* **.1 g**   *Monounsaturated Fat:* **.04 g**   *Polyunsaturated Fat:* **.2 g**

❖ **Fougasse (Provence)** *Kamman*

This Roman flat bread is still made in the Provence and adds an interesting touch to the bread board. The French dough (see recipe on pages 488–489) is shaped into thin, large ovals with elongated holes slashed into the dough, brushed with olive oil, and baked until crisp. An excellent complement to cheeses, it could be displayed on a fruit and cheese tray.

Portions per recipe: 720
Yield: 60 loaves (1 loaf serves 12)
Portion: 1 piece
Serving utensil: knife

Pan: 18″ × 26″ sheet
Oven temperature: 400° F
Time: 20 minutes

Ingredients	Amounts
French bread dough (pages 488–489)	*30 lb.*
Olive oil	*4 oz.*
Fennel seeds	*2 oz.*

Procedure:

1. Weigh dough into 8-ounce balls. Let rest for 10 minutes.
2. Roll into ¼-inch thick oblongs. Make 4 or 5 long slashes in each loaf with a sharp knife.
3. Scatter fennel seeds over dough and press in lightly with rolling pin.
4. Proof for 20 minutes. Brush with olive oil. Bake at 400° F for 20 minutes or until crisp.

Calories: **62**   Protein: **2.0 g (13%)**   Carbohydrates: **12.1 g (78%)**   Sodium: **65 mg**

Total Fat: **.4 g (6%)**   *Saturated Fat:* **.1 g**   *Monounsaturated Fat:* **.2 g**   *Polyunsaturated Fat:* **.1 g**

❖ Health Bread

A round, slightly sweet whole wheat bread that contains eggs, molasses, and honey.

Portions per recipe: 1140
Yield: 76 loaves (1½ pounds each loaf)
*　　(15 slices per loaf)*
Portion: 1 slice
Serving utensil: tongs

Pan: 18″ × 26″ sheet
Oven temperature: 400° F
Time: 25 minutes

Ingredients	Amounts
Non-fat dry milk	3 lb.
Salt	1 lb. 8 oz.
Margarine	5 lb. 4 oz.
Eggs	5 lb. 4 oz.
Dry yeast	1 lb. 8 oz.
Water (100° F)	46 lb.
Whole wheat flour	84 lb.
Black strap molasses	2 lb. 4 oz.
Honey	7 lb. 8 oz.

Procedure:

1. Mix milk powder, salt, and margarine with dough hook for 1 minute.
2. Add eggs and beat for 1 minute. Add yeast and mix for 1 minute.
3. Add water and mix for 30 seconds. Add flour and mix slowly for 1 minute.
4. Add molasses and honey and beat for 10 minutes.
5. Let dough ferment in bowl for 1 hour.
6. Weigh out 2-pound portions of dough and let rest 10 minutes.
7. Form into round loaves and place on parchment-lined sheet pans.
8. Proof until double in size.
9. Bake at 400° F for 25 minutes.

Calories: **148**　Protein: **5.5 g (15%)**　Carbohydrates: **28.1 g (76%)**　Sodium: **244 mg**
Total Fat: **2.5 g (15%)**　*Saturated Fat: **.5 g***　*Monounsaturated Fat: **.9 g***　*Polyunsaturated Fat: **.8 g***

❖ Irish Bread

Caraway seeds and raisins give this bread its great taste. Do not brush with the lemon sugar glaze if the bread will be run through an automatic slicer; it will gum the blades.

Portions per recipe: 1545
Yield: 103 round loaves (1 pound loaves)
   (15 slices per loaf)
Portion: 1 slice
Serving utensil: tongs

Pan: 10" round cake pan
Oven temperature: 390° F
Time: 20–25 minutes

Ingredients	Amounts
Granulated sugar	5 lb. 4 oz.
Non-fat dry milk	5 lb. 4 oz.
Salt	1 lb. 5 oz.
Vegetable shortening	5 lb. 4 oz.
Instant dry yeast	1 lb. 8 oz.
Water (100° F)	45 lb.
Bread flour	74 lb.
Caraway seeds	1 lb. 2 oz.
Raisins	18 lb. 4 oz.

Procedure:

1. Combine sugar, milk powder, salt, and shortening in bowl. Mix at low speed for 2 minutes.
2. Add yeast and water and mix for 1 minute.
3. Add flour, caraway seeds, and raisins. Mix for 15 minutes or until dough comes away from the sides of the bowl.
4. Let dough rise in the bowl for 1 hour.
5. Weigh dough into 1½-pound portions. Let rest 10 minutes. Form into round loaves.
6. Place in greased round cake pans. Proof until double in size.
7. Bake at 390° F for 20 to 25 minutes.

Calories: **122**   Protein: **3.6 g (12%)**   Carbohydrates: **22.7 g (74%)**   Sodium: **159 mg**

Total Fat: **2.0 g (15%)**   *Saturated Fat:* **.5 g**   *Monounsaturated Fat:* **1.0 g**   *Polyunsaturated Fat:* **.4 g**

❖ Kisra—Moroccan Bread *Wolfert*

This anise seed-flavored Moroccan bread is a must at any Moroccan feast to mop up the lovely meat juices of the lamb tagines, but it is also wonderful to eat at any time. I especially like it with jam or cheddar cheese. See color plate **16**.

PRODUCTION NOTE: This dough does not get a rising, it is immediately shaped into small round loaves, which proof for about 1½ to 2 hours.

Portions per recipe: 720
Yield: 72 round loaves (1 pound loaves)
   (10 slices per loaf)
Portion: 1 slice
Serving utensil: bread knife

Pan: 18″ × 26″ sheet
Oven temperature: 400° F
Time: 30 minutes

Ingredients

Ingredients	Amounts	
Low-fat milk (100° F)	10 lb.	
Granulated sugar		10 oz.
Instant dry yeast		15 oz.
Water (100° F)	30 lb.	
Whole wheat flour	12 lb.	
Bread flour	35 lb.	
Salt		10 oz.
Sesame seeds		10 oz.
Anise seeds		10 oz.

Procedure:

1. Place warm milk, sugar, and yeast in mixing bowl. Let ferment for 30 minutes.
2. Add warm water, flours, salt, and seeds. Mix until stiff dough forms and pulls cleanly away from sides of bowl.
3. Let rest for 5 minutes.
4. Weigh out dough into 1 pound 4 ounce portions. Form each portion into a cone shape.
5. Sprinkle sheet pans with cornmeal. Place cone on sheet pan and flatten to a disk 5 inches in diameter with a slightly raised center.
6. Proof for 1½ hours.
7. Using a fork prick bread 3 or 4 times. Bake at 400° F for 30 minutes.

Calories: **115**   Protein: **4.3 g (15%)**   Carbohydrates: **22.6 g (78%)**   Sodium: **18 mg**

Total Fat: **.9 g (7%)**   *Saturated Fat:* **.2 g**   *Monounsaturated Fat:* **.1 g**   *Polyunsaturated Fat:* **.2 g**

❖ Multigrain Bread *Dodge*

Jim Dodge taught us how to make this multigrain bread. The texture and flavor are excellent. It is frequently served on the dinner bread board at UNH and sells well at the bakery outlet. I have modified the saturated fat content of the original recipe by using safflower oil instead of margarine.

PRODUCTION NOTE: The yeast sponge is left to ferment overnight at room temperature. Cover it with a drop cloth.

Portions per recipe: 600
Yield: 40 round loaves (1¼ pounds)
   (15 slices per loaf)
Portion: 1 slice
Serving utensil: serrated knife

Pan: 18″ × 26″ sheet
Oven temperature: 375° F
Time: 35 minutes

Ingredients	Amounts
Water (100° F)	6 lb. 4 oz.
Instant dry yeast	10 oz.
Whole wheat flour	10 lb.
Low-fat milk (100° F)	10 lb.
Blackstrap molasses	5 lb.
Eggs	1 lb. 14 oz.
Eggs, yolks only	15 oz.
Safflower oil	1 lb. 8 oz.
Bread flour	15 lb.
All-Bran cereal	1 lb. 14 oz.
Rolled oats	5 lb.
Yellow cornmeal	4 lb.
Salt	10 oz.
Poppy seeds	5 oz.

Procedure:

1. Mix warm water, yeast, and whole wheat flour. Let sponge ferment overnight.
2. Mix sponge, milk, molasses, eggs, yolks, and safflower oil at low speed for 2 minutes.
3. Add bread flour and mix on medium speed until dough is elastic, about 3 minutes.
4. Add bran cereal, oats, cornmeal, salt, and poppy seeds. Mix at low speed until dough pulls cleanly away from the sides of the bowl.
5. Let dough rise in bowl until double in size.
6. Weigh dough into 1 pound 8 ounce portions. Let rest for 10 minutes. Form into round loaves. Place on oiled and cornmeal sprinkled sheet pans.
7. Proof to double their size. Score top of loaves with a sharp knife.
8. Bake at 375° F for 35 minutes.

Calories: **124**   Protein: **4.3 g (14%)**   Carbohydrates: **22.3 g (72%)**   Sodium: **45 mg**
Total Fat: **2.4 g (17%)**   *Saturated Fat:* **.4 g**   *Monounsaturated Fat:* **.5 g**   *Polyunsaturated Fat:* **1.3 g**

❖ Oatmeal Bread

A slightly sweet loaf that has been enriched with bran and molasses.

Portions per recipe: 2156
Yield: 77 loaves (1½ pounds)
*　(28 slices per loaf)*
Portion: 1 slice
Serving utensil: tongs

Pan: loaf
Oven temperature: 400° F
Time: 25 minutes

Ingredients

Ingredients	Amounts
Granulated sugar	3 lb.
Non-fat dry milk	3 lb.
Salt	1 lb.
Safflower oil	3 lb.
Instant dry yeast	1 lb. 8 oz.
Water (100° F)	52 lb.
Rolled oats	20 lb.
Oat bran	10 lb.
Bread flour	60 lb.
Blackstrap molasses	3 lb.

Procedure:

1. Cream sugar, dry milk, salt, and safflower oil.
2. Add yeast and mix for 1 minute.
3. Add water, oats, and oat bran and mix for 2 minutes.
4. Add flour and mix at low speed while adding molasses.
5. Mix for 15 minutes until dough pulls cleanly away from the sides of the bowl.
6. Let rise in bowl for 1 hour or until double in bulk.
7. Weigh dough into 2-pound portions. Let rest for 10 minutes. Form into long loaves.
8. Place in loaf pans. Proof for 1 hour.
9. Bake at 400° F for 25 minutes.

Calories: **79**　Protein: **2.9 g (15%)**　Carbohydrates: **14.8 g (74%)**　Sodium: **86 mg**

Total Fat: **1.3 g (14%)**　*Saturated Fat:* **.2 g**　*Monounsaturated Fat:* **.3 g**　*Polyunsaturated Fat:* **.7 g**

❖ Pogne *Kamman*

These golden loaves are rich in eggs and butter and are flavored with orange flower water, citrus rinds, and fennel seeds. This bread is baked in the Lower Savoie, Dauphine, and the High Provencal Alps and it was a hit at the French Feast for 5,000. The bread needs no extra butter and is wonderful toasted and spread with orange marmalade or jam.

PRODUCTION NOTES: Bake these loaves in 10-inch round cake pans to help the soft dough keep its shape. Use pastry flour for best results but all-purpose flour will do. Bring the butter to room temperature.

Portions per recipe: *240*
Yield: *20 loaves (1 pound each)*
  (12 slices per loaf)
Portion: *1 slice*
Serving utensil: *serrated knife*

Pan: *10″ round cake*
Oven temperature: *375° F*
Time: *35 minutes*

Ingredients	Amounts
Pastry flour	17 lb. 8 oz.
Instant dry yeast	5 oz.
Low-fat milk (100° F)	2 lb. 8 oz.
Sugar	1 lb. 4 oz.
Salt	1 oz.
Orange flower water	3 oz.
Grated lemon peel	1 oz.
Grated orange peel	1 oz.
Eggs, beaten	1 lb. 4 oz.
Unsalted butter (soft)	2 lb. 8 oz.
Fennel seed	1 oz.

Procedure:

1. Put 2½ pounds of flour in bowl, add yeast, milk, and sugar and let it ferment for 20 minutes.
2. Beat in the rest of the flour, orange flower water, dried peels, and the beaten eggs.
3. Beat for 5 minutes and add soft butter gradually.
4. Let rise in bowl. Dough will be very soft.
5. Weigh out 1 pound 4 ounce portions and form into round loaves.
6. Place loaves into round cake pans and let rise until they have doubled in size.
7. Brush with eggwash and sprinkle with a few fennel seeds.
8. Bake at 375° F for 35 minutes.

Calories: **170**   Protein: **3.4 g (8%)**   Carbohydrates: **28.7 g (67%)**   Sodium: **52 mg**
Total Fat: **4.5 g (23%)**   *Saturated Fat:* **2.6 g**   *Monounsaturated Fat:* **1.3 g**   *Polyunsaturated Fat:* **.3 g**

❖ Russian Bread

This bread has evolved from a recipe given to me by a baker at Brown University. These round loaves are dark, moist, and very flavorful.

PRODUCTION NOTE: The almost finished bread is brushed with a cooked cornstarch wash, which gives the loaves a good crust.

Portions per recipe: 2080
Yield: 104 loaves (1½ pound loaves)
(20 slices per loaf)
Portion: 1 slice
Serving utensil: serrated knife

Pan: 18″ × 26″ sheet
Oven temperature: 400° F
Time: 30 minutes

Ingredients	Amounts
Brown sugar	4 lb.
Vegetable shortening	5 lb.
Salt	1 lb. 10 oz.
Instant dry yeast	3 lb.
Water (100° F)	66 lb.
Cider vinegar	6 lb.
Dry onions, chopped	1 lb. 8 oz.
Instant coffee	10 oz.
Blackstrap molasses	6 lb.
Rye flour	20 lb.
Bread flour	80 lb.
All-Bran cereal	12 lb.
Caraway seeds	1 lb. 4 oz.
Dutch cocoa	2 lb.
Water	2 lb.
Cornstarch	1 oz.

Procedure:

1. Cream sugar, shortening, and salt on high speed.
2. Add yeast and mix for 1 minute.
3. Add water, vinegar, onions, instant coffee, and molasses. Mix at slow speed for 1 minute.
4. Add flours, cereal, caraway seeds, and cocoa. Mix for 10 minutes.
5. Let dough rise in bowl for 1 hour.
6. Weigh out 2-pound portions of dough. Form into round loaves. Sprinkle sheet pans with cornmeal and place 6 loaves on each pan. Proof.
7. Bake at 400° F for 22 minutes.
8. Boil water with cornstarch, brush loaves with this wash, and bake for 8 minutes.
9. This bread can also be shaped into oblong loaves and be baked in lidded bread pans for a sandwich loaf.

Calories: **106**   Protein: **3.3 g (12%)**   Carbohydrates: **20.5 g (77%)**   Sodium: **169 mg**
Total Fat: **1.7 g (14%)**   *Saturated Fat: .4 g*   *Monounsaturated Fat: .7 g*   *Polyunsaturated Fat: .3 g*

❖ **Sourdough Bread** *Dodge*

This is an outstanding bread that gets its wonderful flavor from a sourdough starter made with grapes. This dough can be formed into crisp and soft bread sticks. See color plates **1** and **14**.

PRODUCTION NOTES: Plan to make the starter 7 days in advance of first baking. Use only up to ¾ of the starter. Feed the remaining ¼ of the sourdough starter twice a week with 3 pounds of bread flour and ½ gallon of warm water, and keep it in the refrigerator. The day before baking another batch of bread, feed the starter, and leave it at room temperature. Bruised and loose grapes from your pantry are perfectly fine for this sourdough starter.

SOURDOUGH STARTER

Yield: 6 gallons

Ingredients	Amounts
Green seedless grapes, off the stem	*10 lb. 8 oz.*
Water (100° F)	*5 lb.*
Bread flour	*7 lb.*
Water (100° F)	*16 lb.*
Bread flour	*12 lb.*

One sourdough can take on many forms.

Procedure:

1. Mash the grapes to a pulp. Cover and let ferment for 48 hours at room temperature.
2. Strain the juice. Add 5 pounds of warm water and stir in 7 pounds of flour.
3. Cover and leave at room temperature overnight.
4. Next day stir in 4 pounds of water and 3 pounds of flour. Leave at room temperature overnight. Repeat this process for 3 more days.
5. Sourdough starter is ready to use on the 8th day.

SOURDOUGH BREAD

Portions per recipe: 1632
Yield: 102 loaves (1 pound each)
   (15 slices per loaf)
Portion: 1 slice
Serving utensil: serrated knife

Pan: 18" × 26" sheet
Oven temperature: 425° F
Time: 40 minutes

Ingredients	Amounts
Sourdough starter	36 lb.
Instant dry yeast	10 oz.
Water (100° F)	36 lb.
Kosher salt	12 oz.
Bread flour	82 lb.
Egg whites, beaten with a little salt	1 lb.

Procedure:

1. Place starter in mixing bowl, add yeast, water, and salt. Mix for about 2 minutes.
2. Add bread flour and mix until dough pulls cleanly away from bowl.
3. Let rise in bowl until double in size.
4. Weigh dough into 1 pound 8 ounce portions. Let rest for 10 minutes. Form into round loaves.
5. Place on parchment-lined sheet pans that have been sprinkled with cornmeal.
6. Proof until loaves are 2½ times their original size.
7. Brush risen loaves with egg white and score tops with sharp knife.
8. Place in 425° F oven and open steam (if available) for 10 minutes.
9. Reduce temperature to 375° F and bake for 30 minutes.

Calories: **105**   Protein: **3.5 g (13%)**   Carbohydrates: **21.2 g (81%)**   Sodium: **87 mg**

Total Fat: **.5 g (4%)**   *Saturated Fat:* **.1 g**   *Monounsaturated Fat:* **.04 g**   *Polyunsaturated Fat:* **.2 g**

❖ **Toscano Bread** *Romagnoli*

A very tasty Italian bread made with whole wheat flour.

PRODUCTION NOTES: This bread is made with all-purpose flour, which the Romagnolis believe comes closest to resembling Italian bread flour. This also makes excellent pizza dough. Substitute 1-pound olive oil for 1-pound water. Weigh out 24 ounces of dough for sheet pans and 12 ounces for large 12-inch round pizza.

Portions per recipe: 330
Yield: 22 loaves (1 pound each)
  (15 slices per loaf)
Portion: 1 slice
Serving utensil: serrated knife

Pan: 18″ × 26″ sheet
Oven temperature: 400° F
Time: 25 minutes

Ingredients	*Amounts*
Water (100° F)	*2 lb.*
Instant dry yeast	*9 oz.*
All purpose flour	*2 lb.*
Water (100° F)	*11 lb.*
Whole wheat flour	*7 lb.*
All purpose flour	*12 lb.*
Salt	*3 oz.*

Procedure:

1. Beat together water, yeast, and flour and let ferment for 1 to 2 hours.
2. Add flours, water, and salt and mix for 15 minutes or until dough pulls cleanly away from bowl.
3. Let rise in bowl for 1 hour.
4. Weigh dough into 1½ pound loaves. Let rest for 10 minutes and form into round loaves.
5. Place on parchment-lined pans. Proof until doubled in size.
6. Bake at 400° F for 30 minutes. Bake the first 10 minutes with steam, if your ovens are equipped with steam. Slash top like this #.

Calories: **105**   Protein: **3.6 g (14%)**   Carbohydrates: **22.0 g (84%)**   Sodium: **101 mg**
Total Fat: **.4 g (3%)**   *Saturated Fat:* **.1 g**   *Monounsaturated Fat:* **.04 g**   *Polyunsaturated Fat:* **.2 g**

❖ Triple Fiber Buns

Slightly sweetened with molasses and honey, these soft and airy rolls make a healthy sandwich bun.

Portions per recipe: 180
Yield: 15 dozen rolls
Portion: 1 roll
Serving utensil: tongs

Pan: 18″ × 26″ sheet
Oven temperature: 400° F
Time: 20 minutes

Ingredients

Ingredients	Amounts	
Water (100° F)	12 lb.	
Instant dry yeast		5 oz.
Blackstrap molasses		12 oz.
Honey		12 oz.
Shredded wheat biscuits		15 oz.
Oat bran	2 lb.	
Quick cooking oats	3 lb.	8 oz.
Salt		2 oz.
Eggs	2 lb.	
Safflower oil		8 oz.
Pastry flour	14 lb.	

Procedure:

1. Beat water, yeast, molasses, honey, shredded wheat, oat bran, and oats together. Let mixture ferment for 20 minutes.

2. Add eggs, oil, and flour. Beat for 10 minutes, until dough is smooth and springy.

3. Brush surface with vegetable oil and let dough rise until volume doubles.

4. Divide dough into 3-ounce pieces. Let rest for 10 minutes.

5. Form into large, flat rolls in the shape of hamburger buns.

6. Place 18 rolls on each sheet pan. Brush with egg wash.

7. Proof until rolls have doubled in size and bake at 400° F for 20 minutes.

Calories: **212**　Protein: **6.3 g (12%)**　Carbohydrates: **41.9 g (79%)**　Sodium: **132 mg**

Total Fat: **3.0 g (13%)**　*Saturated Fat: .5 g*　*Monounsaturated Fat: .7 g*　*Polyunsaturated Fat: 1.5 g*

Desserts

Desserts are a treat, but are usually high in sugar and in saturated fat. A daily indulgence in desserts can lead to high cholesterol intake and unwanted weight gain. The desserts in this chapter are no exception. Most of these desserts have been a part of the UNH Great Cooks on Campus special events and they are almost all both very rich and delicious: The perfect ending for a perfect meal. Desserts are a part of pleasurable eating and only strict medical diets need to eliminate them all together.

When we tempt our customers with fabulous desserts, however, we should keep the fresh fruit display nearby.

❖ Almond Cookies   *Hom*

A plain dry cookie that tastes good after a spicy Chinese dinner.

Portions per recipe: 240
Yield: 20 dozen cookies
Portion: 1 cookie
Serving utensil: tongs

Pan: 18″ × 26″ sheet
Oven temperature: 375° F
Time: 18 minutes

Ingredients	Amounts
Blanched slivered almonds	*5 lb.*
Butter (melted)	*5 lb.*
Eggs	*3 lb. 12 oz.*
Granulated sugar	*5 lb.*
Almond extract	*2 oz.*
Bread flour	*5 lb.*

Procedure:

1. Roast almonds until lightly brown, cool, and chop.
2. Melt butter and cool slightly.
3. Beat eggs with butter and sugar until sugar is dissolved.
4. Add almonds and extract and fold in the flour.
5. Scoop with #40 dipper on parchment-lined sheet pans, 2 dozen scoops per pan.
6. Bake at 375° for 18 minutes.

Calories: **170**   Protein: **2.8 g (6%)**   Carbohydrates: **18.4 g (43%)**   Sodium: **10 mg**

Total Fat: **10.5 g (55%)**   *Saturated Fat:* **5.2 g**   *Monounsaturated Fat:* **3.8 g**   *Polyunsaturated Fat:* **.9 g**

❖ Angel Cake

I have included this old-fashioned cake because it is a dessert that contains only a trace of fat and no cholesterol. Serve angel cake with fresh berries or berry sauce.

Portions per recipe: 150
Yield: 15 cakes (10 slices per cake)
Portion: 1 slice
Serving utensil: cake server

Pan: tube cake
Oven temperature: 360° F
Time: 45 minutes

Ingredients

Ingredients	Amounts	
Egg whites	12 lb.	
Salt		1 oz.
Cream of tartar		2 oz.
Vanilla extract		10 oz.
Granulated sugar	6 lb.	
Cake flour	5 lb.	4 oz.
Granulated sugar	6 lb.	

Procedure:

1. Whip egg whites until frothy. Add salt, cream of tartar, and vanilla.
2. Beat at medium speed. Slowly add the first 6 pounds of sugar in a thin stream.
3. Whip until stiff.
4. Sift cake flour with remaining sugar. Fold into stiff egg whites.
5. Pour 1 pound 14 ounces of batter into each ungreased tube cake pan.
6. Bake at 360° F for 45 minutes.

Calories: **145**   Protein: **5.0 g (14%)**   Carbohydrates: **31.0 g (86%)**   Sodium: **189 mg**

Total Fat: **.1 g**   *Saturated Fat:* **trace**   *Monounsaturated Fat:* **trace**   *Polyunsaturated Fat:* **trace**

❖ Apfelkuchen—German Apple Coffee Cake

As a child I ate this cake almost every Sunday from the moment the apples ripened on our tree until my mother found the storage shelf empty in mid-winter.

Portions per recipe: 60
Yield: 1 pan
Portion: 3″ × 2½″ piece
Serving utensil: spatula

Pan: 18″ × 26″ sheet pan
Oven temperature: 375° F
Time: 20 minutes

Ingredients	Amounts	
Margarine	1 lb.	8 oz.
Granulated sugar	1 lb.	8 oz.
Eggs		14 oz.
Almond extract		½ oz.
Cake flour	2 lb.	8 oz.
Baking powder		1 oz.
Low-fat milk		12 oz.
Apples, peeled, cored, sliced ¼″ thick	4 lb.	
Cinnamon		¼ oz.
Ginger		⅛ oz.
Granulated sugar		1 oz.

Apfelkuchen for breakfast or dessert.

Procedure:

1. Cream margarine with sugar, add eggs and extract.
2. Add baking powder and half the flour. Fold in.
3. Add milk and beat until smooth.
4. Fold in rest of flour and beat for 1 more minute.
5. Spread batter on greased sheet pan.
6. Place apple slices close together neatly in 6 rows, pressing lightly into dough.
7. Mix spices with sugar and sprinkle on apples.
8. Bake at 375° F for 25 minutes.

VARIATION: Cut apples into quarters, then core and score deeply lengthwise. Pour cake batter on greased sheet pan and press apples 6 across, 10 down. Sprinkle apples with sugar. Bake.

Calories: **257**	Protein: **4.4 g (7%)**	Carbohydrates: **33.5 g (52%)**	Sodium: **119 mg**
Total Fat: **10.1 g (35%)**	*Saturated Fat:* **1.8 g**	*Monounsaturated Fat:* **4.5 g**	*Polyunsaturated Fat:* **3.1 g**

This wonderful apple cheese tart was inspired by a medieval recipe.

❖ Apple Cheese Tart

This tart evolved from a recipe given to me by a group of students who were interested in serving a medieval feast menu in the dining halls. A moist cream cheese custard is topped with fresh apples and almonds.

PRODUCTION NOTES: The pastry shell is unbaked. Buy a commercially prepared crust or use pie pastry crust from the recipe on page 530 or use one from your own files. Frozen unsweetened apple slices can be used very successfully. The weight of each pastry shell should be about 8 ounces.

Portions per recipe: 80
Yield: 10 pies
Portion: 1/8" wedge
Serving utensil: pie server

Pan: 10" pie pan
Oven temperature: 400° F
Time: 30 minutes

Ingredients	*Amounts*
Cream cheese	5 lb.
Eggs	1 lb.
Granulated sugar	1 lb.
Vanilla	1 oz.
Pastry shell, 10" bottom	5 lb.
Apples, peeled, cored and sliced	10 lb.
Cinnamon	¾ oz.
Granulated sugar	15 oz.
Almonds, unpeeled, sliced	10 oz.

Procedure:

1. Beat cream cheese with eggs, sugar, and vanilla until smooth.
2. Pour 11 ounces of filling into unbaked pastry shell.
3. Top with 1 pound of sliced apples.
4. Mix cinnamon, sugar, and almond slices.
5. Sprinkle 2½ ounces evenly over apples.
6. Bake at 400° F for 25 to 30 minutes, or until cheese filling is set.
7. Cut with a sharp knife that is dipped frequently into hot water.

Calories: **301**   Protein: **4.7 g (6%)**   Carbohydrates: **30.3 g (40%)**   Sodium: **101 mg**

Total Fat: **18.6 g (56%)**   *Saturated Fat:* **8.3 g**   *Monounsaturated Fat:* **7.9 g**   *Polyunsaturated Fat:* **1.6 g**

❖ Baklava

This Greek pastry can be produced in quantity assembly-line fashion. It is so very rich that small portions are satisfactory.

Portions per recipe: *84*
Yield: *7 dozen*
Portion: *1 piece (diamond)*
Serving utensil: *cake server*

Pan: *18″ × 26″ sheet*
Oven temperature: *350° F*
Time: *45–50 minutes*

Ingredients	Amounts
Walnuts	2 lb.
Granulated sugar	4 oz.
Cinnamon	1/4 oz.
Ground cloves	1/8 oz.
Phyllo pastry sheets	2 lb.
Unsalted butter (melted)	8 oz.
Water	1 lb.
Honey	12 oz.
Granulated sugar	2 lb.
Lemon juice	4 oz.
Peel from 1 lemon	
Cinnamon stick, 3″ piece	

Baklava is so rich, most people find small servings very satisfying.

Procedure:

1. Chop walnuts and mix with sugar and spices.

2. Butter bottom and sides of sheet pan. Place 2 phyllo sheets in pan.

3. Brush sheets lightly with melted butter. Repeat until there are 10 sheets.

4. Sprinkle ⅓ nut mixture evenly over phyllo. Cover with 2 phyllo sheets. Repeat once and sprinkle remaining nuts on top of phyllo.

5. Use remaining phyllo leaves, buttering every second sheet very lightly.

6. Brush top with butter and chill for 30 minutes.

7. Cut pastry into 84 diamonds. Bake at 350° F for 45 to 50 minutes.

8. Bring water, honey, sugar, lemon juice, peel, and cinnamon to a boil.

9. Simmer for 10 minutes. Cool slightly. Skim off foam. Remove peel and cinnamon sticks.

10. Pour 3 pints over hot baklava. Let sit overnight so syrup can be absorbed.

Calories: **129**   Protein: **1.8 g (5%)**   Carbohydrates: **23.1 g (71%)**   Sodium: **3 mg**

Total Fat: **3.8 g (26%)**   *Saturated Fat:* **1.5 g**   *Monounsaturated Fat:* **1.0 g**   *Polyunsaturated Fat:* **1.1 g**

❖ **Bourbon Chocolate Pecan Cake**   *Dodge*

This cake is a chocolate addict's dream come true. Serve very small wedges with a dollop of whipped cream and a few fresh peach slices or ripe strawberries on the side.

PRODUCTION NOTES: This is a cake without flour. Jim Dodge recommends freezing the cake for a week and defrosting it in the refrigerator before serving. Oil and line the cake pans with parchment circles. This cake can also be baked in loaf pans.

Portions per recipe: *288*
Yield: *18 cakes (16 pieces)*
Portion: *¹⁄₁₆ pie*
Serving utensil: *pie server*

Pan: *10″ round cake*
Oven temperature: *325° F*
Time: *50 minutes*

Ingredients / Amounts

Ingredients	Amounts
Bittersweet chocolate	6 lb.
Unsalted butter	6 lb.
Dutch cocoa powder	2 lb. 8 oz.
Granulated sugar	6 lb. 12 oz.
Eggs	9 lb.
Bourbon	3 lb.
Pecans, toasted and ground	12 lb.

Procedure:

1. Melt the chocolate with the butter.
2. Sift together the cocoa and sugar. Add cocoa mixture and eggs to the chocolate and mix until well blended.
3. Add the bourbon and pecans and blend well.
4. Pour 2½ pounds of batter into each prepared pan.
5. Set pans in a shallow water bath and bake at 325° F for about 50 minutes, or until the center is set like a custard.
6. Cool in pans, turn out onto cake circles, wrap, and freeze.

Calories: **263**   Protein: **3.6 g (5%)**   Carbohydrates: **20.5 g (31%)**   Sodium: **18 mg**
Total Fat: **19.9 g (68%)**   *Saturated Fat:* **8.4 g**   *Monounsaturated Fat:* **7.3 g**   *Polyunsaturated Fat:* **2.2 g**

❖ **Brioche Bread Pudding** *Dodge*

Jim Dodge has created a luscious bread pudding made with brioche, apples, and raspberries baked in a rich custard sauce.

PRODUCTION NOTES: At the Stanford Court Hotel in San Francisco, Jim served this pudding with fresh raspberries. Use them when they are in season, but frozen (IQF) raspberries can be used, just add them in a barely thawed state.

Portions per recipe: *32*
Yield: *1 pan*
Portion: *3" × 2.5" piece*
Serving utensil: *spatula*

Pan: *12" × 20" × 2"*
Oven temperature: *375° F*
Time: *50–60 minutes*

Ingredients	Amounts
Brioche loaves (2), sliced and trimmed	4 lb.
Eggs	1 lb. 2 oz.
Bread flour	3 oz.
Granulated sugar	6 oz.
Heavy cream	4 lb.
Frozen peeled unsweetened apples	2 lb.
Unsalted butter	4 oz.
Raspberries, IQF	1 lb. 4 oz.

Procedure:

1. Beat eggs with flour, sugar, and cream until smooth. Chill.
2. Sauté apples in butter until slightly soft.
3. Butter the sides and bottom of the pan.
4. Cover bottom with a layer of brioche slices. Spread the apples and raspberries over brioche. Cover with another layer of bread slices.
5. Pour the custard over the brioche. Set the pan on sheet pans.
6. Bake at 375° F for 50 to 60 minutes or until the center is set.
7. Cool slightly before serving.

Calories: **542**   Protein: **9.2 g (7%)**   Carbohydrates: **39.7 g (29%)**   Sodium: **407 mg**
Total Fat: **39.3 g (65%)**   *Saturated Fat:* **23.1 g**   *Monounsaturated Fat:* **11.7 g**   *Polyunsaturated Fat:* **2.0 g**

❖ Cannoli alla Siciliana   *Romagnoli*

Good cannoli shells can be bought from many sources; sample the possibilities and buy the best. Fill them with two different kinds of ricotta creams.

PRODUCTION NOTE: Whip all the heavy cream at once and divide equally.

Portions per recipe: 48
Yield: 24 *chocolate/*24 *candied fruit*
Portion: 1 *cannoli*
Serving utensil: tongs

Ingredients	Amounts
Chocolate	
Ricotta cheese	3 lb.
Granulated sugar	8 oz.
Vanilla extract	½ oz.
Dutch cocoa powder	4 oz.
Heavy cream, whipped	1 lb. 8 oz.
Fruit	
Ricotta cheese	3 lb.
Granulated sugar	8 oz.
Vanilla extract	½ oz.
Heavy cream, whipped	1 lb. 8 oz.
Citron or candied fruit	7 oz.
Cannoli	1 lb. 8 oz.
Chocolate jimmies	6 oz.

Procedure:

1. For the chocolate filling beat ricotta with sugar, vanilla, and cocoa. Fold cream in gently.
2. For the fruited filling beat ricotta with sugar and vanilla. Fold cream and candied fruit in gently.
3. Fill cannoli using a large tube pastry bag.
4. Sprinkle chocolate filling edges with jimmies.

Calories: **320**   Protein: **8.9 g (11%)**   Carbohydrates: **24.4 g (31%)**   Sodium: **157 mg**
Total Fat: **21.8 g (61%)**   *Saturated Fat:* **12.2 g**   *Monounsaturated Fat:* **3.9 g**   *Polyunsaturated Fat:* **.9 g**

❖ Cappuccino Cake   *Dodge*

A coffee lover's delight, this cake is made with two French chocolate cake layers (genoise). For a less rich cake use the wacky cake made with egg whites.

PRODUCTION NOTES: Bake layers in sheet pans for this large cake. If you want to make round cakes, put 10 ounces of dough into 8 round, parchment-lined cake pans to make 8 layers. Heating the eggs with the sugar to 110° F will make the genoise lighter and give it more volume.

Portions per recipe: 60
Yield: 1 two-layer sheet cake
Portion: 3" × 2.5" piece
Serving utensil: spatula

Pan: 18" × 26" sheet
Oven temperature: 375° F
Time: 12 minutes

Ingredients	Amounts
Chocolate Genoise—2 layers	
Eggs	2 lb. 4 oz.
Granulated sugar	1 lb. 8 oz.
Vanilla extract	½ oz.
Baking soda	¼ oz.
Water (cold)	2 oz.
Dutch cocoa	4 oz.
Cake flour	1 lb. 4 oz.
Unsalted butter or margarine, melted	8 oz.
Frosting	
Espresso coffee beans	5 oz.
Instant freeze dried coffee	2 oz.
Water (hot)	1 oz.
Heavy cream	8 lb.
Granulated sugar	3 oz.
Bittersweet chocolate, grated	12 oz.

(continued)

Procedure:

1. Combine eggs and sugar in a mixing bowl and warm to 110° F.
2. With the whip attachment beat warmed eggs and sugar at high speed until they are very light and thick, 10 to 15 minutes.
3. Add vanilla and the soda dissolved in water to the egg foam.
4. Sift flour with cocoa and fold in gently, being careful not to deflate the foam. Do the same with the melted butter. Do not over mix.
5. Pour 2½ pounds into greased sheet pan. Bake at 375° F for 12 minutes.
6. For the frosting, warm the espresso beans in 375° F oven to bring out flavor. Grind to a fine powder.
7. Dissolve the instant coffee in the hot water.
8. Whip the heavy cream with sugar. When it starts to thicken, add the espresso and the dissolved instant coffee. Whip to soft peak stage.
9. Spread a half inch of cream over first layer of genoise. Top with second layer.
10. Cover the top and sides with cream. Sprinkle with grated chocolate.

Calories: **383**   Protein: **5.5 g (6%)**   Carbohydrates: **27.0 g (28%)**   Sodium: **33 mg**

Total Fat: **29.5 g (69%)**   *Saturated Fat:* **17.8 g**   *Monounsaturated Fat:* **6.2 g**   *Polyunsaturated Fat:* **1.5 g**

❖ Cassata alla Siciliana   *Romagnoli*

Pound cake layers are filled with sweet ricotta, whipped cream, citron, and chocolate chips for a great Italian dessert.

PRODUCTION NOTE: Bake the pound cake layers ahead of time. Frost the sides of the cake with whipped cream only.

Portions per recipe: 300	*Pan: 2-pound loaf*
Yield: 12 cassatas (25 slices per cake)	*Oven temperature: 360° F*
Portion: 1 slice	*Time: 1 hour 20 minutes*
Serving utensil: spatula	

Ingredients	Amounts
Granulated sugar	10 lb.
Unsalted margarine	9 lb.
Salt	3 oz.
Eggs	9 lb.
Baking powder	1 oz.
Cake flour	10 lb.
Vanilla extract	3 oz.
Water (warm)	3 lb.
Dry non-fat milk powder	8 oz.

Filling

Ingredients	Amounts
Heavy cream	12 lb.
Plain gelatin	8 oz.
Rum	8 oz.
Ricotta cheese	24 lb.
Granulated sugar	9 lb.
Semi-sweet chocolate chips	6 lb.
Citron, chopped	2 lb. 4 oz.
Almonds, slivered and toasted	1 lb. 8 oz.
Heavy cream, whipped	4 lb.

Procedure:

1. Cream sugar with margarine and salt on low speed for 5 minutes.
2. Add eggs and beat at medium speed for 5 minutes.
3. Mix baking powder with cake flour and add ⅓ of the amount to egg mixture. Blend until smooth.
4. Mix vanilla with warm water and dry milk powder. Add ⅓ of liquid to batter and beat until smooth.
5. Blend in rest of cake flour and slowly add rest of liquid. Mix for 2 minutes or until the batter is smooth and shiny.
6. Pour 3½ pounds batter per oiled pan. Bake at 360° F for 80 minutes.
7. Cool cakes and cut each loaf lengthwise into 3 layers.
8. Beat cream for the filling until stiff.
9. Soak gelatin in rum and heat until dissolved. Cool.
10. Beat ricotta cheese with sugar at low speed for 5 minutes.
11. Fold the stiff cream, gelatin, chocolate chips, and citron into ricotta.
12. Spread bottom cake layer with 14 ounces of filling. Repeat two times.
13. Finish the sides of the loaf cake with 5 to 6 ounces of whipped cream.

Calories: **517**   Protein: **8.6 g (7%)**   Carbohydrates: **51.2 g (40%)**   Sodium: **191 mg**

Total Fat: **29.8 g (52%)**   *Saturated Fat:* **12.3 g**   *Monounsaturated Fat:* **10.5 g**   *Polyunsaturated Fat:* **4.4 g**

❖ Chocolate Mounds *Dodge*

These chocolate cookies are dipped in bittersweet chocolate for a double chocolate treat.

Portions per recipe: 360
Yield: 30 dozen cookies
Portion: 1 cookie
Serving utensil: tongs

Pan: 18″ × 26″ sheet
Oven temperature: 325° F
Time: 15 minutes

Ingredients	Amounts
Baker's unsweetened chocolate	*1 lb. 4 oz.*
Unsalted butter	*3 lb. 2 oz.*
Confectioner's sugar	*1 lb. 14 oz.*
Cake flour	*3 lb. 12 oz.*
Semi-sweet chocolate	*1 lb. 14 oz.*
Unsalted butter	*5 oz.*

Procedure:

1. Melt unsweetened chocolate in steam kettle or warmer.
2. Beat butter, sugar, and flour at low speed to a coarse meal.
3. Add the melted chocolate and mix at low speed until dough forms.

From left to right: hazelnut cookies with a nut in the center, husar's love, chocolate mounds, and hazelnut cookies sprinkled with chopped nuts.

4. Divide dough into 4-ounce pieces. Roll each piece into a cylinder about 10 inches long and ¾ inch in diameter. Chill for about 1 hour.

5. Slice into ¾-inch pieces, and stand cut end down on parchment-lined pan.

6. Bake at 325° F for 15 minutes or until firm.

7. Melt chocolate with butter to make the glaze.

8. Dip ½ of the cooled cookie in glaze. Keep at room temperature until chocolate has hardened.

Calories: **78**   Protein: **.7 g (4%)**   Carbohydrates: **8.5 g (44%)**   Sodium: **1 mg**

Total Fat: **4.2 g (48%)**   *Saturated Fat:* **3.0 g**   *Monounsaturated Fat:* **1.0 g**   *Polyunsaturated Fat:* **.2 g**

❖ Cornmeal Cookies

Cornmeal gives these cookies a pleasant crunchiness.

PRODUCTION NOTE: Instead of dropping these cookies with a scoop, weigh 8-ounce pieces of dough and roll them into 2-inch wide by 16-inch long strips. Place six strips on papered pans and cut each strip into 6 pieces while hot.

Portions per recipe: 432	*Pan:* 18″ × 26″ sheet
Yield: 36 dozen	*Oven temperature:* 385° F
Portion: 1 cookie	*Time:* 10 minutes
Serving utensil: tongs	

Ingredients	*Amounts*
Yellow cornmeal	5 lb. 8 oz.
Granulated sugar	8 lb. 12 oz.
Pastry flour	4 lb. 4 oz.
Bread flour	4 lb. 4 oz.
Baking powder	2 oz.
Salt	2 oz.
Nutmeg, grated	1 oz.
Margarine	6 lb. 8 oz.
Raisins	3 lb.
Eggs	3 lb. 12 oz.
Lemon juice	5 oz.

(continued)

Procedure:

1. Place all dry ingredients with margarine and raisins in mixing bowl.
2. Mix on low speed for 2 minutes. Slowly add eggs and lemon juice.
3. Scrape down mixture and mix on medium speed for 2 minutes.
4. Drop with a #24 scoop onto parchment-lined paper.
5. Bake at 385° F for 10 minutes.

Calories: **153**   Protein: **2.0 g (5%)**   Carbohydrates: **23.0 g (60%)**   Sodium: **82 mg**

Total Fat: **6.2 g (36%)**   *Saturated Fat:* **1.1 g**   *Monounsaturated Fat:* **2.8 g**   *Polyunsaturated Fat:* **2.0 g**

Tasty cornmeal cookies with raisins.

❖ Fresh Orange Slices with Ras el Hanout   *Wolfert*

Ras el hanout is a mixture of freshly ground spices. In Morocco, so Paula Wolfert tells us, secret ingredients purported to have aphrodisiac properties are often mixed into ras el hanout. See color plate **16**.

Portions per recipe: 180   *Serve chilled*
Yield: 6 platters
Portion: 1.5 ounces
Serving utensil: spoon

Ingredients	Amounts
Oranges	*22 lb.*
Fresh lemon peel	*6 oz.*
Fresh lime peel	*6 oz.*
Water	*2 oz.*
Granulated sugar	*14 oz.*
Nutmeg, freshly grated	*¼ oz.*
Whole cloves	*¼ oz.*
White pepper	*⅛ oz.*
Cardamon pods	*½ oz.*
Cinnamon sticks, broken to bits	*¼ oz.*
Ground cayenne	*⅛ oz.*
Mint leaves	*1 oz.*
Dates, pitted and sliced into rounds	*8 oz.*

Procedure:

1. Steam oranges at low pressure for 2 minutes. Peel.
2. Cut into thin slices and layer on platter in circles. Cover and chill.
3. Remove all white membranes from lemon and lime peel and cut into thin slivers.
4. Boil sugar with water. Add peel and cook for 5 minutes. Spread on parchment paper and separate.
5. Pulverize whole spices, add ground spices, and sift over orange slices.
6. Garnish with candied peel, mint leaves, and sliced dates.

Calories: **64**   Protein: **.9 g (5%)**   Carbohydrates: **15.2 g (95%)**   Sodium: **1 mg**

Total Fat: **.3 g (4%)**   *Saturated Fat: .04 g*   *Monounsaturated Fat: .02 g*   *Polyunsaturated Fat: .03 g*

❖ Fried Pastry from Sefrou   *Wolfert*

In Morocco these pastries are eaten with very sweet mint tea. They are also very good with freshly brewed coffee.

Portions per recipe: 720
Yield: 60 dozen strips
Portion: 1 strip
Serving utensil: tongs

Pan: 18″ × 26″ sheet
Oven temperature: 380° F
Time: 1½ minutes

Ingredients

Ingredients	Amounts	
All purpose flour	15 lb.	
Confectioner's sugar	1 lb.	8 oz.
Salt		¾ oz.
Eggs	4 lb.	
Egg yolks		14 oz.
Water	1 lb.	8 oz.
Vegetable oil		8 oz.
Honey	5 lb.	
Confectioner's sugar	1 lb.	

Procedure:

1. Mix flour with powdered sugar and salt. Add eggs, yolks, and water.
2. Beat into a soft dough that is smooth and elastic.
3. Weigh dough into 12-ounce dough balls. Dip in oil and let rest.
4. Roll each ball into a rectangle ⅛-inch thick.
5. Place two rectangles on top of each other. Press together with rolling pin. Cut into ½-inch wide 6-inch long strips. Twist into corkscrew shape and set on sheet pans.
6. Heat oil to 380° F and fry pieces. Turn as they become a pale beige.
7. Heat honey and drizzle strips lightly. Dust with powdered sugar.
8. Serve warm or cold.

Calories: **61*** Protein: **1.5 g (10%)** Carbohydrates: **11.0 g (72%)** Sodium: **15 mg**

Total Fat: **1.2 g (18%)** *Saturated Fat: .3 g* *Monounsaturated Fat: .3 g* *Polyunsaturated Fat: .5 g*

---

*Nutrient values include frying oil.

❖ Ghoriba—Semolina Cookies   *Wolfert*

A Moroccan cookie made with semolina flour.

Portions per recipe: 480
Yield: 40 dozen cookies
Portion: 1 cookie
Serving utensil: tongs

Pan: 18″ × 26″ sheet
Oven temperature: 350° F
Time: 15 minutes

Ingredients	Amounts
Unsalted butter	2 lb. 8 oz.
Vegetable oil	2 lb. 8 oz.
Eggs	5 lb.
Confectioner's sugar	2 lb.
Vanilla extract	2 oz.
Semolina flour	21 lb. 4 oz.
Baking powder	2 oz.
Salt	½ oz.
Confectioner's sugar	8 oz.

Procedure:

1. Melt butter with the oil. Cool slightly.
2. Beat eggs with powdered sugar until light and fluffy.
3. Add melted butter and vanilla and blend.
4. Add semolina, baking powder, and salt. Blend well.
5. Drop cookies (1 ounce each) by hand or machine on sheet pan.
6. Dust with powdered sugar. Bake at 350° F for 15 minutes.

Calories: **128**   Protein: **2.8 g (9%)**   Carbohydrates: **17.9 g (56%)**   Sodium: **36 mg**
Total Fat: **4.9 g (34%)**   *Saturated Fat:* **1.9 g**   *Monounsaturated Fat:* **1.2 g**   *Polyunsaturated Fat:* **1.5 g**

❖ Hazelnut Cookies

A wonderful German cookie that tastes even better when a hazelnut is placed in the center of each cookie before it is baked.

Portions per recipe: 1260
Yield: 105 dozen cookies
Portion: 1 cookie
Serving utensil: tongs

Pan: 18″ × 26″ sheet
Oven temperature: 375° F
Time: 10 minutes

Ingredients	Amounts
Granulated sugar	25 lb.
Unsalted butter	10 lb.
Vegetable shortening	10 lb.
Salt	2 oz.
Baking powder	15 oz.
Vanilla extract	6 oz.
Eggs	12 lb.
Water	2 lb.
Ground hazelnuts	10 lb.
Pastry flour	40 lb.

Procedure:

1. Cream sugar with butter, shortening, salt, baking powder, and vanilla.
2. Add ½ the eggs with the hazelnuts and mix well.
3. Beat in the remaining eggs and the water.
4. Slowly add flour and mix until just combined.
5. Drop by machine or hand on sheet pans. (Each cookie should weigh 1¼ ounces.)
6. Bake at 375° F for 10 minutes.
   Optional: Press a skinless whole hazelnut into the center of each cookie.

Calories: **161**   Protein: **1.9 g (5%)**   Carbohydrates: **20.6 g (51%)**   Sodium: **45 mg**

Total Fat: **8.1 g (45%)**   *Saturated Fat:* **3.0 g**   *Monounsaturated Fat:* **3.9 g**   *Polyunsaturated Fat:* **.8 g**

❖ Honey Nut Brownies

This is a blond whole wheat brownie.

Portions per recipe: *1020*
Yield: *17 pans*
Portion: *3" × 2.5" piece*
Serving utensil: *tongs*

Pan: *18" × 26" sheet*
Oven temperature: *350° F*
Time: *35 minutes*

Ingredients

Ingredients	Amounts
Brown sugar	50 lb.
Salt	10 oz.
Vegetable shortening	15 lb.
Baking powder	3 oz.
Honey	5 lb.
Eggs	20 lb.
Vanilla extract	12 oz.
Whole wheat flour	20 lb.
Bread flour	20 lb.
Walnuts, chopped	8 lb. 8 oz.

Procedure:

1. Beat sugar with salt, shortening, and baking powder until fluffy.
2. Add honey, eggs, and vanilla and beat at medium speed for 1 minute.
3. Add flour and walnuts and blend for 4 minutes at low speed.
4. Pour 8 pounds of batter into each sheet pan. Smooth with spatula.
5. Bake at 350° F for 35 minutes.

Calories: **234**   Protein: **3.5 g (6%)**   Carbohydrates: **36.6 g (63%)**   Sodium: **19 mg**

Total Fat: **8.8 g (33%)**   *Saturated Fat:* **.6 g**   *Monounsaturated Fat:* **4.5 g**   *Polyunsaturated Fat:* **1.8 g**

❖ Hussar's Love   *Dodge*

A hazelnut cookie that you don't have to be a Hussar to love.

Portions per recipe: *300*
Yield: *25 dozen cookies*
Portion: *1 cookie*
Serving utensil: *tongs*

Pan: *18″ × 26″ sheet*
Oven temperature: *350° F*
Time: *10 minutes*

Ingredients	Amounts
Bread flour	1 lb. 6 oz.
Cake flour	1 lb.
Unsalted butter, cold	2 lb. 8 oz.
Granulated sugar	15 oz.
Hazelnuts, toasted and ground	8 oz.
Confectioner's sugar	5 oz.
Seedless raspberry jam	1 lb. 12 oz.

Procedure:

1. Combine all the ingredients except confectioner's sugar and jam and mix to a smooth dough.
2. Divide dough into 4-ounce pieces. Roll into 2-inch long logs. Chill.
3. Cut logs into ⅛-inch-thick circles and place on parchment-lined pans.
4. Bake at 350° F until light brown.
5. Dust with powdered sugar and pipe a small drop of jam in center.

Calories: **58**   Protein: **.5 g (3%)**   Carbohydrates: **6.7 g (46%)**   Sodium: **trace**

Total Fat: **3.3 g (51%)**   *Saturated Fat:* **1.9 g**   *Monounsaturated Fat:* **1.1 g**   *Polyunsaturated Fat:* **.2 g**

❖ Lemon Tart with Candied Ginger *Hom*

Lemon custard with the bite of ginger fills these flaky pastry shells.

Portions per recipe: 96
Yield: 12 pies
Portion: ⅛ pie
Serving utensil: pie server

Pan: 10″ pie
Oven temperature: 350° F
Time: 40 minutes

Ingredients	Amounts
Granulated sugar	3 lb.
Eggs	2 lb. 4 oz.
Egg yolks	12 oz.
Salt	½ oz.
Lemon peel, freshly grated	1 oz.
Heavy cream	6 lb.
Lemon juice	3 lb.
Pie shell, pre-baked	6 lb.
Crystallized ginger, chopped	12 oz.

Procedure:

1. Beat sugar, eggs, yolks, salt, and lemon peel with a wire whip at high speed until thick and lemon colored.

2. Reduce speed to slow and add cream in a steady stream. Then, just as slowly, add the lemon juice.

3. Pour 1 pound 4 ounces into pre-baked shells. Sprinkle each pie with 1 ounce of chopped ginger.

4. Bake at 350° F for 30 minutes or until set. Pies should be puffed but only slightly brown.

Calories: **327**   Protein: **4.2 g (5%)**   Carbohydrates: **31.5 g (38%)**   Sodium: **94 mg**

Total Fat: **21 g (57%)**   *Saturated Fat:* **9.6 g**   *Monounsaturated Fat:* **8.5 g**   *Polyunsaturated Fat:* **.5 g**

❖ **Meringata** *Romagnoli*

This frozen dessert is as light and airy and as cold as snow. It does, however, have more calories.

PRODUCTION NOTES: Buy frozen egg whites for this dessert. Meringue disks and meringue bits are needed for this dessert. This recipe will make twenty-four 9″ disk, four 18″ × 26″ sheets to be broken into small pieces and at least 144 small piped rosettes to decorate the cake. Bake a few extra rosettes, in case they break or are sampled. Bake in advance and store. Broken meringue shells can make an encore appearance with this meringata. The cake can be frozen for up to 3 days.

Portions per recipe: 144
Yield: 12 cakes
Portion: 1 piece/¹/₁₂ of cake
Serving utensil: spatula

Pan: 18″ × 26″ sheet
Oven temperature: 200° F
Time: 1 hour

Ingredients	Amounts
Egg whites	10 lb.
Salt	2 oz.
Granulated sugar	25 lb.
Cornstarch	5 oz.
Cider vinegar	5 oz.
Unflavored gelatin	10 oz.
Water (cold)	1 lb. 4 oz.
Heavy cream	20 lb.
Vanilla extract	1 oz.
Granulated sugar	1 lb. 14 oz.
Almonds, sliced and toasted	1 lb. 14 oz.

Procedure:

1. Whip egg whites until soft peaks form. While beating at high speed add salt and sugar in a slow stream. Beat until glossy and stiff.

2. Mix cornstarch with vinegar and fold into egg whites at low speed for 10 seconds.

3. Take 8 sheets of parchment paper. Draw three 9″ circles on each parchment paper. Place paper on sheet pans and pipe or spread 7 ounces of meringue batter to fill circle.

4. Spread 4 pounds of meringue on lined pan. Pipe 160 (144 are needed) small rosettes on sheet pans.

5. Place in 300° F oven, reduce temperature immediately to 200° F, and let dry for 1 hour. Meringue must be completely dry.

6. Soften gelatin in cold water. Heat until dissolved and clear. Cool to syrupy stage.

7. Whip cream and slowly add sugar. Whip until stiff.

8. Fold in vanilla and gelatin syrup.

9. Spread meringue disk with 9 ounces of cream. Top with 3 ounces of meringue bits and 1 ounce of toasted almond slices. Repeat. Cover sides and top with 12 ounces of cream.

10. Freeze.

11. On day it will be served, decorate meringata with 12 rosettes around edge and sprinkle center with ½ ounce of toasted almonds.

Calories: **614**   Protein: **6.5 g (4%)**   Carbohydrates: **87.7 g (57%)**   Sodium: **222 mg**
Total Fat: **24.6 g (36%)**   *Saturated Fat:* **14.6 g**   *Monounsaturated Fat:* **7.5 g**   *Polyunsaturated Fat:* **.6 g**

❖ Orange Tart *Kamman*

This Provence tart tops buttery orange custard with candied orange slices to cure the winter blahs.

PRODUCTION NOTES: Use small navel oranges and slice, unpeeled, very thinly on a slicer. Steam blanch the slices for 1 minute to soften the rind. Candy in small batches and place on lightly oiled sheet pans to dry. This turned out to be a lengthy and difficult project for the 3,000 portions we needed at UNH. I suggest, although it is not authentic, substituting a fresh, uncandied peeled orange slice instead. Use your own pre-baked pie shell. Cut pie into eighths, and place half of an orange slice on top of each slice.

Portions per recipe: **80**
Yield: **10 pies**
Portion: **1/8th pie**
Serving utensil: **pie server**

Pan: **10" pie**
Oven temperature: **325° F**
Time: **30 minutes**

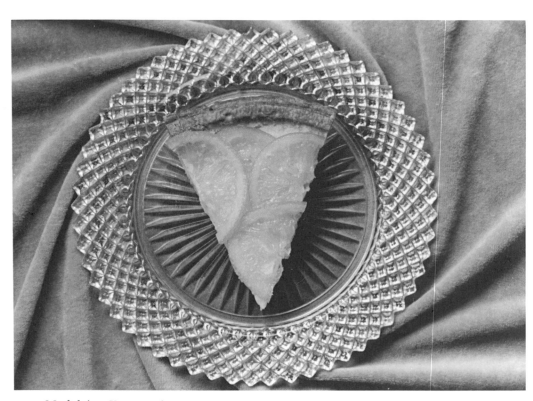

Madeleine Kamman's orange tart.

Ingredients	Amounts		
Unsalted butter	1 lb.	4 oz.	
Granulated sugar	1 lb.	4 oz.	
Cake flour		10 oz.	
Orange rind, freshly grated		2 oz.	
Orange juice	5 lb.		
Orange liqueur		4 oz.	
Eggs	2 lb.	8 oz.	
Egg yolks		12 oz.	
Oranges, seedless	4 lb.		
Water	2 lb.		
Granulated sugar	2 lb.		
Pastry shell, prebaked	5 lb.		

Procedure:

1. Cream butter, sugar, and flour. Add orange rind, juice, eggs, egg yolks, and orange liqueur. Beat at low speed for 2 minutes.

2. Pour a little more than 1 pint into each pie shell.

3. Bake at 325° F for 30 minutes.

4. Slice oranges thinly with electric slicer. Blanch in boiling water for 1 minute or steam for 2 minutes at low pressure.

5. Bring water and sugar to a boil, add a few orange slices at a time and candy until rind is translucent. Let cool on oiled sheet pans.

6. Cover pie with candied orange slices. Cut pie into eighths with a very sharp knife.

❖ Pie Pastry

We used this pie dough at UNH for shells, tops, and turnovers. It is short and flaky and works very well in a pie press.

Portions per recipe: 32	*Pan: 9" pie*
Yield: 332 shells	*Oven temperature: 400° F*
Portion: 1 8-ounce shell	*Time: 14 minutes*

Ingredients	*Amounts*
Vegetable shortening	50 lb.
Granulated sugar	6 lb. 4 oz.
Salt	8 oz.
Dry non-fat milk	6 lb. 4 oz.
Pastry flour	75 lb.
Water (very cold)	28 lb.

Procedure:

1. Combine shortening, sugar, salt, milk powder, and flour for 1 minute or until well blended.

2. Add cold water and mix for 1 minute.

3. Divide into 8-ounce pieces and press into 10-inch tops or turnovers.

4. Pre-bake at 400° F for 15 minutes, or bake according to the recipe. Roll by hand if no machine is available.

---

*Calories: **1040**   Protein: **11.5 g (4%)**   Carbohydrates: **92.9 g (36%)**   Sodium: **312 mg**
Total Fat: **69.3 g (60%)**   *Saturated Fat:* **17.6 g**   *Monounsaturated Fat:* **39.7 g**   *Polyunsaturated Fat:* **8.5 g**

---

*Nutrient analysis based on 1 shell.

❖ Poppyseed Cake

A very moist cake that stays fresh and tasty for about a week.

Portions per recipe: 192
Yield: 12 cakes (16 slices per cake)
Portion: 1 piece
Serving utensil: spatula

Pan: tube cake
Oven temperature: 350° F
Time: 40 minutes

Ingredients	Amounts	
Buttermilk	6 lb.	
Poppy seeds	1 lb.	8 oz.
Margarine	6 lb.	
Granulated sugar	9 lb.	
Baking soda		3 oz.
Baking powder		6 oz.
Salt		1 oz.
Pastry flour	8 lb.	8 oz.
Eggs	6 lb.	12 oz.
Vanilla extract		5 oz.
Granulated sugar	2 lb.	2 oz.
Cinnamon		2 oz.

Procedure:

1. Mix buttermilk with poppy seeds and soak overnight.
2. Cream margarine with sugar until light and fluffy.
3. Blend in dry ingredients.
4. Add eggs and poppy seed mixture and mix until smooth.
5. Pour 1½ pounds into each greased tube pan.
6. Mix sugar with cinnamon. Sprinkle 3 ounces on top of batter, keeping away from the sides of the pan.
7. Top with another 1½ pounds of batter. Smooth the top.
8. Bake at 350° F for 40 minutes. Cool for 5 minutes and dump from pans.
9. Turn upright and sprinkle with powdered sugar.

Calories: **345**   Protein: **4.6 g (5%)**   Carbohydrates: **44.1 g (51%)**   Sodium: **240 mg**
Total Fat: **14.8 g (39%)**   Saturated Fat: **2.7 g**   Monounsaturated Fat: **6.2 g**   Polyunsaturated Fat: **5.0 g**

❖ Raspberry Yogurt Pie

A yogurt cheesecake with less calories than you would expect and a very refreshing taste.

Portions per recipe: *240*	Pan: *10″ pie*
Yield: *30*	Oven temperature: *350° F*
Portion: *⅛th of pie*	Time: *30 minutes*
Serving utensil: *pie server*	

Ingredients / Amounts

Ingredients	Amounts
Eggs	11 lb. 4 oz.
Granulated sugar	6 lb. 14 oz.
Salt	1 oz.
Bread flour	3 lb. 2 oz.
Lemon juice	1 lb. 4 oz.
Vanilla extract	4 oz.
Plain low-fat yogurt	15 lb.
Pastry shells, prebaked	15 lb.
Frozen raspberries	30 lb.
Cornstarch	1 lb. 8 oz.
Water	1 lb.

Procedure:

1. Beat eggs with sugar until thick and lemon colored.
2. Beat in salt, flour, lemon juice, and vanilla. Fold in yogurt.
3. Fill each prebaked pie shell with 1 pound 4 ounces of batter.
4. Bake at 350° F for 30 minutes.
5. Bring raspberries to a simmer. Dissolve cornstarch in cold water.
6. Stir into simmering raspberries and cook until clear. Pour 1 pint on each baked pie. Chill.

Calories: **290**   Protein: **6.9 g (9%)**   Carbohydrates: **41.6 g (57%)**   Sodium: **132 mg**

Total Fat: **11.0 g (34%)**   *Saturated Fat:* **2.8 g**   *Monounsaturated Fat:* **6.0 g**   *Polyunsaturated Fat:* **1.5 g**

❖ Serpent au Pommes et aux Prunes *Kamman*

The Gascony version of the famous strudel, it is indeed a lovely "snake" full of rich fruit surprises.

PRODUCTION NOTES: Soak the prunes overnight in brandy. The apples are briefly sautéed in butter and sugar to caramelize them and deglazed with cognac and lemon juice for a superb flavor. Cook apples quickly in 15-pound batches. Apples should have a firm texture and should not become mushy. To reduce labor we substituted phyllo for strudel dough.

Portions per recipe: *150*
Yield: *15 strudels (10 slices per strudel)*
Portion: *1 slice*
Serving utensil: *spatula*

Pan: *18" × 26" sheet*
Oven temperature: *375° F*
Time: *40 minutes*

Ingredients / Amounts

Ingredients	Amounts
Soft pitted prunes	3 lb. 12 oz.
Brandy	12 oz.
Unsalted butter	1 lb.
Frozen peeled unsweetened apples	30 lb.
Granulated sugar	2 lb.
Lemon juice	8 oz.
Phyllo dough (14" × 18" sheets)	10 lb.
Unsalted butter (melted)	8 oz.
Walnut pieces	1 lb. 4 oz.

Procedure:

1. Soak prunes in brandy overnight. Drain. Reserve liquid.
2. Heat butter, add apples, and gradually add sugar.
3. Cook until browned and slightly caramelized. Add brandy. Cool.
4. Cover workbench with kitchen towels. Stack 3 phyllo sheets on each towel and brush very lightly with melted butter. Repeat 3 more times.
5. Place a row of apple filling (2 pounds) on phyllo dough edge nearest you.
6. Top with 10 prunes and 2 ounces of walnut pieces.
7. Lift the towel edge nearest you and let the dough roll upon itself.
8. Place 3 strudels on each sheet pan, seam side down. Brush with butter and sprinkle with sugar. Bake at 375° F for 40 minutes.

Calories: **234**   Protein: **4.3 g (7%)**   Carbohydrates: **45.2 g (77%)**   Sodium: **129 mg**
Total Fat: **5.3 g (20%)**   *Saturated Fat:* **2.4 g**   *Monounsaturated Fat:* **1.4 g**   *Polyunsaturated Fat:* **.9 g**

❖ Wacky Cake

This is an eggless chocolate cake made with oil. It can be served with whipped cream, frosted, or just dusted with confectioner's sugar. The recipe was developed from a household size version given to us by Raymond Buzzell, a long-time baker at the University of New Hampshire.

PRODUCTION NOTE: Place doilies over tops of cakes and dust with powdered sugar. Remove doilies carefully to preserve the pattern.

Portions per recipe: 180	*Pan: 18″ × 26″ × 3″ cake*
Yield: 3 cakes	*Oven temperature: 350° F*
Portion: 3″ × 2.5″ piece	*Time: 35 minutes*
Serving utensil: spatula	

Ingredients	*Amounts*
Cake flour	*9 lb.*
Granulated sugar	*9 lb.*
Baking soda	*1½ oz.*
Salt	*1 oz.*
Dutch cocoa	*14 oz.*
Water	*8 lb. 6 oz.*
Vegetable oil	*2 lb. 10 oz.*
Cider vinegar	*8 oz.*
Vanilla extract	*1 oz.*

Procedure:

1. Combine dry ingredients in mixing bowl.
2. Combine water, oil, vinegar, and vanilla. Add ½ the liquid to the dry ingredients and beat at low speed for 1 minute, then for 2 minutes at medium speed.
3. Add remaining liquid and beat at low speed for 1 minute. Scrape down bowl. Beat at medium speed for 2 minutes.
4. Pour 10 pounds of batter into each pan. Bake at 350° F for 35 minutes.

Calories: **236**   Protein: **2.2 g (4%)**   Carbohydrates: **41.1 g (70%)**   Sodium: **62 mg**
Total Fat: **7.4 g (28%)**   *Saturated Fat:* **2.1 g**   *Monounsaturated Fat:* **1.4 g**   *Polyunsaturated Fat:* **3.9 g**

❖ Whole Wheat Savory Oil Pastry Crust

This produces a cholesterol free pie or turnover shell. It is a bit difficult to work with, because it sometimes cracks when being rolled. Substitute for any of the pies or turnovers with a savory filling.

Portions per recipe: 24
Yield: 24 shells
Portion: 1 shell

Pan: 10" pie
Oven temperature: 375° F
Time: 20 minutes

Ingredients / Amounts

Ingredients	Amounts
Whole wheat flour	7 lb.
Pastry flour	7 lb.
Salt	1 oz.
Black pepper	1/4 oz.
Dry oregano, crushed	1/4 oz.
Safflower oil	1 lb. 8 oz.
Ice water	3 lb.

Procedure:

1. Blend flours with salt and oregano. Beating on low speed add oil and ice water in a slow stream until it forms a stiff dough.
2. Cover and chill dough.
3. Divide dough into 12-ounce balls. Roll or press out into circles.
4. Pre-bake at 375° F for 20 minutes, or substitute for regular dough and bake according to the recipe.

Calories: **1178**   Protein: **29.0 g (10%)**   Carbohydrates: **195.2 g (66%)**   Sodium: **466 mg**
Total Fat: **33.2 g (26%)**   *Saturated Fat:* **3.2 g**   *Monounsaturated Fat:* **3.8 g**   *Polyunsaturated Fat:* **22.6 g**

APPENDIX A

Dining Services

CYCLE 1

Week of: (DATE)

Items marked with a *V* are vegetarian.

BREAKFAST

Always available	Daily choices	Tuesday	Wednesday	Thursday	Friday	Brunch Service* 10:00 AM to 1:00 PM Saturday	Brunch Service* 10:00 AM to 1:00 PM Sunday	Monday
Orange juice	Juice:	Tomato juice	Cranberry	Pineapple	Grape	Juice: Assorted	Assorted	Cranberry
	Fresh fruit:	Honeydew melon	Banana/kiwi fruit	Grapefruit	Banana	Fresh fruit: Cantaloupe	Kiwi fruit/grapefruit	Honeydew
Hard- and soft-boiled eggs	Entrées:	Poached eggs	Cottage cheese pancakes	Baked potato omelet	Fried egg			Buckwheat cakes with syrup
Cream cheese		Johnny cakes with syrup	Scrambled eggs	Raisin French toast	Yeast pancakes with hot cinnamon apples			Sunshine breakfast drink
Bagel spread		Boston baked beans	Bacon					Ham
Donuts, bagels, toast bread, English muffin		Walnut orange lebani	Herb lebani	Raspberry lebani	Cranberry honey lebani	Herb lebani	Strawberry lebani	Walnut orange lebani
Peanut butter, jam, jelly	Coffee cake/muffin:	Buttermilk scones	Cranberry nut muffins	Zucchini bread	Sweet Georgia muffins	Coffeecake/muffin: Sour cream coffee cake	Blueberry muffin	Raisin scone
Hot cereal								
Assorted cold cereals						Entrées and side dishes: Apple raisin blintzes	French toast with syrup	
Cottage cheese						Ham and cheese omelet	Scrambled eggs	
Yogurt								

LUNCH

Always available	Daily choices	Tuesday	Wednesday	Thursday	Friday	Saturday	Sunday	Monday
Deli— serve 2 kinds of cold cuts and cheeses plus one protein salad.	Soup:	Gazpacho	Fresh garlic	Home style chicken soup	Mulligatawney			Home-style vegetable
	Salad plate:	Cheese salad plate	Chunky chicken plate	Middle Eastern plate	Chilled marinated fish	Italian ricotta torte	Pasta primavera with beef	Prosciutto e melone
Salad bar—serve 3 kinds of greens, 5 kinds of vegetables, 3 dressings, cottage cheese, yogurt.	Entrées:	Muffaletta	Cheeseburger and fries	Pizza rustica with spinach	Shaved roast beef on an onion roll	Home fries	Turkey sausage patty	Beef stew with biscuit**
		Tortellini fiesoli	Garden-style chili with bulgur	Super hero	Vegetarian chow mein			Hummus and cheese pocket
Seasonal fresh fruit	Special salad:	Carrot Salad	Cucumber yogurt salad	Marinated artichokes	Insalata di pasta			Sesame dressed spinach
Fresh fruit/platters	Dessert:	Hazelnut cookies	Snickerdoodles	Nut brownies	Butter cookies	Dessert: Ice cream novelties	Baklava	Double chocolate brownies

DINNER

Always available	Daily choices	Tuesday	Wednesday	Thursday	Friday	Saturday	Sunday	Monday
Salad bar—same as lunch	Entrées:	Chicken parmesan	Grilled rainbow trout	Turkey divan	Flank steak	Chicken teriyaki	Pork loin schnitzel	Grilled veal provolone
		Greek lamb roast	Baked pork chops	Beef burgundy	Mussels with linguini	BBQ ribs with spicy sauce	Monkfish fillet with braised vegetables	Coq au riesling
		Stuffed zucchini V	Tiropita V	Mushroom cakes V	Gateau of crepes V	Tofu stir-fry V	Okra beignet V	Cream cheese soufflé V
Seasonal fresh fruit	Starch:	Steamed rice	German marinated potato salad	Mashed potatoes	Harvest quinoa	Corn and ginger fried rice	Delicious red potatoes	Egg noodles
	Vegetables:	Steamed broccoli	Carrots Vichy	Summer squash casserole	Peas	Oriental vegetable mix	Brussels sprouts	Baked tomato halves
		Sautéed onions	Wilted spinach with lemon	Fresh green beans with red peppers	Asparagus parmesan	Chinese cabbage with 2 kinds of mushrooms	Bajou lima beans	Mushrooms rosemary
	Canned fruit:	Sliced peaches	Applesauce	Pear halves	Fruit cocktail	Plums	Pineapple chunks	Sliced peaches
	Bread board:	Oatmeal and Italian	Anadama and health	Garlic and Kisra	French and multigrain	Assorted	Assorted	Toscano and Russian
	Deserts:	Devil's food cake	Coconut cream pie	Wacky cake	Apple pie	Marble cake	Angel cake	Cherry pie

*Brunch offers a combination of breakfast and luncheon items.   **Creamy yogurt or jalapeño cheese biscuits

Items marked with a *V* are vegetarian.

	Daily choices	Tuesday	Wednesday	Thursday	Friday	Brunch Service* 10:00 AM to 1:00 PM — Saturday	Brunch Service* 10:00 AM to 1:00 PM — Sunday	Monday
BREAKFAST — Always available: Orange juice; Hard- and soft-boiled eggs; Cream cheese; Bagel spread; Donuts, bagels, toast bread; English muffin; Peanut butter, jam, jelly; Hot cereal; Assorted cold cereals; Cottage cheese; Yogurt	*Juice: Fresh Fruit: Entrées:*	V-8 juice; Grapefruit; Mushroom omelet; Cinnamon French toast, hot apple slices; Herb lebani	Apple; Strawberries/kiwi fruit; Buttermilk pancakes with hot raspberries; Fried egg "McMuffin"; Honey nut lebani	Grape; Cantaloupe; Eggs diablo; French toast with maple syrup; Raspberry lebani	Pineapple; Banana; Scrambled eggs; Texas toast with sliced strawberries; Walnut orange lebani	*Juice:* Assorted; *Fruit:* Grapefruit; Strawberry lebani	Assorted; Peaches; Herb lebani	Cranberry; Honeydew Melon; Cheese and ham omelet; French toast with hot blueberry sauce; Honey nut lebani
	Coffee cake/muffin:	Whole wheat bran raisin	Buttery brioche rolls	Banana nut muffin	Apple ginger WW muffin	*Coffee cake/muffin:* Cherry sour cream coffee cake	Sweet Georgia muffin	Kernel corn bread
LUNCH — Always available: Deli—Serve two kinds of cold cuts and cheese plus one protein salad. Salad Bar—Serve 3 kinds of greens, 5 kinds of vegetables, 3 dressings, cottage cheese, and yogurt. Seasonal fresh fruit. Fresh fruit/platters	*Soup:*	Udon noodle soup	Home style beef rice	Lentil soup	Clam chowder	*Entrée and side dishes:* Blueberry pancakes; Poached eggs; Fruit and chicken; Caribbean Black beans Louisiana; Steamed fluffy rice	Fried eggs; Spinach tofu crepes; Sausage Tuscany; Small sub roll; Bacon	Sunny carrot soup
	Salad plate:	Tostada salad plate	Cold marinated picnic chicken	Vegetarian salad	Cold stuffed vegetables			Oriental basket
	Entrées:	Cheeseburger with shoestring potatoes; Empanadas	Penne with ham and asparagus sauce; Sprout & mushroom melt	Turkey chili con carne; Falafel in a pita pocket	Beef and cheese sub; Cheese enchilada casserole			Hot dogs; Noodle Kugel
	Special salad:	Winter salad	Black bean salad	Armenian salad	Delicious salad			Greek salad
	Dessert:	Cornmeal cookies	Chocolate chip cookies	Whole wheat brownies	Granola bars	*Dessert:* Peanut butter cookies	Ice cream smorgasbord	Oatmeal cookies
DINNER — Salad bar—Same as lunch	*Entrées:*	Roast beef pizzaiola; Grilled lamb tips with peppers; Greek bean bake *V*	Turkey paillard; Grilled mahi mahi; Scrambled tofu *V*	Top your own pizza; Garden lasagna *V* (Toppings) Pepperoni, Scrambled beef, Sautéed mushrooms, Sautéed onions, Green and yellow peppers, Grated fontina cheese, Black olives, Anchovies	Djej mechoui; Baked pollock persillade; Spicy vegetables *V*	Greek moussaka; Black forest lamb baeckoffe; Cheese ravioli with mushroom sauce varesa *V*	Sauerbraten; Pollo alla cacciatora; Garden sandwich *V*	Grilled sweet and sour pork tenderloins; Steamed fish with vegetable; Sichuan tofu triangles *V*; Fried rice with whole wheat spaghetti
	Starch:	Rice pilaf	Baked potato with herb yogurt topping		Couscous	Bulgur	Latkes (potato pancakes)	
	Vegetables:	Braised celery; Sautéed Swiss chard	Broccoli al forno; Sautéed red peppers		Italian green beans; Spicy vegetables	Wilted spinach; Primavera vegetables	Pennsylvania cabbage; Peas and lettuce	French style green beans; Ginataan (yams)
	Canned fruit:	Pineapple chunks	Cranberry sauce	Peach halves	Cranberry sauce	Pear quarters	Applesauce	Pineapple chunks
	Bread board:	Italian and health breads	Sour dough and Irish breads	French and Russian breads	Kisra and French breads	Assorted bread	Assorted	Italian and Russian breads
	Desserts:	Cherry crisp	German apple cake	Baked custard	Fried pastry from sefrou	Meringata	Poppy seed cake	Cannoli alla siciliana

Seasonal fresh fruit

*Brunch offers a combination of breakfast and luncheon items.

Dining Services

CYCLE 3

Items marked with a *V* are vegetarian.

BREAKFAST

Always available	Daily choices	Tuesday	Wednesday	Thursday	Friday	Saturday — Brunch Service* 10:00 AM to 1:00 PM	Sunday — Brunch Service* 10:00 AM to 1:00 PM	Monday
Orange juice	*Juice:* / *Fresh Fruit:* / *Entrées:*	Grapefruit / Plum / Scrambled eggs—turkey sausage patty / Cottage cheese pancakes	Tomato / Banana/kiwi fruit / Fresh tomato and green pepper omelet / Warm corn bread / Black-eyed peas	Grape / Peaches / Fried egg / Apple raisin blintzes / Canadian bacon	Grape / Banana / Scrambled eggs / Cottage cheese pancakes	*Juice:* Assorted / *Fruit:* Cantaloupe	Assorted / Kiwi fruit/grapefruit	Cranberry / Blueberries / Vegetable omelet / Apple pancakes with syrup
Hard- and soft-boiled eggs / Cream cheese		Strawberry lebani	Herb lebani	Raspberry lebani	Walnut orange lebani	Herb lebani	Raspberry lebani	Cranberry nut lebani
	Coffee cake/muffin:	Oatmeal scone	Bran muffin	Currant buns	Buttery brioche roll	*Coffee cake/muffins:* Oatmeal scone	Danish	Streusel coffee cake

LUNCH

Always available	Daily choices	Tuesday	Wednesday	Thursday	Friday	Saturday — Brunch	Sunday — Brunch	Monday
Bagel spread / Donuts, bagels, toast bread / English muffin / Peanut butter, jam, jelly / Hot cereal / Assorted cold cereals / Cottage cheese / Yogurt	*Soup:*	Home style chicken soup	Potage parmentier	Zippy avocado soup	Mexican tomato soup	*Entrées and side dishes:* Fried egg / French toast with warm peach and raspberry sauce / Seafood crepes / Hash browns / Bacon	Eggs to order / Asparagus tomato quiche / Chili con queso / Link sausage	Pasta e fagiole
	Salad plate:	Banquet salad plate	Oriental basket	Tortellini salad	Tortellini salad			Cucumber sandwich plate
	Entrées:	Canadian pork pie / Vegetarian sub	Mediterranean seafood sauce with fettucine / Eggplant sandwich	Cheeseburger / Garbanzo casserole	Grilled ham and cheese / Vegetable strudel			Beef & bean quesadilla / Tofu egg salad on rye
	Special salad:	Asparagus salad	Tabouli salad	Insalata riso	Hot and sour cucumber			Cold Sichuan noodles
	Dessert:	Toll house cookies	Ghoriba cookies	Oatmeal cookies	Hazelnut cookies	*Dessert:* Chocolate mounds	Ice cream cones	Double choc. brownies

DINNER

Always available	Daily choices	Tuesday	Wednesday	Thursday	Friday	Saturday — Brunch	Sunday — Brunch	Monday
Seasonal fresh fruit / Fresh fruit/platters	*Entrées:*	Beefsteak au pil-pil / Calif. chicken veronique / Polenta with mushrooms *V*	Herb roasted lamb / Veal sausage cacciatora / Spanakopita *V*	Swiss breast of chicken / Braised pork Caribbean / Eggplant "Mardikian" *V*	Kefta with mint yogurt sauce / Salmon turnover / Celery root with hazelnuts *V*	Carbonade flammande / Rock cornish game hen / Vegetarian stew *V*	Stir-fried beef with orange / Oriental scallops and shrimp / Tofu burger on a whole wheat bun	Roast pork Normandy / Chicken and potato curry / Hawaiian beans *V*
Salad bar—Same as lunch	*Starch:*	Italian potatoes	Barley bake	Rotini or spirale	Mushroom risotto	Parslied boiled potatoes	Corn pudding	Roasted wheat and vegetables
	Vegetables:	Parsnip fritters / Courgettes a la latine	Baked acorn squash rings / Broccoli w. garlic and celeriac	Carrots marsala / Braised beet greens	Peas / Cauliflower milanese	Fresh green beans / Corn on the cob	Vegetable stir-fry / Japanese soybeans	Baby carrots / Curried cucumbers
	Canned fruit:	Cranberry sauce	Pear quarters	Apricots	Fruit cocktail	Pear quarters	Pineapple chunks	Cranberry sauce
	Bread board:	Sour dough and whole wheat	French & multigrain	Pogne and Russian	French and triple fiber bun	Assorted	Assorted	Brioche and Russian
	Desserts:	Cassata (ricotta cake)	Apple cheese tart	Cappuccino cake	Serpent	Lemon tart	Meringata	Peach pie

*Brunch offers a combination of breakfast and luncheon items.

APPENDIX B

DRY HERB AND SPICE OUNCE/MEASURE CONVERSION CHART

1 tablespoon		1 ounce	¼ ounce	⅛ ounce
.2 oz	Allspice, whole	5 Tbs	1 Tbs + 1 tsp	2 tsp
.3 oz	Allspice, ground	3 Tbs + 1 tsp	2½ tsp	1¼ tsp
.33 oz	Aniseed	3 Tbs	2¼ tsp	1 + tsp
.1 oz	Basil	10 Tbs	2 Tbs + 2 tsp	4 tsp
.1 oz	Bay leaf	10 Tbs	2 Tbs + 2 tsp	4 tsp
.33 oz	Caraway seed	3 Tbs	2¼ tsp	1 + tsp
.3 oz	Cayenne pepper	3 Tbs + 1 tsp	2½ tsp	1¼ tsp
.4 oz	Cajun spice mix	2 Tbs + 2 tsp	2 tsp	1 tsp
.3 oz	Cardamom, ground	3 Tbs + 1 tsp	2½ tsp	1¼ tsp
.05 oz	Chervil	20 Tbs	5 Tbs	2 T + 1½ tsp
.3 oz	Cinnamon	3 Tbs + 1 tsp	2½ tsp	1¼ tsp
.3 oz	Chili powder	3 Tbs + 1 tsp	2½ tsp	1¼ tsp
.2 oz	Cloves, ground	5 Tbs	1 Tbs + 1 tsp	2 tsp
.3 oz	Cloves, whole	3 Tbs + 1 tsp	2½ tsp	1¼ tsp
.3 oz	Coriander, ground	3 Tbs + 1 tsp	2½ tsp	1¼ tsp
.2 oz	Coriander seed	5 Tbs	1 Tbs + 1 tsp	2 tsp
.25 oz	Cumin seed	4 Tbs	1 Tbs	1½ tsp
.3 oz	Cumin, ground	3 Tbs + 1 tsp	2½ tsp	1¼ tsp
.2 oz	Curry powder	5 Tbs	1 Tbs + 1 tsp	2 tsp
.1 oz	Dill weed	10 Tbs	2 Tbs + 2 tsp	4 tsp
.25 oz	Fennel seed	4 Tbs	1 Tbs	1½ tsp
.5 oz	Fenugreek seed	2 Tbs	1½ tsp	¾ tsp
.3 oz	Five spice powder	3 Tbs + 1 tsp	2½ tsp	1¼ tsp
.33 oz	Garam masala	3 Tbs	2¼ tsp	1 + tsp
.3 oz	Ginger	3 Tbs + 1 tsp	2½ tsp	1¼ tsp
.2 oz	Gumbo file	5 Tbs	1 Tbs + 1 tsp	2 tsp
.2 oz	Juniper berries	5 Tbs	1 Tbs + 1 tsp	2 tsp
.2 oz	Mace, ground	5 Tbs	1 Tbs + 1 tsp	2 tsp
.05 oz	Marjoram	20 Tbs	5 Tbs	2 T + 1½ tsp
.05 oz	Mint, crushed	20 Tbs	5 Tbs	2 T + 1½ tsp
.2 oz	Mustard, dry	5 Tbs	1 Tbs + 1 tsp	2 tsp
.4 oz	Mustard seed	2 Tbs + 2 tsp	2 tsp	1 tsp
.25 oz	Nutmeg, ground	4 Tbs	1 Tbs	1½ tsp
.1 oz	Oregano	10 Tbs	2 Tbs + 2 tsp	4 tsp
.33 oz	Paprika	3 Tbs	2¼ tsp	1 + tsp
.4 oz	Peppercorns	2 Tbs + 2 tsp	2 tsp	1 tsp
.3 oz	Pepper, black	3 Tbs + 1 tsp	2½ tsp	1¼ tsp
.33 oz	Pepper, white	3 Tbs	2¼ tsp	1 + tsp
.2 oz	Poultry seasoning	5 Tbs	1 Tbs + 1 tsp	2 tsp
.1 oz	Red pepper flakes	10 Tbs	2 Tbs + 2 tsp	4 tsp
.1 oz	Rosemary	10 Tbs	2 Tbs + 2 tsp	4 tsp
.1 oz	Saffron threads	10 Tbs	2 Tbs + 2 tsp	4 tsp
.2 oz	Sage, ground	5 Tbs	1 Tbs + 1 tsp	2 tsp
.1 oz	Savory	10 Tbs	2 Tbs + 2 tsp	4 tsp
.2 oz	Sichuan peppercorns	5 Tbs	1 Tbs + 1 tsp	2 tsp
.08 oz	Tarragon	12 Tbs	3 Tbs	1 T + 1½ tsp
.2 oz	Thyme	5 Tbs	1 Tbs + 1 tsp	2 tsp
.3 oz	Turmeric	3 Tbs + 1 tsp	2½ tsp	1¼ tsp

GLOSSARY

❖

Anise The seed of an annual herb from the carrot family. It flavors Moroccan Kisra bread.

Arborio rice A short, round variety of rice from the Po valley in Italy.

Arugula Also sold as rocket, the small leaves are pungent and slightly bitter. It can be added to salads, and also sautéed or braised.

Asafoetida *See* production note on page 83.

Balsamic vinegar A dark brown Italian wine vinegar from the Modena region. It has a slightly sweet and a very distinct, intense flavor that is excellent with salad greens and roasted vegetables. It is expensive, but a small amount adds lots of taste.

Bean curd *See* **Tofu**.

Belgian endives Sprouts produced by the roots of the witloof plant of the chicory family. The creamy white leaves have light green tips and a slightly bitter taste. Trim stem end and separate spears, discard core.

Black bean sauce *See* **Fermented black beans**.

Bok choy Thick-ribbed Chinese cabbage.

Bonito flakes Tuna flakes dried and shaved paper thin. They are used to make dashi broth.

Buckwheat A plant cultivated for its seeds that is not technically a grain. Used milled as a flour or whole as groats. Toasted and cracked it is known as kasha. Japanese soba noodles are made from buckwheat.

Bulgur Wheat that has been steamed, dried, and ground fine, medium, or coarsely. Soak it for salads, and cook briefly when served as a starch. Do not substitute cracked (uncooked) wheat.

Calvados French apple brandy.

Cannellini White kidney beans that are available canned or dried.

Capers Pickled buds of a Mediterranean shrub. The smaller the buds, the more intense the flavor and the higher the cost.

Cappacola ham An Italian-style ham with a spicy black pepper crust.

Celeriac A specially cultivated celery root, very common in Europe. The knobby brown root must be carefully peeled and trimmed.

Chappatis An Indian whole wheat flat bread not unlike a flour tortilla that must be warmed. It is available from health food purveyors, usually frozen. If placed under a broiler it will puff up and it is called a *phulka*.

Chili bean paste A very spicy thick paste made from ground soy beans and hot red chili peppers.

Chili jalapeño A small, hot pepper that is usually green, but ripens to orange and red. Its "heat" is concentrated in its white membranes. If a milder version is wanted, remove the membrane and the seeds. Hotness can vary dramatically, test by lightly touching a small piece to the tip of the tongue. Canned jalapeños are available peeled, roasted, whole, and diced in no. 10, no. 2, and 4-ounce cans, but do not use canned when fresh is called for. Substitute any other hot chili pepper, such as poblano, serrano, Anaheim chili, or hot Hungarian wax peppers. In an emergency, use bell peppers with a dash of Tabasco sauce. Always protect hands with gloves when handling fiery peppers.

Cilantro The fresh leaves of this strongly flavored herb are used in Indian, Chinese, and Mexican dishes. Readily available all year, it is sometimes sold under the name coriander or Chinese parsley. The dried seeds are available whole and ground as coriander; the seeds are often added to curries and Mexican dishes.

Cloud ear mushrooms Dried frilly Chinese mushrooms that swell like clouds and stay slightly crunchy when cooked.

Concassé Peeled, seeded, and diced tomatoes cooked to a jam-like consistency.

Couscous A very tiny Moroccan pasta; use instant for huge quantities.

Cumin   The seed of an herb belonging to the carrot family that is used whole or finely ground in Indian, Moroccan, and Mexican dishes.

Curry powder   A pungent mixture of herbs and spices that is best made from freshly ground ingredients. Commercially available mixtures usually contain turmeric, cumin, coriander, black, white, and cayenne peppers, and fenugreek.

Daikon   An Oriental radish that has large white roots.

Fennel   Native to the Mediterranean, it tastes faintly of licorice. The cultivated bulb can be eaten raw in salads or cooked. The dried seeds are used in spaghetti sauce and Italian sausage. Do not confuse it with aniseed.

Fenugreek   Fenugreek is a Greek clover seed cultivated solely for curry powder. Do not confuse it with fennel or aniseed.

Fermented black beans   Black beans marinated in soy sauce. Rinse and chop them. Black bean sauce can be substituted, but is much more expensive to use.

Five spice powder   A Chinese spice blend that contains star anise, fennel, cloves, toasted Sichuan peppercorns, and cinnamon.

Garlic   Fresh garlic cloves need to be peeled, crushed (a garlic press is helpful), or chopped. Prepared garlic is available whole or crushed in oil. Refrigerate opened jars.

Genoise   Rich French cake layers, made with eggs and butter.

Ginger   The root of an Oriental lily-like plant that is used fresh, dried, and ground as a spice, and crystallized as a confection. Pickled ginger is served with sushi. Fresh ginger root is usually peeled, then grated or chopped. Do not substitute powdered ginger for fresh root.

Greek Royal olives   Also called Atalanti olives, they are greenish-purple in color. Brandnames: Krinos and Peloponnese.

Hoisin sauce   Made from soybeans, vinegar, sugar, and spices. Do not substitute plum sauce.

Hungarian paprika   Has more flavor and is sweeter than the ordinary type.

Hungarian wax peppers   *See* **Chili jalapeño**.

Italian parsley   A flat leaf parsley with more flavor than the curly variety, but curly may be substituted.

Italian tomatoes   Also called plum tomatoes, they resemble plums in shape and size. They are very fleshy and have few seeds, which makes them a favorite for sauces. Canned, peeled Italian tomatoes are excellent, and they are specified in all recipes using canned tomatoes.

Jicama   A turnip-shaped tuber cultivated in Mexico. Crisp and sweet, it is eaten raw.

Kalamata olives   A medium-sized, dark purple, and pleasantly pungent. Do not substitute domestic black or Greek dry oil-cured olives. The French Niçoise and Greek Royal olives are closer in flavor.

Kombu   Dried seaweed available in health food stores and Asian markets.

Lebani   *See* **Yogurt cheese**.

Lemongrass   An aromatic grass from South Asia. Peel the stem and use the pulp. Dried lemongrass must be soaked and chopped or pulverized before use. Fresh lemon peel can be substituted but it will not come close to the taste of fresh lemongrass.

Marjoram   An herb related to oregano that is sweeter and more delicate in flavor.

Mirin   A sweet rice alcohol flavoring.

Molasses, blackstrap   A very dark, strongly-flavored syrup made from sugar cane. It has slightly more nutritional value than refined sugar.

Mortadella   An Italian sausage similar to bologna with little flecks of fat.

Naan   An Indian quick-bread baked in a tandoor oven. It can be ordered already baked from an Indian restaurant and reheated in a 400° oven. Refer to an Indian cookbook if interested in baking from "scratch."

Nori   Crisp, toasted seaweed sheets, used to wrap sushi. It is high in iodine and vitamin A.

Orange flower water   Available in gourmet shops, pharmacies, and from bakery supply houses.

Oregano A strongly flavored, assertive, and slightly bitter herb from the Mediterranean. Use with discretion.

Pistachio nuts These are bright green when raw and need to be blanched and peeled for cooking.

Phyllo dough Greek strudel leaves available fresh or frozen.

Porcini mushrooms A wild edible mushroom that is widely available fresh or dried. Dried porcini has a strong earthy taste, and must be soaked before using.

Prosciutto An Italian smoke-cured ham. There are some very good domestic brands. Prosciutto should taste mildly smoky and not too salty.

Ras el hanout A Moroccan spice mixture.

Roux Butter, margarine, oils or roasting fats are cooked with flour to thicken soups or sauces. Cook roux slowly to allow the starch particles to swell. In some of the recipes I suggest mixing flour with oil or fat skimmed from the braised meat to make a cold roux. This is similar to using a *buerre manie* (kneaded butter) which has to cook for at least 10 minutes to let the flour cook fully.

Sage Dried sage is the base of poultry seasoning, but the fresh silver-green leaves give a more subtle taste to dishes. Fresh leaves are available year round.

Sake Japanese rice wine with an alcohol content of 10–14%.

Salsa A Mexican tomato and chili sauce ranging from mild to hot (picante) that is available canned. A recipe for fresh salsa can be found on page 46.

Sesame seeds Use hulled seeds because unhulled sesame seeds are not digestible. Toast them briefly to increase flavor.

Shitake mushrooms Very flavorful dried black Chinese mushrooms. Soak and discard tough stems.

Sichuan peppercorns Dried berries from a shrub belonging to the citrus family. Toast for 5–10 minutes in a 350° F oven or on a griddle, and then grind to a fine powder. This can be done ahead of time; place powdered peppercorns in a tightly-closed jar and reduce amount specified in recipe by 10% to allow for moisture lost in toasting.

Sorrel A sour grass that adds a pleasant acidity to green sauce and salad dressings. It is not always available.

Sushi *See* **Nori**.

Straw mushrooms Small and meaty, they are available canned from Taiwan.

Szechuan or **Szechwan** *See* **Sichuan**.

Tahini Sesame seeds ground to a paste. Available in one pound cans.

Tofu Or bean curd. *See* page 288 for a detailed discussion.

Udon noodle A Japanese soft wheat flour pasta, that must be cooked briefly to keep its texture.

Wasabi Available in powdered form from the Japanese wasabi root. It must be moistened with sake, vinegar, or water to make a paste. Like horseradish, its hotness tingles the nose. It is always served with sashimi and sushi. Prepared paste in western markets is made with food coloring, ordinary horseradish and hot chili oil. Use the powder.

Wontons Filled Chinese noodles that are available frozen.

Yellow bean paste A sweet paste made from fermented soy beans.

Yogurt cheese Also called "lebani," is yogurt, drained through a cheese cloth for up to eight hours. Whole milk, low-fat, or non-fat yogurt can be used as long as no stabilizers have been added. Use the whey in breads or cakes. French vanilla-flavored yogurt, when drained, makes an excellent frosting for carrot cake. Ten pounds of yogurt yields approximately 5 pounds/10 ounces of yogurt cheese.

REFERENCES AND SUGGESTED READINGS

❖

Beard, James. *Delights and Prejudices*. New York: Simon & Schuster, Inc., 1964.

Belsinger and Dille. *Cooking with Herbs*. New York: CBI Van Nostrand Reinhold, 1984.

Bjornskov, Elizabeth. *The Complete Book of American Fish and Shellfish Cookery*. New York: Alfred A. Knopf, 1984.

Brody, Jane. *Good Food Book*. New York: W.W. Norton & Company, 1985.

Claiborne, Craig. *Cooking with Herbs and Spices*. New York: Harper & Row, 1963.

Culinary Institute of America. *The Professional Chef*. (4th ed.). Boston: Institutions/Volume Feeding Magazine, 1974.

David, Elizabeth. *Elizabeth David Classics*. New York: Alfred A. Knopf, 1980.

Dodge, Jim. *The American Baker*. New York: Simon & Schuster, Inc., 1987.

Giobbi, Edward. *Eat Right, Eat Well—The Italian Way*. New York: Alfred A. Knopf, 1985.

Hamilton and Whitney. *Nutrition—Concepts and Controversies*. St. Paul: West Publishing Company, 1982.

Heine, Margaret. *Bekannte Gerichte mit Geschichte*. München: Mary Hahn's Kochbuch Verlag, 1985.

Hom, Ken. *Asian Vegetarian Feast*. New York: William Morrow and Company, 1988.

Hom, Ken. *Chinese Cookery*. New York: Harper & Row, 1986.

Hom, Ken. *Chinese Technique*. New York: Simon & Schuster, 1981.

Hom, Ken. *East Meets West Cuisine*. New York: Simon & Schuster, 1987.

Humphrey, Sylvia Windle. *A Matter of Taste*. New York: The Macmillan Company, 1965.

Jones, Evan. *American Food*. (2nd ed.). New York: Random House, 1981.

Kamman, Madeleine. *When French Women Cook*. (2d paperback ed.). New York: Atheneum, 1983.

Kamman, Madeleine. *In Madeleine's Kitchen*. New York: Atheneum, 1984.

Kamman, Madeleine. *Madeleine Cooks*. New York: William Morrow and Company, 1986.

Kittler and Sucher. *Food and Culture in America*. New York: Van Nostrand Reinhold, 1989.

Larousse. *Larousse Treasury of Country Cooking*. New York: Bonanza Books, 1978.

Laurel. *Laurel's Kitchen*. Berkeley: Nilgiri Press, 1976.

Mardikian, George. *Dinner at Omar Khayyam's*. New York: The Viking Press, 1944.

McGee, Harold. *On Food and Cooking*. New York: Charles Scribner's Sons, 1984.

Morash, Marian. *The Victory Garden Cookbook*. New York: Alfred A. Knopf, 1982.

Murdich, Jack. *Buying Produce*. New York: Hearst Books, William Morrow and Company, 1986.

National Institute for the Foodservice Industry. *Foodservice Sanitation*. (3d ed.). Wm. C. Brown Publishers, 1985.

Olney, Richard. *The French Menu Cookbook*. Boston: David R. Godine, Publisher, Inc., 1985.

Pepin, Jacques. *Everyday Cooking with Jacques Pepin*. New York: Harper & Row, 1982.

Pijpers, Dick, Multimedia Publications Ltd. *The Complete Book of Fruit*. New York: Gallery Books, 1986.

Ray, Sumana. *Indian Regional Cooking*. London: Quill Publishing Limited, 1986.

Romagnoli, Margaret and G. Franco. *The New Romagnoli's Table*. New York: The Atlantic Monthly Press, 1988.

Root, Waverley. *Food*. New York: Simon & Schuster, Inc., 1980.

Schneider, Elizabeth. *Uncommon Fruits and Vegetables—A Common Sense Guide*. New York: Harper & Row, 1986.

Thomas, Anna. *The Vegetarian Epicure*. New York: Vintage Books, Random House, Inc., 1972.

West, Bessie Brooks. *Food for 50*. (6th ed.). New York: John Wiley & Sons, 1979.

Wolfert, Paula. *Couscous and Other Good Food from Morocco*. New York: Perennial Library, Harper & Row, 1987.

Wolfert, Paula. *Paula Wolfert's World of Food*. New York: Harper & Row, 1988.

RECIPE CREDITS

❖

Recipes for brioche bread, multigrain bread, sourdough bread, bourbon chocolate pecan cake, brioche bread pudding, cappuccino cake, chocolate mounds, and hussar's loves were adapted from Dodge, Jim, 1987, *The American Baker*, New York: Simon & Schuster.

Recipes for chicken wings in black bean sauce, sweet and sour fish, stir-fried beef with orange, and BBQ ribs with spicy sauce were adapted from Hom, Ken, 1986, *Chinese Cookery*, New York: Harper & Row. Recipes for asparagus salad with mustard dressing, cold green bean salad, cold Sichuan noodle salad, green and white jade salad, hot and sour cucumber salad, tangy tomato soup with lemongrass, sesame dressed spinach salad, Sichuan fried eggplant, and corn and ginger fried rice were adapted from Hom, Ken, 1988, *Asian Vegetarian Feast*, New York: William Morrow and Company, 1988. Recipes for almond cookies and lemon tart with candied ginger were adapted from Hom, Ken, 1987, *East Meets West Cuisine*, New York: Simon & Schuster.

Recipes for soupe au pistou, poulet aux quarante gousses d'ail, beefsteak au pil-pil, rolled leg of lamb Provencale, courgettes a la Latine, wilted spinach with lemon zest, riz à l'Americaine, French bread, and pogne, were adapted from Madeleine Kamman. Recipes for confit of duck legs, magret de canard aux noix, polenta with creamed mushrooms, and serpent aux pommes et aux prunes were adapted from Kamman, Madeleine, 1986, *Madeleine Cooks*, New York: William Morrow and Company. The recipes for fougasse and orange tart were adapted from Kamman, Madeleine, 1983, *When French Women Cook* (2/e), New York: Atheneum.

Recipes for antipasti, marinated kalamata olives, zuppa di Cavolo, pollo con melanzane fritte, triglie e gambaretti arrostiti, agnello di lucca, penne selvaggio, insalata mista, broccoli al forno, and finocchi fritti were adapted from Michela's, Cambridge, Massachusetts.

Recipes for caponata, carrots with marsala wine, cassata alla Siciliana, and tortino di verdure were adapted from Romagnoli, Margaret and Franco G., 1976, *Carnevale Italiano*, Atlantic Monthly Press. Recipes for insalata de riso alla Torinese, cannoli Siciliana, cima alla Genovese, meringata, pollo alla cacciatora, and roast beef with pizzaiola sauce were adapted from Romagnoli, Margaret and Franco G., 1988, *The New Romagnoli's Table*, Atlantic Monthly Press/Little, Brown and Co. Recipes for spuma di fegatini and calamari all'appetitosa were adapted from Romagnoli, Margaret and Franco G., 1980, *The New Italian Cooking*, Atlantic Monthly Press. Recipes for toscano bread, pasta e fagioli, and insalata di pasta were adapted from The Romagnoli's Table, Boston, Massachusetts.

Recipes for fried pastry sefrou, fresh orange slices with ras el hanout, ghoriba, "midway" olives, preserved lemons, spicy eggplant and tomato salad, and spicy vegetables for couscous were adapted from Wolfert, Paula, 1988, *Paula Wolfert's World of Food*, New York: Harper & Row. Recipes for harira soup, djej mechoui, lamb tagine with onions and olives, lamb tagine with raisins and almonds, kefta mkaouara, carrot salad, cucumber salad, Moroccan harissa, and kisra were adapted from Wolfert, Paula, 1987, *Couscous and Other Foods from Morocco*, New York: Perennial Library, Harper & Row.

INDEX

—✦—